EASTERN SEABOARD
NORTHERN GULF COAST
SOUTHEAST AND SOUTH THAILAND
KO SAMUI, KO PHANGAN AND KO TAO
NORTHERN ANDAMAN COAST
PHUKET
KRABI, KO PHI PHI AND KO LANTA
THE DEEP SOUTH
Gulf of Thailand
SOUTH CHINA SEA
Andaman Sea
Myeik Kyunzu (Mergui Archipelago)
Forest Strait
Investigator Channel
Lord Loughborough I.
Lanbi Kyun
Zadetkyi Kyun
Saganthit Kyun
Letsok-aw Kyun
Kanmaw Kyun
Kadan Kyun
Myeik
Tenasserim
Kaeng Krachan National Park
Hua Hin
Pranburi
Nong Sai
Prachuap Khiri Khan
Sattahip
Trat
Ko Chang
Ko Kut
Khlong Yai
Kaôh Kong
Chiméal
Kaôh Rung
Kâmpóng Saôm
Pathiu
Tha Sae
Chumphon
Kra Buri
Kapoe
Tha Chana
Surat Thani
Don Sak
Na Thon
Ko Samui
Kanchanadit
Sichon
Ban Na San
Nakhon Si Thammarat
Pak Phanang
Ron Phibun
Thung Song
Phang Nga
Thalang
Krabi
Ko Surin Nua
Ko Surin Tai
Ko Similan
Ko Similan National Marine Park
Khura Buri
Wiang Sa
Huai Yot
Phatthalung
Trang
Kantang
Ko Lanta
Songkhla
Hat Yai
Pattani
Sai Buri
Narathiwat
Kota Bharu
Tanah Merah
Sungai Kolok
Betong
Yala
Bannang Sata
Na Thawi
Khok Pho
Rattaphum
Khao Chaison
Thung Samet
Satun
Ko Tarutao
Ko Tarutao Marine National Park
Pulau Langkawi
Kangar
Changlun
Jitra
Alor Setar
Pouthisat
Kâmpóng Chhnăng
Kâmpóng Thum
Krâchéh
Mekong
Kâmpong Cham
Suong
Phnom Pénh
Odongk
Kâmpóng Spoe
Srê Ambel
Angk Tasaom
Takev
Kâmpôt
Kâmpóng Trach
Hà Tiên
Du'o'ng Dông
Quân Dao Nam Du
Hòn Thô Chu
Raxh Gía
Ling Xuyên
Cân Tho'
Châu Dôc
Svay Rieng
Banam
Tây Ninh
Trang Bàng
Xa Mát
Bình Long
Thù Dâu Môt
Biên Hòa
HO CHÍ MINH (SAIGON)
Vung Tàu
My Tho
Bên Tre
Trà Vinh
Ba Dông
Sóc Trang
Minh Hai
Cà Mau
Ngoc Hien
Mui Cà Mau
Côn Dao
Cua Sông Cu'u Long (Mouth of the Mekong)
O Rang
Dăc Song
Dak Nong
Du'c Liêu
Cho'n Thành
Ma Da Gui

INSIGHT GUIDES

THAILAND

CONTENTS

Introduction

The Best of Thailand ... 6
The Kingdom of Thailand ... 19
Geography and Landscape ... 22

History & features

Decisive Dates ... 26
Early History ... 29
From Ayutthaya to the 1932 Coup ... 34
Contemporary Thailand ... 43
- A Much-Loved Monarchy ... 44
People and Culture ... 50
- Thailand's Hill Tribes ... 56
A Calendar of Celebrations ... 58
Religion ... 61
Images of the Buddha ... 66
The Performing Arts ... 69
- Thai Literature ... 73
Arts and Crafts ... 75
Cuisine ... 81
- Culture of Rice ... 87
Architecture ... 88
Temple Art and Architecture ... 92

Places

Introduction ... 101
■ BANGKOK AND SUBURBS ... 105
Bangkok ... 109
- Waterways ... 122
- Love for Sale ... 135
Bangkok's Suburbs ... 136
■ CENTRAL THAILAND ... 143
West of Bangkok ... 145
A Feast of Fruits ... 154
North of Bangkok ... 157
South of Bangkok ... 166
■ SOUTHEAST AND SOUTH THAILAND ... 171
Eastern Seaboard ... 173
Northern Gulf Coast ... 185
Ko Samui, Ko Phangan and Ko Tao ... 195
- Full-Moon Party ... 202
Northern Andaman Coast ... 211
- Chao Lay: Thailand's Sea Gypsy Community ... 214

Thailand's Marine Life 220
Phuket 223
Krabi, Ko Phi Phi and Ko Lanta 239
The Deep South 255
NORTH THAILAND 267
Chiang Mai 269
Around Chiang Mai 279
Chiang Rai and East 289
Sukhothai and Surroundings 301
Tak and Mae Hong Son 311
Hill-Tribe Crafts and Clothing 318
NORTHEAST THAILAND 321
Nakhon Ratchasima to Ubon Ratchathani 323
Khmer Legacy 330
North to Loei 337
Along the Mekong River 345

Travel tips

TRANSPORT
Getting There 352
Getting Around 353

A – Z
Accommodation 358
Addresses 358
Admission charges 359
Budgeting for Your Trip 359
Business Hours 359
Business Travellers 359
Children 359
Climate 359
Clothing 360
Crime and Security 360
Customs Regulations 360
Disabled Travellers 361
Electricity 361
Embassies and consulates in Bangkok 361
Emergencies 361
Entry Requirements 361
Etiquette 361
Festivals 362
Health and Medical Care 363
Hospitals 363
Internet 364
Left Luggage 365
LGBTQ Travellers 365
Lost Property 365
Maps 365
Media 365
Money 365
Photography 366
Postal Services 366
Public Holidays 366
Religious Services 366
Shopping 366
Taxes 367
Telephones 367
Time Zone 367
Tipping 367
Toilets 368
Tourist Offices 368
Websites and Apps 368
Weights and Measures 368

LANGUAGE 369
FURTHER READING 371

Maps

Thailand 102
Bangkok 106
Wat Phra Kaew and Grand Palace 111
Bangkok Suburbs 138
Central Thailand 146
Ayutthaya 158
Eastern Seaboard 174
Pattaya 176
Ko Samet 179
Ko Chang 181
Northern Gulf Coast 186
Ko Samui 196
Ko Phangan 204
Ko Tao 207
Northern Andaman Coast 212
Phuket 224
Phuket Town 226
Krabi Province 240
Krabi Beaches 242
Ko Phi Phi 245
Ko Lanta Yai 250
The Deep South 256
Chiang Mai 270
Chiang Mai's Outskirts 275
Around Chiang Mai 281
Northern Thailand 290
Northeast Thailand 324
Inside front cover Thailand
Inside back cover Bangkok

LEGEND
Insight on
Photo story

THE BEST OF THAILAND: TOP ATTRACTIONS

△ **Bangkok**. Thailand's capital is a modern Asian city with an array of hip dining and nightlife options, but thankfully, its more traditional charms – like golden-spired Buddhist temples, serpentine canals and a colourful street life – are still quite evident. See page 109.

◁ **Nakhon Ratchasima (Khorat) Province**. This province in northeast Thailand is a treasure trove of Khmer-era temple ruins and the pristine Khao Yai National Park. See page 326.

△ **Similan Islands Marine National Park**. Easily accessed from Phuket, the crystal-clear waters at this marine park attract both divers and snorkellers. See page 217.

△ **Phuket**. With its spectacular white-sand beaches, luxury resort hotels, plentiful seafood and buzzing nightlife, Phuket is a natural choice for anyone seeking a relaxing holiday. See page 223.

◁ **Mae Hong Son**. Hemmed in by high mountains and bordering Myanmar (Burma), Mae Hong Son in the far north is a good starting point for treks to see colourful hill tribes in the surrounding region. See page 315.

△ **Sukhothai**. This ancient city, to the north of Bangkok, is associated with the golden era of Thai history. This magnificent collection of buildings has been awarded Unesco World Heritage status. See page 301.

◁ **Chiang Mai**. With its distinctive Lanna-style wooden temples, superb handicrafts and gracious people, Chiang Mai in north Thailand is also a centre for treks to hill tribe villages. See page 269.

△ **Ko Samui, Ko Phangan and Ko Tao**. Principal rival to Phuket and the west-coast beaches, the white-sands on the resort island of Ko Samui are lapped by the clear waters of the Gulf of Thailand. Nearby Ko Phangan and Ko Tao offer yet more perfect beaches, wild nightlife and fabulous diving. See page 195.

▽ **Krabi**. This town and its surrounding islands in south Thailand have stunning beaches, lush national parks, excellent diving and snorkelling, and a fiery southern cuisine to sample. See page 239.

▽ **Ayutthaya**. Another Unesco World Heritage site and former capital of Thailand, Ayutthaya is easily accessed from Bangkok by coach or by boat along the Chao Phraya River. See page 158.

THE BEST OF THAILAND: EDITOR'S CHOICE

Beautiful beaches at Ko Tao.

THAILAND FOR FAMILIES

Ancient City: Samut Prakan. See Thailand in a nutshell. Replicas of its most famous sights, some full-size, others scaled down, are strewn around this open-air park. See page 166.
Sampran Riverside Resort: Nakhon Pathom. Traditional dances, Thai boxing *(muay thai)* and other forms of folk culture are performed in a garden setting near Bangkok. See page 145.
Sea Life Ocean World: Bangkok. A giant aquarium with over 30,000 marine creatures will leave the kids spellbound. They can even ride in a glass-bottomed boat. See page 129.

Replica temple at Ancient City: Samut Prakan.

TOP BEACHES

Ao Kantiang: Ko Lanta. No pressing crowds, only pure white sand and clear aquamarine waters. See page 251.
Ao Hin Khok: Ko Samet. One of Samet's less busy beaches, it has a nice laid-back vibe. See page 178.
Hat Kuat: Ko Phangan. It's easy to see why this lovely beach gets so many repeat visitors. See page 205.
Hat Nai Harn: Phuket. Scant development and a broad stretch of white sand make this a clear winner. See page 232.
Hat Tham Phra Nang: Krabi. Utterly gorgeous, this is possibly Thailand's most stunning beach. See page 244.
Ko Nang Yuan: near Ko Tao. Three islets joined by mere wisps of the softest sand guarantee this island beach top billing. See page 208.

Gruesome masks at the Phee Ta Khon Festival.

BEST NATIONAL PARKS

Pha Mak Duk Cliff in Phu Kradueng National Park.

Doi Inthanon National Park: Chiang Mai Province. This natural reserve is centred around Thailand's highest mountain, Doi Inthanon. See page 282.
Erawan National Park: Kanchanaburi Province. The seven-level Erawan Waterfall is the star attraction at this national park to the west of Bangkok. See page 151.
Kaeng Krachan National Park: Phetchaburi Province. Thailand's largest national park is, surprisingly, one of the least explored. See page 188.
Khao Sam Roi Yot National Park: Gulf of Thailand. Expect varied topography, with beaches, marshes, lush forests and mountains at this vast reserve. See page 191.
Khao Sok National Park: Northern Andaman Coast. South Thailand's most popular national park is unique in many ways, and has an amazing variety of flora and fauna. See page 215.
Khao Yai National Park: Nakhon Ratchasima. Although located in northeastern Thailand proper, this popular national park is more usually accessed from Bangkok. See page 323.
Phu Kradung National Park: Loei. This high-altitude forest and mountain reserve is one of the most memorable escapes in northeastern Thailand. See page 342.

BEST SNORKELLING AND DIVE SITES

Burma Banks. Three submerged peaks that provide a superlative diving experience. See page 211.
Chumphon Pinnacle. Famous for frequent sightings of grouper and other large fish. See page 209.
Hin Bai (Sail Rock). Rising like an iceberg out of the water, its highlight is a vertical chimney. See page 206.
Hin Daeng and Hin Muang. These world-class dive sites are located near Ko Rok. See page 252.
Ko Rok. Easily Thailand's best site for snorkelling, with colourful corals and fish found in shallow waters. See page 252.
Richelieu Rock. One of the world's top sites for sightings of whale sharks. See page 213.

Coral formations at Hin Bai, near Ko Tao.

ONLY IN THAILAND

Canal Cruising: Bangkok. Hop on a longtail boat and glide along the canals for a slice of Bangkok's past. See page 117.
Full Moon Parties: Ko Phangan. These wild all-night raves are the island's main claim to fame. See page 202.
Lady-boy (kathoey) cabaret: Bangkok, Pattaya, Phuket, Ko Samui and Chiang Mai. Glitzy cabaret shows by transexual and transvestite performers that would put Vegas to shame. See page 53.
Motorcycle taxis: Bangkok. Fast and furious, these madmen weave through the city's gridlock with knee-scraping accuracy. See page 356.
Thai boxing: Bangkok, Phuket and Chiang Mai. Punishing and brutal, this ancient martial art is more than just sport. See page 138.
Vegetarian Festival: Phuket. There's lots of vegetarian food, but the acts of self-mutilation are only for the robust of heart. See page 363.

Transvestite performer at Simon Cabaret, Phuket.

BEST MARKETS AND BAZAARS

Chatuchak Weekend Market, Bangkok. The biggest market of them all. An unbeatable shopping experience; this has everything. See page 136.

Chiang Mai Night Bazaar. Hundreds of vendors selling everything from cheap trinkets to hand-embroidered hill-tribe clothing. See page 274.

Damnoen Saduak Floating Market: Samut Songkhram. This century-old market has become a bit of a circus, with tourists clamouring to photograph fruit-laden boats paddled by women in straw hats. Still, it's worth seeking out. See page 148.

Pak Khlong Flower Market: Bangkok. A 24-hour market filled with the colour and scent of many thousands of flowers, as well as fruits and vegetables. See page 132.

Patpong Night Market: Bangkok. Surrounded by sleaze and neon, its location is as much the attraction as the fake designer watches, bags, clothes and general tourist tat sold here. See page 132.

Trang Night Market: Trang. One of the largest markets in south Thailand, the offerings run the gamut from handicraft to food, glorious food. See page 256.

Vendor at Damnoen Saduak Floating Market near Bangkok.

Sea canoeing at Ao Phang Nga.

HISTORICAL SITES

Bang Pa-In. The old palaces of the Chakri kings are an interesting hybrid of East-West design. See page 157.

Bridge on the River Kwai: Kanchanaburi. Thailand's haunting memorial to the POWs who died during World War II. See page 149.

Jim Thompson House Museum: Bangkok. Beautiful former home, containing the art collection of the American 'Silk King.' See page 129.

Lopburi. Explore the ruins of the old summer palace of an Ayutthayan king. See page 163.

Phitsanulok. Its Sukhothai-era main temple holds Thailand's second-most important Buddha image. See page 307.

Prasat Hin Khao Phanom Rung. Thailand's largest and best-restored Khmer ruins are in the northeast of the country. See page 329.

Prasat Khao Phra Viharn. Technically in Cambodia, this magnificent cliff-top Khmer temple is only accessible from Thailand. See page 332.

Buddha statue and monkey at Wat Tham Seua, Krabi.

Fun and frolicking at the annual Songkran Festival, Bangkok.

FESTIVALS AND EVENTS

Chinese New Year: Bangkok. Firecrackers, lion and dragon dances, and festival foods herald the start of the new year for Bangkok's Chinese community. Jan/Feb. See page 362.

Fireboat Festival: Nakhon Pathom. This northeastern Thai festival sees gaily decorated "fireboats" being launched on the Mekong River. Oct. See page 363.

Flower Festival: Chiang Mai. The city comes alive in glorious colour with floral floats and flower displays. Feb. See page 362.

Loy Krathong: nationwide. Expect a visual treat as Thais honour water spirits by lighting candles and setting them afloat on tiny baskets along the country's waterways. Nov. See page 363.

Phee Ta Khon Festival: Dansai. Possibly Thailand's most raucous celebration, with people dressed up in colourful costumes and wearing grotesque masks. June/July. See page 363.

Songkran: nation-wide. Pack water pistols (along with a sense of humour) for a three-day orgy of soaking. The Thai Lunar New Year is the nation's largest and wettest celebration. Apr. See page 362.

MOST INTERESTING TEMPLES

Tham Khao Luang: Phetchaburi. More than 100 Buddha images fill this cave temple sanctuary. See page 187.

Wat Chalong: Phuket. Phuket's largest and most important Buddhist temple. See page 233.

Wat Pho: Bangkok. The capital's largest temple is best known for its gigantic statue of the reclining Buddha. See page 115.

Wat Phra Kaew: Bangkok. No one leaves the capital without seeing the Temple of the Emerald Buddha. See page 110.

Wat Phra Mahathat: Nakhon Si Thammarat. One of six royal temples in Thailand. See page 262.

Wat Phra Singh: Chiang Mai. The city's most important temple – and the largest within the old walled city. See page 272.

Wat Phra That Doi Suthep: Chiang Mai. Stunning mountain-top temple just outside of this northern city. Be prepared to climb 290 steps. See page 279.

Wat Phra That Lampang Luang: Lampang. This is a masterpiece of northern-style temple architecture. See page 286.

Wat Phumin: Nan. Most famous for its beautifully rendered 19th-century murals. See page 297.

Wat Rong Khun: Chiang Rai. The "White Temple" appears like a fairytale palace with murals of super heroes. See page 293.

Wat Tham Seua: Krabi. Vast temple complex tucked amid Krabi's forests and cliffs. See page 240.

Doi Suthep, Chiang Mai.

Patong beach, Phuket.

A34

Harvesting rice near Mae Sariang.

Wat Arun and the Chao Phraya River, Bangkok.

Buddha image at Wat Pho, Bangkok.

THE KINGDOM OF THAILAND

Land of the free, land of smiles: the former is a pun on the name Thailand, while the latter is a promotional tourism slogan that is pleasingly truthful. Both define the Thai people and the welcoming nature of their land.

Traditional knife and wooden sheath.

Beneath their graciousness, the Thais have a strong sense of self and tradition. It is this pride in themselves, and in their culture and monarchy, that underpins the Thai sense of identity and an ability to smile at the vicissitudes of life.

The Kingdom of Thailand is ruled by an elected government but retains the tradition of a ruling monarchy, which commands intense loyalty from the people. It has a population of over 69 million and is about the same size as France and twice that of Britain. Its climate is tropical, with three seasons: the hot season (Mar–May), the wet monsoon season (June–Nov) and the cool season (Dec–Feb). The capital city of Bangkok, or Krung Thep in Thai, has at least 10 million people (estimates are, by definition, dubious).

Bangkok is the country's international gateway, and its seat of government, business and the royal family. It is almost a city-state unto itself and bears little similarity to the rest of the nation. When a Thai says, "I'm heading upcountry tomorrow," she or he could mean anywhere outside of Bangkok's city limits. Anywhere is upcountry. Indeed, the second-largest city in Thailand (Udon Thani) has perhaps one-fortieth the population of Bangkok. Most of Thailand is rural, a patchwork of rice fields, villages, plantations and forests.

Parasailing at Pattaya.

Thailand is commonly divided into four regions: the Central Plain, of which Bangkok is a part; the north, including Chiang Mai and Chiang Rai; the northeast, home to three of Thailand's biggest cities, and bordering Laos and Cambodia; and the south, extending from Chumphon down to the Malaysian border. Each region has its own culture and appeal.

Since the East first encountered Siam a millennium ago and Westerners began trickling in during the 16th century, Thailand has been a powerful magnet for adventurers and entrepreneurs. An abundance of resources, a wealth of natural beauty, a stunning cultural tradition revealed in dazzling architecture and art, and a warm, hospitable people have proved irresistible lures.

The country's traditional charms form only one part of the picture, of course. It is a nation in transition, evolving from a developing to a developed country in a rollercoaster of a ride. Since the millennium, economic fortunes have fluctuated, and the country has not been without its share of political turbulence. But true to the people's spirit, consistent throughout the country's history, Thailand has tended to recover quickly from any disruption.

Throughout its history, Thailand has shown a stubborn maverick streak and a sense of pragmatism, both of which have created a determination to chart its own course. The result is a country that has never been colonised by a foreign power and one that has intentionally held onto its past while moving ahead into the future.

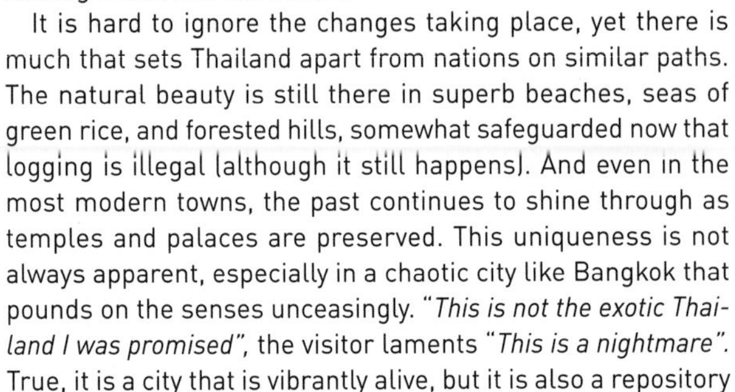

Young monks.

It is hard to ignore the changes taking place, yet there is much that sets Thailand apart from nations on similar paths. The natural beauty is still there in superb beaches, seas of green rice, and forested hills, somewhat safeguarded now that logging is illegal (although it still happens). And even in the most modern towns, the past continues to shine through as temples and palaces are preserved. This uniqueness is not always apparent, especially in a chaotic city like Bangkok that pounds on the senses unceasingly. *"This is not the exotic Thailand I was promised"*, the visitor laments *"This is a nightmare"*. True, it is a city that is vibrantly alive, but it is also a repository of some of the world's most exquisite architecture and historical artefacts.

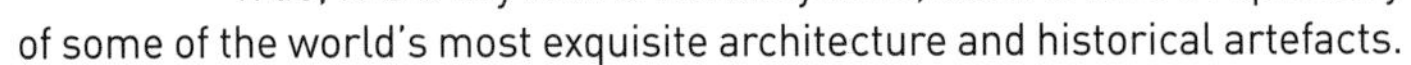

The Thais enjoy life. Something that fails to give personal satisfaction, whether in work or in play, is not worth doing; any activity must have something of this quality within it. Part of this sentiment is distilled from holding on to one's traditions. This may change in Thailand, but for the moment, it is firmly intact, and the visitor cannot help but notice it.

Wat Phra That Doi Suthep, Chiang Mai.

A NOTE ON SPELLINGS AND PRONUNCIATIONS

The transliteration of Thai pronunciation into a Roman alphabet has proved to be a quagmire of phonemes and good intentions. The traveller will encounter several, not just one or two, possible spellings for a single place name. Leaps of linguistic creativity are in order as one negotiates street signs (often Romanised), maps and guidebooks, including this one. As much as possible, this book has sided with common sense and common usage, along with a dose of consistency.

When the letter *h* follows a consonant, it makes the consonant's sound less explosive, softer. Just as Thailand is pronounced *tai-land*, not *thigh-land*, so too the *ph* sound. The pronunciation of *Wat Po* is the same as *Wat Pho*, and, in fact, they are the same temple in Bangkok. Similarly, the island of *Phuket* is always spelled with *ph*, but it is pronounced, always, like *poo-ket*, not *foo-ket* or in other less gracious ways. Other common variations of place-name spellings include *ratcha* and *raja*, and *chom* and *jom*.

The rule of thumb regarding spellings is to be like a Thai when in Thailand: adaptable and tolerant, and with a sense of humour.

Ko Hae, also known as Coral Island, just off Phuket.

GEOGRAPHY AND LANDSCAPE

Although Thailand's wild lands have diminished owing to aggressive development over the past few decades, the country is still endowed with some unique flora and fauna.

From the forested mountains of the northwest to the beaches and plantations of the southern peninsula, Thailand covers some 513,115 sq km (198,115 sq miles), which makes this tropical land roughly equal in size to France. Although Thailand is commonly divided into four regions to reflect cultural influences, it has six areas of distinct geographical character.

In the north, extending along the borders of Myanmar (Burma) and Laos, parallel mountains run from north to south, generally reaching over 2,000 metres (6,500ft) in height. The valleys have been cultivated for centuries, but since the 1950s, the proliferation of slash-and-burn farming techniques has resulted in considerable loss of forest cover in the higher altitudes.

To the south, the vast valley called the Central Plain stretches 450km (280 miles) east to the Gulf of Thailand. The overflowing tributaries of the Chao Praya River deposited rich silt that created large areas of fertile farmland. These days the farms are supported by intensive irrigation, provided by a network of dams.

The Myanmar border to the west is also marked by mountain ranges, which are the source of tributaries of the Mekong, Chao Phraya and Salween rivers. Sparsely populated, this region harbours a rich repository of wildlife.

The northeastern region, known as Isaan, encompasses the broad and shallow Khorat Plateau, which lies less than 200 metres (656ft) above sea level. This is a land of poor soils, little rain, too many people, and more grass and shrub than forest.

On a map, Thailand resembles the head of an elephant, with the narrow southern peninsula forming the trunk. It is sheer coincidence that the elephant is Thailand's national symbol.

Elephants at Chiang Mai.

The hilly southeast coast is bordered on the north by mountains that protrude from Cambodia. It includes some 80 rocky, forested islands along the east coast of the Gulf of Thailand.

Endowed with the heaviest rainfall and humidity, the south covers the narrow Isthmus of Kra all the way to the Malay Peninsula. The south is famous for its beaches on both the Gulf of Thailand (east) and Andaman (west) coasts. Most of the coastal forests here have been cleared to make way for rubber and palm plantations, however some 275 islands scattered in the Andaman Sea support unique marine species and rich coral reefs.

FLORA

In the 1940s, forests still covered about 70 percent of Thailand's land area. By 1960, the figure had dropped to 50 percent. Today, probably only about 15 percent of undisturbed forest remains, although perhaps another 15 percent of it has been replanted, often with non-indigenous species, or else turned into plantations growing palm-oil trees and, especially in the south, rubber and pineapple. Deforestation rates were among the highest in Southeast Asia, but following several fatal landslides, logging was outlawed in 1989, and the situation is now more stable.

Limestone cliffs at Krabi.

Thailand's sheer geographical length gives it some of the most varied forest habitats in the world, although they fall under two broad categories: deciduous and evergreen. Deciduous forests replace most of their leaves in the cool season, whereas evergreens replace leaves all year round, so remain permanently green.

Both have several subcategories, and, as Thailand's terrain is so changeable, a single forest may include several categories of tree, and a single area such as a national park may contain several types of forest.

Deciduous forest (around 70 percent of the total) is found in all regions and has bamboo and mixed deciduous among its main subcategories. Mixed deciduous forest is perhaps the most commercially valuable in Thailand, and in the north includes teak and rosewood.

Among the main evergreen categories are mangrove, beach forest and tropical evergreen forest, the last of which contains another subcategory: tropical rainforest. Tropical rainforests are found predominately in the south and east, where rainfall is above 2,000mm (79 in) a year. They have four separate layers or ecosystems, trees as high as 60 metres (200ft), and one of the most dense concentrations of species in the world.

FAUNA

Of the world's estimated 5,400 species of mammals, 287 have been recorded in Thailand, including 18 hooved species, 13 species of primates, nine types of wild cats (including tigers and leopards), two species of bear, and two of wild dogs. Bats are abundant, with 107 species identified so far. The tiger population has declined, along with the Asian elephant, Thailand's national symbol. From over 200,000 a century ago, fewer than 3,000 wild elephants survive in Thailand today. Khao Yai National Park (see page 323) or the parks close to the Myanmar border offer the best chance of seeing one.

Thailand also harbours four types of reptiles and three of amphibians. Among the 175 species of snakes are deadly cobras, kraits and vipers. Many of the insect species have yet to be identified, but there are 1,200 variegated butterflies alone. Beetle species may number in the tens of thousands, but have been so little studied that entomologists occasionally discover new ones.

Visitors to national parks will be rewarded with bird sightings. There are around 900 species

A school of yellowfin goatfish off Phuket.

permanently resident in the region, while about 240 non-breeding and wintering migratory species pass through Thailand annually.

COASTAL GEOGRAPHY

With over 3,000km (2,000 miles) of coastline and hundreds of islands washed by two seas – the Gulf of Thailand in the east and the Andaman Sea in the west – littoral geography is a significant element in Thailand's environment. Tourists are drawn to the region's powdery, white sand beaches and clear waters that are rich in tropical marine life.

Geologically, the south is noted for its dramatic limestone karst formations jutting out of the sea. Soft and easily eroded, the limestone once formed the seabed. Spectacular caves carved out by underground streams and lagoons hidden within the limestone karsts make for fun-filled exploration on inflatable kayaks. Ao Phang Nga National Park (see page 218) comprises an eye-popping series of crumbly cliffs, jutting islets and karst rocks.

RISKS TO THE COASTAL ENVIRONMENT

Illegal construction, surreptitious land grabs and poor sewage disposal remain a problem at some of the Eastern Seaboard resorts, notably Pattaya. Even national parkland is not sacrosanct. Ko Samet, for instance, is part of a marine national park, but unbridled development along its coast has progressed despite the law. Elsewhere, new legislation, or existing

A DIVER'S HAVEN

With long coastlines skirting either side of the south, Thailand is a major diving and snorkelling destination. The waters are clear and warm year-round, and a plethora of colourful coral reefs attract a huge variety of marine life, including turtles, rays and sharks. With dive shops and live-aboard tours accessing remote dive sites that border Malaysia to the south, Myanmar to the west and Cambodia to the east, Thailand is one of the most affordable places in the world to dive.

The Andaman Sea on the west coast is generally considered better in terms of reef and marine diversity, water clarity and a wealth of idyllic islands at which to drop anchor. The remote Similan and Surin island chains (accessed only by live-aboard dive trips from Phuket) are regarded as the country's premier dive sites, but the waters off Phuket, Krabi, Ko Phi Phi and Ko Lanta are also popular dive havens. More intrepid divers head out to Burmese waters to explore the reefs of the Mergui Archipelago and the Burma Banks, all off the Andaman coast.

Off the Gulf of Thailand, Ko Tao is especially popular among would-be dive enthusiasts. This is Thailand's dive capital, with over 50 dive schools. Also popular are dive trips from Ko Samui and Ko Phangan. Pattaya's waters offer little in terms of marine life and water clarity, but has interesting wreck dives. The Ko Chang Archipelago is still being mapped out as a dive destination.

legislation more rigorously applied, is slowly making a difference.

Following the December 2004 tsunami illegal buildings and ramshackle resorts on the affected areas of the Andaman coast were literally swept away by the gigantic waves. The Thai authorities tried to prevent illegal rebuilding in the aftermath, but this was met with forceful opposition by many displaced locals. Even in a national park like Ko Phi Phi, illegal construction is once again rife.

The marine life of southern Thailand's coastal waters are similarly menaced by human activities, including dynamite and poison fishing – both now strictly outlawed – as well as anchor drag and over-fishing. An additional threat is rising sea temperatures, which can cause coral bleaching. To counter this, "reef balls" of hollow, reinforced concrete that attract coral and offer openings for fish to inhabit are being sunk to rehabilitate reefs in the Andaman Sea off Phuket, and also in the shallower Gulf of Thailand. Some dive sites are now being closed for part of the season. Maya Beach, best known for its central role in the Leonardo DiCaprio film *The Beach*, was closed in 2018 indefinitely, with authorities citing the need for the natural ecosystem to fully recover before it would be reopened. It was a move that suggested authorities have started taking the need for conservation more seriously than ever before.

RISKS TO THAILAND'S INTERIOR

The country's Forestry Department is underfunded and understaffed. In the past few decades, at least 40 rangers have been murdered in the line of duty. Earning less than a factory worker, many rangers also collude with loggers and poachers. The country's poorest people also inadvertently contribute to environmental degradation by farming on protected lands. The endangered populations of tigers and other wildlife are further threatened by the demand for medicinal products among the Chinese.

In the mountainous north of Thailand, deforestation and illegal logging have diminished markedly over the past two decades. Unregistered ownership of power chainsaws is now illegal. However, forest fires, often caused by careless burning of fields or casual disposal of cigarettes, remains a serious problem, and this in turn has led to fire and haze problems during the hot season from March to May.

River flooding can also be a problem. In 2011 the worst floods in decades claimed hundreds of lives and caused economic devastation in northern, northeastern and central Thailand, including much of Bangkok.

In the larger Thai cities like Chiang Mai, Nakhon Ratchasima and Bangkok, attempts are being made, with some degree of success, to limit air pollution caused by vehicular traffic. Two-stroke motorbikes have been largely replaced by less noisy and polluting four-stroke models. Random checks on exhaust emissions and the replacement of old, smoke-belching public transport by newer, greener buses has helped, as has the provision of Bangkok's expanding Metro and Skytrain. All this, however, comes at the cost of the damaging dust caused by constant construction in cities like Bangkok and Chiang Mai.

A white-faced gibbon at Khao Sam Roi Yot National Park.

Tourism undoubtedly plays a part in contributing towards environmental degradation, most visibly when seaside hotels spew untreated sewage. But there are encouraging signs that tourism may become a positive force in the preservation of Thailand's ecology. More enlightened trekking agencies, local green groups and a few progressive politicians are becoming aware that environmental preservation is the key to sustaining the country's booming tourism industry.

DECISIVE DATES

PRE-THAI CIVILISATION

3600–250 BC
Ban Chiang culture flourishes in northeastern Thailand.

AD 6th–9th century
Mon civilisation spreads into Thailand, bringing Buddhism.

9th–13th century
Khmer empire founded at Angkor. Tai peoples migrate south from China into northern Thailand, Burma and Laos.

SUKHOTHAI ERA

1238
As Khmer power wanes, the Kingdom of Sukhothai is founded.

1280–98
Reign of Ramkhamhaeng in Sukhothai. First attempts to unify the Thai people, the first use of the Thai script and the flourishing of the arts.

1281
Chiang Rai kingdom founded in north.

1296
Lanna kingdom founded at Chiang Mai. Mangrai controls much of northern Thailand and Laos.

1298–1347
Sukhothai's early decline.

1438
Sukhothai is now virtually deserted; power shifts to the Kingdom of Ayutthaya.

Sukhothai Historical Park.

KINGDOM OF AYUTTHAYA

1350
City of Ayutthaya founded by Phaya U Thong (Ramathibodi I).

1549
First major warfare with Kingdom of Bago (Burma).

1569
Burmese capture Ayutthaya.

1590
Naresuan becomes king and throws off Burmese suzerainty. Ayutthaya expands rapidly at the expense of Burmese and Khmer empires.

1605–10
Ekatotsarot reigns and begins significant economic ties with Europe.

1628–55
Reign of Prasat Thong. Trading concessions expand and regular trade with China and Europe is established.

1656–88
Reign of King Narai. British influence expands. Reputation of Ayutthaya as a magnificent royal city spreads in Europe.

1733–58
Reign of King Boromakot. A period of peace, and of flourishing arts and literature.

1767
Invading Burmese destroy Ayutthaya.

THE CHAKRI DYNASTY

1767–68
General Phaya Taksin defeats Burmese, establishes new capital in Thonburi, near Bangkok and is crowned King Taksin.

1779
Chiang Mai is captured and the Burmese expelled from the Lanna kingdom. The Emerald Buddha is brought from Vientiane, Laos, to Thonburi.

1782
Taksin is deposed. King Rama I becomes the first ruler of the Chakri Dynasty. The capital is moved across the river to Bangkok.

1868–1910
Chulalongkorn (Rama V) ascends the throne. Schools, infrastructure, military and government are modernised.

1925–32
Reign of Prajadhipok (Rama VII).

END OF ABSOLUTE MONARCHY

1932
A coup d'état ends the absolute monarchy and ushers in constitutional rule.

1941–5
Japanese occupation.

1946
King Ananda is killed by a mysterious gunshot, and King Bhumibol Adulyadej (Rama IX) ascends the throne.

1949
Siam is officially renamed Thailand.

1973
Bloody clashes between army and demonstrating students bring down the military government.

1976
Political and economic blunders bring down the resulting civilian government.

MODERN THAILAND

1992
Another clash between military forces and civilian demonstrators; the military then leaves government to the civilian politicians.

1997
Thailand's banking system and economy in freefall as the baht loses half of its value.

2001
Billionaire Thaksin Shinawatra and his populist Thai Rak Thai Party win the national polls for the Lower House.

2004
In December, a massive tsunami causes devastation along the Andaman Coast. Some 8,000 lives are lost.

2005
The Thaksin administration wins a second four-year term in the general elections.

2006
Thaksin becomes focus of demonstrations by the PAD (known as the Yellow Shirts). He is forced into exile in London by a military coup.

2008
The Yellow Shirts occupy Government House and seize the airport. In December, the courts disband the ruling party. The Democrat Party leader Abhisit Vejjajiva becomes prime minister in a deal seen as being brokered by the army.

2009
In April, Red Shirt protests disrupt the ASEAN Summit in Pattaya, causing several heads of state to be airlifted to safety; Songkran riots erupt in Bangkok; Yellow Shirt leader Sondhi Limthongkul is shot, but survives.

2010
In February the courts find Thaksin guilty of abuse of power. April and May see thousands of Red Shirt demonstrators occupy parts of Bangkok. Banks, department stores and other major buildings are torched. Eighty-five people are killed and nearly 1,500 injured in clashes with the army on April 10 and May 19.

2011
In July, the Thaksin proxy Pheu Thai Party wins a landslide election victory. His sister Yingluck becomes Thailand's first female prime minister.

2014
Coup d'état. General Prayut Chan-o-cha establishes a military junta, the National Council for Peace and Order (NCPO) and is appointed by the king to govern the nation. The army arrests the former PM and other public figures, dissolves the Senate and announces an interim constitution.

2015
On 17 August a bomb explodes at the Erawan shrine, central Bangkok, killing 20 people and injuring 125, mostly tourists. No-one claims responsibility.

2016
King Bhumibol Adulyadej dies, having reigned for 70 years. His son Maha Vajiralongkorn ascends to the throne, but his coronation is delayed to allow for a period of mourning.

2017
King Maha Vajiralongkorn (Rama X) signs a new, military-drafted constitution.

2019
Prayut Chan-o-cha's is re-elected as prime minister. King Maha Vajiralongkorn (Rama X) celebrates his coronation after his marriage to General Suthida Vajiralongkorn Na Ayudhya.

Prime Minister Prayut Chan-o-cha.

Bronze Ganesha, in Sukhothai style.

EARLY HISTORY

Following on from the earliest Ban Chiang and Indic Srivijaya civilisations, the ethnic Thais migrated from southern China into the region in the 10th century AD. Surrounded by powerful neighbours – the Khmers and Mon – they later established the independent state of Sukhothai.

The earliest known civilisation in Thailand dates from around 3,600 BC, when the people of Ban Chiang in the northeast of Thailand developed bronze tools, fired pottery, and began to cultivate wet paddy rice and rear domesticated animals. At this time, the Tai people, who have given their name to the country, did not inhabit the region that makes up present-day Thailand, but were thought to have been living in loosely organised groups in what is now southern China. The identity of the original Ban Chiang people, however, remains a mystery. According to archaeological timetables, the Ban Chiang settlement appears to have lasted until 250 BC, after which the people seem to have faded from history.

Ban Chiang pottery, northeast Thailand.

THE INDIAN INFLUENCE

As early as 300 BC, Indian traders began arriving in Southeast Asia, including peninsular Thailand, in search of fragrant woods, pearls and especially gold – hence the region became known as Suvarnabhumi, or "Golden Land". These traders brought with them both Hinduism and Buddhism, which became established in southern Thailand by the 1st century AD. By about AD 500, a loosely knit kingdom called Srivijaya had emerged, encompassing the coastal areas of Sumatra, peninsular Malaya and Thailand, as well as parts of Borneo. Ruled by *maharajah*, or kings, its people practised both Hinduism and Buddhism. Sustained by brisk trade with India and China, Srivijaya flourished for almost 700 years.

From the 10th century onwards, the power of Srivijaya began to decline, weakened by a series of wars with the Javanese, which disrupted trade. In the 11th century, a rival power centre arose at Melayu, a port believed to have been located further up the Sumatran coast, possibly in what is now Jambi Province. (Melayu's influence is indicated by the fact that the name is the origin of the word "Malay".) The power of the Hindu kings was also undermined by the arrival of Muslim traders and teachers who began to spread Islam in Sumatra along the coast of the Malay Peninsula. By the late 13th century, the Siamese kings of Sukhothai would bring much of the Malay Peninsula under their control. Nevertheless, the great wealth of the region, with its rich resources of aromatic timber, sea products, gold, tin, spices and resins, kept Srivijaya prosperous until its eventual demise in the 14th century.

THE MON KINGDOM OF DVARAVATI

While the Srivijaya kingdom dominated the southern part of the Malay Peninsula, another group, the Mon, established themselves in the northern part of the Thai Peninsula and the Chao Phraya River valley. The Mon's Dvaravati kingdom flourished from the 6th to the 9th centuries, with Nakhon Pathom, U Thong and Lopburi as its major settlements. Like the Srivijaya kingdom, Dvaravati, too, was strongly influenced by Indian culture and religion. Its Mon people

Elephant on an old temple mural.

played a central role in the introduction of Buddhism to present-day Thailand.

It is not clear whether Dvaravati was a single, unitary state under the control of a powerful ruler, or a loose confederation of small principalities. What is documented is that the Mon had succumbed to pressure from the north by the 11th century as the Tai people moved south into Nakhon Pathom and Lopburi, but absorbing much of Mon culture with its dominant Buddhist religion along the way.

THE KHMER EMPIRE

Over in the east, another major power – the Khmer empire of Angkor, forerunner of present-day Cambodia – had begun stamping its

The term "Tai" is used for the original ethnic group believed to have moved south from China into Thailand (and Laos) some time after AD 1000. The ethnic group is sometimes, incorrectly, called "Thai"

influence on what is now eastern Thailand, covering an area that extends all the way from the Chao Phraya valley to the Cambodian frontier, as well as northwards as far as Laos. Strongly influenced by Indian culture, the Khmer civilisation reached its zenith under the reign of Suryavarman II (1113–50), during which time the temple of Angkor Wat in Cambodia was built. Suryavarman united the kingdom, conquering the Dvaravati lands and areas west to the border with the kingdom of Pagan (Bagan), and expanded as far south into the Malay Peninsula as Nakhon Si Thammarat, dominating the entire coast of the Gulf of Siam.

The next great Khmer ruler was Jayavarman VII (1181–1219), who defeated the Cham people, unified the empire and initiated a series of astonishing building projects. His work finally culminated in the construction of Angkor Thom, probably the greatest city in the world at the time, with a population estimated at around 1 million. Yet this was to be the last flowering of Khmer independence until modern times. Like the Dvaravati and Srivijaya kingdoms, the Khmer empire would fall victim to the emerging power that would become known as Thailand.

ARRIVAL OF THE TAIS

There are several interesting theories to explain the arrival of the Tai people in what would eventually become Thailand. The most persuasive one suggests that from as early as the 10th century, various tribes of Tai people living in China's Yunnan region migrated down rivers and streams into the upper valleys of the Southeast Asian river system. The Shan (also known as Tai Yai) settled in Upper Burma; the Ahom settled Assam in northeast India; while other groups settled in Laos and northern Vietnam.

Within Thailand, the first of these groups settled around Chiang Saen in the far north around 1150. They formed themselves into principalities, some of which later became independent kingdoms. The earliest was established in 1238, at Sukhothai. Then came Chiang Rai in 1281, and then Chiang Mai in 1296. Long after the main group of Tais moved further down the peninsula to establish more powerful states, Chiang Mai continued to rule more or less autonomously over the northern region, maintaining the distinctive Lanna culture of its own.

By the 13th century, the Tai had begun to emerge as the dominant rulers of the region, and slowly started to absorb the weakened empires of the Mon and Khmers.

SUKHOTHAI, THE FIRST TAI/ THAI KINGDOM

Sukhothai, roughly halfway between Bangkok and Chiang Mai, was part of the Khmer empire until 1238, when two Tai chieftains seceded and established the first independent Tai kingdom. This event is considered to mark the founding of the modern Thai nation, and from this point we can begin to speak of "Thais" rather than "Tais". Rather confusingly, for all of Thai history from this point until the modern era, "Thai" is broadly interchangeable with "Siamese", and "Thailand" with "Siam".

Praying deities, c.13th–15th century.

THE LEGEND OF SUKHOTHAI

Siamese tradition attributes the founding of the kingdom of Sukhothai to Phra Ruang, a mythological hero. Prior to his time, according to historical legend, the Tai people were forced to pay tribute to the Khmer rulers of Angkor. This tribute was exacted in the form of sacred water from a lake outside Lopburi; the Khmer god-king needed holy water from all corners of the empire for his ceremonial rites, a practice later adopted by Thai kings.

Every three years, the water tribute was sent by bullock carts in earthenware jars. The jars cracked en route, compelling the tribute payers to make second and third journeys to fill the required quota. When Phra Ruang came of age, he devised a new system of transporting water in sealed woven bamboo containers, which arrived in Angkor intact. This success aroused the suspicion of the Khmer king. His chief astrologer said the ingenious Thai inventor was a person with supernatural powers who posed a threat to the empire. The king at once resolved to eliminate the Thai menace, and sent an army westwards.

Phra Ruang perceived the danger and went to Sukhothai, where he was a monk at Wat Mahathat. The Khmers were defeated, and Phra Ruang's fame rose. He left the monkhood, married the daughter of Sukhothai's ruler, and when that monarch died, he was invited to the throne. Fact and fiction are inseparable in this account.

Sukhothai represents the birth of the Thai nation, although other less well-known Tai states, such as Lanna, Phayao and Chiang Saen, were established at about the same time. Sukhothai was able to expand by forming alliances with the other Tai kingdoms and adopted Theravada Buddhism as the state religion with the help of Sri Lankan monks.

Under the rule of King Ramkhamhaeng (1280–98), Sukhothai enjoyed a golden age of prosperity. During his long reign, the present Thai alphabet evolved, Theravada Buddhism became more entrenched, and the foundations of present-day Thailand were securely established. King Ramkhamhaeng expanded his control over the former Mon and Khmer territories in the south as far as the Andaman Sea and Nakhon Si Thammarat on the Gulf of Thailand coast, as well as over the Chao Phraya valley and southeast into present-day Cambodia.

With the creation of the kingdom of Sukhothai, a new political structure came into being across mainland Southeast Asia. A new and

Wat Mahathat, Sukhothai.

KING RAMKHAMHAENG'S LEGACY

King Ramkhamhaeng (1280–98) was a devout Buddhist of the Theravada school that was practised in Sukhothai. Exchanges were initiated with Sri Lankan monks that resulted in a purification of texts and an adoption of Sinhalese influences in the design of the *chedi*. There remained, however, a trace of animism in Thai Buddhism. Ramkhamhaeng wrote about a mountain-dwelling ghost named Phra Khapung Phi. If correctly propitiated, the spirit would bring prosperity to the country. The idea of a superior spirit looking after the Thai nation survives today in the image of Phra Siam Devadhiraj, Siam's guardian angel.

Sukhothai Buddha images, characterised by their refined facial features, fluidity and harmony of form, are perhaps the most beautiful of Thai artistic expressions.

One of the keys to King Ramkhamhaeng's political success lay in his diplomatic relations with China. The Mongol court in China pursued a divide-and-rule policy and supported the Thais' rise, but at the expense of the Khmers. Ramkhamhaeng was said to have gone to China himself – the *History of the Yuan* records seven missions from Sien (Siam) between 1282 and 1323. Chinese craftsmen came to teach the Thais their secrets of glazing pottery, resulting in the ceramic ware of Sawankhalok, whose products were shipped to China on Siamese junks.

vigorous state subdued the Mon and absorbed broad swathes of territory from both Srivijaya and the Khmer empire. At the same time, the Thai newcomers, an ethnically Sinitic people, intermarried with the inhabitants of the states they had supplanted, and adopted their Indianised culture.

THE KINGDOM OF LANNA

Long after the main group of Thais moved further down the peninsula to establish Ayutthaya, Chiang Mai remained independent as the King-

A 15th-century Lanna gold crown, complete with rubies and pearls.

dom of Lanna, or "One Million Rice Paddies", maintaining a distinctive culture of its own. With its capital at Chiang Mai, the "New City" founded by King Mangrai (1259–1317) in 1296, Lanna's territorial limits extended far beyond present-day northern Thailand, into Burma's Shan State, China's Xishuangbanna region, and western Laos.

For the next two and a half centuries, Lanna flourished as an independent state, trading and exchanging goods and ideas with neighbouring countries. Links were established with distant Sri Lanka via the Burmese port of Martaban, and Theravadan monks travelled between the great Sri Lankan Buddhist centre

> *King Mangrai of Lanna was struck by lightning in the year 1317. By this time he had founded not just a kingdom, but a dynasty that would rule northern Thailand for the next two centuries.*

of Anuradhapura and Chiang Mai. As a result of these links, King Tilokaraja sponsored the Eighth Buddhist Council at Chiang Mai in 1477. Delegates travelled to the council from Pegu,

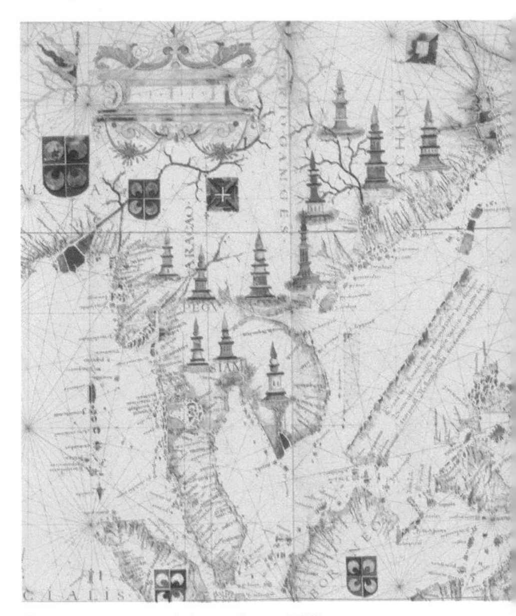

Portuguese map of the region, c.1575.

Sri Lanka and all over the Buddhist world. Lanna was in its prime, a respected regional power able to deal on equal footing with both Burma and Ayutthaya.

Inevitably, there were wars too. The kings of Chiang Mai were under constant pressure from the Siamese to the south, and during the century of decline that followed the death of King Tilokaraja in 1487, the Lanna kingdom suffered attacks not just from Ayutthaya, but also from Burma, Laos and even Vietnam. In 1558, King Bayinnaung of Pegu succeeded in occupying Chiang Mai, and for the next two centuries Lanna became a tributary province of Burma, although it still remained very much part of the Thai world.

FROM AYUTTHAYA TO THE 1932 COUP

The rulers of Ayutthaya oversaw the increasing influence of European traders in the region. Brief subjugation by the Burmese was followed by the emergence of the long-lasting Chakri Dynasty, before the absolute power of the kings was brought to an abrupt end by the 1932 coup d'état.

The glories of Sukhothai, the first Tai kingdom, were to be short lived. During the early 14th century, a rival state began to develop in the lower Chao Phraya valley, centred on the ancient Khmer city of Lopburi, close to present-day Bangkok. In 1350, the ambitious ruler, known as Phaya U Thong, moved his capital from Lopburi to a nearby island in the river, which would be more defendable, giving the new city the name Ayutthaya, and proclaiming himself King Ramathibodi (1351–69). He declared Theravada Buddhism the state religion, invited Buddhist monks from Sri Lanka to help purify and spread the faith, and compiled a legal code based on the Indian Dharmashastra which would remain largely in force until the 19th century.

Ayutthaya soon eclipsed Sukhothai as the leading Thai kingdom, and by the end of the 14th century it had become the strongest power in Southeast Asia, even though it lacked the manpower to dominate the region fully. In the last year of his reign, Ramathibodi seized Angkor during what was to be the first of many successful Thai assaults on the Khmer capital. The weakened Khmer periodically submitted to Ayutthaya's suzerainty, but efforts to maintain continued control over Angkor were repeatedly frustrated. Forces were also diverted to suppress rebellion in Sukhothai and to campaign against Chiang Mai, where Ayutthaya's expansion was tenaciously resisted. Eventually, Ayutthaya subdued Sukhothai, and after Ramathibodi died in 1369, his kingdom was recognised by the Hongwu emperor of China's newly established Ming Dynasty as Sukhothai's rightful successor.

Ayutthaya at this time was not a single, unified state but rather a patchwork of self-governing principalities and tributary provinces owing allegiance to the king. These states were ruled by members of the royal family of Ayutthaya who had their own armies and warred among themselves. The king had to be vigilant in order to prevent royal princes from combining against him or allying with Ayutthaya's enemies.

Crypt mural detail, Wat Rachaburana, Ayutthaya.

During the 15th century, most of Ayutthaya's energies were directed southwards, towards the Malay Peninsula, where the great trading port of Malacca contested its claims to sovereignty. Malacca and other Malay states to the south of Nakhon Si Thammarat had become Muslim early in the century, and thereafter Islam served as a unifying symbol of Malay solidarity against the Thais. Although it failed to make a vassal state of Malacca, Ayutthaya established control over much of the peninsula, making both the Andaman Sea and the Gulf of Siam coasts definitively Thai as far south as Hat Yai, and extending its authority further south over the Malay regions of Pattani and Kelantan.

EUROPEANS AND BURMESE

The 16th century was marked by the first arrival of Europeans, as well as by almost continual conflict with the Burmese. The Portuguese had conquered Malacca in 1511, and soon thereafter their ships sailed to Siam. King Ramathibodi II (1491–1529) granted the newcomers permission to reside and trade within the kingdom in return for arms and ammunition. Portuguese mercenaries fought alongside the king in campaigns against Chiang Mai and taught the Thais the arts of cannon foundry and musketry.

In 1569, Burmese forces captured the city of Ayutthaya and exiled the royal family to Burma. A vassal ruler, King Thammaracha (1569–90), was appointed king, before his son, King Naresuan the Great (1590–1605) succeeded in restoring Siamese independence for a further century and a half. The reign of Naresuan's brother, Ekatotsarot (1605–10) coincided with the arrival of the Dutch, who opened their first trading station at Ayutthaya, in 1608. Keen to promote commercial relations, Ekatotsarot sent emissaries to The Hague, the first recorded appearance of Thais in Europe.

During the reign of Songtham (1610–28), the English arrived bearing a letter from King James I. Like the Dutch, they were welcomed and allotted a plot of land on which to build.

Following the death of Songtham, Prasat Thong (1629-1656) ascended the throne after a power struggle and ruled for 27 years, during which foreign trade continued to develop. Europeans were primarily attracted to Siam as a gateway to the riches of China. The nature of

Burmese and Siamese armies engaged in combat, c.1593.

AYUTTHAYA'S FOUNDER

Legend has it that the king of Traitrung unhappily discovered that his unmarried daughter had given birth after eating an aubergine, which a vegetable gardener had fertilised with his urine. The culprit – Nai Saen Pom, or Man With a Hundred Thousand Warts – was banished from the city, along with the princess and their son. The god Indra took pity on the trio and granted the gardener three wishes. Saen Pom first asked for his warts to disappear. Next, he prayed for a kingdom to rule over. Finally, he asked for a cradle of gold for his son. The child, named Phaya U Thong (Prince of the Golden Crib), later became the first ruler of Ayutthaya, taking the name Ramathibodi I.

seasonal monsoons made direct sailing to China impossible, so Ayutthaya and its ports became entrepôts for goods travelling between Europe, India and the East Indies, China and Japan. The Siamese home market was also quite substantial. The peace initiated by Naresuan had given rise to a surplus of wealth, which created a demand in Thai society for luxury items like porcelain and silk. The Japanese, who had already established a sizeable community of traders at Ayutthaya, paid in silver for local Siamese products such as hides, teak, tin and sugar.

It was the French who gained the greatest favour in Narai's court. French Jesuit missionaries first arrived at the court of Ayutthaya in 1665. The king's friendliness and religious tolerance were taken by the bishops as a sign of his imminent conversion. Their exaggerated accounts excited the imagination of Louis XIV, who hoped that the salvation of Siamese heathens could be combined with French territorial acquisition. Narai was delighted to receive a personal letter from the Sun King in 1673, but he did not convert and would remain a good Buddhist all his life.

Mural image of a 17th-century European adventurer.

The Dutch established maritime dominance in the East when they drove the Portuguese out of Malacca in 1641. Seven years later, they made a show of naval force in the Gulf of Thailand, thereby persuading the Ayutthaya court to agree to certain trade concessions and giving the Dutch virtual economic control in Siam.

KING NARAI

The new king, Narai (1656–88), mistrusted the Dutch and welcomed the English as a European ally to counter Holland's influence. But another Dutch blockade, in 1664, this time at the mouth of the Chao Phraya River, won them a monopoly on the hide trade and, for the first time in Thai history, extraterritorial privileges.

The presence of Europeans throughout Narai's reign – including that of Constantine Phaulkon – gave the West most of its early knowledge of Siam. Western visitors to Narai's court generated much literature and their attempts at cartography left a record of Ayutthaya's appearance, though few maps exist today. Royal palaces and hundreds of temples crowded the area within the walls around the island on which the capital stood. Some Western visitors called Ayutthaya "the most beautiful city in the east".

The kings who succeeded Narai ended his open-door policy. A modest amount of trade was maintained and missionaries were permitted to remain, but Ayutthaya embarked on a course of isolation that lasted about 150 years.

THE KINGDOM OF THONBURI

In 1767, the Burmese armies once again invaded, destroying the capital and scattering the defending forces. Ayutthaya's art treasures, the libraries containing its literature and the archives housing its historic records were looted, and the city was left in ruins.

Against the odds, Siam made a rapid recovery. A noble of Chinese descent named Taksin led the resistance. From his base at Chanthaburi on the southeast coast, he defeated the Burmese within a year and re-established the Siamese state with a capital at Thonburi on the west bank of the Chao Phraya River. In 1768, he was crowned King Taksin, and would posthumously become Taksin the Great. Taksin rapidly reunited the central Thai heartlands under his rule, and in 1769 conquered Cambodia. He then marched south and re-established Siamese rule over all southern Thailand and the Malay States as far south as Penang and Terengganu.

18th-century illustrated manuscript from Thonburi.

Although a brilliant military strategist, by 1779 Taksin was in trouble. He alienated the Buddhist establishment by claiming to be in the possession of divine powers, and attacked the economically powerful Chinese merchants. In 1782, he sent his armies under General Chao Phaya Chakri to invade Cambodia, and while they were away, a rebellion broke out near the capital. The rebels, who commanded widespread popular support, offered the throne to General Chakri, who accepted. Taksin was subsequently executed, an ignominious end to an able leader.

THE CHAKRI DYNASTY

After ascending the throne on 6 April 1782 – a day commemorated today in Thailand as Chakri Day – Chao Phaya Chakri took the name Phra Phutthayotfa. Later known as Rama I (1782–1809), he became the founding father of the

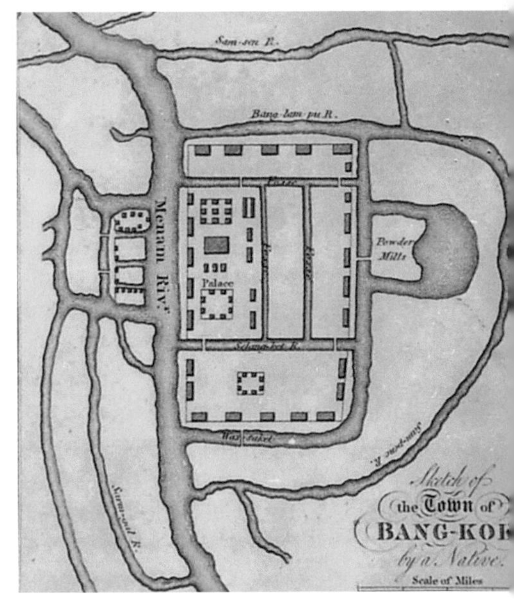

Early map of Bangkok.

PHAULKON THE GREEK

Constantine Phaulkon was a Greek who began his career as a cabin boy with the East India Company. He arrived in Siam in 1678, quickly learnt Thai and rose through Thai society to the rank of Phaya Vijayendra. In this powerful position, he had access to King Narai. The crafty Phaulkon also ingratiated himself to the French by promising to convert the Thais to Roman Catholicism (which, of course, never came to pass). In the meantime, high-ranking Thai court officials became irked by Phaulkon's extravagant lifestyle and his influence on King Narai. When Narai fell ill in 1688, an anti-French faction of the court took over. Phaulkon was arrested for treason and executed.

Chakri Dynasty – which continues in place to this day. Uniquely in this part of Asia, the dynasty managed to maintain formal Thai independence (albeit somewhat compromised at times) from the European colonial powers.

During his rule, Rama I would prove to be a strong and far-sighted king who not only laid firm foundations for modern Thailand's security and prosperity, but also launched an assiduous cultural revival programme. One of his first decisions was to move the capital across the Chao Phraya River from Thonburi to a small settlement on the east bank called Bang Makok, the "place of olive plums". Here he built a new grand palace and laid out the ground plan for an artificial island, protected from attack by the river to the west and by a series of canals to the north, east and south. Called Ko Rattanakosin, it would become the heart

> *After his abdication, Taksin was executed in the traditional manner reserved for royals; a blow to the neck by a sandalwood club concealed in a velvet bag.*

19th-century Siamese women.

CHAKRI KINGS TIMELINE

Since 1782, the Chakri Dynasty has lorded over Thailand.

Reign Title *Name*

1782–1809 Rama I *Chakri*

1809–24 Rama II *Phuttayotfa*

1824–51 Rama III *Nangklao*

1851–68 Rama IV *Mongkut*

1868–1910 Rama V *Chulalongkorn*

1910–25 Rama VI *Vajiravudh*

1925–35 Rama VII *Prajadhipok*

1935–46 Rama VIII *Ananda Mahidol*

1946–2016 Rama IX *Bhumibol Adulyadej*

2016–present Rama X Maha Vajiralongkorn

of the Chakri realm and contain the principal components of the Thai nation: those representing religion, monarchy and administration.

The lofty Wat Phra Kaew, or the "Temple of the Emerald Buddha", was constructed in 1784 to house the country's most revered Buddha image, which was brought from Thonburi earlier. Next on Rama I's agenda was the Grand Palace. He also restored much of the social and political system of Ayutthaya, promulgating new law codes, reinstating court ceremonies and imposing discipline on the Buddhist *sangha* (monkhood).

RAMA II AND RAMA III

King Rama I's successors, Rama II and Rama III, completed the consolidation of the Siamese kingdom and the revival of Ayutthaya's arts and culture. Best remembered as an artist, Rama II (1809–24) was responsible for building and repairing numerous Bangkok monasteries. His most famous creation was Wat Arun, or the Temple of Dawn, on the Thonburi side of the Chao Phraya River. He is also said to have carved the doors of Bangkok's Wat Suthat. Rama II also reopened relations with the West, which had been suspended since the time of King Narai.

Rama III (1824–51) continued his predecessor's policy of opening Siam's doors to foreigners. An extremely pious Buddhist, he was considered to be "austere and reactionary" by Europeans. One thing he is remembered for is encouraging missionaries to introduce Western medicine, including the smallpox vaccine, to Thailand.

KING MONGKUT (RAMA IV)

King Rama IV (1851–68), loosely represented in the Hollywood film *The King and I*, was a modern-minded and learned scholar who studied English and Latin as well as Pali and Sanskrit. A monk for many years before his accession

Wat Arun, legacy of Rama II.

THE LONGEST PLACE NAME IN THE WORLD

When King Rama I established the new capital on a bend in the Chao Phraya River in 1782, he wisely chose an easily defendable site where an old settlement, called Bang Makok – or Bangkok for short – already existed. The name translates as "place of olive plums", and King Rama I deemed it insufficiently noble for a royal city.

Hence, the capital was given a new name (take a deep breath): *Krung Thep Mahanakhon Amon Rattanakosin Mahinthara Yuthaya Mahadilok Phop Noppharat Ratchathani Burirom Udomratchaniwet Mahasathan Amon Phiman Awatan Sathit Sakkathattiya Witsanukam Prasit*, which is officially the longest place name in the world. And yes, it is written in Thai script without a single break. In English, the name may be rendered: "Great City of Angels, City of Immortals, Magnificent Jewelled City of the God Indra, Seat of the King of Ayutthaya, City of Gleaming Temples, City of the King's Most Excellent Palace and Dominions, Home of Vishnu and All the Gods".

How do the Thais get around the verbiage? Quite simply, they style their capital city Great City of Angels, etc. in official usage, but quite practically refer to it by just the first two syllables, Krung Thep – City of Angels – in everyday speech. Whatever you call it, Bangkok or Krung Thep is today the thriving metropolis that dominates Thailand, and is 40 times larger than any other city in the kingdom.

to the throne – which had given him a unique opportunity to roam as a commoner among the populace – he studied history, geography and the sciences, especially astronomy.

Better known as King Mongkut, Rama IV realised that traditional Thai values alone would not save his country from Western encroachments. Instead, he made the momentous decision to Westernise many of the country's institutions, believing that modernisation would bring Siam in line with the West and reduce hostilities with foreigners.

Rama V (King Chulalongkorn) r.1868–1910.

DEATH OF AN ASTRONOMER

Mongkut's beloved hobby, astronomy, was the indirect cause of his death. From observatories at his favourite palaces, the Summer Palace at Bang Pa-In and the Palace on the Hill, at Phetchburi, he successfully calculated and predicted a total eclipse of the sun in 1868. European and Asian sceptics joined him on the southeastern coast of the Gulf of Thailand to await the event. As the moon blocked the sun's light, both the Europeans and the scoffers among the royal astrologers raised an exclamation of admiration, raising the king's esteem among both parties. But his triumph was short-lived. The king contracted malaria during the trip, and died two weeks later from it.

Britain was the first European country to benefit from this policy, when an 1855 treaty – not gained entirely without coercion by the British – granted extraterritorial privileges: a duty of only three percent on imports, and permission to import Indian opium duty-free. Other Western nations, including France and the United States, followed suit with similar treaties.

Together with his son and successor Chulalongkorn, this approach means that he can be considered chiefly responsible for Thailand's continued independence throughout the colonial period. To this day Thais reserve a special place in their hearts for both these monarchs.

KING CHULALONGKORN (RAMA V)

King Mongkut's son, King Rama V (1868–1910), also widely known as King Chulalongkorn, ascended the throne in 1868 when he was only 15 years old. By the time of his death, 42 years later, he had become the "Beloved Great King", a father-figure for his people and perhaps the most popular Thai monarch ever. A man of remarkable foresight, Chulalongkorn instituted a veritable revolution from above, abolishing serfdom and ending the ancient custom of ritual prostration in the presence of the ruler. He brought in foreign advisers and sent his sons to study at universities across Europe.

Chulalongkorn's contributions to the cultural heritage of Bangkok included the construction of Dusit Palace, Rajadamnoen Avenue and the palace and pleasure-gardens of Bang Pa-In. When he died in 1910, a grieving nation posthumously awarded him the title *Phya Maharaj*, or "Beloved Great King".

In the area of foreign relations, however, Chulalongkorn had to compromise and give up parts of his kingdom in order to protect Siam from foreign colonisation. When France conquered Annam (Vietnam) in 1883 and Britain annexed Upper Burma three years later, Siam found itself sandwiched between the two rival powers. It was forced to surrender to France its claims to Laos and western Cambodia. Similarly, in 1909, certain Malay territories were ceded to Britain in exchange for renunciation of British extraterritorial rights in Siam. But that was a small price for maintaining the country's peace and independence. Unlike its neighbours, Siam was never under colonial rule (unless one counts the Japanese occupation of 1941–5).

Before the reign of King Rama VI (Vajiravudh) most Thai people did not have surnames, a practice that the king considered to be uncivilised. (Even today, it is common practice to refer to Thai people by their first names only.)

RAMA VI AND RAMA VII

King Rama V was succeeded by King Vajiravudh (Rama VI), who reigned from 1910 to 1925. Being Oxford-educated and thoroughly Anglicised, he introduced Western-inspired reforms to modernise his country. Primary education was made compulsory throughout the kingdom; Chulalongkorn University, the first in Siam, was founded, and schools for both sexes flourished during his reign. Vajiravudh was, however, criticised as autocratic and lacking in coordination. His extravagance soon emptied the funds built up by Chulalongkorn; near the end of Vajiravudh's reign, the national treasury had to meet the deficits caused by his personal expenses.

Following his brother's early death in 1925, King Prajadhipok (Rama VII) succeeded the throne. Unlike the former, he tried to cut public expenditure by drastically reducing civil service and royal household expenses. Prajadhipok's economic policies, combined with increased revenue from foreign trade, amply paid off for the kingdom.

The worldwide economic crisis of the 1930s, however, affected Siam's rice export. Prajadhipok dropped the gold standard, linking the Thai baht to the pound sterling, but it was too late to stem the financial crisis. The government was forced to implement further measures, such as cutting the salaries of junior personnel and retrenching the armed forces, which fuelled much discontent in the process.

Royal barges along the Chao Phraya River at Prajadhipok's (Rama VII) 1925 coronation.

COUP D'ÉTAT AND WORLD WAR II

In 1932, a coup staged by the People's Party – a military and civilian group masterminded by foreign-educated Thais – ended the absolute power of the Thai monarchs. The chief ideologist was Pridi Panomyong, a young lawyer trained in France. On the military side Plaek Phibunsongkhram (Pibul) was responsible for gaining the support of important army colonels. At the time, King Prajadhipok was in Hua Hin, a royal retreat to the south. Perceiving he had little choice and to avoid bloodshed, he agreed to accept a provisional constitution by which he continued to reign. For the next 14 years, Siam would be without a resident monarch, and power would lie with the military.

On the edge of Bangkok, 1950.

CONTEMPORARY THAILAND

The constitutional monarchy that followed the 1932 coup d'état has proved a stabilising anchor amid the upheavals that continue to characterise the country's modern history.

The years leading up to World War II were characterised by a number of political power struggles. Following the 1932 coup, the power of Plaek Phibunsongkhram (Pibul) and the army was further strengthened by the decisive defeat of a rebellion in October 1933 led by Prince Boworadet, who had been the war minister under King Prajadhipok. The king had no part in the rebellion, but had become increasingly dismayed by quarrels within the new government. He moved to England in 1934 and abdicated in 1935. Ananda Mahidol (Rama VIII), a 10-year-old half-nephew, agreed to take the throne, but remained in Switzerland to complete his studies.

After a series of crises and an election in 1938, Pibul became prime minister. His rule, however, grew more authoritarian, and he was famous for whipping up sentiment against the Chinese. Borrowing many ideas from European fascism, he attempted to instil a sense of mass nationalism in the Thais. In 1939, Pibul ordered the name of the country to be officially changed from Siam to Thailand, and adopted the current national flag.

POST-WORLD WAR II

On 7 December 1941, the Japanese bombed Pearl Harbor and launched invasions throughout Southeast Asia. Resistance lasted less than a day, despite a decade of military build-up and Thailand was overrun. Pibul acceded to Japan's request for "passage rights", but Thailand was allowed to retain its army and political administration. By 1944, Thailand's initial enthusiasm for its Japanese overlords had evaporated. The country faced runaway inflation, food shortages, rationing and black markets.

King Maha Vajiralongkorn.

In 1946, while on a visit to Thailand from Europe, the now-adult King Ananda was found shot dead in his bedroom. He was succeeded by his younger brother, Bhumibol Adulyadej (Rama IX), who returned to Switzerland to complete law studies. He did not, however, take up active duties until the 1950s.

The first few years after the end of World War II were marked by a series of democratic civilian governments. In 1948, under threat of military force, Pibul assumed power again, ushering in a period marked by strife, failed coup attempts and corruption. In 1957 he was overthrown by a clique of one-time protégés. The leader, General Sarit Thanarat, and two crony generals, Thanom Kittikachorn and Prapas Charusathien, ran the

A MUCH-LOVED MONARCHY

King Bhumibol reigned as Thailand's monarch for seven decades, remaining incredibly popular throughout the country, as well as exercising considerable influence.

Ever since the first independent Thai kingdom was established more than seven centuries ago, Thailand has been ruled by kings. Although the 1932 revolution ended absolute monarchy and replaced it with the constitutional variety, Thais continue to love and honour their royal family.

King Bhumibol Adulyadej's coronation, 1946.

Most Thais are confirmed monarchists, with the throne making up one of the three central pillars of the national polity: – in Thai, *chat*, *sat* and *prama-hakasat* – Thai Nation, Buddhist Religion and Chakri Dynasty. It is hard to overestimate the affection and respect Thais and non-Buddhish minorities feel for their kings.

KING BHUMIBOL

Thailand's former monarch, King Bhumibol Adulyadej, acceded to the throne in 1946. Born in Massachusetts, Bhumibol proved to be an able leader. Perhaps because of his ability to reach the common man, he was extremely popular, shared only by his grandfather, King Chulalongkorn.

Although Bhumibol was a constitutional monarch, because of the affection in which he was held by Thais, he played a political role, occasionally intervening when he felt politicians had got out of hand. In May 1992, when military strongman Suchinda Krapayoon seized power in a coup, the king intervened to end three days of riots and killings when soldiers fired on demonstrators. Suchinda was forced to resiqn in disgrace, and democracy was restored.

King Bhumibol made it clear on a number of occasions that he disapproved of ex-Prime Minister Thaksin Shinawatra's executive style of government. In 2008, two years after the military coup that removed Thaksin from power, Queen Sirikit presided at the funeral of a People's Alliance for Democracy street protestor, which was generally regarded as a tacit admission of support. The general acceptance in the media and among Thaksin supporters that "the traditional elite" were behind the coup led to unprecedented public criticism of "the highest institution" in some quarters. The country's lèse-majesté laws were used widely to silence political rivals from all sides.

KING MAHA VAJIRALONGKORN

On 13 October 2016, aged 88, King Bhumibol passed away. A period of national mourning ensued. As the only son of King Bhumibol and Queen Sirikit, Maha Vajiralongkorn took the throne in December 2016, as Rama X. He made a big impact, endorsing a military-backed constitution in April 2017, but not before requesting amendments. He celebrated his coronation in May 2019.

The monarchy costs the Thai treasury nothing, at least not directly, since the royal family pays its own way with income from property holdings and investments. The royal family earns their respect through its own enterprise. The king's grandmother initiated a series of agricultural projects that reduced opium production in the north, while his mother worked to preserve Thai traditional arts and crafts and led a programme to provide rural folk with the skills to produce these crafts. There are numerous royal ceremonies, such as the seasonal robing of the Emerald Buddha, and various traditional Buddhist holy days.

Bangkok's Democracy Monument was built in 1939 to commemorate the 1932 revolution. Since the 1970s it has been the focus of many pro-democracy protests, and the scene of much bloodshed.

government until 1973 under martial law. All three men used their power to amass huge personal fortunes, but they also deserve some credit for developing Thailand. Health standards improved, the business sector expanded, construction boomed and a middle class began to emerge. These socio-economic changes would, in turn, lead to new aspirations among the Thais.

Anti-government protests in 1975; the banners read "Return my people to me", referring to arrested students.

STRING OF GOVERNMENTS AND COUPS

On 13 October 1973, a demonstration in Bangkok to protest against the military dictatorship turned violent, and at least 100 students were shot by riot police. With the country in turmoil, the army switched sides and the generals fled into exile. For the next two decades, Thailand was chronically unstable: a succession of governments were ousted after periodic clashes with protesting students and a succession of military coups.

In April 1992, public discontent grew when a former coup leader, General Suchinda Krapayoon, assumed the prime ministership without having stood for election. In May 1992, another violent clash between military forces and civilian demonstrators, dubbed "Bloody May" by the media, took place in Bangkok, near Sanam Luang and the Democracy Monument. Killings, beatings and riots went on for three days and only ended when the leaders of both factions were summoned before King Bhumibol. The military bowed out and an unrepentant Suchinda left the country. In the September 1992 re-elections, the Democrat Party and other prominent critics of the military prevailed.

DEMOCRACY IS USHERED IN

Prime Minister Chuan Leekpai, considered honest but ineffectual, held office from 1992 to 1995, and can be credited with diluting the power of military officers in many state enterprises. But for many, he was too passive a leader. No one was held responsible for the 1992 clashes, and the numbers and identity of those who died or disappeared are still in dispute. His coalition finally collapsed in 1995 when wealthy members of Chuan's own party were discovered profiting from a land-reform programme.

Two subsequent elections brought a provincial businessman, Banharn Silpa-archa (1995–6), and a former general, Chavalit Yongchaiyudh (1996–8), to the highest office for brief terms. Both were lambasted for their incompetent handling of the economy, which suddenly went into freefall in 1997, setting off an Asian economic crisis and a massive devaluation of the baht.

In 1998, a Democratic government led by former Prime Minister Chuan Leekpai replaced the Chavalit administration. After two years of hard work and changes in banking and investment laws, the economy began to recover.

Ex-Prime Minister Thaksin Shinawatra.

THE THAKSIN ADMINISTRATION

In 2001, general elections saw the leader of the Thai Rak Thai (TRT) Party, billionaire entrepreneur Thaksin Shinawatra, replace Chuan as premier, amid allegations of vote-buying and rigging. Thaksin's governance proved controversial. He faced corruption charges and was condemned for suppressing the media and for his "War on Drugs", in which hundreds were killed. He is roundly regarded as a self-serving politician who changed laws to further his business interests, although this is far from unusual in Thailand.

Foreign media reported the People's Alliance for Democracy (PAD) or Yellow Shirts were offering cash to mothers and children to join the 2008 airport protest, though this was strenuously denied by party spokesmen.

To Thaksin's credit, his government dealt swiftly and decisively with the fallout from the tsunami on 26 December 2004, which left some 8,000 people dead. He also introduced loans and cheap health care for the poor, and he became wildly popular in poorer rural areas.

But he was irritating traditional powers in Bangkok, and in 2005, anti-Thaksin demonstrators adopted the colour yellow to show allegiance to the monarchy, and became known as the Yellow Shirts. In January 2006, Thaksin was accused of tax evasion after selling his stake one of Thailand's largest telecommunications companies, to Temasek Holdings in Singapore for US$1.9 billion.

THE 2006 COUP AND ITS AFTERMATH

In September 2006, when Thaksin was in New York, the army seized power in a bloodless coup. They instigated a new Constitution and dissolved Thaksin's TRT party.

In the meantime, Thaksin had been working behind the scenes from exile in London. His supporters, calling themselves the United Front for Democracy Against Dictatorship (UDD), and wearing red shirts, launched their own protests. They regrouped politically under the banner of the People's Power Party (PPP), and won the December 2007 general election. In February 2008 Thaksin returned to Thailand, but facing corruption charges, skipped bail and fled abroad.

TURBULENT TIMES

The period from 2008 to 2014 was one of Thailand's most turbulent. In May 2008 the Yellow Shirts took to the streets of Bangkok and later invaded Government House. Street clashes in September left one dead and 43 injured, and Thaksin's puppet Prime Minister, Samak Sundaravej, was forced out to be replaced by Somchai Wongsawat, Thaksin's brother-in-law. In November the Yellow Shirts occupied Suvarnabhumi International Airport, which severely damaged Thailand's reputation around the world and disrupted travel for thousands of passengers.

In December, the courts disbanded the ruling party, and, in a deal largely seen as being brokered by the army, the Democrat Party took office with Abhisit Vejjajiva as prime minister.

In April 2009, Thaksin's Red Shirt supporters disrupted the ASEAN Summit in Pattaya, causing several heads of state to be airlifted to safety, Songkran riots erupted in Bangkok, and Yellow Shirt leader Sondhi Limthongkul was shot, but survived the assassination attempt.

In February 2010, Thaksin was found guilty of abuse of power and had assets of 46 billion baht confiscated. In April and May, thousands of Red Shirt demonstrators occupied parts of Bangkok, closing Pathumwan shopping malls for several weeks. Many buildings were torched, 85 people were killed and nearly 1,500 injured in clashes with the army, mainly on April 10 and May 19.

In 2011, the Thaksin proxy Pheu Thai Party, led by his sister Yingluck, won a landslide election victory and Yingluck became Thailand's first female prime minister.

During 2012 the government pushed for a change to the Constitution and a general amnesty for post-coup events, seen as an attempt to return Thaksin's confiscated assets and allow him a comeback to the country. Opposition came not only from anti-Thaksin quarters wary of a long-term political change away from the traditional ruling elite, but also from red shirts who were against making deals with the elite.

The protests resumed in 2013. About 100,000 people protested on the streets when the blanket amnesty for those involved in 2010 protests was altered to include all political crimes, which critics contended would allow human rights abuses – such as the killing of civilian protestors – to go unpunished. The bill was not passed, but the protests did not stop. A new movement called the People's Democratic Reform Committee (PDRC) emerged and as it gained popularity, it made new demands. Parliament was dissolved and a new election scheduled for February 2014. However, voting was disrupted by the PDRC and the election was annulled. Yingluck was summarily removed from office on 7 May 2014.

On 22 May, two days after the Royal Thai Army introduced martial law, General Prayuth Chan-o-cha assumed power in a military coup. The junta dissolved the government and senate, and repealed the constitution. On 26 May, King Bhumibol formally acknowledged the coup and appointed General Chan-o-cha to run the country as prime minister. An interim constitution was introduced.

Protest in Bangkok.

Immensely popular, King Bhumibol Adulyadej died on 13 October 2016, aged 88, ushering in a period of national mourning and dousing any hopes of a fresh election. He was succeeded by his only son Maha Vajiralongkorn, who became Rama X, the tenth monarch of the Chakri Dynasty.

Meanwhile the post-coup military regime employed stringent measures to crack down on dissent. In August 2016 the Thai people voted for, and in April 2017 King Maha Vajiralongkorn signed, a new, military-drafted constitution, the country's 20th since 1932. A general election was announced for February 2019, with General Chan-o-Cha extending his tenure as prime minister.

Directing the Bangkok traffic.

PEOPLE AND CULTURE

Warm-hearted smiles, a pleasant disposition and a sense of calm: these are the qualities that are readily discerned by visitors to Thailand. But Thais can also be fiercely patriotic; criticisms against the Thai monarchy are not easily tolerated.

Travellers to Thailand are generally struck by the smiles, warmth and friendliness of the local people. There is always amiable concern – not to be interpreted as nosiness – and an openness seldom found elsewhere in the world. The standard greeting is *pai nai*, or "Where are you going?" But this is not meant to be interpreted literally; rather, it is the approximate equivalent of "Hello" or "How are you?" One of the guiding precepts of Thai life is *sanuk*, which means fun or joy. The quantity and quality of *sanuk* in both work and play will often determine whether something is worth pursuing.

Almost as important is the concept of *sabai*, best translated as "comfortable" or "contented". As far as Thai people are concerned, in the best of all possible worlds, life should be both *sanuk* and *sabai*. The antithesis of *sanuk* is *seriat*, a borrowing from the English word "serious". Life just isn't meant to be taken too seriously. Underpinning this light-hearted pursuit of happiness are the Buddhist values of tolerance and acceptance.

Thai children at school.

ETHNIC MIX

Thailand has a population of over 67 million people, more than 90 percent of whom are Theravada Buddhists. Muslims make up around 12 percent of the population and, though they live all over the country, are mostly concentrated in the southern peninsular regions.

Around 14 percent of the population are descendants of Chinese immigrants who mainly relocated from China during the 19th and first half of the 20th century. The Chinese have assimilated remarkably well into local society and have intermarried freely with the Thais. There is no deep-rooted anti-Chinese bias, in contrast with some other parts of Southeast Asia. Living mostly in urban areas and involved in trade and commerce, the Chinese knack for entrepreneurial know-how has ensured that much of the country's wealth is controlled by Sino-Thai families. Other, much smaller, immigrant groups in Thailand include Indians, Khmer, Vietnamese and the various hill tribes (see page 56) living in the north.

Thailand can be divided into four regions: central, north, northeast and south. Each of the regions has its own language variant, cultural traits and distinctive cuisine. Bangkok is the geographical and commercial heart of the country, home to around one in five Thais. It is located in the Central Plain, Thailand's linguistically dominant region. The central Thai dialect is the language spoken by educated Thais from all over the country.

In the mountainous north, once the seat of the ancient Lanna kingdom, people speak a Thai variant called *kham meuang* and share culinary similarities with neighbouring Myanmar. People in the northeast speak Isaan, a language closely related to Lao, and eat their meals with sticky rice. The northeast also happens to be Thailand's poorest region, often subject to debilitating droughts. Many northeasterners leave to seek work as migrant labourers in Bangkok.

The south is a more prosperous region; its beautiful coastal scenery attracts tourists and there are significant fishing and fruit-growing industries. Aside from a small group of Malay-speaking Muslims, most people in this region speak a southern dialect of Thai. Travellers should be aware that in the three southernmost provinces of Yala, Pattani and Narathiwat, civil unrest between Muslims and the Thai government has been rumbling on for many years.

A REVERED MONARCH

At the heart of Thai society is the kingdom's reverence for the Thai monarch, His Majesty King Maha Vajiralongkorn (see page 44). Visitors will be struck at how the national anthem is played before cinema screenings and the audience will stand as a mark of respect to the king. Even when the anthem is played at 8am and 6pm on radio and TV each day, many Thais stop whatever they are doing and stand erect. At offices, shops and houses throughout the land, the king's portrait is prominently portrayed; such is the measure of respect accorded to the Thai monarch.

In fact, on celebratory occasions such as the late King Bhumibol's 80th birthday in 2007 and the anniversary of his ascension, millions of people across the country jam the roads leading to the Royal Plaza during official Bangkok ceremonies. Despite recent political upheavals, overt criticism of the king and royal family is still extremely rare. *Lèse-majesté* laws prevent public critique of the royal institution in the local media and carry a maximum penalty of seven years imprisonment.

HI-SO

Thai society is fiercely hierarchical, with an individual's roles and duties defined by his or her social status. In fact the Thai language uses personal pronouns which indicate whether the speaker is addressing a younger or elder person, or a person of lower or higher status.

The top end of Thai society is known as "Hi-So", a Thai slang abbreviated from "high society", and comprises Thai nobility and wealthy Sino-Thai families. Being Hi-So is as much about glamour and wealth as it is about pedigree (their ranks were swelled by the *nouveaux riches* created during the economic boom of the 1980s and early '90s, but reduced somewhat in the 2008–2010

A Muslim man outside a mosque in Khao Lak.

THAI-STYLE GREETING

Thais greet each other by raising and clasping their hands together in a prayer-like gesture called the *wai*. While the *wai* may look like a simple movement, it is loaded with social nuances. The hands must be held at certain levels between the chest and the forehead, depending on the relative social standing of each person. When greeting a person of higher rank, for instance, the hands must be raised higher to show respect. In response to a child's greeting, an adult may keep his or her hands at the chest level. Modern-day adaptations include the informal one-handed *wai*, used among friends, and no one bats an eyelid when a mobile phone is held in the other hand.

downturn). The Hi-So scene is confined mainly to Bangkok and is frequently depicted in the society pages of the city's newspapers and magazines, like *Thailand Tatler*, with the immaculately attired women sporting big hair and big jewels.

Thailand's growing middle class is largely made up of educated urbanites living on suburban housing estates and working at corporate jobs in the city. Billboards advertising these housing estates are everywhere; they often depict Western-style houses complete with two children and a dog playing in the garden.

Four generations of a Thai family.

The majority of Thai people make up the agrarian segment living in villages and farming the land. The village idyll, however, has changed radically over the past few decades as environmental degradation and poverty have forced many villagers to find work in the big cities as taxi drivers, construction workers and prostitutes. The rural-urban divide is stark, and it is only in recent years that the problems of rural Thailand have been brought to the fore in the capital through the political conflict surrounding ex-Prime Minister Thaksin Shinawatra and coalitions like the Forum of the Poor, which organised protest movements in the capital, striking out at the building of dams and other ruinous government policies.

WOMEN IN THAI SOCIETY

There is an old Thai saying that women are the hind legs of the elephant. And it does hold true to a certain extent; while most of the legal discrimination against women has been largely eliminated, women are still expected to be socially submissive to Thai men. Still, many women maintain power behind the scenes as matriarchs and holders of the family purse-strings. For years, women have also been at the helm of large private businesses as men customarily go into government or the military. Today, Thai women are prominent in the hotel trade, tourism, real estate, advertising, the export trade, banking, medicine and the law. The university population is almost equally male and female, while the government bureaucracy attracts large numbers of women.

In relationship stakes, women generally don't fair too well. It is a well-accepted fact that most Thai men are *chao choo*, or adulterers. The law favours male promiscuity; if a woman is unfaithful, it is ample grounds for divorce but it is not, however, when a man cheats on his wife. The extra-marital affair is semi-formalised in the practice of keeping a *mia noi*, literally "minor wife" or mistress.

SEXUAL ATTITUDES

Thailand has unfortunately acquired a reputation as a sexual playground and although forced prostitution and the exploitation of children is less of a problem than previously, Thailand is still a conduit for trafficked women and minors. Foreign sex tourists might gain most headlines abroad, but most of the clients are in fact Thais. Outside of Bangkok areas like Patpong and Nana Plaza, or Pattaya's more tawdry scene, prostitution in Thailand is similar to elsewhere in the world: brothels exist in almost every medium-sized town, but the rest of society is fairly conservative where sex is concerned.

Tradition still dictates a certain propriety of dress, and public displays of affection are rare. While Western influence has meant that young Thai couples hold hands in public, it is unusual to see anything but very chaste interactions.

Thai people are generally sympathetic in their attitude towards sexuality. Consensual adult homosexuality is tolerated, and *kathoey*, or "lady-boys" – transvestites or men who have undergone a sex change – while discriminated against legally and often the brunt of jokes in TV soap operas, are more accepted and receive more understanding than they do in most societies.

A protestor in Bangkok.

SOCIALISING AND ETIQUETTE THE THAI WAY

The Thai love of fun, or *sanuk*, infuses all social gatherings. They enjoy group activities, and it's always a case of the more the merrier. Generally speaking, Thais hate to be alone, and most are puzzled by the average foreigner's need for occasional solitude.

Thais greet each other with a *wai*, but may use the more intimate *hom kaem* (to smell the cheek), which is simply a sniff against someone's face. Surnames are rarely used, and even relative strangers will refer to each other by their nickname, or *cheu len* (play name). These are most often one-syllable monikers based on animals like Moo (pig), Noo (mouse), or Poo (crab), or are more modern adaptations from English, such as X, Boy or Benz.

There is a sense of family about Thai activities, a gathering that does not exclude outsiders. For the visitor invited to join, there is no automatic expectation of reciprocation, although it is always much appreciated. It is not unusual for a visitor to stray into a small city lane and be invited to join a partying group. Such activities are usually accompanied by music, alcoholic drinks and small snacks. Drunkenness is frowned upon, but a certain tipsiness is acceptable in such circumstances.

Aside from *sanuk*, there are a few particularly Thai concepts that are helpful in understanding Thai culture. One key emotion is *kraeng jai*, which denotes an unwillingness to impose on other people. This often means that emotions such as anger or displeasure are hidden away, and tension and conflict avoided at all cost. Thais place a high value on equanimity and will go to great lengths to prevent confrontation. Neither do they like saying "no" too directly for fear of causing offence.

Connected to this is the idea of *jai yen*, or "cool heart": it is imperative for Thais to keep a cool

Thai policeman.

and calm heart in all situations. To lose your temper or to raise your voice in public is seen as a severe loss of face; problems should always be dealt with in a friendly manner and with equanimity. Those unable to maintain this cool veneer are considered to be *jai ron*, or "hot-hearted".

It is difficult to stir a Thai to real anger. A smile and an apology should deflate almost any tense situation. Anger, demonstrated by physical violence or raised voices, can provoke serious hostility, however, and an angry Thai can be aggressive indeed. For example, touching a Thai (especially on the top of the head), shouting, or threatening the strong sense of independence that Thais have may effect an immediate and often hostile response. Visitors should also avoid pointing their

The three colours of the Thai flag represent the key components of the Thai kingdom: red is symbolic of the blood of the Thai people, white is Buddhism and blue is the monarchy.

feet at Thais, for example, when crossing their legs. The foot is considered unclean, and pointing it at someone is thought to be a great insult.

Closely allied with *jai yen* is a concept that provides the answer to all of life's vicissitudes: *mai pen rai*, a phrase best translated as "never mind." Most Thais would rather shrug their shoulders in the face of adversity than risk escalating a difficult situation. Solutions that contribute to restoring or maintaining calm are welcomed. In fact, one reason the Thais have survived intact as a sovereign nation is by adopting a superb sense of compromise, putting trifling or trivial matters in perspective, or else ignoring them.

SOME SOCIAL PROBLEMS

Beneath the placid and happy-go-lucky surface of Thai society lies a darker underbelly. Organised crime is prevalent throughout the country as powerful mafia clans thrive on illegal gambling, drugs and prostitution. Known as *jao phor*, the godfathers often operate legal businesses as well and may even participate in provincial politics. Gangland-style assassinations by hired hitmen are not uncommon in Thailand.

Corruption is rife in politics and daily life, and a 2011 poll revealed that only 35.5 percent of people think it unacceptable. Government and big businesses have nepotistic values; construction contracts, for instance, will often be offered to favoured companies, while a traffic policeman will usually collect an on-the-spot "fine" for perceived misdemeanours.

As traditional family networks are broken down by the rural-to-urban demographic shift, people no longer have the safety net of family and community. The side-effects of rapid modernisation can be seen by the rising number of slum-dwellers and beggars who live in Bangkok.

ADAPTING TO NEW INFLUENCES

The effects of globalisation have profoundly altered Thailand. Bangkok is in a constant state of renewal. Skyscrapers filled with apartments, offices and shopping malls have sprouted throughout the city with alarming speed. Life in the rural villages, too, is being transformed. Not so long ago, villagers might gather around the communal well at sunset to collect water and catch up on village gossip; now, many have water piped into their homes and they gather instead around their TV sets or chat on mobile phones.

Historically, Thailand has always welcomed outside influences – such as those of Western countries in the 19th century – rather than fought them. The Thais have traditionally preferred to adapt or accept, influenced in part by their Buddhist faith. Today, this mentality can be seen all over the country. International chainstores mushroom in the cities, and trends, like the recent nationwide obsession with Korean soap operas, have gripped the population. Even beauty is now personified by the *luk kreung* – literally "half child" – mixed-race children who have one Thai and one Caucasian parent. Their perfectly formed features dominate the world of music, soap operas and advertising today.

The universal 'wai' greeting is loaded with social nuances.

A resident of Hua Hin.

THAI SOAP MELODRAMAS

The national obsession with soap operas provides an entertaining window into the Thai psyche. *Lakhorn teewee*, or TV plays, occupy the prime-time slots on national Thai television, and there are over 40 companies producing more than 200 soap operas each year.

The reel-life soaps present an idealised and highly dramatised depiction of Thai life. Important social problems such as HIV/AIDS or extreme poverty are seldom touched upon, and the plots are superficial, mainly revolving around melodramatic love stories and convoluted family sagas. There is always an innocent female heroine who is the personification of the perfect Thai woman; beautiful, demure and diligent, and portrayed quite often these days by a near-perfect *luk kreung* mixed-race beauty. The male lead will be dashingly handsome and incredibly wealthy. Added to the mix are a plethora of jealous male suitors, evil sisters, mean mothers and overly protective fathers. For comic relief there may be a *kathoey* or "lady-boy" transvestite character or a dark-skinned goofy-looking maid from Thailand's poor northeast region.

This basic mix of characters is repeated through a variety of historical, urban and rural settings. Supernatural tales are popular, and ghosts can make cameo appearances in any genre. Rags-to-riches tales are a sure-fire hit. And, not surprisingly, in the rarefied world of Thai soaps, the hero and heroine almost always live happily ever after.

THAILAND'S HILL TRIBES

The colourfully clad minorities who inhabit the forested hills of northern Thailand are a major tourist draw.

An Akha man in Chiang Rai Province.

The tribal people of Thailand – referred to as "hill tribes" or *chao khao* (literally, mountain people) – make up less than 2 percent of the total population. There are at least 20 distinct hill tribes, which belong to six principal groups: Karen, Hmong, Lahu, Mien, Akha and Lisu. They mainly originate from Tibet, Myanmar (Burma), Laos and China. Virtually all live in the mountainous areas of Chiang Mai, Chiang Rai, Mae Hong Son and Nan provinces.

KAREN

With a population of over 320,000, the Karen are by far the largest hill tribe in Thailand. They comprise two subgroups, the Sgaw and Pwo, whose dialects are not mutually intelligible. The Karen have been settling in Thailand since the 18th century and they are still trickling in, fleeing human-rights abuses in neighbouring Myanmar, where they have been fighting for independence for over 50 years. Early converts to Christianity when Myanmar was a British colony, the Karen place a great emphasis on monogamy and trace their ancestry on the maternal side of the family.

HMONG

Numbering around 120,000, the Hmong are the second-largest hill tribe in Thailand. The majority arrived in the 1950s and 1960s, fleeing the civil war in Laos. On the alert for communists at the time, the Thai military regarded them as subversives, and Hmong relations with Thai officialdom still remain edgy – despite the fact that in Laos they are known for their anti-communist stance, having been allied with the Americans during the Vietnam War. Kinship is patrilineal and polygamy is permitted. The White Hmong and Blue Hmong can be identified by their dialects and clothing. Blue Hmong women wear indigo pleated skirts and tie their hair up in huge buns, while White Hmong women wear white hemp skirts and black turbans.

LAHU

Some of the 73,000 Lahu in Thailand are Christian, but they are also animists and have a long history of messianic leaders who are believed to possess supernatural powers. The traditional dress of the four groups – Red Lahu, Black Lahu, Yellow Lahu and Lahu Sheleh – are all slightly different, but red and black jackets are common. Lahu are skilled makers of baskets and bags. The Lahu are famed for their hunting prowess with both rifles and crossbows. Although leopards and tigers no longer roam the northern hills, the Lahu continue to hunt bear, wild pigs, deer, squirrels, birds and snakes.

MIEN

Like the Hmong, most Mien (also known as Yao) probably came to Thailand from Laos, but there are large numbers in Myanmar, Vietnam and China's Yunnan Province. Many Chinese elements, such as ancestor worship and Taoism, are evident in their animist religious beliefs. Kinship is patrilineal and polygamy is practised. Though many of Thailand's 40,000 Mien wear modern garments, women traditionally wear black jackets with red fur-like collars and large blue or black turbans. They also create dense, intricate embroideries on bags and clothing.

AKHA

Probably the poorest of the hill tribes, the 48,000 Akha have been the most resistant to assimilation with the Thais. Tourists are drawn by the ornate headdress of silver discs, coins, beads and feathers worn by the Akha women. Unlike other tribeswomen who save their finery for ceremonies, Akha women wear their headdress even while tending the fields. Animist beliefs are mixed with ancestor worship, and the Akha can trace their ancestry back 20 generations.

LISU

The 28,000 Lisu in Thailand are easily identified by their penchant for bright colours. Women wear long green or blue cotton dresses with striped yokes. Men wear baggy trousers of the same colours. Animist beliefs are combined with ancestor worship. The Lisu are good silversmiths and make jewellery for the Akha and Lahu. They are regarded by other tribes as sharp businesspeople, and have a strong sense of self-esteem.

OTHER MINORITIES

Two other groups deserve mention as their villages are frequent stops on trekking tours, though strictly speaking they are not Thai hill tribes. The Shan are very similar to the Thais with their settled communities, rice-growing practices and Theravada Buddhist beliefs. They are an ethnic Tai group and their language is close to the northern Thai dialect. Many Shan have immigrated to Thailand in recent times to escape the upheavals in Myanmar. The Shan may have been the first Tai inhabitants of northern Thailand in the 9th or 10th century.

The Kayan (also known as Padaung) are a Karennic people residing in Myanmar. Kayan women are famous for the heavy brass neck rings they wear; these typically weigh 5kg (11lbs) and make their necks appear elongated. The money generated from tours to view the so-called "Giraffe Women" is so lucrative that Thai officials have allowed three tourist villages to be set up just west of Mae Hong Son. Though the practice had almost died out in Myanmar, a number of Padaung women there, forced by grinding poverty to chase the tourist dollar, have since donned the coils.

THREATS TO TRIBES

The cultures of Thailand's hill tribes are threatened by shortage of land, resettlement, lack of land rights and citizenship, illiteracy and poor medical care. Living in villages at higher elevations, most hill-tribe farmers practise slash-and-burn agriculture and traditionally grow opium. The Thai authorities have been discouraging such practices. Some of the crop-substitution programmes sponsored by the Thai government, the UN and foreign governments have been very successful. Tribal people now grow coffee, tea and fruit. The idea is that if villagers can make a living from more profitable crops, they would not need to grow and sell opium in order to buy rice. But some have resisted switching to non-opium cash crops because of the capital investment involved.

Lisu girls near Mae Hong Son.

A CALENDAR OF CELEBRATIONS

Whether religious or secular, national or local, festivals in Thailand are almost always an occasion for celebration.

There can be no doubt that the Thais place great importance on their festivals. Some are of venerable vintage, such as Loy Krathong, which began in the 13th century. Others, like Lamyai Fruit Festival, are recent creations. In fact, new festivals are thought up every year, sometimes to promote tourism and often just for a bit of *sanuk* (fun). Some festivals are weighty matters upon which the future of the nation depends. Some are more spiritual, allowing one to make merit and ensure a better karmic rebirth, while others are purely secular celebrations of the joy of living. Note: As Buddhist festivals rely on the lunar calendar, their exact dates vary each year.

The Surin Elephant Festival in northeast Thailand takes place over the third weekend of November, attracting visitors from all over the country.

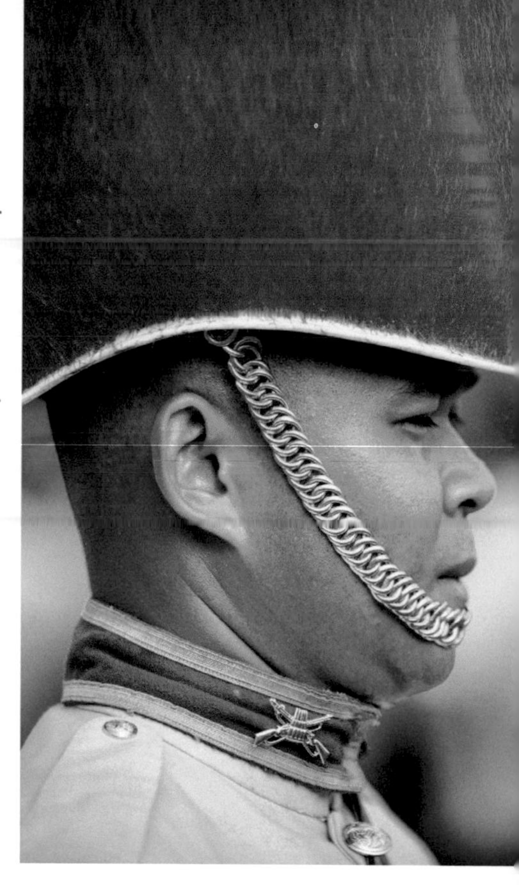

3 December is the Trooping of the Colours, held outside the old Thai Parliament in Bangkok. The king and members of the royal family review the elite Royal Guard.

Magha Puja is observed on the full moon of the third lunar month, to mark one of the Buddha's most important sermons.

Thais mark Songkran, the lunar new year, on 13 April with good-humoured water-throwing throughout the country.

The Vegetarian Festival

The Phuket Vegetarian Festival is one of Thailand's most famous and extreme celebrations. It's a Chinese Taoist event held in the first nine days of the ninth month of the Chinese lunar calendar, usually in late September or early October.

Adherents avoid eating meat, drinking alcohol or indulging in stimulating acts such as sex. They also make temple offerings, stage cultural shows, consult with mediums and perform extraordinary acts of self-mortification. These include walking on red-hot coals, climbing ladders of sword blades and piercing their flesh with all manner of sharp objects, such as stakes, spears and daggers.

Thousands of locals and visitors line the streets to observe the events, which are accompanied by loud music, frenzied dancing and the constant noise of exploding firecrackers.

During the festival, spectators and participants enjoy specially prepared vegetarian food at street stalls and markets. Often these vegetarian dishes, cooked in Thai or Chinese style, are fashioned to look like chicken legs or pork steak, and taste like it, too. The festival also occurs – without the mutilation – in other locations, including Bangkok.

The three-day Phee Ta Khon Festival at Dan Sai in Loei Province takes place each summer and features devilish masks. It is possibly the most riotous festival in the Thai calendar.

Perhaps Thailand's most picturesque festival, Loy Krathong is celebrated on the full-moon night in November to pay respects to Mae Khongkha, goddess of the country's life-bringing rivers and lakes.

Worshippers at Wat Bowonniwet, Bangkok.

RELIGION

All over Thailand, the visitor will see saffron-clad Buddhist monks, and hear the soft chanting of Pali scriptures and the tinkling of temple bells. Yet a strong thread of animism and superstition persists, as seen in the use of amulets and the presence of spirit houses and city pillars.

Thailand is an overwhelmingly Buddhist nation. Over 87 percent of the population follow Buddhism, and its influence is apparent throughout the country. About 12 percent of the Thais are Muslims, and they live mainly in the far south, close to the border with Malaysia, while the remainder is made up of a sprinkling of Christian, Hindu and Sikh communities.

Over the centuries, Buddhism has played a profound role in shaping the Thai character. The Buddhist concept of the impermanence of life and possessions, and of the necessity to avoid extremes of emotion or behaviour, has done much to create the relaxed, carefree charm of the Thai people.

Flower garland at the Erawan Shrine, Bangkok.

THERAVADA BUDDHISM

Most of the Thai population are followers of the Theravada school of Buddhism, which is also the main Buddhist form practised in neighbouring Laos, Cambodia and Myanmar (Burma), as well as Sri Lanka. Nevertheless, even a casual visitor to temples in these countries will quickly notice differences between them. In the same way that they have adapted other external cultural influences – Khmer temple decorations and Chinese food, for instance – into a unique Thai form, the Thais have evolved their own interpretation of Buddhism over the centuries.

Theravada Buddhism is a mixture of Buddhist, Hindu and animistic beliefs. It is the oldest of all Buddhist faiths, and it is the only one to trace its origins directly back to the teachings of Gautama Buddha in the 6th century BC. The central doctrines are based on the temporary nature of life and the imperfections of all beings.

With the help of a complicated system of rules, each Thai, whether layperson or monk,

INDIAN INFLUENCE

Many of the Thais' non-Buddhist beliefs are Brahman in origin, thanks to Indian influence in early Thai history. Even today, Brahman priests officiate at major ceremonies. The Thai wedding ceremony is almost entirely Brahman, as are many funeral rites, while the rites of statecraft pertaining to the royal family are presided over by Brahman priests. One of the most popular of these, the Ploughing Ceremony takes place each May in Bangkok. To signal the start of the rice-planting season, sacred oxen are offered a selection of grains. The grains they choose will determine the amount of rainfall to come, and the success or failure of the crops in the year ahead.

tries to achieve spiritual merit in the present life so that it will favourably influence their next life – thus permitting an existence that will be characterised by less suffering and ultimately lead to the final goal of nirvana, or enlightenment. To this end, almost all the religious activities that a traveller will experience in Thailand have to do with the concept of merit-making. Therefore, a man who spends some part of his life as a monk will earn merit by living in accordance with the strict rules governing monastic life. Similarly, a person who supports the monks on a daily basis

Nearly every Thai male spends part of his lifetime as a monk, regardless of age.

by donating food, or who visits a temple to pray for a sick person, gains merit.

The Buddha image in front of which the prayers are offered provides only a formal background for these activities. It is important to note that neither the statue, nor the Buddha himself, is worshipped.

MAHAYANA BUDDHISM

Mahayana Buddhism is practised mainly by those of Chinese descent, and visitors are most likely to spot Mahayana temples in Bangkok's Chinatown district. Mahayana literally means "Greater Vehicle". The defining belief, according to this doctrine, is that those who have attained nirvana return to earth to help others reach the same state. The various Buddhist sects and practices that predominate in countries like China, Tibet, Taiwan, Japan, Korea and Vietnam are classified as Mahayana.

This form of Buddhism is characterised by the use of lucky charms and talismans. The visitor entering a *sanjao*, or inner shrine, of a typical Mahayana temple will have a chance to shake sticks out of a canister, from which their fortune can be told. At funerals, paper money and doll-sized cardboard houses (complete with paper Mercedes-Benz cars) are burnt to assist the deceased in his or her next life.

TEMPLE LIFE

Most of Thailand's 300,000 or so monks live in wat (temples), practising and teaching the rules of human conduct laid down by the Buddha. There are literally hundreds of Buddhist temples in the cities and suburbs, usually sited in serene pockets of densely packed neighbourhoods and serving as hubs for the spiritual and social life of the community.

The term wat defines a large, walled compound made up of several buildings, including a *bot* or hall where new monks are ordained, and one or more *viharn* where sermons are delivered. It may also contain a bell tower, a *ho trai* (library) and *guti*, or monks' living quarters, as well as a domed edifice, called *chedi* in Thailand, or *stupa* on the

Indian subcontinent. The *chedi* sometimes contains relics of the Buddha, but in most instances the relics are of wealthy donors or holy people.

Tradition requires that every Buddhist male enter the monkhood for a brief period before marriage, and companies customarily grant paid leave for male employees wishing to do so. The entry of a young man into monkhood is seen as repayment to his parents for his upbringing, and for bestowing special merit on them, particularly his mother.

Despite the ascetic nature of monastic life, a Buddhist wat in Thailand is by no means isolated from the outside world. In addition to the schools that are attached to most wat (for centuries, the only schools were those run by monks), the temple has traditionally been the centre of social and communal life. Monks also double up as herbal doctors, psychological counsellors and arbitrators of disputes in the villages. They also play an important part in daily life, such as blessing a new building, or at birthdays and funerals.

SPIRITS AND AMULETS

It is not known exactly when the Thai people first embraced a belief in spirits, but it was most probably long before their migration south into present-day Thailand, and certainly long before their gradual conversion to Buddhism around AD 800–1200. Even after Buddhism took root in Thailand, the people continued to worship their old deities and spirits to fill in what they saw as gaping holes in Buddhism.

Most Thais widely accept that there are spirits everywhere; spirits of the water, wind and woods, and both locality spirits and tutelary spirits. These spirits are not so much good or bad, as powerful and unpredictable. Moreover, they have many of the foibles that plague humans, being capable of vindictiveness, lust, jealousy, greed and malice. To appease them, offerings must be made, and since spirits display many aspects of human nature, these offerings are often what people would value themselves.

> *Thailand differs from most other Buddhist countries in that women cannot be ordained into the priesthood. It is thus the duty of a son, as a monk, to earn merit on behalf of his mother and other female relatives.*

To counteract the spirits and potential dangers that lurk in life, protective spells are often cast and kept in small amulets, mostly worn around the neck. Curiously, the amulets cannot be bought or sold, but rather rented on an indefinite lease from "landlords", who are often monks considered to possess magical powers.

Some monasteries have been turned into highly profitable factories for the production of amulets. There are amulets that offer protection

Amulets protect from misfortune and evil.

against accidents during travel or against bullet and knife wounds; some are even said to boost sexual attraction. All this, however, has no more to do with Buddhism than the intricate blue-patterned tattoos sported by some rural Thais in an attempt to ward off evil.

THE CITY PILLAR

When the first Thai communities established themselves in the north of the country, their basic unit of organisation was the *muang*, a group of villages under the control and protection of a *wiang*, or fortified town. Of crucial importance was the *lak muang*, or city pillar, located at the centre of each *wiang*. This structure remains a feature of many towns throughout Thailand. Generally a rounded pole – thought to represent a rice shoot – it is the home of the guardian spirits of the city and surrounding district. It is venerated on a regular basis, and an annual ceremony, with offerings of incense, flowers and candles, is held to ensure the continuing prosperity and safety of the *muang*.

SPIRIT HOUSES

Traditionally, offerings are made when land is cleared for agriculture or building. After all, the spirits of a place are its original owners, and their feelings have to be taken into consideration. At some point, it was decided that an effective way of placating a locality spirit was to build it a small house of its own. That way, it would be comfortable and contented.

Today, no building in Thailand, not even the humblest wooden hut, will be seen without a spirit house, or at least a house altar. In ordinary residences, the small doll-like house may resemble a Thai dwelling; in hotels and offices, it is usually an elaborately decorated mini-temple.

Thai Buddhist temples have also accommodated the practice of spirit worship. There is

A spirit house.

Phalluses at Swissôtel Nai Lert Park in Bangkok.

CONSECRATING A SPIRIT HOUSE

Setting up a spirit house is not a casual undertaking, but one that requires the services of an experienced professional. Usually this is a Brahman priest called a *phram* (clad in white, in contrast to the Buddhist saffron robes), or at least someone schooled in Brahman ritual.

The consecration ritual is commenced by scattering small coins around the site chosen for the new spirit house, and in the soil beneath the foundations. The spirit house is then raised, and offerings are made. These include flowers, money, candles and incense; the last is often stuck into the crown of a pig's head.

The *phram*, together with the householder and his various relatives and friends, then pray to the spirits, beseeching the local *chao thii*, or lord of the locality, to take up residence in the new spirit house.

Spirit houses are often beautifully decorated with statues of dancers, ponies, servants and other items made of plaster or wood. In more recent times, contemporary offerings like replica cars and other modern consumer desirables have been offered as well, each carefully chosen to placate the resident spirit. In the grounds of Bangkok's Swissôtel Nai Lert Park is an unusual spirit house that is filled with offerings of phalluses, from tiny to gargantuan, sculpted from wood, wax, stone and cement, and with startling fidelity to real life. These are left by women hoping to conceive a child.

hardly a wat anywhere in the country that does not incorporate an elaborate spirit house in its grounds, built at the same time as the consecration of the temple in order to accommodate the displaced locality spirits.

Thais also erect spirit houses along the roads linking their settlements, paying particular attention to threatening or ominous landscapes or features. Every pass or steep section of road is marked by a spirit house to accommodate the inconvenienced locality spirit. Passing drivers lift their hands from the wheel and wai in salutation, and many stop to make offerings. Spirit houses are also raised in the fields to ensure the safety of the crop.

Muslim children from Hat Yai in the far south.

ISLAM IN THE SOUTH

It is only in the southernmost regions of peninsular Thailand, in Malay-speaking territory, that temples and spirit houses disappear, replaced by minarets and mosques. Islam first came to this region in the 8th century. Carried across the Indian Ocean by Arab and south Indian traders, it found fertile ground among the region's Malay-speaking people. The Muslims of Thailand's deep south, as in neighbouring Malaysia, follow the Sunni Islam branch of the Shafi'i school.

When the first Muslims arrived, they settled and intermarried with the local Malays, most of whom practised a syncretic Hindu-Buddhist religion. By Islamic law, the children of such unions were raised as Muslims, and over the centuries a combination of intermarriage and proselytising led to the conversion of almost all the indigenous Malay population.

Comprising about 12 percent of the national population, Thai Muslims are dominant in the four southern provinces of Satun, Pattani, Yala and Narathiwat. In this region, most people work as farmers or fishermen, studying the faith in religious schools, and saving up to go on the *haj*, or pilgrimage, to Mecca. The Shafi'i school is not overly rigorous, although in recent times, there has been growing fundamentalist influence from foreign Muslim radicals from Malaysia and Indonesia, fuelling the separatist movements and constant unrest in Pattani, Yala and Narathiwat provinces. Satun Province, although largely Muslim, has steered clear of such strife, and is currently safe to visit.

A spirit tradition is also practised by some southerners, although it is officially condemned by orthodox Muslim teachers. This tradition is represented by the *bomoh*, or Malay "witch doctor", who can foretell future events, cure physical, mental and spiritual diseases, curse individuals or lift such curses.

IMAGES OF THE BUDDHA

From the gigantic seated Buddhas to tiny Buddhas worn as amulets, these religious icons rank among the world's greatest expressions of Buddhist art.

Images of the Buddha are devotional objects and are not considered to be works of art by their makers. When artists create an image of the Buddha, they follow a set of specific rules that have been laid down for generations. The Buddha is defined by a set of peculiar characteristics, a particular monastic garb and a series of *mudras* (attitudes, postures or gestures). The 32 bodily marks, evident at the time of the Buddha's birth, include hands that reach the knees without bending, a lion-like jaw and wheel marks on the base of the feet. Buddhist artists have interpreted these marks according to the era in which they were working and the school of interpretation they had chosen to follow.

Wat Suthat in Bangok is known for its fine statuary. The large ordination and sermon halls are surrounded by cloisters of gilded Buddha images.

SUKHOTHAI SCHOOL

Thai Buddhist imagery was at its artistic height during the Sukhothai period (early 13th–early 15th centuries), when the smoothness and sheen of cast metals matched the graceful, elongated simplicity of the basic Buddha form perfectly. During this era, the Buddha was usually represented sitting cross-legged or with one foot forward in the "striding" position. One hand is raised in the *abhayamudra* (dispelling fear) action. Slightly androgynous in appearance, the Buddha images also feature a flame-like *ketumula* on the crown of the head, protruding heels, flat soles and toes all of the same length.

Thai artists simplify anatomical details in their images of the Buddha to emphasise the spiritual qualities of Buddhism.

Buddha at Wat Ko Loi in Si Racha.

A seated Buddha in the bhumisparsamudra position.

Symbolism of the mudra

The Buddha can be seen sitting, standing, lying or walking. Every image of the Buddha is represented in a particular mudra or attitude. Hand gestures in particular are key iconographical elements in representations of the Buddha:

Abhayamudra is the *mudra* of dispelling fear or giving protection: the Buddha is usually in a standing position, the right hand raised and turned outwards to show the palm with straightened fingers.

Bhumisparsamudra, or calling the earth as witness: this is made by a seated figure, with the right hand on the knee and the fingertips pointing towards the ground.

Dharmacakramudra means spinning the Wheel of Law: both hands are held in front of the body, with the fingertips of the left hand resting against the palm of the right hand.

Dhyanamudra is the meditation *mudra*: the hands rest flat in the lap, one on top of the other.

Varamudra, giving blessing or charity: made by the seated or standing Buddha with the right arm pointing downwards, the palm open and fingers more or less straightened.

Vitarkamudra is the preaching mudra: the end of the thumb and index finger of the right hand touch to form a circle, symbolising the Wheel of Law.

Seated Buddha at the feet of the Big Buddha Temple on Ko Samui.

The standing Buddha on Khao Takiab (Chopstick Hill) towers 20 metres (66ft) above the southern end of Hua Hin beach.

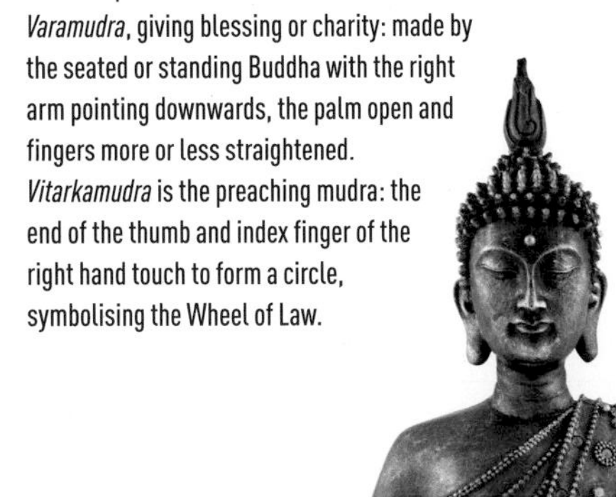

A depiction of the meditation mudra; the hands are laid flat on the lap.

A traditional Thai performance, featuring Khon dancers.

THE PERFORMING ARTS

Thailand's traditional dance-dramas are an entrenched part of its performing-arts scene. Lesser known, but just as engaging, are its shadow-puppet theatre, a cutting-edge movie industry, contemporary theatre and dance, and a popular music scene.

The Thai people have combined a lively imagination and a superb sense of the aesthetic to produce some of the most arresting performing arts found in Asia. Thai dance-dramas, for instance, with their elaborate and colourful costumes, and graceful, enchanting movements, are among the world's most dazzling and stylistically challenging dance forms.

But there's more to Thai performing arts than traditional dance and drama. Several genres of indigenous music and contemporary theatre, as well as a vibrant independent movie scene, contribute to the cultural landscape. Underpinning all this is a strong body of Thai literature that acts as both a creative source and an inspiration for the performing arts.

THAI DANCE DRAMA

Traditional theatre is still the most recognised performing-arts genre in Thailand, and comprises six main forms: *khon*, *lakhon*, *likay*, *manohra*, *lakhon lek* and *nang*. Both dance and drama are inextricably linked in traditional Thai theatre. In effect, the actor is a mime, with the storyline and lyrics provided by a singer and chorus to the side of the stage. A traditional *phipat* orchestra creates not only the atmosphere, but also an emotive force.

A phipat orchestra.

KHON

The most identifiable form of dance-drama is the *khon*, traditionally performed by a troupe of male dancers, some of whom wear beautifully crafted masks. Originally staged for the royal court, these days a condensed version of several episodes from the *Ramakien* – based on the Hindu epic *Ramayana* – is adapted into a short medley of palatable scenes for tourist dinner shows in Bangkok, Phuket and Chiang Mai. More elaborate *khon* performances are staged occasionally at Bangkok's National Theatre and weekly at the Royal Chalermkrung Theatre, but even these are abridged versions as the entire *Ramakien* would take up to 720 hours to perform.

Four types of characters make up a *khon* performance: men and women, monkeys and demons. Only the monkeys and demons wear masks during the performance. The expressionless masks force the viewer to focus attention on the dancers' movements, whether it's a dismissive flick of the hand, a finger pointed in accusation, or a foot stamped in anger.

LAKHON

The most graceful Thai dance-drama is the *lakhon*. There are two main forms: *lakhon nai* ("inside" *lakhon*), once performed only within palace walls by women, and *lakhon nawk* ("outside" *lakhon*), performed beyond the palace by both sexes. Resplendent in costumes as elaborate as their movements, the performers glide slowly about the stage, their stylised movements conveying the plot. The dance's rich repertoire includes scenes from the *Ramakien*, and Thai folk tales, with their romantic storylines. These days, a simpler version called *lakhon chatri* can be seen at temple festivals and shrines throughout Thailand. A variation of this dance is *lakhon kae bon*, which consists of a 20-member ensemble of dancers and musicians who perform at shrines as a form of thanksgiving. Performances can be seen at Lak Muang (City Pillar) shrine and the Erawan Shrine.

LIKAY

There have always been two cultures in Thailand: palace and village. The village arts are often parodies of the palace arts, but more burlesque, with pratfalls and bawdy humour. *Likay* is the village form of *lakhon*, played out against gaudy backdrops to an audience that walks in and out of the performance at will, eating and talking, regardless of what happens on stage.

Hun lakhon lek puppeteers at Bangkok's Joe Louis Theatre.

> **OPERA AND CLASSICAL MUSIC**
>
> Multi-talented Cambridge graduate Somtow Sucharitkul, writer of Hollywood scripts and several books in English, set up the Bangkok Opera in 2002. In addition to its three or four yearly productions of mainstream Western classics are Somtow's own works (written in English) such as *Mae Naak*, which is based on a Thai ghost story. His works are mainly staged at the Thailand Cultural Centre in Bangkok.
>
> In addition to providing many of the musicians for the Bangkok Opera, the Bangkok Symphony Orchestra plays regular concerts throughout the year, often at the Thailand Cultural Centre. They also perform at Lumphini Park on Sundays during the cool season.

Likay has lost some of its audience in recent years, but it still remains a vital art form in some parts of Thailand. It is usually staged by troupes of performers who travel from village to village. The performances could be excerpts from the *Ramakien*, but they are more likely to be stories incorporating elements of melodrama, slapstick comedy, sexual innuendo and the occasional stab at Thai politics and society.

SHADOW-PUPPET THEATRE

Traditional Thai shadow-puppet theatre is something of a declining art. Two forms still exist, mainly in the south of Thailand. The *nang thalung* form is what visitors will most likely encounter in places like Nakhon Si Thammarat. Originating from Malaysia and Indonesia, *nang thalung* recounts excerpts from the *Ramakien*.

Puppeteers manipulate figures made from *nang* (dried buffalo hide) against a translucent screen, which is backlit by torches, to relate complex tales of good and evil. A rarer version of shadow-puppet play in south Thailand, known as *nang yai*, uses life-size puppets but is seldom practised due to the lack of expertise.

MARIONETTE THEATRE

Visually mesmerising and based on *khon* masked dance-drama, the art of *hun lakhon lek* requires three puppeteers who manipulate sticks attached to the 1-metre (3ft) tall marionettes to bring them to life. Once only performed for royalty, this endangered art was revived by Sakorn Yangkeawsot, who goes by the moniker Joe Louis.

This revival has updated *hun lakhon lek* by allowing freer movement and more detailed costuming, and also by incorporating contemporary themes and modern speech. You can see these elaborately costumed puppets twist and turn nightly at Bangkok's riverside Asiatique.

CONTEMPORARY DANCE AND THEATRE

The main venue for quality modern productions is the partly open-air Vic Hua Hin Theatre in Hua Hin, run by Patravadi Mechudhon, whose adaptations of classic Thai tales meld traditional local dance and theatre with modern Western styling. Some of its works fuse elements of diverse Asian dance forms such as the Japanese *butoh* and Indonesian *wayang kulit*.

In Bangkok, try and catch a show by B-floor Theatre, who stage performances at Bangkok's Pridi Banomyong Institute or Democrazy Theatre Studio.

THAI CLASSICAL MUSIC

To the uninitiated, classical Thai music sounds like a jarring and ear-piercing mishmash of contrasting tones without any fixed pattern. The key is to listen to it as one might listen to jazz, picking out one instrument and following it, switching to another as the mood moves you. The music is set to a scale of seven full steps, with a lilting and steady rhythm. Each instrument plays the same melody, but in its own way and seemingly without regard to how others are playing it. Seldom does an instrument rise in solo; it is always challenged and cajoled by the other constituent parts of the orchestra.

King Bhumibol Adulyadej knew how to swing on the saxophone, and cut several records influenced by the bebop genre during his life. A song that only he could write is entitled "H.M. Blues."

Khon Thai classical masked dance at the Sala Chalermkrung.

A classical *phipat* orchestra is made up of a single reed instrument, the oboe-like *phinai*, and a variety of percussion instruments. The pitch favours the treble, with the pace set by the *ching*, a tiny cymbal, aided by the drums beaten with the fingers. The melody is played by two types of *ranat ek*, a bamboo-bar xylophone, and two sets of *khlong wong*, which are tuned gongs arranged in a semicircle around the player.

Another type of *phipat* orchestra employs two violins, the *saw-oo* and the *saw-duang*, which usually accompany a Thai dance-drama. A variation of the *phiphat* orchestra performs at a Thai boxing (*muay thai*) match to spur the combatants to action.

> *Bangkok's National Theatre is one of the best places in Thailand to see traditional dances, as well as music and drama.*

MODERN MUSIC AND FILM

Apart from the vibrant Thai pop scene, full of plastic-looking *luk kreung* (half-Thai and half-Caucasian) stars singing bubblegum tunes, there are several genres of popular music worth mentioning. Love songs and colloquial storytelling are at the heart of *mor lam* music, which is played on the *khaen* instrument, a type of mouth organ. *Mor lam* music comes from Laos and northeast Thailand and is based on traditional poetry (known as *glawn*), which emphasises local folklore, struggle and political sentiment. The tempo is rapid and accompanied by staccato vocals. Modern versions of *mor lam* use electronic instruments and are more structured, often blending with other traditional forms of music. Purists have criticised the shift, but the offshoot has its own devout circle of fans.

Thai actors and director at the Busan International Film Festival in South Korea.

Luk thung (literally "child of the fields") is Thai country music, peppered with tales of hardship, poverty and despair. It is very popular with working-class Thais. Vocals are usually drenched with vibrato and feature slow, steady tempos and the use of electric guitars, keyboards and drums. This genre of music is so in demand it has spawned several magazines and TV programmes, its own dedicated radio station and even a few films.

Plaeng phua chuwit (songs for life) are protest songs that originated in the 1970s and became the voice of student movements rebelling against the brutal military government of the time. The most famous contemporary practitioner is Aed Carabao.

CINEMA

Of the few talented Thai directors receiving acclaim on the international circuit, Apichatpong Weera-sethakul leads the way. He followed Cannes Film Festival successes for *Blissfully Yours* (*Prix Un Certain Regard* 2002) and *Tropical Malady* (Jury Prize 2004) with the ultimate Palme d'Or in 2010 for *Uncle Boonmee Who Can Recall His Past Lives*. His film *Cemetery of Splendour* (2015) was also shown at many festivals, including at Cannes and Toronto.

In common with practically everywhere else in the world, though, Hollywood blockbusters dominate cinemas in Thailand and even high-profile works by local filmmakers don't get the airing they deserve. The only real indie cinema is House RCA, with occasional screenings at Lido in Siam Square. Many Thai films do make it to film festivals though, including the World Film Festival and the EU Film Festival.

A rating system introduced in 2009 has seen a slight relaxing of censorship that has stifled local creativity by banning films dealing with sensitive issues such as charlatan monks and southern unrest or containing political content that "threatens national security". In 2010 a rating was allowed for Wisit Sasanatieng's *The Red Eagle*, which, although politically mild, features a Thai superhero who fights a corrupt prime minister, and was considered at risk of censorship.

THAI LITERATURE

For years accessible to the aristocracy alone, Thai literature did not come of age until the 20th century.

The Thai literary tradition is both absorbing and rich in its history, and includes a complex oral tradition of storytelling that dates back centuries and predates written text.

Nearly all forms of early Thai writing were lost in 1767 when Burmese invaders burnt down the old capital of Ayutthaya, along with its wealth of literature. After this tragic event, the rewriting of the old texts became primarily a royal task, as until the mid-19th century all literature was written in verse form, only known to royalty and the aristocratic classes.

THE RAMAKIEN

The rewrite was further necessitated by the loss of the *Ramakien*, the piece of literature at the heart of all Thai oral and transcribed history. It is based on the Indian classical tale *Ramayana*, an enduring story that has found a home in the literature of almost every country in Southeast Asia. In retelling the *Ramayana*, the Thais made it their own and gave a Buddhist spin to what was essentially a Hindu text. Understanding the *Ramakien* allows one to comprehend a wide variety of Thai dramatic forms, including dance-drama, its significance for Thai monarchs (who have adopted the name Rama as their own) and its role as model for exemplary social behaviour. In fact, the *Ramakien* is part of the Thai school curriculum.

INDIGENOUS LITERATURE

Exceptional among 19th-century writers is Thailand's best-known poet, Sunthorn Phu. He was the first commoner to be celebrated as a writer, and he abandoned the verse form used by the aristocratic classes for his works. His epic poem *Phra Aphaimani* follows Prince Aphaimani, a flawed hero, in his adventures in ancient Thailand.

It wasn't until the 1920s that Thai novels were published, with themes touching mainly on social or political issues. In the 1950s, however, censorship became so heavy and writers so harshly persecuted that quality fiction practically disappeared. Since the 1980s, writers have recovered a measure of political freedom. While they remain social critics, there are efforts to write fiction of literary merit. The late prime minister and cultural advocate Kukrit Pramoj's *Many Lives*, gives a good introduction to the Buddhist way of thinking. His *Four Reigns* is a fictional, yet accurate, account of court life in the 19th and 20th centuries. Pramoj, who died in 1995, was hugely influential.

Contemporary Thai writers have shown a tendency to pontificate on societal ills in their writing; among the least sanctimonious is Pira Sudham. His books are available in English, and notable works include *Tales of Thailand* and *The Force of Karma*.

'Ramakien' mural, Wat Phra Kaew, Bangkok.

In modern times the highest literary honour for a Thai writer is the annual SEA Write Award. Recent winners include Jadet Kamjorndet in 2011 for books such as his short story collection *This Morning's Sun is Too Hot to Sit Sipping Coffee*, Veeraporn Nitiprapha in 2015 for her debut novel *Saiduan Ta Bod Nai Khaowongkot* (A Blind Earthworm In A Labyrinth), inspired by the 2010 political crisis, and Jidanun Lueangpiansamut for *Singto Nok Khok* (The Lion Out Of Its Den), a collection of short stories challenging social norms.

Expatriate writers have published novels set in Thailand. Alex Garland's *The Beach* is the most famous, but most are forgettable detective romps. The most widely acclaimed of such writing is probably *Bangkok 8*.

Mudmee silk from northeast Thailand.

ARTS AND CRAFTS

With numerous cultural and aesthetic influences from around Asia, it's little wonder that Thailand's traditional arts and crafts have an almost universal appeal. No less absorbing is Thai contemporary art, which is inspired by a heady mix of spiritual and modern metaphors.

As with its architecture, music, religion, and cuisine, Thailand's visual arts and handicrafts are the product of an inventive amalgamation of various regional influences. People with some knowledge in the field may say, "Hmm... that bit's Chinese... and that bit's Indian... and that bit's European," yet it must also be concluded that the sum of all the parts is entirely home-grown and uniquely Thai.

Thailand is renowned worldwide as a centre of flourishing arts and crafts, one of the reasons why it's such a shopper's delight. But Thai artistry is found almost everywhere if you open your eyes to it, adorning temple walls in the form of murals and gold and lacquer paintings, and in the palaces filled with ornate furniture and fabrics. It's even found in food, with fruit and vegetables carved into the shapes of intricate flowers, fish and birds.

High-quality lacquerware.

LACQUERWARE AND POTTERY

Thailand's traditional crafts have a rich heritage that dates back centuries. While each region has its own specialities, the largest variety for sale (and the best prices) are found in Bangkok and Chiang Mai, and to a lesser extent in Phuket. The range on offer at both the large malls and street vendors is astounding.

Lacquerware is a Burmese-Chinese import, and much of that made today, mainly in north Thailand, is fashioned by highly skilled and patient artists who laboriously apply layer after layer of a resin to containers most often made from wood or woven bamboo. Some of the finest work may take several weeks or months to complete.

Another craft from China, related to lacquering, is mother-of-pearl decoration. Thai craftsmen are supremely skilled at setting the

RELIGIOUS ANTIQUES

Thai and Burmese antiques are among the finest in Asia, but the real thing is hard to come by these days. For the tenacious and well informed, though, treasures can still be unearthed. The centre of Thailand's antiques trade is located in Bangkok's River City shopping centre, which contains a sprawling array of shops selling genuine antiques as well as look-alike *objets d'art*.

Note that the Ministry of Culture's Fine Arts Department maintains strict control over the export of religious antiques. Genuine antiques dealers will be able to obtain the export permits required to take a true antique out of Thailand.

iridescent oyster shells aglow in black lacquer backgrounds to create scenes of enchanting beauty on boxes, furniture and statuary.

The earliest pottery discovered in Thailand dates back to 3600 BC and was discovered in Ban Chiang in the northeast. While original antiques are rare, most ceramics are still fashioned along the same shapes and designs of their time-honoured counterparts. Among the most well-known pottery are Sawankhalok ceramic plates from the Sukhothai era with their distinctive twin fish design. Celadon is a beautiful stoneware with a light jade-green or dark-brown glaze, and is used to make dinnerware, lamps and statuary.

During the Ayutthaya period, generals would ride into battle on elephants, wearing sashes encrusted with jewels that they believed would give them protection from injuries and the strength to wage war.

The dazzling colours of Thai silk.

The fine art of *bencharong* ceramics originated in China and was later developed by Thai artists. The five colours of *bencharong* – red, blue, yellow, green and white – appear on delicate porcelain bowls, containers and decorative items. Blue-and-white porcelain, which also originated in China, has been produced in Thailand for centuries.

WOODCARVINGS

Another distinctly Thai handicraft is ornamental woodcarving. Traditional motifs include the lotus and other flowers, mythological creatures from India, and serpents and dragons from China. Usually, decorative woodwork is found on furniture and in the adornment of religious and royal buildings, royal barges and carriages, and even in the humblest homes, albeit in a more modest style. Teak is seldom used in carving nowadays as it is very expensive; most of the woodwork sold today is made from rattan, bamboo and cheaper woods.

TEXTILES

The glamour of Thai silk was first recognised in the late 1940s by American entrepreneur Jim Thompson. He promoted it abroad, where it quickly gained favour for its slightly bumpy texture and shimmering iridescence. While Jim Thompson outlets all over Thailand offer an excellent range of silks and ready-made products, better bargains can be had at the Jim Thompson Factory Outlets in Bangkok, Phuket,

Pattaya and Nakhon Ratchasima. Most of the Thai silk these days is produced in the northeast, and the northeastern city of Khon Kaen celebrates an annual silk festival each November.

A variation is *mudmee*, a silk from northeast Thailand that is characterised by subtle zigzagging lines and comes in more sombre hues such as dark blue, maroon and deep yellow.

Dazzling embroidery can be found in the modern-day versions of *teen chok*, a method with which women of the ancient Lanna kingdom in the north of Thailand symbolically wove their family histories into their silk or cotton sarongs. The country's northern hill tribes also have their own distinctive patchwork and embroidery designs on cotton, mainly in bright blues, magentas and yellows.

At shops all over Thailand, hand-woven silks and cottons are sold in lengths, or ready-made as cushion covers, tablecloths and clothes. Bangkok and other cities have excellent tailors who can whip up elegant dresses made of Thai silk and embellished with appliqué and beadwork.

JEWELLERY AND GEMSTONES

Thailand is also famous for its gold and silver jewellery and gemstones. It is a major player in the global jewellery market, rivalled only by Sri Lanka and India. In the Ayutthaya and early Bangkok eras, the use of gold in royal household items, such as cosmetic jars and tableware, as well as on thrones and ceremonial objects, brought honour to the artisans who were commissioned by royal families. Today, most of the gold jewellery sold is unimaginative, taking the form of thick and heavy chains purchased mainly as a guarantee against a fluctuating currency.

More affordable (and fashionable) is jewellery fashioned from silver. Most of the silver is imported and then pounded into delicate jewellery and ornately crafted trays, boxes, bowls and other containers. The finest pieces are from north Thailand and usually sold at shops in cities like Chiang Mai and Chiang Rai.

Bangkok is home to the world's leading cutters of coloured gems. Both the International Colored Gemstone Association (ICA) and the Asian Institute of Gemological Sciences (AIGS) are based here. Most of the gems sold in Thailand today are imported from neighbouring Myanmar and Cambodia, some of which arrive in Thailand by questionable means. Rubies range from pale to deep red (including the famous "pigeon's blood" rubies); sapphires come in blue, green and yellow, as well as in the form most associated with Thailand, the star sapphire. Thai jewellers can turn gold, white gold, silver and platinum into delicate jewellery settings and are able to produce both traditional and contemporary designs.

Be careful when shopping for gems and jewellery; on the streets and in some small shops, the stones may not be of the quality and weight advertised. The Tourism Authority of Thailand has joined hands with gem-trading organisations to provide quality control through the Jewel Fest Club; look for the ruby-ring logo on shopfronts in the major cities. Border markets in Mae Sot, Mae Hong Song and Mae Sai in the north are also good bets for gems and offer an exciting alternative to the high-pressure Bangkok "factories", where quality is often questionable and the prices can be ridiculous.

Hill-tribe-influenced fashion accessories at Chiang Mai's vibrant night market.

OTHER HANDICRAFTS

There is a whole range of handicrafts that do not belong to any of the categories discussed above. Teakwood is carved into practical items such as breadboards and salad bowls, as well as more decorative trivets and statues of mythical gods, angels and elephants. Bronze statues of classical drama figures, like the recumbent deer from the *Ramakien,* make elegant decorations. Brassware, like the large noodle cabinets which street vendors sling on bamboo poles, can double up as small side tables. Natural fibres woven into products like placemats, laundry baskets and handbags also make great buys.

Street markets all over Thailand sell umbrellas made of *sah* paper (from Chiang Mai), silk fans, linen bedspreads, and mango and coconut wood utensils and receptacles. One of Thailand's lesser-known arts is nielloware, which involves applying an amalgam of black metal onto etched portions of silver or, to a lesser extent, gold.

Thai craftsmanship and creativity extends far beyond the realm of the traditional; Bangkok is fast becoming a hub for contemporary design, while local designers are also making waves in the area of home decor. Thai cosmetics-makers are busily reinventing natural Thai beauty products like jasmine rice soap and tamarind facial scrubs, and packaging them in elegant rattan baskets. Walk into any of the major malls and you will encounter shops selling trendy home accessories that often use indigenous materials. Bangkok's sprawling shopping zone, Chatuchak Weekend Market, is an alternative treasure trove for all crafts traditional and contemporary (and cheap).

Buddha images, Leng Noi Yee temple, Bangkok.

BUDDHA IMAGES

The focal point of the *bot* and *viharn* (ordination and sermon halls) of a Thai temple is the magnificent Buddha image. The image is not considered to be a representation of the Buddha, but it is supposed to serve as a reminder of his teachings. Buddha images cast in bronze, or alternatively carved in wood or stone, constitute the bulk of classical Thai sculpture. They employ some of the finest artistry (and some of the highest prices) of any arts. Fantastic examples of bas-relief sandstone carving can be located around the base of the *bot* of Wat Pho, situated in the capital of the country.

TEMPLE ART

The inner walls of the *bot* (ordination halls) and *viharn* (sermon halls) in Thai temples are traditionally covered with murals. In the days before public education, the temple was the principal repository of knowledge for the commoners. The principal themes are the life of Buddha, with the back wall generally depicting stories from the *Maravijaya*, in which all earthly temptations are united to break the meditating Buddha's will and prevent him achieving nirvana.

The murals at Buddhaisawan Chapel in Bangkok's National Museum are among the finest examples of Thai painting. Others include the murals at Wat Suthat and the 19th century paintings at Wat Bowonniwet, both in Bangkok. Although restored several times with less than perfect accuracy, the *Ramakien* murals in the walls surrounding Bangkok's Wat Phra Kaew include wonderful scenes of village and palace life.

Traditional art is also executed in the form of lacquer and gold paintings found on the shutters of most Thai temples. The best examples of lacquer painting can be found on the walls of the Lacquer Pavilion at Suan Pakkad Palace in Bangkok. Equally stunning is the intricate mother-of-pearl work by Thai artisans.

CONTEMPORARY ART

At the turn of the 20th century, King Chulalongkorn commissioned several European artists to embark on art projects in Bangkok, a trend the government continued in 1923 when they hired Italian sculptor

Corrado Feroci. The Florentine artist was a catalyst for the development of modern Thai art right through to the 1960s; locals even gave him the adopted name Silpa Bhirasri. He is attributed as being the forefather of modern art in Thailand, and established the country's first School of Fine Arts, which later became Silpakorn University.

Spirituality and Buddhism have been, and still are, major precepts in contemporary art – whether created by neo-traditionalist painters like Thawan Duchaneeand Chalermchai Kositpipat, or the meditative installations of the late Montien Boonma.

THE FUTURE OF CONTEMPORARY ART

Despite having a wealth of talented young artists, Thailand is struggling to find its feet and voice as an artistic centre in Southeast Asia. Lack of funding and proper infrastructure are the primary problems.

The works of Thailand's most famous contemporary artist, Rirkrit Tiravanija – who divides his time between Berlin, New York and Thailand (and was born in Buenos Aires) – have been favourably received in the West but, unfortunately, he has not shown locally for many years.

Art for sale at Chiang Mai night market.

Sakarin Krue-on uses spiritual metaphors as his basis, appropriating traditional imagery to question the blind adoption of Western trends. Also of note is Bangkok artist Jakkai Siributr, who weaves giant textile pieces using bright silk, which he then pastes, cuts and mutilates using cartoons. The result is a comment on the perversities of modern Buddhism as well as Thai society.

Aside from the spiritual, many local artists question the effects of globalisation on the Thai identity. The artist Vasan Sitthiket blurs his art with faux political campaigning to highlight his contempt for national policies, while conceptual photographer Manit Sriwanichpoom ridicules the Thai urbanite's consumerist compulsions with his satirical *Pink Man* series.

Meanwhile, contemporary art exhibitions are regular and sometimes outstanding at the galleries of the Silpakorn and Chulalongkorn universities and at a small number of private galleries in Bangkok, like H Gallery and 100 Tonson Gallery. The Bangkok Art and Culture Centre (see page 128), which opened its doors in 2008, has staged several good international exhibitions. A significant addition was the Museum of Contemporary Art (MOCA), which, despite a remote Bangkok location, is well worth a visit for the city's best public displays of modern Thai art. In 2016 the MAIIAM Contemporary Art Museum opened in Chiang Mai showcasing the work of modern-day Thai artists.

Gourmet Thai cuisine.

CUISINE

Thai cuisine is not just about tongue-numbing and tear-inducing spices. Regional, ethnic-migrant and fusion styles of cooking combine to create a variety of exciting and complex flavours that appeal even to the serious gourmand.

Thai food is expanding faster globally than any other cuisine, and it's easy to see why. Less a dining experience than a sensory overload on different levels, it's one of the few cuisines in the world capable of drawing people to a country purely on its own merit.

It may be the explosive spiciness of Thai food that initially overwhelms, but what's most impressive is the extraordinary complex balance of flavours that lie underneath. And contrary to what most people think, Thai cuisine is not all blatantly spicy; most Thai meals will include a sampling of less aggressive dishes, some subtly flavoured with only garlic and mild herbs.

The variety of foods and cooking styles is immense, as each of Thailand's four regions have given rise to distinct cuisine variations. The northeast is influenced by Laos, the south by Malaysia and Indonesia, the central area by the cuisine of the Royal Thai kitchens (the one foreigners are probably most familiar with) and the north by Myanmar and Yunnan (in China).

Tourist centres such as Bangkok, Chiang Mai, Pattaya, Phuket and Ko Samui have restaurants as diverse as Brazilian, French, Japanese and Italian (the country's favourite Western food). Adding excitement, especially in Bangkok, are restaurants experimenting boldly with Asian and Western ingredients and methods of preparation.

HOW TO EAT THAI FOOD

Most Thai meals have dishes placed in the middle of the table to be shared by all; the larger the group, the more dishes you get to try. For novices to Asian-style dining, the proper etiquette is to dish out a heap of rice onto your plate together with small portions of various dishes at the side (it's polite to take only a little at a time).

Chillies add the all-important fire.

DINING OPTIONS AND COSTS

The country's major cities have a range of international cuisine, but elsewhere the options will be almost exclusively Thai. If you're anywhere near the coast, check out the local seafood for the giant prawns, crab and lobster. Eating out is still cheap. Roadside stalls can serve up delicious noodle soup, or *kuaytiaw*, for 30–50 baht, while the bill for a full meal with alcohol at most restaurants will rarely exceed 1,000 baht (around US$30) per head. Expect to pay around 400 baht (around US$12) per head on average. Service charges are sometimes included; if not, a 10 percent tip is appreciated. Most restaurants are open throughout the day, closing around 11pm.

Eat with a fork and spoon, using the fork in the left hand to push food onto the spoon. Chopsticks are only for Chinese and noodle dishes. For soupy noodle dishes, use the chopsticks to pile noodles onto the spoon with a little broth.

Rice is the staple (see page 87), in the past it sustained workers throughout the day with just small portions of chilli, curry or sauce added for flavour. Even now, many rural Thais eat large helpings of rice with just small morsels of dried or salted fish. Jasmine-scented Thai rice is one of the most delicious varieties found in Asia.

Isaan food featuring gai yang (fried chicken) and som tam papaya salad.

Condiments on the table usually include such items as dried, ground red chilli, sliced chilli with vinegar, sliced chilli with the ubiquitous *nam pla* (fish sauce), and white sugar. These are mainly used to add extra flavour to noodle dishes.

NORTHERN CUISINE

This is the mildest of Thai food. Northerners generally eat *khao nio* (sticky rice), kneading it into a ball to dip into sauces and curries such as the Burmese-inspired *kaeng hanglay*, a sweet-and-tamarind-sour pork dish. The noodle dish called *khao soi* is also found in Myanmar, but it is possibly of Chinese origin. Usually made with chicken, it has fresh egg noodles swimming in a mild coconut curry, with crispy noodles sprinkled on top.

> *The small but very fiery Thai chillies (prik) come in red or green forms, but both pack a potent punch. When sliced and served in fish sauce (nam pla) as a condiment, it's called prik nam pla.*

Other northern Thai specialities include sausages, such as the spicy pork *sai oua* (roasted over a coconut husk fire to impart aroma and flavour) and *naem* (fermented raw pork and pork skin seasoned with garlic and chilli). *Laab* is a popular salad dish of minced pork, chicken, beef or fish served with mint leaves and raw vegetables to reduce the heat of the spices. It's also commonly served in the northeast region.

Northern-style dipping sauces include *nam prik ong* (minced pork, mild chillies, tomatoes, garlic and shrimp paste), and the potent classic, *nam prik noom* (grilled chillies, onions and garlic). Both are eaten with the popular snack called *khaep moo* (crispy pork rind).

NORTHEASTERN CUISINE

The food of the northeastern (Isaan) region is generally simple peasant fare, usually spicy, and eaten with mounds of sticky rice kept warm in bamboo baskets. Spicy dishes include the ever-popular *som tam* (shredded green papaya, garlic, chillies, lime juice, and variations of tomatoes, dried shrimp, preserved crab and fermented fish) and a version of *laab* sausage, which is spicier and more sour than its northern counterpart.

But perhaps the most popular Isaan food, *gai yang*, is not spicy at all. This is chicken grilled in an aromatic marinade of peppercorns, garlic, fish sauce, coriander and palm sugar, then chopped into bite-sized pieces and served with both spicy and sweet dipping sauces.

SOUTHERN CUISINE

The south – notable for some of Thailand's most fiery dishes – also has gentler specialities such as *khao yam*, a mild salad of rice, vegetables, pounded dried fish and a southern fish sauce called *budu*. Slightly spicier is *phad sataw*, a stir-fry usually of pork or shrimp, and *sataw*, a large lima bean look-alike with a strong flavour and aroma. *Khao moke gai* is delicious roasted chicken with turmeric-seasoned yellow tinted rice, like an Indian-style *biryani*, often sprinkled with crispy fried onions.

Spicy southern dishes include *kaeng tai plaa*. Fishermen who needed food that would last for days out at sea are said to have created this dish by blending the fermented stomachs of fish with chillies, bamboo shoots, vegetables and an intensely hot sauce. An even hotter dish is *kaeng leuang* (yellow curry), a variant of the central Thai *kaeng som* curry, with fish, green papaya and bamboo shoots or palm hearts.

CENTRAL CUISINE

Central cuisine influenced by the royal palaces, includes many of the dishes made internationally famous at Thai restaurants abroad. It's notable for the use of coconut milk and garnishes such as grapes, which mellow the chilli heat of the fiery dishes and add a tinge of sweetness. Trademark dishes include *tom kha gai* (a soup of chicken, coconut milk and galangal) the celebrated *tom yum goong* (hot and sour shrimp soup) and *kaeng khio waan* (green curry with chicken or beef, basil leaves and pea-sized

Tom yum goong soup.

Kaeng massaman, a southern Thai Muslim-style curry.

ORIGINS OF ROYAL THAI CUISINE

The so-called Royal Thai cuisine has had an enormous influence on the food of central Thailand, with popular dishes such as green curry or *kaeng khio waan* (made with beef or chicken) and the hot-and-sour shrimp soup called *tom yum goong* originating in the royal kitchens. The great-grandson of King Rama IV, MR Sorut Visuddhi, co-owner of Bangkok's Thanying restaurant, a Royal Thai restaurant that serves the recipes of his mother, Princess Sulap-Walleng Visuddhi, explains: "In the palace it was considered bad manners to perspire at the table or to eat foods that had strong smells. So we would use coconut milk to cut down on these tastes. This had a big influence on Central cooking."

The Grand Palace had many residences where *ahaan chawang* (food for the palace people) was prepared. Recipes were spread through the wealthy classes via palace finishing schools and publications such as *Mae Krua Hua Baak*, the country's first cookbook, written by a descendant of King Rama II. Later, when the royal families moved out of the palaces, the kitchen hands they had hired began cooking the royal dishes for their own families. A number of royally connected restaurants began to open from the 1980s onwards, but few authentic ones remain today. The intricate fruit and vegetable carving you will see at fine Thai restaurants – like the Sala Rim Naam at the Mandarin Oriental hotel – is also a legacy of Royal Thai cuisine.

aubergines). Another influence on the regional cuisine is the large Chinese presence; stir-fries and noodle dishes are commonplace.

LOCAL SPECIALITIES

A lack of rural transport infrastructure until the late 20th century and geographical obstacles, such as the mountains in the north, have resulted in significant local variations within the four regions of Thailand, often forged by ingredients available locally or the cultural character of village communities. Some towns are celebrated for "the best" version of a particular dish or product.

Phetchaburi, a coastal city south of Bangkok, is reputed to have the best palm sugar in Thailand. Consequently, it is famous for desserts, notably a legendary yellow bean pudding called *khanom mor keng*. Phetchaburi's central market also has stalls selling *khao chae*, which is rice in chilled water flavoured with fragrant herbs. The dish originated from the Mon, who populated areas mainly in the west of Thailand, from around the 6th century AD. Traditional Mon dishes are still found in stalls around Kanchanaburi, and in Bangkok, on the island of Ko Kret.

Street food at a Khon Kaen market.

Fried crickets are a local delicacy.

Close to the borders with Myanmar, near the towns of Sangklaburi, Mae Sot and Mae Hong Son, tea-leaf salads are common, along with a snack called *miang*, consisting of chopped ingredients like grated coconut, dried shrimp and chilli wrapped in tea leaves. By talking to locals while travelling, you will find some less well-known culinary gems.

Kaeng is usually loosely translated as curry, but it covers a broad range, from thin soups to near-dry dishes such as the northern *kaeng ho*. Many *kaeng* are made with coconut cream, like *kaeng ped* (red curry), *kaeng khio waan* (green curry) and *kaeng massaman*, a rich, spicy-sweet dish of

EATING INSECTS

Farmers in Thailand's northeast region make extra income by catching insects to sell to local food stalls. They may look gruesome and even revolting to the uninitiated, but these spiky and multi-legged creatures are rich in nutrients. The *takkatan* (grasshopper) has the flavour of deep-fried crispy pork skin, the *mawn mai* (silkworm) is somewhat nutty, and if you fancy a *maeng da* (water beetle), the females displaying bright orange eggs are said to be the tastiest. Be sure to rip off the legs and shell first: they slide down your throat more easily. Insect cuisine is now also found in tourist areas, and insects are even canned for export, mainly to Japan.

Persian origin with meat, potatoes and onions. *Kaeng* without coconut milk include what are known as "jungle curries", which are very spicy.

Fish and seafood often feature in Thai cooking. Trang is famous for its soft-shell crab, and if you're visiting Satun, be sure to try the speciality black fried squid (cooked in its own ink). Other dishes to try are *hoi malaeng poo op maw din* (mussels in their shells, steamed in a clay pot with lime juice and herbs) and *poo pat pong karee* (steamed chunks of crab in an egg-thickened curry with crunchy spring onions). Mud crabs caught fresh on the Gulf coast beyond Chonburi are said to be the best in Thailand.

MEAT

Meat – usually chicken, pork or beef – is cooked in all manner of styles, such as *muu thawd kratiam prik Thai* (pork fried with garlic and black pepper) or the sweet-and-sour pork dish called *muu pad prio waan*, probably of Portuguese origin, although brought to Thailand by Chinese immigrants. *Neua pad nam man hoi* is beef fried with oyster sauce, spring onions and mushrooms. The popular and spicy *pat pet pat bai kaprao* dishes include meat stir-fried with chillies, garlic, onions and holy basil *(bai kaprao)*. The main ingredients to note in Thai cuisine are: chicken *(gai)*, pork *(moo)*, beef *(neua)*, duck *(ped)*, seafood *(talay)* and shrimp *(goong)*. In remote northern villages you can still find wild foods such as snake, turtles and deer, while in the northeast, frogs, lizards and insects are commonly eaten.

A noodle stall on Bangkok's Khao San Road.

NOODLES AND RICE

Noodles – a Chinese import – are ubiquitous all over Thailand, and come in two types: *kuay tiaw*, made from rice flour, and *ba mee*, from wheat flour. Both can be ordered broad *(sen yai)*, narrow *(sen lek)* or very narrow *(sen mee)*, and with broth *(sai naam)* or without *(haeng)*.

Common dishes are *kuay tiaw raad naa* (rice noodles flash-fried and topped with sliced meat and greens in a thick, mild sauce) and *paad thai* (narrow pan-fried rice noodles with egg, dried and fresh shrimp, spring onions, tofu, crushed peanuts and bean-sprouts) – one of the best-known Thai dishes in the West. In *mee krawp*, the rice noodles are fried crispy, tossed in sweet-and-sour sauce and topped with sliced chillies, pickled garlic and slivers of orange rind.

Many lunchtime rice dishes are of Chinese origin. They include the popular *khao man gai* (chicken with rice cooked in chicken broth), *khao moo daeng* (with Chinese red pork) and *khao kaa moo* (with stewed pork leg and greens).

At night and in the early morning, two soup-like rice dishes are favoured by Thais: *khao tom*, which comes in the water it was boiled in (with additions such as garlic-fried pork, salted egg or pickled ginger), and the close relative *joke*, which is porridge-like rice seasoned with minced pork, chopped coriander leaves and slivers of fresh ginger.

> *If you sample nothing else in Thailand, don't miss the heavenly khao niao ma-muang (sweet mango with sticky rice and coconut cream).*

THAI DESSERTS

Khanom (desserts) come in a bewildering variety, from feathery light concoctions with crushed

Rice cakes.

Thai desserts often feature fruit and a savoury item such as sticky rice.

ice and syrup, to custards, ice creams and an entire category of cakes based on egg yolks cooked in flower-scented syrups. After-meal desserts, served in small bowls, are generally light and elegant. *Kluay buat chee* has banana slices in sweetened and salted warm coconut cream. *Kluay kaek* uses bananas sliced lengthwise, dipped in coconut cream and rice flour, and deep-fried until crisp. Another favourite is *taap tim krawp* (water chestnut pieces covered in red-dyed tapioca flour and served in coconut cream and crushed ice), and *sangkhaya ma-praoawn*, a coconut cream custard steamed in a coconut or a small pumpkin.

Many desserts are inventive – you may finish a rich pudding before realising that its tantalising flavour comes from crisp fried onions. Look out for vendors who sell *khanom beuang*, crispy shells filled with strands of egg yolk cooked in syrup with shredded coconut, sweet and spicy dried shrimp, coriander and coconut cream.

REFRESHMENTS

With meals, Thais drink locally brewed beers such as Singha, Kloster and the stronger Chang. Many city restaurants have a decent selection of wines (although they are very expensive, due to high taxes), with the wine lists in the top Bangkok restaurants being particularly eclectic.

Among Thailand's working classes, rice whisky brands like Maekhong and Saeng Thip are popular, usually served as a "set" with ice, soda and lime. Fresh fruit juices and iced drinks will often get a good splash of syrup (and salt) unless you request otherwise.

CULTURE OF RICE

A central pillar of Thai culture, the planting and harvesting of the staple crop has an important, unifying role in rural society.

The Thai expression *kin khao* is translated as "to eat", but it actually means "to eat rice". Indeed, in this land where rice has been a staple for centuries, the two are synonymous.

Cultivating rice is by necessity a cooperative effort, tightening the bonds of family and community. According to tradition, a farmer can ask fellow villagers to help with the work, and without having to pay for their labour. All that is expected from the host is a meal during the day, and perhaps some rice liquor in the evening. In the countryside, nearly everyone is drafted in to help with the preparation of paddy fields and the sowing of seeds. Children are on holiday from school, as they will be when harvesting begins later in the year.

The social importance of this cooperation can hardly be exaggerated. It has a direct influence on individual behaviour, because if there are problems between individuals, families and communities, the work may not get done. Moreover, it is believed that quarrelling will upset the rice spirit and the crop may fail.

THE YEAR IN RICE

The main rice-planting season – although the most fertile lands manage two harvests – begins in May, when the king presides over the ancient ploughing ceremony at Sanam Luang, in Bangkok. This Brahmanic rite symbolises the attention that the spirits give to the prospects for the forthcoming rice harvest. Soon after the rice seedlings are transplanted into the paddy fields, villagers leave token packets of rice and other food in the fields, as offerings to the rice spirit.

Another rice-related ceremony is the Boon Bang Fai, or skyrocket festival, which takes place at the start of the monsoon season to encourage abundant rains. It has Buddhist origins, although there are also elements of Brahmanism and animism. The traditional Buddhist account is that Boon Bang Fai began at the death of the Lord Buddha, when one of his grieving disciples, unable to reach his torch to the top of the funeral pyre, hurled it up to the top in a manner similar to the appearance of skyrockets being launched. Villagers make their own rockets with gunpowder, firing them from a ladder-like structure, or from a very tall tree. Monks are involved, and if the rockets do not go off properly, the monks will lose prestige.

The cooperative effort given to the rice crop continues through the growing months: one of the most onerous tasks is keeping birds away from the ripening grain. By early December, the rice is ripe enough for harvesting in the central plains and the north. The harvest comes later in the south. Harvesting schedules are fixed by common consent within each village.

A traditional rice farmer.

Finally, when the rice has been harvested and is safely stored away, the farmers can relax and enjoy themselves. And it is then that they celebrate Songkran, the most joyous festival of the year, which marks the beginning of the traditional Thai new year, in April.

Yet there are, inevitably, some changes to this age-old ritual. Large-scale commercial farmers and agribusiness companies produce rice on an industrial scale and even smallholders are now experimenting with genetically modified (GM) rice. Former farmers have left their fields altogether, and instead work on roads, drive trucks and maintain tractors. Rice is no longer the top Thai export, although it is still a vital one – Thailand continues to remain the world's top rice exporter, earning over US$2 billion annually.

ARCHITECTURE

The stunning temples of Thailand are a microcosm of the Buddhist world, while the traditional Thai house – many of which have been turned into museums – reflects a near-perfect adaptation to the environment.

As is the case for much of Thailand's artistic expression, many of the country's finest temples, palaces and other noteworthy buildings show the influences of several cultures, yet at the same time are all identifiably Thai. Indian, Khmer, Burmese and Chinese architectural styles have all had substantial impact on Thai design through the centuries, but there is no mistaking the bright colours, the swooping multi-tiered roof lines, the ornamental decorations, the stunning interior murals and the lovingly crafted gold-adorned Buddha images that define the Thai style.

TEMPLE ARCHITECTURE

Any study of Thai architecture begins with the temple, or wat (see page 92), which assumed a traditional role as school, community centre, hospital and entertainment venue, as well as a place of community worship and where lessons on Buddhism were taught. There are approximately 32,000 temples in Thailand today.

Temple compounds can be vast like Wat Pho in Bangkok, or modest, as is the case in most villages. Whatever their size, temples usually include a *bot* (ordination hall), a *viharn* (sermon hall) and dome-shaped *chedi*, where relics of the Buddha or other holy people may be housed (in Khmer influenced temples these are phallic-like spires called *prang*, epitomised by Wat Arun) (see page 118) in Bangkok. In addition, there might be ancillary temple structures such as a *sala* (open-sided pavilion), *guti* (living quarters for monks) and a *ho trai* (Buddhist scripture library).

Symbolism abounds in the ornate decoration found in Thai temples. The ends of temple columns are often shaped like water lilies or lotus buds: the lotus symbolises the purity of the Buddha's thoughts in the same way it pushes through the mud to burst forth in extraordinary beauty. The *bot* is always bounded by eight stones, believed to keep away evil spirits, an example of how animist beliefs coexist with Buddhism. Roof peaks are often adorned with *chofa*, the curling, pointed extensions at each end that represent the *garuda*, the vehicle of Vishnu. Thai palace architecture too is fairly similar to that of the temple, employing many of the same motifs and construction materials.

Wat Thammamongkol in Bangkok.

REGIONAL INFLUENCES

Regional influences have also left their mark on Thai temples. Northeastern Thailand was once part of the sprawling Khmer empire of Cambodia. Hence temples like Prasat Hin Khao

Phanom Rung (see page 329) and Prasat Khao Phra Viharn (see page 332) are boldly Khmer in style. In the north, many of the older and less well-known temples are Burmese in style, constructed during the Burmese occupation of what was then the Kingdom of Lanna.

Window panels and murals in Bangkok's old temples cross many cultural and international boundaries, and are often decorated with Chinese dragons, mythological figures from the Indian *Ramayana* and foreign merchants wearing distinctly European garb.

The Jim Thompson House.

TRADITIONAL HOUSES

Homes for ordinary Thai people share the same sensitive treatment as those for the wealthy. Thai-style teak houses, with their inward-sloping walls and steep roofs, seldom fail to impress with their airiness and their adaptation to the tropical climate.

Like the temple, the Thai house has gone through centuries of evolution. Some trace the style to southern China, the origin of much of today's Thai population. Steep roofs, sometimes multi-layered like the temples that dominated village life, with a few rooms or one large divided room elevated on pilings, characterised the earliest homes. The structures were positioned to shed rain and take advantage of the prevailing winds, and many of the components were prefabricated, then fitted together with wooden pegs.

Over time, the houses were raised higher on stilts to protect the home from flooding and wild animals, while creating a space beneath the house for keeping livestock or to be used for daily work such as weaving. Such homes are common in villages throughout Thailand today, although in urban areas, nearly all houses are more Western in design and steadfastly anchored to the ground with brick and mortar. Most of the early homes were made

Central chedi at Wat Phra Mahathat, Nakhon Si Thammarat.

DOMESTIC DESIGN

The architectural styles of traditional homes vary from one region to another, although some characteristics are common throughout. In the flat Central Plain north of Bangkok, an open veranda is often the focus of home life as it becomes an outside living space. In north Thailand, where dry-season temperatures are lower, the ventilation and living spaces are designed to retain warmth. In most traditional dwellings, the central innermost room is both a sleeping area and the abode for any ancestral spirits.

Outside most Thai homes and commercial buildings stands the spirit house (see page 64), varying between plain and modest, or gaudy and large.

of native woods such as teak, which is rarely used today as it is expensive and hard to come by, or bamboo, which is making a small comeback as it is eco-friendly. The Jim Thompson House (see page 129), Suan Pakkad Palace (see page 129) and Kamthieng House (see page 134) are fine examples of grand Thai houses. Numerous, albeit humbler, examples line the banks of the canals that crisscross Bangkok's Thonburi suburbs.

In south Thailand, a different design evolved, featuring shorter pillars, no exterior veranda, and windows with hinged shutters that closed from the top during torrential monsoon rains.

WESTERN INFLUENCES

With the arrival of Western traders and missionaries in Bangkok in the 18th century, elements of Western architectural design started to make an appearance. This was further bolstered by trips to Europe by the Thai monarchy in the 19th century. By the mid-19th century, Western-style buildings were being built alongside traditional Thai structures on both sides of

Kamthieng House, Bangkok.

HOTEL HIGH STYLE

Thailand is a cut above the rest of Asia when it comes to design and high style, evident in the raft of hotels that continue to open. It's almost impossible to come up with a definitive list of the country's best hotels and resorts, as the choices are just too varied and too many. Most will agree that the ones listed here are worthy of mention, having been lavishly awarded or praised in the international media.

Bangkok: Urbane **COMO Metropolitan** (www.comohotels.com/metropolitanbangkok), resort-like **The Sukhothai** (www.sukhothai.com), chic **Conrad Bangkok** (www.conradhotels.com) and The **Peninsula** (www.peninsula.com) are all high-end options. Cheaper but just as stylish is the **Arun Residence** (www.arunresidence.com).

Chiang Mai: The Four Seasons Chiang Mai (www.fourseasons.com) has always been a hip outpost. Newer places include **The Rachamankha** (www.rachamankha.com) and **Anantara** (http://chiang-mai.anantara.com).

Beaches: Closer to Bangkok, the best luxury boltholes are **Aleenta** (www.aleenta.com) in Pranburi and **SO Sofitel** (www.accorhotels.com) at Cha-am. In Phuket is the much-lauded **Amanpuri** (www.amanpuri.com) and more affordable **Twinpalms** (www.twinpalms-phuket.com). North of Phuket on Ko Racha is the minimalist **The Racha** (www.theracha.com). Other contenders are **Rayavadee** (www.rayavadee.com) in Krabi, **Zeavola** in Ko Phi Phi (www.zeavola.com) and **Four Seasons** in Koh Samui (www.fourseasons.com).

the Chao Phraya River, the centre of Bangkok's government and commerce.

Some of this early architecture still stands today, including the original Author's Wing of the Mandarin Oriental hotel (see page 131) as well as the French Embassy, the East Asiatic Company and the Old Customs House, all designed by European architects and found within walking distance of each other along the riverside near Thanon Silom. The Vimanmek Mansion (see page 123), in Bangkok's Dusit district, built entirely of teak but decidedly more Western than Thai; the monumental Grand Palace (see page 112), with its Western neoclassical features; and the Italianate palace built by King Chulalongkorn at Bang Pa-In (see page 157), near Ayutthaya, offer ample evidence of Thailand's passionate embrace of Western styles, which continues to this day.

Another legacy of this era are the shophouses built in the Sino-Portuguese style. These narrow and long two-storey linked buildings with ornate window and roof treatments can still be seen near the Tha Chang boat landing along the Chao Phraya River in Bangkok, as well as Thanon Thalang in Phuket and Thanon Charoenrat in Chiang Mai. As in the past, the ground floor of the structure serves as a shop, while the family lives on the floor above.

CONTEMPORARY ARCHITECTURE

Most contemporary architectural efforts show little regard for the past. Hundreds of functional high-rises appear each year in the cities, while cardboard-copy rows of townhouses are erected for the country's growing middle class in the suburbs and small towns. During the building boom of the 1980s and '90s, many architects tried to outdo each other and some fairly quirky designs evolved in Bangkok. Some of the more successful designs include the UOB Building at the corner of Thanon Sathorn and Soi Pikun, designed by one of the country's foremost modern architects, Dr Sumet Jumsai. It looks more like the creation of a child's fantasy than a stuffy bank headquarters, and, complete with eyes and antennae, it is affectionately dubbed the "robot building." The robotic appearance is a symbol of modernisation in Thai banking.

Also of note in the north Bangkok business district at Soi Pahon Yothin is the whimsical Elephant Tower, which has three towers connected to form the shape of Thailand's national animal, while the extraordinary 314-metre (1,030ft) -high MahaNakhon skyscraper, completed in 2014, has a "pixelated" exterior that resembles uneven stacks of glass Lego bricks. It houses the Ritz-Carlton residences.

In 1997 Bangkok's then tallest building, the 90-storey Baiyoke Tower II, on Thanon Ratchaprarop, was completed, with a revolving observation deck on the 84th floor that provides an eye-popping 360-degree view of the city.

Bangkok's landmark Elephant Tower.

Since then, rooftop panoramas, usually accompanied by wining and dining, have become a major feature of the city, as seen from the hotel "lebua at State Tower," on Thanon Silom.

Since the 1997 crash, economic stability has largely returned to Thailand, and today, as well as the creation of new buildings clad in steel and glass, there is a greater awareness of conservation, as seen in the 2011 restoration of the shop houses opposite Bangkok's Grand Palace.

Some old residences have been restored and converted to boutique hotels or museums, and another trend is the construction of luxurious new hotels consciously designed to incorporate or recreate traditional Thai aesthetics. One spectacular example is the Dhara Dhevi Chiang Mai Resort.

TEMPLE ART AND ARCHITECTURE

The temple, or wat, plays a vital role in every community, large and small. For many visitors, they are the country's most enduring and iconic sights.

A typical Thai wat (temple) has two enclosing walls that separate it from the secular world. The monks' quarters are situated between the outer and inner walls. In larger temples, the inner walls may be lined with Buddha images and serve as cloisters for meditation. This part of the temple is called *buddhavasa* or *phutthawat*. Inside the inner walls is the bot or *ubosot* (ordination hall), surrounded by eight stone tablets and set on consecrated ground. This is the most sacred part of the temple – ordinations and special ceremonies are held here – and only monks can enter. The *bot* contains a Buddha image, but it is the *viharn* (sermon hall) that contains the principal Buddha images. Also in the inner courtyard are the bell-shaped *chedi* or *stupa* (relic towers), which contain the relics of the Buddha, renowned monks or benefactors. Some have Cambodian-style spires called prang, which are a variation of the *chedi*.

Sala (open-sided pavilions) can be found all around the temple; the largest of these is the *sala kan prian* (study hall), used for afternoon prayers. Apart from Buddha images, various mythological creatures are found within the temple compound.

Gilded chofa (the curling, pointed roof extensions), intricately carved gables, and green- and ochre-coloured tiles are common features of Thai temple roofs.

Buddha statues at Wat Pho.

Temple exteriors are often very ornate, such as the Emerald Buddha at Wat Phra Kaew. Gold tiles, glass mosaic, lacquer and mother-of-pearl are some of the materials used.

An example of the late 18th-century art style.

Temple murals

Thai temple murals are created on a background that has been prepared and dried before the artist paints on it using coloured pigments mixed with glue. Often featured on the interior of temple walls, such murals depict the classic subjects of Thai painting, including tales from the Jataka (Buddha's birth and previous lives) and other Buddhist themes, and also vignettes of local life.

During the reign of Rama III (1824–51), mural painting reached its peak, with artists not only following the principles of traditional Thai art, but also introducing new elements, like Western perspective. The mural from Wat Suthat in Bangkok, is an example of the late 18th-century art style (better known as the Rattanakosin period).

Wat Si Sawai, Sukhothai, an example of the Khmer temple style that dominated the region during the years of Khmer hegemony.

The Sri Lankan-influenced 15th-century chedi at Wat Sorosak at Sukothai is supported by a parade of elephants. Considered sacred, the elephant is an important motif in Thai (and Khmer) religious architecture.

These towering chedi at Wat Pho sit on square bases and have graceful and elegant proportions, reminiscent of the Lanna-style architecture of north Thailand.

Erawan National Park, Kanchanaburi Province.

Wat Phra Kaew, also known as the Temple of the Emerald Buddha, Bangkok.

View of Bangkok from the Sirocco Restaurant.

Krabi, located on Thailand's west coast.

INTRODUCTION

A detailed guide to the entire country, with principal sites cross-referenced by number to the accompanying maps.

A gibbon, near Phuket.

Thailand has good roads and transport systems linking all four regions, so getting around is pretty easy to arrange, whatever your budget. And there's plenty of variety, from tropical rainforests to temple ruins and beautiful palm-lined beaches to the energy of bustling Bangkok. Under the rainforest canopies you'll find iridescent kingfishers, flying squirrels, gibbons, nearly 1,000 varieties of orchid, and, if you're really fortunate, maybe even a tiger. The beaches are known for spa retreats and mayhem at infamous full moon parties, while offshore are some of the world's best dive sites.

The mountainous north, with the nation's second capital, Chiang Mai, at its centre, offers trekking to hill tribe villages, elephant camps and white water rafting, and dotted all around are old temples and buildings portraying the distinct Lanna culture.

The people of the poorest region, the northeast, are traditionally farmers. They speak Lao and Khmer dialects and have some of the bawdiest and most politically pointed performance arts. The region also has some of the country's best silk weavers and 1,000 year-old ruins of old temples left over from the Khmer empire.

The triple chedi of Wat Phra Sri Sanphet, Ayutthaya.

The fertile central plains are packed with the evidence of royal heritage, from Bangkok's ornate Grand Palace to the historic old capital Ayutthaya and coastal summer retreats still used to this day. Bangkok has wonderful restaurants, shops and a steamy mix of nightlife options, while close by are floating markets and the national parks around Kanchanaburi.

The south – as well as hundreds of islands, powdery sands and eerie limestone karsts that tower from the water – has a Malay-influenced culture. Many of the people are Muslim; the traditional arts include shadow puppetry; and among spectator sports is buffalo fighting.

Whether you're looking for relaxation, adventure travel or cultural enlightenment, Thailand has it.

Gulf of Tonkin
VIETNAM
LAOS
THAILAND
BURMA
(MYANMAR)
Gulf of Martaban
Hue
Dong Ha
Thanh Hoa
Vinh
Ha Tinh
Xam Nua
Nam Noen
Louangphabang
Muang Souy
Muang Khun
Xaignabouli
Huoi Mo
Phôn Hông
Mouang
Pakxan
Viangchan (Vientiane)
Lak Sao
Katèp
Nyommalat
Khe Ve
Savannakhet
Muang Phin
Salavan
Attapu
Pakxé
Champasak
Khôngxédôn
Muang Pakxong
Muang Không
Siempang
Bung Lum
Bâ Kêv
Thalabâriyat
Stoĕng Trĕng
Choâm Khsant
Sâmraông
Ânlung Vêng
Kulen
Sisophon
Krâlânh
Thakek
Nakhon Phanom
Sakhon Nakhon
Mukdahan
That Phanom
Nong Khai
Tha Bo
Chiang Khan
Udon Thani
Ban Chiang
Loei
Phu Kradung National Park
Ubon Ratana Dam
Khon Kaen
Kalasin
Maha Sarakham
Roi Et
Yasothon
Khemmarat
Amnat Charoen
Ubon Ratchathani
Warin Chamrap
Phibun Mangsahan
Si Saket
Surin
Buri Ram
Nakhon Ratchasima (Khorat)
Khao Yai National Park
Pak Chong
Chaiyaphum
Phetchabun
Lom Sak
Phitsanulok
Sukhothai
Sawankhalok
Uttaradit
Phrae
Nan
Doi Phu Kha N.P.
Sirikit Dam
Phayao
Chiang Rai
Chiang Saen
Mae Sai
Tachilek
Fang
Chiang Mai
Lamphun
Lampang
Doi Suthep-Doi Pui N.P.
Doi Inthanon N.P.
Huay Nam Dang N.P.
Sri Lanna N.P.
Mae Hong Son
Mae Sariang
Bhumiphol Reservoir
Tak
Mae Sot
Lang Sang N.P.
Kamphaeng Phet
Khlong Lan N.P.
Mae Wong N.P.
Nakhon Sawan
Uthai Thani
Chai Nat
Sing Buri
Lopburi
Saraburi
Ayutthaya
Nakhon Nayok
Prachin Buri
Aranyaprathet
BANGKOK
Min Buri
Chachoengsao
Chonburi
Samut Prakan
Samut Sakhon
Nakhon Pathom
Pathum Thani
Suphan Buri
Ang Thong
Kanchanaburi
Ban Pong
Ratchaburi
Srinagarind National Park
Sri Nagarind Reserv.
Sangkhlaburi
Thong Pha Phum
Thiu Khao Phetchabun
Khao Phanom Dongrak
Hsi-hseng
Loikaw
Hpa-an
Thaton
Mawlamyaing
Mudon
Kyaikkami
Thanbyuzayat
Ye
Tavoy
Launglon
Launglon Bok. Islands
Thanlwin Myit (Salween)
Khong
(Mekong)

Thailand
0 100 km
0 100 miles
N
Gulf of Thailand
Andaman Sea
Myeik Kyunzu
(Mergui Archipelago)
Cua Sông Cu'u Long
(Mouth of the Mekong)
MALAYSIA
HỒ CHÍ MINH
(SAIGON)
Phnom Penh
Vung Tàu
Biên Hòa
Thu Dâu Một
My Tho
Bên Tre
Trà Vinh
Cân Tho'
Ling Xuyên
Châu Dôc
Raxh Gia
Cà Mau
Ngọc Hiên
Sóc Trang
Long My
Vi Thanh
Minh Hai
Gia Rai
Ba Dông
Côn Dao
Mui Cà Mau
Hà Tiên
Du'o'ng Dông
Quân Dao Nam Du
Hòn Thô Chu
Kâmpôt
Kâmpong Saôm
Kaôh Rung
Kaôh Kong
Kâmpong Cham
Kâmpong Chhnang
Mekong
Basak
Takev
Svay Rieng
Tây Ninh
Binh Long
Krâchéh
Trat
Chanthaburi
Rayong
Sattahip
Ko Samet
Ko Samet National Park
Ko Chang
Ko Kut
Khlong Yai
Hua Hin
Pranburi
Nong Sai
Prachuap Khiri Khan
Thap Sakae
Bang Saphan
Pathiu
Tha Sae
Chumphon
Sawi
Lang Suan
Ko Tao
Ko Phangan
Ko Samui
Surat Thani
Kanchanadit
Sichon
Nakhon Si Thammarat
Pak Phanang
Ron Phibun
Hua Sai
Ban Na San
Thung Song
Phatthalung
Thale Luang
Songkhla
Hat Yai
Pattani
Yala
Sai Buri
Narathiwat
Sungai Kolok
Betong
Kota Bharu
Tanah Merah
Kampung Buloh
Alor Setar
Sungai Petani
Kangar
Jitra
Satun
Pulau Langkawi
Ko Tarutao
Ko Tarutao Marine National Park
Trang
Kantang
Huai Yot
Krabi
Ko Phi Phi
Ko Lanta
Phang Nga
Thalang
Phuket
Ko Phuket
Tha Chat Chai
Takua Pa
Ko Similan
Ko Similan National Marine Park
Khao Sok National Park
Ko Phra Thong
Ko Surin Nua
Ko Surin Tai
Kapoe
Ranong
Isthmus of Kra
Kra Buri
Khura Buri
Chiaw Lan Lake
Thanboke Koranee National Park
Wiang Sa
Myeik
Tenasserim
Lenya
Kawthaung
Zadetkyi Kyun
Lord Loughborough I.
Lanbi Kyun
Investigator Channel
Forest Strait

Yaowarat Road, Chinatown, Bangkok.

BANGKOK AND SUBURBS

As Bangkok reinvents for the modern age it offers the best of both worlds: hot clubs and Michelin-tinged restaurants with traditional markets and the world's best street food.

One of Bangkok's many street markets.

Bangkok is in constant motion, a city racing into the 21st century. Frenzied building sends ever more towers of gleaming glass up onto the skyline, housing ritzy hotels, shopping malls, and glamorous apartments catering to a growing middle class that is fast becoming "ample rich", as former Prime Minister Thaksin Shinawatra so memorably called his offshore company.

The shopping malls are filled with famous labels. If your desire is Gucci, Porsche or Jimmy Choo you'll find it here, and young Thai designers, too, are building names with bold themes in clothing, fashion accessories and home decor.

As motorbikes and tuk-tuks weave between the traffic, the expanding Skytrain and Metro systems drill their way to all corners of the capital, old and new, the only sure-fire ways to beat Bangkok's notorious gridlock.

A frenetic bout of muay thai kick-boxing – Thailand's most popular sport.

Though conservation and city planning have never been high on the Bangkok agenda, between the modern façades lovely reminders of history remain. Wooden houses teeter on stilts on the banks of canals, dragon costumes hang in Chinatown alleys, and picture postcard golden spires shade saffron monks in the Old Town temples.

The traditional goods for which Thai artisans are famous are still here, too; textiles, silverware, tribal handicrafts... now as likely found in air-conditioned shops as the street stalls of Chatuchak, said to be Asia's biggest flea market.

At night, from beers at Cheap Charlie's to rooftop champagne cocktails at the Sky Bar and international DJs at the elegant Levels Club, the city pulses with energy. And everywhere the glorious smell of Thai food fills the air as diners sit at street-side eateries over bowls of *tom yum goong*, curries and spicy salads. In this modern age, though, you can also choose from a large range of top Thai and international restaurants, including branches of Michelin-starred outfits such as the French D'Sens and the molecular Thai Sra Bua.

But as the city hurtles on, one constant remains; the Thai ability to enjoy it. The overriding concept of fun, or *sanuk*, is never far away.

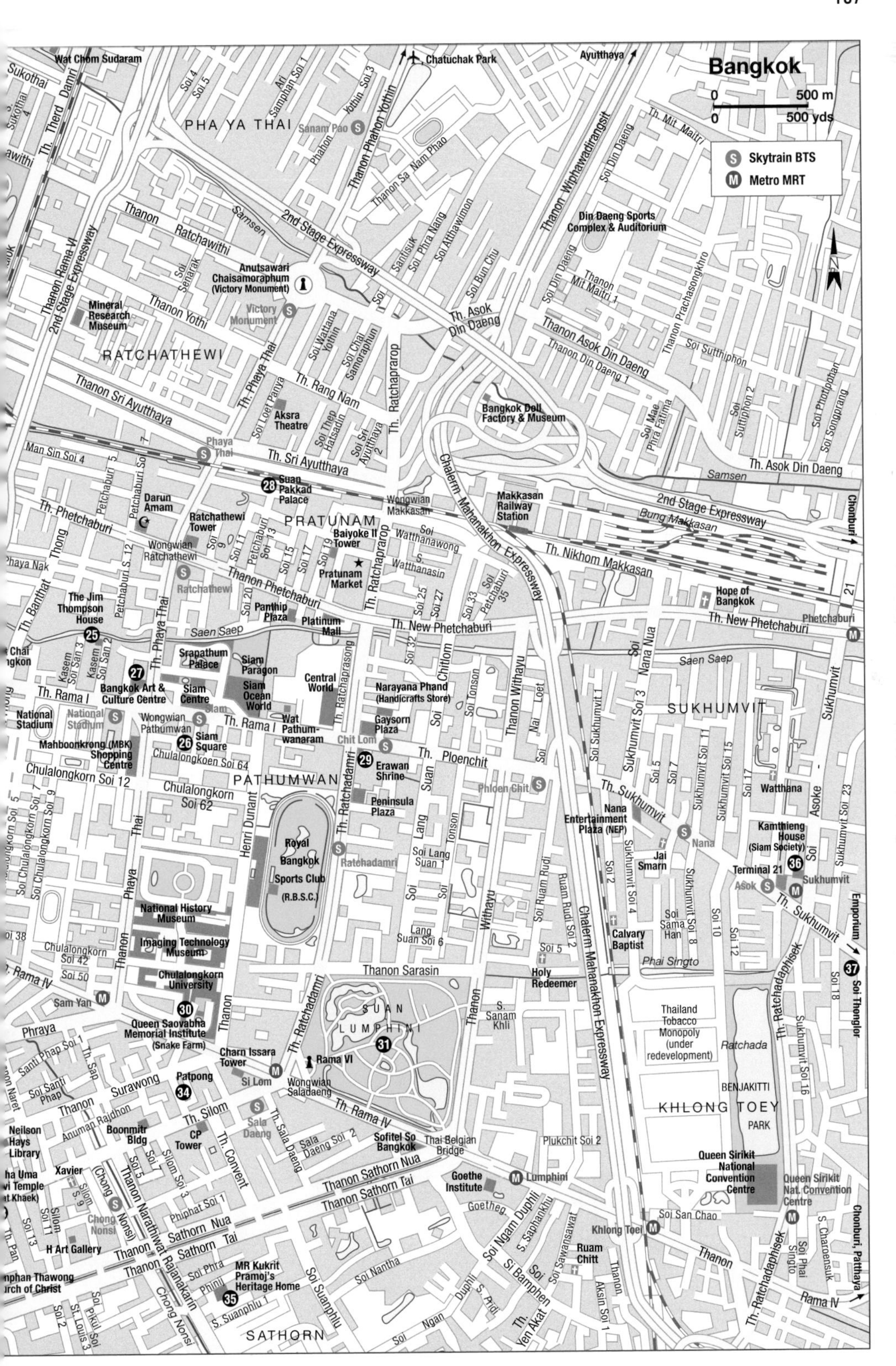
Bangkok
0 500 m
0 500 yds
Skytrain BTS
Metro MRT
Chatuchak Park
Ayutthaya
Wat Chom Sudaram
PHA YA THAI
Sanam Pao
Thanon Phahon Yothin
2nd Stage Expressway
Din Daeng Sports Complex & Auditorium
Anutsawari Chaisamoraphum (Victory Monument)
Victory Monument
Mineral Research Museum
RATCHATHEWI
Thanon Sri Ayutthaya
Aksra Theatre
Bangkok Doll Factory & Museum
Phaya Thai
Th. Sri Ayutthaya
Suan Pakkad Palace
Darun Amam
Makkasan Railway Station
Th. Asok Din Daeng
Chalerm Mahanakhon Expressway
Ratchathewi Tower
PRATUNAM
Baiyoke II Tower
Pratunam Market
Th. Nikhom Makkasan
Hope of Bangkok
Ratchathewi
Thanon Phetchaburi
The Jim Thompson House
Panthip Plaza
Platinum Mall
Th. New Phetchaburi
Phetchaburi
Saen Saep
Srapathum Palace
Siam Paragon
Siam Ocean World
Central World
Narayana Phand (Handicrafts Store)
SUKHUMVIT
Bangkok Art & Culture Centre
Siam Centre
Th. Rama I
National Stadium
Wat Pathumwanaram
Gaysorn Plaza
Siam Square
Mahboonkrong (MBK) Shopping Centre
Chit Lom
Th. Ploenchit
Erawan Shrine
PATHUMWAN
Phloen Chit
Peninsula Plaza
Th. Sukhumvit
Nana Entertainment Plaza (NEP)
Nana
Watthana
Kamthieng House (Siam Society)
Royal Bangkok Sports Club (R.B.S.C.)
Ratchadamri
Jai Smarn
Terminal 21
Asok
Sukhumvit
National History Museum
Imaging Technology Museum
Calvary Baptist
Emporium
Chulalongkorn University
Thanon Sarasin
Holy Redeemer
Phai Singto
Soi Thonglor
Sam Yan
Queen Saovabha Memorial Institute (Snake Farm)
SUAN LUMPHINI
Thailand Tobacco Monopoly (under redevelopment)
Ratchada
Charn Issara Tower
Rama VI
Si Lom
Patpong
BENJAKITTI PARK
KHLONG TOEY
Th. Rama IV
Th. Silom
CP Tower
Sala Daeng
Sofitel So Bangkok
Thai Belgian Bridge
Neilson Hays Library
Boonmitr Bldg
Queen Sirikit National Convention Centre
Xavier
Thanon Sathorn Nua
Thanon Sathorn Tai
Goethe Institute
Lumphini
Chong Nonsi
Khlong Toei
H Art Gallery
Ruam Chitt
MR Kukrit Pramoj's Heritage Home
Chonburi, Pattaya
Rama IV
SATHORN
Chonburi

Skytrain station.

BANGKOK

Thailand's capital offers a mind-blowing array of experiences: royal architecture at Rattanakosin, spirituality at ancient Buddhist temples, shopping at raucous street markets and hip mega malls. Come evening, there are eateries and nightspots galore.

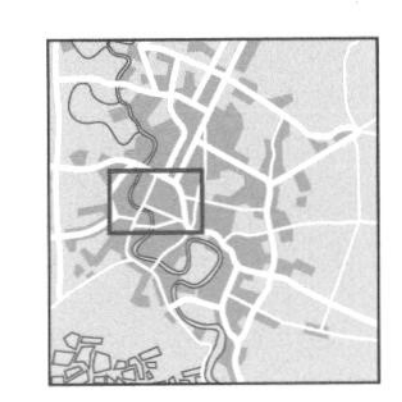

At first glance, this Asian super-city of 8.5 million people seems like a bewildering amalgam of new, old and indeterminate, as well as exotic, commonplace and indescribable, all tossed together into a gigantic urban maze. It's hardly surprising that Bangkok should convey this impression, considering that only a little more than half a century ago, much of what makes up the Thai capital was farmland. Despite the construction of the Skytrain and Metro mass transit networks, which have done much to make this vast city more navigable (and comprehensible), the traveller's mental map of Bangkok needs a few pointers in order to aid orientation.

The long and winding Chao Phraya River is the city's most obvious landmark, and cradles many of the city's most important sites on its eastern bank. On the western side of the river, Thonburi's canals thread through colourful residential neighbourhoods.

In the late 18th century Bangkok's founding king, Rama I, ordered the construction of a canal between two of the river's bends and sliced off a parcel of land into an artificial island called Rattanakosin. This is the location of the glittering Grand Palace and Wat Phra Kaew, an essential part of any city tour.

Just south of Rattanakosin are the enclaves where foreigners originally settled: Chinatown, Little India (or Pahurat) and Thanon Silom. Today, Silom Bangkok, together with Thanon Sathorn and Thanon Sukhumvit further east, have become important business and commercial centres.

RATTANAKOSIN

The establishment of the old city of **Phra Nakorn** marked Bangkok's rise in 1782 as the new capital of Thailand. It was based spiritually and geographically on the former capital of Ayutthaya, which was abandoned after being invaded by the Burmese in

Main attractions

- Wat Phra Kaew and Grand Palace
- National Museum
- Wat Pho
- Wat Arun
- Thonburi Canals
- Khao San Road
- Ananta Samakhom Throne Hall
- Chinatown
- The Jim Thompson House
- Patpong Night Market

Maps on pages 106, 111

Kinnaree statue at Wat Phra Kaew.

Tip

The dress code for Wat Phra Kaew and the Grand Palace is strict. Visitors must be dressed smartly: No shorts, short skirts, sleeveless or revealing shirts and tops, and no sandals or flip-flops. Suitable clothing may be hired from an office near the entrance, so unless you want to don stale rubber slip-ons and a gaudy sarong, dress conservatively.

1767. The royal district of Phra Nakorn was the island of **Rattanakosin**, with its majestic Grand Palace. Moats and ramparts created a stronghold, while canals were dug to transport people across marsh and swampland.

Rattanakosin brims with architectural grandeur; it contains many government offices as well as two of Thailand's most respected universities: Thammasat and Silpakorn. It is also the religious and ceremonial nucleus of the country. Best explored on foot, the area's proximity to the river means that it can be conveniently accessed by water transport.

WAT PHRA KAEW AND GRAND PALACE COMPLEX

The exotic splendour of Bangkok's most important attractions – Wat Phra Kaew and the Grand Palace – is breathtaking despite the pressing crowds. These fabulously ornate buildings are an arresting spectacle of form and colour, glistening golden *chedi*, pillars of mosaic glass, and towering mythological gods.

The Wat Phra Kaew and Grand Palace complex.

The site originally spread over 160 hectares (400 acres) around this strategic locale by the banks of the Chao Phraya River. It was initiated by King Rama I in 1782, who ordered a new residence built to house the Emerald Buddha, the country's most revered religious image, as well as a palace befitting the new capital of Bangkok. The entire compound is surrounded by high crenellated walls, securing a self-sufficient city within a city.

The only entrance (and exit) to the **Wat Phra Kaew and Grand Palace** ❶ **complex** (daily 8.30am–3.30pm; charge includes entry to Queen Sirikit Museum of Textiles; www.royalgrandpalace.th) is along Thanon Na Phra Lan to the north. Make sure you are dressed appropriately and disregard touts outside the complex telling you that it is closed for a major festival (it's a scam usually ending in a jewellery shop).

On the right after you walk in is the **Queen Sirikit Museum of Textiles** Ⓐ, (www.qsmtthailand.org). It has four galleries showing traditional Thai textiles and items from the queen's personal collection of haute couture. Entrance is included with the Grand Palace ticket, although it is possible to visit this spot alone for a lower fee, without admission to the Grand Palace Complex.

The ticket office for the whole complex is 50 metres/yards further on. It's worthwhile hiring the informative audio guide. If you prefer, official guides are also available near the ticket office.

The complex is loosely divided into two, with Wat Phra Kaew (Temple of the Emerald Buddha) encountered first to the left, and the Grand Palace and its peripheral buildings to the right. Most of the Grand Palace's interiors are not open to the public, but the exteriors are an impressive blend of East and West.

WAT PHRA KAEW

Wat Phra Kaew (Temple of the Emerald Buddha) serves as the royal chapel of the Grand Palace. The magnificent temple compound is modelled after palace chapels in the former capitals of Sukhothai and Ayutthaya, and contains typical monastic structures, apart from monks' living quarters, a feature found in most Thai temples.

At the main entrance to the temple compound is the statue of Shivaka Kumar Baccha, reputed to be the Buddha's private physician. First to catch the eye on the upper terrace on the left are the gleaming gold mosaic tiles of the Sri Lankan-style **Phra Si Rattana Chedi** Ⓑ, said to enshrine a piece of the Buddha's breastbone.

In the centre of the compound, the **Phra Mondop** Ⓒ (Library of Buddhist Scriptures) is a delicately beautiful building, studded with blue-and-green glass mosaic and topped by a multi-tiered roof fashioned like the crown of a Thai king. The library is surrounded by statues of sacred white elephants.

Next door, the **Prasat Phra Thep Bidom** Ⓓ (Royal Pantheon) contains life-size statues of the Chakri kings and is open to the public only on Chakri Day (6 April). Around the building stand marvellous gilded statues of mythological creatures, including the half-female, half-lion *aponsi*. The original pantheon was built in 1855, but was destroyed by fire and rebuilt in 1903. Flanking the entrance of the Prasat Phra Thep Bidom are two towering gilded *chedi*.

Behind the Phra Mondop is a large **sandstone model of Angkor Wat**, built during King Rama IV's reign when Cambodia was a vassal Thai state. Just behind this, along the northern edge of the compound, the **Viharn Yot** (Prayer Hall) is flanked by the **Ho Phra Nak** (Royal Mausoleum) on the left and the **Ho Phra Montien Tham** (Auxiliary Library) on the right.

The walls of the cloister enclosing the temple courtyard have murals depicting the *Ramakien* epic, the Thai version of the Indian *Ramayana*, these were originally created during the reign of King Rama III (1824–50), and have been restored.

Around the cloisters, six pairs of towering *yaksha* (demons), characters

Yaksha, a half-demon, half-god protector at Wat Phra Kaew.

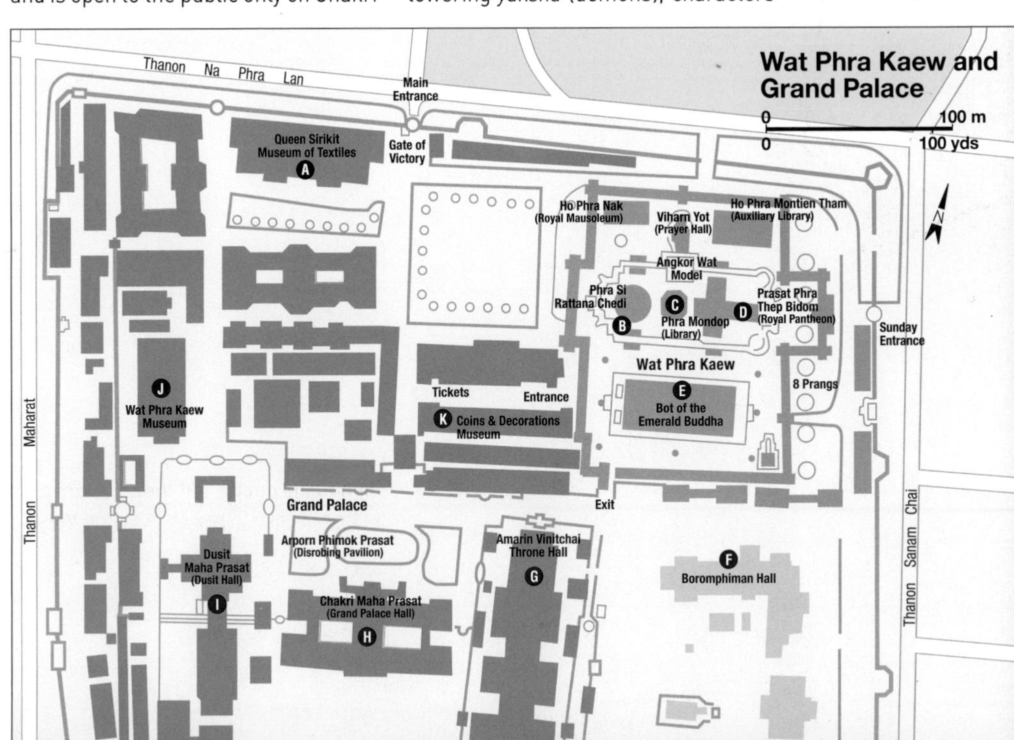

Worshipper outside the Bot of the Emerald Buddha

from the *Ramakien*, stand guard, armed with clubs, protecting the Emerald Buddha. At the complex's eastern edge are eight Khmer-style *prang* structures, which represent Buddhism's Eightfold Path.

THE EMERALD BUDDHA

Wat Phra Kaew's most sacred structure is the **Bot of the Emerald Buddha** E. Outside, at the open-air shrine, the air is always alive with supplicants' murmured prayers and heavy with the scent of floral offerings and smouldering joss sticks.

At the top of the elaborate golden altar, in a glass case under an ornate nine-tiered umbrella, sits the country's most celebrated image, the diminutive 75-cm (30-inch) -tall Emerald Buddha. Despite the name, it is not emerald, but carved from a solid block of green jade. Many non-Buddhists are disappointed by the size of the statue (it's hard to get a clear view of it from ground level), but its power and importance should be instantly apparent from the demeanour of the pilgrims inside the hall.

The Emerald Buddha is of unknown origin. Legend claims it was carved in India, but stylistically it is more likely 13th- or 14th-century Thai. The story says the statue was discovered in Chiang Rai in 1434 hidden inside a *chedi* that was struck by lightning. It was taken to Luang Prabang and remained in Laos until the Thais seized it back in 1779. King Rama I brought the statue, which is said to bestow good fortune on the kingdom that possesses it, to Bangkok in 1784.

THE GRAND PALACE

Adjoining Wat Phra Kaew, the **Grand Palace** embodies Thailand's characteristic blend of temporal and spiritual elements, and has been added to or modified by every Thai king since it was first built. The result is a mélange of architectural styles, from traditional Thai, Khmer and Chinese to British, French and Italian Renaissance. In 1946, following the mysterious death of his brother King Ananda in the Grand Palace, the current king moved permanently to the more private Chitralada

The large grounds fronting the Chakri Maha Prasat.

Palace in Dusit district. The Grand Palace is now used for special ceremonies and state visits.

PALACE BUILDINGS

Exiting Wat Phra Kaew, immediately to the left and tucked behind a closed gate guarded by a sentry is the French-inspired **Boromphiman Hall** Ⓕ. It was built in 1903 as a residence for King Rama VI but is now reserved as a state guesthouse for dignitaries.

To the west, the **Amarin Vinitchai Throne Hall** Ⓖ is part of the three-building Phra Maha Montien complex. Originally a royal residence, it contains the bedchamber of King Rama I.

In a large courtyard adjacent to the throne hall stands the triple-spired former royal residence, and the grandest building in the complex, the **Chakri Maha Prasat** Ⓗ (Grand Palace Hall). This two-storey hall was constructed during King Chulalongkorn's reign (1868–1910) to commemorate the 100th anniversary of the Chakri Dynasty in 1882. An impressive mixture of Thai and Western architecture, it was designed by British architects. The Thai spires, however, were added at the eleventh hour, following protests that it was improper for a hallowed Thai site to be dominated by a European-style building.

The top floor contains golden urns with ashes of the Chakri kings; the first floor still functions as an audience chamber for royal banquets and state visits, while the ground floor is now a **Weapons Museum**. Outside, the courtyard is dotted with ornamental ebony trees pruned in the Japanese *bonsai* style.

The next building of interest is the **Dusit Maha Prasat** Ⓘ (Dusit Hall), built in 1789 by King Chakri (Rama I) to replace an earlier wooden structure. A splendid example of classical Thai architecture, its four-tiered roof supports an elegant nine-level spire. To its left stands the exquisite **Arporn Phimok Prasat** (Disrobing Pavilion). It was built to the height of the king's palanquin so that he could alight from his elephant and don his ceremonial hat and gown before proceeding to the audience hall.

Bangkok's Lak Muang (or City Pillar) houses the city's guardian spirits.

Gilded garuda images encircle the exterior of the Bot of the Emerald Buddha.

Shop

Amulets on display at Wat Mahathat's amulet market come in myriad forms and serve a variety of purposes, from religious or spiritual to the more practical, such as ensuring sexual potency.

Opposite, don't miss the collection of small but exquisite Buddha images made of silver, ivory, crystal and other materials at **Wat Phra Kaew Museum J**. On the way out, next to the ticket office, the **Coins and Decorations Museum K** has coins that date from the 11th century, royal regalia, decorations and medals made of gold and precious stones.

LAK MUANG

Every Thai city has a foundation stone or city pillar, known as the *lak muang*, around which the city's guardian spirits are believed to gravitate, protecting and bringing good fortune to worshippers. Bangkok was officially founded in 1782 when King Rama I erected the **Lak Muang 2** (daily 5am–7pm; free), located across Thanon Sanam Chai from the eastern wall of the Grand Palace.

The gilded wooden pillar resembles the Hindu Shiva *lingam*, which represents strength and potency. It accompanies the taller Lak Muang of Thonburi, which was moved here when that district (and former capital) became part of Bangkok.

Another view of Wat Phra Kaew.

SANAM LUANG

North of Wat Phra Kaew and the Grand Palace, **Sanam Luang 3** (Royal Field; daily 5am–10pm; free) is the site of royal cremations and other important ceremonies such as the birthday of King Maha Vajiralongkorn (28 July), Songkran (New Year) festival in April and the Ploughing Ceremony in May. Kite-flyers also use the grounds in November and from February to April.

NATIONAL MUSEUM

To the west of Sanam Luang at Thanon Na Phra That, the **National Museum 4** (Wed–Sun 9am–4pm; guided tours 9.30am on Wed and Thu) houses a vast collection of antiquities from all over Southeast Asia.

The museum has an interesting history of its own. Its grounds and some of the principal rooms were part of the former Wang Na (Front Palace) that belonged to the king's second-in-line, called the Prince Successor – a feature of the Thai monarchy until 1870.

The oldest buildings in the museum compound date from 1782, including the splendid **Buddhaisawan Chapel**. Built by the Prince Successor as his private place of worship, it contains some of Thailand's most beautiful and best-preserved murals (dating from the 1790s) as well as Thailand's second-most sacred Buddha image, Phra Buddha Sihing, which dates back to 13th-century Sukhothai.

To the left of the museum entrance, the **Sivamokhaphiman Hall** was originally an open-sided audience hall, but now houses a prehistoric art collection. The front of the building is devoted to the **Thai History Gallery**, documenting the country's history from the Sukhothai period (13th century) to the present Rattanakosin period (1782 onwards).

Also on site is the **Red House** (Tamnak Daeng), an old golden teak dwelling that once belonged to King Rama I's elder sister. Built in the Ayutthaya style, the house has an ornate wood finish and elegant early Bangkok-style furnishings.

The central audience hall of the Wang Na is divided into rooms (Nos. 4–15) containing various ethnological exhibits like elephant *howdah*, woodcarvings, ceramics, palanquins, royal furnishings, weapons, *khon* masks, musical instruments and other treasures. Temporary exhibits are displayed in the Throne Hall.

WAT MAHATHAT

Nestled between Thammasat and Silpakorn universities, **Wat Mahathat** ❺ (daily 7am–5pm; free) can be accessed from Thanon Na Phra That or Thanon Maharat. Founded in the 1700s, the temple also houses the **Maha Chulalongkorn Rajavidyalaya University,** one of the two highest seats of Buddhist learning in the country, where King Rama IV spent almost 25 years studying as a monk before acceding to the throne in 1851.

Wat Mahathat exudes a more genuine, working temple atmosphere than the more ceremonial temples in the area, and the temple interior is closed to visitors. Those who are keen to get in tune with their inner selves may do so at the temple's **International Buddhist Meditation Centre** (www.mcu.ac.th/IBMC), which conducts classes and meditation retreats in English.

Across Thanon Maharat, a busy warren of lanes runs from Trok Wat Mahathat to Tha Phra Chan pier. This is the amulet market, where people bargain for religious items ranging from large Buddhas to tiny carvings that one might wear around the neck to bring good fortune.

WAT PHO

South of the Grand Palace and Wat Phra Kaew complex, on Thanon Thai Wang, **Wat Pho** ❻ (daily 8am–5pm; www.watpho.com) is the city's largest and oldest surviving temple. Apart from its historic significance, visitors come to Wat Pho to pay homage to

Amulets on display at Wat Mahathat's amulet market. These come in myriad forms and serve a variety of purposes, from religious or spiritual to the more practical, such as ensuring sexual potency.

Wat Pho's main chedi are dedicated to the Thai monarchs.

Fact

It was an ancient Hindu belief that 108 represented the universe. The numbers signify: 1 – a single entity; 0 – nothing or emptiness; and 8 – infinity. Subsequently the number was incorporated into related religions such as Buddhism in areas like the number of identifying marks on a buddha, the number of prayer beads, the number of temptations, and so on.

the monumental Reclining Buddha, and unwind at its traditional massage centre.

Also known as Wat Phra Chetuphon, the temple dates back to the 16th century. However, it did not achieve real importance until the establishment of Bangkok as the capital. Wat Pho was a particular favourite of the first four Bangkok kings, all of whom added to its treasures. The four towering, coloured *chedi* to the west of the *bot* (ordination hall) are memorials to the past monarchs, and around the hall are some 90 other *chedi*.

The temple cloisters contain almost 400 bronze Buddha images, retrieved from ancient ruins in Sukhothai and Ayutthaya. One of the most important additions was the Reclining Buddha, donated by King Rama III in 1832, who also instructed that the walls be inscribed with lessons on astrology, history and archaeology. The temple became known as Thailand's first university.

Wat Pho's giant Reclining Buddha, 46 metres (150ft) long and 15 metres (50ft) high, depicts the Buddha passing into nirvana, having achieved enlightenment. The flat soles of the feet are inlaid with 108 mother-of-pearl auspicious signs for recognising Buddha. Also numbering 108 are the metallic bowls that line the wall; a coin dropped in each supposedly brings good luck.

Wat Ratchabophit.

WAT PHO MASSAGES

Wat Pho became, and still is, the place to learn about traditional medicine, particularly massage and meditation. The temple's medicine pavilion displays stone tablets indicating beneficial body points for massage. Skirting the temple grounds, several small rock gardens contain statues of hermits striking poses; these were used as diagnostic aids. The **Watpo Thai Traditional Massage School** (Mon–Sat 10am–5pm; www.watpomassage.com) also offers cheap hour-long massages.

MUSEUM OF SIAM

Just south of Wat Pho on Thanon Sanam Chai, the **Museum of Siam** ❼ (Tue–Sun 10am–6pm) has interactive multimedia displays and tableaux explaining what it is to be "Thai". It starts 2,000 years ago and runs through historical eras and population shifts, including the periods of Khmer, Sukhothai and Ayutthayan dominance.

THONBURI

Established by King Taksin after the fall of Ayutthaya in 1767, Thonburi, accessed by ferry or bridge across the Chao Phraya River, served as Thailand's capital for 15 years prior to the establishment of Bangkok in 1782. Fancy riverside condos are starting to appear but there remain few high-end hotels, although those that exist benefit from views to the city across the river. The tourist attractions are largely confined to areas close to the old palace grounds, but one of the most pleasing activities in Bangkok is a tour of Thonburi's canals.

These include **Khlong Bangkok Noi**, which winds into **Khlong Bangkok Yai** and **Khlong Om**. With rickety teak houses, vendors selling produce from boats, fishermen dangling rods out of windows and kids frolicking in the water, the sights along Thonburi's canals are reminiscent of a more peaceful bygone era. The floating markets at **Wat Sai** (daily) and **Taling Chan** (Sat and Sun), once the daily source of fresh produce for local communities, are now little more than tourist souvenir stops.

CANAL AND RIVER CRUISING

Thonburi's major canals are serviced by public longtail boats. But as services can be erratic at certain times of the day, it is better to hire your own private longtail boat for a more leisurely exploration.

There are several good places to visit within easy reach on Khlong Bangkok Noi. Leaving the Royal Barge Museum, nearby on the left is Baan Bu, where craftsmen have made bronzeware bowls called *khan long hin* since their descendants fled Ayutthaya after it was destroyed by the Burmese in 1767. Today Jiam Sangsajja (Mon–Fri 9am–5pm) is the only remaining workshop. Traditionally, *khan* were used to keep drinking water cool and to carry food as alms to monks, but most bowls here sell as decorative items. Next, the delightful Wat Suwannaram (daily 8am–4pm; free), once an execution site for Burmese prisoners of war, is known for the only surviving murals by artists Thongyu and Kongpae. Slightly further is Wat Sisudaram (daily 6am–5pm; free), where you can feed fish and see a small shrine to Thailand's greatest poet, Sunthorn Phu (1786–1855), who studied here.

Getting from pier to pier along the Chao Phraya River is best done by the **Chao Phraya Express** boats, which operate from the southern outskirts all the way up to Nonthaburi in the north. For shuttling from one side of the river to the other, make use of the cheap cross-river ferries; these can be boarded at the many jetties close to those servicing the Chao Phraya Express boats.

Tip

When having a Thai massage, try to relax completely. The massage will involve some contortionist-like poses, and the natural inclination is to resist when you are sometimes bent into awkward positions. Don't resist – just go with the flow.

The National Museum.

Tip

If you've a night to spare and want to cruise the Chao Phraya in style, book a cabin on the Anantara Bangkok Riverside's converted rice barge that sails from Bangkok to Ayutthaya (www.anantara.com/en/cruises-bangkok).

WAT ARUN

When King Taksin first moored at the Thonburi bank of the Chao Phraya River at sunrise after sailing down from the sacked capital of Ayutthaya in 1768, he found an old temple called Wat Magog and thought it a fitting place for the sacred Emerald Buddha. He renamed it Wat Jaeng (The Temple of Dawn), which King Rama IV eventually changed to Wat Arunratchawararam. Now it's known simply as **Wat Arun** ❽ or the Temple of Dawn (daily 8.30am–5.30pm).

After Taksin's demise, the new king Rama I, moved the capital (along with the Emerald Buddha) to Bangkok, but Wat Arun held the interest of the first five kings. In the early 19th century King Rama II enlarged the structure and raised the central *prang* (Khmer-style tower) to 104 metres (345ft), making it the city's tallest religious structure. The great *prang* represents the Hindu-Buddhist mythological Mount Meru, home of the gods with its 33 heavens.

Four smaller *prang* stand at the cardinal points with niches containing statues of Nayu, the god of wind, riding on horseback. The entire complex is guarded by mythical giants called *yaksha*, similar to those at Wat Phra Kaew.

Rama III introduced the colourful fragments of porcelain that cover most of the temple's exterior using broken ceramics that were leftover ballast from Chinese merchant ships.

MUSEUM OF ROYAL BARGES

On the north bank of Khlong Bangkok Noi is the **National Museum of Royal Barges** ❾ (daily 9am–5pm). The dry dock displays eight vessels from a fleet of over 50 that only sails on auspicious occasions. Their last outing – to celebrate the king's 80th birthday in 2007 – saw 2,000 oarsmen, musicians and guards in traditional dress sailing in 52 barges to Wat Arun for a *khatin* ceremony, in which robes are presented to monks.

The original Royal Barge fleet dates back to 14th-century Ayutthaya, while the present craft were constructed in the early 20th century. The king travels in the largest of the barges, the

The giant Reclining Buddha at Wat Pho.

Suphannahongse, made in 1911 from a single trunk of teak stretching 46 metres (151ft).

THE OLD CITY

Dominated by the wide boulevard of Thanon Ratchadamnoen, this section of the "Old City" of Bangkok contains all the peripheral buildings and temples that lie outside the island of Rattanakosin. Khlong Banglamphu and Khlong Ong Ang acted as city moats and ferried supplies from the surrounding countryside. Preservation orders have maintained a strong sense of the past, making this one of the city's most rewarding areas to explore. Aside from tourist attractions, most foreigners head to the district of Banglamphu for cheap accommodation and entertainment in the well-known backpackers' quarter of Thanon Khao San.

WAT RATCHABOPHIT

Located on Thanon Fuang Nakhon, **Wat Ratchabophit** ⑩ (daily 8am–5pm; free) is recognisable for its characteristic amalgamation of Thai temple architecture and period European style. An unusual design places the main circular *chedi* and its circular cloister in the centre. Commissioned in 1869 by King Chulalongkorn (Rama V), the complex took well over two decades to complete.

The ordination hall is covered in brightly patterned Chinese ceramic tiles, known as *bencharong*, while the windows and entrance doors to the hall are exquisite works of art, with tiny pieces of mother-of-pearl inlaid in lacquer. The doors open into one of the most surprising temple interiors in Thailand; a Gothic-inspired chapel of solid columns that looks more like a medieval cathedral than a Thai temple.

WAT SUTHAT

Standing behind the **Giant Swing**, once the venue for a now-outlawed Brahmin ceremony, **Wat Suthat** ⑪ (daily 8.30am–9pm) is considered one of the country's six principal temples. Begun by Rama I in 1807, it took three reigns to complete. The temple is noted for the dimensions of its *bot*, or ordination hall, said to be the tallest in Bangkok, and its *viharn* (sermon hall). They are surrounded by cloisters lined with gilded Buddha images. The 8-metre (26ft) -tall Phra Sri Sakyamuni Buddha, one of the largest surviving bronze images from Sukhothai, was transported by boat from the northern kingdom. The temple courtyard is a virtual museum of statuary, with stone figures of Chinese generals and scholars, which originally came as ballast in rice ships returning from deliveries to China and were donated to temples.

THANON RATCHADAMNOEN

Stretching east and then northeast from the Grand Palace **Thanon Ratchadamnoen** (Royal Passage) splits into three sections eventually reaching Dusit Park. Built at the turn of the 20th century, the tree-lined avenue was modelled on the boulevards of Paris

Fact

The Giant Swing was the venue of an annual Brahman ceremony in former times. Four men would set the swing in motion, trying to grab with their teeth a bag of coins suspended on a pole.

Wat Arun at dusk.

Fact

Bangkok's most famous temple fair is held at Wat Saket each November. Temple fairs are raucous occasions with market stalls, games, fortune telling and theatre.

and has some of the city's widest and least cluttered pavements. On royal birthdays, the area is turned into a sea of fairy lights, flags and royal portraits.

DEMOCRACY MONUMENT

At the crossroads with Thanon Dinso, **Democracy Monument** ⓬ was designed by Italian sculptor Corrado Feroci (also known as Silpa Bhirasri) in 1939. The monument is a celebration of Thailand's transition from absolute to constitutional monarchy in 1932. Marked by four elongated wings, the central metal tray contains a copy of the Constitution. Almost every detail of the monument has symbolic relevance.

The monument was the rallying ground for demonstrations in 1973, 1976, 1992, 2010 and 2014 that led to many civilian deaths.

Further east on Thanon Ratchadamnoen Klang, the **Rattanakosin Exhibition Hall** ⓭ (Tue–Sun, 10am–7pm; www.nitasrattanakosin.com) exhibits the official history of the area from a mainly royal perspective, with multimedia displays including architecture, traditional arts and the Grand Palace. Visitors can also learn some *khon* masked dance and puppetry skills.

Touring Bangkok's canals.

LOHA PRASAT AND WAT RATCHANATDAM

On the right just before the point where Thanon Ratchadamnoen Klang crosses the Pan Fah Bridge, the **Loha Prasat** ⓮ (Metal Palace) shares the grounds of **Wat Ratchanatdam** and is the main attraction here (both daily 8am–5pm; free).

Originally meant to be the temple's *chedi*, Loha Prasat's unusual architecture is said to draw on a Sri Lankan temple design from the 3rd century BC. Commissioned by Rama III in 1846, two tiers square the central tower, peaked by 37 iron spires, which symbolise the virtues needed to attain enlightenment. Just behind the temple is a thriving **amulet market**, similar to the one close to Wat Mahathat.

GOLDEN MOUNT

South of the ruins of Mahakan Fort, and just beyond the old city walls, is the **Golden Mount** ⓯ (Phu Khao Thong; daily 8am–4pm). Started by Rama III as a huge *chedi*, the city's soft earth made it impossible to build on, and the site became an artificial hill overgrown with trees and shrubbery. Rama IV finally added a *chedi* in 1865, when it became Bangkok's highest point.

Visitors take the gentle climb past rock gardens, ringing temple bells and enjoying 360-degree views of the city as the path spirals upwards. There's a refreshment stop halfway.

At the foot of the mount, Wat Saket (free entry), one of Bangkok's oldest temples, is notable for a seated Buddha and murals in the ordination hall and a beautiful Rama I era wooden scripture library.

KHAO SAN ROAD

Located in Banglamphu to the north of Thanon Ratchadamnoen Klang,

Khao San Road ⓰ has been a backpacker hangout since the early 1980s, and was once a rather seedy gathering of cheap guesthouses, noodle shops and poky bars, as portrayed in Alex Garland's novel *The Beach*. In the late 1990s, after local film and TV shows began using the street as a location, young Thais craving a sympathetic ambiance for their own growing indie lifestyle started opening places to hang out in. The result is now a mix of East and West twentysomething culture that stretches over several blocks and is among the most vibrant areas of the city. Recent years have seen an upgrade, with the arrival of boutique hotels like Buddy Lodge, sleek bars and international chains like Starbucks. Although that seedy edge has not been eradicated entirely.

All the needs of the 'alternative' traveller are here; tattooists, hair braiders and body piercers, jugglers and buskers, tarot readers, used books and dealers in fake IDs. And of course, a perpetual party atmosphere.

WAT BOWONNIWET

Just to the north is **Wat Bowonniwet** ⓱ (http://watbowon.org; daily 8am–5pm; free), a modest-looking monastery with strong royal bonds. It was built during the reign of Rama III in 1826, and King Mongkut (Rama IV) served as abbot of the temple for a small portion of his 27 years as a monk. More recently, the former King Bhumibol (Rama IX) donned saffron robes here after his coronation in 1946. Home to Thailand's second Buddhist university, the temple is known for its extraordinary murals painted by monk-artist Khrua In Khong.

DUSIT

From the bridge beside Mahakan Fort, Thanon Ratchadamnoen Klang turns northeast to become Ratchadamnoen Nok, a pleasant, tree-lined boulevard that ends at **Royal Plaza**, which has a bronze equestrian **Statue of King Chulalongkorn** (Rama V) at its centre. The king was responsible for the construction of much of this part of Bangkok, which was then a royal retreat from the city.

The Giant Swing was the venue of an annual Brahman ceremony in former times. Four men would set the swing in motion, trying to grab with their teeth the bag of coins suspended on a pole.

The Museum of Royal Barges.

WATERWAYS

The old thoroughfares of Bangkok were water- rather than land-based. Those that remain reward exploration by boat.

For centuries, the rivers and *khlongs*, or canals, were the main transportation routes. In a land that flooded whenever the monsoon-swollen rivers overflowed their banks, it made little sense to build roads that would be washed away. Rivers and canals also provided natural defences as moats against invaders.

ENGINEERING FEATS

In the 16th century a canal was dug across a loop of the Chao Phraya River, between the present site of Thammasat University and Wat Arun, to cut the distance from the sea to the then Thai capital at Ayutthaya, 85km (55 miles) north. On its banks, two towns rose; Thonburi on the west and Bangkok on the east. Erosion gradually widened the canal, which became the river's main course, while the original river loop became the *khlongs* of Bangkok Noi and Bangkok Yai.

When King Rama I established Bangkok as the new capital, he built concentric canals, turning the city into an island. The most extensive rural canal expansion was ordered by King Chulalongkorn in the late 19th century, and within a few years, thousands of miles of canals crisscrossed central Thailand. Houses were built on bamboo rafts and it was estimated that more than 100,000 boats plied Bangkok's waterways.

A khlong to the west of Bangkok.

BANGKOK'S KHLONG

Zipping along in a *reua haang yao*, or longtail boat, is one of the most pleasant ways to see Bangkok (although it's also noisy, so sit at the front). The low, narrow boat has a truck engine mounted at the stern and a long shaft with a propeller on the end that extends into the water. The boat moves rapidly on the river, and in the narrow canals, where they move more slowly, the shaft allows the craft to turn in a very tight circle.

A lovely 90-minute route wends upriver to Khlong Bangkok Noi. Arrange beforehand a price and any stops you want to make, such as the Royal Barge Museum. Continue up the canal, turning left into Khlong Chak Phra, which soon changes its name to Bang Kounsri and eventually to Bangkok Yai.

The main cross-Bangkok canal is Khlong Saen Saep, dug in 1837 to carry troops to the east, and to join the Bangpakong River for a journey to the sea. It begins in the Old City, but only becomes scenic when it reaches eastern Bangkok, where it passes through lovely rice country.

In the mid-20th century, Bangkokians began leaving boats for cars. Canals were filled in to make roads, and houses were built on land. The congested streets that are sweltering in the hot season become flooded in the monsoon season. Many of the floating markets that closed once goods were transported by road, have now started re-opening as they have become such a hit with tourists.

As well as the *khlongs*, many people enjoy travelling on the Chao Phraya River, not only to escape the roads, for the cool breeze and the cleaner air, but because numerous sites are best seen from the water. There are beautiful colonial-style structures and early European churches and back doors to markets, where water borne goods are still loaded from boats; and not very far north you're into the green countryside. The river is not just a means to get from A to B; it can be a very satisfying tour in itself and well worth an hour or two of your time.

At the time of writing, many of the sights around Dusit were closed after King Maya Vajiralongkorn took up official residence in Amphorn Sathan Residential Hall. His late father, King Bhumibol, had resided previously in the nearby **Chitralada Palace**. As a result, many of the Dusit sites are either closed or being refurbished. Please see below for specific information on the sites affected and check online for the latest updates before attempting to visit.

ANANTA SAMAKHOM

At the north end of the Royal Plaza, the **Ananta Samakhom Throne Hall** is an Italian Renaissance-style hall of grey marble crowned by a huge dome. It was closed to the public at the time of writing.

Started in 1907 by King Chulalongkorn as a grandiose hall for receiving visiting dignitaries and other state ceremonies, the Throne Hall became the country's first parliament after the end of absolute monarchy in 1932. The highlights now are the domed ceiling, with frescoes depicting the Chakri monarchs from Rama I to Rama VI, and an exhibition hall showing beautiful reproductions of classical Thai craftsmanship called Arts of the Kingdom.

VIMANMEK MANSION

The Throne Hall is the largest building in the manicured gardens of **Dusit Park** (Suan Ambhorn, daily 9.30am–4pm; appropriate smart dress is required, no photos allowed), parts of which remain open, and which is home to several museums and former royal buildings. The next most important is **Vimanmek Mansion**, which was also closed to the public at the time of writing.

Originally built in 1868 as a summer house for King Chulalongkorn on the east-coast island of Ko Si Chang, the king had the three-storey mansion dismantled and reassembled on the Dusit grounds in 1901. It is billed as the world's largest golden-teak building, and is constructed without a single nail. The gingerbread fretwork and octagonal tower of this 72-room mansion look more Victorian than period Thai.

Fact

The royal areas of Dusit have a completely different atmosphere to the rest of Bangkok as they are influenced by King Chulalongkorn's visits to Europe at the end of the 19th century. Many buildings have European architecture, the pavements are wider and there is more green space.

Seated Buddha statues at Wat Suthat.

Tip

It's an armchair on a motorbike – or an alfresco oven. Tuk-tuks are Bangkok's signature transport, great for short trips but, once the novelty has worn off, not really one of delight. If you do board, bargain hard for the fare before setting off.

Vimanmek (meaning Palace in the Clouds) offers an insight into how the royal family of the day lived.

ABHISEK DUSIT THRONE HALL

To the right of Vimanmek, the **Abhisek Dusit Throne Hall** was constructed in 1903 for King Chulalongkorn as an accompanying throne hall to Vimanmek; the ornate building is another sumptuous melding of Victorian and Moorish styles, but retains a distinctly Thai sheen. The main hall was used as a showroom-cum-museum for the SUPPORT foundation, a charitable organisation headed by Queen Sirikit that helps preserve traditional arts and crafts. A shop next door sold the handiworks of village artisans. This site was also closed to the public at the time of writing.

DUSIT ZOO

To the east, the grounds of **Dusit Zoo** were originally part of the Royal Dusit Garden Palace, the site of King Chulalongkorn's private botanical garden. In October 2018 the 19-hectare (47-acre) public zoo was closed down, with the roughly 300 species of mammals, almost 1,000 bird species and around 300 different kinds of reptiles relocated to other museums around the country. A new replacement zoo is planned in the Thanyaburi District in the suburbs of Bangkok.

WAT BENJAMABOPHIT

Southeast of the King Chulalongkorn statue along Thanon Rama V, **Wat Benjamabophit** ⓲, more popularly known as the Marble Temple (daily 6am–5pm), is the most recent major temple to be built in central Bangkok and the best example of modern Thai religious architecture.

Started by King Chulalongkorn at the turn of the last century, the wat was designed by the king's half-brother Prince Naris together with Italian architect Hercules Manfredi, and completed in 1911. The collaborators fused elements of the East and West to dramatic effect. The most obvious are the walls of Carrara marble from Italy, the cruciform shape of the main temple

The Democracy Monument.

building and the unique European-crafted stained-glass windows depicting Thai mythological scenes. The *bot*'s principal Buddha image is a replica of the Phra Buddha Chinarat of Phitsanulok, with the base containing the ashes of King Chulalongkorn.

Behind the *bot*, a fascinating gallery holds some 53 original and copied Buddha images from all over Asia, providing a useful educational display. In the early morning, merit-makers gather before its gates to donate food and offerings to monks. This contrasts with other parts of the city, where monks generally conduct alms rounds by visiting communities.

CHINATOWN

The area to the southeast of Rattanakosin was settled by Chinese merchants, who were relocated so the Grand Palace could be built. In 1863, King Mongkut built Thanon Charoen Krung (New Road), the first paved street in Bangkok, and Chinatown soon mushroomed from the original dirt track of Sampeng (now officially Soi Wanit 1). Other adjacent plots of land were given to the Indian and Muslim communities.

With narrow roads and lanes teeming with commercial bustle, this is one of the capital's most traffic-clogged districts. Exploring on foot allows you to soak up the atmosphere. Away from Downtown's plush mega malls, Chinatown is a raw experience of traditional Bangkok: old shophouses, *godowns* (warehouses), temples and shrines, all teeming with life and activity.

SAMPENG LANE

Sampeng was the original mercantile area, where early Chinese immigrants toiled as labourers, rickshaw runners and also dock workers at a time when the river was filled with wooden shops and houses floating on bamboo platforms. It inevitably had its raunchy element and by 1900 was known as "Sin Alley", with lanes leading to opium dens, gambling houses and also brothels. The stretch of **Sampeng Lane** ⓳ that lies between Thanon Ratchawong and Thanon Mangkon sells everything from cheap clothing and footwear to

Khao San Road, backpacker central.

Shop

The main shopping areas in downtown Bangkok are linked by the Skywalk – a covered elevated walkway beneath the Skytrain tracks – connecting Chit Lom, Siam Square and National Stadium Skytrain stations and others along Sukhumvit. This means you can walk from one mall to another under shade and without having to cross the streets.

Chinese confectionery, cosmetics and gems for making your own jewellery.

PAK KHLONG TALAD

With floral garland offerings at temples and shrines all over the city, Bangkok needs a constant supply of fresh blooms for its worshippers. Situated on the riverfront west of Sampeng, **Pak Khlong Talad** ⑳ (Flower Market) serves as the capital's flower and vegetable garden (daily 24 hours). The bargain-priced bunches are a riot of fragrance and colour. The market is a great place for taking photographs. Just to the east from 7pm to 2am each night, the pavements around the Phra Buddha Yodfa Monument host Saphan Phut Market, which is particularly good for clothing and accessories.

PAHURAT MARKET

North of Pak Khlong Talad, **Pahurat Market** ㉑ (daily 8am–6pm) is a two-level bazaar sometimes known as Bangkok's Little India. In the late 19th century, Indian migrants converged here, and their presence is still strongly felt today. It is filled with merchants selling all manner of colourful fabrics and clothes, as well as Hindu deities, wedding regalia and traditional Thai dance costumes. On Thanon Pahurat and parts of Thanon Chakraphet, cheap curry eateries and Indian tea and spice stalls do a roaring trade. Nearby at Thanon Chakraphet, the golden-domed **Sri Guru Singh Sabha** gurdwara (daily 8am–5pm; free) is the focal point of Bangkok's Sikh community.

WAT MANGKON KAMALAWAT

North of Pahurat, one of Chinatown's two main thoroughfares Thanon Charoen Krung, links the old city with the new. It contains the most revered temple in Chinatown, **Wat Mangkon Kamalawat** ㉒ (daily 8am–6pm; free), also known as Leng Noei Yee (Dragon Flower Temple). Built in 1871, the wat is one of the most important centres for Mahayana Buddhism in Thailand, and elements of Taoist and Confucian worship are also prevalent. The temple is also the centre point for the Vegetarian Festival each October.

Women praying at Wat Mangkon Kamalawat.

SOI ITSARANUPHAP

Chinatown's most interesting lane, **Soi Itsaranuphap** (Soi 16), runs south from Thanon Phlab Phla Chai all the way to Sampeng Lane, although it changes names a couple of times along the way. It is packed with stalls and shops selling all manner of items, including miniature paper houses, cars, even mobile phones, and "hell money", all items that the spirits of deceased relatives might need in the afterlife. They are burnt as offerings at temples in Chinese *kong tek* ceremonies.

TALAD KAO AND TALAD MAI

Soi Itsaranuphap contains two of the city's best-known markets. Between Thanon Charoen Krung and Thanon Yaowarat, **Talad Mai** (New Market) has been plying goods until sundown for more than 100 years. The two-century-old **Talad Kao** ㉓ (Old Market) lies close to Sampeng, and usually wraps up by late morning. Both have a reputation for high-quality meat, fish and vegetables, with the latter being a place to find more unusual ingredients. Both markets overflow with crowds during the Chinese New Year.

Running parallel to Sampeng Lane, **Thanon Yaowarat,** with its forest of neon signs looks much like a busy Hong Kong street. It is best known for its gold shops and its name, 'Yaowarat', which is what the locals call Chinatown.

WAT TRAIMIT

Just east of the point where Thanon Yaowarat meets Thanon Charoen Krung, across from the China Town Gate, stands the unremarkable-looking **Wat Traimit** ㉔ (www.wattraimitr-withayaram.com; daily 8am–5pm; heritage centre closed on Mon). It is also known as the Temple of the Golden Buddha, because on the left as you enter the grounds, a huge marble *mondop* (pavilion) houses the world's largest solid-gold Buddha. The 5.5-ton, 3 metre (10ft) Sukhothai-era statue is believed to date from the reign of King Ramkhamhaeng the Great (c.1279– 98). It was discovered by accident in the 1950s when a stucco figure during transportation

The China Town Gate, with Wat Traimit in the background.

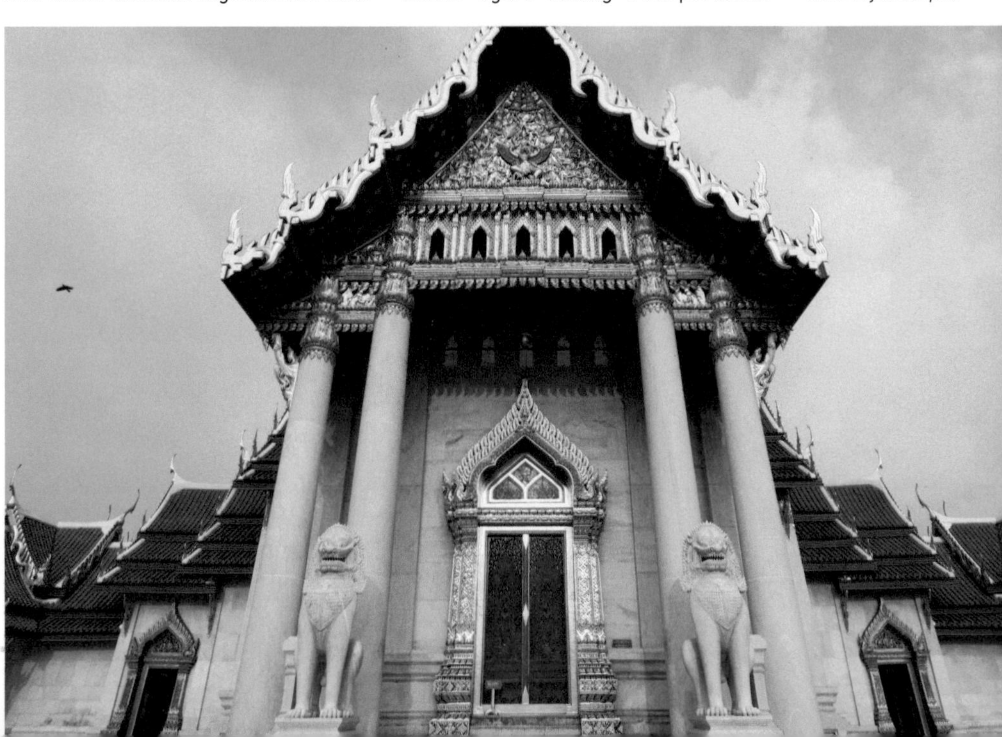

Wat Benjamabophi.

Lumphini Park, a rare open space in a busy city.

crashed to the ground, revealing the solid gold image under the cracked surface. The *mondop* is also the location of the Yaowarat Chinatown Heritage Centre, which has old photos, prints of period paintings and tableaux.

PATHUMWAN AND PRATUNAM

The heart of downtown's shopping area is **Pathumwan,** a sprawl of malls connected by the Skytrain and an expanding skywalk that allows you to avoid the cracked pavements and steaming heat of traffic. One sight harking back to a more traditional city is The **Jim Thompson House** ㉕. It stands near the banks of **Khlong Saen Saep**, the construction of which in the early 19th century enabled the capital to spread further east from the old city. This area extends east as far as Thanon Withayu (Wireless Road), a major thoroughfare lined with embassies and upmarket housing.

THANON RAMA I

Siam Square ㉖, along Thanon Rama I, is another example of downtown Bangkok losing its character to air-conditioned malls. Its once maverick air of teen-friendly low-rise shops, cafés and restaurants is fast disappearing, although it remains a favourite hangout for students from the nearby Chulalongkorn University, which owns the land.

Cross the footbridge over Thanon Phaya Thai from Siam Square and head into the mayhem of **Mahboonkrong** (www.mbk-center.co.th), better known as the MBK Center. It's always busy with teens, but it has appeal for all ages, with goods ranging from cosmetics to cameras, art fakes to clothes and jewellery.

Close by, north of Thanon Rama I, the 11-storey **Bangkok Art and Culture Centre** ㉗ (BACC; Tue–Sun 10am–9pm; free except for special events; www.bacc.or.th) has regular contemporary art and multimedia shows. The retail outlets on the lower floors have been issued to small independent galleries or organisations such as the Thai Film Foundation and Bangkok Opera. Art markets feature regularly on the concourse and there are performances in a small auditorium.

A traditional tea shop in Chinatown.

East along Thanon Rama I, the **Siam Discovery Centre** and **Siam Centre** are interconnected. Both stock local designer wear, sports and surf clothing shops, plus interior decor and electronics. Bangkok's outlet of Madame Tussaud's (daily 10am–8pm; www.madametussauds.com/bangkok/) is on the 6th floor of **Siam Discovery Centre**.

Continuing east, next is the swanky **Siam Paragon** with its glut of chichi designer shops and numerous restaurants and cafés. In the basement is Bangkok **Sea Life Ocean World** (daily 10am–9pm; www.sealifebangkok.com), where you can swim with sharks and view over 30,000 marine creatures.

At the corner of Thanon Rama I and Thanon Ratchadamri is **Central World,** which at 550,000 sq metres (5.9 million sq ft) is Bangkok's largest mall. It includes the department store Isetan, along with a staggering array of shops, restaurants and two enormous cineplexes. The adjoining Centara Grand Hotel has an open-air bar-restaurant, Red Sky, on the roof.

PRATUNAMAREA

Northwards, past the Khlong Saen Saep canal and Thanon Phetchaburi, is the somewhat dingy **Pratunam Market.** This bustling warren of stalls is more a lure for residents than tourists, with piles of cheap clothing, fabrics and assorted fashion accessories. The area is shadowed by the **Baiyoke II Tower** (309 metres/1,014ft), whose 84th floor observation deck (daily 10.30am–10pm) offers excellent views of the city and beyond. Across Thanon Phetchaburi from Pratunam, Platinum Fashion Mall (daily 9am–8pm) is home to hundreds of small clothes, textiles and accessory stalls and **Panthip Plaza** (daily 10am–9pm) is devoted to IT.

SUAN PAKKAD PALACE

Most tourists make a beeline for the Jim Thompson House, missing out on an equally delightful abode, the **Suan Pakkad Palace** ㉘ (daily 9am–4pm; charge includes guided tour; www.suanpakkad.com). Located a short walk along Thanon Sri Ayutthaya from Phaya Thai Skytrain station, the name Suan

Drink

In the cool season, the square outside Central World becomes a beer garden with rock bands and large-screen TVs. This is also the location for Bangkok's New Year Countdown, similar to the one held in London's Trafalgar Square.

The Jim Thompson House offers respite from the cacophony of the city.

THE JIM THOMPSON HOUSE

The oasis of the Jim Thompson House is a principal downtown attraction on most tourist itineraries (daily 9am–6pm; entry fee includes compulsory guided tours of the museum; www.jimthompsonhouse.com). Its former occupant was the American entrepreneur responsible for the revival of Thai silk. An architect by training, Thompson first came to Thailand at the end of World War II, later returning to Bangkok to live. He became interested in the almost redundant craft of silk weaving and design, which he subsequently (and profitably) reinvigorated. He mysteriously disappeared in the Malaysian jungles in 1967, but his well-preserved house still stands today by the banks of the Khlong Saen Saep. Thompson was an enthusiastic collector of Asian arts and antiquities, many of which adorn his traditional house-turned-museum.

The house museum comprises six teak structures, which were transported from Ayutthaya and elsewhere to the silk-weaving village of Ban Khrua, just across Khlong Saen Saep, before being reassembled at their present site in 1959. From the windows of the house, it's easy to imagine how scenic the view would have been some 50 years ago, looking across the lush gardens, or "jungle" as Thompson called it. Next to the old house is a pondside café, while opposite is the Jim Thompson Art Center, a contemporary gallery that holds exhibitions of local and international arts and crafts.

Pakkad, or "Cabbage Patch", refers to its former use as farmland before the palace was constructed here in 1952. The former residence of the late Prince and Princess Chumbhot, both of whom were prolific art collectors and gardeners, Suan Pakkad comprises five teak houses set amid a beautiful, lush garden and lotus pond. Converted into a museum, the wooden houses display an eclectic collection of antiques and artefacts.

THANON PLOENCHIT MALLS

Further south where Thanon Rama I morphs into Thanon Ploenchit, there are yet more malls, including the **Erawan Bangkok**, a boutique mall connected to the Grand Hyatt Erawan hotel. Across the street, the **Gaysorn** is a designer mall that is relatively quiet save for the trickle of "Hi-So" spenders and window-shoppers. A large treasure trove of Thai arts and crafts can be found to the north along Thanon Ratchadamri, just opposite Central World, at the three-floor emporia of **Narayana Phand**. At the southeast corner of Ratchadamri and Ploenchit is the atmospheric **Erawan Shrine** ㉙.

SNAKE FARM

For an encounter with dangerous reptiles, visit the **Queen Saovabha Memorial Institute** ㉚, popularly called the **Snake Farm** (www.saovabha.com; Mon–Fri 8.30am–4.30pm, Sat–Sun 8.30am–noon). Located on Thanon Rama IV, it was founded in 1923 as the Pasteur Institute. The institute's principal work lies in the research and treatment of snakebites. Venom-milking sessions (Mon–Fri 11am; slide show 30 mins before) are the most popular times to visit, when the snakes are pulled from the pit and mercilessly goaded for the audience. Every day at 2.30pm the audience have an opportunity to hold the snakes and take pictures with them.

LUMPHINI PARK

Green spots are few and far between in Bangkok, but in the southeast of the downtown area, at the junction of Thanon Rama IV and Thanon Ratchadamri, **Lumphini Park** ㉛ (daily 4.30am–9pm;

Offerings at the Erawan Shrine.

ERAWAN SHRINE

The **Erawan Shrine** (daily 8am–10pm) sits at one of Bangkok's busiest intersections, yet it's the aromatic haze of incense that hits you rather than exhaust fumes. The shrine is dedicated to the four-headed Hindu god of creation, Brahma. It was erected in 1956 after an astrologer recommended it would ward off bad luck plaguing construction of the Erawan Hotel (now the Grand Hyatt Erawan), after which it was named. The bad luck ceased and the shrine has since been revered for its powers. So revered, in fact, that when a mentally disturbed man smashed it with a hammer in 2006, an angry mob beat him to death. Photographs of the shrine were displayed so that people could still worship until a new one was erected: 1,000 people attended the unveiling. Underlining the influence of supernatural belief in Thailand, an opposition leader accused supporters of then Prime Minister Thaksin Shinawatra of being responsible for the destruction, saying they wanted to maintain power over the country through black magic. On 17 August 2015, a bomb exploded at the shrine, killing 20 and injuring 125, mostly tourists. No group or individual has since claimed responsibility for the attack.

People walking by or travelling in cars press their palms together to *wai* the shrine as they pass, and supplicants line up to buy offerings in return for good fortune. Those whose wishes are granted might give thanks by paying the on-site dance troupe to perform.

free) is the city's premier green lung. The park was bequeathed to the public in 1925 by King Vajiravudh (Rama VI), whose memorial statue stands in front of the gates. Embellished with lakes (pedal boats for hire) and a Chinese-style clock tower, the park sees elderly Chinese practising t'ai chi and sweaty joggers at sunrise or sunset. The park hosts outdoor classical concerts in the cool season.

BANGRAK AND SILOM

Bangkok's main business district, Bangrak, lies to the south of Pathumwan's shopping malls. Gravitating eastwards from some of the Chao Phraya River's premier riverfront real estate, Thanon Silom is the principal thoroughfare, ending at Thanon Rama IV with Lumphini Park beyond. Parallel to Silom are Sathorn, Surawong and Si Phraya roads.

Thanon Silom and **Thanon Sathorn** are considered the city's main business arteries, but at dusk, the trade on Silom moves to market stalls and sex.

But it's not all starchy office blocks and unbridled sleaze that make up Bangrak. Between the River City shopping centre and the luxury Shangri-La hotel is what is regarded as the old *farang* (foreigner) district. Easily navigable, the lanes in this part of town still hold a few buildings from its days as a 19th-century port settlement, although even some of the best are in poor repair.

ASSUMPTION CATHEDRAL

Down a side road on Oriental Avenue opposite the **Mandarin Oriental** 32 a small square is dominated by **Assumption Cathedral** (daily 6am–7.15pm; free; www.assumption-cathedral.com). Built in 1910, the red-brick cathedral's ornate interior is topped by a beautiful domed ceiling towering over a large sacristy with gilded pillars. Take a breather here and mull over Bangkok's secluded architectural delights.

ASIATIQUE

A ten-minute boat shuttle south along the river from Saphan Taksin pier, Asiatique (daily 4pm–midnight; www.asiatiquethailand.com) is one of the city's

Fact

Silom is in an area called Bangrak, which means 'Village of Love.' Consequently, every St Valentine's Day the district office is besieged by hundreds of couples wanting to be married in a lucky place on an auspicious day.

A LUXURIOUS RETREAT

Founded back in the 1870s, the riverside Mandarin Oriental Hotel has consistently been rated as one of the world's best. A retreat for the influential and wealthy, its grandeur has endured through the years. However, the uninspiring exteriors of two newer extensions, the Garden Wing (1958) and the River Wing (1976), added to the original Author's Wing, somewhat detract from its classic feel. To imbibe its old-world atmosphere fully, sit down to afternoon tea in the elegant Authors' Lounge and muse over the literary greats who have passed through its doors, such as Somerset Maugham, Noël Coward and Graham Greene. As well as partaking of first-class wining and dining, guests can also ride the shuttle across the river to the Oriental's spa, in a traditional house carved from golden teak.

The Mandarin Oriental hotel by the Chao Phraya River.

Motorcycle taxis waiting for passengers.

few pedestrian friendly waterfront spaces and has many restaurants and stalls, including some relocated from the now-closed Suan Lum Night Market. They sell a wide range of items such as handicrafts, home decor and clothes. Also here are *katoey* (ladyboy) shows at Calypso Cabaret (shows 7.30pm and 9pm; www.calypsocabaret.com) and the **Joe Louis Theatre** (one show nightly at 8.00pm; www.joelouistheatre.com). Joe Louis was the working name of Sakorn Yangkeawsot, who revived the fading art of *hun lakhon lek*, a unique form of traditional Thai puppetry.

MAHA UMA DEVI TEMPLE

Looming behind the Assumption Cathedral at the corner of Silom and Charoen Krung is the faux-classical **State Tower** and its fashionable rooftop drink-and-dine venue, **Sirocco**.

Continuing further along Thanon Silom, the lively Hindu **Maha Uma Devi Temple** ㉝ (daily 6am–8pm; free), on the corner of Soi Pan, is named after Shiva's consort, Uma Devi. It was established in the 1860s by the city's Tamil community, who maintain a strong presence in the area. It is known to Thais as Wat Khaek, meaning "guests' temple" (*khaek* is also a less welcoming term used by locals for people from the Indian Subcontinent). The temple and surrounding streets are particularly busy during the Navaratree Festival in September–October.

KHWAENG SILOM GALLERIES

In the streets around Chong Nonsi and Surasak stations are some of the best exhibition spaces for modern Thai art. Two spaces to check out are H Gallery Bangkok (www.hgallerybkk.com; Wed–Mon 9am–6pm) housed in an old mansion building, and Number 1 Gallery (Mon–Sat 11am–7pm), which also has a good little café on site. Wander the streets between Silom and N Sathom roads and you are likely to come across many more.

PATPONG

Come nightfall, the upper end of Thanon Silom transforms as stall holders set up a **night market** commandeering the narrow pavements from Soi 2 to

Shoppers at the MBK shopping centre.

Soi 8. The main focus of the market is **Patpong** ㉞ (Soi 1 and Soi 2) where the main goods are counterfeit watches, fake name-brand bags and clothes, and bootleg CDs. Prices will start high, so bargain low.

Patpong became one of Bangkok's first Western-oriented red-light areas when it opened in the 1960s to cater to US GIs on R&R from the Vietnam War. Depending on your tolerance levels, there is a surprisingly unsleazy ambience here and the two sois are prime tourist attractions.

Nevertheless, you will be hassled by touts flashing menu cards with a list of notorious ping-pong acrobatics, and these – along with ground floor go-go bars with girls pole dancing in bikinis – are accessed by some women tourists, too, who drop in for a peek at Bangkok's seamier side. In fact, this type of invitation card has a long history. In 1923 the writer Somerset Maugham recorded a man giving him a card offering the services of 'Miss Pretty Girl,' who would 'put him in dreamland with perfumed soap.'

A few lanes east, **Silom Soi 4** is a compact street of dance clubs, restaurants and bars that is largely but not exclusively gay. Nearby the expensive hostess bars along **Soi Thaniya** cater for mainly Japanese clientele, and further on still Silom Soi 2 is dedicated to full-on gay party goers.

KUKRIT PRAMOJ'S HOME

Halfway down Thanon Sathorn, **MR Kukrit Pramoj's Heritage Home** ㉟ (daily 10am–4pm) is tucked away on Soi Phra Phinij. The late Kukrit Pramoj, born of royal descent (signified by the title Mom Ratchawong – MR), was briefly prime minister during the disruptive 1970s, but is better remembered as a prolific author and cultural preservationist.

His home – now a museum – comprises five stilt buildings that recall the traditional architecture of the Central Plain. The *bonsai* garden adds a sense of serenity, and the home has displays of beautiful *objets d'art*, antique pottery and an ornate bed that belonged to Rama II.

The Chong Nonsi intersection in the southern suburbs.

SUKHUMVIT

The eastern extension of Thanon Rama I/Ploenchit is **Thanon Sukhumvit**, a bustling, traffic-clogged road that actually runs all the way to the Cambodian border. The Skytrain is the fastest way between its quickly multiplying malls, restaurants, and entertainment venues. Although thin on major tourist attractions, Thanon Sukhumvit is where most of the city's growing expatriate community lives and is one of Bangkok's main nightlife areas.

A mall of go-go bars on Soi 4, Nana Entertainment Plaza gives a lascivious veneer to Sukhumvit's energetic early blocks. Opposite, Soi 3 (known as "Soi Arab" for its shisha cafés), marks the start of a night market that crowds the pavement all the way to Soi 19, where, across Asoke intersection, are more red lights on Soi Cowboy.

Nonetheless, Sukhumvit overall is far from sleazy, and has many of the city's best nightspots, including **Q Bar** and **Bed Supperclub** on Soi 11.

Sukhumvit night market.

KAMTHIENG HOUSE

One of Sukhumvit's oldest buildings is the headquarters of the **Siam Society** at Sukhumvit Soi 21 (Soi Asoke), founded in 1904 to promote the study of Thai culture. There's an excellent library full of rare books on Thai history, old manuscripts and maps.

In the same grounds, **Kamthieng House** 36 (Tue–Sat 9am–5pm; www.siam-society.org) is an authentic 150-year-old wooden home transplanted from Chiang Mai and carefully reassembled here as an ethnological museum.

EMPORIUM AREA

On the corner of Soi 24, near Phrom Phong Skytrain station, stands one of Sukhumvit's premier shopping malls, **Emporium**. Big on interiors and fashion it also hosts several cinemas and the excellent Thailand Creative & Design Center, with a design reference library and regular exhibitions (daily 10am–9pm; www.tcdc.or.th).

Further east is **Soi Thonglor** 37, lined with restaurants, cafés and nightspots (see box).

THONGLOR NIGHTLIFE

One of Bangkok's liveliest neighbourhoods is Soi Thonglor, a rapidly developing area with low-rise malls, funky bars and clubs and a wide choice of restaurants, many located in old town houses. It's where increasing numbers of 20 to 50-something "creatives" head for a night on the town.

Notable bars include Iron Fairies (www.theironfairies.com) for burgers and jazz, and Fat Gut'z (www.facebook.com/FatGutzSaloonEastville) for fish and chips with RnB. There's a buzz around the cocktails and Thai food at Soulfood Mahanakorn (www.soulfoodmahanakorn.com); upmarket cocktails can be found down the Rabbit Hole (www.facebook.com/rabbitholebkk/) and gourmet fusion at Water Library (www.waterlibrary.com) with a mere 10 seats. For affordable wines go to Wine Republic (tel: 0-2714 7599) and for late clubbing it's Demo (www.facebook.com/demobangkok).

LOVE FOR SALE

Bangkok has a complex historical relationship with its sex workers: the trade is both illegal and openly tolerated, a source of shame to some, and of income to others.

Thailand made prostitution illegal in 1960, although the law is rarely enforced, and sex is openly for sale not only in the country's many girlie bars, brothels and massage parlours, but also by freelancers in the bars of five-star hotels. In part this openness is because it is an accepted practice for Thai men to patronise prostitutes or have a *mia noi*, literally "little wife" or mistress on the side. Thais usually patronise more discreet brothels or, at the higher end, plush members-only clubs, while tourists go to a town's red light districts such as Patpong and Nana Entertainment Plaza.

Most Bangkok sex workers, both male and female, come from northeast Thailand, where incomes are the lowest in the country, although local press reports of middle-class students feeding a consumer lifestyle are also common. Sex workers from poorer regions regularly send money home to support their families. Many cross-cultural marriages have started in a Bangkok brothel, and government figures have cited foreign husbands in Northeastern villages on GDP statistics.

NGOs estimate there are between 200,000 and 300,000 sex workers in Thailand, and, having found that few are motivated to leave the business, no longer focus their efforts on extricating them. Organisations such as the Thai NGO Empower (www.empowerfoundation.org/index_en.html) instead educate sex workers about the dangers of HIV and how to protect themselves from sexually transmitted diseases, teach them English, campaign for equal status with other workers, and promote a sense of dignity within their members.

The non-voluntary side of the sex trade is infinitely grimmer. While enforced prostitution in Thailand is less common generally than at its height in the 1990s, there are still an estimated 60,000 child prostitutes in the country, many willingly sold by their parents, against whom convictions are very rare. Other vulnerable groups affected are stateless hill tribe girls and illegal immigrants from neighbouring Laos, Burma and Cambodia. Thailand is also an established conduit for trafficking to other countries. Lured by promises of factory jobs or waitress work, girls unwittingly sell themselves into lock-up brothels, where they must work until they have earned back the price the brothel-owner paid for them.

New laws are occasionally mooted. The latest attempt at legalising prostitution, in 2004, foundered largely on moral objections, while the 1997 law, the Prevention and Suppression of Trafficking in Women and Children Act, focuses on prosecuting traffickers rather than prostitutes. It promises, at least on paper, the confiscation of assets to provide compensation for trafficked women and girls. In reality, traffickers are rarely affected and Empower claims that, due to overzealous policing and entrenched attitudes towards prostitutes, sex workers are now more victimised by authorities pursuing the act than by traffickers.

The highly visible nature of sex work in Thailand is at odds with the otherwise high moral code of behaviour in the country. Women especially are expected to deport themselves modestly, and the Ministry of Culture (much to the outrage of many) constantly pronounces about appropriate behaviour and dress.

Neon lights and working life in the infamous Patpong neighbourhood.

BANGKOK'S SUBURBS

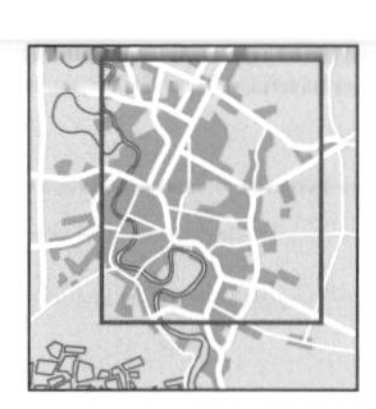

Accessible getaways from the big city's relentless pace are sleepy Nonthaburi by the river, delightfully green Rama IX Royal Park, child-friendly Dream World and the sprawling Chatuchak Weekend Market; highly recommended for incurable shopaholics.

Main attractions
Chatuchak Weekend Market
Nonthaburi
Ko Kret
New Lumpini Boxing Stadium

Map on page 138

There are some surprisingly rural retreats very close to the city centre, where the pace of life is a slow amble. But first there are the strobe lights of Bangkok's biggest dance clubs.

RATCHADAPHISEK

North along Sukhumvit Soi 21 is Ratchadapisek, an area served by Pra Ram 9 MRT station, and one of the city's designated Nightlife Zones. Most revellers head to the huge clubs of Royal City Avenue (RCA), although a few smaller bars along Thanon Ratchadapisek also draw young Thais. People come here, too, for the cultural shows of Siam Niramit (daily shows at 8pm; www.siamniramit.com) and the Thailand Cultural Centre, one of Bangkok's major venues for classical music.

Souvenir shopping at the Chatuchak Weekend Market.

MARKET CHATUCHAK WEEKEND MARKET

Next to Kamphaeng Phet MRT station, and also the final stop on the Skytrain's northern line at Mo Chit station is **Chatuchak Weekend Market** ❶ (Sat–Sun 9am–6pm; www.chatuchakmarket.org). Reputed to be Asia's biggest flea market, Chatuchak's sheer scale and variety awes even the least enthusiastic of the estimated 200,000 shoppers that weave through the maze-like alleys every weekend.

It's a heady assault on the senses, so an early start (arrive by 9am) is recommended to beat the soaring heat and crowds. Although the market is loosely partitioned into sections, stumbling across gems of kitsch or culture is a great adventure, and you will find anything from crafts, home decor and clothing, to flowers, snakes and violins. Wherever you are, beware of pickpockets, who can spot a distracted cashed-up shopper at 100 paces.

Free maps of the market are available at the **Chatuchak Information**

Counter at the entrance near Section 27 along Thanon Kamphaengphet 3.

Numerous cafés, snack and juice bars are dotted throughout the market, with many staying busy long after the stalls pack up for the day. After sunset, the outer edge of the market on Thanon Kamphaengphet comes alive with a string of bars and coffee shops.

If the market is simply too overwhelming, retreat to the nearby **Chatuchak Park** (Queen Sirikit Park; daily 5am–6.30pm; free). Nearby, on Srinakarin Soi 51, just behind the Seacon Square, the night market Talad Rod Fai (The Train Market; Thu–Sun 5pm–1am) is popular for vintage items, from cameras to car parts, furniture and fashion.

NONTHABURI

The riverside town of **Nonthaburi** ❷, around 45 mins north of Bangkok by express boat, feels a world away from the hectic city. The journey weaves past tiny tugboats, gilded temples and communities of stilted houses. At Nonthaburi, it's worth exploring the streets and markets, or charter a longtail boat to visit the island of Ko Kret or the scenic Khlong Om. A canal trip along it will take you past durian plantations and water-based communities. Five minutes upriver from Nonthaburi pier brings you to the beautifully restored 19th-century temple of **Wat Chalerm Phra Kiet**.

KO KRET

Further upstream from Nonthaburi, the car-free island of **Ko Kret** ❸, best reached by chartered longtail boat from Nonthaburi, makes for a laidback half-day. The island is encircled by a path you can walk in about three hours or in half that time by rented bicycle. The islanders are primarily the ethnic Mon group, who migrated to central Thailand from Burma. The ferry stops beside Wat Poramaiyikawat (Mon–Fri 1–4pm, Sat–Sun 9am–5pm; free), where a small museum displays amulets, a hem (monk's coffin) and other old accoutrements of monastic life. The island also has a couple of pottery villages, where you can watch all the processes in action and buy items such as bowls, incense burners and ornate vases.

DREAM WORLD

Bangkok's **Dream World** ❹ (Km 7, Thanon Rangsit Nakornnayok; Mon–Fri 10am–5pm, Sat–Sun 10am–7pm; www.dreamworld.co.th) comprises Dream World Plaza, Dream Garden, Fantasy Land and Adventure Land.

A sightseeing train circles Dream Garden, while a cable car and monorail offer views of the park and surrounding rural areas. Thrill-seekers should head for the stomach-churning Adventure Land for rollercoasters, a swinging Viking ship, a Super Splash log flume and the Grand Canyon water ride. In Snow Town, locals experience frosty weather, with sledge rides down a slope made of artificial snow.

AIR FORCE MUSEUM

Plane spotters will appreciate the **Royal Thai Air Force Museum** ❺ (171 Thanon

Allow a sufficient amount of time to browse the gargantuan Chatuchak Market.

A Mon potter at Ko Kret.

Eat

En route to Dream World, stop off at one of the restaurant barges that moor up along Khlong Rangsit canal beside Thanon Rangsit Nakorn Nayok. They all specialise in a delicious noodle dish found only in this area.

Phahonyothin; http://rtaf.mi.th/; daily 8am–4pm; free). Exhibits include the only Model I Corsaire and one of only two Japanese Tachikawas in existence, plus Thailand's first domestically built aircraft, the 1920s Model II Bomber Boripatr. There are also helicopters and jetfighters on display. With little English-language signage, the museum is geared more towards organised groups.

SAFARI WORLD

Some 45km (28 miles) northeast of Bangkok near Minburi, **Safari World** ❻ (99 Thanon Ramindra; www.safariworld.com; daily 9am–5pm) contains a safari park and a marine park. You can either drive in or take an organised minibus tour with an English-speaking guide. Animals include giraffes, zebras, ostriches, rhinos and camels, while dolphins and sea lions perform acrobatics. Other attractions include water and jungle rides, stunt shows and animal feeding. While these practices have been criticised by animal-rights groups, the park nevertheless retains its popularity.

LUMPINEE BOXING STADIUM

New Lumpini Boxing Stadium ❼ (Thanon Ram Intra; www.lumpineemuaythai.com; matches on Tue, Fri and Sat at 6pm) is the country's premier venue for the sport of *muay Thai* (Thai boxing). The sport, although brutal – arms, elbows, knees and feet are all used – is highly ritualised, with the contestants initially performing a *wai kru kru* dance of respect for their trainers. A traditional Thai *pipat* band sits ringside accompanying the action with a wailing of pipes and reeds. The crowd becomes increasingly animated as the punches rain in and the betting action is a whirlwind of arms signalling odds and wagers across the arena.

PRASART MUSEUM

The **Prasart Museum** ❽ (9 Soi 4A Thanon Krungthep Kreetha; tel: 02-379 3601/7; visits only by appointment Tue–Sun 10am–3pm) contains owner Prasart Vongsakul's collection of antique Thai arts and crafts in several beautiful buildings, all replicas inspired by classic architectural styles. They include a European-style mansion, a

Go karting at Dream World Amusement Park.

Khmer shrine, central and northern Thai teak houses, plus Thai and Chinese temples, all set in a lush garden.

BANGKRAJAO

Although just 30 minutes from town, **Bangkrajao** ❾ is a protected green haven of mangrove and palm plantations that could be miles away. Get there by boat from Wat Khlong Toei Nok Pier and explore the charms of Ban Nam Pueng Floating Market and Suan Si Nakhon Keun Kan (also known as Central Park) by bicycle, either with outfits such as Spice Roads (www.spiceroads.com) or hired at rental shops by the arrival pier. You can also stay at the Bangkok Tree House (tel: 082-995 1150; www.bangkoktreehouse.com), which is much more stylish (and expensive) than the name implies.

WAT THAMMAMONGKHON

At the easternmost reaches of Thanon Sukhumvit at Soi 101, **Wat Thammamongkhon** (daily 6am–6pm; free) has a 95-metre (312ft) -high *chedi*, which is the tallest in Bangkok and offers commanding views of the low-rise eastern suburbs. Built in 1963, the *chedi* is modern in design, containing study rooms for novice monks and a lift to the top-most circular shrine room.

At the *chedi*'s base, the Will Power Institute runs classes in Buddhist meditation. The three-level glass pavilion beside the temple houses a 14-tonne Buddha image and a 10-tonne sculpture of the Chinese goddess Guanyin, both carved from a solid slab of jade.

RAMA IX ROYAL PARK

One of the city's largest green spaces, the 81-hectare (200-acre) **Rama IX Royal Park** ⓫ (daily 5am–7pm) offers a delightful escape from the city. Unfortunately, the park's suburban locale in Sukhumvit 103 entails taking a 20-minute taxi ride from Udom Suk Skytrain station. In a city desperately thin on public greenery, the park's opening in 1987 as a 60th birthday tribute to the king was a welcome addition.

With a dome-covered botanical garden, canals and bridges, water-lily pond, Chinese and Japanese ornamental gardens, the park is a delight.

Enjoying a picnic at Rama IX Royal Park.

Feeding the giraffes at Safari World.

Erawan Waterfall at Erawan National Park, Kanchanaburi.

Damnoen Saduak Floating Market.

CENTRAL THAILAND

When Bangkok overwhelms, easy escapes within a few hours' drive from the city provide welcome relief. Choose from ancient monuments, sandy beaches or verdant national parks.

Wat Phra Sri Rattana Mahathat, Lopburi.

Bangkok has much to offer, but when you tire of its charms, there is an array of attractions within just a few hours' drive. Some are strictly day trips but several, especially beach destinations, can be extended into leisurely week-long stays. Getting around in Thailand is relatively easy and cheap, with a good network of domestic flights, a regular, if slow, rail network, and frequent inter-city buses, although drivers can be reckless. The roads, themselves, are generally decent, if you want to drive yourself.

The nearest and most accessible areas from Bangkok are in the flat, fertile Central Plains, which contain the remnants of former kingdoms and several expansive national parks. To the west are attractions like the Rose Garden cultural shows, the world's largest Buddhist shrine, at Nakhon Pathom and Kanchanaburi, with its legendary Bridge on the River Kwai. The area around Kanchanaburi has river rafting, trekking and waterfalls. Further west are the ancient Khmer ruins at Prasart Muang Singh, while due north are the rainforests at Erawan and Sai Yok national parks.

Bang Pa-In Palace.

The area immediately south of Bangkok is scant on tourist sights; the main attractions are the Ancient City, where you can see Thailand in miniature, and the Crocodile Farm and Zoo.

Heading into the Gulf of Thailand coast, Hua Hin is where royalty and wealthy Thais have kept holiday homes for over a century.

The Eastern Seaboard has beach escapades, all the way from scandalous Pattaya, through Ko Samet, to the white sands of Ko Chang. And north, the ancient city of Ayutthaya is a grand repository of faded ruins, dating to the 14th century, when it functioned as Thailand's capital. Some say the best part about Ayutthaya is getting there; on a teakwood barge winding up the sinuous Chao Phraya River. Still further north is Lopburi, the old summer retreat of the Ayutthayan kings.

To the northeast of Bangkok, the main attraction is Khao Yai National Park, a favourite spot for Thais seeking picturesque mountains, waterfalls and a break from the city heat.

Phra Pathom Chedi.

WEST OF BANGKOK

Home to the world's tallest Buddhist monument, the historic River Kwai Bridge and spectacular waterfalls in rainforest-clad national parks, this region offers history, culture and nature in equal measure.

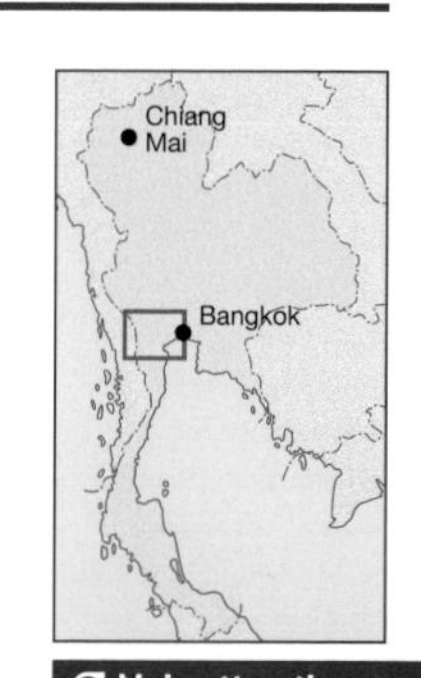

Main attractions

- Sampran Riverside
- Phra Pathom Chedi
- Sanam Chandra Palace
- Damnoen Saduak Floating Market
- Kanchanaburi
- Erawan National Park
- Prasat Muang Singh
- Sai Yok National Park

Map on page 146

The provinces west of Bangkok have a number of attractions in range of a day trip or a pleasant overnight break, but the closer you get to the border with Myanmar (Burma) it is worth considering a couple of nights or more. Most people heading in this direction make a brief stop in Nakhon Pathom to see the huge *chedi* that dominates the town, before heading on to Kanchanaburi famous for its so-called "Bridge on the River Kwai", with its tragic wartime associations. However, also fascinating are the seldom-visited coastal provinces of Samut Sakhon and the lush lowlands of Samut Songkhram.

NAKHON PATHOM

SAMPRAN RIVERSIDE

Some 32km (20 miles) west of Bangkok on Route 4 towards Nakhon Pathom is **Sampran Riverside** ❶ (www.sampranriverside.com; daily 8am–6pm), formerly the Rose Garden. It features well-landscaped gardens with roses and orchids, as well as a resort-style hotel, a cultural centre, restaurants, tennis courts, an artificial lake with paddleboats, a spa and an excellent golf course.

The main draw for tourists here are the cultural and nature-based activities. These include daily Thai cooking classes, Rim Klong Art, which explores aspects of traditional creativity like coconut leaf weaving, silk pressing and clay figurine making. There is also a tour of an organic farm and a weekend farmers' market. Otherwise, spend time browsing the Cultural Village and take part in the morning workshops scattered around the village.

SAMPHRAN ELEPHANT GROUND

Just a stone's throw from the Sampran Riverside is **Samphran Elephant Ground & Zoo** (www.elephantshow.com; daily 8.30am–5.30pm), another

Manicured grounds at the Sampran Riverside Resort.

> **Fact**
>
> The Jumbo Queen contest that takes place at Samphran Elephant Ground annually on 1 May seeks a "well-padded lady" who "best exhibits the characteristics of the majestic pachyderm to persuade people to support the cause of elephant conservation in Thailand". Strange but true. More details at www.jumboqueen.com.

family-oriented attraction where visitors can ride an elephant and learn about its importance in traditional Thai culture. Other animals include gibbons, macaques, pythons, crocodiles and birds.

Samphran Elephant Ground is a very popular attraction, but controversial too, with a number of critics claiming there's mistreatment of the animals. In recent years animal rights groups have correctly called attention to the questionable use of practices like elephant performances and crocodile wrestling.

PHRA PATHOM CHEDI

Beyond the Sampran Riverside on Route 4, 56km (35 miles) west of Bangkok, is the town of **Nakhon Pathom ❷**, known for the colossal **Phra Pathom Chedi** (daily 8am–5pm). Measuring 120 metres (390ft), the site of this landmark is believed to have had an association with the Buddhist faith from around 150 BC based on Indian-style Buddhist artefacts found locally. Later, from the 6th–11th centuries, Nakhon Pathom was the centre of Dvaravati, an affiliation of city-states populated by ethnic Mon. There has been a *chedi* on this site since the 6th century, although the original was devastated in a Burmese attack in 1057 and lay in ruins until King Rama IV built a new one over the remains in 1860 and constructed a replica of the original a few metres to the south.

The temple that surrounds the *chedi* is one of the most important in Thailand. It has four *viharns* (prayer halls) marking the cardinal compass points, each with a Buddha image. The northernmost, containing a standing Buddha, holds the ashes of King Rama VI (1910–25). The outer terraces are notable for Chinese statuary and a large reclining Buddha.

Nearby is the **Phra Pathom Chedi National Museum** (Wed–Sun 9am–4pm), which has artefacts including tools, carvings and statuary from the Dvaravati period.

West along Thanon Rajamankha Nai, King Vajiravudh (Rama VI) commissioned **Sanam Chandra Palace** (daily 5–9am and 4–8pm) in 1907 for royal visits. Although the grounds are open to the public, the palace buildings,

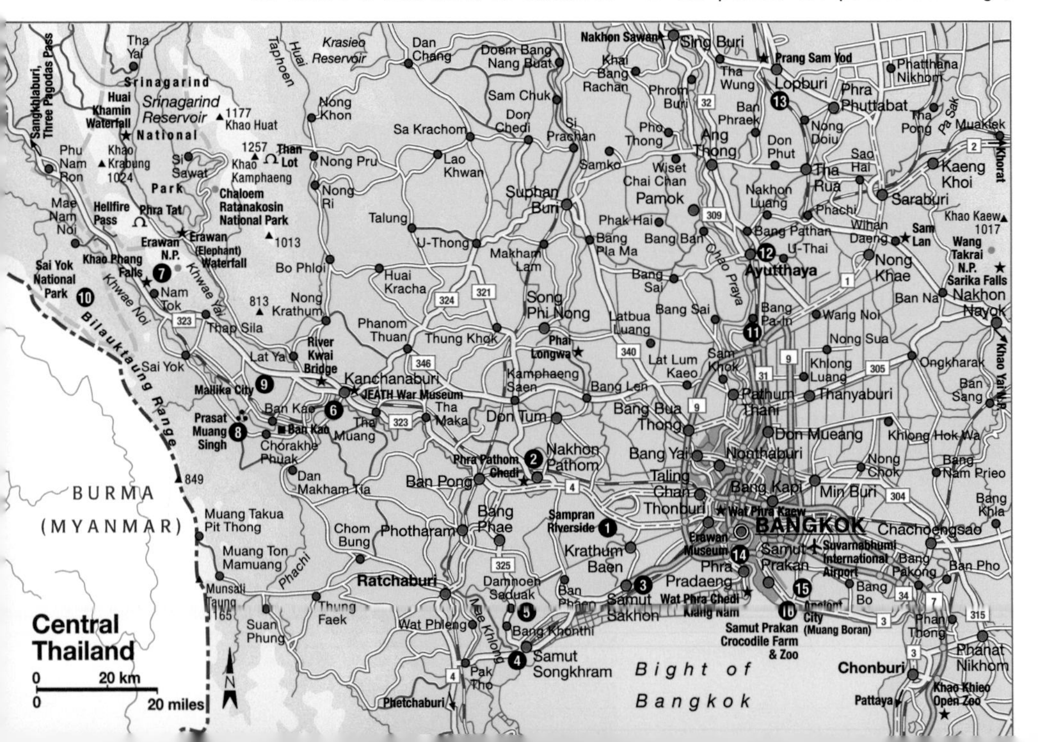

which include a Thai-style pavilion and an idiosyncratic structure in English Tudor style, are off-limits apart from a small museum that contains memorabilia of King Vajiravudh. Nevertheless, their fairy tale castle-style architecture is easily appreciated from the outside.

SAMUT SAKHON

A good way to approach the coastal port of **Samut Sakhon** ❸, 28km (17 miles) southwest of Bangkok, is by the Mae Khlong railway line that connects to Thonburi in Bangkok. The line carries passengers on a 40-minute journey through the capital's suburbs, then through thriving vegetable gardens, groves of coconut and areca palms, and rice fields. A busy fishing port, Samut Sakhon (still often called by its previous name Mahachai) lies at the confluence of the Tachin River, the Mahachai Canal and the Gulf of Thailand. The main landing stage on the riverbank is marked by a clock tower and a seafood restaurant.

At the fish market pier, it's possible to hire a boat for a round trip to Samut Sakhon's principal temple, **Wat Chong Lom**, at the mouth of the Tachin River. Most of the temple structures are modern, except for an old *viharn* immediately to the right of the temple's river landing. The *viharn* dates back about a century. The grounds overlooking the river are laid out with shrubs and flowering trees. There is also a bronze statue of King Chulalongkorn commemorating his visit to the temple.

SAMUT SONGKHRAM

From Samut Sakhon, cross the river to the railway station on the opposite side. Here, board a second train for another 40-minute trip to **Samut Songkhram** ❹, 74km (46 miles) from Bangkok, on the banks of the Mae Khlong River. The route passes by broad salt flats, with their picturesque windmills slowly turned by the sea breezes.

The smallest province in Thailand, Samut Songkhram has abundant fruit orchards. Pomelo, jackfruit, rose apple, lychee, mango, as well as the ubiquitous bananas and coconuts, are harvested here before being sent to Bangkok to be loaded onto the ice-packed vending carts that trundle the streets of the capital. Samut Songkhram itself is just another fishing town; wandering around its wharf is an olfactory and visual experience. Teak barges can be hired for private dinner cruises up the river (ask at riverside restaurants), a trip made more picturesque by the swarms of fireflies that magically illuminate the shoreline of *lamphu* trees in the evenings.

DON HOI LOT

Another option, accessible by either car or longtail boat from Samut Songkhram, is **Don Hoi Lot**, at the mouth of the Mae Khlong River. Don Hoi Lot is, in fact, a bank of fossilised shells that has become a popular attraction with locals. It's a great place to enjoy fresh seafood and tube-like clams (*hoi lot* in Thai means "straw clams"). In the late afternoon when the tide is low,

Tip

If you see an elephant being made to beg in the street, don't be tempted to hand over any cash. Your money will be better spent if donated to a registered charity, rather than to a possibly unscrupulous *mahout*.

Catching razor clams at Don Hoi Lot.

Rose apples harvested in the orchards of Samut Songkhram.

villagers enthusiastically search the muddy estuary for their quarry.

KING BUDDHALERTLA NAPHALAI MEMORIAL PARK

From Samut Songkhram, you can detour to Amphawa district to visit the **King Buddhalertla Naphalai Memorial Park**, also known as King Rama II Memorial Park (Mon–Fri 8.30am–5pm, Sat and Sun until 5.30pm), situated at the birthplace of Rama II. This small museum houses arts and crafts from the early Rattanakosin period in four beautifully reconstructed teakwood stilted houses, illustrating how Thai people lived during the rule of King Rama II. Rare trees, some of which are mentioned in classical Thai literature, flourish in gardens around the museum. A fair here every February celebrates Thai music, dance and drama.

Nearby, the **Amphawa Floating Market** anchors in front of the old Wat Amphawa each Friday, Saturday and Sunday afternoon (2–10pm). It's located about a 10-minute walk from the historical park. Many communities in the area had floating markets until roads superseded waterways over the last 30 years, and Amphawa was reopened following the tourism success of Damnoen Saduak. However, it is smaller and has a more authentic atmosphere.

Also close, just off Route 325, is Ban Pinsuwan Benjarong (Ben Ja Rong; tel: 034-751 322; Mon–Sat 8am–noon and 1pm–5pm, Sun 8am–noon), a family workshop making traditional Benjarong pieces. You can watch craftsmen and buy from a small selection of items. There is also a small ceramics museum.

Produce for sale at Damnoen Saduak.

DAMNOEN SADUAK

From Amphawa, hire a longtail boat for a trip up the Mae Khlong River to the **Damnoen Saduak Floating Market** ❺ (daily 6am–noon) in Ratchaburi Province. If travelling directly from Bangkok, an early morning departure is necessary to beat the tour buses that flock here by 10am.

While it is possible to walk along the bankside lined with souvenir stands, it's far more fun to hire a longtail boat and float between the colourful fruit- and vegetable-laden wooden vessels, paddled by smiling women in wide-brimmed straw hats. Traditionally, smallholders would take their wares by boat to their local floating markets and sell them directly, while still bobbing on the water.

If you've hired your own longtail boat, you could ask the boatman to take you deeper into the countryside for a better view of canal-side communities.

KANCHANABURI

Located around 130km (81 miles) west of Bangkok, the provincial town of **Kanchanaburi** ❻ is well worth the two-to-three hour drive. You can also travel by train or bus, either for a busy day trip or a relaxing overnight stay.

Kanchanaburi is known primarily for its bridge over the infamous "Death Railway" built during World War II by Allied POWs and Asian labourers under the watch of the occupying Japanese army. Thousands of lives were lost as the malnourished and ill-equipped prisoners struggled under appalling conditions to complete over 400km (250 miles) of railway track linking Thailand with Burma.

Despite these associations, Kanchanaburi has a laidback feel and has several interesting temples, as well as nearby caves, waterfalls, forests and the remnants of a 13th-century Khmer palace.

RIVER KWAI BRIDGE

The latticed steel **Bridge on the River Kwai** (also known as Khwae Yai) can be reached by boat or road from Kanchanaburi. Period steam trains are parked close by, including an ingenious Japanese supply truck that could run on both road and rail. There are more exhibits at the main railway station on Saeng Chuto Road.

You can walk across the bridge, but gaps in the planking reveal long drops into the river, so people have to shuffle carefully around each other on the firm central plates between the tracks. Niches between the spans provide a refuge in case a rare train happens along.

The bridge itself was the second of two structures, built side by side across the river; the earlier wooden bridge was completed in 1942, with the sturdier steel structure erected by May 1943. Both were a constant target for Allied bombers and were eventually bombed out of action in 1945. Only the eight curved segments on each side of the current structure are original; the rest was rebuilt after the war as part of Japan's wartime reparations.

The tragic saga was represented in the 1957 film *The Bridge on the River Kwai*, directed by David Lean and starring Alec Guinness. The movie won seven Academy Awards, although it contained several historic inaccuracies – most blatant of which was that the bridge was destroyed by commandos, when in fact it was bombed by Allied planes.

Today, most of the old railway tracks have been removed, although three trains run daily from the bridge, on a sheer-drop narrow track past jungle and limestone cliffs to the terminus at Nam Tok about two hours away, where you can swim in a nearby waterfall during the rainy season. Some remnants of the track can also be seen at **Hellfire Pass**, about 14km (9 miles) from Nam Tok, the longest of several mountain cuttings hacked out by the POWs and Asian labourers. The **Hellfire Pass Memorial Museum** (daily 9am–4pm; free) has several exhibits and a film about the railway.

WORLD WAR II MUSEUM

Located beside the bridge is the **World War II Museum** (daily 8am–5pm), also known as the Art Gallery & War Museum. It contains an odd mixture of exhibits, most of which have nothing at all to do with the war. But if you are into kitsch, there's plenty of interest. Around the building's exterior are life-size sculptures of significant figures involved in the war; the likes of Hitler, Churchill,

Tip

Instead of staying at a land-based hotel in Kanchanaburi, opt for a floating guesthouse moored by the river bank. Be warned, though; while these are atmospheric, they can also get very noisy during weekends, thanks to loud music and karaoke boats packed with young Thais.

Damnoen Saduak Floating Market.

Tip

Kanchanaburi town is quite small but too big to walk everywhere. You can get around town by tuk-tuk or *songthaew* (open-backed taxi vans) for around B30, or hire motorbikes and bicycles along River Kwai Road.

Einstein and Hirohito are among those given an almost comic treatment.

JEATH WAR MUSEUM

The small but informative **JEATH War Museum** (daily 8am–6pm), just before the gate of Wat Chaichumpol on Thanon Pak Phraek at the southern end of Kanchanaburi, grants a better appreciation of the enormous obstacles the prisoners faced. Its peaceful locale on the banks of the Mae Khlong River (the larger river formed by the merge of the Kwae Yai and Kwae Noi), shadowed by a 500-year-old *samrong* tree, provide for a quiet moment of reflection.

The acronym JEATH comes from the first letter of some of the principal countries that were involved in this regional conflict during World War II, namely Japan, England, America, Thailand and Holland. The museum is split into two buildings, the larger of which is a long bamboo hut similar to those that housed the POWs during their construction of the Siam–Burma railway. Inside is a collection of poignant photographs, sketches, paintings, newspaper clippings and other war memorabilia illustrating the harsh conditions the POWs endured during their period of enforced labour and incarceration.

DEATH RAILWAY MUSEUM

The town's most coherent WWII displays are at the Death Railway Museum in the **Thailand-Burma Railway Centre** (www.tbrconline.com; daily 9am–5pm), adjacent to the Allied War Cemetery. The museum within has eight galleries tracing the history and sufferings of the people involved in the Death Railway, including a replica of the original wooden bridge, a timeline and useful maps plotting Japanese expansion in Asia, videos and prisoners' personal items such as diaries.

ALLIED WAR CEMETERY

The **Kanchanaburi Allied War Cemetery** (daily 8.30am–5pm; free) opposite the museum holds the graves or memorials of 6,982 Allied soldiers, representing less than half of the 16,000 soldiers who lost their lives building the railway. Immaculate green

JEATH war museum.

DEATH RAILWAY

The Japanese began work on a railway line between Thailand and Burma in 1942 to link supply lines between Burma and Japanese positions in the rest of Asia. For most of its 400km (250-mile) length from Bangkok to the Burmese border, the railway followed the valley of the Kwai Yai River, with construction taking place simultaneously in different areas. In the end, nearly 15km (9 miles) of bridges were completed. The Japanese forced some 250,000 Asian labourers and 61,000 Allied POWs to construct 260km (160 miles) of rail on the Thai side, leading to the Three Pagodas Pass on the Thai-Burmese border. It is estimated that 100,000 Asian labourers and 16,000 Allied POWs lost their lives between 1942 and 1945 from beatings, starvation and disease.

lawns planted with colourful flowers add a sense of serenity to the graves of the British, Australian and Dutch soldiers lined row after row. The American casualties were repatriated.

Located in a more tranquil setting is the **Chung Kai Allied War Cemetery** (www.cwgc.org; daily 9am–5pm; free), situated across the river just southwest of Kanchanaburi town. Another 1,690 POWs are said to be buried at this site.

AROUND KANCHANABURI

For those who opt to stay overnight in Kanchanaburi, the surrounding countryside holds plenty of interest. The limestone crags on the southern outskirts of town are home to cave temples. Some nimble legwork is required in order to navigate the claustrophobic passageways that lead to the eerily lit meditation cells filled with Buddha images. While generally safe, don't venture into the more remote caves unaccompanied.

One of the most frequently visited cave temples is **Wat Tham Mangkhon Thong** (daily 8am–5pm), primarily known for its "floating nun". An old nun, who has since died, used to float on her back and in sitting position in a large pool of water while in a state of meditation. Today, a young disciple gives her own interpretation of the ritual – in return for a fee – for busloads of tourists.

ERAWAN NATIONAL PARK

Other trips in the vicinity include the spectacular seven-tiered **Erawan Waterfall**, found in **Erawan National Park** ❼ (http://portal.dnp.go.th; daily 8am–4.30pm) and best visited during – or just after – the rainy season (May–Nov), when the water is at full flow. Situated some 70km (40 miles) north of Kanchanaburi, it is a popular sight and can become quite congested with locals at weekends and on public holidays.

The route to the waterfall starts from the national park office. The climb up the first few levels is manageable, but getting up to the slippery sixth and seventh levels is not recommended unless you are fit and reasonably agile. You can cool off at the inviting natural pools (don't forget your swimsuit) at the base of each of the tiers. The

The Bridge on the River Kwai.

thundering water flow from the highest level is said to take on the shape of the three-headed elephant, Erawan, hence its name.

There are several hiking trails in the park, which covers some 550 sq km (212 sq miles) and comprises mainly deciduous forests with limestone hills rising up to 1,000 metres (3,300ft). One of the most popular hiking options is the 90-minute Khanmak-Mookling trail; the 1,400-metre (0.85-mile) circular route starts from the national park office. Also taking approximately 90 minutes, the Wangbadan Cave trail takes you through bamboo and evergreen forest along a 1,350-metre route.

PRASAT MUANG SINGH

Located 43km (27 miles) west of Kanchanaburi off Route 323, the Khmer ruins of **Prasat Muang Singh** 8 (daily 8am–4.30pm) are situated in a manicured park. The site makes for a great picnic spot as it is located beside the picturesque Khwae Noi River (a smaller tributary of the Khwae Yai). The central sanctuary of this 13th-century temple complex points east, and is in direct alignment with its more grandiose sister, Angkor Wat in Cambodia. Although nowhere near as impressive or intricate as Angkor Wat, Prasat Muang Singh is still a fascinating testament to just how far west the Khmer empire stretched at the height of its power.

On the same site is a small exhibition hall containing duplicates of Khmer sculptures, while near the river is a Neolithic burial site displaying partially uncovered skeletons.

MALLIKA CITY

Just over 7km (4.5 miles) northeast of Prasat Muang Singh is the period village of **Mallika City** 9 (www.mallika124.com; daily 9am–8pm), which is designed to look like a Siamese settlement at the turn of the 20th century. The site includes curious buildings like a turntable bridge, which can be moved to allow larger boats to pass through, traditional wooden stilt houses, and a farm and floating market where you can buy snacks and souvenirs. It is

Prasat Muang Singh Historical Park.

also possible to dress up, and wander round, in traditional clothing.

With the arrival of evening, a dinner and cultural show spectacle begins, featuring *khon* and *satchatri* dancing, among other events. Dinner starts at 6pm, while the show starts at 7pm daily.

SAI YOK NATIONAL PARK

Less visited is Sai Yok Waterfall in **Sai Yok National Park ⑩** (http://portal.dnp.go.th; daily 8am–6pm). The cascade here (again best seen in the rainy season, or just after) is a little more remote at 100km (62 miles) northwest of Kanchanaburi and best undertaken on an overnight tour.

The national park covers over 500 sq km (193 sq miles) of forest – predominantly teak – with one side bordering Myanmar. The park is also known as the habitat of the smallest known mammal in the world, the bumblebee bat. Found in Sai Yok's limestone caves in 1974, the creature, which weighs a mere 2 grams (3/4oz) – and is hardly larger than a bumblebee – has been declared an endangered species. An interesting sight is Tham Daowadung, a cave filled with eerie stalactites.

To the north of the park is Hin Dat Hot Springs (daily 8am–6pm), another worthy stop. Just metres away from the cold rushing waters of the river, bathers can soak in the steaming-hot mineral waters.

SANGKHLABURI

If you have an extra day to spare, a beautiful 230km (140 miles) drive west of Kanchanaburi is the small town of Sangkhlaburi, set on a man-made lake. The population includes Karen, Mon and Burmese, as well as Thai, so Burmese dishes and goods are sold in local cafés and at the dry market. Thailand's longest wooden bridge links to a Mon village across the lake. Guest houses can arrange boating, fishing and trekking trips to national parks, and day passes into Burma are available at the Three Pagodas Pass border post, nearby. Sangkhlaburi is also accessible via jungle trek from Um Phang.

Sangkhlaburi, Kanchanaburi Province.

The Erawan Waterfall is best visited after the rainy season.

A FEAST OF FRUITS

There is a sizeable range of fruits in Thailand, many of which may be unfamiliar. As well as bananas and pineapples, there are all kinds of brilliantly coloured and strangely shaped produce to sample.

Thai people love food, and during the afternoon they snack on an incredible variety of fruits. For visitors who are in need of a boost, fruit can be a great source of refreshment and energy. Traditional fruit sellers have glass-fronted carts stacked with blocks of ice and peeled pieces of seasonal fruit. Choose a selection of what you want to eat and the vendor will pop it into a bag for you along with a toothpick for spearing the slices. Some fruits, like pineapple, are eaten with a little salt and ground chilli, a twist of which is supplied separately. Don't be afraid of this combination; the natural sweetness of the pineapple is enhanced by these salty and spicy additions.

One of the best ways to cool down is to drink a delicious fruit juice or *naam phon-la-mai*. To order, say the Thai word for water (*naam*) in front of the name of the fruit, or just point to your selection from the fruits on display. Another favourite drink is fruit juice blended with ice; known as a *naam pan* or "smoothie". You can have syrup mixed in to sweeten your juice or salt added (as the Thais like it) to bring out the flavour of the fruit.

CONTROVERSIAL DURIAN

People either love or hate durian. Ask any visitor in Thailand to recall the first time they came across it and they will describe, in detail, its "perfume." To most *farang* (Europeans or Caucasians), the durian's odour is repugnant, but for the Thais the fruit commands the utmost respect.

According to devotees, the rewards of eating durian far outweigh any objections to its smell. The only way to enter the great durian debate is to try it for yourself. If you can't face eating the fruit *au naturel* there is durian cake, ice cream and chewing gum.

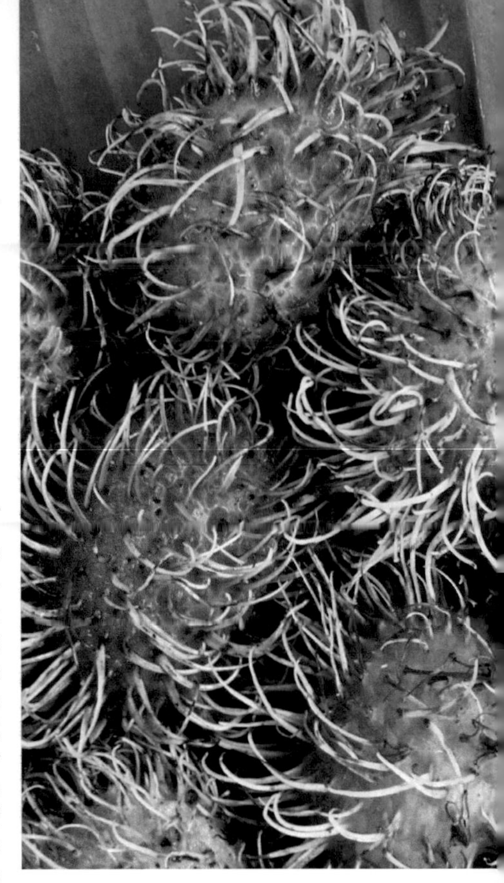

Rambutan (ngaw). The hairy rambutan (rambut means hair in Malay) is a close relative of the lychee and has a similar taste. There is a technique to squeezing it open to avoid squirting yourself with its juices; as any Thai will happily show you.

Snake fruit (ra-gahm or salak). Easily peeled, this unusua dry fruit has a pleasant flavour. The leathery skin varies from bright red to brown.

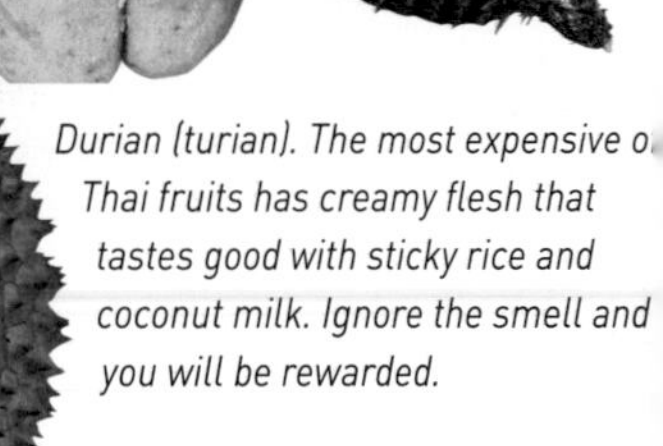

Durian (turian). The most expensive o Thai fruits has creamy flesh that tastes good with sticky rice and coconut milk. Ignore the smell and you will be rewarded.

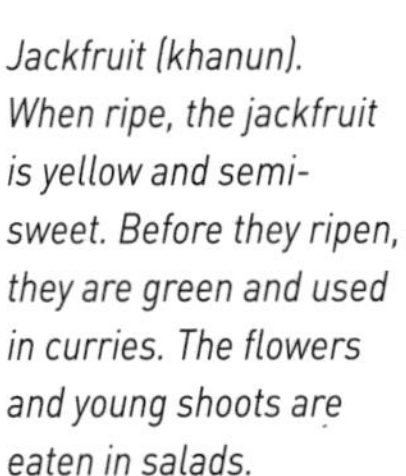

Jackfruit (khanun). When ripe, the jackfruit is yellow and semi-sweet. Before they ripen, they are green and used in curries. The flowers and young shoots are eaten in salads.

Crops: a growing concern

Farming and fishing have always been at the centre of Thai life. Despite rapid industrialisation, this is still the case. Thailand is self-sufficient in food, and agribusiness is an important pillar of the Thai economy, claiming nearly a quarter of GDP and making Thailand the only net food exporter in Asia. Thailand is the world's leading exporter of canned pineapple and has big overseas markets in canned logans and rambutans.

Fruit production is expected to increase as available land and labour resources dwindle and farmers switch from producing staple crops, such as rice and cassava, to cash crops like soya beans, fruits, sugar cane and rubber. Large fruit farmers are starting to process their products before they reach the consumer, and many are now applying for loans to invest in equipment to dry and freeze their produce. Although some of this produce will be sold to Thailand's neighbours, much of it will end up in the snack-food departments of Japanese supermarkets; Japanese businesses have already set up factories in Thailand to process fruits, vegetables and nuts for their home market.

Mangosteen (mangkhut). Thais believe durian requires the cool, refreshing sweet taste of the mangosteen as a chaser. See if you can guess how many sections your mangosteen has before you break it open.

Dragonfruit (gaeo mang gawn). The common name for the pitaya, whose bright magenta skin makes it very striking. It grows best in dry areas.

Pomelo (som). At up to 30cm (12ins) in diameter, this is the world's largest citrus fruit. It is related to the grapefruit, although it has a sweeter flavour. Used in Thai salads.

Golden Buddha at Wat Phra Mahathat, Ayutthaya.

NORTH OF BANGKOK

Ayutthaya – the capital city of the Thai kingdom in the 14th–18th centuries – is a time capsule that captures the faded grandeur of that era. Further north is Lopburi, where the Ayutthayan kings retired to during the hot summers.

Main attractions

Bang Pa-In
Ayutthaya Historical Park
Lopburi

North of Bangkok in the Central Plains, watered by the Chao Phraya River and a network of tributaries and canals, lie two important sites that played a central role in Thai history. The first is Ayutthaya, Thailand's fabled capital from 1350 to 1767; the second is Lopburi, a former Khmer stronghold and part of the ancient Mon Dvaravati kingdom from the 6th to 9th centuries.

BANG PA-IN

Bang Pa-In ⓫ (daily 8am–5pm), some 60km (37 miles) north of Bangkok, is an eclectic collection of palaces and pavilions once used as a royal summer retreat. Most people make a stop here before continuing another 25km (16 miles) north to Ayutthaya.

The palace buildings date from the late 19th- and early 20th-century reigns of King Chulalongkorn (Rama V) and King Vajiravudh (Rama VI), who came here to escape the mid-year rains in Bangkok. Following the wishes of Chulalongkorn, the buildings that are dotted around the manicured grounds feature Italian Baroque, European Gothic, Victorian and Chinese architectural styles. Only parts of the royal quarters are open to public view, but they provide a glimpse into Chulalongkorn's penchant for European furniture and decor.

The **Aisawan Thipphaya-at**, an 1876 Thai-style pavilion in the middle of the lake adjacent to the main entrance, is regarded as one of the finest examples of Thai architecture. Other buildings of note include the two-storey Chinese-style **Wehat Chamrun Palace** and the red-and-yellow **Ho Withun Thatsana** observation tower, both situated on islets, and the Italianate **Warophat Phiman Hall**.

Across the river and slightly south of the palace, **Wat Niwet Thammaprawat** is surmounted by a spire and as a result looks more like a Gothic

Maps on pages 146, 158

A mix of Thai and Western-influenced architectural styles at Bang Pa-In.

The lookout tower known as Withun Thasana.

Christian church than a Buddhist temple. The pleasant gardens are embellished with canals, fountains, bridges and quirky elephant-shaped hedges.

AYUTTHAYA

The ruined old city of the former capital **Ayutthaya** ⓬ now forms Ayutthaya Historical Park and is tantalisingly suggestive of the 18th century when it had 2,000 golden temples, a population of 1 million, and trade links from Holland to China. It is a Unesco World Heritage site, but suffered badly, with 158 monuments damaged, in the country's worst floods in decades in 2011. This, coupled with urban development and encroachment from vendors feeding the tourism industry, led the Global Heritage Fund to name Ayutthaya as one of the top 10 sites in Asia facing "irreparable loss and destruction." It is still an arresting sight, but more government funds are needed to ensure its future.

Located 85km (55 miles) north of Bangkok, Ayutthaya was built at the confluence of three rivers with a canal dug to create an island. Palaces and temples were erected alongside a further network of canals, few of which exist today. Europeans dubbed it the "Venice of the East." Even today, chartering a longtail boat around the moat is the best way to see many of the riverbank ruins. Several boat operators from Bangkok organise regular trips from the capital in either modern express boats or traditional teakwood barges.

AYUTTHAYA'S FOUNDATIONS

Ayutthaya was founded around 1350 by Prince U Thong (later known as King Ramathibodi I). Thirty years later, the northern kingdom of Sukhothai was placed under Ayutthayan rule, which then extended its control east to Angkor and west to Pegu in Burma. By the 1600s, it was established as one of the richest and most cosmopolitan cities in Asia – exporting rice, animal skins and ivory – and had a population of 1 million, greater than that of London at the time. Merchants came from Europe, the Middle East and elsewhere in Asia to trade in its markets, with many eventually settling there.

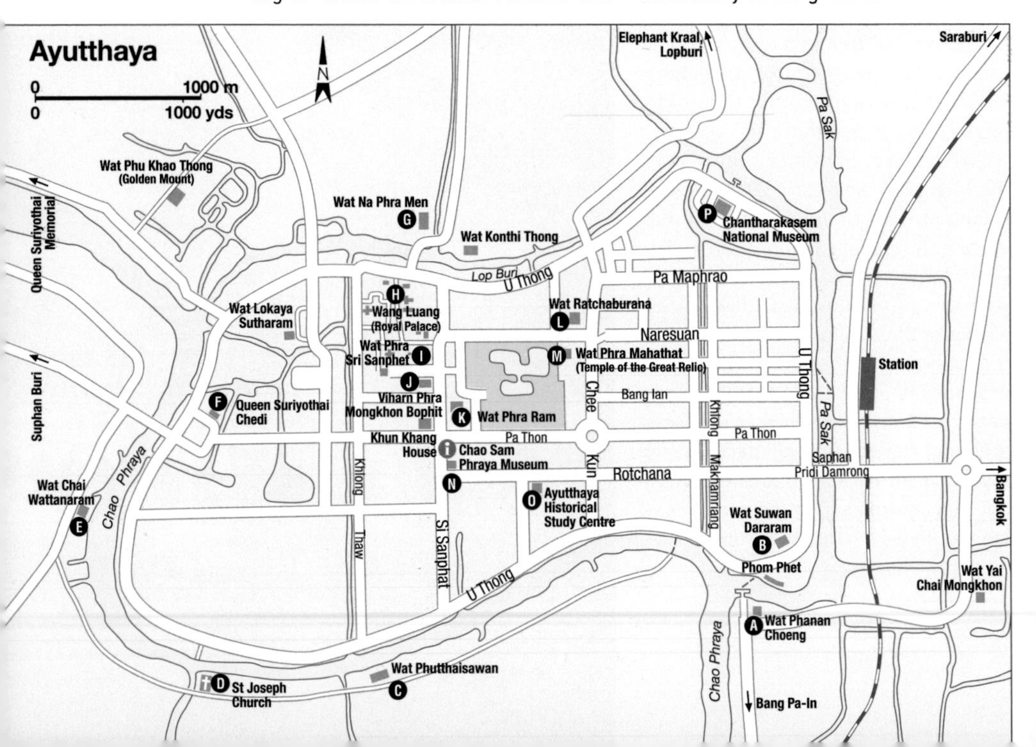

Today, there is a plaque to mark Ayutthaya's former Portuguese settlement and a memorial hall and gate at the Japanese settlement. Europeans at the time wrote accounts eulogising the fabulous wealth of the courts. Thirty-three kings left their mark on the old capital.

Although in ruins, very impressive remnants of Ayutthaya's rich architectural and cultural achievements can still be seen today. As swiftly as it rose to greatness, it collapsed, suffering destruction so complete the original city was never rebuilt. Burmese armies had been pounding on its doors for centuries before occupying the city for a period in the 16th century. Siamese kings then expelled them and reasserted independence. In 1767, however, the Burmese triumphed again. In a mad rampage, they burnt and looted, destroying most of the city's monuments, and killing, enslaving and scattering the population.

Within a year, Ayutthaya had been reduced to a ghost town; its population had diminished to under 10,000 as the royal court resettled south near the mouth of the Chao Phraya River in what today is Bangkok. By the time the Burmese were eventually defeated, Ayutthaya was beyond repair, a fabled city left to crumble into dust.

AYUTTHAYA HISTORICAL PARK

Today the ruins, collectively known as the **Ayutthaya Historical Park** (http://ww2.ayutthaya.go.th; daily 8.30am–4.30pm, times vary for individual sites), stand on the western half of the island, with the modern city of Ayutthaya on the eastern side. Some of the more centrally located ruins can be visited on foot, but it is best to rent a bicycle or a tuk-tuk for the further-flung sights. As several of the major temples are located along the edge of the riverbank or close to it, longtail boats can be hired from the pier outside the Chantharakasem National Museum for a two-hour trip.

Begin close to the junction of the Pa Sak and Chao Phraya rivers, passing by the imposing **Wat Phanan Choeng** Ⓐ (daily 8am–5pm). Records suggest that the temple was established 26 years prior to Ayutthaya's foundation around 1350. It houses the statue of a

Tip

One of the best ways of exploring the widely spread-out ruins of Ayutthaya is by bicycle. These can be rented for about B50 a day at many guesthouses in Ayutthaya. If you are disinclined to expend your energy, hire a motorised tuk-tuk with driver for about B180 an hour. Bear in mind that exploring the ruins can be tiring on hot days; take along sunscreen, a hat or umbrella, as well as something to eat and drink.

Wat Chai Wattanaram, Ayutthaya.

giant seated bronze Buddha, so tightly pressed against the roof that the statue appears to be holding it up. With an unmistakably Chinese atmosphere, Wat Phanan Choeng was a favourite with the Chinese traders of the time, who prayed there before setting out on their long sea voyages. The temple also holds the Mae Soi Dok Mak shrine, a tribute to a Chinese princess who supposedly killed herself on this spot after receiving an icy reception from her suitor, an Ayutthayan king.

Ayutthaya was at one time surrounded by fortress walls, of which only a few sections remain today. One of the best preserved is at **Phom Phet** (daily 7am–6pm), across the river from Wat Phanan Choeng. Nearby is the restored **Wat Suwan Dararam** B (daily 8am–6pm), built towards the end of the Ayutthaya period. Destroyed by the Burmese in 1767, the temple was rebuilt by Rama I. The murals date from the reign of Rama III, with the more unconventional mural depicting King Naresuan's famous battle with the Burmese added between 1925–35. The temple is magical when the monks chant prayers in the early evening.

Upstream from Wat Phanan Choeng by the riverbank is the restored **Wat Phutthaisawan** C (daily 8.30am–5pm). Seldom visited, it is quiet, and the landing is an excellent place to enjoy the river's tranquillity in the evenings. Further upstream, the Catholic **St Joseph Church** D is a reminder of the large European population that lived in the city in its prime.

Where the river bends to the north stands one of Ayutthaya's most romantic ruins, **Wat Chai Wattanaram** E (daily 8am–6pm), erected in 1630 and restored in the 1990s. Modelled after the Angkor Wat complex in Cambodia, the dramatically placed temple is a photographer's favourite, especially at sunset. It was built by King Prasat Thong, and has a large central Cambodian-style *prang* fringed by several smaller *chedi*. Perched high on a pedestal in front of the ruins, a Buddha keeps solitary watch. With its rows of headless Buddhas, this extraordinary temple makes a fine contrast to the somewhat less

Wat Phra Sri Sanphet, Ayutthaya Historical Park.

impressive **Queen Suriyothai Chedi** ⓕ (daily 8.30am–4.30pm) on the city side of the river. The shrine commemorates the life of Suriyothai, an Ayutthayan queen who, dressed as a male soldier and riding an elephant into battle, sacrificed herself by intervening in a duel between her husband King Maha Chakraphet and a Burmese prince. The stuff of legend, her passionate act was immortalised in the 2001 film *Suriyothai*, one of Thailand's most lavish and expensive movies. For a more impressive homage, head northwest up the river to the **Queen Suriyothai Memorial**, a large statue of her atop an elephant.

Across a river bridge from the palace of Wang Luang stands the restored temple of **Wat Na Phra Men** ⓖ (daily 8am–6pm). Used as a strategic attack post by the Burmese when they descended on the old city, the temple is one of Ayutthaya's few monasteries not to have been ransacked. Here, a large stone Buddha is seated on a throne, a sharp contrast to the yoga position of most seated Buddhas. Discovered in the ruins of Wat Phra Mahathat, the statue is believed to be one of five that originally sat in the Dvaravati-period complex in Nakhon Pathom. The main hall or *bot* contains an Ayutthayan-style seated Buddha in regal attire, which is very unlike the more common monastic dress of Buddha representations.

THE PALACE AND SURROUNDINGS

The palace of **Wang Luang** ⓗ (Royal Palace) (daily 6am–6pm) was substantial, if the foundations for the stables of some 100 elephants are any indication. Established by King Borommatrailokanat in the 15th century, it was later razed by the Burmese. The bricks were removed to Bangkok to build the city's defensive walls, so only remnants of the foundations survive today to mark the site.

A part of the original palace grounds, the three Sri Lankan-style *chedi* next door belong to **Wat Phra Sri Sanphet** ⓘ (daily 8am–6pm). The royal temple would have held as much importance in its heyday as the Temple of the Emerald Buddha (Wat Phra Kaew) does in Bangkok today. Two of the *chedi* were built in 1492 by King Borommatrailokanat's

Fact

In the 1950s, unscrupulous locals plundered Ayutthaya's hidden treasures and Buddha images. The Thai government recently realised that some of Ayutthaya's most important treasures are now housed in overseas museum collections, and they are trying to reclaim these stolen artefacts. Even today some temple abbots in Ayutthaya are forced to stand guard and sleep beside their precious Buddha images.

Exploring the ruins of Ayutthaya.

A stone Buddha at Ayutthaya.

son, Ramathibodi II, to hold the ashes of his father and brother, while the third was added in 1540 by Ramathibodi II's son to hold the ashes of his late father. The three spires have become the iconic image of Ayutthaya.

For two centuries after Ayutthaya's fall, a huge bronze Buddha – over 12 metres (39ft) tall – sat unsheltered near Wat Phra Sri Sanphet. Its flame of knowledge (on the top of its head) and one of its arms had been broken when the roof, set on fire by the Burmese, collapsed. Based on the original, a new building called **Viharn Phra Mongkhon Bophit** Ⓙ (daily 8am–4.30pm) was built in 1956 around the restored statue. As one of Thailand's largest bronze images, it seems rather cramped in its new sanctuary.

Across the road to the east, **Wat Phra Ram** Ⓚ (daily 8am–6pm, 7.30–9pm) is one of Ayutthaya's oldest temples. Founded in 1369 by the son of Ayutthaya's founding king, Prince U Thong, its buildings dating from the 1400s have been restored twice. Elephant gates punctuate the old walls, and the central terrace is dominated by a crumbling *prang* to which clings a gallery of stucco *naga*, *garuda* and Buddha statues. The reflection of Wat Phra Ram's *prang* shimmers in the pool that surrounds the complex, making it one of Ayutthaya's most tranquil settings.

Buddha head enveloped by the gnarled roots of a banyan tree at Wat Phra Mahathat.

AYUTTHAYA'S BEST TEMPLES

Two of Ayutthaya's finest temples stand side by side across the lake from Wat Phra Ram. The first is known as **Wat Ratchaburana** Ⓛ (daily 8am–6pm), and was built in 1424 by the seventh king of Ayutthaya, King Borom Rachathirat II (1424–48) as a memorial to his brothers who died as a result of a duel for the throne. Excavations during a 1957 restoration revealed a crypt below the towering central *prang*, containing a stash of gold jewellery, Buddha images and other artefacts, among them a magnificent ceremonial sword and an intricately decorated elephant statue – all likely to have been the property of the interred brothers. The narrow, claustrophobic and dimly lit crypt can be accessed through a doorway in the *prang*, leading down steep stairs to some barely visible wall paintings.

The second temple, **Wat Phra Mahathat** Ⓜ (Temple of the Great Relic; daily 8am–6pm) was once one of the most beautiful temple complexes in Ayutthaya, and one of its oldest, dating from the 1380s. The site, across the road from Ratchaburana, was the focal point for religious ceremonies and reverence, and the residence of King Ramesuan (1388–95). Its glory was its huge laterite *prang*, which originally stood at 46 metres (150ft) high. The *prang* later collapsed, but its foundations are still there, surrounded by several restored *chedi*. A much-revered symbol here is a stone Buddha head that has been embedded in the gnarled roots of an old banyan tree. Next door, the government has built a model of how the royal city may have once looked.

AYUTTHAYA'S MUSEUMS

While looters quickly made off with a great deal of Ayutthaya's glories, the surviving highlights of Thailand's greatest archaeological treasure chest are now displayed at the **Chao Sam Phraya Museum** N to the south of Rama Public Park (www.virtualmuseum.finearts.go.th; daily 9am–4pm).

The **Ayutthaya Historical Study Centre** O (daily 9am–4.30pm) nearby, was funded by the Japanese government. Sitting on land that was once part of Ayutthaya's Japanese quarter, the modern building houses excellent hi-tech exhibits that guide visitors through 400 years of the development, trade, administration and social changes of the Ayutthayan period. There are also models of the city in its glory days, a Chinese junk, and small tableaux of village life.

To the east, **Chantharakasem National Museum** P was formerly known as the Chantharakasem Palace (www.virtualmuseum.finearts.go.th; Wed–Sun 9am–4pm). It was originally constructed outside the city walls, close to the confluence of the rivers and the canal. King Maha Thammaracha built it for his son Prince Naresuan (later king), and it became the residence for future heirs apparent. In 1767, the Burmese destroyed the palace, but King Mongkut (Rama IV) resurrected it in the 19th century as a royal summer retreat. Today, it looks out on the noisiest part of modern Ayutthaya. The palace's collection isn't notably impressive but it is still worth perusing.

To its rear, the European-style four-storey **Pisai Sayalak** tower was built by King Mongkut for stargazing. Across the street from the palace is the boat pier for trips around the island, and a night market with food stalls set up beside the water.

LOPBURI

Lopburi 13 lies 150km (100 miles) north of Bangkok, a two- to three-hour drive through the fertile rice bowl of Thailand. Centuries before it became the favoured summer residence for Ayutthayan King Narai, the strategically located town was known as Lavo and lay within the Mon Dvaravati kingdom (6th–10th centuries). From the 10th–13th centuries, it became

Fact

Elephantstay (www.elephantstay.com) in Ayutthaya is a village where guests can spend a few days and learn more about Asian elephants, a fascinating experience and one that helps the animals, too.

Phra Narai Ratchanivet, Lopburi.

A fleet of tuk-tuks at Ayutthaya.

an outpost of the Angkor empire, before falling under the influence of the Sukhothai kingdom to the north.

Lopburi enjoyed its heyday in the mid 1600s when King Narai retreated here each summer to escape Ayutthaya's heat. When the Dutch imposed a naval blockade on Ayutthaya from the Gulf of Siam, King Narai decided to install Lopburi as a second capital, running his court from there. It was said that while his throne was in Ayutthaya, his heart belonged to Lopburi; he spent more and more time here after his new palace was completed.

WAT PHRA SI RATTANA MAHATHAT

Just across from Lopburi's main train station, **Wat Phra Si Rattana Mahathat** (daily 6.30am–6pm) was originally a simple Khmer temple with a tall stucco-decorated laterite *prang*. Around the 12th century, King Narai added a large *viharn* (sermon hall) that infused elements of European and Persian architecture, the latter influence coming from the strong Persian presence at the Ayutthayan court: the Ayutthaya period was notable for the number of influential foreign visitors arriving in Thailand, including Indians, Chinese, Japanese, Persians and Europeans.

PHRA NARAI RATCHANIVET

Just northwest, the grounds of **Phra Narai Ratchanivet** (or Lopburi Palace) (daily 8.30am–4.30pm; free but permission needed – obtain from the Office of His Majesty's Principal Private Secretary, Grand Palace) are enclosed by massive walls that still dominate the centre of the modern town. Built between 1665 and 1677 in a mélange of Thai, Khmer and European styles, the palace grounds are divided into three sections enclosing the complex of official, ceremonial and residential buildings.

The outer grounds contained facilities for utilities and maintenance. The middle section enclosed the **Chanthara Phisan Pavilion**, the first structure built by King Narai, and later restored by King Mongkut. On the south side is the **Dusit Maha Prasat Hall**, built for the audience granted by King Narai in 1685 to the French ambassador of Louis XIV.

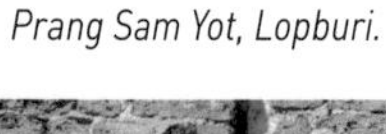

Prang Sam Yot, Lopburi.

To the left is the **Phiman Mongkut Pavilion**, a three-storey colonial-style mansion. It was built in the mid-19th century by King Mongkut, who wanted to restore the entire palace. The immensely thick walls and high ceilings went some way to averting the summer heat in the days before air-conditioning.

The mansion, small but full of character, now functions as the **Narai National Museum** (Wed–Sun 9am–4pm). It contains a display of bronze statues, Chinese and Sukhothai porcelain, coins, Buddhist fans and shadow-play puppets. Some of the pieces, particularly the Ayutthaya bronze heads and Bencharong porcelain, are superb. The inner courtyard housed the private chambers of King Narai, but not much is left except for the foundations and the **Suttha Sawan Pavilion**, nestled amid gardens and ponds.

BAAN VICHAYEN

North of Phra Narai Ratchanivet are the remains of **Baan Vichayen** palace (Wed-Sun 7am–5pm), said to have belonged to Constantine Phaulkon, the Greek adventurer who arrived in Siam in 1678 to work for the British East India Company and gained favour with King Narai. As a foreigner, Phaulkon's mercurial rise aroused a great deal of suspicion and resentment, and he was eventually executed. The period following his demise saw the Siamese court become more xenophobic towards foreign influence.

The palace buildings of Baan Vichayen show strong European influences, with their straight-sided walls and stucco decorations embellishing Western-style windows.

PRANG SAM YOT

To the east are the three laterite towers of **Prang Sam Yot** (Wed–Sun 6am–6pm). This much-photographed sight is of interest as the towers were built by the Khmers as a Hindu shrine to honour the gods Brahma, Vishnu and Shiva. It was later converted into a Buddhist shrine, incorporating a hotchpotch fusion of Brahman, Khmer and Buddhist elements that is often dubbed as the Lopburi style. Beware of the persistent and rather aggressive monkeys at this site.

Ban Vichayen, Lopburi.

SOUTH OF BANGKOK

This area is scant on sights, but those available – whether a quirky museum or a beautiful park – make a very pleasant break from the chaos of the city.

Main attractions
Erawan Museum
Ancient City

Map on page 146

Samut Prakan Province, around the river-mouth town of Paknam, is 30km (20 miles) – or about half an hour's drive – southeast of Bangkok. It is home to three prime attractions: two superb cultural museums, including one of the world's largest, in Muang Boran, and a much-touted crocodile farm.

ERAWAN MUSEUM

The **Erawan Museum** ⓮ (daily 9am–7pm) at Sukhumvit Soi 119 is housed in an extraordinary 43m (141ft) -high, three-headed elephant that represents Erawan, the animal ridden by the god Indra in Hindu mythology. It was created by businessman and philanthropist Lek Viriyaphant, whose other projects include the Ancient City and the Sanctuary of Truth, in Pattaya.

The museum is divided into three sections. The basement, 'Underworld,' contains mainly Chinese and Thai pieces from the founder's private antiques collection. The middle section, 'Earth,' has a stained-glass domed ceiling and examples of Thai art styles from the country's most celebrated craftsmen. These include stucco work from Phetchaburi, hammered tin plating from Nakhon Si Thammarat and ceramics from Amphawa. In the hollow interior of the elephant's belly, 'Heaven' is an odd, hippie-esque purple room with abstract murals and antique Buddha statues dating to the Dvaravati period from the 6th–9th centuries AD.

Because the museum contains many Buddha images it has assumed the status of a holy place for many Thais, who make the pilgrimage to a shrine in the gardens to earn merit and pray for good luck.

ANCIENT CITY

One of Bangkok's best-value (and surprisingly under-visited) tourist

A reproduced monument at Ancient City.

attractions is the **Ancient City** ⓯ or Muang Boran (daily 9am–7pm; www.ancientcity.com), located 33km (21 miles) southeast of Bangkok. This open-air site, roughly the shape of Thailand, has over 100 monuments, palaces and other buildings placed as close as possible to their real sites. The result is an architectural splendour that covers 15 centuries of Thai history.

There are replicas of famous monuments and temples from all parts of the kingdom, some full-sized, most one-third the size of the originals. Some are reconstructions of buildings that no longer exist, such as the Grand Palace of Ayutthaya, some are copies of buildings such as the temple of Khao Phra Viharn on the Thai-Cambodian border. Others are salvaged antiquities.

Experts from the National Museum worked as consultants to ensure the historical accuracy of the reproductions.

There is a lot to see and you could spend a whole day here. The grounds are landscaped with small waterfalls, ponds, and lush greenery, while deer graze among the sculptures representing figures from Thai literature and Hindu mythology. The site also has regional variations of traditional wooden houses, and markets where you can watch craftsmen carve puppets from buffalo hide and buy handicrafts and sculptures.

At 129ha (320 acres) it is not practical to tour the Ancient City on foot. You can drive around it, rent bicycles or golf carts at the gate, or take a tram tour, which is available with an English-speaking guide.

CROCODILE FARM & ZOO

Samut Prakan's **Crocodile Farm & Zoo** ⓰ (daily 8am–6pm; charge; www.worldcrocodile.com) is located a short distance from the Ancient City on the old Sukhumvit Highway (Route 3).

The farm is home to more than 60,000 freshwater and saltwater local crocodiles from 28 species, as well as some South American caimans and Nile River crocodiles. Chai Yai, the world's largest captive crocodile at 1,114kg (2,456lb) and 6 metres (20ft) (listed in the *Guinness Book of World Records*), also lives here.

The Crocodile Farm has eight daily shows (hourly from 9am–4pm, reptile feeding 4–5pm), during which handlers wrestle with the (very sleepy looking) crocodiles and place their heads in their mouths. The farm's shops sell crocodile skin handbags, belts and shoes certified by CITES (Convention on International Trade in Endangered Species), and stewed crocodile meat, which is used in traditional Chinese medicine, purportedly as a tonic and aphrodisiac. This is another popular site that feels increasingly outdated, and frequent accusations of animal cruelty are made against the elephant and crocodile shows.

Suvarnabhumi (pronounced "su-wa-na-poom") Airport.

Inside the Erawan Museum in Bangkok.

Ko Tao.

Wai beach on Ko Samet.

SOUTHEAST AND SOUTH THAILAND

For many, Thailand is synonymous with paradise islands, and for those, the south, with miles of unspoilt beaches by the emerald waters of the Gulf of Thailand and the Andaman Sea, is the place to head.

Longtail boats are a common method of transport in this part of the world.

Blessed with some 3,000km (2,000 miles) of stunning coastline and more than 30 beautiful islands washed by the Gulf of Thailand and the Andaman Sea, this is a region that attracts everyone, from gregarious party animals to reclusive honeymooners.

A short way from the capital, the brash coastal resort of Pattaya has been dubbed (somewhat hopefully) the "Riviera of the Eastern Seaboard". Further east, the pretty island of Ko Samet is a favourite weekend escape for young Bangkokians, while Ko Chang, Thailand's second-largest island, is part of an extensive marine national park that's woken up to its tourism potential.

Heading south, the Gulf of Thailand coast is fringed with sandy beaches and backed by mountains. The most accessible and popular is family-friendly Hua Hin, but further south, Pranburi is fast making a name for itself too, with its clutch of design-conscious resorts. Offshore, Ko Samui, the largest of some 80 islands comprising the Samui Archipelago, is the main tourist hub and can be combined with visits to neighbouring Ko Phangan, notorious for its anything-goes full-moon raves, and Ko Tao, a renowned hub for diving.

Hat Na Ko, Ko Kradan.

Lapped by the blue-green waters of the Andaman Sea on the west coast, Thailand's largest island, Phuket, is the kingdom's premier holiday spot. It hosts some of the world's most luxurious hotels, which contrast with rustic fishing villages and mangrove forests. Further east lie Ao Phang Nga and Krabi, and islands like Ko Phi Phi and Ko Lanta with their amazing limestone towers that reach skyward above azure waters. The spectacular dive sites near Similan and Surin islands are another major lure.

Heading south, Trang, Satun, Songkhla and Nakhon Si Thammarat are all breathtakingly beautiful but less touched by tourism. For the present, this guide omits the restive Muslim-dominated provinces – Pattani, Yala and Narathiwat – in the deep south of Thailand. Everything else, as they say, is fair game.

Fishermen returning to Bang Bao Bay, Ko Chang.

EASTERN SEABOARD

Miles of sandy beaches, dozens of tiny offshore islands, dense forests and hidden waterfalls... all these and more await on Thailand's easily accessible Eastern Seaboard.

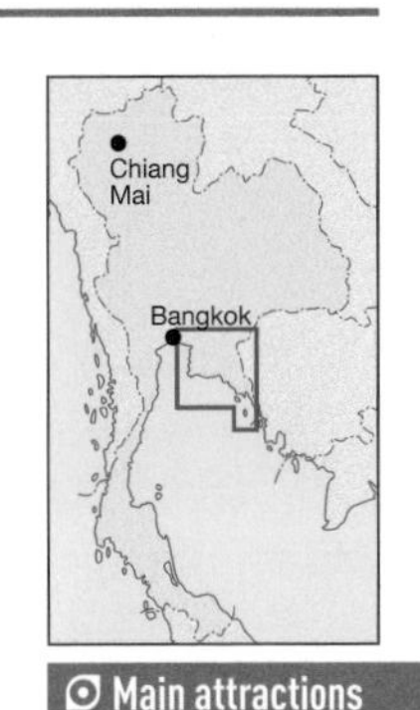

Main attractions

Bang Saen
Ko Si Chang
Pattaya
Ko Samet
Ko Chang
Ko Kut

The Eastern Seaboard has numerous factories and oil refineries between Bangkok and Rayong. Thankfully, it also has miles of sandy beaches, dozens of islands and relatively calm seas all year. Pattaya and the islands of Ko Samet and Ko Chang abound with activities, the region is speckled with national parks, and over 20 international-standard golf courses surround Pattaya.

Highway 3 is the principal road through the provinces of Chonburi, Rayong, Chantabhuri and Trat, all the way to Cambodia. There is a (slow) rail line as far as Pattaya, and two small airports, U-Tapao, near Pattaya, and Trat, the arrival point for passengers en route to Ko Chang.

BANG SAEN

Just south of Chonburi, the 2km (1.5-mile) long beach at **Bang Saen** ❶ springs to life each weekend with hordes of Bangkokians. The nearest beach from the capital, it is covered with beach umbrellas and inflatable inner tubes, and the surf is filled with bodies fully dressed to avoid a tan (in addition to concern about UV rays, many Thais associate tanned skin with working folk who toil in the sun).

SI RACHA

The port town of **Si Racha** ❷, about 100km (62 miles) from Bangkok, nestles between two ranges of hills. The town's signature tangy red sauce – *nam prik si racha* – can be enjoyed at waterfront restaurants, where it's used to spice up fresh shrimp and crab.

KO SI CHANG

A 45-minute boat ride from Si Racha, the island of **Ko Si Chang** ❸ (not to be confused with the far larger Ko Chang, further east) was once a coastal retreat for King Chulalongkorn (Rama V). The king built his summer palace here in the 1890s, only to abandon

Maps on pages 174, 176, 179, 181

Fishing boat in Si Racha Thailand.

Wat Atsadang Nimit on Ko Si Chang features a mix of Thai and European architecture.

it after the French briefly occupied the island a few years later. Busy on weekends with Thai day-trippers, the island has a few passable beaches, though not Thailand's best or cleanest. For a slice of island living without the tourism onslaught, you can visit Ko Si Chang as a day trip from Bangkok or en route to Pattaya.

SIGHTS AND ACTIVITIES

After exploring **Tha Bon**, the island's main fishing town, most visitors head for the grounds of Rama V's **Judhadhut Palace** (daily 8am–6pm; free), which double as an oceanfront park. The rebuilt **Atsadang Bridge** is actually a wooden pier once used as Chulalongkorn's landing stage. Now kids like to leap from it and swim around the moored fishing boats.

While the main teak palace was dismantled and rebuilt in Bangkok as the Vimanmek Mansion, several other structures have been remodelled, including the green wooden house **Ruen Mai Rim Talay**, once used as a convalescent home for Western visitors. Pretty gardens extend up the hill towards the white spire of **Wat Atsadang Nimit**, with a Thai-European design fusion popular at the time. The circular *chedi* has stained-glass panels.

The island's principal beach, **Hat Tham Pang** (Fallen Cave), on the west coast, is usually crowded and has food shacks located behind.

Over on steep Kayasira hill, the gaudy Chinese temple **Sanjao Pho Khao Yai** (daily 8am–5pm; free) has great views overlooking the port. It's a popular stop for Chinese visitors who pay homage at the cave shrines before hiking up further to a *sala* (pavilion) said to contain a Buddha's footprint.

PATTAYA

Located 147km (91 miles) from Bangkok, or around two hours by road, **Pattaya**'s ❹ notoriety for sex workers dates back to the Vietnam War, when it was an R&R stopover for American troops. Consequently most people have formed an opinion before they even arrive.

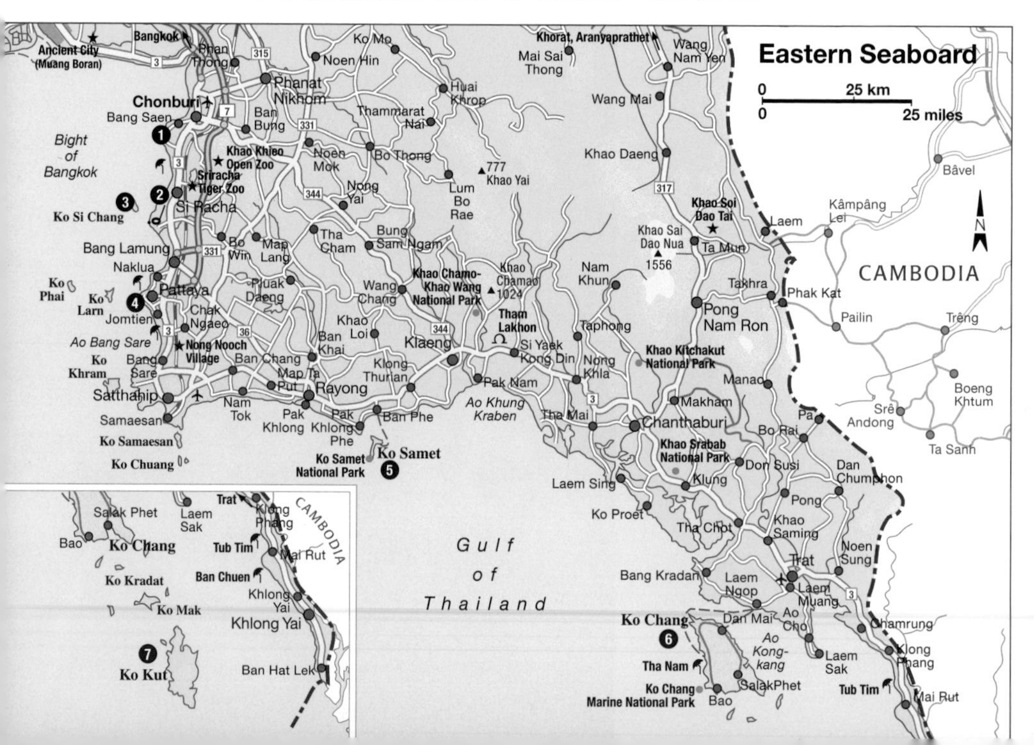

But Pattaya has long been popular with Thai families and it has many facilities to cater to both them and foreign tourists. The town has a raft of good-value accommodation and restaurants, and if Pattaya's salacious nightlife scene is not your thing, there's a wide range of outdoor and indoor activities, and several cultural attractions.

There is a high demand for property in Pattaya. Many foreigners own beach condos and houses; Bangkok expats use them as weekend getaways, while European retirees escape the northern winter. Improvements to infrastructure, especially international schools, also help to draw more respectable residents. But the city's seedy reputation also attracts a strong criminal element. Thankfully, this is rarely visible to the average visitor, and Pattaya usually feels as safe as anywhere else in Thailand.

PATTAYA'S BEACHES

The nicest-looking, least populated of Pattaya's three beaches, with fewest umbrellas, is found to the north, rounding the headland at **Hat Naklua** Ⓐ towards the fishing village of the same name.

The least attractive is the middle beach, the 3km (2-mile) long crescent-shaped **Hat Pattaya** Ⓑ, with only a narrow, umbrella-crammed wisp of yellow sand backed by a palm-lined promenade that is a pitching point for working girls. The Phra Tamnak hill area separates the main action from a number of mid- and high-end hotels (like the InterContinental and Royal Cliff) on small, pleasant beaches.

Just a short ride south, the 6km (4-mile) long **Hat Jomtien** Ⓒ is only marginally cleaner and better than Hat Pattaya.

BEACH ACTIVITIES

Pattaya and Jomtien are good locations for watersports, with windsurfing and sailing equipment available for rent, along with jet skis, waterscooters and waterskiing equipment.

Offshore, **Ko Larn** – identified in brochures as **Coral Island** but whose name actually translates as Bald Island – is one of Pattaya's most popular day-trips. Dynamite fishing has destroyed its once-pristine reefs, yet glass-bottomed boats still ferry visitors peering in vain at the dead grey coral. Ko Larn, however, has the wide, soft sand beaches that Pattaya lacks and is a great place to spend a day. Seafood restaurants line the shore and there are watersports aplenty.

Several scuba schools run dive trips to outlying islands. Four sunken vessels make up some of Thailand's best wreck dive sites between Pattaya and Satthahip. Nearby isles like **Ko Sak** and **Ko Krok** have waters, though not crystal clear, that are protected from currents, and so suitable for beginners. Further out, **Ko Rin** and **Ko Man Wichai** are better dive spots with clearer visibility and abundant marine life, including sharks and turtles.

Tip

Pattaya has a bad reputation for con artists – collecting donations for spurious causes, selling precious stones at "bargain" prices, or offering "free" trips to touristic sights. Keep your wits about you.

Out and about in Pattaya.

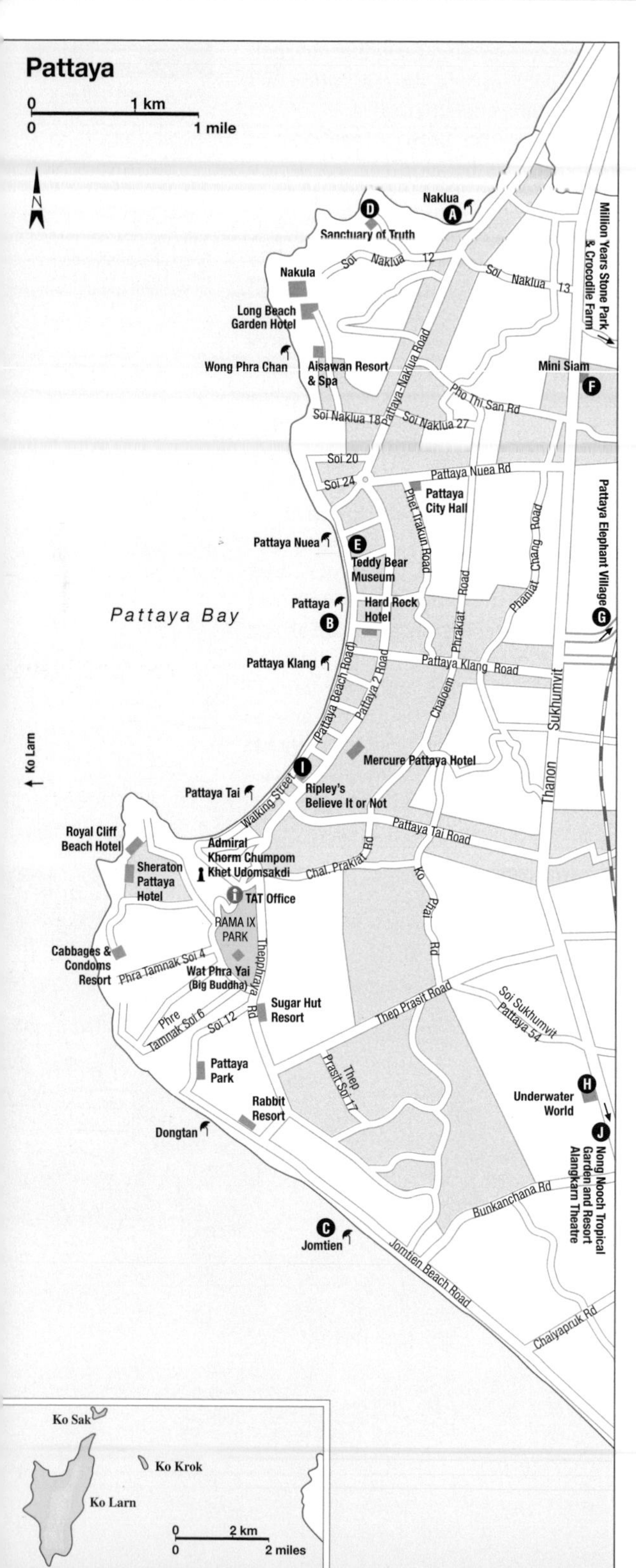

LAND ATTRACTIONS

Back on land, the **Sanctuary of Truth** D (daily 8am–6pm; www.sanctuaryoftruth.com) on Naklua Soi 12 is an awe-inspiring carved teak structure dramatically perched on the seafront. Begun in 1981 and expected to take another 10 years to complete, it blends ancient religious iconography from around Asia, and is intended to act as a spiritual beacon and preserve traditional artisan techniques.

Along Beach Road by North Pattaya Beach is one of the city's more kid-oriented attractions. The 2000-plus cuddly toys of the **Teddy Bear Museum** E (daily 9am–8.30pm; http://teddybearmuseumpattaya.com) are a great diversion from the busy streets outside. There are stuffed animals everywhere and plenty of spots for good photo opportunities. This site is aimed primarily at younger children. There is a dance show with, inevitably, performers dressed as teddy bears at 2, 3, and 4pm every Saturday and Sunday.

Other family-oriented attractions include **Mini Siam** F (daily 7am–10pm; www.minisiam.com) at Thanon Sukhumvit in North Pattaya, where you can step around tiny scale models of many of the world's architectural landmarks. The **Pattaya Elephant Village** G on Thanon Sukhumvit (daily 8am–5.30pm; charge; www.elephant-village-pattaya.com) offers a daily elephant show and rides into the countryside. However, treatment of the elephants may not sit well with most animal lovers. For a land-based view of marine wonders, **Underwater World** H (daily 9am–6pm; www.underwaterworldpattaya.com), just after the Thanon Thep Prasit junction with Thanon Sukhumvit has a viewing tunnel, a touch pool for hands-on interaction with small marine animals, and a shark and ray tank. There is also a **Ripley's Believe It or Not** I (daily 11am–11pm; www.ripleysthailand.com) at the Royal Garden Plaza.

South of Pattaya at Km 163 of Thanon Sukhumvit, **Nong Nooch Tropical Garden & Resort** ❹ is a 243-hectare (600-acre) landscaped parkland enclosing two lakes (daily 8am–6pm; www.nongnoochtropicalgarden.com). It has an extensive collection of orchids and palms, a butterfly garden, mini-zoo and a daily cultural show with traditional dancing and Thai boxing. **Cartoon Network Amazone** (daily 10am–6pm; www.cartoonnetworkamazone.com), opposite Nong Nooch on Thanon Sukhumvit, has a beach and 150 features based on characters such as Ben 10, with a wave pool, an "adventure river" and a speed slide falling from a six-storey tower.

PATTAYA'S NIGHTLIFE

Pattaya's main nightlife zones cluster around Thanon Hat Pattaya (Beach Road) and Walking Street in **South Pattaya**. There is a staggering range of bars, Irish pubs, German brew houses, live-music venues, nightclubs, plus many go-go bars, open-air "beer bars" and massage parlours. The strip called **Boyz Town** (Pattayaland Soi 3) follows the same theme for gay men. The town also has lip-synching Vegas-style cabaret featuring *kathoey* or "lady-boys" (transsexuals). The best is Tiffany's, on Pattaya 2 Road (daily shows at 6pm, 7.30pm and 9pm; www.tiffany-show.co.th).

Pattaya has its own mini Chatuchak at Thepprasit Market (Fri–Sun 5pm–11pm), close to the junction of Thepprasit and Sukhumvit roads, selling the usual knock-off watches, bags, T-shirts and homewares.

KO SAMET

Located 200km (124 miles) or three hours by road from Bangkok and a short boat trip across from the fishing harbour of **Ban Phe**, the postcard-perfect island of **Ko Samet** ❺ is a popular weekend getaway. The island is known as the place where Sunthorn Phu (1786–1855), a flamboyantly romantic court poet, retired to compose some of his works. Sunthorn called the island Ko Kaew Phisadan, or "island with sand-like crushed crystal", and it was here that his best-known poem, *Phra*

Tip

For those who do not want to get wet, book a trip with the Yellow Submarine. The 2-hour trip involves a boat ride to Ko Sak, southwest of Pattaya, where the submarine is moored. Climb aboard and the vessel will sink up to 30 metres (98ft) for a close-up view of marine life; visibility will vary depending on the time of year.

TROUBLED TROUBADOUR

Poster boy for Ko Samet, Sunthorn Phu was a Byronic hero if ever there was one. Thailand's most famous poet was born a commoner in 1786. He fell in love with a woman named Jun who was related to the royal family. Their affair scandalised protocol, but they were later pardoned and Sunthorn was subsequently appointed court poet. Later, a descent into alcoholism, violence and adultery led to a divorce and a prison sentence. He was stripped of his title, but later won his way back into royal favour.

Sunthorn Phu died in 1855, leaving his historical poems, including the romantic epic *Phra Aphaimani*, as a lasting legacy. Thailand celebrates his poetry every year on 26 June with public recitals, and the cultural significance of his works has been recognised by Unesco.

Nong Nooch Tropical Garden.

Tip

While the regular fishing-boat ferries are much cheaper, taking a speedboat across to Ko Samet (around B800) from the mainland port is much faster, drops you on the bay of your choice, and usually means you escape the national park entry fee of B200 per foreign person, which is steep compared to the B20 that Thais are charged.

Aphaimani, a tale about a prince and a mermaid, was set.

Today the island is a laid-back resort with fine white sand beaches and clear turquoise-blue waters. As part of a national marine park, technically, most of the resort operations are illegal. Thankfully, development remains fairly unobtrusive, with single-storey huts and bungalows.

KO SAMET'S BEACHES

Almost all the sandy beaches run down the east coast, gradually getting more isolated as the island narrows to the southern bay of Ao Karang. Most infrastructure – school, clinic, temple, market and a few shops – are near **Na Dan** pier Ⓐ and along the paved road to Hat Sai Kaew.

The island is only 6km (4 miles) long and 3km (2 miles) wide and you can hike from end to end, in a few hours, though the coastal track cuts across several rocky headlands. A single road down the centre of the island turns into a bumpy dirt track along its outer reaches.

Ao Phrao Ⓑ, the only beach on the west coast, is the most exclusive, with just a few hotels on the small scenic bay. On the east coast, **Hat Sai Kaew** Ⓒ (Diamond Sand) – a short walk from Na Dan pier – is the most developed and congested spot on the island, blessed as it is with powdery white sands. This is where most Thai and packaged-tour visitors stay.

Further south, the bay of **Ao Hin Khok** Ⓓ is separated from Hat Sai Kaew by a rocky promontory marked by a weathered mermaid statue inspired by Sunthorn Phu's poem. Foreigners tend to stay here and at the next bay, **Ao Phai** Ⓔ, which has an equally nice white sandy beach. Hotels like Naga Bungalows (Ao Hin Khok) and Silver Sand (Ao Phai) frequently host late night parties.

The next white-sand bay is small and intimate **Ao Tub Tim** Ⓕ, with only two places to stay here, but with the attractions of Ao Phai a short walk away. There are two more quiet bays, **Ao Nuan** and **Ao Chao**, until you hit the picturesque, crescent-shaped **Ao**

LADY-BOYS

There is no Western equivalent to the term *kathoey*, as it describes a wide range, from men who merely dress as women to transgendered people who have undergone complete sex-change surgery.

Kathoey are highly visible, most obviously on TV game shows and as a flamboyant presence around red-light districts, but also as waitresses, shop assistants and business executives. In 2012, Yollada 'Nok' Suanyos, who had a sex-change operation at 16, became the country's first transgender politician. Famous sporting *kathoey* include Parinya 'Nong Tum' Charoenphon, who was a male kick boxing champion undergoing hormone therapy. She wore make-up in the ring and would kiss her defeated opponents.

Many *kathoey* are apparent from a young age. Former Miss Tiffany Universe Nalada Thamthanakorn says she knew from the age of seven, and high schools throughout Thailand have *kathoey* students. Although not allowed to wear women's clothes, they are unashamed in extravagantly feminine gestures. Some will be taking hormones to help form a more shapely body, although implants will probably come later. One school poll found 10 percent of students identified as transgender, and several educational establishments have installed a third set of toilets to accommodate them.

Transgender individuals are legally regarded as men, but debates in parliament about recognising a third sex may address this issue.

Pattaya's nightlife has a sleazy edge to it.

Wong Deuan G, which is becoming increasingly spoilt by boats, noisy jet skis and the clutter of bars and accommodation (mostly middle- to upper-end price range). The facilities are good, with minimarts, motorcycle rental and internet cafés.

After Ao Wong Deuan, the bays become very peaceful. Scenic **Ao Thian H** (Candlelight Beach) is actually a series of small beaches separated by rocky outcrops, while the southern **Ao Kui I** is little more than a quiet beach and the location of the island's most exclusive accommodation the Paradee Resort.

SIGHTS AND ACTIVITIES

Most activity at Ko Samet is relaxed and beach-bound – sunbathing, beach strolls, swimming and snorkelling – though jet skis and inflatable banana boats do occasionally interrupt the tranquillity. Vendors hawk fruit, beer, ice cream, snacks and sarongs, and there's an army of women offering massage and hair-braiding on the busier beaches. There isn't much by the way of reef around the shoreline and what little there is has been badly damaged, but you will still encounter colourful varieties of fish.

Several resorts offer snorkelling trips by speedboat around Ko Samet and to nearby islets. A few places offer scuba-diving off the beach at Ao Phrao, while boat trips head out to nearby islands such as **Ko Talu**, where visibility is clearer. Off the island's southern tip, **Shark Point** can experience strong currents and is best suited to experienced divers.

Ko Samet is best avoided on public holidays, when visitors outnumber beds, and tents are pitched on any spare patch of land. Evenings are relatively low-key; restaurants set up fresh seafood beach barbecues, while some eateries entertain the impecunious backpacker crowd with the latest pirated Hollywood flicks.

KO CHANG

At 492 sq km (190 sq miles) Thailand's second-largest island after Phuket, **Ko Chang 6** (Elephant Island) is part of

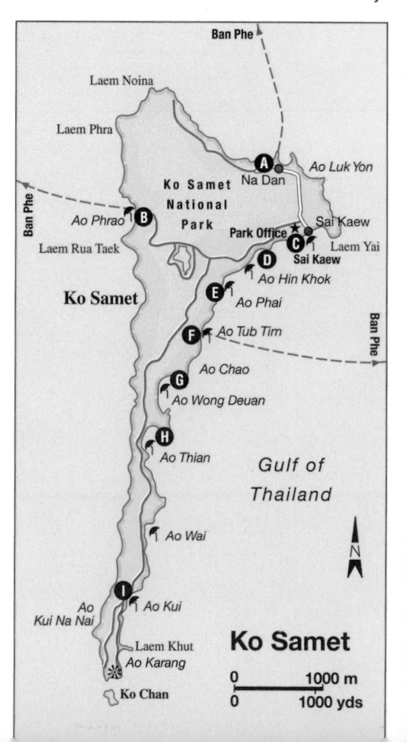

Hat Sai Kaew, Ko Samet, is the busiest beach on the island.

Poolside at The Emerald Cove Koh Chang resort at Hat Khlong Phrao.

a national marine park that includes some 52 islands. Around a five-hour drive from Bangkok (or 45 minutes by air to Trat on the mainland, then a 45-minute transfer by boat), the verdant island is part of Trat Province close to the Cambodian border. Located 20km (12 miles) southwest of Trat town, the mainland pier of **Laem Ngop** is the main jumping-off point to the island.

For years Koh Chang escaped the rapid development of islands like Phuket, and remained a favourite almost exclusively with low budget travellers. However, expansion began after former Prime Minister Thaksin Shinawatra promoted Ko Chang as a playground for the rich in 2003. The official plan has since been abandoned, but the legacy is a boom in construction around the single road, which will eventually loop the island.

While the upsurge detracts from Ko Chang's untouched appeal, there is a wider range of accommodation, including stylish hotels with spas. There's a wider range of tourists too, as despite higher prices than of old, several beaches still attract the budget crowd. Car ferries from the mainland are also more numerous and the loop road busier. It has several hazardous hill passes with sharp bends, so take care if exploring on motorcycle.

KO CHANG'S BEACHES

Despite the incursions of the modern world, the island's size means that it has retained its relatively untouched interior, areas of mangrove forest and some lovely beaches. The main ones are along the west coast, with **Hat Sai Khao** Ⓐ (White Sand Beach) the most developed (and longest) stretch. Its swathe of powdery sands is framed by a backdrop of casuarina trees.

To the south, **Hat Khlong Phrao** Ⓑ is one of the most picturesque and quietest beaches on the island. It is effectively divided into the northern, central and southern sections by canals. Beyond, **Hat Kai Bae** Ⓒ has seen much recent development. Unfortunately, parts of its beach disappear when the tide is high. Next up is the last vestige

Beach bungalows on Klong Prao beach, Koh Chang.

of Ko Chang's hippie traveller scene, the lovely stretch of **Hat Tha Nam** D, or Lonely Beach; it's no longer such a haven of solitude as plush resorts have edged in. Just over 1km (0.6 mile) long, this fine-sand beach gets a little coarser towards the south. It's the island's best beach for swimming, although there is a steep shelf at the northern tip. Next is **Ao Bai Lan** E, a bay with rocks and reef but no beach.

At the southern end of the west coast, the fishing village of **Ban Bang Bao** F has become little more than a concrete pier devoted to tourism, with seafood restaurants, dive shops, souvenir shops and guesthouses. This is also the departure point for dive and snorkel trips to surrounding islands. The next bay along the south coast – accessed from the east coast – contains **Salak Phet** G fishing village, which has a more authentic and less developed feel than Ban Bang Bao.

Ko Chang's eastern shoreline has few beaches and is largely ignored by most visitors. This makes a leisurely drive along the plantation- and hill-backed road a real pleasure, with few vehicles and the reward of a seafood lunch at Salak Phet. An alternative route runs east of Salak Phet, where a winding road continues all the way to **Hat Yao** H, or Long Beach, on the southern tip.

SIGHTS AND ACTIVITIES

The lush forests that clothe the mountainous backbone of Ko Chang are home to many birds (including hornbills), macaques, pythons and cobras, monitor lizards, deer and boar, as well as striking wild flora.

There are several companies operating elephant treks into the interior: the best one is **Ban Kwan Chang** (tel: 081-919 3995), which conducts half-day treks and feeding sessions with the elephants. Other popular activities include kayaking and treks to the island's numerous waterfalls. The two most visited are **Khlong Phu** and **Than Mayom**.

Snorkelling and diving trips usually head to the smaller outlying islands off the southern end of Ko Chang. There is fine diving at reasonably shallow

Tip

Hat Tha Nam (also known as Lonely Beach) is one of Ko Chang's nicest beaches, but beware of the strong undertow and currents at its northern end. A number of drownings have occurred in these treacherous waters.

Young Thais at Hat Sai Kaew, Ko Samet.

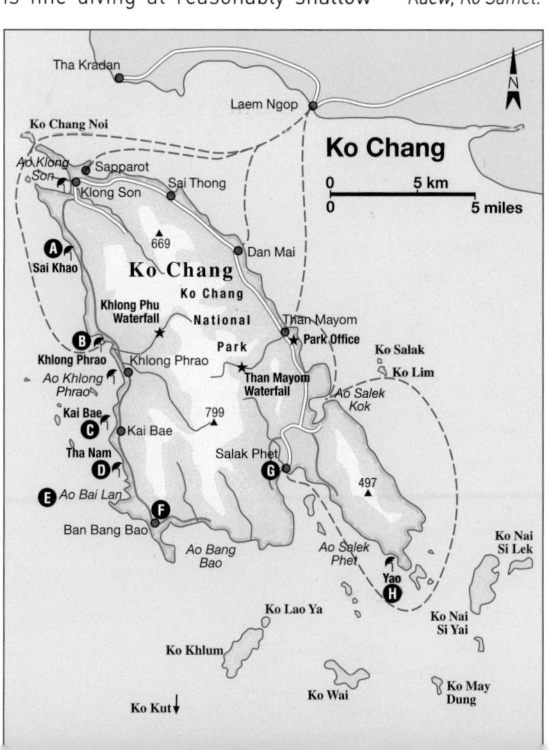

depths, at its most enjoyable between November and March, when the sea is calmer and visibility clearer. Some of the best sites include the pinnacles off **Ko Rang**, the reefs around **Ko Wai**, the shallow dives off **Ko Khlum** and **Hin Luk Bat**, a rock pinnacle 30 minutes south by boat from Ban Bang Bao. The **Thonburi Wreck** off Ko Chang's south-eastern tip is another highlight.

NIGHTLIFE

Ko Chang's nightlife is subdued compared to that of Ko Samui or Phuket, with each beach having its own preferred watering holes. **Hat Sai Khao** hosts the main action. Lying on beach mats is the typical set-up, and live music features at many bars. As a sign of things to come, there is a block of raucous "beer bars" on the road at the southern end of Hat Sai Khao.

Further down the west coast, **Hat Kai Bae** has a small nightlife scene with a couple of unassuming bars along the road. **Hat Tha Nam** has its own pockets of entertainment, with a couple of bars that close by midnight.

KO CHANG ARCHIPELAGO

Around 10km (6 miles) off Ko Chang, the tiny island of **Ko Wai** has limited and basic accommodation, but the views of surrounding islands are spectacular, and there's a lovely coral reef just a short swim from the main beach.

An hour by speedboat from the mainland pier of Laem Ngop, **Ko Mak** is dense with coconut trees and has two lovely, quiet beaches, **Ao Kao** and **Ao Suan Yai**. Both beaches have some basic accommodation and restaurants.

The southernmost island in the archipelago is **Ko Kut** ❼, Thailand's fourth largest island and 2.5 hours away by speedboat. Some 25km (16 miles) long and 12km (7 miles) wide, the island is inhabited partly by people of Khmer origin, with most inhabitants earning a living off fishing or agriculture.

Aside from several fine beaches and clear seas, attractions include **Khlong Chao Waterfall** and the fishing village at **Ao Sa Lad**. Due to its remote location, the island's development has been fairly low-key, and it attracts mainly organised tour groups.

Idyllic beach scene.

Than Mayom Waterfall, Ko Chang.

Frangipani on a pathway at Phra Nakon Kiri Temple Complex, Phetchaburi.

NORTHERN GULF COAST

This narrow strip of land hosts sandy beaches, good weather, interesting towns and two national parks. Popular destinations include historic Phetchaburi, beach getaways such as Cha-am and Hua Hin, and celebrity-friendly Pranburi.

Chiang Mai
Bangkok

Main attractions

- Phetchaburi
- Kaeng Krachan National Park
- Cha-am
- Hua Hin
- Pranburi
- Khao Sam Roi Yot National Park
- Prachuap Khiri Khan

Map on page 186

Wedged between the Gulf of Thailand and the Andaman Sea, southern Thailand resembles an elephant's trunk snaking down from below the Central Plain to the tip of the Malay Peninsula. The Isthmus of Kra, as this land bridge is named, connects mainland Asia with the Malay Peninsula, and at its narrowest point in Chumphon, is only 44km (27 miles) from coast to coast.

The 600km (373 miles) or so from Bangkok to Surat Thani (main jumping-off point for Ko Samui) is blessed with miles and miles of sandy beaches and equable weather, together with lush, forested interiors and historic towns that harbour plenty of attractions worth exploring. The southern rail line and Highway 4, also known as Petchkasem Highway, are the two principal links to the south, although there are also airports in Surat Thani and Hua Hin.

The upper section of the Gulf coast is home to two of the country's best-known national parks: Kaeng Krachan and Khao Sam Roi Yot. Phetchaburi, with its ancient temples, is a worthy stop before travellers continue to Cha-am and Hua Hin, both popular with Bangkokians as weekend beach getaways. Further south, Pranburi has a good reputation as a high-end boutique resort. Prachuap Khiri Khan and Chumphon see few tourists, except those departing from Chumphon's port for the boat ride to Ko Tao; the latter is more easily accessed from Ko Samui.

PHETCHABURI

Historically rich **Phetchaburi ❶** is one of Thailand's oldest towns and has been an important trade and cultural centre since the 11th century. Lying on the Phetchaburi River some 120km (75 miles) south of Bangkok, the town has come under the influence of the Mon, Khmers and Thais at various times, and has over 30 temples that reflect the differing cultures and architectural

Tham Kao Luang Cave, Phetchaburi.

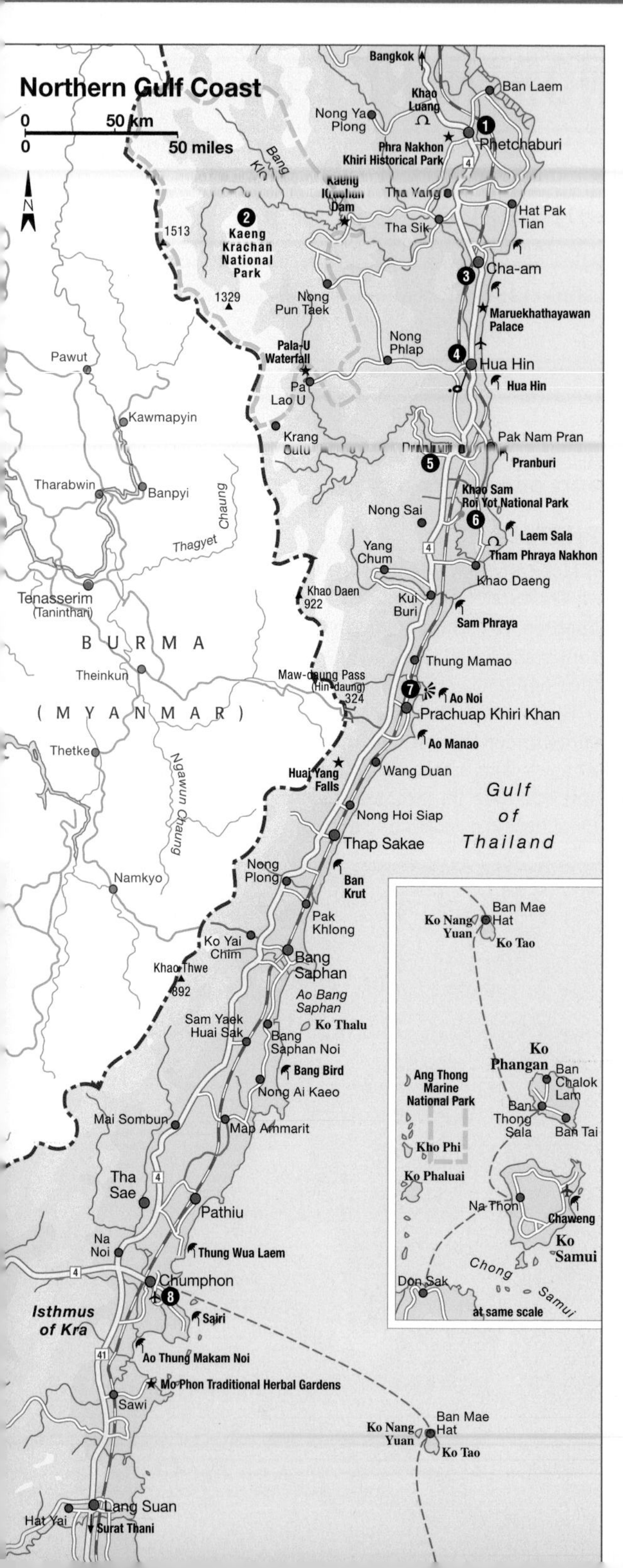

styles of its past invaders. A pleasant place to while away a day or two, Phetchaburi is easily navigable on foot.

KHAO WANG

Just west of town, the 92-metre (302ft) hill called **Khao Wang** (Mount Palace) provides a useful landmark. Commissioned in 1860 as the summer residence of King Mongkut (Rama IV), the complex is known as **Phra Nakhon Khiri Historical Park** (daily 8.30am-4pm; www.phranakhonkhiri.com). It is a curious mélange of Thai, Chinese and Western architectural styles taking the form of shrines, temples, pagodas and other structures. Many of these offer fabulous panoramas of the vicinity, especially at sunset.

The hilltop buildings include three throne halls (two of which have been turned into a museum for furniture and collectables belonging to King Mongkut), a neoclassical observatory (the king was an avid astronomer), a large white *chedi* and the **Wat Maha Samanaram**. The steep cobblestone trail to the peak winds through forest and gardens populated by monkeys. An easier option is to take the cable car (daily 8am–5pm) on the Petchkasem side of the hill; its entrance is marked by a line of souvenir shops.

PHETCHABURI'S OTHER TEMPLES

The former Hindu **Wat Kamphaeng Laeng** (daily 6am–5pm; free) with its five laterite Khmer *prang* is one of Phetchaburi's key religious sites. Located on Thanon Phra Song, it is thought to have marked the southernmost point of the Khmer empire. The temple dates from the 12th century. Although the towers have undergone some restoration, they are still dishevelled enough to look authentic.

Just around the corner on Thanon Phongsuriya, the 17th-century **Wat Yai Suwannaram** (daily 6am–5pm; free) is best known for its fading murals of Hindu gods that date back to the 18th century. The temple's ample grounds hold a lovely teak pavilion, as well as a catfish-filled pond. Jutting out into the pond is a small stilted *ho trai*, or scripture library.

Back across the river and along Thanon Damnoenkasem, five white stucco-covered *prang* make **Wat Mahathat** (daily 8am–4.30pm; free) the town's most dominant temple. As with any Mahathat (Great Relic) place of worship, the 14th-century site enshrines relics of the Buddha, but is probably better known for the intricate depictions of angels and other mythical creatures in low-relief stucco on the gables of the main buildings.

THAM KHAO LUANG

Just 5km (3 miles) from town, **Tham Khao Luang** cave (daily 7am–6pm) makes an interesting excursion. Shafts of sunlight filter down from naturally formed holes in the cave roof, creating a splendid visual effect. The rays illuminate some of the 100 or more Buddha images that rest in the three main chambers of the cave. Beside the entrance, **Wat Bunthawi** showcases wonderfully carved wooden door panels. Unofficial guides wait near the approach to the cave, offering to turn on the cave lights for a fee.

BAN PUEN PALACE

As the railway line brought greater access to this part of Thailand, a number of palaces were erected for the royal family in times past. Right beside the Phetchaburi River, about 1km (0.6 mile) from the city centre, along Thanon Ratchadamnoen, **Ban Puen Palace** (Mon–Fri 8.30am–4pm, Sat–Sun until 4.30pm) would look more at home in Germany's Black Forest than here in the coastal flats of Phetchaburi. Built in 1910 for King Rama V (the same year he died), this stately home was designed by a German architect, a grandiose two-storey palace intended as a rainy-season hideaway. Although little in the way of furniture remains to convey its original splendour, the porcelain-tiled dining room and inner courtyard with its pond and fountain are interesting to explore, as are the expansive gardens by the riverbank.

Fact

The Gulf of Thailand coast covered in this chapter has weather similar to that of the rest of Thailand. However, although the rains here continue well into November, the effects of the monsoon are milder. The best months of the year are from December to March, while April and May are the hottest months. The rainy months stretch from July to November.

Phra Nakhon Khiri.

Hua Hin is known for its fine seafood restaurants.

KAENG KRACHAN N P

Around 60km (37 miles) southwest of Phetchaburi Town, **Kaeng Krachan National Park** ❷ (daily 6am–6pm; http://portal.dnp.go.th) is the largest in Thailand. It is the source of the Phetchaburi and Pranburi rivers and a haven for numerous large mammals, including elephants, leopards, bears, deer, gibbons, monkeys and a few tigers. With around 300 species of resident and migratory birds, it is also a prime bird-watching spot. Considering its proximity to Bangkok, surprisingly few tourists venture here. Trekking is the main activity; guides can be hired at the park's headquarters at the end of the road beyond the dam. Accommodation consists of basic park lodgings. The easiest way to visit is on a tour organised by hotels in Hua Hin.

The topography varies between rainforest and savannah grasslands, rugged mountain ranges and a freshwater lake. It is possible to ascend the tallest peak, the 1,207-metre (3,960ft) **Phanoen Tung**, for superb views of the lush countryside, or trek to the 18-tier **Tho Thip Waterfall**. Swimming and boating in the vast reservoir created by **Kaeng Krachan Dam** are other popular activities.

On the southern edge of Kaeng Krachan, towards the mountain range that divides Thailand from Myanmar, is the spectacular 11-tier **Pala-U Waterfall,** surrounded by dense forest. It is best seen during the rainy season.

Seafood vendor at Cha-am.

CHA-AM

The long stretch of sand at **Cha-am** ❸, around 40km (25 miles) south of Phetchaburi, is a popular weekend getaway from Bangkok. The beach is fairly quiet during the week, but at weekends the mood is more raucous as families and students arrive in droves, picnicking (and boozing) under the casuarina trees and riding banana boats. The sand underfoot is a bit rough and the waters are less than pristine, but Cha-am offers good value for money when it comes to hotels and food, with plenty of seafood stalls and cheap restaurants along the waterfront on Thanon Ruamchit. In recent years chic minimalist hotels like the **Veranda** and **So Sofitel Hua-Hin** have varied the accommodation options.

MARUEKHATHAYAWAN PALACE

Just south of Cha-am, the seaside **Maruekhathayawan Palace** (Thu–Tue 8.30am–4pm; www.mrigadayavan.or.th) was built in 1923 from teak, and served as a retreat for King Vajiravudh during the last two years before his death in 1925. The airy stilted structures were designed by an Italian architect and are European in style, supposedly based on sketches made by King Vajiravudh (Rama VI). Beautifully renovated in summery pastel shades, the three palace wings are interconnected by long raised covered walkways. The magnificent audience chamber is the centrepiece of the palace structure.

HUA HIN

Prachuap Khiri Khan is Thailand's narrowest province and its coast is fringed with mountains and beaches, the most popular of which is the 5km (3-mile) stretch at **Hua Hin** ❹, just three to four hours by road or rail from Bangkok. Hua Hin, like many locations on this coast, has attracted Thai royalty; Bangkok's wealthy elite followed suit, and Hua Hin has many upmarket residences. Partly because of this, it retains a slightly more genteel ambience than some other beach destinations in Thailand, although it also has excesses if you look for them.

The royal connection can be seen at the seafront teak summer residence **Klai Kangwon Palace**, which means "Far from Worries". Built in 1926 for King Rama VII, the Spanish-style villa is still used by the royal family and is not open to the public.

One of the country's first rail lines linked Bangkok to Hua Hin at the start of the 20th century, transporting the capital's wealthy to the southern shores. Hua Hin thus assumed the aura of a European spa town, with the royals coming here for the clean air. Today, the coastal town has several exclusive spa retreats, like the award-winning **Chiva Som**.

HUA HIN SIGHTS

Today, some visitors still choose to take the train to Hua Hin, and the railway station is a beautiful place at which to arrive: built in the early 1920s, it evokes the romance of a bygone era, complete with a station library and a still-intact cream-and-red royal waiting room, once used by King Rama VI.

Thanon Damnoenkasem leads from the railway station directly to the beach and another historic landmark, the colonial-style **former Railway Hotel**. Dating from 1923, the Victorian-inspired building was Thailand's first resort hotel, and has been restored to its original wood-panelled glory as the **Centara Grand Beach Resort & Villas Hua Hin**. Even if you don't stay here, try to have afternoon tea or dine at one of its eateries, then stroll through its large manicured gardens filled with animal-shaped topiary creations.

The sweep of Hua Hin beach is backed by the lavish summer homes of Bangkok's elite, along with a series of faceless condo developments. Some of the homes, which fuse elements of Thai and Western architecture, date back almost

Tip

Avoid feeding the monkeys at Khao Wang, even if they seem tame; this helps to protect them from eating unsuitable food and also minimizes the chance of being on the receiving end of some simian attitude.

PHETCHABURI TRANSPORT

The best way to get around Phetchaburi town is by hiring a *pok pok* (a squat open-sided minivan), a *samlor* (a three-wheeled bicycle rickshaw) or a motorcycle taxi. You can find them at the train and bus stations or the Day Market, on Thanon Phanit Charoen, or you can flag one down on the road. It should cost around B20 for each hop, but bargain a price before you set off and ask the driver to wait while you tour each site. In Hua Hin, the central areas are achievable on foot. Otherwise, there are cars (B1,300/day) and motorbikes (B200/day) to rent opposite the Centara hotel. If you're stuck for somewhere to park, the grounds of Wat Hua Hin, on Phetchakasem Road, charge a small fee.

Green and white broadbill.

Tip

Despite the convenience of the road and airport, travelling by train to Hua Hin, following the route taken by the royal family who initially popularised the resort, is possibly the most pleasant way of getting to the resort.

a century. A few have been restored and converted into boutique resorts, like **Baan Bayan** (www.baanbayan.com) and **Baan Talay Dao** (www.baantalaydao.com).

The beach, although punctuated by occasional boulders, lacks the character of Thailand's palm-lined island bays. But it is good for long strolls. Further south, **Suan Son** and **Khao Tao**, are nicer and more secluded, but again not the best. While the sea is generally calm during the low season from May to September (with jellyfish an occasional problem), the winds can whip up the water towards the end and start of the year. This is when windsurfers and kite-surfers take to the water.

OUTSIDE HUA HIN

For some of the best panoramas of Hua Hin beach, head up steep **Khao Hin Lek Fai** hill. Around 3km (2 miles) west of town, turn down Soi 70 and follow the signposts to any of the six viewpoints. Dawn and sunset are the best times.

A few kilometres south of town is **Khao Takiab** (Chopstick Hill), a rocky outcrop which marks the end of Hua Hin beach. It is a steep climb to the top, but the views of the surrounding coast are worth the sweat. The hill is split into two windswept peaks; the nearest has several small shrines and a steep staircase that leads down to a 20-metre (66ft) tall Buddha image. Standing dramatically just above the crashing surf, the image looks back towards Hua Hin beach with its hands outstretched. On the other brow is **Wat Khao Lad**, with its lofty pagoda up a long flight of stairs.

ACTIVITIES

While Hua Hin was always known as a place for wonderfully fresh seafood, the diversity of culinary options has expanded to Japanese, Korean, Scandinavian, German, French and Italian eateries, reflecting the nationalities of the major tourist arrivals. The restaurants and bars are all clustered into a small area around Thanon Naresdamri and behind on the parallel Thanon Phunsuk. Soi Bintabaht has the highest concentration of beer bars, and the pier area along Naresdamri serves some of the best grilled seafood in town.

Limestone pinnacles at Khao Sam Roi Yot National Park.

CLAIM TO FAME

When the producers of Roland Joffe's Academy Award-winning movie *The Killing Fields* – depicting Pol Pot's murderous takeover of Cambodia in 1975 – were looking for a suitable location, their eyes fell on the former Railway Hotel at Hua Hin. The hotel's fleeting appearance in the film – it mainly features during the scenes when the foreign correspondents are holed up in the Cambodian capital in the wake of the Khmer Rouge revolution – gave it an added lustre both in the eyes of film buffs around the world and guests who enjoyed its gracious architecture and beautifully manicured grounds.

Hua Hin's other claim to celluloid fame is a short scene in the German film *Devil's Paradise*, which was loosely based on Joseph Conrad's novel *Victory*.

Golfers have access to several courses within striking distance of Hua Hin, with more on the drawing board. The oldest is the **Royal Hua Hin Golf Course**, built in the 1920s, and used by the Thai royalty.

Hua Hin sees a lot of weekend activities and events catering to the Bangkok crowds. These include the annual **Hua Hin Jazz Festival** (www.huahininterjazz.com), usually held in May. It mainly consists of Thai bands, many of which would struggle to justify the jazz moniker, but has included the likes of Bill Bruford's Earthworks in the past. The Hua Hin Regatta falls in July or August and attracts sailors from around the region to compete in several classes. There may be crewing opportunities if you want to sail but have no boat. The **Hua Hin Vintage Car Parade** celebrates its 20th anniversary in 2022.

PRANBURI

Around 20-minute's-drive south of Hua Hin towards **Pranburi** ❺, Paknampran, the mouth of the Pranburi River, marks the beginning of a clean but unremarkable beach. It is home to some of Thailand's most exclusive beachfront hideaways, including the **Evason,** its sister property **Evason Hideaway** and celebrity-friendly **Aleenta**.

About 63km (39 miles) south of Hua Hin, **Khao Sam Roi Yot National Park** ❻ (daily 8.30am–5pm; http://portal.dnp.go.th) translates as "Three Hundred Mountain Peaks", referring to the dramatic limestone pinnacles jutting up from the park's mangrove swamps. Carved from the rugged coastline, the 98-sq-km (38-sq-ft) park features beaches, marshes and brackish lagoons, forests, caves and offshore islands. Wildlife includes migratory birds that congregate on the marsh and mudflats, crab-eating macaques and the rare serow (a mountain goat-antelope). At certain times, pods of dolphins also swim along the park's shores.

Reached by boat or by foot along a steep half-hour trail from Hat Laem Sala, **Tham Phraya Nakhon** is the park's most famous attraction; the huge cave has a large sinkhole that allows shafts of light to enter and illuminate the grand Thai-style pavilion or *sala* called

The plush Aleenta resort in Pranburi.

Signalling the arrival of the train at Hua Hin's picturesque railway station.

Phra Thinang Khuha Kharuhat. It was built in the 1890s for a visit by King Chulalongkorn (Rama V). Other noteworthy caves are **Tham Sai** and **Tham Kaew** (Jewel Cave), the latter with glistening stalactite and rock formations.

Most Hua Hin and Pranburi hotels organise day trips to the park, but travellers can also catch a train or bus to Pranburi, and from there take a *songthaew* to the fishing village of Bang Pu. From here, take a short boat ride to the park checkpoint on **Hat Laem Sala** beach. The Forestry Department runs accommodation here, but a better option is to stay at a hotel, like the **Dolphin Bay Resort**, located at **Hat Phu Noi** beach a few kilometres north of the park.

SOUTH OF PRANBURI

The coastline south of Khao Sam Roi Yot is lined with miles of sandy beaches, yet most foreign tourists go directly to Chumphon for ferry connections to Ko Tao (see page 207), or to Surat Thani and then by boat to either Ko Samui (see page 195) or Ko Phangan (see page 201). While this stretch of the Gulf of Thailand coast is not being geared towards pampering foreign visitors, you benefit from less tourist-oriented commercialism.

Prachuap Khiri Khan ❼, 85km (53 miles) from Hua Hin, is an interesting town to explore, as are the beaches of **Ao Manao**, 4km (3 miles) south of Prachuap Town, and **Ban Krut**, 70km (43 miles) south, although both have limited facilities by way of accommodation and restaurants. Further south, offshore from the town of **Bang Saphan Yai**, is the island of **Ko Thalu** one of the first south of Bangkok that is good enough for snorkelling and diving.

About 184km (114 miles) from Prachuap Khiri Khan, **Chumphon** ❽ is considered by many to be the start of southern Thailand. It has several good beaches, including **Thung Wua Laem**, 12km (7 miles) north of Chumphon Town, and **Ao Thung Makam Noi**, about 25km (16 miles) to the south. Some 20km (12 miles) offshore, the reef-fringed islands of **Ko Ngam Yai** and **Ko Ngam Noi** are popular with divers, while 80km (50 miles) away **Ko Tao** is another diving hotspot.

One of the many resorts at Phrachuap Khiri Khan.

Divers observe a whaleshark in the waters just off Ko Tao.

Ang Thong National Marine Park.

KO SAMUI, KO PHANGAN AND KO TAO

The spa-laden paradise of Ko Samui shares the Gulf of Thailand waters with Ko Phangan, equally idyllic, and known for its anything-goes, all-night Full Moon Parties. If you prefer to dive or snorkel, head to the pristine waters off Ko Tao.

Palm-fringed **Ko Samui** is the biggest of 80 islands that make up the Samui Archipelago, which also includes the party isle of **Ko Phangan**, the dive mecca of **Ko Tao** and pristine **Ang Thong Marine National Park**. Some 80km (50 miles) from the mainland town of Surat Thani in the southern Gulf of Thailand, and with only a handful of islands hosting any significant settlement, much of the area remains unspoilt, with perfect white-sand beaches ringed by colourful coral reefs and rugged forested interiors.

For over a century, the people of the islands – largely immigrant Chinese and Muslim communities – derived their incomes from coconut plantations and fishing. And although tourism dominates today, many of Ko Samui's poorer islanders still make their living from the coconut plantations.

The Samui Archipelago saw a significant jump in tourists from 2005, as holiday makers scrambled to find alternative destinations away from the tsunami-hit resorts along the Andaman coast. Development mushroomed, particularly on Ko Samui, during the following years and the island remains a very popular holiday spot.

However, while Samui increasingly tailors itself to the higher end of the market, Ko Phangan and Ko Tao still gear themselves to backpackers. Samui is an hour's flight from Bangkok, 644km (400 miles) away. Convenient ferry connections between the three islands make it easy to sample the unique pleasures of each.

KO SAMUI

When foreign backpackers first began travelling to Ko Samui in the 1970s, travellers' tales of this island paradise soon surfaced; it was only a matter of time before the secret was out. The simple A-frame huts that once sheltered budget travellers can still

Main attractions

- Ko Samui's Fisherman's Village
- Ko Samui's Hat Chaweng
- Ko Samui's Hat Lamai
- Ang Thong Marine National Park
- Ko Phangan's Ban Tai
- Ko Phangan's Hat Kuat
- Ko Tao
- Ko Nang Yuan

Maps on pages 196, 204, 207

On the streets of Bo Phut, Ko Samui.

Seated Buddha image at Hat Bangrak.

be spotted on the island's peripheral beaches, but nowadays the most scenic bays have been taken over by luxury boutique resorts that blend in with the palm-lined beachfronts.

But Ko Samui's raw beauty is still largely intact, and this coupled with a laidback vibe is one reason the island attracts so many repeat visitors. Many have secured their own piece of this 247-sq km (95-sq mile) tropical paradise by buying holiday houses or condos here.

The island has also become one of Thailand's hottest spa destinations, with a wide variety of extravagant hotel-based pampering, as well as independent day spas and retreat centres that claim to restore both physical and spiritual health. For those who tire quickly of the soft sandy beaches, the verdant jungles and waterfalls of the interior offer a different kind of escape.

Ko Samui still has some way to go before matching the yachting marinas and theme parks of Phuket, but with an 18-hole golf course and two large supermarket chains among its list of amenities, it looks destined to follow in the same footsteps. The rapid rise of tourism has brought some problems, however. Severe water shortages are becoming

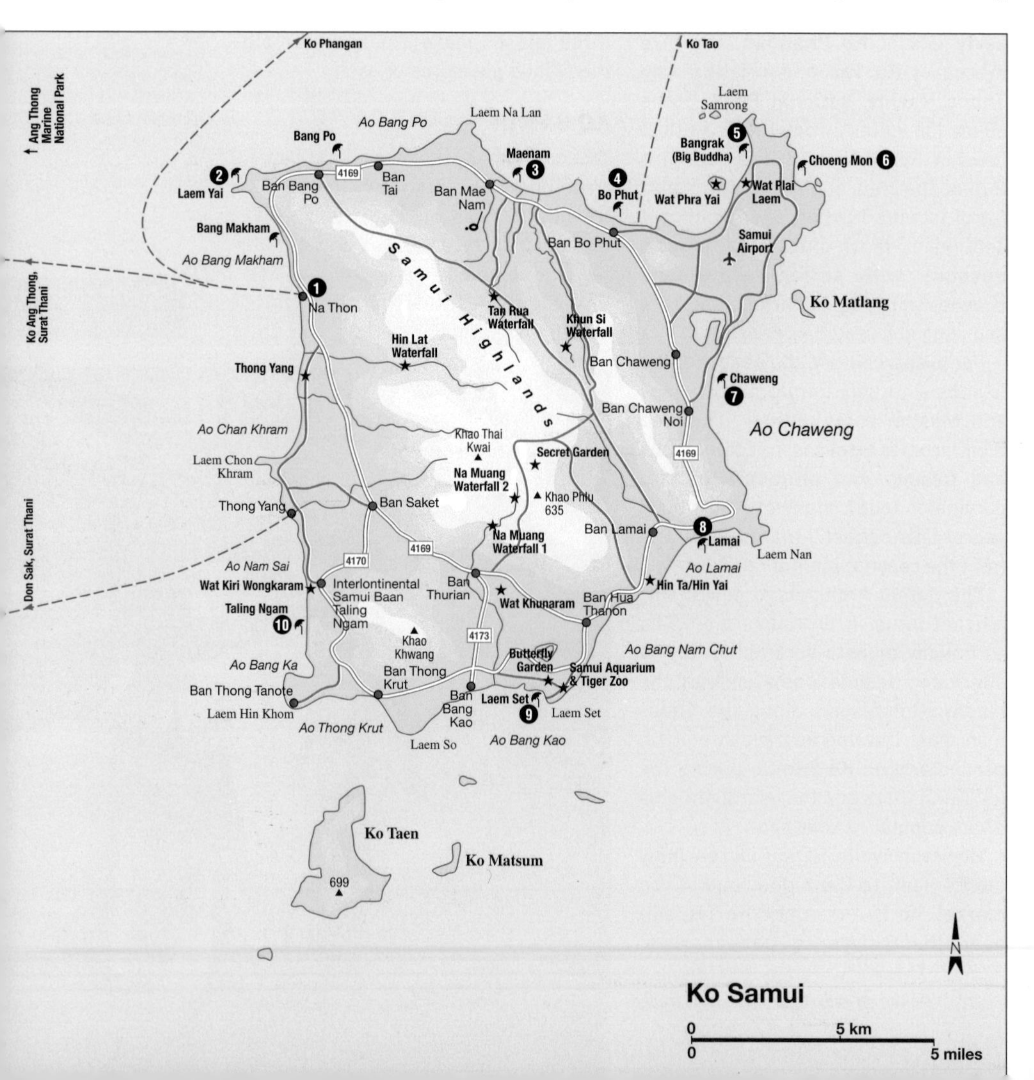

a regular occurrence during the driest months, while the rainy season sometimes brings flood waters rushing down from deforested hills to many of the island's roads and beachfront properties.

For better or worse, Ko Samui is becoming increasingly cosmopolitan. Dining choices are ever more varied and upscale, with more design-conscious eateries independent of hotels opening by the month. While the nightlife scene is always busy, the island is short on stylish bars and clubs, with most socialising taking place in "beer bars", Brit-style pubs and throbbing clubs.

GETTING TO KO SAMUI

Direct flights link Ko Samui's airport (located on the northeastern tip of the island) with Bangkok, Phuket and Krabi, as well as some international destinations. The tropical escape begins the minute you touch down; with its quaint open-plan buildings and manicured gardens, this airport is one of Thailand's most picturesque arrival points. Many people also travel by boat from mainland Surat Thani (Ban Don pier) to the busy port town of **Na Thon** ❶ on Ko Samui's northwest coast.

Na Thon, which is also the island's commercial centre, has little of interest to visitors, save for a few vintage Chinese-influenced wooden shophouses, souvenir shops for last-minute purchases, banks, restaurants and cafés, travel agents, a few faceless hotels, and an immigration office for visa extensions.

Ko Samui's roads are generally well paved, and the two-lane highway that loops around the island – Route 4169 – is eminently drivable. Yet accidents are frequent (mainly caused by intoxicated drivers), and great care should still be taken if you are driving your own vehicle.

LAEM YAI AND HAT MAENAM

The secluded beach of **Laem Yai** ❷, located on a headland with a steep hillside rising behind it, is home to one of Ko Samui's most exclusive resorts, the all-villa **Four Seasons Koh Samui**.

The second beach of note on the north coast is **Hat Maenam** ❸, about

Fact

The southwest monsoon brings light intermittent rains to the Samui archipelago from June to Oct. From Nov to Jan, the northeast monsoon takes over: the heaviest rains fall during this period, with Nov being the wettest month. Given the rather unpredictable wet-weather pattern, the best time to visit the islands is from February to May – although there are plenty of fine days right through to September.

Grandfather Rock, Hat Lamai.

KO SAMUI'S SPAS

Few aspects of Thailand sum up the national predilection for having a good time and taking it easy (*sanuk* and *sabai*) as a trip to a spa, a pastime that has become an integral part of many Thai vacations. The industry has grown exponentially, partly because many native ingredients are incorporated in spa treatments, additionally because the Thais' gentle nature lends itself naturally to what is universally referred to as pampering, and also because the kingdom's climate and architecture both lend themselves to designing out-of-this-world-class spas.

Tamarind Retreat is a prime example, a bucolic haven that opened in the late 1990s and which now incorporates a swathe of villas where guests can stay just steps away from their next treatment. All over Ko Samui, spas have sprung up in imitation, either attached to hotels or as independent concerns. The real delight of this sybaritic industry is that it's supremely adaptable. Customers can drop in for a quick massage, work out a day-long programme, or go the whole hog and move in for a series of treatments that include several days' fast and come out feeling utterly rejuvenated. First-timers should put aside any doubts – staff are universally considerate and caring, and the sheer delight of lying back and healthily doing nothing for a couple of hours has very few equals.

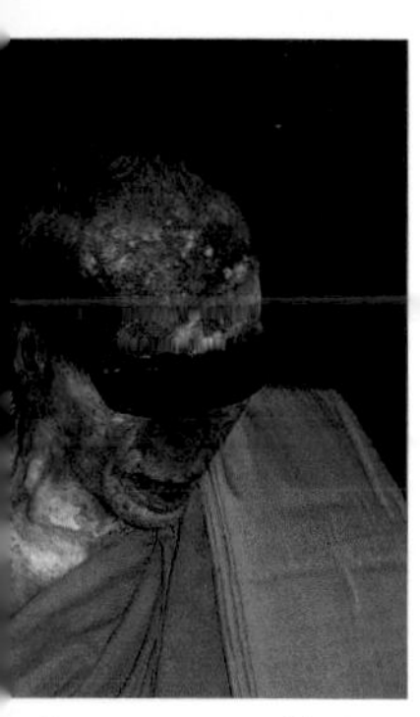

Famous mummified monk Luang Phor Daeng at Wat Khunaram, Ko Samui.

13km (8 miles) from Na Thon and 6km (4 miles) from the airport. The 4km (2.5-mile) long stretch is fairly isolated and quiet. The golden yellow sand underfoot is a little coarse and the beach is pleasant but quite narrow. Numerous budget hotels have sprung up here in addition to the deluxe-class **Santiburi**. Nights can be quiet in Maenam due to the near-absence of bars and clubs; for that you have to head south to Chaweng.

HAT BO PHUT

East of Maenam is **Hat Bo Phut** ❹. While the beach is nice enough and of similar standard to Maenam, the 2km (1.5-mile) strip is better known for the quaint seafront lane of old wooden shophouses, known as **Ban Bo Phut** or **Fisherman's Village**. The old timber shacks have been tastefully converted into restaurants, bars and shops, making this one of the most attractive places on the island to wander around. There are several resorts here, the top-of-the-line place being **Anantara Bophut Ko Samui**, a short distance west of Fisherman's Village.

Of all the islands in the Gulf of Thailand, Ko Samui has the most off-beach attractions. There are many waterfalls cascading down from the Samui Highlands that are worthy of the trip from the island's north coast, including **Tan Rua**, **Khun Si** and **Hin Lat**. These tend to see a lot less traffic than the tourist bus-packed falls further south on the island. Roads are particularly severe and winding in places though, so take extra care if navigating them on your own by car or motorbike. Largely set up for tourists, but a nod to the island's coconut plantation heritage, the trained "monkey work coconut" shows at the **Samui Monkey Theatre** in Bo Phut (daily 10.30am, 2pm, 4pm; charge) reveal how southern Thais use simian labour to assist in harvesting coconuts. Like many animal entertainment places, concerns have been expressed about the treatment of the animals here.

HAT BANGRAK

On the headland to the northeast of Bo Phut, **Hat Bangrak** ❺ is better known

Tropical beach on the Bo Phut coastline.

locally as **Big Buddha beach** due to the presence of **Wat Phra Yai**, or Big Buddha Temple (daily 8am–5pm; free) on a small islet across the bay. The 12-metre (39ft) golden Buddha image is linked by a causeway to the end of the beach.

At low tide, the water can retreat quite far out, exposing a swathe of mud. There is some budget accommodation set behind the beach but most of it isn't particularly nice. As the Big Buddha statue is a popular photo stop for island tours of Ko Samui, swarms of vendors hawking souvenirs frequently crowd the path leading to the entrance of the temple.

A short hike and a northwards turn from the temple entrance is the much more intriguing **Wat Plai Laem** (daily 8am–5pm), a small, colourful temple set in the middle of a large fish-filled pond, with a base in the form of a giant lotus flower. There are two large statues either side of the Goddess Guanyin and the Laughing Buddha. Remember that at all temples it is required that everyone dress in polite attire, which means no shorts, vests, short skirts, crop-tops or sandals.

HAT CHOENG MON

On the other side of the headland is **Hat Choeng Mon** ❻, a small but serene white-sand bay backed by casuarina trees. It has a relatively undeveloped ambience, save for a couple of upmarket resorts. There is hardly any nightlife here, but then busy Chaweng beach is only a short drive away. Several of the island's premier beach resorts, like the **Imperial Boathouse**, **Tongsai Bay** and the all-villa **SALA Samui Choengmon Beach Resort** occupy prime positions along this scenic stretch.

HAT CHAWENG

The 6km (4-mile) long **Hat Chaweng** ❼ on the east coast is by far the busiest beach on Ko Samui. It is roughly divided into three sections: North Chaweng, Central Chaweng and South Chaweng. The stunning powdery white-sand beach facing clear turquoise waters follows the shore from the headland in the north near the small island of **Ko Matlang**, all the way down to the curving bay and rocky end point of South Chaweng.

North Chaweng beach is sheltered by a coral reef, which means that while the sea is sheltered from strong winds during the monsoon season the waters can also be still as a millpond at other times of the year. It is also less crowded than **Central Chaweng**, which is the most built up. Behind the rather cramped line of beach resorts, Chaweng Beach Road is a rather faceless sprawl of somewhat tacky tourist-oriented shops, restaurants and bars. However, recent upmarket shopping arcades like **Iyara Plaza**, **Central** and **Living Plaza** are a sign of things to come. Past a tiny spit of land is the relatively quiet **South Chaweng**, which is not much thinner on accommodation and restaurants.

HAT LAMAI

Further south, over a rocky ridge that has stunning viewpoints back towards

Fact

Getting to Talay Nai lagoon involves a 20-minute trek, but the vista of waters encircled by limestone cliffs is worth the effort.

Wat Phra Yai.

Getting to Talay Nai lake involves a 20-minute trek, but the vista of limestone cliff-encircled waters is worth the effort.

the Chaweng shoreline, is Samui's second most populous beach, **Hat Lamai** ❽. It is lovely and far less hectic compared to its northern neighbour, with better accommodation choices for budget travellers, although there are also several boutique resorts. Lamai is also the home of the island's original wellness centres, namely **The Spa Resort** and **Tamarind Springs**.

A little beyond the beach's southern tip are two natural rock formations known as **Hin Ta** (Grandfather Rock) and **Hin Yai** (Grandmother Rock). As they resemble male and female genitalia, the rocks are the subject of much photo-taking, and not a little sniggering.

Dining at Lamai doesn't have Chaweng's breadth and quality, and unfortunately, gets a bad rap for its slightly lascivious nightlife scene, with its stretch of raunchy girlie bars.

INLAND FROM LAMAI

Taking Route 4169 inland from Hat Lamai leads to one of the temples featured on most around-the-island tours, **Wat Khunaram** (daily 8am–5pm; free). The temple is famed as the home of mummified monk Luang Phor Daeng. His body is still seated in the same meditating position he held when he died decades ago.

Continuing past the village of Ban Thurian is **Na Muang Waterfall 1**: in the wet season, a cascade of water plunges some 20 metres (66ft) into a large pool. Getting to **Na Muang Waterfall 2** (part of the same falls further up) involves a fairly strenuous 1.5km (1-mile) trek.

Another of Lamai's attractions is the **Samui Aquarium & Tiger Zoo** (daily 9.30am–4.30pm, daily show at 1.30pm; charge; www.samuiaquariumandtigerzoo.com), located within the Samui Orchid Resort in south Lamai. The aquarium exhibits are nothing to write home about; more entertaining is the daily bird and Bengal tiger show. Like many of the wildlife entertainment venues in Thailand, numerous concerns have been expressed about the welfare of the animals here.

Sea kayaking at Ang Thong National Marine Park.

SOUTH AND WEST COASTS

The south- and west-coast beaches aren't as pretty, although a few beautiful resorts can be found along these shores. If you are intent on a secluded holiday, the beach at **Hat Laem Set** ❾ (also sometimes referred to as **Hat Na Thian**) could be the place. The stylish **Centara Villas Samui** with its elegant rooms is a popular accommodation choice here. Not far around the bay from Centara Villas you come to **The Butterfly Hill** (daily 8.30am–5.30pm), where the rainbow-coloured wings of myriad butterflies flutter within its net-covered compound.

Over on the west coast is **Hat Taling Ngam** ❿, the site of the stylish **Inter-Continental Samui Baan Taling Ngam Resort**. Occupying a vantage position on a steep hill, the views of the coast here partly compensate for the rather ordinary beach.

ACTIVITIES

Ko Samui has plenty of options for those who seek more active pursuits.

On land, hire a four-wheel-drive jeep, or mountain bike, and explore the dirt trails that lead up into the verdant hills of the interior. There are also a host of watersports; jet skiing, kayaking, windsurfing, waterskiing, parasailing, deep-sea fishing and sailing. The annual Ko Samui International Regatta (www.samuiregatta.com), usually from May to June, has helped establish the island as a yachting base and a few companies now charter luxury boats.

Although the island has numerous dive shops, the surrounding waters are not particularly good for diving and snorkelling. Most dive trips head out to the nearby **Ang Thong Marine National Park**, **Hin Bai** and **Ko Tao**.

ANG THONG MARINE NATIONAL PARK

Although Ko Phi Phi's Maya Bay was the chosen location setting for the 2000 film *The Beach*, it was the dramatic scenery of **Ang Thong Marine National Park** (http://portal.dnp.go.th) that was Alex Garland's original inspiration for his best-selling novel.

Ang Thong, or "Golden Bowl", Marine National Park lies some 31km (19 miles) west of Ko Samui. These 42 virtually uninhabited islands make up an archipelago that stretches over 100-sq-kms (39-sq-miles), an expanse of land and sea that forms a pristine environment for a wide diversity of flora and fauna, including macaques, langurs and monitor lizards. Pods of dolphins are known to shelter in the waters late in the year.

A principal visit on any day trip to the island chain is to the Talay Nai (inland sea), an emerald-green saltwater lagoon on Ko Mae Ko encircled by sheer limestone walls covered with vegetation. The picturesque lake can be reached by a trail from the beach.

Several tour companies on Ko Samui operate day trips, including kayaking expeditions to the archipelago, which usually include a stop on the largest island, **Ko Wua Talab** (Sleeping Cow Island). Aside from a beach and the park's headquarters, there is a steep 400-metre (1,300ft) climb up to a lookout point that has unrivalled views of the surroundings, with Ko Samui and Ko Phangan in the distance. Also involving an arduous climb is Ko Wua Talab's other highlight, **Tham Bua Bok**, or Waving Lotus Cave. It is named after lotus-shaped rock formations.

Diving and snorkelling at Ang Thong are usually best experienced at the northern tip, around the islet of **Ko Yippon**. Although visibility isn't crystal-clear, the shallow depths make it easy to view the colourful coral beds, which are inhabited by sea snakes, fusiliers and stingrays. There are also shallow caves and archways to swim through.

KO PHANGAN

The second-largest island in the Samui Archipelago, **Ko Phangan** is blessed with numerous seductive white-sand beaches and richly forested mountains, yet its current international reputation stems almost exclusively from the infamous Full Moon Party, which takes

Tip

There are no official tourism offices in Ko Phangan. A decent source for information is the website www.phangan.info, which has information and useful tips on what to do on the island.

The island-studded Ang Thong National Marine Park.

FULL-MOON PARTY

Ko Phangan has long been known for its wild beach parties. Despite official disapproval, the money they generate has guaranteed their survival.

An essential stop on any backpacker's tour of Southeast Asia, the Full Moon Party is dubbed the "world's biggest beach party", and, despite the Thai government's intermittent calls for the event to be scrapped, this Ko Phangan cash cow is too vital for the tourism industry to stop milking. The party takes place on Hat Rin Nok, or Sunrise Beach, with the focal point of the all-night rave at the southern end of the beach in front of Paradise Resort.

The event itself builds in momentum from sunset to sunrise, and Paradise Resort is regarded as the main hub of this no-holds-barred party. This is where the party circuit's most popular DJs spin, although there are DJs vying for attention at the main bars all along the beach. Each bar leans towards a different groove, and the dance hotspots shift periodically, depending on who is spinning what, where and when – or on the inclinations of the hell-bent-on-partying crowd in that particular year.

Having fun at the Full Moon Party.

The Full Moon Party (aka F-M) draws thousands of global revellers throughout the year, though the peak season of December and January sees the wildest action. Guesthouses charge high-season rates and the rooms fill up quickly as the moon waxes, with some places only taking bookings for a minimum of four or five nights. Those craving beauty sleep should choose accommodation well away from Hat Rin Nok as the party scene can be loud on most nights, cranking up to an eardrum-bursting crescendo on full-moon night.

For those who desire distance from the monthly mayhem, transport from other beaches to the party is plentiful. And if you prefer to nurse a post-party hangover within the confines of a luxury hotel in Ko Samui, numerous boats make the night-time crossing between the two islands.

ANYTHING (AND EVERYTHING) GOES

Generally, people spend the night getting wasted on cheap booze concoctions and being painted up in fluorescent ink. Aside from all the music, dance, booze and fleeting romances, a lot of partygoers are there to sample what first gave F-M its notoriety, namely illicit substances. However, today's F-M is no longer an open display of magic-mushroom teas and omelettes, or speed and ecstasy punches. Drug-taking is still prevalent, but there are many plain-clothed and uniformed police on patrol, so purveying or indulging of drugs is done with discretion. Penalties for possession of, or being under the influence of, illegal drugs are extremely harsh in Thailand.

The Full Moon Party is a bane for international embassies in Bangkok as every month at least one excessive partygoer loses the plot after ingesting some psychotropic cocktail, and officials are left to piece together the patient's fractured mind before shipping him or her back home. The local methamphetamine *yaa baa* (crazy drug) is one of the most common yet most addictive drugs around.

Sunrise is met by cheers, and the chance to raise the tempo for anyone who might have been thinking about collapsing into bed. The beach party winds up late morning, but the traditional after-party kicks off at Backyard Bar up the hill.

For more info and current F-M dates, check out www.fullmoon.phangan.info.

place at Hat Rin Nok on the island's southern tip. With an infamy that rivals that of Ibiza and Goa, the lunar gathering has steadily grown since the first party back in the late 1980s.

Lying around 20km (12 miles) north of Ko Samui, and 40 minutes by boat, Ko Phangan became an outpost on the shoestring traveller's map in the 1980s, around the same time as Ko Samui. But while the latter rapidly developed into a hub for package holidaymakers and flashy beach homes for the wealthy, Ko Phangan has largely remained an enclave of backpackers, revellers and New Age *nirvana*-seekers. However, pockets of the 193-sq-km (75-sq-mile) island are becoming built up, particularly Hat Rin and its vicinity, which now looks and feels very different to the rest of the island.

While most revellers confine themselves to the southern cape beaches of Hat Rin Nok (Sunrise Beach), Hat Rin Nai (Sunset Beach) and nearby Leela Beach, there are plenty of other more isolated bays that skirt the mountainous interior. Increasingly serviceable roads have made the furthest reaches of the island more accessible, but even so, a couple of coves, such as Hat Kuat (Bottle Beach), can be reached only by boat or on foot.

Located halfway along the west coast, the island's administrative centre and main arrival point is the small town of **Thong Sala ❶**. Apart from fishing boats unloading their daily haul, the port is usually busy with ferries and boats travelling to and from Ko Samui, Ko Tao and Surat Thani. Thong Sala has all the usual tourist-friendly services; internet cafés, banks, shops and a few restaurants and bars, plus a morning and night market mainly patronised by locals.

BAN TAI AND BAN KHAI

East of Thong Sala, the south coast is endowed with a continuous stretch of white-sand beach running all the way up to the Hat Rin cape, though the shallow reefs make the water often unfavourable for swimming. The most popular beaches here are between the villages of **Ban Tai ❷** and **Ban Khai ❸**.

Tip

Lots of vendors offer cheap massages by the beach at Hat Rin Nok and Hat Rin Nai on Ko Phangan.

A beach on Ko Phangan.

> **Tip**
>
> The advantages of staying on any of the west-coast beaches on Ko Phangan are fewer crowds and beautiful sunset views with the islands of the Ang Thong Marine National Park framed against the horizon.

Both basic and more comfortable family-run bungalow accommodation runs along the length to Thong Sala, with Ban Khai, the closest to Hat Rin, the only spot that offers any night-time activity.

HAT RIN

East of Ban Khai is where all the beach action lies. **Hat Rin** is certainly not Ko Phangan's most serene destination, but its original appeal remains; it hosts two beaches within easy walking distance across a flat headland, both with sensational sunrise and sunset views.

Hat Rin Nok ❹, or Sunrise Beach, is the wider, more popular bay, and is where the main nightlife cranks up, climaxed by the monthly Full Moon party. Hat Rin attracts a global melting pot of young clubbers and alternative lifestyle devotees, who find this tiny pocket of Thailand the perfect place to express their inner selves, helped along by alcohol and other – less legal – substances.

The less attractive of the two beaches is **Hat Rin Nai** ❺, or Sunset Beach, a thinner stretch of sand lined with beach huts that offer respite from the late-night cacophony over at Hat Rin Nok. The walk between the two beaches is jam-packed with accommodation, shops, restaurants, internet cafés and travel agents.

Further towards the island's southern tip is pretty **Leela** beach. It is around a 15-minute walk from Hat Rin Nai, and has a more peaceful atmosphere.

EAST-COAST BEACHES

There are several small but fine bays that run north up the east coast from Hat Rin, but a lack of roads means taking a boat (from Hat Rin) is the only way to venture there and as a result, development is patchy. **Hat Yuan** ❻ and **Hat Yao** (not to be confused with the longer Hat Yao on the west coast) and particularly **Hat Thian** ❼ are popular with travellers who seek isolated beaches.

At the top of the east coast are the increasingly popular twin bays of **Ao Thong Nai Pan Noi** ❽ and **Ao Thong Nai Pan Yai** ❾, described by many as the island's most beautiful coves. Getting up here is now easier, as the 12km

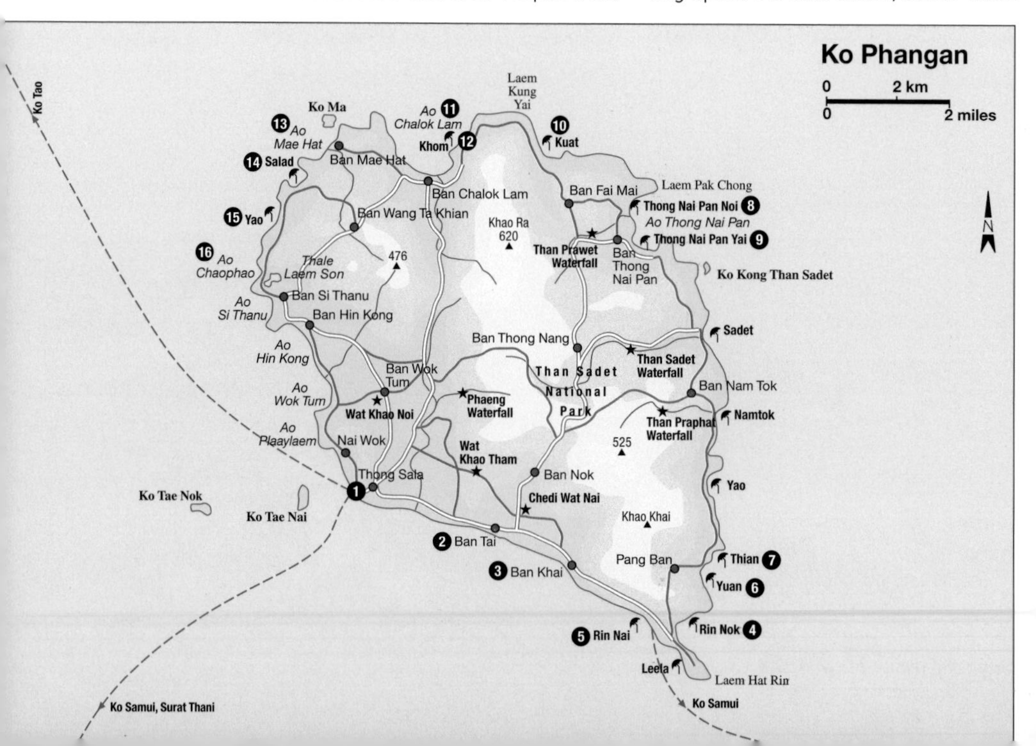

(8-mile) road from Ban Tai in the south has been paved, and the accommodation choices are increasing in range and price. The bays are separated by a headland that can be traversed in about 20 minutes.

Ao Thong Nai Pan Noi was a favourite stop-off for King Chulalongkorn, who made numerous visits to Ko Phangan between 1888 and 1909, when just a few hundred Thai and Chinese islanders eked a living from coconuts, fishing and mining tin.

NORTH-COAST BEACHES

The north coast has two bays that are worth seeking out. The first of these is **Hat Kuat** ⑩, or Bottle Beach. Get there on a decent road from Thong Sala up to Ao Chalok Lam, from where you can take a boat. This is one of Ko Phangan's best bays, the splendid white sands backed by steep hills. Accommodation is at the budget end.

The second bay to the west, **Ao Chalok Lam** ⑪, is occupied by a large fishing village which functions as the island's second port. The pier in the centre of the large curving bay is usually busy with fishermen who supply the seafood restaurants here with the freshest catch. The small white-sand cove, called **Hat Khom** ⑫, along this stretch and closer to the headland east, is the best bit of beach here, ringed by a coral reef offshore. The 10-km (6-mile) road from Thong Sala in the south to Ao Chalok Lam is one of the island's best, so access is not a problem.

WEST-COAST BEACHES

The west-coast beaches stretching from Ao Mae Hat all the way to Thong Sala in the south are more attractive than those along the southeastern shores, yet see fewer visitors compared to the Hat Rin area.

Starting from the northwest corner is **Ao Mae Hat** ⑬, which has a sandbank at low tide that connects to the tiny reef-fringed island of **Ko Ma** (Horse Island). The reef that runs up the coast from Ao Chaophao all the way to Ko Ma is considered the island's best snorkelling and diving site.

Further down the coast is scenic **Hat Salad** ⑭, with good snorkelling just off the northern edge of the beach. Next is an attractive 1km (0.6-mile) sandy stretch called **Hat Yao** ⑮, or Long Beach. It has become very popular in recent years and is giving Hat Rin a run for its money, with its range of accommodation, bars, restaurants and other facilities. Further south is a small bay called **Ao Chaophao** ⑯, which has a decent range of facilities. Further down the coast still are four more beaches of note: **Ao Si Thanu**, **Ao Hin Kong**, **Ao Wok Tum** and **Ao Plaaylaem**.

INLAND ATTRACTIONS

Phangan's thickly forested interior has a number of attractions. When King Chulalongkorn used to visit the island, one of his favourite haunts was **Than Sadet Waterfall**, which flows out to **Hat Sadet** beach in the next cove down the east coast from Ao Thong

Lots of vendors offer cheap massages by the beach at Hat Rin Nok and Hat Rin Nai on Ko Phangan.

Crossing the wooden rope bridge at Chalok Lam beach.

Tip

Although Ko Tao mainly appeals to divers, those who want to spread their adventure can abseil, rock climb or go wakeboarding, among many others. Contact Goodtime Thailand, http://goodtimethailand.com.

Nai Pan Yai, some 12km (7 miles) up from Hat Rin. The island's other cascades are **Than Praphat Waterfall** on the way to the east-coast beach of Hat Namtok, **Than Prawet Waterfall** located near Ao Thong Nai Pan Noi, and **Phaeng Waterfall** found halfway across the island en route from Thong Sala to Ban Chalok Lam village. All these waterfalls come under the umbrella of the 65-sq-km (25-sq-mile) **Than Sadet National Park** (http://portal.dnp.go.th).

A cave monastery on a hill near the village of Ban Tai, **Wat Kow Tahm International Meditation Center** (www.watkowtahm.org) holds silent retreats lasting from 10-days taught by an Australian-American couple.

DIVING AND SNORKELLING

Ko Phangan has some coral reefs, but most diving happens at a few sites some distance out at **Ang Thong Marine National Park, Hin Bai** (Sail Rock) and around **Ko Tao**. Snorkelling and diving closer to Ko Phangan is best along reefs on the northwest tip of the island, around **Ko Ma, Ao Mae Hat** and **Hat Yao**. Ko Ma is Ko Phangan's best dive site, with fairly shallow depths up to 20 metres (66ft). The area is frequented by blue-spotted stingrays, giant grouper and reef sharks.

Located about halfway between Ko Phangan and Ko Tao, **Hin Bai** (Sail Rock) is regarded as one of the best dive sites in the Samui Archipelago and is suitable for all levels. The rugged rock emerges like an iceberg from the water; most of its bulk is hidden below the surface, reaching depths of more than 30 metres (100ft). The granite pinnacle is circled by large schools of pelagic fish, but the highlight is a dramatic vertical chimney that can be entered at 19 metres (62ft) underwater, with an exit at 6 metres (20ft) from the surface.

NIGHTLIFE AND OTHER ENTERTAINMENT

Apart from the notorious Full Moon Party, Ko Phangan has plenty of other regular weekly and monthly party

Diving among the coral reefs off Hin Bai (Sail Rock).

nights to keep the backpackers bouncing. Those who like commercial dance music will have to make do with a mix of trance, techno and drum 'n' bass, the music of choice at the island's main nightspots. The so-called **Half Moon** parties shape up twice a month, a week before and after full moon, held at a hypnotically lit outdoor venue in Ban Tai.

For more information on the island's entertainment scene, pick up a copy of *Phangan Info* (www.phangan.info).

KO TAO

You don't have to be a diver to enjoy Ko Tao, but it helps. Around 40km (25 miles) northwest of Ko Phangan and 60km (37 miles) from Ko Samui, **Ko Tao**, or Turtle Island, is the northernmost inhabited island in the Samui Archipelago. The remote and tiny 21-sq-km (8-sq-mile) island, topped with tropical forest and fringed with some picturesque secluded bays, is said to draw its name from its rather loose geographical shape of a diving turtle; others have attributed its name to the once-abundant turtles that swam in these waters. Today, this laidback outpost might just as well be called "aqualung" island for the density of affordable dive schools that operate expeditions to its coral-abundant waters, making this one of the world's best places to learn to scuba dive.

Less than a decade ago, Ko Tao consisted solely of rustic backpacker huts. More recent development, however, has seen better accommodation options and entertainment venues. And the bonus of a large percentage of visitors studying in dive schools or out on dive trips is that the island's beaches are relatively peaceful during the day.

WEST-COAST BEACHES

Ko Tao is accessed by ferries and speedboats from the mainland port of Chumphon, located some 80km (50 miles) to the east, as well as from Ko Samui, Ko Phangan or Surat Thani to the south. The main arrival point is the small but lively village of **Ban**

Tip

Ko Tao is too tiny and undeveloped to have a tourism office. A good bet for information and tips on the island is www.kohtaotoday.com.

Taking the plunge off Ko Tao.

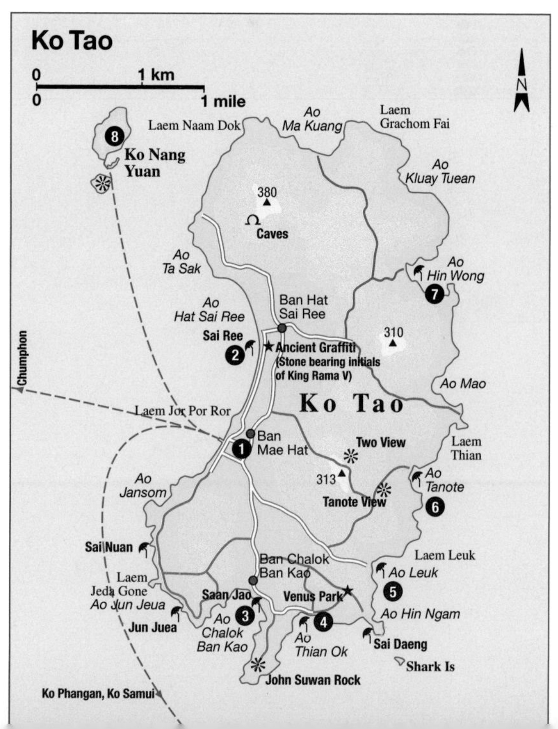

Tip

Dive shops are plentiful on Ko Tao, but as most offer more or less the same services, it's best to shop around and ask people for recommendations.

Mae Hat ❶ on the west coast. It is little more than a one-street village lined with a post office, banks, shops, cafés, bars and other tourist-related infrastructure.

There are good small bays at Hat Sai Nuan and Ao Jansom south of the village, while north is the small, shallow bay of **Ao Hat Mae**. There is some accommodation here, but it may be too close to the village for some. Much nicer is the 2km (1.5-mile) long **Hat Sai Ree** ❷, the island's longest and most popular curve of white sand. Sai Ree is lined with hotels to suit most budgets, getting gradually quieter further north with the ever-growing **Ban Hat Sai Ree** village backing the beach just over the halfway mark. Beyond Sai Ree, the road makes an incline up towards the northern tip of the island, with several more out-of-the-way cliff-top resorts, including attractive **Thipwimarn**, whose restaurant offers stunning sunset views.

SOUTH-COAST BEACHES

Ko Tao's southern shores are home to a few small, pretty beaches that lie either side of the island's second-busiest beach, **Ao Chalok Ban Kao** ❸, a well-protected bay that is jammed with resorts, dive shops, eateries and bars. The large headland at the eastern end of Ao Chalok Ban Kao features a viewpoint atop the **John Suwan Rock**, which has incredible views in either direction. To the east of the promontory is the long yet quiet **Ao Thian Ok** ❹, and further still is **Hat Sai Daeng**.

Within walking distance to the west of Ao Chalok Ban Kao is the small scenic bay of **Ao Jun Jeua**. Unfortunately, the monsoon season from June to October brings strong winds and heavy seas, causing disruptions to ferry schedules, and a lot of flotsam gets washed up here.

EAST-COAST BEACHES

The east coast of the island is characterised by several isolated inlets with scant sleeping options; although none have outstanding beaches, there are plenty of good snorkelling and diving spots here. The dirt trails to the eastern shores can be treacherous (the only other way is by boat) and once you are there, it can be difficult (and expensive) to venture back west. Most lodgings along this coast offer basic facilities. Heading north from Hat Sai Daeng, the bays include the lovely **Ao Leuk** ❺, the scenic horseshoe-shaped **Ao Tanote** ❻, the tiny cape of **Laem Thian**, and eventually the remote **Ao Hin Wong** ❼.

THE NORTH COAST

A short boat ride off the island's northern tip is the picture-perfect **Ko Nang Yuan** ❽, a gathering of three small islets joined together by mere wisps of sand that can be walked across at low tide. The setting, both above and below sea level, is incredible, so much so that dive trips and boat tours from around the island, as well as from Ko Samui and Ko Phangan, all converge here, somewhat spoiling the idyll. With

Stunning Ko Nang Yuan is a must-see.

simple bungalows spread across the three outcrops, only the **Nangyuan Island Dive Resort** (www.nangyuan.com) has the rights to operate here, with outside visitors charged B100 just to set foot on the island.

DIVING AND SNORKELLING

Ko Tao's reputation as a premier dive destination has diminished slightly in recent years, mainly due to the hefty increase in the number of divers; at the more popular sites the undersea human traffic can be annoying. Even so, visibility in the warm water is usually very clear – sometimes over 30 metres (100ft) – and there are a variety of dive sites to choose from. While sightings of giant groupers and turtles are not uncommon, and territorial disputes with toothy triggerfish best avoided, an encounter with an underwater giant such as a whale shark or a manta ray is still a special event.

Unlike the lengthy journey times to dive sites from Ko Samui and Ko Phangan, Ko Tao has more than 25 dive sites close by that can be reached in less than 30 minutes. Both the proximity and favourable conditions (outside the November–December monsoon) make the island's waters an ideal place to learn diving.

Some of the best dive sites are found off Ko Nang Yuan, including the granite boulder and swim-throughs of **Nang Yuan Pinnacle**. About 5km (3 miles) northwest of Ko Tao, the **Chumphon Pinnacle** is a very popular site, with depths of up to 38 metres (125ft) and regular sightings of large groupers and other sizeable fish. In the opposite direction, the **Southwest Pinnacle**, some 7km (4 miles) from Ko Tao, is rated as one of the best soft-coral reefs in the Gulf of Thailand, with currents that attract large schools of pelagic fish.

Ko Tao has nearly 50 dive schools that offer competitive dive packages that include accommodation; in fact, a few resorts refuse to take in non-divers during the peak season. Advance reservations are advised. The majority of schools offer PADI open-water certification, with rates averaging B8,500–B10,000.

ACTIVITIES AND NIGHTLIFE

Ko Tao's compact size makes the island an ideal place for walking, with the reward of panoramic hilltop views or a hidden pristine cove at the end of your journey. Day-long boat trips around the island can be chartered with longtail boat operators at most of its beaches and piers, or through your guesthouse. Watersports like kayaking, wakeboarding and waterskiing can be enjoyed on Ao Tanote or Hat Sai Ree beaches. On land there are increasing options like Flying Trapeze Adventures at Hat Sai Ree.

As Ko Tao develops, its nightlife is moving from basic beach bars to the fire-jugglers and cheap Thai whisky scene of Ko Phangan, and there are regular party nights with guest DJs.

Fact

Buying a villa, or land to build on, is a tempting prospect – but can be fraught with difficulty. Those who have done so successfully suggest engaging a trusted lawyer, and reading the small print carefully, with particular regard to Thailand's foreign ownership laws. However, the rewards, both financial and otherwise, can be more than satisfying.

Taking a break at Ko Nang Yuan.

A sea gypsy child at Ko Surin.

NORTHERN ANDAMAN COAST

This region is well known for its diving and snorkelling hotspots – the Similan and Surin islands – as well as the limestone formations at Phang Nga Bay. Also worth exploring are its land-based waterfalls, hot springs and jungle trails.

Main attractions

Ko Chang
Surin Islands Marine National Park
Khao Sok National Park
Khao Lak
Similan Islands Marine National Park
Ao Phang Nga Marine National Park

Map on page 212

The spectacular Andaman Coast of western Thailand stretches from Ranong on the Isthmus of Kra all the way south to the Malaysian border. This chapter covers only the land and sea attractions as far south as Phang Nga. Highlights include the renowned scuba and snorkelling hotspots of the Similan and Surin islands, and the dramatic limestone formations towering out of the waters around Phang Nga Bay.

RANONG AND SURROUNDINGS

Ranong Province – some 600km (370 miles) from Bangkok and 300km (185 miles) north of Phuket – is thin on attractions. Despite its coastal location, it is not blessed with beautiful beaches, and the main points of interest lie offshore. The province records the highest rainfall in Thailand, which accounts for the lush greenery and many waterfalls. There are a few inland attractions, as well as the undeveloped islands of Ko Chang and Ko Phayam.

There is not much to see or do in **Ranong Town**, a large port filled with fishing boats. Divers mainly use it as a launch point for dive trips to the **Burma Banks**. Because of its proximity to **Myanmar** (25 minutes by boat), many foreigners in south Thailand also use Ranong Town as a base to leave the country to renew their visas. The harbour is filled with companies offering to make the border run and sort out the paperwork.

Punyaban Waterfall ❶, about 15km (9 miles) north of Ranong Town and off Highway 4, is worth seeing for its cascading waters that plunge down several levels. Access to its base is possible by scaling a few boulders, while a 300-metre (330yd) nature trail leads to an elevated lookout; from here the water below hits the rocks in spectacular fashion before dispersing into a fine mist.

About 2km (1.5 miles) southeast of town, **Raksawarin Park ❷**, Ranong's

Punyaban Waterfall in Ranong.

most famous attraction, is home to natural **Hot Springs** (daily 10.30am–7.30pm; free). Heated to around 65°C (150°F), the water is, however, too hot to bathe in. There are concrete pools circled by stone seals where people can stop, sit and inhale the reviving steam. To experience a hot spring bath, head to the **Tinidee Hotel@Ranong**, where the water is piped directly in from the hot springs.

Ngao Waterfall ❸, located 13km (8 miles) south of Ranong, lies within **Khlong Phrao National Park** (daily 9am–5pm; http://portal.dnp.go.th). Its source is deep in the dense forest, and the water pouring down the cliff can be seen from a long way off.

KO CHANG

The quiet island of **Ko Chang** ❹ is part of **Mu Ko Phayam National Park** (http://portal.dnp.go.th), and home to a population who moved here from Surat Thani and Ko Phangan decades ago and now live in small fishing communities. It is accessible by boat from both Ranong (2.5 hours) and Laem Son National Park (1 hour). During the monsoon season from May to October, vessels stop operating as the seas are too dangerous to cross, and accommodation on the island shuts down.

Most of Ko Chang's golden-sand beaches extend along the west coast, the longest being **Ao Yai**, which has most of the basic beach huts. Calm waters and shallow coral reefs mean safe swimming and snorkelling, and as there is no pier, beach access is only possible by longtail boat, wading through the water on nearing the shoreline. There are no cars on the island, and two concrete tracks lead to Ko Chang's only village, which contains a shop and restaurant. There are smaller beaches, such as **Ao Lek** on the east coast, but they require a 5km (3-mile) trudge.

KO PHAYAM

Smaller but more developed than Ko Chang is **Ko Phayam** ❺, 15 minutes away by boat. A backdrop of forested hills shadow white sandy beaches. There is a population of around 500,

Tip

Because the famous Burma Banks dive site is located within the territorial waters of Myanmar (Burma), the only way to visit it is by travelling onboard a live-aboard dive-cruise boat that would have the required papers to be granted access.

A Moken village in the Surin Islands National Marine Park.

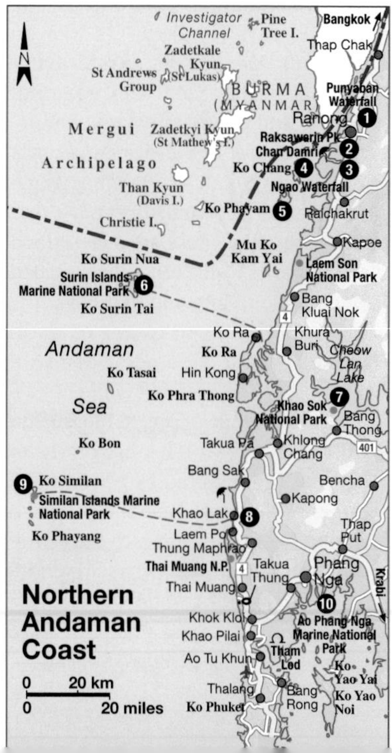

who mainly eke a living by growing cashew nuts and coconuts.

The two main beaches are on opposite sides of the island, so the pier is fairly quiet with just a handful of convenience stores and an internet café. As the walk to the other side of the island can take a good hour, motorcycle taxis do a brisk trade. There are just a couple of restaurants on both of the beaches, so most hotels also offer meals as well.

The most popular beach is **Ao Yai** on the southwest coast. Most of the beach huts (some with 24-hour electricity) are set slightly back from the white-sand beachfront behind a border of palm and pine trees. **Ao Khao Khwai** on the northwest coast is smaller and has fewer lodgings. Nonetheless, it has clear water, a fine stretch of sand and colourful coral close to the shore, making it good for snorkelling. Its nickname, Buffalo Bay, comes from the curvature of its two sides, resembling a pair of buffalo horns.

SURIN ISLANDS

The five islands that make up **Mu Ko Surin National Park** ❻ (Nov–May daily 9am–5pm; http://portal.dnp.go.th) lie some 55km (34 miles) from the coast and are renowned for their superlative diving and snorkelling. Because of the distance, the islands are mainly visited by divers on live-aboard boats. The scenery above water is equally spectacular, with numerous sandy bays and coves backed by verdant jungle. The ecology of the islands has suffered badly over the years due to fishermen using dynamite to blast fish up to the water's surface. Mooring posts to prevent anchor damage have helped coral re-growth in recent years, while dynamite fishing has been banned.

The two main islands, **Ko Surin Nua** and **Ko Surin Tai**, are separated by a narrow 200-metre (660ft) channel of small beaches and pockets of mangroves that can be forded at low tide. These islands are largely uninhabited, although Ko Surin Tai is home to a small community of *chao lay* or sea gypsies, and Ko Surin Nua houses the park's headquarters and the island's only accommodation – rustic bungalows and a campsite. The other three islands, **Ko Ri**, **Ko Khai** and **Ko Klang**, are just small islets covered with sparse vegetation and are not worth exploring.

DIVE SITES

The Surin Islands' most popular dive site, **Richelieu Rock**, is only just exposed at low tide. It is one of the world's top locations for sighting whale sharks, with February to April being the best time. On average, 10 percent of all dives in a year at Richelieu result in an encounter with this 20-metre (65ft) behemoth.

Around 60km (37 miles) northwest of the Surin Islands lie the renowned **Burma Banks**, where the three submerged peaks of **Silvertip**, **Roe** and **Rainbow** rise from 300-metre (980ft) deep waters to within 15 metres (50ft) of the sea's surface. Encounters with

Tip

From May to October, the southwest monsoon brings heavy rain to the entire Andaman Coast. While this means that some of the islands further away cannot be accessed because of rough seas, it's not unusual to get days of intermittent sunshine even during the peak rainy-season months.

Snorkelling in the clear waters of the Surin Islands.

CHAO LAY: THAILAND'S SEA GYPSY COMMUNITY

Outside the mainstream of Thai society, the sea gypsies are content to continue in their traditional ways.

The "sea gypsies" of southern Thailand, known in Thai as *chao lay* or "people of the sea", are divided into three groups, though they sometimes intermarry and generally consider themselves as one kindred people. Numbering between 4,000 and 5,000, they live either in huts by the shore, or on itinerant craft that ply the coastal waters south from Ranong all the way to Ko Tarutao close to the border with Malaysia.

The **Urak Lawoi**, numbering around 3,000, form the largest sea-gypsy group. They live in simple shacks on beaches from Phuket to Ko Tarutao and make a living by fishing and beachcombing. The two largest Urak Lawoi settlements are at Ko Sireh and Rawai in the southeast of Phuket, but smaller communities are also found on the islands of Ko Lanta, Ko Phi Phi, Ko Jum and Ko Lipe. The Urak Lawoi group are fairly well integrated into Thai society and are registered as citizens.

Less numerous than the Urak Lawoi, the 1,000-strong **Moklen** community live between Ko Phra Tong near Takua Pa and Phuket, including the Surin Islands, while the 500 or so **Moken** live north from Ko Phra Thong to the Burmese frontier. Of the three *chao lay* groups, the Moken are the least adapted to modern life; they still use dugout canoes rather than motorised longtail boats, and avoid all contact with settled people – especially local authorities – as much as possible. They are not registered as citizens and the Thais distinguish them from the other groups by calling them *chao ko tae* or "real island folk". The Moken rarely build huts on dry land, preferring to live a completely nomadic existence on the waters of the Andaman Sea.

Regarded as an indigenous people of Thailand, it seems likely the *chao lay* were among the earliest inhabitants of the region, predating the arrival of the Tais from the north by many centuries. They are shorter, stockier and darker than the Tais, and are more closely related to the *orang laut*, or "sea people", of Malaysia, and perhaps also to the Mani or Negrito peoples who inhabit the southern Thai interior. Little is known of the *chao lay*'s past as they have no written language or records. Their spoken languages are related to Malay, though the Moken, living furthest from Malaysia, have borrowed a much larger vocabulary from the Thais and Burmese.

Chao lay venerate tutelary spirits, especially those associated with wind, water and islands. The Moken are strictly animist and worship the sea. Twice a year, during the full moon of the sixth and 11th lunar months (usually June and November), they stop working for three days and nights to feast, dance, sing and drink alcohol, often entering into a trance. The Moken believe that their earliest ancestor was washed ashore, but on landing refused to become Muslim or Buddhist, choosing instead to return to the sea. Certainly, the sea gypsies remain a people apart, living on the fringes of southern Thai society, with few material possessions and little inclination to use technology.

Yet, while they may be ill-equipped to deal with modern life, the *chao lay* have some natural advantages. During the December 2004 tsunami, although more than 1,000 sea gypsy households sustained damage and some loss of life, they seemed to have instinctively realised the danger better than their Thai neighbours, as many saved themselves by moving early to higher ground.

A Mokien Surin islander taking a break.

silvertip, nurse and, occasionally, grey reef sharks are a near certainty. The only way to dive these sites is from a live-aboard dive charter arranged out of Khao Lak, Phuket or Ranong.

KHAO SOK NATIONAL PARK

Easily accessible from Phuket and Surat Thani, **Khao Sok National Park** ❼ (daily 7am–6pm; http://portal.dnp.go.th) is often dismissed as simply another national park. However, alongside the usual flora, fauna, rivers and forests are some features that make Khao Sok unique. It is home to one of the world's oldest evergreen rainforests – approximately 160 million years – and its location on the mountain ridge between the east and west coasts makes it the wettest area in Thailand – rains from both the Gulf of Thailand and the Andaman Sea coasts deposit as much as 3,500mm (138in) of rainfall annually. Within the park's dense rainforest, the world's second-largest flower, the *Rafflesia Kerrii*, grows up to 80cm (31ins) in diameter when in bloom.

Geographically, much of the 740-sq-km (285-sq-mile) park comprises limestone mountains, most in the 400–600-metre (1,300–2,000ft) range, with the highest at 960 metres (3,150ft). Lowland rainforest dominates, but there are also many towering trees, some reaching heights of around 65 metres (215ft). Large mammals, including elephants and leopards, roam free (though they are rarely seen) while cobras, tarantulas and scorpions are common.

JUNGLE TRAILS

Of the nine trails in the national park, eight follow the same route for the first 5km (3 miles) along the **Sok River**, after which they split. One continues a further 2km (1.5 miles) to the **Ton Gloy Waterfall** which is great for a dip, another to the **Bang Leap Nam Waterfall**, which is not as large but easier to reach. **Sawan Waterfall** is the most difficult to access, and involves clambering over the river across slippery and sometimes steep rocks. The ninth trail leads in a different direction altogether,

Scenery at Khao Sok National Park.

A beach at Khao Lak.

following the **Bang Laen River** all the way to **Sip-et Chan Waterfall**.

You can tackle these jungle trails yourself, but half-day tours booked from Phuket or Krabi are led by experienced guides who will point out rare flora and signs of animal life that the untrained eye could easily miss.

Another popular day trip takes in **Cheow Lan Lake**, some 60km (37 miles) from the main accommodation area. It is home to over 100 small islands and was formed in the 1980s when the **Ratchprabha Dam** was built to construct a hydroelectric power plant. Activities include boat trips, fishing and canoeing, as well as walks around the lake to locations such as **Tham Nam Talu** cave. The lake is at its most beautiful in the early morning, when gibbons call from deep within the mists hanging over the lakes and mountains.

KHAO LAK

Frequented primarily by diving enthusiasts, sleepy **Khao Lak** ❽ is the closest access point to the marine-life paradise of the **Similan Islands**, some 60km (37 miles) offshore. It is seen by many as a pleasant, less frenetic alternative to Phuket, although development is increasing rapidly, with hotels, shops and restaurants spreading back on the side roads leading from the beach to the main Highway 4 to Phuket. But the beach is beautiful and local bye-laws that restrict building to below tree level help maintain the overall charm of the area.

KHAO LAK'S BEACHES

The view over Khao Lak when arriving from Phuket, located 80km (50 miles) to the south, is quite stunning. As the narrow mountain road winds down to the beaches below, turquoise waters lapping against the sand give an impression of a postcard-perfect tropical scene. Khao Lak is, in fact, made up of a string of beaches extending in a very long shallow arc along the bay, each separated by rocky outcrops, offering many places of relative seclusion even in the peak season.

From north to south, the beaches run as follows: **Bang Sak**, **Pakarang**

Beautiful scenery at the Similan islands.

Cape, **Khuk Khak**, **Bang Niang**, **Nang Thong** and finally, **Khao Lak**. The last is a relatively small stretch of sand extending 800 metres (2,625ft). Before the tsunami hit southern Thailand in 2004, most of the development in the area was centred on Bang Niang, which took the longest to recover. Nang Thong and Khao Lak beaches also have a good number of hotels. Swimming conditions in the high season are excellent on all beaches, but during the monsoon season it is better to keep to the north towards the rocky headland where the currents are not so strong.

SIMILAN ISLANDS

Promoted in nearly every dive shop and diving website and mentioned in countless brochures throughout Thailand is the beautiful **Mu Ko Similan National Park** ❾ (Nov–May; https://similan-islands.com). The islands are 100km (62 miles) northwest of Phuket but are most easily accessible from the nearest mainland point Khao Lak, 60km (37 miles) away.

Similan, derived from the Malay word *sembilan*, means nine, in reference to nine islands that originally made up this 128-sq-km (50-sq-mile) marine national park. For easy reference, the islands are numbered from north to south in descending order, starting with **Ko Bon** (No. 9), **Ko Ba Ngu** (No. 8), **Ko Similan** (No. 7), **Ko Payoo** (No. 6), **Ko Miang** (collective name for islands No. 4 and 5), **Ko Pahyan** (No. 3), **Ko Phayang** (No. 2) and **Ko Hu Yong** (No. 1). In 1998 the Park expanded to include two more islands: Ko Tachai and Ko Bon.

With the exception of Ko Ba Ngu and Ko Miang, the Similan group is uninhabited; for years, prior to their rise in popularity among the dive fraternity, the islands were visited only by sea gypsies. Today, the most frequent visitors are day-trippers from Phuket and Khao Lak, and divers on multi-day live-aboard boats.

Like many such sites in Thailand, the reefs have suffered greatly from the effects of dynamite fishing and the indiscriminate anchoring of boats and trawlers. Since 1987, however, fishing has been banned and boundaries set for moorings so that the reefs can return to their former pristine state. The authorities are now also closing many dive sites for a period each year to attempt some recuperation of resources.

DIVING THE SIMILANS

There are more than 20 dive sites around the Similan Islands. The eastern side of the archipelago features hard coral gardens where the most popular activity is drift diving along slopes that lean dramatically from the surface down to depths of 30–40 metres (100–130ft). Popular sites include **Christmas Point** and **Breakfast Bend**, both at Ko Ba Ngu, where soft coral growth and colourful sea fans are among the largest found in Thailand. The Napoleon wrasse, a rare sight in Thailand, is occasionally glimpsed at

Speedboat on clear water in the Similans.

Tip

The Ao Phang Nga Marine National Park also includes the islands of Ko Yao Yai and Ko Yao Noi. Of the two islands, Ko Yao Noi is the more popular as it has nicer beaches and better accommodation. Since Ao Phang Nga itself has few decent hotels, staying at Ko Yao Noi is more advisable. There is a string of budget places, but surprisingly, the island is host to one of Thailand's most expensive beach resorts, the Six Senses Hideaway Ko Yao Noi (www.sixsenses.com).

Breakfast Bend, along with leopard sharks resting on the sands beneath.

The western side of the Similan Islands offers faster-paced and more exhilarating diving, with currents swirling around huge granite boulder formations, and dramatic holes and overhangs. Colourful soft corals grow so thick on many of these boulders that the rock is no longer visible. Most dive sites on the west coast are best seen with a guide, since navigation can be tricky. Popular sites include **Fantasy Reef** and **Elephant Head** at Ko Similan where clownfish, lionfish and, occasionally, turtles can be seen.

AO PHANG NGA

Less than an hour by road from Phuket Airport, the mainland town of **Phang Nga** has few attractions of interest. There are a few caves and waterfalls nearby, but none are overly impressive. For the main attraction in the area, head south from Phang Nga to reach **Ao Phang Nga**, the site of Thailand's most striking jungle-clad limestone rock formations, monoliths and cliffs. Spread over a coastal area of 400 sq km (155 sq miles) between Phuket and Krabi, the islands are part of the **Ao Phang Nga Marine National Park** ⑩ (daily 8am–5pm; http://portal.dnp.go.th/).

While impressive by day and evocative of a Chinese brush painting, the spectacular vistas of towering karsts are especially captivating on moonlit nights, when the silvery light casts haunting shadows off the eerie rock structures into the watery depths around them. Sheltered from both northeast and southwest monsoon seasons, the blue-green waters around the bay are calm year-round.

Trips to the bay are mostly arranged from either Phuket or Krabi, but they can also be booked in Phang Nga Town itself. A more interesting way of exploring Ao Phang Nga is by sea canoe. At low tide these low-lying craft can slip through sea tunnels beneath the limestone karsts, which shelter hidden lagoons (called *hongs*) within. The karsts support their own mini ecosystem, including small troops of monkeys; it has been reported that they

James Bond Island is a favourite with tourists.

even swim from island to island. The *hongs* are truly magical, lost worlds that seem totally remote from the surrounding area. The better sea-canoe operators run trips in the late afternoon and evening, when there are fewer boats around: check to ensure your trip is to one of the more remote areas, as large tour groups can blight the *hongs*' serene ambience.

KO PING KAN (JAMES BOND ISLAND) AND KO PANYI

Thailand has long been in demand as an exotic film locale, and in 1974, one of the rocky pinnacles of Phang Nga was featured in the film *The Man with the Golden Gun*. As a result, **Ko Ping Kan** is better known internationally as **James Bond Island**.

The small beach here is perpetually crowded with day-trippers who pose for pictures with the geological oddity called **Ko Tapu**, meaning Nail Island, behind them. Rising from a precariously thin base 200 metres (650ft) out of the water, the rocky outcrop seems destined to tip into the water at some point. Bond fans are smitten, though, and there is something undeniably cool about standing on the same spot as 007.

All tours of Ao Phang Nga also make a stop at nearby **Ko Panyi**, a Muslim village built entirely over the water and nestled against towering cliffs. Come lunchtime each day, it transforms from a quiet fishing community into a bustling hive of restaurants and souvenir shops with the arrival of 3,000 or so tourists on their way to or back from James Bond Island. Overnight tours of Ao Phang Nga stop here for the night, but the accommodation is basic.

Apart from stopping off at James Bond and Ko Panyi islands, most tours will pass by a number of rocks and uninhabited islands named after the strange shapes they resemble. One popular stop is **Khao Khien** (Painting Rock) to see ancient cave art painted on its inner walls. An array of animals, including monkeys, elephants, fish and crabs are depicted alongside human stick figures. Another stop is **Tham Lod**, a narrow sea-cave tunnel filled with strangely shaped stalactites.

View of Ko Tapu from James Bond Island.

Ao Phang Nga National Park.

THAILAND'S MARINE LIFE

The coral reefs that fringe Thailand's coasts are an outstanding wonderland of colour, home to a variety of vivid marine life.

Thailand's underwater world is rewarding to explore from both sides of the country, but each coast is quite different in terms of what you can see. The flora and fauna of the Andaman Sea are characteristic of the Indian Ocean, while Gulf of Thailand species are typical of the Pacific. However, the Andaman Sea is deeper and clearer than the Gulf, and overall its coral reefs are more extensive.

The reefs of both waters have been only patchily surveyed, but they support at least 400 species of fish and 30 kinds of sea snake. Bottlenose dolphins and the occasional whale are found in Thai waters, but the gentle dugong, or "sea cow", is increasingly hard to find among the sea grasses of Phang Nga, Phuket, Trang and Satun provinces. Thailand's coral species number almost 300, with the Andaman Sea boasting an even greater diversity. Intact reefs, however, survive only in areas far from human habitation, such as the vicinity of the Surin and Similan islands.

Cuttlefish are among the most intelligent invertebrates in the animal kingdom. Like their close relatives, the squid and octopus, they can expel "ink" when threatened.

Thai waters are home to four species of turtle – green, leatherback, hawksbill and Olive Ridley. All are endangered, especially the hawksbill.

The scorpionfish camouflages itself innocuously on the seabed, but can deliver an extremely poisonous sting if stepped on.

Lagoon triggerfish are frequently seen in Thai waters. The larger titan triggerfish can be very aggressive.

Scuba diving in the Andaman Sea.

Exploring the reefs

Thailand has long been considered a great dive destination. Not only does the region offer clear, accessible water and some outstanding coral, it has (in most cases) modern, international-standard dive services at competitive prices.

Phuket is a regional leader in diving. There are extensive, prime dive areas not far from shore, plus an abundance of dive shops competing for business. Any level of diver can enjoy themselves here.

Increasingly, divers are looking to give something back to mother earth and you can search online resources such as www.responsibletravel.com for a list of dive companies that include conservation initiatives as part of their itinerary. The national parks authorities also have a more responsible line, closing some sites to foster recovery. This is particularly true of the closure of Maya Bay in 2018, which was the finest demonstration to date that Thai authorities are taking the threat to their ecosystems very seriously.

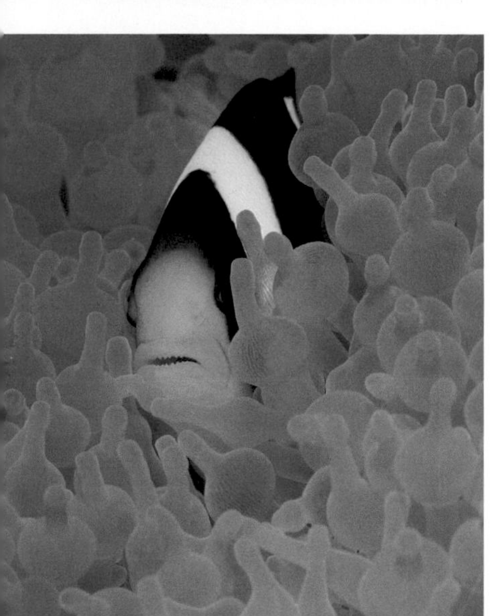

Clownfish are found throughout the warm waters of the Indian and Pacific oceans. These colourful fish live in a symbiotic relationship with sea anemones or stony corals.

The poisonous crown of thorns starfish can grow to over 30cm (1ft) in diameter.

Beach volleyball on Patong beach.

PHUKET

Thailand's largest – and richest – resort island caters to a broad range of holidaymakers. Bars and beaches draw the biggest numbers, but there is a lot more to Phuket's diverse ethnic and geographical make-up, as veering just a short way off the beaten track will show.

Main attractions

- Chinatown (in Phuket Town)
- Hat Kamala
- Hat Patong
- Hat Kata Yai and Noi
- Kata Hill Viewpoint
- Hat Nai Harn
- Laem Prompthep
- Wat Chalong
- Ko Bon and Ko Hae
- Wat Phra Thong

Maps on pages 224, 226

Phuket is no longer just an island, it has become a brand. In the space of a generation, the country's smallest province (587 sq km/225 sq miles) went from growing coconuts for local consumption to welcoming tourists from all over the world. With tourism came development, driving Phuket's dramatic growth from a sleepy little island in the 1970s to today's full-on resort destination synonymous with hedonism. There are now hotels to suit all budgets, but recent development has seen the construction of boutique properties and upmarket villa-style houses, along with shopping complexes, schools and hospitals of international standard. Not surprisingly, all this has encouraged many foreigners to take up permanent residence in Phuket.

The stunning white-sand beaches along the 48km (30-mile) long west coast are separated by picturesque headlands. Some are small and pristine with intimate hidden coves, while others teem with noisy jet skis and vendors hawking sarongs and souvenirs.

Phuket is a base for dive trips to several renowned sites in the surrounding seas, and a number of operators offer courses, organised dive excursions and live-aboard trips. Phuket is also an excellent base for exploring nearby islands, national parks and mainland areas like Khao Lak and Krabi.

PEOPLE AND ECONOMY

The majority of Phuket's 300,000 or so people are Buddhist, with Muslims comprising around 35 percent. A number of locals make their living from the island's rubber and pineapple plantations, but since the 1980s, tourism has overtaken agriculture as the main source of income. When the tsunami hit Phuket and surrounding areas on 26 December 2004 – the peak of the high season – Phuket suffered badly. While some beaches escaped relatively unscathed, others (like Patong

Extracting rubber latex.

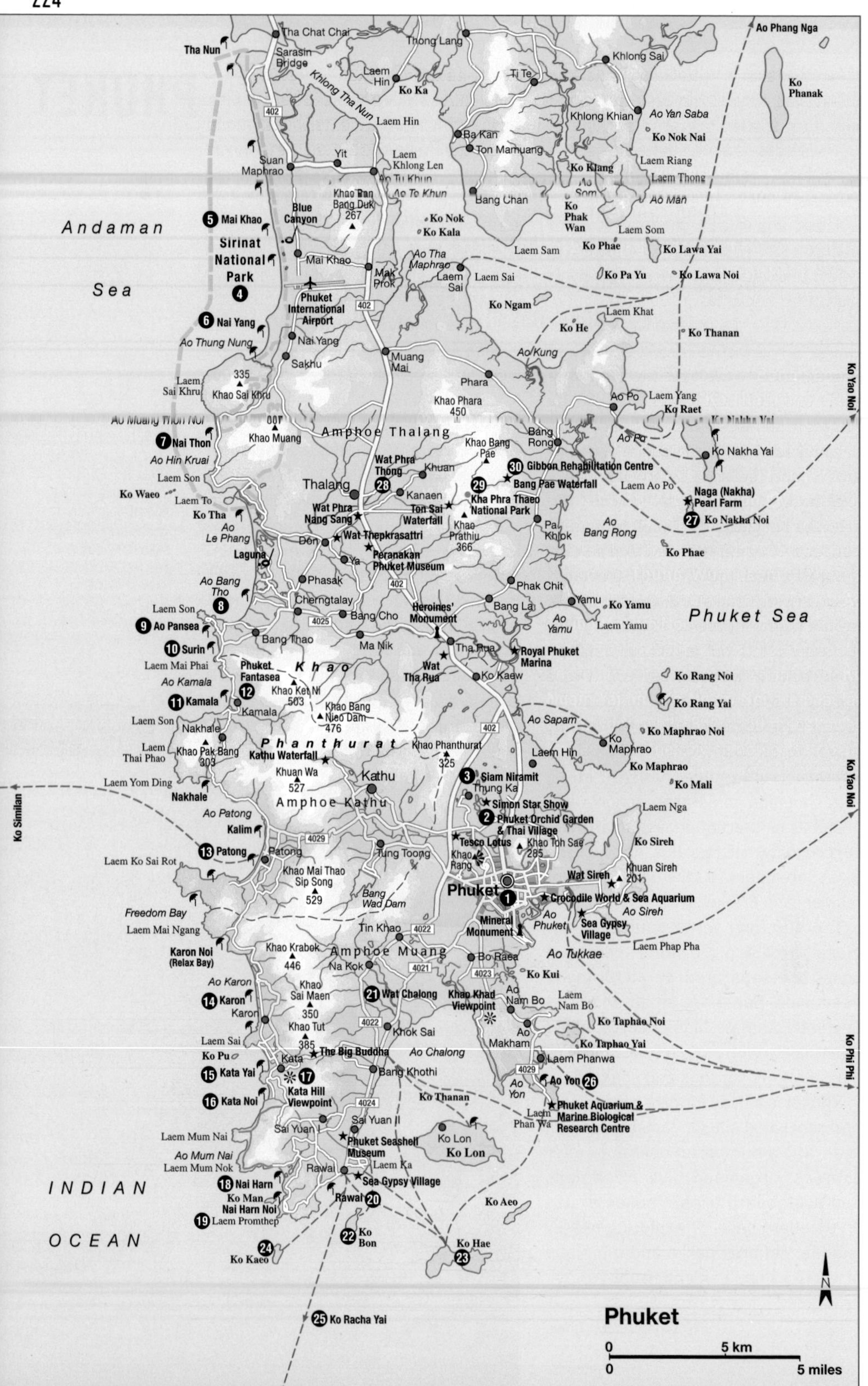

Phuket
Andaman Sea
Phuket Sea
INDIAN OCEAN
Tha Nun
Tha Chat Chai
Sarasin Bridge
Thong Lang
Khlong Sai
Ao Phang Nga
Ko Phanak
Laem Hin
Ko Ka
Ti Te
Khlong Tha Nun
Khlong Khian
Ao Yan Saba
Ko Nok Nai
Ba Kan
Ton Mamuang
Laem Riang
Laem Thong
Ao Man
Suan Maphrao
Yit
Laem Khlong Len
Ao Tu Khun
Ko Klang
Ko Som
Khao Ban Bang Duk 267
Ao To Khun
Bang Chan
Ko Phak Wan
Blue Canyon
Ko Nok
Ko Kala
Laem Som
5 Mai Khao
Sirinat National Park 4
Mai Khao
Ao Tha Maphrao
Laem Sam
Ko Phae
Ko Lawa Yai
Mak Prok
Laem Sai
Ko Pa Yu
Ko Lawa Noi
Phuket International Airport
Ko Ngam
Laem Khat
6 Nai Yang
Ao Thung Nung
Nai Yang
Ko He
Ko Thanan
Muang Mai
Ao Kung
Sakhu
335
Laem Sai Khru
Khao Sai Khru
Phara
Ko Yao Noi
Khao Phara 450
Ao Po
Laem Yang
Ko Raet
Ao Muang Thon Noi
007
Khao Muang
Amphoe Thalang
Bang Rong
Ao Po
7 Nai Thon
Khao Bang Pae
Ko Nakha Yai
Ao Hin Kruai
Wat Phra Thong
Khuan
30 Gibbon Rehabilitation Centre
Laem Son
Thalang 28
29 Bang Pae Waterfall
Laem Ao Po
Ko Waeo
Kanaen
Kha Phra Thaeo National Park
Naga (Nakha) Pearl Farm
Laem To
Wat Phra Nang Sang
Ton Sai Waterfall
27 Ko Nakha Noi
Ko Tha
Khao Prathiu 366
Pa Khlok
Ao Bang Rong
Ao Le Phang
Don
Wat Thepkrasattri
Ko Phae
Laguna
Ya
Peranakan Phuket Museum
Phasak
Phak Chit
Ao Bang Tho 8
Cherngtalay
Yamu
Ko Yamu
Laem Son
Bang Cho
Heroines' Monument
Bang La
9 Ao Pansea
4025
Ao Yamu
Laem Yamu
Bang Thao
Ma Nik
Tha Rua
10 Surin
Royal Phuket Marina
Laem Mai Phai
Phuket Fantasea
Khao
Wat Tha Rua
Ko Kaew
Ko Rang Noi
Ao Kamala
12
Khao Ket Ni 503
Ko Rang Yai
11 Kamala
Kamala
Khao Bang Nieo Dam 476
Ao Sapam
Laem Son
Nakhale
Ko Maphrao Noi
Laem Thai Phao
Khao Pak Bang 303
Phanthurat
Kathu Waterfall
Khao Phanthurat 325
Ko Maphrao
Laem Hin
Ko Maphrao
Khuan Wa 527
Kathu
3 Siam Niramit
Thung Ka
Laem Yom Ding
Ko Similan
Ko Mali
Nakhale
Amphoe Kathu
Simon Star Show
Laem Nga
Ao Patong
2 Phuket Orchid Garden & Thai Village
Kalim
Tesco Lotus
Khao Toh Sae 285
Ko Sireh
13 Patong
4029
Patong
Tung Toong
Khao Rang
Laem Ko Sai Rot
Khao Mai Thao Sip Song 529
Wat Sireh
Khuan Sireh 201
Phuket 1
Crocodile World & Sea Aquarium
Bang Wad Dam
Ao Phuket
Ao Sireh
Freedom Bay
Mineral Monument
Sea Gypsy Village
Laem Mai Ngang
Tin Khao
4022
Laem Phap Pha
Karon Noi (Relax Bay)
Khao Krabok 446
Amphoe Muang
Ao Tukkae
Na Kok
4021
Bo Raea
4023
Ko Kui
Ao Karon
Khao Sai Maen 350
21 Wat Chalong
Khao Khad Viewpoint
Ao Nam Bo
Laem Nam Bo
14 Karon
Karon
Ko Taphao Noi
Khao Tut 385
Khok Sai
Ao Makham
Ko Taphao Yai
Laem Sai
Ko Phi Phi
Ko Pu
The Big Buddha
Ao Chalong
Laem Phanwa
Kata
15 Kata Yai
17
Bang Khothi
4029
Ao Yon 26
Kata Hill Viewpoint
Ao Yon
16 Kata Noi
Ko Thanan
4024
Phuket Aquarium & Marine Biological Research Centre
Laem Phan Wa
Sai Yuan II
Sai Yuan I
Laem Mum Nai
Phuket Seashell Museum
Ko Lon
Ko Lon
Ao Mum Nai
Laem Mum Nok
Rawai
Laem Ka
18 Nai Harn
Sea Gypsy Village
Ko Man
Nai Harn Noi
Rawai 20
Ko Aeo
19 Laem Promthep
22 Ko Bon
Ko Hae 23
24 Ko Kaeo
25 Ko Racha Yai
N
0 5 km
0 5 miles

and Kamala) were hit hard. The loss of life, injuries and damage to property were considerable.

Due to rapid rebuilding and focused tourism campaigns overseas, Phuket soon got back on its feet again. Indeed, with beaches swept clean of debris and buildings renovated and given a fresh lick of paint, the island is literally sparkling once more.

PHUKET TOWN

Unsurprisingly, many people head straight for the beaches and give **Phuket Town** ❶ a miss. But, although it can seem busy and unattractive, especially given its confusing one-way traffic system, it is only 20 minutes' drive from Patong, and worth at least a day trip. Getting about on foot, with a good map, is the best way to go. There are plenty of sights and shops, as well as a sprinkling of good bars and restaurants.

CHINATOWN

In the heart of Phuket Town, between Thanon Thalang and Thanon Deebuk, lies the **Chinatown** Ⓐ area, where old colonial houses and Sino-Portuguese-style mansions dominate. Originally built by Europeans, they were designed for Chinese sensibilities. The combination of Eastern and Western influence has produced some fine architecture, recognisable by tiled roofs, artistically chiselled exteriors and tall, spiralling pillars at the front. Many are privately owned, but some have been turned into museums, galleries and restaurants.

Once regarded as Phuket's most beautiful home, and formerly the Governor's Mansion, Phra Pitak Chinpracha Mansion on Krabi Road was restored and reopened in 2010 as a branch of the international Thai restaurant chain **The Blue Elephant**. Next door is Chinpracha House, which is open for tours (tel: 076-211 167; Mon–Sat 8am–4pm).

The **Thai Hua Museum** (daily 9am–5pm; www.thaihuamuseum.com) also on Krabi Road has exhibits that include Phuket traditional ceremonies, Sino-Portuguese buildings and local cuisine, while the quirky **Thavorn Hotel Lobby Museum** on Rassada Road (daily 8am–5pm; www.thavornhotel.com)

Tip

The southwest monsoon brings heavy rain from May to Oct to the Andaman Coast, including Phuket. Nov is the start of the dry season but it can be unstable; Dec to Feb is best. Apr and May are the hottest months and Sept the wettest. Hotel rates in Phuket are the lowest from May to Oct, and many people take advantage of this as there can be intermittent days of sunshine between rainy spells.

PHUKET'S CHINESE

Phuket's Chinese population (now standing at 35 percent by some estimates) originally came as labourers to work in the tin mines in the 18th and 19th centuries. They mainly originated from Penang, Malaysia, the region's major port and the destination for most of the tin. By the late 19th century the Chinese dominated the tin mining trade and many became wealthy. They intermarried and currently play a significant part in the everyday life of the island. They carry Thai passports but are still very much aware of their ethnic heritage. The Chinese influence on architecture and religion is especially evident in Phuket Town. You will see a Chinese influence on the design of doors. The thick walls on many of Phuket Town's buildings are typically Chinese too.

Devotees seeking their fortunes at Put Jaw Temple.

Tip

Avoid taxi touts at the airport; their prices tend to be misleading, their navigational skills hazy, and they are unlikely to be insured. Metered taxis are available outside.

is a small family-run hotel museum with historical items ranging from tin mining paraphernalia to toy trains and opium beds.

CHINESE TEMPLES

Due to the strong Chinese presence in Phuket, a number of temples are Taoist in character. A few in particular stand out. **Sanjao Sam San** B (aka Jor Ong Shrine; daily 8am–6pm; free) at Thanon Krabi, erected in 1853 in dedication to Tien Sang Sung Moo, the patron saint of sailors and goddess of the sea, is recognisable by the gold statues that stand proudly outside and intricate carvings that adorn the inner walls.

Put Jaw Temple C (daily 6.30am–8pm; free) on Thanon Ranong, is dedicated to Kwan Im, the Chinese goddess of mercy. Standing for over 200 years, this is the oldest Chinese Taoist temple in Phuket. In the middle hall, before an image of Kwan Im, are wooden fortune-telling blocks, which when dropped to the floor imply a "yes" or "no" answer to a question. Your fortune can also be told by the aid of divining sticks.

Jui Tui Temple (daily 8am–8.30pm; free), next door, is more ornate. On the altar stands the red-faced statue of Kiu Ong Ya, one of Nine Emperor Gods to whom the temple is dedicated. This temple is the main location for the annual **Vegetarian Festival** when thousands pack the streets to witness devotees perform acts of self-mutilation.

PHUKET TRICKEYE MUSEUM

For something a bit different while in Phuket Town, this interactive 3D museum D (daily 10am–7pm, last entry at 6pm; www.phukettrickeyemuseum.com), located near the Pear Hotel, offers loads of family fun. The exhibition features around 100 paintings created using the trompe-l'oeil technique, which encourages interaction and is a gift when it comes to great photo opportunities.

PHUKET ORCHID GARDEN AND THAI VILLAGE

About 2.5km (1.5 miles) out of town at Thanon Thepkrassatri, the **Phuket Orchid Garden and Thai Village** 2 (daily 9am–9pm) has a collection of

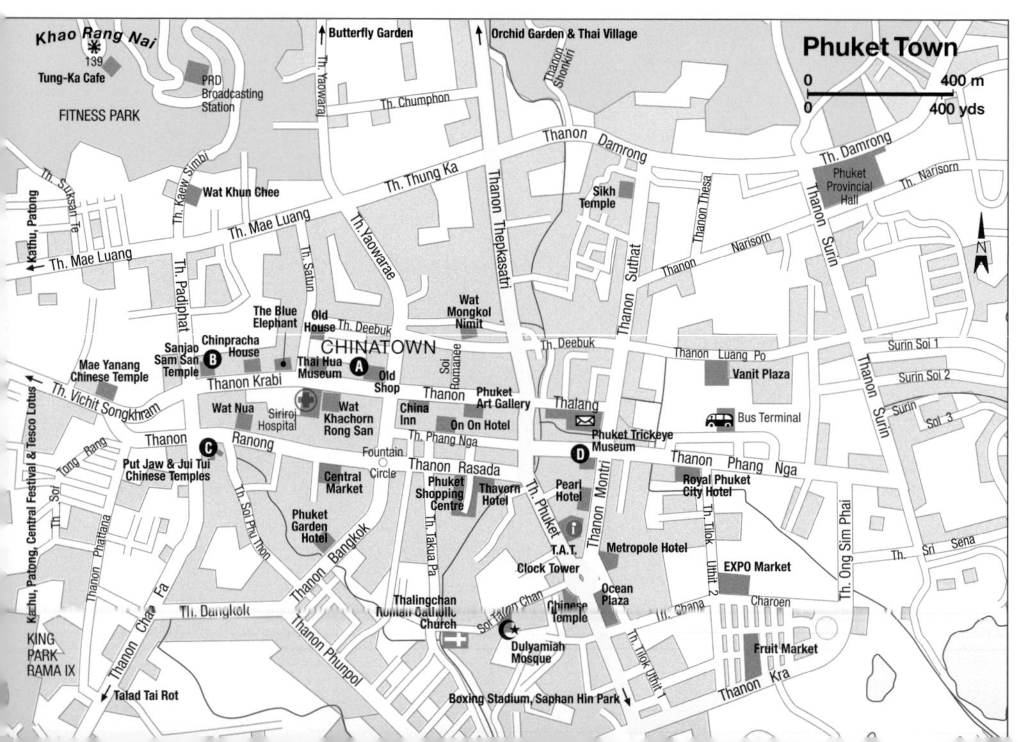

rare orchids and a cultural centre with traditional dances, staged wedding ceremonies, a handicraft centre and Thai restaurants.

SIAM NIRAMIT

Slightly further north, a Phuket version of Bangkok's cultural attraction **Siam Niramit** ❸ (Wed–Mon 5pm–11pm; www.siamniramit.com) explores Thailand's cultural heritage and history. As well as facilities such as a floating market, restaurants and tableaux of village life, a spectacular one-hour show starts at 8.30pm that creatively portrays the country's present in the context of its past.

WEST COAST

Phuket's prime western coastline is a string of beautiful secluded coves covered in fine white sand.

SIRINAT NATIONAL PARK

A large chunk of the northwest cape is given over to the 90-sq-km (35-sq-mile) **Sirinat National Park** ❹ (http://portal.dnp.go.th), of which three-quarters is sea. It encompasses the beaches at **Hat Nai Yang** and **Hat Nai Thon** as well as the mangroves of **Hat Mai Khao**.

Casuarinas are the most common tree found in the park, and many species of bird, mammal and insect live in its mangrove forests. The park's marine environment is diverse and its coral reefs are among the most pristine around Phuket. Located in water between 4–7 metres (12–23ft) deep are extensive plate and tree corals, as well as sea fans and sea anemones.

HAT MAI KHAO

The sands of the secluded **Hat Mai Khao** ❺, the longest of Phuket's beaches at over 17km (11 miles), are more golden than white and a little coarse underfoot. But the waters are very clean. As the beach is part of the protected Sirinat National Park, development has been low-key, which is perhaps why hundreds of Olive Ridley sea turtles, as well as the odd giant leatherback, come ashore to lay their eggs here between November and February each year.

For years, the only hotel on this beach was the luxury **JW Marriott**

Fact

Following the catastrophic tsunami of 2004, Phuket is now equipped with an early-warning system and clearly marked evacuation routes in the event of a similar natural disaster.

MARKETS AND MALLS

Phuket Town is home to the cheapest markets around. The undercover EXPO Market on Tilok Uthit 2 Road changes its stock of clothes and accessories on a regular basis. Phuket's oldest fresh produce market is a daily bustle on Ranong Road for fruit, vegetables, herbs, meat and fish. And the popular Talad Tai Rot (Sun, 4pm–9pm) is a Sunday night market just outside town near the junction of Chao Fa East and Chao Fa West roads. It sells everything ranging from food and clothing to household items and even pets. North of Phuket Town, Central Festival Phuket (daily 11am–10pm) is a very-large shopping complex of global brands featuring a supermarket, department store and also includes a cinema.

A Sino-Portuguese-style mansion in Phuket.

Turtle being released.

Resort & Spa. Initially criticised for encroaching on national park land, the hotel changed public perception by initiating the **Marine Turtle Foundation** (www.maikhaomarineturtlefoundation.org), encouraging all its guests to donate US$1 a day to support local conservation. The Marriott has since been joined by other hotels, and Mai Khao's profile is gradually being raised.

HAT NAI YANG

Despite housing the headquarters of Sirinat National Park and being a protected area, **Hat Nai Yang** ❻ hosts a few hotels. Still, it is very laidback and quiet. In the low season it is virtually deserted, but high season sees a strip of thatched wooden beach huts serving cold beer and seafood. The beach is a beautiful curving bay lined with evergreen trees that provide visual relief and shade. A large coral reef around 1km (2/3 mile) offshore is home to several species of fish.

HAT NAI THON

The smallest of Sirinat National Park's three beaches is **Hat Nai Thon** ❼, which, due to its position at the foot of a series of high hills, is harder to reach and requires a journey on a long and winding road, passing jungle and rubber plantations. The beach is not totally deserted, however, and a few sun beds are available for hire. Nai Thon offers good swimming and snorkelling along rocky headlands that attract rich marine life year-round. Offshore, the remains of a wrecked tin dredger is a favourite spot with divers.

AO BANG THAO

The 8km (5-mile) stretch of beach at the gently curving **Ao Bang Thao** ❽ is dominated by the Laguna Resort, a cluster of five luxury hotels, the most exclusive being the **Banyan Tree Phuket**, with its own 18-hole golf course. Bang Thao is one of the loveliest beaches on the island, but beware of the strong undertow during the monsoon season. All accommodation is found at the northern end of the beach, so a walk south will often lead to a deserted patch of sand.

Poolside gardens at JW Marriott Resort & Spa.

TURTLE PRESERVATION

The Marine Turtle Foundation at Hat Mai Khao strives to keep the area free from development to ensure the safe return of Olive Ridley and endangered giant leatherback sea turtles. The species return here between November and February each year to lay their eggs on the beach where they were born. If you are lucky, you can witness the hundreds of hatchlings dashing across the sand to the sea. Villagers record the number of eggs laid each year and patrol the beach to guard the nesting sites. A number of eggs are taken to a hatchery to ensure their survival in case of human or natural disturbance, and the baby turtles are released to the sea during a special ceremony in April which takes place each year.

AO PANSEA AND HAT SURIN

Thailand's most senior exclusive resort, the luxury **Amanpuri**, occupies prime position at **Ao Pansea ❾**, with Thai-style pavilions interspersed in a coconut plantation on a sea-facing headland. The beach runs for only 300 metres (984ft) and is very private, as it's closed off by headlands on either side of the bay. The other end of Ao Pansea is anchored by the expensive **Surin Phuket** resort.

Beyond the Surin Phuket resort, the beach becomes **Hat Surin ❿**. It is popular with locals, but not as pristine as Phuket's other beaches; again, beware of the undertow during the monsoon season. Vendors frequently set up makeshift stalls at the beach car park and sell freshly grilled prawns and barbecued mackerel.

HAT KAMALA

Kamala ⓫ is only a few minutes' drive from the hustle of Patong, yet it could not be more different. The lovely beach is calm, relaxed and peaceful, with few vendors touting for business. The inhabitants are mainly Muslim.

In the heart of Kamala, **Phuket Fantasea ⓬** (Fri–Wed 5.30–11.30pm, showtime 7.30pm and 9pm; www.phuket-fantasea.com) is a night-time cultural theme park with fun show for seven-year-olds of all ages, combining acrobatics, pyrotechnics and illusions. The vast menagerie of performing animals includes over 40 elephants on stage at the same time. As ever though, time is rendering the sorts of sites that force animals to perform daily to people as somewhat outdated.

HAT PATONG

Love it or hate it, brash **Hat Patong ⓭** is the driving force behind Phuket's tourism success. The 3km (2-mile) stretch of beach is strewn with sunburnt bodies sheltering under rows of umbrellas, and even in the low season it is virtually impossible to find a quiet spot. But the location is naturally beautiful and the sea is usually clear outside the monsoon season. It is good for swimming or snorkelling, too, as long as you can avoid the jet skis and banana boats whizzing close to the shore.

Fact

Inside Put Jaw Temple are two cans filled with numbered sticks. Say your problem aloud and then shake the cans, picking up the first stick that falls out. The number on the stick will correspond to a pigeon hole in the adjacent hall. Inside you will find a piece of paper with your fortune written on it. Fortunes are told for free (you need an interpreter), but you are expected to leave a donation.

Tourists flock to Patong beach.

Tip

To see the lady boys at Simon Cabaret without sitting through the show, head to the car park around 11pm when they all come out and line up for photos. This is a better opportunity to see them up close and personal.

Patong has a multitude of shops, restaurants, street stalls, neon lights, flashy bars and clubs. Touts from restaurants and tailors go overboard enticing you into their shops, but at least there is plenty to buy and the variety is good, especially in malls like Jungceylon. Visit Baan Saan Market where you can try decent street food including seafood, as well as shop for clothes and souvenirs.

Patong restaurants have an immense range of cuisines for every palate. And while the nightlife in certain areas is seedy and the prostitution blatant (notably along Th. Bangla), you can have a fun and entertaining night out in Patong if you don't take it all too seriously.

PATONG NIGHTLIFE

In the heart of Patong is **Thanon Bangla**, the epicentre of the sex trade, with bar after bar of prostitutes, *katoey* or "lady-boy" transsexuals, and explicit "ping-pong" sex shows. Despite the blatant commercial trade, the atmosphere is relaxed and feels safe. Single men may get hassled to buy drinks for the bar girls, and families and women on their own may not feel entirely comfortable away from the main street.

Heading south out of Patong is **Simon Cabaret** (showtime nightly at 6pm, 7.30pm and 9pm, www.phuket-simoncabaret.com) on Thanon Sirirat. It's popular for Las Vegas-style shows featuring extravagant routines of lip-synching song and dance by Thailand's infamous lady boys. There are LGBTQ-friendly bars, hotels and clubs around the **Paradise Complex** near the Royal Paradise Hotel on Thanon Raja Uthit.

HAT KARON NOI AND HAT KARON

Beyond Hat Patong is **Hat Karon Noi**, sometimes referred to as Relax Bay. Although it is a public beach, this beguiling crescent of white sand is dominated by a single hotel, **Le Meridien Phuket**, which can make access a little difficult.

The 4km (3-mile) long beach at **Hat Karon** ⓮ is Phuket's second-most popular beach after Hat Patong. The sand is golden in colour and the beach is rarely packed, and it is screened from the road by a line of sand dunes and a grassy

"Lady-boys" perform nightly at Simon Cabaret.

embankment. During the rainy season, large waves make Hat Karon excellent for surfing, although unsafe for swimming. There is a good range of hotels, most of which, like in Patong, are tucked behind the beachside Thanon Karon.

HAT KATA YAI AND HAT KATA NOI

Just past the headland from Karon is **Hat Kata Yai** ⓯ (mostly referred to only as Kata), arguably one of the most scenic of Phuket's beaches as it looks out towards the small uninhabited Ko Poo (Crab Island). Kata's lovely beach is blessed with white sand and clear waters that are good for swimming and snorkelling, but can get quite busy. The southern end of the beach is home to **The Boathouse** hotel, which has a well-known fine-dining restaurant. At night, the beach is quiet and romantic, and there are a number of seafood restaurants lit by fairy lights overlooking the waves lapping the shore. To the far south a casual beach bar has chunky wooden tables above the sand. The food isn't great, but they have fire-juggling shows and a reggae soundtrack.

Separated by a rocky headland is **Hat Kata Noi** ⓰, which shares the same white sand and clear blue-green waters but is even prettier and more peaceful. The sprawling **Katathani Resort** has almost complete run of this beach. At the southern end of the beach are some decent corals for snorkelling.

KATA HILL VIEWPOINT

A sharp, steep mountain road leads out of Kata that cars and motorbikes sometimes struggle on; on a sunny day, the view from it is breathtaking. The After Beach Bar, a small, reggae-type place with a simple wooden platform jutting over the hillside, is good for watching the sunset. A little further, and opposite, is Kok Chang Elephant Camp (www.kokchangsafari.com) where you can feed the elephants, arrange treks or stop for a drink at the bamboo bar at the front of the park, often accompanied by the two resident monkeys. At the peak is the **Kata Hill Viewpoint** ⓱, from which the three stunning bays of Kata, Karon and Patong can be seen at one fell swoop. This famous scene

Eat

The views at Promthep Cape Restaurant (tel: 076-288 656; daily 10am–10pm) are better than the food, of which the fresh oysters, reared in the owner's farm, are the most impressive. Service can be slow, but the staff are usually friendly and the prices reasonable.

Fishing boats off Kata beach.

appears on postcards island-wide. Photography conditions are better in the morning, as even on a seemingly perfect day the clouds can roll in by mid afternoon and block the view.

HAT NAI HARN

South of Kata and lying between two ridges is the stunning white-sand **Hat Nai Harn** ⓲, relatively undeveloped despite its charms. For this it can thank the **Samnak Song Nai Harn Monastery**, which occupies a large portion of the beachfront land and has thwarted development. Nai Harn is a quieter alternative to the island's other beaches. It's popular with expats who are often seen exercising their dogs and offers some conveniences in the form of a few small bars, restaurants and shops.

SOUTH COAST

The south coast beaches from Laem Promthep onwards are largely mediocre at best and mainly used as a staging point for explorations of the islands off the southern coast.

LAEM PROMTHEP

Leading up the mountain from Nai Harn, **Laem Promthep** ⓳ (Promthep Cape) overlooks a splendid headland stretching into the blue Andaman Sea. When the conditions are right, the sunset vistas here are breathtaking, and it's packed almost every evening with tourists gazing at the horizon. Promthep Cape Restaurant serves cheap Thai food, and is an ideal spot for dinner and drinks.

HAT RAWAI

A base for a great number of Phuket's foreign residents, **Hat Rawai** ⓴ offers all the attractions of island life but without the intrusive tourist facilities of Kata, Karon and Patong. Rawai is often picturesque with its rows of small fishing and longtail boats waiting to journey to the nearby islands, but at low tide, the exposed rocks make it unsuitable for swimming and snorkelling. Rawai is popular for its street vendors who barbecue freshly caught seafood along the beach road throughout the day, and the fresh seafood restaurants that open in

Laem Promthep at sunset.

the evenings. To the south of the beach is a small *chao lay* (sea gypsy) village.

The most exclusive hotel in the area is the **Rawai Palm Beach Resort**, which maintains its own private beach for its guests' use.

Nearby on Thanon Viset the **Phuket Seashell Museum** (daily 9am–5.30pm), has an interesting display of over 2,000 different species of shells and fossils; some of the latter are reputedly over 380 million years old.

AO CHALONG

North of Rawai, **Ao Chalong**, has an important temple and a pier from which many dive expeditions and boat trips to nearby islands depart daily. The island's latest sailing facility is the Chalong Bay Marina.

Wat Chalong ㉑ (daily 7am–5pm; free; www.wat-chalong-phuket.com), located inland of Rawai on Route 4021, is Phuket's largest and most important Buddhist temple. It is also one of the most ornate and is well visited by both Thais and foreigners. Wat Chalong is associated with the revered monks Luang Pro Chaem and Luang Pho Chuang, famous herbal doctors and bone-setters who tended to the people of Phuket during the tin miners' rebellion of 1876. In another traditional role of monks they also mediated in the conflict, bringing both parties together to resolve disputes. Today, many Thais visit the temple to pay homage to the two statues that honour the monks.

One of Phuket's most impressive viewpoints is Ko Nakkerdwhich overlooks Ao Chalong and the small islands in the Andaman. At the peak of the mountain the 45-metre (148 feet) -high Big Buddha statue was officially completed in 2011 following years of construction.

SOUTHERN ISLANDS

The waters around Phuket's southernmost tip are dotted with islands, all of which can be reached by the longtail boats lining Hat Rawai beach or the pier at Ao Chalong. If you are staying overnight at islands like Ko Racha, the resort will arrange the boat transfers.

KO BON

Nearest to shore is the small but pretty **Ko Bon** ㉒, which can be reached in just 10 minutes, but has no fresh water or electricity and no accommodation.

Most day-trippers head for the side where **Sit Lo Chia**, a small Thai and seafood restaurant, is all that rests on the sandy beachfront, with the water in front good for snorkelling. There is also some coral in the deeper waters offshore.

KO HAE AND KO KAEO

About 20 minutes from Phuket, and often combined on a day trip with Ko Bon, is **Ko Hae** ㉓ (Coral Island). Amenities are better than at Ko Bon, with a number of restaurants, a few small shops and some watersports. Overnight stays are possible at the **Coral Island Resort**, the island's only accommodation. The crystal-clear turquoise waters around the island make it particularly good for both swimming

Snorkelling in the waters of Ko Racha.

Wat Chalong.

Gibbons kept as pets are reintroduced to the wild by Phuket's Gibbon Rehabilitation Centre.

and snorkelling, and there is a shallow coral reef within easy swimming distance of the beach.

Known to locals as Buddha Island, **Ko Kaeo** ㉔ is by far the least visited by day-trippers due to its lack of facilities. But it offers the chance of your own private beach for the day. Only a 10-minute boat ride from mainland Phuket, the island is home to a number of Buddha statues and shrines, hence its name.

KO RACHA

Approximately 20km (12 miles) off the coast of Rawai are **Ko Racha Noi**, a small uninhabited island with more rocks than beaches, and the larger **Ko Racha Yai** ㉕. Ko Racha Yai is the site of a stunning luxury resort known simply as **The Racha** on the northeast coast along **Ao Batok**. High season sees the island transform into a bustling hotspot, with day-trippers arriving on longtail boats and filling out the beaches. The picturesque shoreline in front of The Racha has talcum powder sand and crystal-clear turquoise waters. Watch out for small corals and rocks, however, when you wade into the waters.

Scuba-divers at Ko Hae.

Both Racha islands offer some of the best diving in the Phuket area and are often compared to the waters around the Similan Islands. On **Ko Racha Yai**, the **Bungalow Bay** reef offshore of Ao Batok has clear waters and soft coral gardens, with good visibility and currents that allow gentle drift diving along sloping reefs. Elsewhere on the island are more white-sand beaches and snorkelling spots.

Along the eastern coast is **Ao Kon Kare**, a small sandy beach with **Lucy's Reef** within swimming distance, a nickname given to the staghorn coral found here. Further up the east coast, a submerged wreck lies off **Ao Ter** at depths of 25–35 metres (80–115ft).

On the northern coast is **Ao Siam**, where shallow waters not only make for good snorkelling but also prevent boats from docking, keeping this beach less busy than those on other parts of the island.

The smaller **Ko Racha Noi** also has a few good dive sites for experienced divers; depths here are generally greater and currents stronger. On the southwest side of the island, lots of reef fish are drawn to a 27-metre (88ft) shipwreck, while a large pinnacle at the northern tip attracts stingrays and reef sharks.

Numerous dive sites are scattered around the Andaman Coast.

EAST COAST

The east coast of Phuket was once the bank of a flooded river and, unlike the west, comprises mainly limestone shoals, with virtually no sandy beaches.

LAEM PHAN WA

The only decent beach on the eastern coast of Phuket is **Laem Phan Wa**, 10km (6 miles) southeast from Phuket Town. This quiet cape is frequently filled with yachts sailing around **Ao**

Yon ㉖, where a totally unspoilt stretch of sand sheltered by headlands on both sides makes it good for swimming year-round. Only a handful of hotels and restaurants are found in the Laem Phan Wa area, and as tuk-tuk and motorcycle taxis rarely journey over the winding mountain road to get here, the beach is often deserted.

Khao Khad Viewpoint (reached by following signs along Thanon Sakdidej that lead through Muang Tong village) is one of the island's best-kept secrets and a beautiful spot from which to gaze out to the sea. From this elevated point, Phuket Town lies to one side, Chalong Bay to the other, and the shadowy outline of Ko Phi Phi island can be seen in the distance.

On the southernmost tip of Laem Phan Wa on Route 4129 is the **Phuket Aquarium and Marine Biological Research Centre** (daily 8.30am–4.30pm; http://phuketaquarium.org). The impressive display of sharks, tropical fish, reefs and a touch pool with starfish and sea cucumbers is an excellent primer before one takes that first diving or snorkelling trip.

THE MARINA

A fair number of holidaymakers have decided that a fortnight a year on Phuket is simply not enough, and have either retired to the island or set up a business here, running everything from humble beach bars to condominiums. One prime example is Karachi-born mobile-phone tycoon Gulu Lalvani, the brains (and money) behind the Royal Phuket Marina located on the east coast of Phuket. His vision resulted in the transformation of a muddy backwater into a lifestyle destination, complete with condos, restaurants and shops selling everything from beachwear to boats. The Marina has become a regular stage for international events as well as a haven for the region's yachting aficionados and is still expanding.

KO SIREH

A small bridge separates Phuket from the tiny island of Ko Sireh, which is home to a community of sea gypsies *(chao lay)*. Otherwise, Ko Sireh has a small beach, Hat Teum Suk, mainly visited by Thai families.

NAGA PEARL FARM

There's another sailing facility, Ao Po Grand Marina (www.aopograndmarina.com) in the northeast of the island, and the nearby Ao Po jetty is the departure point for the 30-minute boat ride to **Ko Nakha Noi** ㉗. Here you will find the **Naga Pearl Farm** (daily 9am–3.30pm), where full-sized South Sea pearls worth thousands of dollars are cultivated. It also displays a replica of the world's largest pearl, the original of which is currently housed at the Mikimoto Pearl Museum in Japan.

Visitors can wander round and see pearls at various stages of cultivation, from the nurturing of the baby oysters to the extraction of pearls from their shells years later. Longtail boat operators at Ao Po can arrange a boat ride to

Fact

The east coast is popular with sailors and has four of the island's five marinas. The Royal Phuket Marina (www.royalphuketmarina.com) is located roughly in the centre of Phuket's eastern coast, and next to the longer-established Phuket Boat Lagoon (www.phuketboatlagoon.com). Both are huge developments boasting exclusive bars and restaurants and luxury waterfront accommodation.

A sea gypsy mending nets.

A rubber plantation.

the island (about B300 per person for a return trip) or else book a guided tour directly with the Naga Pearl Farm.

PHUKET'S INTERIOR

Most visitors confine themselves to Phuket's beaches and see little else of the island. This is a pity, as the interior is filled with lush, jungle-covered hills interspersed with rubber and pineapple plantations. Phuket's compact size and relatively good roads will allow you to access trails through rainforest to take a dip at hidden waterfalls and still be back at your beachside hotel come nightfall.

THALANG

About 12km (7 miles) north of Phuket Town is a large roundabout along Thanon Thepkrasattri (Route 402), with the striking statues of two women encircled by flags. Called the **Heroines' Monument**, these figures stand proud with drawn swords, honouring Lady Chan and Lady Muk, the widow of the governor of Phuket and her sister, who led the successful defence of the island against the invading Burmese in 1785.

The statues mark the entry into the **Thalang** district. Thalang Town itself is rather run-down, but it is steeped in history and was the administrative centre of Phuket until the emergence of Phuket Town in the mid-19th century. Roughly 5km (3 miles) northwest of the monument is **Peranakan Phuket Museum** (daily 9am–6pm; free; http://peranakanphuketmuseum.com). It recounts Phuket's past through exhibitions of jewellery, clothing photography and historical information.

Continue north on Route 402 through **Thalang Town**. Just beyond the main crossroads is one of Phuket's most famous temples, **Wat Phra Thong** 28 (daily 7am–7pm; free). Inside is the statue of a golden Buddha that is half buried in the ground. From the chest up it measures about 2 metres (7ft). Over the years, thanks to stories circulating that the Buddha image was cast in gold, many people, including an invading Burmese army, have tried to dig it out of the ground. The legend says that to date none have succeeded in unearthing it, and

Blue skies and clear waters at Ko Racha Yai.

most have met with grisly deaths, as a result of a curse associated with the image. The statue is, in fact, made of brick and plaster, with a thin layer of gold covering it.

KHAO PHRA THAEO NATIONAL PARK

East of Thalang Town is **Khao Phra Thaeo National Park** ㉙ (daily 8am–5pm; http://portal.dnp.go.th), a pretty but hardly spectacular protected reserve. This is Phuket's largest tract of virgin rainforest and covers an area of 22 sq km (8.5 sq miles). A leisurely 20-minute walk from the park's entrance leads to **Bang Bae Waterfall**. It's a nice spot for lunch and a swim, but not overly remarkable, as it's neither high nor does it carry much water; indeed, at certain times of year it is totally dry. A further 3km (2 miles) along the same route is **Ton Sai Waterfall**, which, although more impressive, is also at risk of drying up during the summer months.

The rainforest is particularly lush during the rainy season when the greenery is more vibrant. Guides are available at the information centre at the park entrance and should be used for treks; unless you are an expert, the tell-tale signs of wildlife are easy to miss. Tigers and bears once roamed the park, but today it is far more common to see monkeys, civets and other small animals.

GIBBON REHABILITATION CENTRE

A 15–20-minute walk from Bang Pae Waterfall leads to the **Gibbon Rehabilitation Centre** ㉚ (Sun–Fri 9am–4.30pm, Sat until 3pm; free; www.gibbonproject.org). This is a non-profit organisation that aims to stop the poaching of Thailand's gibbons for tourist attractions and the pet trade. The gibbons are kept in large enclosures, but as the whole purpose is to reintroduce them to the wild, it's not possible to see them up close. Although located within the national park, the Gibbon Rehabilitation Centre receives none of the money from park fees and relies solely on donations from visitors.

Tip

The juice and flesh of a fresh coconut – sold all over the island and served in the shell ice-cold – is a sovereign remedy for both hangovers and jetlag, as it contains natural sugars. And you don't have to be suffering from one or the other to enjoy them!

People relaxing and under Bang Pae Waterfall.

Railay Bay, Krabi.

KRABI, KO PHI PHI AND KO LANTA

Visually striking, yet still off the beaten track, Krabi and its islands present one of the more charming and intriguing facets of Thailand.

KRABI PROVINCE

The lush and sprawling 4,708-sq km (1,818-sq mile) Krabi Province, just east of Phuket, embraces both the mainland and some idyllic islands. It is famous for sheer-sided limestone outcrops known as karsts. Their formation began millions of years ago as a result of limestone created by seashell deposits when parts of mainland Krabi were submerged under water. Subsequent continental shifts bulldozed the limestone into the towering peaks that are now scattered in the waters of the Andaman Sea, including at Ao Phang Nga (see page 218). As a result, Krabi is a popular destination for sports enthusiasts who come here to scale these challenging rock faces.

Many of the islands around Krabi Province are tiny or uninhabited, although the best known, **Ko Phi Phi** and **Ko Lanta**, are both inhabited and extremely popular with tourists for their legendary beaches.

Krabi mainland is also blessed with a string of white-sand beaches that attracts thousands during the dry season from November to April. Inland there are lush rainforests that harbour rare birds and wildlife. Camera crews often travel miles to take advantage of the idyllic surroundings for commercials, television shows and movies, including the blockbusters *The Beach*, *Around the World in 80 Days* and *Star Wars III*. While Krabi has its own airport, the area is still less developed than Phuket, and getting off the beaten track (with the exception of Phi Phi) is a lot easier than might be expected.

KRABI TOWN

Located some 180km (112 miles) from Phuket, **Krabi Town** ❶ is the main jump-off point for travellers en route to the beaches and islands of Krabi Province. Thanon Maharat, which is the central point in the busy and compact

Main attractions

- Wat Tham Seua
- Khao Phanom Bencha National Park
- Thanboke Koranee National Park
- Hat Railay West
- Hat Tham Phra Nang
- Ko Phi Phi Don
- Ko Phi Phi Ley
- Ko Lanta
- Mu Ko Lanta National Park

Biker family.

Tip

The southwest monsoon brings heavy rain from May to Oct to the Andaman Coast, including Krabi, Ko Phi Phi and Ko Lanta. Room rates can drop by as much as half during the wet months, so some people take advantage of this and hope for the best. There can be intermittent days of sunshine between rainy spells.

town, hosts both the main market and most of the restaurants and shops. The concentration of guesthouses and hotels on Thanon Chao Fa are just a few minutes' walk from **Chao Fa Pier**. The pavements around the pier are a bustling hub in the evenings when grills are fired and saucepans and woks clatter up a feast of freshly caught seafood.

At the bottom of Krabi Town, **Thara Park** overlooks **Krabi River** and the opposite bank, where there is a thicket of dense mangroves and a small fishing community lives in wooden huts raised on stilts. You can hire longtail boats at Chao Fa Pier to explore the mangroves, which shelter many types of fish, crabs, shrimps and shellfish, and are important nesting grounds for hundreds of bird species.

Most tours of the mangroves will stop at **Khao Khanab Nam** ❷, two 100-metre (328ft) limestone pinnacles that rise dramatically from the side of Krabi River. They have come to represent both the town and Krabi Province. Legend has it that two ceremonial *krabi* (swords) were discovered here in ancient times. Inside one of the peaks a series of caves reveal impressive formations of stalactites and stalagmites. Skeletons – thought to be the remains of people who took refuge here before being cut off by a massive flood – were discovered in one of the caves, though they have long since been removed.

KRABI'S INTERIOR

WAT THAM SEUA

"Tiger Cave Temple", or **Wat Tham Seua** ❸ (daily 8am–5pm), was founded by Jamnien Silasettho, a monk and teacher of meditation. Set amid forests and cliffs 9km (6 miles) from Krabi Town, it is easily reached by car or motorbike. At the rear of the temple a concrete staircase comprising 1,272 steps leads to the top of the 600-metre (1,970ft) peak where a small shrine contains a footprint of the Buddha in a flat rock. The hour-long ascent is exhausting, but the fantastic view of the surrounding area at the top makes up for it. A second staircase, next to a

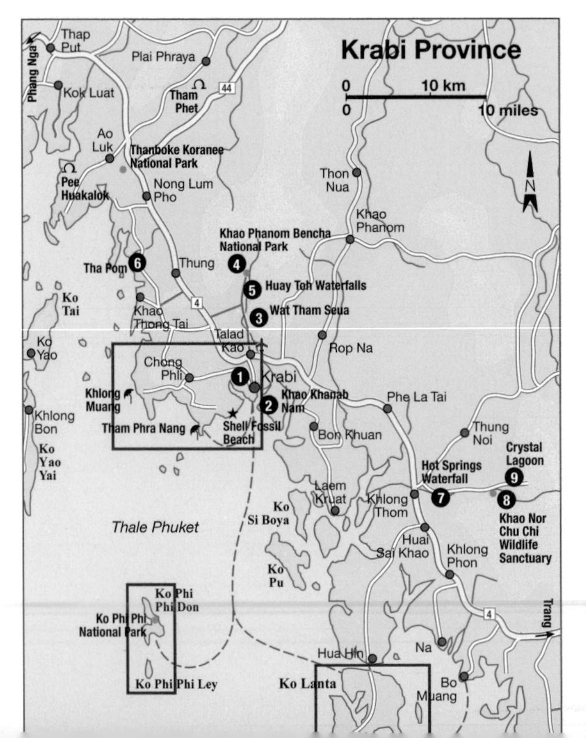

Rowing through mangroves in Krabi.

large statue of Kwan Im, the Chinese goddess of mercy, takes you on a different route up 1,237 steps.

KHAO PHANOM BENCHA N P

Covering an area of about 50 sq km (19 sq miles), **Khao Phanom Bencha National Park** ❹ (daily 8am–4.30pm; http://portal.dnp.go.th) lies some 20km (12 miles) to the north of Krabi Town. The park is the site of the dramatic 1,397-metre (4,583ft) limestone karst called **Khao Phanom Bencha**. The reserve lists 218 species of birds and 32 mammals including leopards, Asiatic black bears and even tigers, although sightings of the last are rare. The waterfalls flowing down the mountain slopes are another of the park's attractions, the main one being the 11-tiered **Huay Toh Waterfalls** ❺. Situated near the park headquarters, the tiers are at varying heights, with the highest at 80 metres (262ft).

THA POM

Some 34km (21 miles) north from Krabi Town is an unusual canal often referred to as **Tha Pom** ❻ (daily 8.30am–4.30pm). On signage leading to this attraction, however, the name appears as **Tha Pom Khlong Song Nam**, which translates as "Canal of Two Waters". A 700-metre (2,300ft) boardwalk takes you on a trail past mangrove and forest, eventually leading to the main attraction, a stream of clear water with two distinct colours. The water will appear colourless in poor weather, but on a good day, when the sun's rays penetrate, it creates a seemingly invisible line between its turquoise-blue and emerald-green layers. This phenomenon apparently occurs during high tide when tidal seawater meets fresh spring water running off the mountainside.

HOT SPRINGS WATERFALL

Some 55km (34 miles) southeast of Krabi Town, past the town of Khlong Thom on Highway 4, is another unusual phenomenon, the **Hot Springs Waterfall** ❼ (daily 8.30am–5pm). This is where an underground hot spring

GHOST'S SKULL CAVE

About 45km (28 miles) northwest of Krabi Town, Thanboke Koranee National Park (daily 8.30am–4.30pm; http://portal.dnp.go.th) has many caves and waterfalls, but one of its main highlights is Ghost's Skull Cave, or Tham Pee Huakalok. Locals believe that an oversized human skull found over half a century ago belongs to a ghost who dwells within the cave, hence its name (*pee* is Thai for ghost, *hua* means head and *kalok* is skull). The walls of the cave also have hundreds of colourful cave paintings and prehistoric drawings, estimated by archaeologists to be 2,000 to 3,000 years old. The cave burrows into a hill surrounded by water and mangroves, but is accessible by boat from Bor Tor Pier, 7km (4 miles) south of Ao Luk.

Wat Tham Seua.

leaks water through the earth's surface to cascade down smooth boulders. It is quite an experience to let the soothing warm water wash over you before you take a dip in the cool waters of the stream, a sort of a natural hydrotherapy in the middle of the jungle. It's a popular place to relax in but is relatively small and can get crowded around lunchtime when large tour groups arrive.

KHAO NOR CHU CHI WILDLIFE SANCTUARY

A 10-minute drive east of the Hot Springs Waterfall, the **Khao Nor Chu Chi Wildlife Sanctuary** 8 (daily 8am–5pm; http://portal.dnp.go.th) is also known as Khao Pra Bang Khram Wildlife Sanctuary. This is said to be the last patch of lowland rainforest in Thailand and one of the few locations in the world where the endangered bird species *Gurneys Pitta* can be found.

A 3km (2-mile) trail from the park leads through a shaded path to **Crystal Lagoon** 9 (also known as Emerald Pool). Bacteria and algae living in this emerald-coloured pond cause a variation of colours, ranging from pale green where the temperature is cooler to a greenish blue where the temperature peaks at around 50°C (122°F). It's safe to swim here, but the calcium carbonates in the water make it unsuitable for drinking, and a sign at the entrance asks bathers to refrain from using shampoo or soap. Enter the pond slowly and be careful of slippery moss at the water's edge.

KRABI'S BEACHES

HAT KHLONG MUANG AND HAT NOPPHARAT THARA

Only a handful of small hotels are fortunate enough to share the secluded beach of **Hat Khlong Muang** A Rocky in parts and backed by lush vegetation, this beach is very quiet. Set outside Krabi Town (but only a 30-minute drive away), it has clean waters that are pleasant to swim in year-round. Most of the accommodation at Hat Khlong Muang is simple, with notable exceptions being the five-star **Dusit Thani**

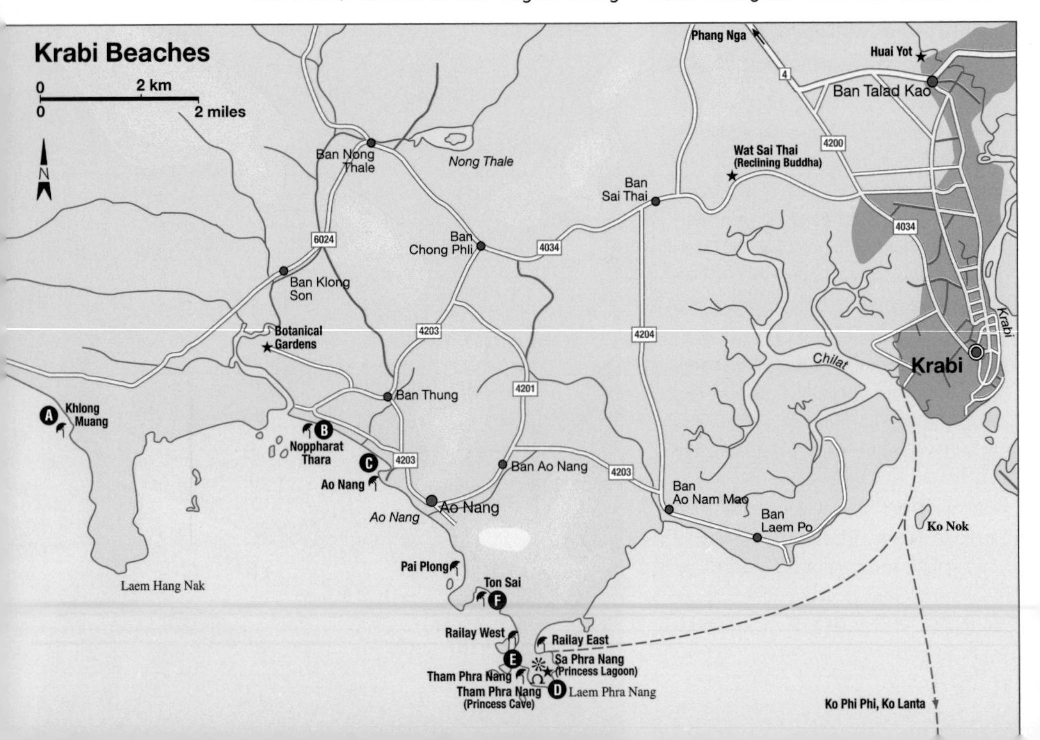

Krabi and the boutique-style luxury **Nakamanda** resort.

A finger of land called Hang Nak Cape separates Hat Khlong Muang from **Hat Noppharat Thara** B, the next beach, which enjoys uninterrupted views out towards a cluster of limestone islands. Shady casuarinas back this 2km (1-mile) long beach, and seafood vendors gather around the car park. The western end of the beach is quiet and, because it is separated by a canal, can only be accessed by longtail boat. The middle section is similarly peaceful, with a visitors' centre and the park headquarters, while the eastern section is the busiest.

AO NANG

A few minutes' drive from Hat Noppharat Thara, and sharing a similar view of the limestone cliffs in the distance is **Ao Nang** C. It is a very ordinary beach, located 22km (14 miles) east of Krabi Town, but would be nicer were it not for the longtail boats congesting its shore, which allow very little space to relax at high tide. The quiet is also shattered by the piercing drone of the longtail boat engines. Ao Nang is also the most commercial and developed beach on mainland Krabi, so it gets a little crowded in the high season. But it is not yet so built up as to be totally ruined, and the development at least means facilities like bars and restaurants for those who prefer a little action.

North of the beach is a cluster of open-air seafood restaurants, mainly owned by the small hotels behind them. Other restaurants, serving mostly Thai and Italian food, are found along the main beach road.

LAEM PHRA NANG (RAILAY BAY)

Surrounded by sheer limestone cliffs on three sides and only accessible by boat, the peninsula of **Laem Phra Nang** D, better known as **Railay Bay**, feels more like an island paradise than the mainland beach that it actually is. This stunning peninsula has four beaches, each with crystal-clear turquoise waters, powder-white sands and sheer-sided limestone cliffs that seemingly melt into the waters below, making it one of the world's leading rock-climbing destinations (look out for the Krabi Rock and Fire International Contest every April).

HAT RAILAY WEST AND HAT RAILAY EAST

Most arriving boats head straight to the western side of the peninsula, to **Hat Railay West**. The absence of a pier demands a short wade to the shore, but this has fortunately also prevented ferry-loads of day-trippers landing on its pristine white sands. Although still developing, Railay West is a world away from nearby Ao Nang. Its lodgings are of a better class (no ramshackle guesthouses here), which has helped prevent it from turning into a busy backpacker haunt. Accommodation is more expensive than on the other Krabi beaches, but that is the premium

Tip

Check the tide before scaling the cliff towards the viewpoint high above Hat Tham Phra Nang. When the tide is in at Hat Railay East, it makes for much more stunning views from the top.

The Krabi coastline is strewn with islands which make for fun excursions.

The Shell Fossil Beach at Krabi.

to be paid for direct access to such a lovely beach.

On the opposite side of the peninsula is **Hat Railay East**. Backed by dense mangroves, this is a less scenic beach and is unsuitable for swimming due to the incredibly low tides and the jagged rocks along the foreshore. Still, the lower-priced bungalows here get their fair share of trade. Access between the two Railay beaches is easy – a 5-minute walk along a flat paved pathway takes you from one beach to the other. The same people appreciating the mango-streaked sunsets on Railay West are often seen a few hours later enjoying fire shows and all-night parties at Railay East.

HAT THAM PHRA NANG

The prettiest beach on Railay Bay, if not the whole of Thailand, is **Hat Tham Phra Nang** E, where the extravagant and ultra-expensive **Rayavadee Resort** (www.rayavadee.com) occupies prime position (there is no other accommodation here). Set amid 11 hectares (26 acres) of coconut groves and surrounded by towering limestone cliffs, Tham Phra Nang is endowed with the softest of white sands, limpid turquoise-blue waters and beautiful coral reefs offshore. Although staying at the Rayavadee gives you the most direct access to this beach, many day-trippers from Railay West and Railay East flock to Tham Phra Nang to sunbathe, swim and snorkel.

Hat Tham Phra Nang is named after a princess *(phra nang)* who locals believe resides in the area. Near the Rayavadee Resort, at the beach's eastern end, is **Tham Phra Nang** (Princess Cave), where a collection of wooden phallic-shaped objects sit as an offering to her, its supplicants hoping she will bestow the surrounding mountains and sea with fertility. The cave is not as spectacular as it's made out to be, and is actually little more than a series of small overhangs, but a map at its base highlights the way towards a **viewpoint** and **Sa Phra Nang** (Princess Lagoon), which are both far more impressive.

The route to each of these sights is straightforward, but neither is suitable

Hat Tham Phra Nang beach, Railay.

SHELL FOSSIL BEACH

You will discover the entrance to **Shell Fossil Beach** (which is also known as Susan Hoi Shell Cemetery) marked by a small Chinese temple, approximately 17km (11 miles) from Krabi Town. Extending right to the edge of the sea are the remnants of sea shell deposits that have accumulated over 75 million years. Approaching from a distance, they appear to look like large concrete slabs. But while the site is not extraordinarily beautiful to look at, many people appreciate being a witness to evidence of life that existed millions of years before humans. This phenomenon can only be witnessed at two other locations in the world. One exists in Japan while the other stands in the US; the one in Krabi is the only coastal site around.

for the young, elderly or unfit, and good footwear is a must. The most challenging part of the walk is at the beginning, which involves clinging to ropes to clamber up a fairly steep incline; after this, the pathway becomes easier to follow. Veering to the left as the pathway splits leads to a viewpoint with spectacular vistas of the east and west bays of Railay. Continuing straight leads to a sharp rock face with yet more ropes, this time used almost to abseil down into the Princess Lagoon. The lagoon is suit-able for swimming, but it is not crystal-clear and does contain some rocks.

HAT TON SAI

From Hat Railay West, it is possible at low tide to walk to the nearby **Hat Ton Sai** Ⓕ. Longtail boats can also be hired to make the 5-minute journey, or if you are feeling energetic, you may simply swim to the beach. Budget travellers are attracted to Ton Sai by its cheaper accommodation and convivial atmosphere. Of all the beaches on the Laem Phra Nang headland, Ton Sai has the most vibrant nightlife, with beach bars open until the early hours and monthly full-moon parties. The view out to sea is as beautiful as that of Railay's, with limestone monoliths in the foreground and to the sides, but the sand is not as white, and at low tide the beach becomes muddy and makes swimming difficult.

ROCK CLIMBING

Sheer limestone cliffs facing mile upon mile of tranquil sea make Railay Bay a favoured spot for rock climbers. Most of the 650 or so routes that have developed since Krabi's cliffs were first scaled by sports climbers in the late 1980s are located in this peninsula. Among the most popular climbs is the challenging yet phenomenal **Thaiwand Wall** on the southern end. There are a range of other climbs suited for beginners right through to professionals, involving limestone crags, steep pocketed walls, overhangs and hanging stalactites.

Any of the climbing operations around Railay will advise on the best climbs, some of which are accessed

Fact

The Krabi coastline is strewn with islands, and most tour agencies sell the "Krabi Four Islands" tour of Ko Poda, Ko Tup, Ko Kai and Phra Nang Cave. The opening of Krabi Boat Lagoon Marina has been a boon to sailors.

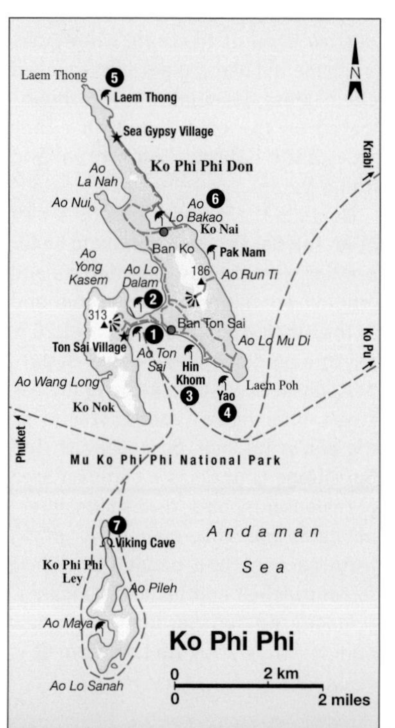

Rock climbing at Railay Bay.

by a combination of boat and a hike through the jungle.

KO PHI PHI

Lying in the Andaman Sea between the main hubs of Phuket and Krabi (about two hours by boat from either location) are the twin islands that make **Ko Phi Phi**. The two islands – the larger **Ko Phi Phi Don** and the smaller **Ko Phi Phi Ley** – are part of the protected **Mu Ko Phi Phi National Park** (http://portal.dnp.go.th), but somehow development, especially on Ko Phi Phi Don, seems to have run wild over the years, playing havoc with its natural beauty. From afar though, the islands are still stunning with their mountains and lovely arcs of soft white sand washed by gin-clear waters. Ko Phi Phi Don hosts all the accommodation and facilities, while Ko Phi Phi Ley is uninhabited and mainly visited on day trips.

The islands' rise to fame is characterised by both fortune and tragedy. As recently as in 1998, Ko Phi Phi was still considered a quiet, idyllic retreat. Turquoise waters bordering limestone cliffs and palm-tree-filled interiors made it a postcard-perfect location. Then came the major blockbuster film *The Beach*, which was shot mainly at **Ao Maya** (Maya Bay) on Ko Phi Phi Ley in 1998. Within one year, thousands were flocking to Ao Maya in the hope of seeing this Utopian image of the perfect unspoilt beach. While Ko Phi Phi Ley was spared development, it suffered from overcrowding and this took a toll on its ecology. The larger Ko Phi Phi Don also saw a rash of construction – resorts, restaurants and bars built quickly to cater to the constant onslaught of tourists. Finally in 2018, Thai authorities began to take the impact seriously and took the unprecedented decision to close Ao Maya to allow the coral reefs time to recover.

There are no roads on the island, so walking is generally the only way to get around. Most dive sites around Ko Phi Phi were unaffected by the 2004 tsunami, and it remains one of Thailand's most popular diving locations.

Beach life on Ao Lo Dalam.

KO PHI PHI DON

Ko Phi Phi Don is made up of two elongated islands joined together by a narrow isthmus to create what looks from the air like a giant high-backed chair. Most development is concentrated on the bays found on either side of the isthmus; Ao Ton Sai and Ao Lo Dalam.

Boats to the island dock at the pier at **Ao Ton Sai** ❶ a bay that would be far prettier were it not for the ferries and longtail boats lining it from one end to the other. An entrance fee of B20 is payable on disembarking, which purportedly goes towards keeping the bay clean. Information booths cluster at the end of the pier, beyond which **Ton Sai village** comprises a compact area of restaurants, bars, dive shops, internet cafés and stalls selling everything from sarongs and beaded jewellery to sandwiches and banana pancakes. Opposite Ao Ton Sai and only a few minutes' walk away, **Ao Lo Dalam** ❷ is a quieter and prettier bay with a lovely curve of white sand skimming clear blue waters. What makes it even nicer is that, following the tsunami, reconstruction along Ao Lo Dalam has been slower compared to Ao Ton Sai.

Although **Hat Hin Khom** ❸, located at the eastern end of Ao Ton Sai, and scenic **Hat Yao** ❹ (Long Beach), at the southeastern tip of the island, were similarly hit by the tsunami, the damage was less severe and the hotels were able to rebuild more quickly. Access to Hat Yao is either by longtail boat (10 minutes) from Ton Sai or a 40-minute walk.

All the beaches along the eastern side of Ko Phi Phi Don were left unscathed by the tsunami. The best snorkelling and the most exclusive resorts are found to the northeast of the island on **Hat Laem Thong** ❺, where the majority of visitors are either honeymooners or those seeking a more isolated beach. The beach is beautiful and quiet, but as boat transportation is scarce, it is difficult to get to the other parts of the island. There is a morning ferry between here and Ton Sai, otherwise all transport is by hired longtail boat. Hat Laem Thong is also the home of a small community of *chao lay* or sea gypsies.

South of Hat Laem Thong, **Ao Lo Bakao** ❻ contains mainly upmarket accommodation on its quiet beach, including the luxury all-suite **Zeavola Resort**. Further south is **Hat Pak Nam** and **Hat Ranti**, which are very low key and have scant accommodation.

Inland attractions are limited but many people take the 30-minute hike over to the **viewpoint** located high on a bluff at the southern end of Ao Lo Dalam. To get there, follow the path eastwards towards Hat Hin Khom and turn left when it forks inland. Understandably, the scenic point is at its busiest around sunrise and sunset; from here the vista of the twin bays of Ao Ton Sai and Ao Lo Dalam, separated by a thin band of land with the mountain behind, is simply breathtaking.

KO PHI PHI LEY

Uninhabited **Ko Phi Phi Ley** is a mere speck at 6.5 sq km (2.5 sq miles). It lies about 4km (2 miles) south of Ko Phi Phi Don. Formed entirely from limestone, the island is surrounded by steep karsts rising out of the sea that circle it almost completely. Of the picturesque bays around the island, the most visited are **Ao Pileh** to the east and the aforementioned **Ao Maya** on the west coast. Ao Maya is a beautiful spot often spoiled by the sheer volume of daytrippers who descended in droves and frequently left their litter behind. The result was the closure of the beach; a necessary but unfortunate move. The impact on the local tour operators may be short term, but the long-term protection of the coral reefs will prove to be a crucial decision for decades to come. Since the announcement, local authorities in Indonesia and the Philippines have followed suit at sites heavily affected

Fact

Several companies operate regular ferry services to Ko Phi Phi Don from Phuket and Krabi. The more expensive ones justify their higher prices with indoor air-conditioned areas. However, if the seas are rough, it's better to be on the outdoor decks with the bracing salty air blowing against you.

Approaching Ko Phi Phi Don island.

by tourism, highlighting the significance of the decision.

One of the major draws of Ko Phi Phi Ley is the **Viking Cave** 7 at the northeastern end of the island. The cave walls are inscribed with coloured chalk drawings of various boats, believed to have been sketched hundreds of years ago by pirates who used the cave as a shelter. Today, the pirates have been replaced by hundreds of swifts, which build their nests in crevices high up on the steep cave walls. These nests are collected by local villagers who climb the tall rickety ladders, risking life and limb, to collect the birds' nests, which are so highly prized by certain Chinese restaurants for their supposed health-giving properties. Swarms of swifts descend on the caves of Ko Phi Phi Ley every year between January and April and build their nests using their saliva as a bonding material.

DIVING AND SNORKELLING

Many of the dive sites around Ko Phi Phi are the same ones that can be visited from Phuket, Krabi and Ko Lanta. Around Ko Phi Phi itself, the best diving and snorkelling sites are **Hin Bida** (Phi Phi Shark Point), **Ko Pai** (Bamboo Island), and **Ko Yung** (Mosquito Island). The **King Cruiser** wreck between the waters of Phuket and Ko Phi Phi is another favourite dive site.

KO LANTA YAI

Ko Lanta is the most remote, and as a result perhaps the most pleasant, part of Krabi Province. Stretching 27km (17 miles) in length and 12km (7 miles) in width, it is one of only three inhabited islands in an archipelago of over 50. Originally named Pulao Satak, meaning "Island with Long Beaches" by the *chao lay* (sea gypsies) who first settled on the island, the term Ko Lanta generally refers to the largest of these islands, Ko Lanta Yai.

Most people travel to Ko Lanta direct from Krabi, where public ferries leave twice daily on a journey that takes about two hours and terminates at **Ban Sala Dan** village on Ko Lanta's northernmost tip. Running from north

Children at Ko Lanta.

KO LANTA COOL

Bangkok's smart set – that is to say, its wealthy rather than merely its famous – has always had a weekend retreat. The location has changed over the years: at one stage it was Hua Hin; Ko Samet has also played its part for A-lister R&R; while Chiang Mai enjoyed a brief period in the top spot. But the popularity of Krabi, and specifically Ko Lanta, has proved enduring. All it takes is a Friday afternoon flight to the airport, followed by a speedboat transfer, and then you can spend a day or more away from the frantic carryings-on in the capital, well out of the gaze of prying paparazzi, and enjoy the luxury of first-rate accommodation and excellent food. Sundays see a northward-exodus, when Ko Lanta returns to its more usual status as backwater.

to south, the island's single main road passes along the western beaches while a few smaller roads lead inland towards the southeastern coast, where there are small settlements of sea gypsies. Development has mainly been confined to the west coast, where spectacular sunsets viewed from along a number of striking white-sand beaches are a near-daily certainty. The east coast is fringed by long stretches of mangroves and swimming is not advisable.

Ko Lanta is developing. The red-earth dirt tracks are slowly being replaced by tarred roads, making access easier for both visitors and developers. But so far the island has managed to retain its sleepy feel. Phone reception is patchy, internet connections are slow and beach bungalows dominate. What development has brought is a greater range of accommodation and an increase in activities. Many resorts have in-house spa treatments to offer, some have Thai cooking lessons, and there are some with on-site dive operations.

BAN SALA DAN

Whether arriving by passenger or car ferry, the first stop for most visitors is the main village of **Ban Sala Dan ❶**. Guests at the more exclusive resorts on Ko Lanta have the luxury of being delivered right to the doorstep, or rather shorestep, of their hotel by high-speed private boat transfers. Concrete posts and overhead electrical cables make Ban Sala Dan a rather unsightly place, but for a relatively small island, it is well equipped with a police post, clinic, convenience stores, tour agents and internet facilities. Along the pier, a number of seafood restaurants display freshly caught seafood on beds of ice to draw customers.

HAT KHLONG DAO

A few kilometres south of Ban Sala Dan, **Hat Khlong Dao ❷** is the first of the island's westerly beaches. Shallow waters and safe swimming conditions make this 3km (2-mile) stretch of beach a preferred choice with families, and there is plenty of mid-range accommodation. Its proximity to the

Free diving in Krabi.

pier at Ban Sala Dan also appeals to scuba-divers seeking easy access to nearby dive sites. Despite its attractions – white sand, picturesque hilly backdrop and some of the most dramatic sunsets along the western coast – Khlong Dao rarely seems crowded. The beach is wide enough that even in the peak season it's always possible to snag a relatively secluded spot.

AO PHRA AE

Equally popular to Khlong Dao, neighbouring **Ao Phra Ae** ❸ (Long Beach) is slightly longer at 4km (3 miles) and shaded by vast stretches of tall coconut and pine trees. Phra Ae is fine for swimmers and sunbathers, but parts of the seabed are a little steep, so families with small children should be wary. There are lots of accommodation choices, including the luxury **Layana Resort & Spa**, and an ample variety of restaurants.

HAT KHLONG KHONG

Just south of Ao Phra Ae is laidback **Hat Khlong Khong** ❹. Although not great for swimming, it is one of the island's best beaches for snorkelling; at low tide the rocky underlay reveals a rich assortment of fish and other marine life. Accommodation is generally cheaper than on the more northern beaches, with an emphasis on clean but basic beachfront bungalows. Most have attached restaurants and beach bars that spring to life in the evenings, with tables set on the sand.

HAT KHLONG NIN AND HAT KHLONG HIN

If you turn right about 4km (2.5 miles) from Hat Khlong Khong the road leads past a few convenience stores and restaurants before emerging at **Hat Khlong Nin** ❺. This lovely beach has a relaxed feel and the atmosphere of a small, intimate village. The powdery white sands of Hat Khlong Nin stretch about 2km (1 mile) and calm waters – outside of the monsoon – make it excellent for swimming. Accommodation consists primarily of stylish resorts like **Sri Lanta** and

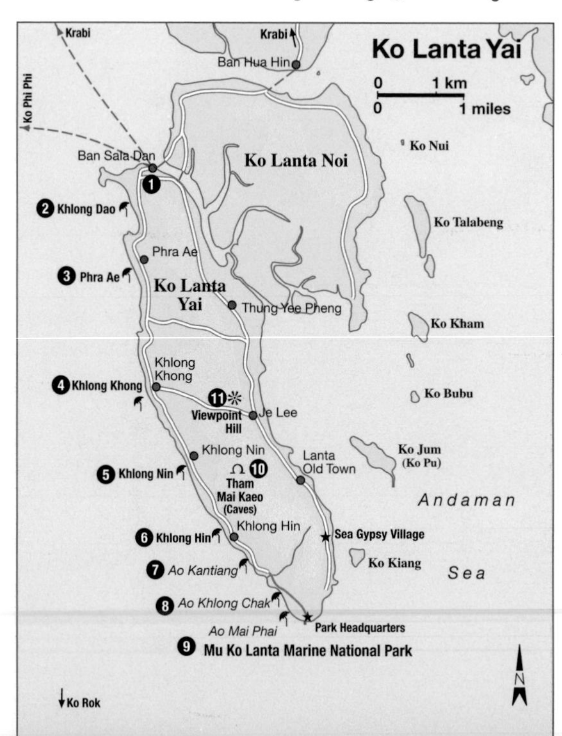

Ko Lanta fisherman.

the **Rawiwarin**, most with in-house restaurants and beach bars. At the start of Hat Khlong Nin is the popular reggae-style **Rasta Baby Bar**. A stroll along the beachfront reveals more of the same; at night, the next buzzing bamboo beach bar is never more than a short walk away.

At its southern end, Hat Khlong Nin merges with the much smaller and secluded **Hat Khlong Hin** ❻. Separated from the former by a cluster of trees, the waves here are rough during the monsoon season.

AO KANTIANG

About 6km (4 miles) from Hat Khlong Hin lies the picturesque bay of **Ao Kantiang** ❼. It has a secluded and private feel as the bay is framed on both sides and to the rear by jungle-covered hills. To the north and high up on the hill are a handful of small stilted bungalows; there are lovely views from the top, but you need to climb a considerable number of steps to get there. The southern end of this bay is anchored by the luxury **Pimalai Resort and Spa**. This five-star resort is set in 40 hectares (100 acres) of natural tropical surroundings and has direct access to the 1km (0.6-mile) long stretch of white-sand beach.

AO KHLONG CHAK AND AO MAI PHAI

Beyond Ao Kantiang, the further south one ventures, the more remote and consequently harder to reach the beaches become. Shortly after the Pimalai Resort, the road comes to an abrupt halt before morphing into a rugged dirt track; navigating it without the assistance of a four-wheel-drive vehicle is a near-impossibility. The reward is a cluster of some of the most scenic and underdeveloped beaches on the island, including **Ao Khlong Chak** ❽, one of Ko Lanta's smallest beaches at just 400 metres (1,310ft) long.

Only a small handful of budget to mid-range resorts are found here. During the monsoon season, Ao Khlong Chak is most rewarding for its waterfall, found 1.5km (1 mile) inland.

Beyond this is a short but even bumpier drive leading to **Ao Mai Phai**

Tip

If you plan to rent a jeep or a motorbike and explore Ko Lanta yourself, be sure to fill up with enough petrol before leaving the main village of Ban Sala Dan. The few petrol stations on Ko Lanta are expensive, difficult to find and shut annoyingly early.

The picturesque Ao Kantiang beach is anchored by Pimalai Resort and Spa at one end.

Tip

Longtail boatmen tend to be long on boat-handling skills and fairly short on general cheeriness. Don't hesitate to bargain hard for fares, and make sure the destination you want is clear.

(Bamboo Bay). This is the last beach before reaching the headquarters of Mu Ko Lanta Marine National Park on the southernmost tip. Its difficulty of access and geography – Ao Mai Phai is backed by mountains on three sides – gives this bay a real sense of isolation. The beach is only 500 metres (1,640ft) in length, but is ideal for swimming; a shallow boulder-strewn stretch at the northern edge is more suited to snorkelling. Only a few resorts are to be found here.

MU KO LANTA M N P

Declared a national park in 1990, **Mu Ko Lanta Marine National Park** (http://portal.dnp.go.th) 9 comprises the southern tip of Ko Lanta Yai and 15 small surrounding islands. The southernmost tip of Ko Lanta comprises two beaches: **Laem Tanode** and the rocky **Hat Hin Ngam**; the latter hosts the park headquarters. A 2.5km (1.5-mile) hiking trail leading along a cliff begins here and offers the chance of spotting local fauna like fruit bats, deer, wild pigs and reptiles. Also here is a small white lighthouse, from which there are scenic views out to the sea and mountains.

SNORKELLING AND DIVING

Some of Thailand's finest spots for snorkelling and scuba-diving are found in the waters off Ko Lanta. The most visited site for snorkelling, and considered by many to be one of Thailand's best, is **Ko Rok**, about 47km (29 miles) south of Ko Lanta. There are actually two islands, **Ko Rok Nai** and **Ko Rok Nok**, graced with powdery white-sand beaches and an extensive patch of coloured coral in between. Visibility is mostly very good, and many interesting types of reef fish can be found in these waters.

Approximately 20km (12 miles) from Ko Rok, the twin peaks of **Hin Daeng** and **Hin Muang** – frequently rated one of the world's top 10 dive sites – pierce the surface of the water. An incredible variety of marine life thrives at this site. As the only outcrops in this area of deep open sea, the peaks also attract many pelagics, as well as large tuna and barracuda. Schools of grey reef

A beach on Ko Lanta.

sharks often approach divers, and the area has one of the highest incidences of whale-shark sightings in the world.

INLAND DIVERSIONS

There are limited attractions on Ko Lanta apart from its stunning beaches. Some 4km (2.5 miles) south of Hat Khlong Khong, the road splits into two. The left fork leads all the way to the east coast of the island, where few tourists venture.

A turn-off at the 3km (2-mile) mark to the right leads to **Tham Mai Kaeo** ⑩ caves. It is best to get your hotel to organise this trip, as finding the caves on your own is a bit of a challenge; you need to clamber up a steep hill, often with the help of tree branches. The combination of slippery paths, rickety bamboo ladders and confined spaces makes this an inadvisable activity for the physically challenged. The expedition leads through a labyrinth of winding tunnels and caverns, past dramatic rock formations. At the end, after negotiating a steep slope with the aid of a rope, is a deep pool, where you can cool off.

For early risers, a sunrise trip to the central peak referred to simply as **Viewpoint Hill** ⑪ is worth the effort. To get there, continue on the road heading east, following signs that are set at intervals along the way. The near-360-degree panoramic vista amid the crisp morning air is truly breathtaking. The experience can be enjoyed over a "sunrise breakfast" at the café high on the hill. The food is nothing to tweet about, but gazing out towards the sea, you will barely notice it. If the thought of rising before dawn fills you with dread, you could go at sunset and have cocktails at Cliff Sunset Restaurant, which has good Thai food and a few Western fusion dishes.

KO BUBU AND KO JUM

Those seeking an even quieter retreat should consider the smaller islands nearby. At 7km (4 miles) off the east coast of Ko Lanta, tiny **Ko Bubu** takes just 30 minutes to circumnavigate by foot. This essentially uninhabited isle only has a basic restaurant and a few simple bungalows on the western coast, where the small but stunning gently sloping beach is ideal for swimming. Boat transfers can be arranged for guests of **Bubu Island Resort** (tel: 0-7561 8066) the only resort on the island; there is no other regular service. Longtail boats at Krabi and Ko Lanta can, however, be chartered for the journey.

Larger than Ko Bubu is **Ko Jum** (Ko Pu), to the northwest of Ko Lanta. While facilities are increasing here it has yet to sustain much impact from tourism and is still pleasantly underdeveloped. The island has powdery white-sand beaches and clear waters with plenty of healthy coral reefs. Some 3,000 permanent residents earn a living mainly from fishing and the island's rubber plantations. Accommodation now runs from budget to expensive resorts like the stylish Koh Jum Beach Villas.

Tip

Buying seashells, or taking them from the shore, strips Thailand's ecology, and encourages greedy entrepreneurs. Take a photo instead.

Tropical beach in the Mu Ko Lanta National Park.

Sivalai Beach Resort, Trang.

THE DEEP SOUTH

Here you will find picture-perfect beaches and be able to sample Thai-Muslim culture. Trang and Satun provinces shelter pristine islands, and historic Nakhon Si Thammarat was once capital of an ancient kingdom.

Main attractions

- Trang Town
- Hat Chang Lang
- Tham Morakot
- Ko Kradan
- Ko Libong
- Ko Tarutao Marine National Park
- Songkhla Town
- Nakhon Si Thammarat

Map on page 256

Misconceptions abound when it comes to Thailand's southernmost provinces. Among Thais, the predominantly Muslim residents are regarded as rough and prone to violence. The region is also one of the poorest in Thailand, with scant tourist infrastructure. Therefore, comparatively few outsiders, foreign or Thai, visit the area. The provinces of Narathiwat, Yala and Pattani, which continue to suffer the effects of a Muslim separatist insurgency, should be expressly avoided and, at the time of writing, most Western embassies were also advising against travel to Songkhla. Check for updates if you decide to travel there. The other provinces covered in this chapter, especially Trang and Satun, are perfectly safe to visit. While the population in the countryside is mainly Muslim, there are large Chinese communities in the cities of all these provinces.

North of Songkhla along the Gulf of Thailand is Nakhon Si Thammarat Province, technically speaking not part of the Deep South and therefore spared from the violence experienced by the more southerly provinces.

The Deep South has some of Thailand's most fascinating highlights, including Thai-Muslim culture and cuisine, the pristine islands of Ko Tarutao Marine National Park, and a chance to avoid the tourism crowds.

TRANG

Trang Province holds what is probably the greatest variety of attractions of any of the provinces in the Deep South. In the north are pretty beaches and islands with ample accommodation, a wealth of outdoor activities and good food. To the south of Trang, the beaches and islands are more isolated but still offer some fascinating wildlife and the rhythms of rural island ways.

A coffee shop in Trang Town.

Fact

The southwest monsoon brings heavy rain from May to Oct to the Andaman Coast, including Trang and Satun. The Gulf of Thailand coast, which includes Songkhla, experiences the worst rains from Nov to Jan.

TRANG TOWN

Trang Town ❶ is a pleasant place with a predominantly Chinese population and enough attractions to warrant at least an overnight stay. While Trang is well known among Thais as the birthplace of Chuan Leekpai, a former prime minister, travellers will be more taken by another legacy; from Chinese-style coffee shops to one of Thailand's best **night markets** (along Thanon Ruenrom), the food in Trang is one of its highlights. Trang Town also has a colourful morning market on Thanon Ratchadamnoen and Thanon Sathani, where vendors sell a deluge of fresh produce. Meanwhile, seafood stalls line the streets behind the Ko Teng Hotel.

TRANG'S BEACHES

Trang's 119km (74-mile) coastline from Hat Pak Meng to Hat Chao Mai, plus a number of islands nearby, are part of the **Hat Chao Mai National Park** (http://portal.dnp.go.th). The line of secluded beaches along the mainland coast and several of the islands are worth seeking out.

Some 40km (25 miles) west of Trang Town, **Hat Pak Meng** is a shallow beach that gets muddy at low tide. There is a row of seafood restaurants and a pier at the northern end where boats depart for trips to nearby islands. Apart from these, Pak Meng is very much a local scene, bolstered by Thais picnicking at weekends.

South of Hat Pak Meng, **Hat Chang Lang** ❷ is a lovely and isolated beach with greyish-white sands backed by casuarina trees. The beach is only swimmable at high tide; when the tide is low it exposes large sandbanks, which are great to walk on. When the conditions are right, the sunsets can be truly spectacular here, the orange glow bathing limestone crags and islands studded across the horizon.

Beyond Hat Chang Lang are more beaches – **Hat Yong Ling**, **Hat Yao** and **Hat Chao Mai** – but facilities and accommodation both become very sparse. Nearby Ban Chao Mai is where the harbour is located, a jump-off point for island tours.

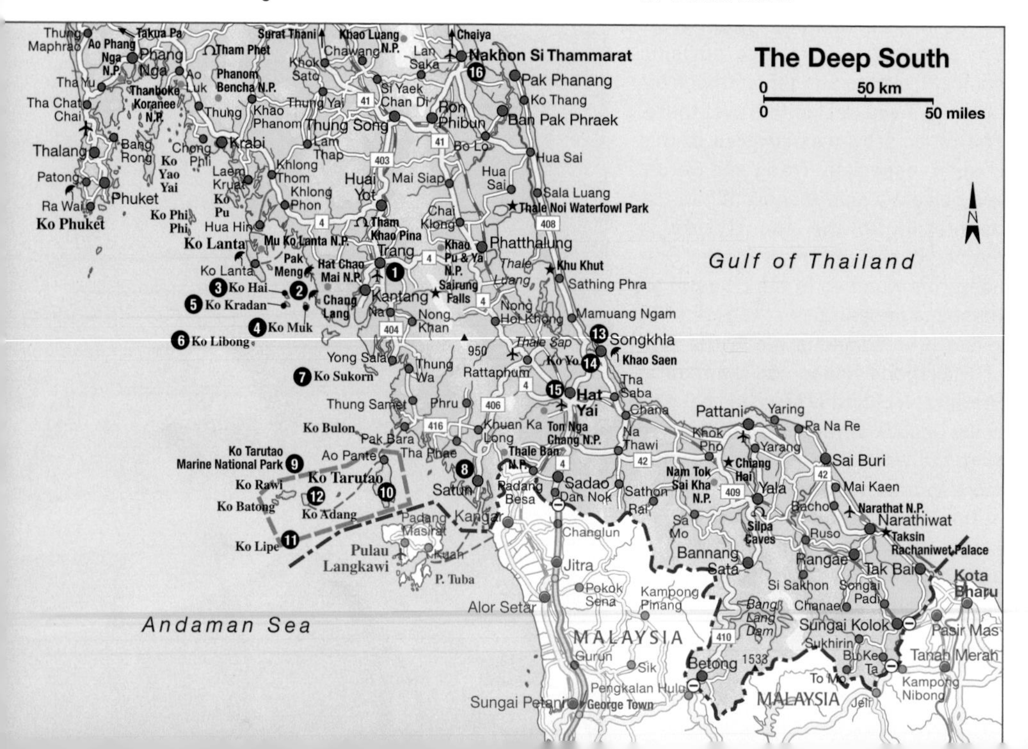

Inland from Hat Yao, the caves at **Tham Lod** are best reached by kayak; the journey winds its way past mangrove forests and enters a cave through a tiny gap. A 10-minute paddle in darkness follows until you emerge into a scenic hidden lagoon surrounded by mangroves and towering limestone walls.

TRANG'S ISLANDS

Some 16km (10 miles) southwest of Hat Pak Meng is **Ko Hai** ❸ (also known as Ko Ngai). It actually lies in Krabi Province, but is more accessible from Trang. Ringed by clear water and coral reefs, it has several low-key resorts and a near-perfect swimming beach on its eastern side.

Approximately 8km (5 miles) south of Ko Hai is **Ko Muk** ❹. Boats to Ko Muk usually arrive at the small fishing village of Hua Laem, on the east side of the island, which is home to a small local population and rubber plantations, giving it a rural atmosphere. Ko Muk's finest beach is the secluded **Hat Farang** on the west coast, a cove-like inlet ringed by limestone cliffs, not unlike Railay Bay in Krabi. The highlight of Ko Muk is **Tham Morakot**, or "Emerald Cave", in the northern part of the island. During low tide, it's possible to swim through this partially submerged cave, the last few metres in complete darkness, to emerge at a hidden beach surrounded by tall limestone cliffs and lush greenery.

Ko Kradan ❺, about 6km (4 miles) southwest of Ko Muk, is considered by some to be the most beautiful island in the area. The beaches are blinding white and there are some nice reefs offshore. Accommodation on the island is getting better, and includes the luxury Seven Seas Resort, but Kradan is still widely visited by day-trippers who come to laze on its beaches, to snorkel and dive.

Southwest of Ko Kradan are two less frequently visited islands. The first is **Ko Libong** ❻, the largest island in the group and known for its wildlife. The waters around the island constitute one of Thailand's remaining habitats of the dugong. **Libong Beach Resort** (one of few resorts on the island) offers

The streets of many towns in the Deep South are lined with elaborate wooden birdcages holding doves.

The dugong is an endangered species.

DUGONG

Sometimes dubbed "sea cow", reputed to be the origin of legends about mermaids, the dugong is one of the strangest-looking creatures in the ocean.

Found in tropical waters from Australia to East Africa, the vegetarian dugong is sometimes confused with the manatee, a related but separate species (both are related to the elephant). Dugongs graze on underwater grasses day and night, and can stay beneath the surface for up to six minutes before coming up for air. Endowed with a certain graceless beauty, these languid animals are often targeted by coastal hunters, and they were long sought for their meat, oil, skin, bones and teeth. Dugongs are now legally protected, but their populations remain endangered. Sighting one while diving or snorkelling is to be transported back to prehistoric times.

Eat

Trang is also well known for its old-world Chinese-style coffee shops, known as *raan kopi*. Try Tubtieng Oldtown Cafe on Huai Yod 2 (daily 11am–9pm), or the Green House (10am–7pm).

snorkelling trips to the waters populated by the dugongs.

Ko Sukorn ❼, southeast of Ko Libong, is home to nearly 3,000 people, and just a handful of motor vehicles. The island's beaches are concentrated on the western shore, the most attractive being **Hat Talo Yai**, where there are some of the island's sprinkling of budget resorts.

SATUN

Remote and mountainous **Satun Province** shares a border with Malaysia, and is in many ways more Malay than Thai in terms of culture. Despite this, Satun has managed to avoid the conflicts of neighbouring provinces to the east, and is a safe area to travel.

SATUN TOWN

Set in a lovely green valley walled by limestone cliffs, **Satun Town** ❽ is pleasant enough for a quick tour. The town's only real tourist attraction is the elegant Sino-Portuguese **Kuden Mansion**, originally built to accommodate King Rama V for a visit that, ironically, never materialised. In 1902, the building became the governor's mansion before it was turned into Satun **National Museum** (Wed–Sun 9am–4pm). The restored building mainly features exhibits on southern Thai life.

KO TARUTAO M N P

Ko Tarutao Marine National Park ❾ (mid-Nov–mid-May; http://portal.dnp.go.th) is the province's principal claim to fame. It encompasses more than 1,400 sq km (541 sq miles) of the Andaman Sea and comprises 51 islands. Only three of the islands are inhabited, mainly by *chao lay* sea gypsies. Established as a national park in 1974, the forests and seas that comprise Tarutao are home to Thailand's healthiest coral reefs – said to harbour 25 percent of the world's tropical fish species – and an incredible variety of fauna.

The Tarutao islands support creatures such as langurs, crab-eating macaques and wild pigs, as well as aquatic mammals including dolphins and dugongs. Several kinds of turtle lay their eggs on the largest island, Ko

Life on Ko Libong island.

Tarutao, and especially along Ao Sone beach on the west coast. This spectacle can be witnessed every January.

The marine park is divided into two parts: the **Tarutao Archipelago** located 45km (28 miles) off the coast of mainland Satun, and the **Adang-Rawi Archipelago**, about 50km (30 miles) west of Ko Tarutao itself. The islands of the latter group are known for their excellent dive spots, and include the park's most popular island, Ko Lipe. The park is only open during the dry season, typically mid-November to mid-May. Boat trips to the islands set off from the fishing town of **Pak Bara**, 60km (40 miles) north of Satun Town.

KO TARUTAO

Imposing **Ko Tarutao ⑩**, the largest of the park's islands, is an excellent place for hiking and exploring caves, or to simply relax on its wide beach. The 152-sq-km (59-sq-mile) island is home to the park headquarters, behind the vast stretch of fine white sand on the western shore known as **Ao Phante Malacca**. Behind the park office, at the end of a short path, **Toe Boo Cliff** has great views over the bay from its craggy summit, which can be reached in a 30-minute climb.

To the south of Ao Phante Malacca lie two scenic beaches, **Ao Jak** and **Ao Molae**. To get to the next beach, **Ao Sone**, an important nesting ground for endangered turtles from September to May (and especially in January), requires a good two-hour walk.

On the island's eastern side, **Ao Taloh Wow** was a place of exile for Thai prisoners in the 1930s and 40s. Ko Tarutao made the news again in 2002 when **Ao Rusi**, on the northeast coast of the island, was used as the backdrop for the American reality television show *Survivor*. It caused some controversy as Thai environmentalists feared that the virgin environment would be irrevocably harmed. In the end, hard business won out. But to its credit, CBS, the show's producers, left the area more or less in the same pristine condition as when the film crew first arrived.

KO LIPE AND KO ADANG

Tiny **Ko Lipe ⑪**, 40km (25 miles) from Ko Tarutao, is the most popular and also the most developed island. Despite the fact that Ko Lipe lies within the national park boundaries, the 1,000 or so *chao lay* sea gypsies who inhabit the island have gained the right to develop sections of it. This accounts for the largely disorganised and often unattractive development that has taken root. Fortunately, there isn't enough of it to detract from the natural beauty of the island.

Boats from Pak Bara arrive at **Hat Na Ko** ("front of the island") in the north, where there is some accommodation. A short walk from Na Ko via a dirt path leads to **Sunset Beach**, probably the most beautiful of Ko Lipe's beaches. It plays host to only a few small-scale resorts and offers a wonderful view of the neighbouring islands.

Bay view from Toe Boo Cliff on Ao Phante Malacca.

Fact

The streets of many Deep South towns have elaborate wooden birdcages holding *merbok*, or zebra doves, which are famous for their singing. Contests may draw over 1,000 regional entries from as far away as Indonesia.

On the southern side of Ko Lipe is a bay called **Ao Pattaya**. With its long sandy coastline and clear water, this is easily the most popular beach and home to the majority of the island's accommodation and bars.

For those interested in diving and or snorkelling, Ko Lipe's prime position in the middle of the Adang-Rawi Archipelago makes for easy access to nearby dive sites. Popular spots in this area include the reefs surrounding **Ko Rawi**, **Ko Yang** and **Ko Hin Sorn**.

Visible from the shores of Sunset Beach and less than 2km (1 mile) away, towering **Ko Adang** ⓬ has a densely forested hilly interior, beautiful white-sand beaches and basic national-park accommodation. It is popular with day-tripping snorkellers, and jungle trails inland lead to waterfalls (during the wet season) and scenic viewpoints.

SONGKHLA

Songkhla Province is often overlooked. Although the flashy border city of Hat Yai draws thousands of Malaysian and Singaporean tourists each year, visitors from other countries typically give the province a wide berth. This is unfortunate, as Hat Yai isn't nearly as seedy as it's thought to be, and offers great food and bargain shopping, as well as a chance to see the southern Thai pastime of buffalo fighting. Hat Yai has been the victim of bomb attacks and at the time of writing most Western governments were advising against travel to Songkhla. Check for updates.

Directly east of Hat Yai, the tiny provincial capital, Songkhla Town, is a fascinating melting pot of southern Thai culture, with decent beaches, interesting temples and what is probably the best night market in the entire Deep South region.

SONGKHLA TOWN

Little-visited **Songkhla Town** ⓭, 25km (16 miles) east of Hat Yai, is one of the Deep South's nicer towns. Predominantly Chinese, but with a visible Muslim minority, Songkhla Town is located on a finger of land separating the Gulf

Buying dinner at Songkhla's extensive night market.

of Thailand from the Thale Sap Songkhla, a large brackish lake. On the north coast of this promontory is **Hat Samila**, a long sandy beach marked by a bronze mermaid statue, making it a popular photo spot. While not great for swimming, the beach is nice enough for a stroll to watch the sun set or for a meal at one of the many beachside restaurants.

The town's charming old enclave, found between Thanon Nakhorn Nok and Thanon Nang Ngaam, has a number of Sino-Portuguese buildings, as well as numerous Chinese-style restaurants and old coffee shops that haven't changed in decades. **Songkhla National Museum** (Wed–Sun 9am–noon, 1–4pm), housed in an elegant Sino-Portuguese mansion, is worth seeing for its exhibits of art, sculpture, pottery, ceramics and furniture from all the major periods of Thai history.

Songkhla's most famous temple, **Wat Matchimawat** (Wed–Sun 1pm–4pm; free), is located directly west of the Old Town. Its highlights are the beautiful temple paintings, probably executed in the early Rattanakosin period more than 200 years ago. Another worthwhile temple to visit is the hilltop compound of **Khao Tang Kuan** (Mon–Fri 10am–7pm, Sat–Sun 8am–7pm). Accessible by air-conditioned tram, the quasi European-style temple complex was originally commissioned by King Rama V. It offers great views over Songkhla Town and Ko Yo island.

AROUND SONGKHLA

To the west of Songkhla, in the salty waters of the Thale Sap, is the island of **Ko Yo** ⓮, which can be visited as a day trip from Songkhla or Hat Yai. In recent years it has become something of a cultural tourism hotspot, and is famous for its hand-loomed cotton weaving called *phaa kaw yaw*. The best place to buy it, either in lengths or as clothing, is at the central market.

Also on Ko Yo is the interesting **Thaksin Folklore Museum** (daily 8.30am–5pm), which highlights the history, architecture, traditions and handicraft of the people of south Thailand. The Muslim fishing village of **Khao Saen**, about 5km (3 miles) from Songkhla Town, is also worth seeing for its rows of colourful prawn-fishing boats docked every evening along the beach. The highly decorated boats, embellished with dragon prows, make for great photos.

HAT YAI

Sprawling **Hat Yai** ⓯ is the third-largest city in Thailand, and predominantly Chinese in character. Unfortunately, it has become a tourist destination for all the wrong reasons; it attracts busloads of Malaysians and Singaporeans who travel across the border from Malaysia to frequent its numerous sleazy massage parlours and nightclubs. There are no real draws in Hat Yai, but the shopping and great food

Chinese temple in Songkhla.

plus ample accommodation options will appeal to those who have just come from an island.

If in Hat Yai during the first Saturday of the month, make sure to catch the colourful southern Thai spectacle of **buffalo fighting**. This is held at **Noen Khum Thong Stadium**, about 10km (6 miles) west of Hat Yai. Unlike the Western, rather more bloodthirsty, version of the sport, Thai buffalo fights involve two bulls locking horns and trying to force the other into submission.

NAKHON SI THAMMARAT

Beyond the Deep South region and north of Songkhla is **Nakhon Si Thammarat Province**. It is home to an excellent national park and Nakhon Si Thammarat Town, the second-largest city in south Thailand and known for its excellent southern food, important Buddhist temples and the art of *nang thalung*, or leather shadow puppets. The terrain is mainly mountainous, but there are some nice beaches to the north of the province.

Wat Phra Mahathat, Nakhon Si Thammarat.

NAKHON SI THAMMARAT TOWN

Nakhon Si Thammarat Town ⓰, usually referred to simply as "Nakhon", has a rich history dating back to the 2nd century when it was known as Ligor, the capital of the ancient kingdom of Tambralinga. It later became an important port and the centre of the Sumatra-based Srivijaya empire, at least until the 10th century. Today, Nakhon is often regarded as a bastion of traditional southern Thai culture. For most tourists, the city is a mere transport hub to Ko Samui or the beaches of Ao Khanom to the north. But Nakhon has several attractions that make it worthy of at least an overnight stay.

The physical aspects of Nakhon's history are extensively displayed in its **National Museum** (daily 8am–5pm) at the southern end of Thanon Ratchadamnoen. It houses one of the most important historical collections of Thailand outside of Bangkok's National Museum.

At the northern end of Thanon Ratchadamnoen is **Wat Phra Mahathat** (daily 8am–6pm), one of six royally sanctioned temples in the country, and regarded as one of the most important temples in southern Thailand.

PUPPET SHOW

Another must-see in this town is **Suchart Subsin's Shadow Puppet Workshop** (daily 8.30am–5pm; free) along Thanon Si Thammasok. The art of using carved leather shadow puppets to perform tales from the Hindu *Ramayana* epic that originated in India can be found all over Southeast Asia, including Thailand, where Suchart is the most famous *nang thalung* exponent. His family has been making puppets and giving performances for over 60 years, and Suchart has even performed for King Bhumibol. The family sells puppets, and for a small donation may put on a private performance.

Nakhon Si Thammarat puppet show.

Working in the rice paddies.

Phu Chi Fa, Chiang Rai Province.

NORTH THAILAND

The north is an area of high mountains, colourful hill tribes and outdoor adventure. Very different from the rest of Thailand, this is a world unto itself.

Sukhothai Historical Park.

An extensive region of mountains, valleys and rivers, northern Thailand straddles an important historical junction where peoples from China, Laos, Myanmar, Thailand and beyond have long traded commodities and ideas. The blend was further enlivened by the migrations of tribes like the Akha, Karen, Lisu, Hmong and Yao, whose ethnic heritage knows no political boundaries.

Until the early 20th century, the north was accessible from Bangkok only by a complicated river trip, or by several weeks on elephant back. It is not surprising, then, that the region has retained a distinct flavour all its own, one still so strong that tourists from other parts of Thailand come here almost as if to visit another country. They marvel at the beauty of the temples, with their splendid teak carvings and intricate Burmese-inspired decorations; the wild orchids that grow profusely in the hills; the gentle manners of the people (among whose hospitable habits it is to place a basin of cool water outside their gates for thirsty strangers); and the novelty of having to bundle up in a sweater in the cool season.

Waiting for the annual flower parade, Chiang Mai.

The north is a region of great natural wealth and scenic beauty. Although decades of deforestation have reduced the hardwood forests, a logging ban has ensured the remainder should survive. The mountains are home to Thailand's hill tribes, now a tourist industry in their own right. Still an exotic thread on the fringe of Thai life, the hill tribes are gradually being woven into the national fabric, and more and more of them are migrating to the larger cities of the north.

It is hard for the authorities to patrol this wild terrain adequately, but easy for smugglers to slip back and forth across the borders with Myanmar and Laos in the notorious Golden Triangle. Although there has been some success in introducing alternatives to opium as a cash crop, the smuggling of contraband drugs is still a major factor in the northern economy.

The school run in Chiang Mai.

CHIANG MAI

Chiang Mai, the capital of north Thailand, is regarded as the cultural heart of the country. With its lovely Lanna-style temples, museums and a market where one can indulge in night-time shopping, this is a city of diverse charms.

Main attractions

Wat Chiang Man
Wat Phra Singh
Wat Chedi Luang
Wat Bupparam
Chiang Mai Night Bazaar
Wat Suan Dok
Wat U Mong
Wat Jet Yot
Chiang Mai National Museum
Tribal Museum

Maps on pages 270, 275

It has become trendy to bemoan the supposed demise of **Chiang Mai ❶**, Thailand's "Rose of the North". Noisy tuk-tuk replaced silent *samlor* pedicabs years ago, concrete buildings have ousted traditional wooden housing, and high-rise condominiums now mark the skyline. And, above all, the traffic has increased exponentially.

In recent years, however, there has been a revival of sorts. In the beautiful, historically important Old City, new construction is limited to three storeys. Old streets have been cobbled in red brick, concrete lamp standards replaced with ornate Parisian-style lanterns, and the city walls restored. The polluted city moat has been dredged and cleaned up, and is now populated by fish and turtles.

NORTHERN HOSPITALITY

Despite rapid urbanisation, 700-year-old Chiang Mai remains a pleasant, balmy escape from Bangkok's humidity. Situated 300 metres (1,000ft) above sea level in a valley divided by the picturesque 560km (350-mile) long **Ping River** (Mae Nam Ping), the city was for seven centuries the capital of the Lanna (Million Rice Fields) kingdom. Its remoteness ensured significant isolation from Bangkok – 700km (400 miles) south – well into the 20th century.

This isolation allowed Chiang Mai to develop a culture removed from that of the Central Plain, characterised by its exquisite wooden temples and unique crafts like lacquerware, silverwork, woodcarvings, ceramics and umbrella-making. Although the city is somewhat strained by masses of visitors, the people are more gracious than in other Thai cities.

Thai and foreign visitors alike will find that Chiang Mai has perhaps the strongest sense of place of any Thai city. Keenly aware of its glorious past, it clings to its northern Thai identity. Obvious manifestations of this are the numerous modern

Chiang Mai Night Bazaar.

> **Fact**
>
> During north Thailand's winter months (December to early February) a jacket or pullover will come in handy at night – but the days are warm and clear. From March to May, a haze of dust and smoke (from the burning of rice fields and agricultural land in the north) often forms over Chiang Mai and the surrounding region: temperatures rise quickly, and overall this is not the best time to visit.

office buildings that bear stylised *kalae* (X-crossed, carved gables typical of traditional northern-style roofs).

Various hill tribes, called *chao khao* (literally "mountain people"), often travel into town from the highlands to trade, adding another element to Chiang Mai culture. One can see their colourful garb and distinctive faces at the Chiang Mai Night Bazaar (see page 274), where they have dealt with Thais and foreign traders for centuries.

Northern Thai cuisine will keep gourmands busy with its exciting blend of Thai, Lao, Shan and Yunnanese elements, and an abundance of cookery courses means that Chiang Mai also caters to those who want to learn Thai culinary arts.

Onward travel options from Chiang Mai are plentiful, with good connections to the rest of Thailand by plane, train and bus, while bicycles, motorcycles and cars are easily arranged through rental agencies, hotels or guesthouses.

ORIGINS

Long a major entrepôt along caravan routes from China's Yunnan Province to the port of Mawlamyine (Moulmein) in Myanmar, Chiang Mai first gained prominence in the 13th century. The northern Thai kingdoms of Lanna and Sukhothai arose in this region and are still widely recognised as sources of Thai nationhood. As Lanna's capital, Chiang Mai became the religious and cultural centre for the entire region.

The city's founder, Mangrai, ruled an empire that ran as far north as Chiang Saen, on the Mekong River. When the Mongol ruler, Kublai Khan, sacked the Burmese city Bagan in 1287, Mangrai formed an alliance with the rulers of Sukhothai to secure his southern boundaries. In 1296, he set up a new base in the Ping valley, and named it Chiang Mai, or "New City". Legend has it that the site was chosen for the auspicious sighting of white deer and a white mouse (with a family of five) at the same time. As the Ping River often floods, Mangrai had 90,000 labourers build his brick-walled city half a kilometre west of the river.

Within a century of Chiang Mai's founding, however, Ayutthaya had replaced Sukhothai as the Thai capital.

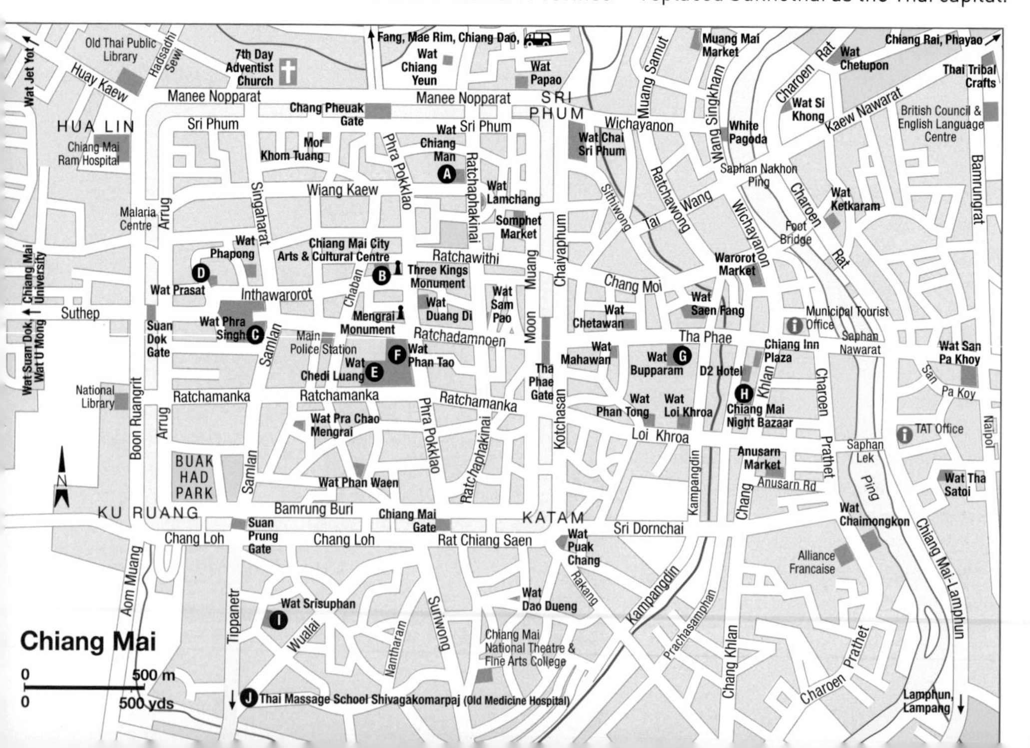

This new kingdom had its own expansionist plans, including designs on its northern neighbour. For 400 years, there was fierce rivalry and sometimes open warfare between the two. In 1515 Ayutthaya crushed an army from Chiang Mai in retaliation for earlier attacks by the Lanna kingdom. And then, in 1556, the Burmese invaded the city, and proceeded to control it for over 200 years.

Under the Thai warlord (and later king) Phaya Taksin, the Thais recaptured Chiang Mai in 1775 and made the Lampang chieftain Chao Kawila the viceroy of Lanna. In 1800, Kawila ordered the massive city walls to be built and began restoring the city to its former prominence. Regional trade also flourished. Chiang Mai continued to enjoy autonomy from Bangkok, at least until the railway facilitated the arrival of central government officials in 1921. In 1932, following the death of the last king of Chiang Mai and the end of absolute monarchy in the country, the north was finally fully incorporated into Thailand.

THE GATED CITY OF CHIANG MAI

The Old City quadrangle, bounded by canalised moats and crumbling brick city walls, is filled with historic temples, shops, old hotels and guesthouses. Away from the main avenues and tourist districts, the narrow, winding *soi* (lanes) of the moated city draw the visitor into an atmospheric world populated by cobblers and other tradespeople, noodle shops and over 30 Lanna-style temples.

WAT CHIANG MAN

The city's spiritual history began with **Wat Chiang Man** Ⓐ (daily 8am–5pm; free), which translates as "steadfast city". Located on Thanon Ratchaphakinai in the northeast part of the old walled city, it is the oldest of Chiang Mai's 300-plus temples, and the first to be built by Mangrai, who lived there during Chiang Mai's construction in 1296. *Lai kham* (gold-leaf stencil designs on red lacquer) on the walls of the main *viharn* (sermon hall) illustrate scenes from the king's life. Two ancient Buddha images are kept

Fact

The northern Thai dialect has its own Lanna script, which is commonly used on monastery signs. Even though many northerners may speak northern Thai as a first language, few today know how to read it as central Thai has become the standard.

ETHNIC DIVERSITY

Chiang Mai's strong sense of identity is apparent to many visitors. Although the locals refer to themselves as "Khon Muang" ("people of the principality"), suggesting a homogeneous people, the city's unique character is in fact born of its ethnic diversity. Particularly during the period of Burmese rule (1556–1775), skilled artisans were resettled here. From Bagan in Burma came temple craftsmen who produce the lacquerware found in the Night Bazaar. From the Shan State of northern Burma came the Yong, talented weavers, and the Kheun, skilled silversmiths, who settled in the Wua Lai district of the city. Colourful hill tribes such as the Akha and Lisu, as well as the Chinese and Pathan Muslims, add further depth to this ethnic mosaic, reflected in the city's festivals, handicrafts and architecture.

Chedi and roof details at Wat Chiang Man.

in a small sanctuary nearby. The first of these, **Phra Satang Man**, is 10cm (4ins) tall and made of crystal, which Mangrai brought to Chiang Mai from Lamphun, where it had reputedly resided for 600 years. Apart from a short time in Ayutthaya, the image has remained in Chiang Mai ever since. During the Songkran festival in April, the tiny statue is paraded through the city streets.

The second image, a stone **Phra Sila Buddha** in bas-relief, is believed to have originated in India around the 8th century. Both statues are said to bring rain and to protect the city from fire.

The other important structure in Wat Chiang Man worth seeing is the **Phra That Chang Lom**, a 15th-century Lanna-style *chedi* buttressed by rows of stucco elephants.

CHIANG MAI CITY ARTS AND CULTURAL CENTRE

Close to Wat Chiang Man, on Thanon Phra Pokklao, is the **Chiang Mai City Arts and Cultural Centre** B (Tue–Sun 8.30am–5pm). It occupies the former Provincial Hall. Built in 1924, this is a good example of European-influenced Thai secular architecture. The centre has interactive displays on Chiang Mai's history and culture and is a useful first stop for visitors wanting to familiarise themselves with the city's heritage.

In a brick plaza in front of the building stands the **Three Kings Monument**, bronze sculptures depicting Phaya Ngam Muang, Phaya Mangrai and Phaya Khun Ramkhamhaeng, the three Thai rulers from whose alliance the Lanna kingdom was formed. Locals still place flowers, incense and candles at the kings' feet in tribute to their powerful spirits.

Ho trai (Buddhist library) at Wat Phra Singh.

WAT PHRA SINGH

Chiang Mai's most important temple, **Wat Phra Singh** C (daily 8am–5pm; free), is imperiously positioned close to Suan Dok Gate at the head of the Old City's principal east–west thoroughfare, Thanon Ratchadamnoen. It was founded in 1345 and is the largest temple within the Old City. The magnificent Lanna-style *ho trai* (Buddhist library), on the north side of the compound, is an elaborate wooden affair raised on a high brick-and-stucco base decorated with bas-relief deities. Behind the main *viharn*, built in 1925, is a wooden *bot* (ordination hall); behind that is a *chedi* built by King Pha Yu in 1345 to store his father's ashes.

Wat Phra Singh's most beautiful building is the small **Phra Viharn Lai Kham** to the left of the *bot*. Built in 1811, the wooden structure's front wall has *lai kham* flowers on red lacquer. Intricately carved wooden frames accent the doors. Its interior is decorated with murals commissioned by Chao Thammalangka, ruler of Chiang Mai from 1813 to 1821. Focusing on the Buddhist stories of Prince Sang Thong (north wall) and the *Heavenly Phoenix* epic (south wall), they also record in fascinating detail aspects of early 19th-century Lanna society, with clear indications of Burmese cultural influence.

The Phra Viharn Lai Kham houses one of Thailand's most famous bronze Buddha images, the **Phra Singh Buddha**. Thai folk tales claim that the Phra Singh Buddha came from Sri Lanka, but its stylistic features suggest a northern Thai, Lanna-era origin. It is almost identical to two other images, one in Nakhon Si Thammarat and the other in Bangkok, whose origins are also shrouded in myth.

WAT PRASAT, WAT CHEDI LUANG AND WAT PHAN TAO

Across from the north side of Wat Phra Singh stands **Wat Prasat** Ⓓ (daily 8am–6pm; free), whose original *viharn* is a well-kept example of Lanna temple architecture. The walls behind the principal Buddha image depict scenes from the Buddha's life.

Calamity is associated with **Wat Chedi Luang** Ⓔ (daily 8am–5pm; free), built in 1441 east of Wat Phra Singh on Thanon Phra Pokklao. King Mangrai was reportedly killed nearby by lightning. The temple is named after the monumental royal *chedi luang* in the central courtyard. A 16th-century earthquake reduced the 90-metre (295ft) *chedi* to 42 metres (140ft). It was never rebuilt, but the base and reliquary were restored in the 1990s with financing from Unesco and the Japanese government. The colossal monument is majestic even in its damaged state.

For 84 years from 1475, Thailand's most revered image, the Emerald Buddha, was housed in the temple's eastern niche before being moved to Vientiane, and later to Wat Phra Kaew in Bangkok (see page 110). A replica was installed in the same niche in 1995 for the city's 700th anniversary.

Close to the temple entrance stands a tall ancient gum tree. According to legend, when it falls, so will the city. As if serving as counterbalance, the *lak muang*, or city pillar, in which the spirit of the city is said to reside, stands near its base.

The *viharn* of **Wat Phan Tao** Ⓕ (daily 8am–5pm; free), next to Wat Chedi Luang, was assembled from the teak pillars and panels of a former palace, and is a masterpiece of wooden construction.

Tip

Red *songthaew* pick-ups may be hailed all over town; fares are a fixed B20 for most journeys. More expensive, but still quite cheap, noisy tuk-tuk carry passengers to any point around town. Expect to pay B40 for short tips.

Tuk-tuks transporting passengers through streets of Chiang Mai.

Its doorway is crowned by a beautiful Lanna peacock framed by *naga*, or mythical serpents. The temple has a collection of rare palm-leaf manuscripts and lacquer manuscript cabinets.

OUTSIDE THE CITY WALLS

Thanon Tha Phae, the street running from the Old City's eastern gate to the Ping River, acts as an extension of the Old City, and is lined with travel agencies, antique shops and restaurants. After it crosses the Ping River via Nawarat Bridge, it becomes Thanon Charoen Muang, leading to the main post office and railway station.

WAT BUPPARAM

Built by Shan and Burmese artisans and financed by Burmese teak merchants who lived in Chiang Mai over a century ago, **Wat Bupparam** G (daily 8am–6pm; free), on Thanon Tha Phae about 500 metres/yds east of the eastern city gate, features a small, ornate Lanna-style ordination hall of carved teak, a larger, modern *viharn* and a Shan-style *chedi*. Guardian deity sculptures surrounding the complex take on whimsical animal forms; look for dogs playing with lions and the mythical *mom*, part-lizard and part-dog.

CHIANG MAI NIGHT BAZAAR

Ancient trade caravans between Yunnan and the Gulf of Martaban stopped Ban Haw market, which is close to the current site of **Chiang Mai Night Bazaar** H (daily 5–11pm), now one of Chiang Mai's best-known tourist attractions. The bazaar covers several blocks of Thanon Chang Khlan between Thanon Tha Phae and Thanon Sri Dornchai, with more stalls offering handicrafts and a good selection of restaurants on nearby side streets, such as the Anusarn Market lane (perpendicular to Thanon Chang Khlan).

Every day, at around 4pm, hundreds of vendors begin lining the street with their huge steel carts. The carts' upper doors swing open to reveal the vendors' wares, which can range from woodcarvings and inexpensive silk and cotton clothing to elaborate Thai- or hill-tribe-inspired home accessories. Colourfully

A mural inside the Phra Viharn Lai Kam, Wat Phra Singh.

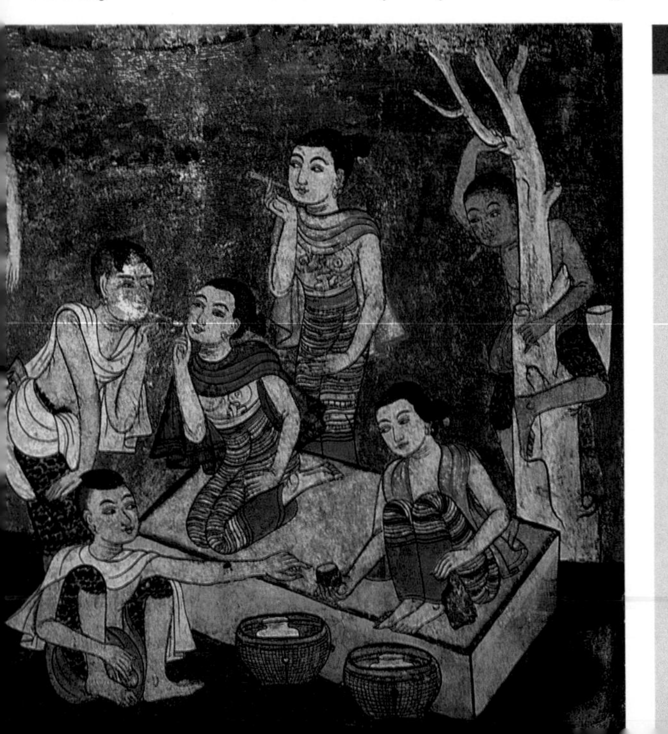

WAT U MONG

South of the Chiang Mai University grounds, the 15th-century Wat U Mong (daily 8am–5pm; free) is set amidst grand teak trees on a flat-topped hill. All but abandoned for years, it was revived in the 1960s under a famous reformer monk, the late Than Ajahn Buddhadasa. A large Lanna-style *chedi* stands on the hill, and a lake on the grounds is surrounded by rustic *guti* (monastic huts). It is one of the few truly quiet spots left in Chiang Mai. The hill beneath the wat contains a honeycomb of underground brick-lined tunnels and meditation cells. Resident foreign monks give free English-language talks on Buddhism at Wat U Mong on Wednesdays and Sundays.

clad traders from various northern hill tribes are usually present at the market.

WAT SRISUPHAN

The early 16th century **Wat Srisuphan** ❶ (daily 8am–5pm; free), south of the Old City walls on Thanon Wualai, was founded by the Thai Khün people who migrated to Chiang Mai from Kengtung in Burma's Shan State. Many silversmith workshops established by the Thai Khün can still be seen along Thanon Wualai.

The temple compound houses several structures including a school, a *chedi* and a large and attractive *viharn*. Most interestingly, the original *ubosot* has been replaced by a strikingly unique example built of pure silver, tin, and silver mixed with aluminium. Silversmiths from the neighbourhood and throughout the country have contributed their labours both in the form of repoussé panels portraying scenes from the Jatakas (tales of the life of Buddha) and intricate silver alloy panels from which the entire structure is fashioned.

Wat Srisuphan is known for its annual Poy Sang Long festival, a Shan-style group ordination of boys as novices, which usually takes place in March. One of the highlights is the colourful street procession, when the boys are garbed in princely regalia before donning the saffron robes of monkhood.

NORTHERN TRADITIONAL HEALING HOSPITAL

Further along Thanon Wualai, at 78/1 Soi Siwaka Komarat, is the **Thai Massage School Shivagakomarpaj** ❶ (better known as Old Medicine Hospital; www.thaimassageschool.ac.th). This is Thailand's main centre for the healing art known as *nuat phaen bohraan* (traditional northern Thai massage therapy and herbal medicine). Many foreigners enrol here for two-week massage courses.

WAT SUAN DOK

About 1km (2/3 mile) west of the western old wall gate on Thanon Suthep is one of Chiang Mai's most impressive temple complexes, **Wat Suan Dok** (daily 8am–6pm; free). The temple dates back to 1373 and was built by the sixth Lanna king, Phyaa Keu Na. At

Fact

Part of Mahachulalongkorn Buddhist University's efforts to spread Buddhism is a forum known as Monk Chat (Mon–Fri 4–7pm; free; www.monkchat.net). A few rooms have been set aside at Wat Suan Dok so that visitors can discuss Buddhism with monastic residents.

Toy stall at the Chiang Mai Night Bazaar.

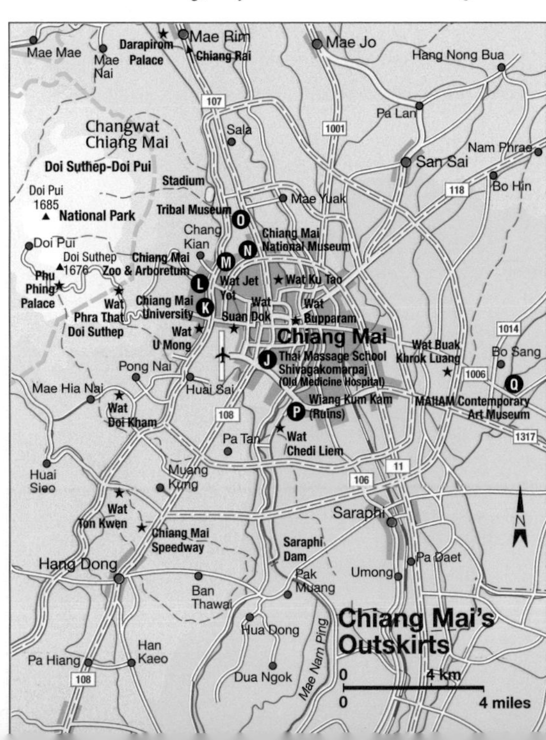

Chedi and Buddha image at Wat Jet Yot.

its northwest corner is a whitewashed *chedi* with the ashes of Chiang Mai's royal family, and a larger central *chedi,* said to hold eight Buddha relics. The monastery grounds also host a branch of the **Mahachulalongkorn Buddhist University** attended by monks and novices from all over Thailand.

CHIANG MAI UNIVERSITY

Further west just off Thanon Suthep is the sprawling 1,412-hectare (3,490-acre) campus of the **Chiang Mai University** Ⓚ. Established in 1964, it is the largest educational institution in the north, and has about 18,000 students in 108 departments, including highly rated faculties of medicine, dentistry and engineering. There are several entrances along Thanon Suthep, and a single entrance on Thanon Huay Kaew to the north. Recreational facilities open to the public include a fitness park (free), swimming pool (charge) and sports track (free). The bucolic **Ang Kaew Reservoir**, at the east end of the campus, is a favourite with strollers and joggers.

CHIANG MAI ZOO AND ARBORETUM

Thanon Huay Kaew, which leads from the northwest corner of the Old City out to Doi Suthep is lined with modern high-rise hotels, shopping centres and apartment buildings. But as the road approaches the mountain these give way to gently rolling hills and expanses of greenery.

This is where **Chiang Mai Zoo and Arboretum** Ⓛ (daily 8am–5pm; additional fee for some facilities, including panda-viewing; www.chiangmai.zoothailand.org) spreads over a well landscaped terrain on Thanon Huay Kaew. It has a wide range of mammals (including two giant pandas), reptiles, birds (over 5,000 birds representing 150 species), a large aquarium and trees – both local and imported.

WAT JET YOT

King Trailokaraja completed **Wat Jet Yot** Ⓜ (daily 6am–6pm; free) in 1455 about 1km (0.6 mile) northwest of the city walls. As its name "Seven Spires" suggests, its roof is topped with seven

Wat Suan Dok, which dates back to 1373.

chedi replicating the Mahabodhi Stupa found in India's Bodh Gaya, where the Buddha gained enlightenment after spending seven weeks in its gardens.

The striking stucco images of the *bodhisattva* (Buddhist saints) that decorate the temple walls are said to be the faces of Trailokaraja's family. Its similarity to a temple in Burma's then-capital of Bagan did not stop invading Burmese from severely damaging it in 1566.

CHIANG MAI NATIONAL MUSEUM

Northeast of Wat Jet Yot is the **Chiang Mai National Museum** ⓝ (Wed–Sun 9am–4pm), established in 1954. The museum has a collection of almost one million artefacts, including precious Buddhist art, northern Thai celadon, historic weaponry, costumes and other items of ethnological interest. Most of the collection is labelled in Thai and English. Exhibits are rotated with its sister museums in the nearby northern cities of Lamphun, Chiang Saen and Nan.

TRIBAL MUSEUM

Ethnology enthusiasts should not miss the smaller but equally fascinating **Tribal Museum** ⓞ (daily 9am–4pm), set in the picturesque gardens of Suan Ratchamangkhala to the north, just off Thanon Chotana. The museum has informative displays labelled in Thai and English of hill-tribe jewellery, costumes, handicrafts, household utensils, architecture, tools and musical instruments set out on its three floors.

Video shows on the tribes are presented at regular intervals throughout the day. The museum is a good first stop for understanding the lifestyles of the various northern hill tribes before setting out on a trek.

WIANG KUM KAM

The Mon people established a satellite capital of the Hariphunchai kingdom in the 11th and 12th centuries close to the southern reach of the Ping River, 5km (3 miles) south of Chiang Mai. Heavy flooding led to the abandonment of **Wiang Kum Kam** ⓟ (daily 8am–5pm) in the 18th century, but the partially restored ruins are still visible.

The most impressive remains include a rectilinear Mon-style *chedi* (part of the more modern Wat Chedi Si Liam) and the brick foundations of several Mon temples, the most complete of which belongs to Wat Kan Thom. In addition, some 1,300 stone inscriptions have been found here. One of the more interesting is an 11th-century slab of stone, whose proto-Thai script predates the better-known Ramkhamhaeng inscription of Sukhothai by a century or more.

MAIIAM ART

Chiang Mai's **MAIIAM Contemporary Art Museum** ⓠ (Wed–Mon 10am–6pm; www.maiiam.com) lies to the east of the city and displays contemporary artworks by Thai and Southeast Asian artists.

Flamingos at the Chiang Mai Zoo.

Intricately carved wooden doorway at Wat Phra That Doi Suthep.

AROUND CHIANG MAI

The area surrounding Chiang Mai provides plenty of opportunities for day trips. There are mountains, lush valleys and national parks, the majestic cliff-top temple of Wat Phra That Doi Suthep and the historic towns of Lamphun and Lampang.

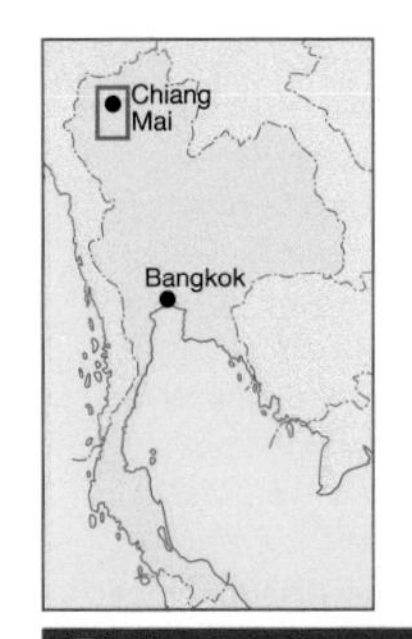

Main attractions

Wat Phra That Doi Suthep
Doi Pui
Bo Sang
Ban Thawai
Wat Phra That Si Chom Tong
Doi Inthanon National Park
Lamphun
Lampang
Mae Sa valley
Tham Chiang Dao

Map on page 281

Some of northwest Thailand's most intriguing attractions are in the surrounding mountains and valleys. To the northwest of the city are the mountains of Doi Suthep and Doi Pui, while southwest is Thailand's highest peak, Doi Inthanon. But the most striking mountain scenery is northwards, around the country's third-highest peak, Doi Chiang Dao (also known as Doi Luang), where forested limestone cliffs and caves stand alongside craggy ranges.

The valley plains south of Chiang Mai contain two of Thailand's most historic towns, Lamphun and Lampang. Both are endowed with lovely Lanna-period Buddhist monasteries, and are not yet swamped by tourism.

WAT PHRA THAT DOI SUTHEP

A steep series of hairpin curves climb the 1,676-metre (5,497ft) **Doi Suthep** Ⓐ, along Thanon Huay Kaew, 15km (9 miles) northwest of the city. Chiang Mai's best-loved temple, **Wat Phra That Doi Suthep** (daily 6am–5pm) lies halfway up the mountain, and was sited here, according to legend, in the mid-1300s by an elephant that was turned loose with a Buddha relic strapped to its back. It climbed then would climb no more. The temple was built at the spot where it halted, and consecrated in 1383.

The road up to the temple passes the entrance to the Chiang Mai Zoo, where red *songthaew* pick-up trucks ply the route to the temple (and to Phu Ping Palace, and a hilltribe village). The scenery is spectacular as the road winds through **Doi Suthep/ Doi Pui National Park** to a large car park across the road from the entrance to Wat Phra That Doi Suthep. Seven-headed *naga* undulate down the balustrades of a 290-step stairway from car park to temple. For the weary, an enclosed cable car makes the ascent for B30. From Wat Phra That Doi Suthep, Chiang Mai is spread out below.

The stairway to the wat.

Fact

Khru Ba Sriwichai (1878–1938) was a charismatic monk who organised the building of a road to Doi Suthep temple as well as many other temple constructions and renovations. Because of his superior ability to organise the local people, he was often in conflict with the Bangkok authorities. Today he is viewed as a *nak bun*, or saint, in Chiang Mai, and a shrine dedicated to him at the foot of Doi Suthep is regularly visited by devotees.

In the temple grounds, beyond cloisters decorated with murals depicting scenes from the Buddha's life, is a 24-metre (80ft) high gilded *chedi*, partially shaded by gilded parasols. The *chedi* is surrounded by an iron fence topped with praying *thewada*, or angels. At the eastern end of the compound, a sermon hall, or *viharn* shelters nuns in white robes chanting prayers each dawn. At sunset, monks chant from a similar hall in the west.

PHU PHING PALACE

From the parking area of Wat Phra That Doi Suthep a road ascends 5km (3 miles) to **Phu Phing Palace** (daily 8.30am–3.30pm; closed when the royal family uses the palace from Jan to early March; www.bhubingpalace.org). Constructed in 1961 as the royal family's winter residence, the palace has audience halls, guesthouses, dining rooms, kitchens and official suites, but only the beautiful gardens are open to the public. It also serves as headquarters for the royal family's agricultural and medical projects in aid of the hill tribes and people living in the nearby villages. Shorts are not allowed, but you can rent trousers at the gate.

DOI PUI

From the palace entrance, the road continues through pine forests to the commercialised Hmong hill-tribe village of **Doi Pui**. Tourism has brought material benefits to the village, including a paved street lined with souvenir stands. Once subsistence farmers, the tribespeople have long since become wise to the tourist dollar, and the sight of a camera may trigger a hand extended for a donation. The Hmong, whose population straddles Thailand, Myanmar and Laos, once grew opium for their livelihood; despite government efforts to steer them towards other crops, many still cultivate small patches of the lucrative poppy deep in the hills.

For those who lack the time to go deeper into the northern hills, Doi Pui offers an example of hill-tribe life, albeit in rather ersatz form. An interesting insight into opium farming is provided by Doi Pui's **Opium Museum**

Doi Pui Hmong village.

CHIANG MAI NIGHT SAFARI

Just before the climb to Doi Suthep, on Thanon Ratchapreuk, **Chiang Mai Night Safari** (daily 11am–10pm; www.chiangmainightsafari.com) is one of Chiang Mai's top visitor attractions. The night safari is more exciting than the day safari, so it's best to arrive an hour before sunset to look around the zoo attractions before taking a tram ride safari, which start from 7.45pm and come with English speaking guides. The safari rides through open land where animals such as giraffes and zebras run free. Tigers, lions and other fascinating creatures are located behind a ditch. You can pet, feed and hold some of the animals. The complex also has restaurants, cabaret and laser shows.

(daily 9am–5pm), which details the process of cultivation and harvest.

A well-worn hiking trail leads to the summit of 1,685-metre (5,525ft) **Doi Pui** **B**, a much-favoured picnicking spot among Chiang Mai residents. Maps of other hiking trails are available at the Doi Suthep/Doi Pui National Park headquarters (daily 8am–6pm; http://portal.dnp.go.th). Two waterfalls, **Sai Yai** and **Monthathon**, can easily be visited in the park.

EAST OF CHIANG MAI

Heading east out of Chiang Mai leads to a handicraft village and a sacred Buddhist cave, but first you will pass **Wat Buak Khrok Luang** **C** (daily 8am–5pm; free) located about 300 metres/yards south off Route 1006, just before the km 4 marker en route to Bo Sang. This is a 19th-century monastery with a charming set of Shan and Lanna murals in remarkably good condition.

BO SANG

About 9km (5.5 miles) east of Chiang Mai on Route 1006 is **Bo Sang** **D** (or Bor Sang), known as the "Umbrella Village" because much of the village is devoted to the crafting of painted paper umbrellas made from the bark of the mulberry tree. But umbrellas are not the only products sold here; there are variety of other handicrafts, including lacquerware, silverware, hill-tribe jewellery, silk, bronze sculptures, woodcarvings and ceramics.

THAM MUANG ON

Some 28km (17 miles) east from Chiang Mai, off Route 1317, on a scenic country road that parallels Route 1006, is **Tham Muang On**, a sacred Buddhist cave set into a huge limestone cliff. A large stalactite found in the cave's main chamber is worshipped as a natural *chedi* by Buddhist visitors.

Close to the cave is a set of steep cliffs known as **Crazy Horse Buttress**, with 16 crags and over 100 popular rock-climbing routes.

The zip-line park **Flight of the Gibbon** (www.flightofthegibbon.com) lies another 20km (12 miles) to the east in the village of Mae Kompong.

Umbrella painter at work in Bo Sang.

Wat Phra That Doi Suthep is located near the summit of Doi Suthep mountain.

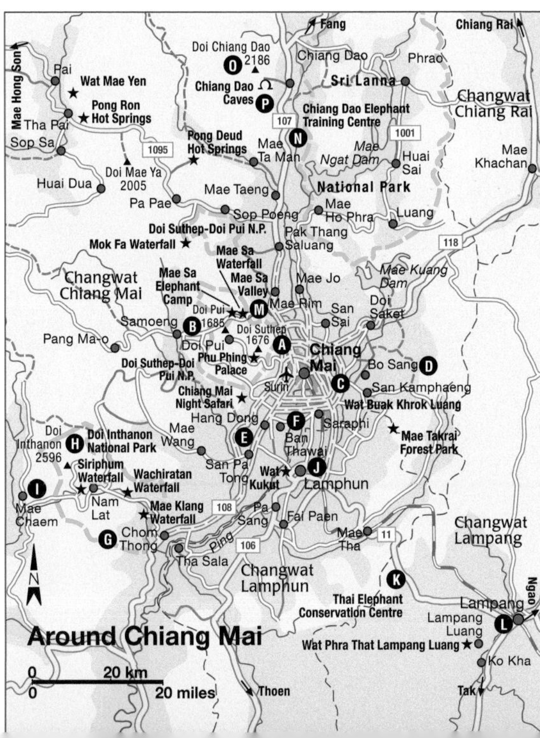

SOUTH OF CHIANG MAI

Route 108 heads south from Chiang Mai to a cluster of three small towns noted for their handicrafts and antiques.

HANG DONG, BAN WAN AND BAN THAWAI

About 15km (9 miles) south of Chiang Mai is **Hang Dong** Ⓔ, a burgeoning centre for ceramics, antiques, wooden furniture and crafts made from woven bamboo, cane and rattan. Shops along Route 108 sell to both retail and wholesale buyers. Either way, bargain for a price.

Ban Wan, to the immediate east of Hang Dong, is a village with a small selection of relatively high-quality antique and furniture shops. A few kilometres further east, its larger, more famous sister **Ban Thawai** Ⓕ has shops and factories of woodcarvings and made-to-order furniture. Even if not buying, Ban Wan and Ban Thawai are worth visiting to watch artisans at work.

WAT PHRA THAT SI CHOM THONG

Route 108 leads to the district of **Chom Thong** Ⓖ, 58km (34 miles) further southwest. This is the jump-off point for Doi Inthanon National Park. The pride of Chom Thong is the elegant temple of **Wat Phra That Si Chom Thong** (daily 7am–6pm), where subdued light accentuates a beautiful collection of bronze Buddhas. The gilded *chedi* dates from 1451, and the sanctuary from 65 years later. The large cruciform *viharn* – deeply incised with floral patterns entwined with birds and *naga* serpents – dominates the temple compound. Four standing Buddhas, clothed as celestial kings, flank the *viharn*.

While much of the temple decoration reflects a Shan/Burmese penchant for elaboration, the central Buddha image, with its protective *naga*, seems eminently Lanna, and resembles the image at Wat Phra Singh in Chiang Mai. On either side of the *viharn* are enshrined miniature gold and silver Buddha images, some bejewelled and metallic, others carved from crystal. Behind the main compound, a large **meditation centre** (tel: 0-5382 6869) offers 10- to 26-day courses in *vipassana* (insight meditation).

Giant yang trees line the road from Chiang Mai to Lamphun.

DOI INTHANON N P

From Chom Thong, the gateway to **Doi Inthanon National Park** Ⓗ (daily 5am–6pm; http://portal.dnp.go.th), is another 47km (28 miles) up steep, forest-clad slopes to the top of **Doi Inthanon**, which at 2,596 metres (8,516ft) is Thailand's highest peak. The ashes of Chiang Mai's last king are enshrined on its mist-shrouded summit. Hmong and Karen villages have been allowed to remain in the reserve since they take part in temperate-weather vegetable farming – part of the Royal Project's opium cultivation eradication program.

Of the trio of waterfalls along the way to the summit – **Mae Klang**, **Wachiratan** and **Siriphum** – Mae Klang is the most popular and most accessible, as a footbridge links the viewpoints at various elevations. By making prior arrangements with park authorities, visitors can take a three- to five-day trek up the mountain on foot or by pony. Several campsites (B40) and bungalows (B800–1,000) provide simple accommodation for trekkers (tel: 0-5328 6730 for reservations).

MAE CHAEM

Visitors to Doi Inthanon can take a side trip to secluded **Mae Chaem ❶**, famous for the distinctive weaving used to make the *pha sin*, a skirt worn by northern Thai women.

A few kilometres south of Mae Chaem is **Wat Pa Daet** (daily 8am–5pm; free). Thai art historians admire the temple's rare, post-Lanna murals for their velvety blues and reds, accented by bold black outlines that lend a poetic rusticity to the art. The murals provide a rich source of detail on traditional clothing, with vivid depictions of the loom-woven, horizontal-striped women's skirts, and intricate waist-to-knee blue tattoos once worn by virtually all northern Thai men.

LAMPHUN

Straddling the Ping River 25km (15 miles) south of Chiang Mai along tree-lined Route 106, the town of **Lamphun ❶** is said to date back to the 8th century. It was a centre of Mon culture until King Mangrai overran the city in 1281. Highway 11, the main road from Chiang Mai to Lampang, bypasses Lamphun, which has enabled the town to preserve its mellow, upcountry quality. Today, it is famed for its attractive, confident women, succulent *lamyai* fruit and two elegant temples. It has also become a popular place of residence for Thai artists seeking peace from city life.

WAT PHRA THAT HARIPHUNCHAI

Lamphun houses two of the most famous temples in Thailand. **Wat Phra That Hariphunchai** (daily 6am–6pm) has one of the eight holiest *chedi* in the country. For the best perspective of the temple, enter through its riverside gate, where statues of mythical lions guard the portals. Inside the large compound, monks study in a Buddhist

Fact

For one week every August, Lamphun's streets fill with floats decorated with *lamyai* fruit to celebrate the annual harvest. Other Lamyai Festival activities include a Miss Lamyai beauty contest, boisterous night markets and live street concerts.

Wachiratan Waterfall, Doi Inthanon National Park.

Tip

Don't miss seeing Baan Sao Nak, or "Many Pillars House" (daily 10am–5pm; tel: 054-227 653). Located in the northern part of Lampang town, this Lanna-style house built in 1895 is supported by an astonishing 116 teak pillars.

school set amidst monuments and buildings that date back to the 11th century, making this temple one of the oldest in northern Thailand. **Chedi Suwan**, the 50-metre (165ft) high gold-topped tower in the centre of the courtyard was built in 1418 and may in fact have been constructed over an older, smaller *chedi*.

A gilt-roofed *ho trai* (library) stands to the left of an open-air pavilion that shelters one of the world's largest bronze gongs. The temple museum contains several styles of old Buddhist art.

WAT CHAMA THEWI

A kilometre (0.6 mile) west of Lamphun's old moat stands **Wat Chama Thewi** (daily 8am–6pm; free), also known as **Wat Kukut**. It was originally built by the Dvaravati Mon in the 8th or 9th century and rebuilt by the Hariphunchai Mon in 1218. The monastery contains a superb and unusual tower called Chedi Kukut. The rectilinear *chedi* consists of five tiers, each of which has three niches. Each niche houses a Buddha statue, making for an impressive display of 15 Buddha images on each side. The overall plan is very similar to Sri Lanka's Satmahal Prasada, which is approximately a century older, suggesting a Buddhist link between Hariphunchai and Sri Lanka.

HARIPHUNCHAI MUSEUM

At nearby Thanon Inthayongyot is the **Hariphunchai National Museum** (Wed–Sun 9am–4pm), which has a very good collection of historical artefacts on the surrounding region. These mainly focus on the Hariphunchai kingdom, along with a number of items from the Dvaravati and Lanna kingdoms.

THAI ELEPHANT CONSERVATION CENTRE

Off Highway 11, southeast towards Lampang from Lamphun or Chiang Mai, is the royally sponsored **Thai Elephant Conservation Centre** Ⓚ (daily 8am–3.30pm; charge; www.thailandelephant.org). It stages shows three times a day a day (10am, 11am and 1.30pm) to demonstrate how elephants were

Horse-drawn carts are a feature of Lampang.

QUEEN CHAMADEVI

The first ruler of the Mon statelet of Hariphunchai, later to become Lamphun, was a woman called Chamadevi. She ruled the city wisely, and spread the Buddhist faith. Local legend recounts that she received the unwelcome attentions of King Viranga, the ruler of the indigenous Lawa, an uncivilised, animist people from the nearby hills. Protocol demanded that she agree to the marriage, but she added a condition; he must hurl a spear from his native Chiang Mai to Lamphun. His first effort landed just outside her city's walls. Queen Chamadevi then sent him a gift of a hat, which he immediately placed on his head. The hat, however, was made from her petticoat and this sapped Viranga of his supernatural powers and his subsequent efforts fell short of his target.

once used as work animals for logging and agriculture. The elephants have been trained to play music together on gigantic Thai musical instruments. They can also hold brushes in their trunks.

For an additional fee, visitors can take elephant rides through the grounds, lasting from 15 minutes to one hour. An on-site hospital treats sick or injured animals. You can learn to be an elephant handler *(mahout)* here, with courses lasting one to three days. They also have homestay facilities. While these practices have been criticised by animal-rights groups, the centre nevertheless retains its popularity.

LAMPANG

About 30km (18 miles) further to the southeast, Highway 11 enters the provincial capital of **Lampang** ⓛ. Although much of its bucolic tranquillity has disappeared, it retains one relic found in no other Thai city: horse-drawn carriages. These can be hired by the journey or by the hour. There are few more romantic experiences in Thailand than clip-clopping down a moonlit backstreet.

WAT PHRA KAEW DON TAO

Several unique temples in Lampang, each showing various degrees of Burmese, Shan and Lanna influence, are worth seeing. On the right bank of the Wang River, **Wat Phra Kaew Don Tao** (daily 8am–6pm) is a striking fusion of Burmese and Lanna architecture. In the *mondop* (square pavilion), teak columns soar to a ceiling covered in a kaleidoscope of inlaid enamel, mother-of-pearl and cut glass, depicting mythical animals.

WAT CHEDI SAO

Surrounded by rice fields 6km (4 miles) north of town, the 20 chalk-white *chedi* of **Wat Chedi Sao** (daily 8am–6pm; free) occupy lovely monastery grounds landscaped with casuarinas and bougainvillea. A 15th-century solid gold Buddha image weighing 1,507kg (3,311lbs) is on display in a glass-encased room built over a pond.

Fact

Horse-drawn carts are a feature of Lampang. A 15-minute jaunt around town will cost you B150. They can usually be found near the big hotels in town.

Wat Phra Kaew Don Tao.

Chiang Dao Cave, Chiang Mai Province.

WAT PHRA THAT LAMPANG LUANG

A masterpiece of northern Thai temple architecture, **Wat Phra That Lampang Luang** (daily 8am–5pm; free) is situated 20km (12 miles) south of town in Ko Kha district. Cherished by scholars for its antiquity and delicate artwork, the temple compound is all that remains of a fortress city that flourished more than a millennium ago. Some of the temple murals are the only existing examples in the north of the traditional local technique of *lai khram*, in which drawings are etched onto a gold coating. But skill in the technique is fading and restoration work in 2012 has been much criticised. The temple's triple-roofed, open-sided main chapel, **Viharn Luang**, was built in 1476 and is thought to be the oldest existing wood building in Thailand. A large gilded and enclosed shrine in the back of the hall displays a venerable 16th-century bronze Buddha image. Other important structures include the 45-metre (147ft) **Phra That Lampang Luang** (a copper-plated, Lanna-style *chedi*) and the diminutive **Viharn Nam Taem**, a 16th-century Thai Lü-style building famous for its surviving pastel-hued murals.

NORTH OF CHIANG MAI

Northwest of Chiang Mai is **Mae Sa** Ⓜ, a valley that was once a thriving agricultural region. Today, a variety of tourist developments have taken hold, including resorts; elephant camps; butterfly farms; orchid nurseries; animal exhibitions; and adventure parks.

One of the most visited is **Mae Sa Elephant Camp** (shows at 8am, 9.40am and 1.30pm daily; charge; www.maesaelephantcamp.com), near the **Mae Sa Waterfall**. Visitors can watch elephant activities, ride them and take an elephant training course. While these practices have been criticised by animal-rights groups, the centre nevertheless retains its popularity.

Sai Nam Phung Orchid and Butterfly Farm (daily 7.30am–5pm) is the better of two orchid options. About 2km (1.6 miles) away are the **Queen Sirikit Botanic Gardens** (daily

Visit to the Sai Nam Phung Orchid and Butterfly Farm.

8.30am–5pm; www.qsbg.org), developed with the help of Britain's famous Kew Gardens and including a 5km (3-mile) nature trail.

To reach the popular town of Pai take Route 107 north from Chiang Mai and then Route 1095 to the left. Route 107 continues towards Chiang Dao past rice fields and small villages, then climbs past Mae Taeng into the Mae Ping Gorge, which forms the southern end of the Chiang Dao valley. On the left, as you follow the river bank, is the silhouette of Doi Chiang Dao mountain. The road continues to the northern town of **Fang.**

CHIANG DAO ELEPHANT TRAINING CENTRE

At the km 56 marker is the **Chiang Dao Elephant Training Centre** N (daily 8am–15pm; charge; www.chiangdaoelephantcamp.com) on the bank of the Ping River, which has elephant training routines daily at 10am. You can ride the elephants (mornings only), including to a hilltribe village, and take a bamboo raft for a 45-minute trip down the river.

DOI CHIANG DAO

About 60km (40 miles) north of Chiang Mai on Route 107, a dirt road branches left to **Doi Chiang Dao** O, which at 2,186 metres (7,175ft) is Thailand's third-highest peak. A jeep or a trail bike is needed to negotiate this 9km (6-mile) long track up to the Hmong village of Pakkia on the mountain. Entry to the sanctuary is restricted, and permission must be obtained from the wildlife headquarters near **Tham Pha Plong Monastic Centre** at the foot of the mountain.

THAM CHIANG DAO

Further north, Route 107 enters the quiet town of **Chiang Dao**, located 70km (45 miles) from Chiang Mai. At the far end of town, a road leads off west and to the left for 5km (3 miles) to the caves at **Tham Chiang Dao** P (daily 7am–5pm; www.chiangdaocave.com). Guides lead visitors deep into high caverns that contain Buddha statues. Further down is a large, reclining limestone Buddha.

Tip

A good day trip from Chiang Mai, either by car or motorcycle, is the "Samoeng Loop", a journey of just under 100km (60 miles). Head north towards Mae Rim (Route 107), then follow the winding road (Route 1096) up the Mae Sa valley around the back of Doi Pui. The road emerges near Hang Dong and continues north back to Chiang Mai.

Wat Pra That Lampang Luang.

Wat Tha Ton, Chiang Mai.

CHIANG RAI AND EAST

The mere mention of the "Golden Triangle" – the point where Thailand, Laos and Myanmar meet – evokes thoughts of uncertain frontiers and illicit smuggling. There's romance, adventure and much else to enjoy in this little-visited area of north Thailand.

Like other cities of the north, **Chiang Rai** has undergone rapid development in recent years, not only in the town itself but also in the surrounding hills, where holiday homes for affluent Thais are springing up. Disappointingly for travellers seeking the picturesque, little of Chiang Rai's rich past is still extant. Outside the provincial capital, however, there are many rewarding sights, both historical and natural. To the east, the seldom-visited provinces of Phrae and Nan reveal aspects of northern Thai life and culture that only a small percentage of tourists ever encounter.

CHIANG MAI TO CHIANG RAI

For most visitors, the trip to Chiang Rai begins in Chiang Mai, along Route 118. The 183km (114-mile) journey takes about three hours, meandering through hills and valleys.

But for those with more time, it is recommended to take the longer route on Route 107 due north past Chiang Dao to **Fang** ❷ 150km (94 miles) from Chiang Mai. Fang was established by King Mangrai in the late 1260s, but after being destroyed by the Burmese in the early 1800s, it remained uninhabited until the 1880s. During the 1950s, the district witnessed a black-gold rush following a minor discovery of crude oil. Production never matched expectations, but "nodding donkey" pumps still groan and grind in the fields to the west of town. Fang has a rough reputation for *yaa baa* (amphetamine) smugglers, although nothing in its seemingly benign appearance would suggest it.

DOI ANG KHANG

Some 40km (25 miles) west of Fang **Doi Ang Khang** ❸, at an altitude of 1,935 metres (6,348ft), has a pleasant year-round climate (albeit with temperatures as low as freezing in winter). The

Main attractions

Doi Ang Khang
Mae Salong
Chiang Rai
Chiang Saen
Chiang Khong
Sop Ruak
Hall of Opium
Mae Sai
Tham Luang
Nan
Phrae

Map on page 290

Sakura trees line the roads at Doi Ang Khang.

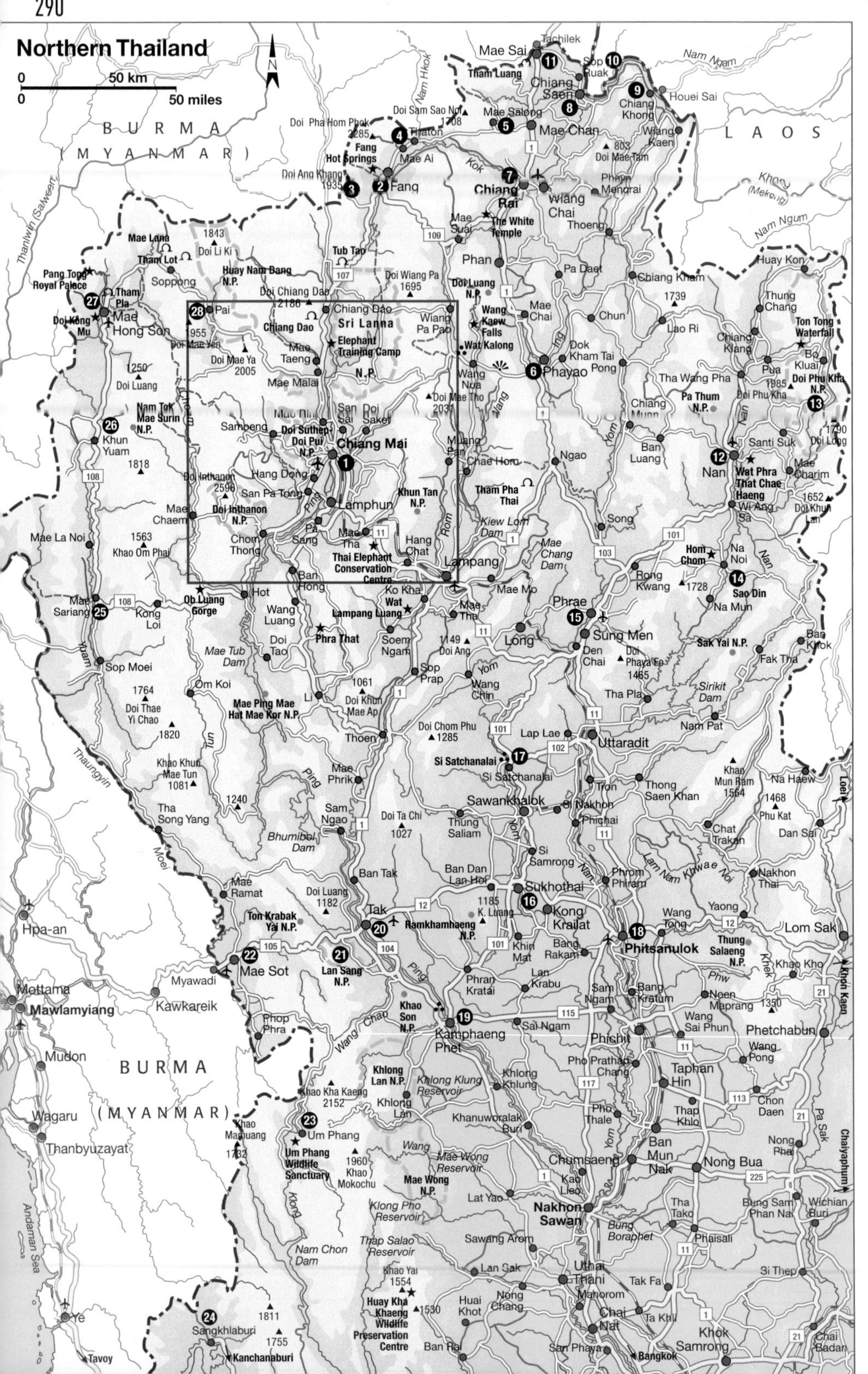
Northern Thailand
0
50 km
0
50 miles
N
BURMA
(MYANMAR)
LAOS
Mae Sai
Tachilek
Tham Luang
Sop Ruak
Chiang Saen
Chiang Khong
Houei Sai
Nam Ngam
Doi Sam Sao Noi
1708
Mae Salong
Mae Chan
Wiang Kaen
803
Doi Mae Tam
Doi Pha Hom Phok
2285
Thaton
Fang Hot Springs
Mae Ai
Doi Ang Khang
1935
Fang
Kok
Chiang Rai
Wiang Chai
Phaya Mengrai
Khong (Mekong)
Nam Ngum
Thoeng
Mae Suai
The White Temple
Mae Lana
1813
Doi Li Ki
Tham Lot
Soppong
Huay Nam Dang N.P.
Tub Tao
Doi Wiang Pa
1695
Phan
Pa Daet
Chiang Kham
Huay Kon
Pang Tong Royal Palace
Tham Pla
Mae Hong Son
Doi Kong Mu
Pai
1955
Doi Mae Yen
Doi Chiang Dao
2186
Chiang Dao
Sri Lanna N.P.
Elephant Training Camp
Wiang Pa Pao
Doi Luang N.P.
Wang Kaew Falls
Wat Kalong
Mae Chai
Chun
1739
Thung Chang
Lao Ri
Ton Tong Waterfall
Chiang Klang
Doi Mae Ya
2005
Mae Taeng
Mae Malai
Wang Nua
Dok Kham Tai
Phayao
Pong
Tha Wang Pha
Pua
Bo Kluai
1985
Doi Phu Kha
Doi Phu Kha N.P.
1250
Doi Luang
Doi Mae Tho
2031
Pa Thum N.P.
Chiang Muan
Nam Tok Mae Surin N.P.
Samoeng
Mae Rim
San Sai
Doi Saket
Doi Suthep-Doi Pui N.P.
Chiang Mai
Muang Pan
Chae Hom
Ngao
Yom
Ban Luang
Santi Suk
1790
Doi Long
Khun Yuam
1818
Hang Dong
Doi Inthanon
2596
San Pa Tong
Lamphun
Khun Tan N.P.
Tham Pha Thai
Nan
Wat Phra That Chae Haeng
Mae Charim
1652
Doi Khun Lan
Wi Ang Sa
Mae Chaem
Doi Inthanon N.P.
Pa Sang
Mae Tha
Kiew Lom Dam
Song
Mae La Noi
1563
Khao Om Phai
Chom Thong
Thai Elephant Conservation Centre
Hang Chat
Lampang
Mae Chang Dam
Hom Chom
Na Noi
Rong Kwang
1728
Sao Din
Na Mun
Mae Sariang
Kong Loi
Ob Luang Gorge
Hot
Ban Hong
Ko Kha
Wat Lampang Luang
Mae Mo
Mae Tha
Phrae
Sung Men
Long
Den Chai
Sak Yai N.P.
Fak Tha
Ban Khok
Wang Luang
Phra That
Soem Ngam
1149
Doi Ang
Doi Phaya Fo
1465
Mae Tub Dam
Doi Tao
Sop Moei
Yuam
Sop Prap
Wang Chin
Tha Pla
Sirikit Dam
1764
Doi Thae Yi Chao
Om Koi
1061
Doi Khun Mae Ap
Li
Mae Ping Mae Hat Mae Kor N.P.
Nam Pat
1820
Doi Chom Phu
1285
Lap Lae
Uttaradit
Thoen
Si Satchanalai
Si Satchanalai
Thaungyin
Khao Khun Mae Tun
1081
Mae Phrik
Khao Mun Ram
1564
Na Haew
Tron
Thong Saen Khan
1468
Phu Kat
Dan Sai
Loei
1240
Tha Song Yang
Sam Ngao
Doi Ta Chi
1027
Thung Saliam
Sawankhalok
Si Nakhon
Phichai
Chat Trakan
Bhumibol Dam
Si Samrong
Moei
Ban Tak
Ban Dan Lan Hoi
Phrom Phiram
Lam Nam Khwae Noi
Nakhon Thai
Mae Ramat
Doi Luang
1182
1185
K. Luang
Sukhothai
Kong Krailat
Yaong
Wang Tong
Lom Sak
Hpa-an
Ton Krabak Yai N.P.
Tak
Ramkhamhaeng N.P.
Phitsanulok
Thung Salaeng N.P.
Mae Sot
Lan Sang N.P.
Khiri Mat
Bang Rakam
Khek
Khao Kho
Myawadi
Kawkareik
Mottama
Mawlamyiang
Phran Kratai
Lan Krabu
Sam Ngam
Bang Kratum
Noen Maprang
1350
Khon Kaen
Khao Son N.P.
Kamphaeng Phet
Sai Ngam
Phichit
Wang Sai Phun
Phetchabun
Phop Phra
Wang Chao
Mudon
Pho Prathap Chang
Wang Pong
BURMA
(MYANMAR)
Khlong Lan N.P.
Khlong Klung Reservoir
Khlong Khlung
Taphan Hin
Khao Kha Kaeng
2152
Khlong Lan
Chon Daen
Wagaru
Khao Mamuang
1732
Um Phang
Khanuworalak Buri
Pho Thale
Thap Khlo
Pa Sak
Thanbyuzayat
Um Phang Wildlife Sanctuary
1960
Khao Mokochu
Wang
Mae Wong Reservoir
Mae Wong N.P.
Chumsaeng
Ban Mun Nak
Nong Bua
Nong Pha
Chaiyaphum
Andaman Sea
Klong
Klong Pho Reservoir
Lat Yao
Kao Lieo
Nakhon Sawan
Tha Tako
Bung Sam Phan Nai
Wichian Buri
Bung Boraphet
Phaisali
Thap Salao Reservoir
Nam Chon Dam
Sawang Arom
Khao Yai
1554
Lan Sak
Uthai Thani
Tak Fa
Si Thep
Manorom
Huai Khot
Nong Chang
Huay Kha Khaeng Wildlife Preservation Centre
1530
Chai Nat
Ta Khli
Ye
1811
Sangkhlaburi
1755
Ban Rai
San Phaya
Khok Samrong
Chai Badan
Tavoy
Kanchanaburi
Bangkok
Thanlwin (Salween)
Nam Hkok
Ing
Lao
Ping
Wang
Rom
Tun
Nan
Phw
1
11
12
21
101
102
103
104
105
107
108
109
113
115
117
225
1
2
3
4
5
6
7
8
9
10
11
12
13
14
15
16
17
18
19
20
21
22
23
24
25
26
27
28

agricultural station here, supported by the Thai monarchy, specialises in the research of temperate fruit trees, vegetables, herbs and flowers. One of the best accommodation options on the mountain is **Angkhang Nature Resort** (www.mosaic-collection.com/angkhang), with private balconies and mountain views.

THATON AND MAE SALONG

A few kilometres south of Fang, Route 109 cuts east towards Chiang Rai. Alternatively, north from Fang, a rough road leads 25km (15 miles) to **Thaton ❹**, on the banks of the **Kok River**. Here, you can rent a boat for an exciting three-hour journey down the Kok River to Chiang Rai.

From Thaton, the unusual hill town of **Mae Salong ❺** (also known as **Santikhiri**) is to the north, on a dusty, but wide, paved road. It climbs a ridge along the Myanmar border, emerging at the small hillside town where the walls are decorated with red banners covered in gold Chinese characters and everyone speaks Chinese.

Many residents are descendants of Kuomintang soldiers given refuge in Thailand after China's Communist takeover. Many became involved in the opium trade, but, under pressure from the Thai military and with incentives from the monarchy, they gradually converted to other crops, and by the late 1980s large-scale poppy cultivation was finished. Many of the locals now tend tea plantations and brew potent rice wines.

ROUTE 118 VIA PHAYAO

Route 118 from Chiang Mai leads northeast via **Doi Saket**, a community where Thai-style retirement homes are popular with Westerners. About 74km (44 miles) further on, a detour to Wang Nua (Route 120) leads east for 59km (35 miles) across rolling hills to **Phayao ❻**, focal point of the hugely fertile **Ing River** basin. The province encompasses an extensive network of ponds, swamps and waterways and was part of Chiang Mai Province until 1977, when it gained independent provincial status.

Although relatively small (pop. approximately 21,000) and undistinguished, the provincial capital and nearby districts hold considerable interest for archaeologists, who believe that an unbroken series of at least four former settlements existed in the area before the Lanna period. From the remains of a moat and eight city gates, they estimate the oldest site may predate the Bronze Age.

KWAN PHAYAO AND ENVIRONS

Phayao's landmark lake **Kwan Phayao** covers 18 sq km (7 sq mile) at the eastern edge of town. It is a source of livelihood for farmers and fishers and the main local source of recreation. Among its resident fish is the sailfin shark (actually related to the carp), which is also found in the Salween and Mekong rivers. Restaurants line a scenic promenade on the lake's east side.

Tip

It's possible to travel from Thaton to Chiang Rai by boat via the Kok River. Either take the public boat (departure daily 12.30pm; B350 per person) or hire a boat (B2,300 for the entire boat). The ride will take about three hours during the rainy season, but can take longer if water levels are low.

A farmer picking strawberries on Doi An Khang Mountain, Chiang Mai.

On the southern edge of the lake, **Wat Si Khom Kham** (daily 8am–6pm; free) is considered the area's most important temple because it houses a 400-year old, 16 metre (55ft) high Buddha image called Phra Chao Ton Luang. Artist Angkarn Kalayanapongsa uses bright colours and modern brush techniques to cleverly reinterpret traditional mural themes into contemporary Buddhist ones in a new *bot* (ordination hall) on the lake's edge.

Next to Wat Si Khom Kham, the well-designed **Phayao Cultural Exhibition Hall** (Wed–Sun 9am–4pm) contains a collection of historic sandstone sculptures from pre-Lanna cultures in Phayao, along with lacquerware, ceramics, textiles and other handicrafts.

CHIANG RAI

From Phayao, Highway 1 continues north for some 100km (62 miles) towards **Chiang Rai ❼**, the capital of Thailand's northernmost province. King Mangrai, who also established Chiang Mai, founded the city in 1292. He is commemorated by a much-venerated statue in the northeast of the city, next to a reconstructed stretch of the old city wall.

Buddhist monks sweeping the street outside Wat Phra Kaew, Chiang Rai.

WAT PHRA SINGH AND WAT PHRA KAEW

Despite its exotic location at an elevation of 580 metres (1,900ft), Chiang Rai itself is short on ambience and historic ruins. Two of the town's most important temples, Wat Phra Singh and Wat Phra Kaew, share the distinction of having once sheltered famous images.

The *chedi* and *viharn* (sermon hall) at **Wat Phra Singh** (daily 8am–5pm; free) have been restored too many times to allow accurate dating, but documents suggest it was built in the 15th century or earlier. **Wat Phra Kaew** (daily 8am–5pm; free), founded in the 13th century on Thanon Trairat behind Wat Phra Singh, was the original residence of Thailand's holiest Buddha image, now housed in the temple of the same name in Bangkok. Local chronicles say its *chedi* was struck by lightning in 1434, revealing a jadeite Buddha image that became known as the Emerald Buddha. A close copy carved of Canadian jade, commissioned in 1990 and called the Phra Yok Chiang Rai (Chiang Rai Jade Buddha), occupies an ornate shrine, the **Haw Phra Kaew**, on the temple grounds.

HILL TRIBE MUSEUM

Another worthy stop is the **Hill Tribe Museum and Education Centre** (Mon–Fri 8.30am–6pm, Sat–Sun 10am–6pm; www.pdacr.org) on Thanon Tanalai. It provides a useful overview of hill-tribe community life and sells ethnic handicrafts at its gift shop. All proceeds go towards supporting hill tribe community projects.

MAE FAH LUANG ART & CULTURE PARK

About 5km (3 miles) west of town, the Mae Fah Luang Art & Cultural Park (Tue–Sun 8am-6pm; www.maefahluang.org) has three pavilions containing permanent and visiting exhibitions of rare Lanna cultural artefacts, including architectural styling and sacred and ritual objects such as Buddha images and candelabra.

THE BLACK HOUSE

North of Chiang Rai along Highway 1, celebrated Thai artist Thawan Duchanee has run Baandam, or Black House (daily 9am–5pm; free; www.thawan-duchanee.com), for over 30 years. The compound and the 40 huts inside hold weird and wonderful exhibits of artefacts, oddities and contemporary art from around the world, including many of Thawan's own pieces.

THE NORTHERN BORDER AND GOLDEN TRIANGLE

The **Mekong River** is the 12th-longest river in the world at 4,000km (2,500 miles), and passes through six countries on its way to the South China Sea. It also defines much of the remote border area between Thailand and Laos.

CHIANG SAEN

The ancient capital of **Chiang Saen** ❽ – 60km (37 miles) northeast of Chiang Rai – nestles near the point where Myanmar, Laos and Thailand meet. For years this area, known as the Golden Triangle, produced a considerable portion of the world's opium. Thailand's contribution has dropped greatly in the past 25 years, but Laos, and especially Myanmar, continue to produce opium in large quantities. These days Thai border patrols are often in armed conflict with amphetamine smugglers running drugs made in factories in Myanmar.

Scholars believe Chiang Saen was founded around the end of the 13th century and heavily fortified about 100 years later by a grandson of King Mangrai. The Burmese captured it in the 16th century. Rama I retook it in the early 1800s, but ordered the town abandoned. It remained deserted for nearly a century. Today, it is a thriving river port for barges from China carrying all manner of Chinese exports. Passengers can now travel up the Mekong by boat on an express passenger boat to the Chinese town of Jinghong (a visa must be obtained in advance at any Chinese consulate, such as in Chiang Mai or Bangkok).

Quote

"Necessity knows no law. We fight the evil of Communism, and to fight you must have an army, which must have guns that are bought with money. In these mountains, the only money is opium, which is why we deal in it."

KMT General Duan Shi Wen, interviewed in Doi Mae Salong, Thailand, 1967.

WAT RONG KHUN

As if in answer to the Black House, one of Thailand's most extraordinary temples, Wat Rong Khun, or the White Temple (temple daily 6.30am–6pm, gallery Mon–Fri 8am–5.30pm, Sat–Sun until 6pm), appears off Highway 1, 13km (8 miles) south of Chiang Rai. Its pure white spires look like a fairytale palace from *Snow White*. Artist Chalermchai Kositpipat doesn't expect the temple, which opened to the public in 1997, to be fully complete until 2070. The entrance is across a bridge, below which 500 sculpted hands reach skywards, seemingly from hell, to implore salvation. Among the offerings inside, suppurating hands hold burning cigarettes and the murals common to most temples are here of a modern bent, including planes hitting New York's Twin Towers, satellites in outer space, and super heroes from the Matrix's Neo to Batman. It's a must-see.

Wat Pa Sak, Chiang Saen.

Chiang Saen's setting on the Mekong River strongly enhances the charm of its old temples. Moreover, it is one of the few ancient towns in Thailand to have retained most of its lovely old trees. The remains of its once-formidable wall and moat can be seen at its perimeter, and the ruins of ancient monuments are scattered every-where.

CHIANG SAEN NATIONAL MUSEUM AND WAT CHEDI LUANG

Along the main street Thanon Phahonyothin is **Chiang Saen National Museum** (Wed–Sun 8.30am–4.30pm; www.virtualmuseum.finearts.go.th), with a good assortment of Lanna-period Buddha images and northern Thai ceramics as well as prehistoric and hill-tribe artefacts. Behind are the ruins of **Wat Chedi Luang**. The 60-metre (200ft) tall, 13th-century *chedi* stands out in style as well as size; its bricks rise from an octagonal base to a bell-shaped top.

WEST OF CHIANG SAEN

Just west of town stands **Wat Pa Sak** (daily 8am–5pm; free), whose name is derived from the 300 teak, or *sak*, trunks used for its original enclosure. The temple's foundation was laid in 1295, during the reign of King Mangrai. Earlier Srivijaya and Dvaravati influences, along with the then-prominent Sukhothai style, are evident in the *that* (reliquary), as well as the clothing worn by the deities.

Located about 1km (0.6 mile) west of the town gate, **Wat Phra That Chom Kitti** (daily 8.30am–5pm; free) occupies a hill commanding a good view of Chiang Saen. Chronicles suggest that the old *that*, with a leaning top, was built around the 10th century and restored at least twice. Below it lies a ruined *chedi* of **Wat Chom Chang**. From here, a staircase leads further downhill and back to town.

CHIANG KHONG

A scenic excursion from Chiang Saen is by longtail boat down the Mekong as far as **Chiang Khong** ❾, a three-hour trip possible after the rainy season, when the water level is high. The river follows an approximately S-shaped

Monument beside the Mekong at Sop Ruak.

course, first flowing southeast to the mouth of the Kok River, then curving north between hills and mountains, before finally heading south again. Then for a thrilling last 20km (12-mile) the boats ride down narrow stomach-churning rapids beneath steep, jungle-clad mountains.

At Chiang Khong, the river widens slightly. The Lao town of **Houei Sai** lies opposite, and ferries carry both passenger and vehicular traffic across the river, including large trucks with shipping containers headed for China, which lies a mere 250km (150 miles) to the north, on what are now quite passable roads. The towns on both sides of the river owe their vibrancy to this border traffic, which increased further with the fourth Friendship Bridge between Thailand and Laos. Visas for Laos are now available on arrival in Houei Sai.

SOP RUAK

Head north for around 9km (6 miles) from Chiang Saen to reach the small town of **Sop Ruak** ⑩, which proudly promotes itself as the "Heart of the Golden Triangle". In recent years, the town has heavily cashed in on the wild mystique of the area, and is home to several good resorts and hotels. The main street is lined with souvenir shops that sell a variety of local textiles and plastic kitsch, as well as numerous food stalls and restaurants.

Several boat trips are possible from Sop Ruak, including ferries to Chiang Saen and Chiang Khong, as well as round trips on the Mekong and Ruak rivers skirting the Myanmar and Lao frontiers.

HALL OF OPIUM

In reality, Sop Ruak has little to hold the traveller's attention, aside from views of neighbouring Myanmar and Laos. Worth a visit, though, is the impressive **Hall of Opium** (Tue–Sun 8.30am–4pm; www.maefahluang.org), just opposite the luxury **Anantara Golden Triangle Elephant Camp & Resort** to the southwest of town. This small but well-designed museum has multi-media displays and implements relating to the history,

The Hall of Opium in Sop Ruak.

THE GIANT FISH

In the deep, narrow Mekong River channels between Chiang Khong and Houei Sai swims the giant Mekong catfish, considered the largest freshwater fish in the world. Known to the Thais as *plaa beuk* (giant fish), and to zoologists as *Pangasianodon gigas*, it can reach up to three metres (10ft) in length and weigh as much as 300kg (660lbs).

Local Thai and Lao anglers are permitted to catch the hefty catfish using heavy rope nets only during two weeks each year. This is in early May, when the river reaches its lowest depth and the species is moving upriver to spawn in China.

Even though a breeding programme has had some success in keeping the fish from the brink of extinction, the annual *Pangasianodon* count appears to be on a downward curve.

A ferry on the Mekong.

Fact

There are now eight official international border crossings between Laos and Thailand, four of which will use bridges across the Mekong. One of the most recent bona fide crossings is from the village of Huay Khon in the far north of Nan Province to the remote Sayaboury Province of Laos. The roads on the Lao side are still very rough, but magical Luang Prabang is only 70km (42 miles) away.

cultivation and trade of *Papaver somniferum*, the opium poppy from which heroin is extracted, and which has given the Golden Triangle its notoriety. Most exhibits are labelled in English.

MAE SAI

Continuing 35km (22 miles) northwest from Sop Ruak, the road finally reaches **Mae Sai ⓫**. This busy border town, Thailand's most northerly, has a real frontier feel. **Tachilek** is clearly visible on the Myanmar side of the small Sai River.

In the shops and stalls along the main streets of Mae Sai, Burmese, Thai, Shan and hill-tribe traders sell gems, lacquerware and antiques – both new and old – along with imported whisky, cigarettes and medicinal herbs.

To the west of the main street, close to the border, a flight of steps ascends a hill to **Wat Phra That Doi Wao (daily 8am–6pm)**. This temple was purportedly constructed in memory of several thousand Burmese soldiers who died fighting Chiang Kai-shek's Kuomintang army, which in turn was fighting Mao Zedong's Communists for control of southern China. The temple grounds have splendid views over Mae Sai and Myanmar.

The entrance of a cave in Tham Luang.

THAM LUANG

About 6km (4 miles) south of town is **Tham Luang** (daily 9am–5pm), or Great Cave, reached via a turn-off to the west of Route 110 heading back to Chiang Rai. The cave burrows for several kilometres into the hills. Gas lanterns can be hired at the entrance.

NAN PROVINCE

Due east of Chiang Mai, **Nan Province** may be northern Thailand's last great undiscovered tourist territory. The province has lovely mountains, the full complement of hill tribes, a newly designated national park, and a friendly population not yet jaded by exposure to foreign travellers. The principal roads are sealed and offer excellent mountain biking and motorcycling, since they are hilly rather than mountainous and seldom disrupted by traffic. Not many people speak English, few signs are romanised, and there is barely any accommodation outside of the provincial capital.

The first Nan Dynasty emerged in the mid-1300s, and later became one of the first 10 Thai-Lao states to merge and form the first Lanna empire. The town was later conquered by the Burmese and the next few hundred years were tumultuous, but in 1788 Nan allied with Siam. Because Nan's rulers cooperated in the drive by Chulalongkorn to unite a mismatched quilt of vassal states into a modern nation, the province retained its special status as a semi-independent principality until the death of the last Nan prince in 1931.

With its cement-block architecture, the town of **Nan ⓬**, 320km (200 miles) from Chiang Mai, initially appears to be yet another nondescript upcountry backwater. A stroll beyond the downtown area, however, soon reveals plenty of old wooden houses, of which three different upraised provincial styles can be discerned.

NAN NATIONAL MUSEUM

Exhibits of the three styles of Nan-style houses can be seen at the **National Museum of Nan** (Wed–Sun 9am–4pm). Make this your first stop. Located on Thanon Pha Kong, in the 1903 former palace of the last two Nan princes, the museum offers information on the hill tribes, crafts and history of this region, including displays of rare Lanna- and Lao-style Buddha images. A 300-year-old black elephant tusk on display is said to have magical powers.

WAT PHRA THAT CHANG KHAM

The allegiances and influences of 600 years are evident in the temples of Nan, which display the architectural styles of Lanna, Sukhothai, northern and southern Laos, the Thai Lü people, and in various combinations. Styles of the Sukhothai period are prominent at **Wat Phra That Chang Kham** (daily 6am–6pm; free), across the street from Nan National Museum. Elephants, seven on each side, supporting the second tier of the square *chedi*, are a Sukhothai motif. The standing Buddhas in the 15th-century *viharn* are also Sukhothai. The scripture library, with its high ceiling, was once the largest in Thailand, though it is now empty.

Next to the Nan National Museum is the even older **Wat Hua Khuang**, with a wooden veranda in the Luang Prabang (or northern Lao) style. Although it's often closed, lucky visitors may catch the weekend painter who has spent years restoring the murals.

Mural at Wat Phumin.

WAT PHUMIN

Nan's most famous murals are found a short walk south at **Wat Phumin** (daily 8am–5pm; free), which was first constructed in 1596 and features a *bot* with an unusual cruciform layout. The 19th-century murals depict episodes from the *Jataka,* the chronicle of Buddha's previous incarnations. If the great carved doors of the *viharn* wing are fully open, make sure to peek behind them to see the murals that decorate the front wall: there are rowing boats

TACHILEK (MYANMAR)

From Mae Sai, visitors are allowed to cross the small bridge to Myanmar for the day to take a quick stroll around Tachilek, which really has little to offer except for the claim of visiting Myanmar. Alternatively, longer journeys of up to two weeks or more can be made by those already holding a 28-day Myanmar tourist visa, perhaps travelling as far as Kengtung, midway between Thailand and China. Frontier regulations between Thailand and Myanmar are prone to change, so check before crossing. And note that the bridge closes in the evening, so be sure not to get stranded overnight on the wrong side of the river.

Shopping seems to be the main lure of Tachilek, mainly fake designer bags, cheap handicrafts, gems of dubious quality and pirated DVDs. And that carton of Marlboros is probably filled with Burmese cigarettes.

Mae Sai.

loaded with bearded foreigners who smoke pipes and wear naval caps, among them a few heavily-dressed *farang* (European) women. At the centre of the hall is a four-sided sitting Buddha in the Sukhothai style.

WAT PHRA THAT CHAE HAENG

Standing on a hill about 3km (2 miles) southeast of town and across the Nan River, where large "dragon boats" race for a week every autumn, is **Wat Phra That Chae Haeng** (daily 6am–6pm; free). You'll recognise the temple by the lengthy *naga* serpent snaking down the hill. The striking 55-metre (180ft) gilded *chedi* is classic Lanna. The *bot*, however, shows Thai Lü influences, such as the sweeping, five-layered wooden roof, the low ceilings and the intertwined *naga* carved in stucco over the entrance. Regarded as a minority, but not a hill tribe, the Thai Lü are ethnic Thais who settled in the Nan valley about 150 years ago.

DOI PHU KHA N P

One can arrange one- to three-day hill treks in Nan, but it is also possible to visit tribal (as well as Thai Lü) villages on the 80km (50-mile) journey to **Doi Phu Kha National Park** ⓭ (daily 8am–5pm; http://portal.dnp.go.th). The majestic mountains along this route are some of the most beautiful in Thailand.

The national park has some undisturbed areas, but they are not served by trails. Park rangers can direct you to some scenic spots, such as the 1,300-metre (4,300ft) peak of **Don Khao** and **Ton Tong Waterfall**.

SAO DIN

About 60km (37 miles) south of Nan are the strange **Sao Din** ⓮ earth pillars. Carved by the wind, these bare, pointed projectiles form desolate canyons. Getting there by public transport is quite an effort; the easiest way is to rent a motorbike.

SOUTHWEST TO PHRAE

A walled, moat-encircled city like Chiang Mai and Lamphun, **Phrae** ⓯ is a sleepy provincial capital full of old teak mansions and historic temples. Founded in the 15th century, it established itself as an important centre of the teak trade in the 19th and early 20th centuries.

The city's best-known temple, **Wat Phra That Cho Hae** (daily 8am–5pm; free), is an important pilgrimage site. Perched on a low hill 9km (5 miles) southeast of town off Route 1022, it features a 33-metre (108ft) gilded *chedi* at its centre. Just outside the Old City, the towering wooden roofs of 19th-century **Wat Chom Sawan** (daily 8am–4.30pm) demonstrate obvious Burmese/Shan influence, a legacy of the once-thriving teak merchants, most of whom hailed from Burma.

The best surviving example of local teak architecture is **Vongburi House** (daily 9am–5pm). Completed in 1907, the two-storey mansion, which once housed Luang Phongphibun, Phrae's last monarch, is now a museum filled with the prince's antique furniture and personal effects.

Four-sided seated Buddha in the centre of the ordination hall at Wat Phumin.

A rickshaw driver.

Wat Mahathat, Sukhothai Historical Park.

SUKHOTHAI AND SURROUNDINGS

Sukhothai was the centre of the first independent Thai kingdom, considered to be the golden era of Thai history. Its magnificent temple and palace ruins vie for attention with the nearby monuments at Phitsanulok and Kamphaeng Phet.

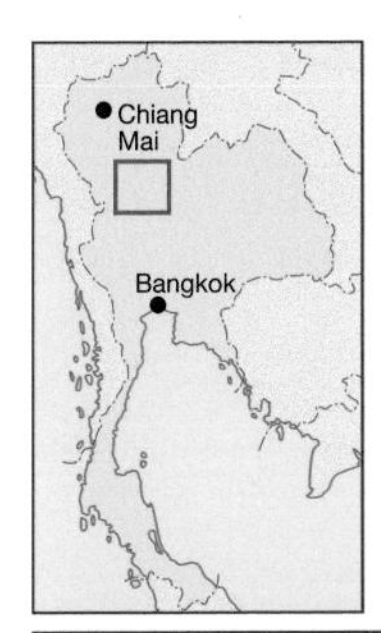

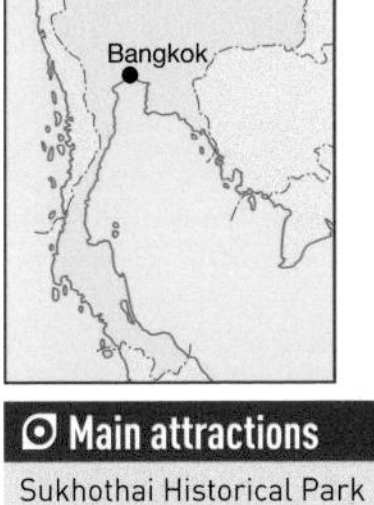

Main attractions

Sukhothai Historical Park
Si Satchanalai-Chaliang Historical Park
Phitsanulok
Kamphaeng Phet Historical Park

Map on page 290

The ancient city of **Sukhothai** ⓰ is set on a broad plain between the mountains of Tak Province and Burma to the west, and the mountains of Phetchabun, facing Laos to the east, depriving potential invaders of an element of surprise. Some 460km (275 miles) north of Bangkok and 330km (200 miles) south of Chiang Mai, the area is well fed by rivers – ideal for rice cultivation – which allowed Ramkhamheang, the kingdom's most famous monarch, to proclaim, "There is fish in the water and rice in the fields," to describe this bounteous environment. To the Thais, the magnificent site represents the heritage of their people.

The route from Phitsanulok passes through New Sukhothai with its concrete shophouses, hotels and restaurants. About 10km (7 miles) further, the road enters the limits of old Sukhothai through **Kamphaenghak Gate**.

The Sukhothai kingdom was founded in 1238 following King Intharathit's assertion of independence from the Khmer empire. The kingdom, which at one time included most of modern Thailand, plus parts of the Malay Peninsula and Burma, is synonymous with some of the finest artistic endeavours in Thai history, including the most exquisite Buddha images. Unfortunately, this golden age was relatively short-lived, lasting just two centuries: by 1438, it had been consumed by the kingdom of Ayutthaya. The most notable of the Sukhothai kings was Ramkhamhaeng, who, among other noted accomplishments, reformed the Thai script, promoted Theravada Buddhism and established links with China.

SUKHOTHAI HISTORICAL PARK

The remains of ancient Sukhothai's massive walls reveal that the inner city was protected by three rows of earthen ramparts and two moats. The city was previously ruled by the Khmers, and

Presenting alms to monks.

Tip

Large open-air ruins like those at Sukhothai and its surroundings are best explored during the cool season from November to February. But even then, either plan for an early morning or evening exploration, when the air is cooler.

the most visible remainder of their presence are the three Hindu *prang*, in the centre of Wat Si Sawai, which the Thais converted to a Buddhist temple. When the Angkor empire began to contract, the Khmers abandoned Sukhothai and the Thais began to build their own structures. In place of the intricate Khmer irrigation network, they installed a less complex system, and a lack of water eventually contributed to the city's demise.

The **Sukhothai Historical Park** (daily 6am–9pm) was designated as a Unesco World Heritage site in 1991, and for good reason. Inside the walls of the Old City are the magnificent ruins of 21 temples and monuments, and there are another 70 monuments within a 5km (3-mile) radius of the park. The ruins are divided into five zones – north, south, east, west and central – with the most important sites found within the Old City walls of the central zone. Tickets are sold separately for each zone at a daily price of B100, with an additional B50 charge for motor vehicles.

RAMKHAMHAENG NATIONAL MUSEUM

A short distance from Kamphaenghak Gate is the **Ramkhamhaeng National Museum** (daily 9am–4pm), a good starting point for a tour of the historical park. The museum has a fine collection of Sukhothai sculpture, ceramics and other artefacts, plus exhibits from other periods.

The entrance hall is dominated by an impressive bronze image of a walking Buddha, regarded as the finest sculptural innovation of the Sukhothai period. Local sculptors were the first to make statues of the walking Buddha in the round. The image also has features that typify the Sukhothai style, including fluid lines, a somewhat androgynous figure, and an interpretation of the 32 *raksana*, or characteristics, by which a Buddha would be recognised, such as wedge-shaped heels, arms down to the knees, and fingers and toes of equal length.

During the Sukhothai period, the Thais definitively embraced Theravada Buddhism and invited monks from Sri

Wat Mahathat.

Lanka to teach scripture. Yet, as Buddhism blossomed, Hindu influence remained strong, indicated by the two bronze images of Hindu gods flanking the bronze walking Buddha. The figure on the right, combining the attributes of Vishnu and Siva, is especially fine.

On the mezzanine floor of the museum is a copy of the famous stone inscription of King Ramkhamhaeng; the original is the single most prized exhibit of the National Museum in Bangkok.

CENTRAL ZONE: WAT MAHATHAT

The central zone, contained within the walls of the Old City, covers about 3 sq km (1 sq mile). The sights can be explored on foot, but a bicycle is perhaps the best option.

The largest and most important temple here is **Wat Mahathat**, in the centre of the Old City and surrounded by a moat. It's not certain who founded this temple, the spiritual centre of the kingdom, but it is presumed to be Intharathit, Sukhothai's first king. Wat Mahathat's present form is due to a remodelling commissioned by Ramkhamhaeng's son King Lo Thai (1298–1347), around 1345.

The original design, before Lo Thai's restoration, was a typical Khmer-style "quincunx", with one central tower and four axial towers resting on a laterite platform. When the structure subsequently collapsed, Lo Thai restored it, adding four brick towers, alternating with the four Khmer laterite towers around a new central "lotus bud" tower, with its distinctive bulbous ornamentation at the top. The brick towers erected by Lo Thai stand at the four corners and look quite different; some experts say they show Lanna influence, others Mon. The entire structure rests upon a square platform with a stucco frieze of walking monks around the base. Scattered around Wat Mahathat are several monumental Buddha images.

WITHIN THE CENTRAL ZONE

Familiar architectural themes are repeated among the 20 other shrines within the walls of the central zone (and some 70 more scattered in the other zones). The following

Fact

The annual Loy Krathong festival in November, when tiny boats decorated with flowers, incense and small coins are set afloat in the country's waterways, is celebrated in Sukhothai in especially grand fashion. There is a spectacular fireworks display, folk dances and an excellent sound-and-light show highlighting Wat Mahathat. Loy Krathong is said to have originated in Sukhothai.

Wat Si Sawai, Sukhothai Historical Park.

monuments found within the central zone are of special interest.

Wat Si Sawai: Southwest of Wat Mahathat, it was originally a Hindu shrine with an image of Shiva. Triple towers built in a modified Khmer style remain, with fine stucco decoration of mythical birds and divinities, added in the 15th century.

Wat Chana Songkhram and **Wat Trakuan:** Located just north of Wat Mahathat, both have notably attractive Sri Lankan-style *chedi,* of which only the lower parts still stand. Wat Trakuan has many bronze images of the Chiang Saen period.

Wat Sa Si: Found to the north on the other side of the highway, on the way to the southern gate, it has a Sri Lankan-style *chedi*. The *bot* (ordination hall) lies on an island to the east of the spire. The ruins of the main shrine consist of six rows of columns, which lead to a well-restored seated Buddha image. As Achille Clarac, author of *Discovering Thailand*, puts it: "The detail, balance and harmony of the proportions and decoration of Wat Sa Si, and the beauty of the area where it stands, bear witness to the unusual and refined aesthetic sense of the architects of the Sukhothai period."

NORTH ZONE: WAT PHRA PHAI LUANG

Leave the walled city (or central zone) by the northern San Luang, or Royal Shrine gate, and travel 1km (0.6 mile) or so to the important shrine of **Wat Phra Phai Luang**. Located within the north zone, it originally consisted of three laterite towers covered with stucco, probably built in the late 12th century when Sukhothai was still part of the vast Khmer empire.

This shrine might have been the original centre of Sukhothai, as Wat Mahathat is of a later period. A fragmentary seated stone Buddha image, dating to 1191 and the reign of the Khmer king Jayavarman VII, was found here. It is now housed in the grounds of the Ramkhamhaeng Museum. During restoration in the mid-1960s, a stucco Buddha image in the central tower collapsed, revealing many smaller images

Excavations at Si Satchanalai-Chaliang Historical Park.

SAWANGKHALOK POTTERY

The town of Si Satchanalai is associated with Sawankhalok, one of the core Thai ceramic styles, which was fired in hundreds of kilns around central Thailand from the 14th century. Si Satchanalai was known for fine clay that produced the best wares. The glazed brown or green pieces had many designs, but most famous are double-fish motifs. Many ended up in China, among Thailand's first exports, and remains have been found in sunken ships in the Gulf of Thailand. Thais have been crafting pottery for over 5,000 years, and while original antiques are rare, most ceramics are still thrown along the same shapes and designs of their age-old counterparts. Another famous style, celadon, was also traditionally thrown in the kilns of this area.

inside. Some date these images to the second half of the 13th century.

East of the main shrine is a pyramidal brick *chedi* with several seated stucco Buddha images from the late 13th century. The niches, which were walled up with bricks later, were removed during restoration work in 1953.

When heads of the stucco images from this *chedi* appeared in the antique market in Bangkok, authorities realised that the shrine was being pillaged. A government team was sent to the site, but the damage was already done. Those Chiang Saen-style heads that have not left the country are in private Thai collections, and also in the National Museum in Bangkok.

NORTH ZONE: WAT SI CHUM

Beyond Wat Phra Phai Luang to the west is **Wat Si Chum**, with one of the largest seated Buddha images in Thailand. The *mondop*, or enclosing shrine, was built in the second half of the 14th century, but the 15-metre (49ft) image itself, called Phra Achana (The Venerable), is believed to be the one mentioned in King Ramkhamhaeng's inscription, which would date it somewhat earlier as Ramkhamheang reigned from 1280–98.

There is a stairway within the walls of the *mondop* to the roof. The ceiling of the stairway is made of over 50 slate slabs carved with scenes from Buddhist folklore. These turn the climbing of the stairs into a symbolic ascent to Buddhahood. Because of the precarious nature of the stairway, and also to stop people disrespectfully standing above the Buddha's head, climbing is no longer permitted.

There is a story of troops gathered here before a battle who heard an ethereal voice that came from the Buddha. This is attributed to a cunning ploy by a general who hid a man on the stairway and told him to speak through a window concealed by the image; the effect was inspiring, however, and the soldiers routed the enemy.

SOUTH ZONE: WAT CHETUPON

South of the walled city is another group of shrines and monasteries. One of the most interesting is **Wat Chetupon**, where the protecting wall of the

Fact

Ban Hat Siaw, a village southeast of Si Satchanalai, is famous for its hand-woven textiles, characterised by horizontal stripes bordered with rich brocade. The Thai Phuan people, who live in this area, migrated to Si Satchanalai from Laos around a century ago when Vietnamese invaders occupied their Xieng Khuang homeland.

The huge seated Buddha at Wat Si Chum.

The Phra Phuttha Chinnarat is Thailand's second-most important Buddha image.

viharn is of imitation wood made from slabs of slate. The gates are also huge plates of slate mined from nearby hills. Some say they resemble the megaliths of Stonehenge, but on a smaller scale.

The bridges over the moat surrounding the temple are also made of stone. The central tower has Buddha images in the standing, reclining, walking and sitting postures. The walking Buddha here is said to be one of the finest of its kind.

WEST ZONE: WAT SAPHAN HIN

"To the west of the city of Sukhothai," says Ramkhamhaeng's inscription, "is a forested area where the king has made offerings. In the forest is a large, tall and beautiful *viharn* which contains an 18-cubit image of the standing Buddha." This was identified as **Wat Saphan Hin**, the Monastery of the Stone Bridge, named because it is approached by a stairway of large stone slabs. The 12-metre (40ft) image stands on the crest of a low hill, and can be seen from a distance. Its hand is raised in the attitude of giving protection, and is almost certainly the image described by Ramkhamhaeng.

Wat Phra Si Rattana Mahathat.

WAT PA MAMUANG

There are other monuments in this western area, probably built by Sri Lankan monks, who preferred to locate their monasteries in the forest. Near the road, not far from the western gate of Sukhothai, is **Wat Pa Mamuang**, or Temple of the Mango Grove, where Ramkhamhaeng's grandson King Lu Thai (1347–68) is said to have installed a famous Theravada monk in 1361. Still standing are the shrine foundations and the ruins of the main *chedi*.

SI SATCHANALAI

About 50km (31 miles) north of Sukhothai, just off a highway and on the banks of the Yom River, lies the venerable city of **Si Satchanalai** ⓱. Founded in the 13th century, like Sukhothai, it was the seat of the viceroys of Sukhothai, and has been mentioned in ancient history books as the twin city of the capital. Whereas restoration, the removal of trees and the installation of lawns have eroded some of Sukhothai's grandeur, Si Satchanalai's setting gives it an aura attained in few other ancient sites. It is a pleasure to wander through the wooded complex, and turn a corner to be surprised by a wat or monument.

SI SATCHANALAI-CHALIANG HISTORICAL PARK

Si Satchanalai and Chaliang, an old city 1km (0.6 mile) to its east, together form **Si Satchanalai-Chaliang Historical Park** (daily 8am–5pm). The most important monument within the 720-hectare (1,780-acre) site is **Wat Chang Lom**. There is little doubt that this is the "elephant-girdled shrine" in Ramkhamhaeng's inscription, which records that construction began in 1285 to house holy relics of the Buddha, and was finished six years later. It is the only surviving *chedi* that can be attributed with certainty to King Ramkhamhaeng. Made of laterite and stucco, its large bell-shaped spire in the Sri Lankan style stands on a two-storey, square basement. The upper tier has mostly empty niches for images, while the lower level has 39 elephant-shaped laterite buttresses.

South of the Elephant Shrine are the ruins of **Wat Chedi Jet Thaew**, which include seven rows of *chedi*, believed to contain the ashes of the viceroys of Si Satchanalai. One *chedi* has a stucco image of the Buddha sheltered by the *naga* serpent, and is in unusually good condition. Further south, close to the massive city walls, are the remains of **Wat Nang Phya**, Temple of the Queen. It has fine stucco decoration on one external wall, which probably dates from the 16th century and is vaguely reminiscent of European Baroque.

Other temples worth visiting include **Wat Khao Phanom Pleung** and **Wat Khao Suwan Khiri**, located on scenic hills linked by a walkway. **Wat Phra Si Rattana Mahathat** in Chaliang, a lovely temple, lies a couple of kilometres southeast of the Old City in a setting overlooking the Yom River.

PHITSANULOK

Located some 50km (31 miles) east of Sukhothai, **Phitsanulok** ⓲ today has few mementoes of the past; a fire in the 1950s razed most of the old town. The new city is quite dull, although nothing can detract from its superb location along the Nan River, with quays shaded by flowering trees, and houseboats and floating restaurants moored by its steep riverbanks. Phitsanulok is an alternative base to Sukhothai for exploring the region.

WAT PHRA SI RATTANA MAHATHAT

Fortunately, the fire spared **Wat Phra Si Rattana Mahathat**, also called Wat Yai (daily 6.30am–6pm), is Phitsanulok's main monastery. The **Phra Phuttha Chinnarat** (or Chinnarat Buddha) image in the main *viharn* is considered Thailand's second-most important, after Bangkok's Emerald Buddha. The seated Sukhothai-style bronze image has a flame-like bronze halo following the outlines of the head and torso and end in *naga* heads near the base.

Fact

Phitsanulok serves as the economic capital of Thailand's lower north. With its position at the geographical crossroads of three regions – northern, northeastern and central Thailand – it is also of major strategic importance to the kingdom in terms of national communications, transport, trade and defence.

Wat Chang Lom, Si Satchanalai-Chaliang Historical Park.

Laterite Buddha images at Wat Phra Kaew, Kamphaeng Phet Historical Park.

The temple does brisk business in Chinnarat Buddha amulets and other religious souvenirs. The Lanna-style chapel that enshrines the image comprises a three-tiered roof that drops steeply to head-high side walls, drawing attention to the gleaming image at the end of the nave. Two wooden pulpits of superb late-Ayutthaya workmanship flank the image. The large one on the left is for monks, who chant the ancient Buddhist texts; the smaller pulpit on the other side accommodates a single monk who translates the Pali chants into Thai for the congregation. Note the late 18th-century main doors, inlaid with mother-of-pearl. Behind the chapel is a lofty *chedi* topped by a *prang* (Khmer-influenced tower).

A **bronze foundry** on nearby Thanon Wisut Kasat casts copies of the Chinnarat Buddha, and Buddhas in other styles. Visitors can see photographs of the painstaking process, and watch the Buddha images being cast and polished (Wed–Sun 8.30am–4.30pm; free).

Buddha casting foundry.

KAMPHAENG PHET

The city of **Kamphaeng Phet** ⓳, on the Ping River 77km (48 miles) southwest of Sukhothai, was built by King Lu Thai (1347–68), Ramkhamhaeng's grandson, to replace the older town of Chakangrao on the opposite bank. Both served as garrison towns for the Sukhothai kingdom.

KAMPHAENG PHET HISTORICAL PARK

A visit to King Lu Thai's fortifications reveals why the town was called Kamphaeng Phet, or "Diamond Walls": the massive earthen ramparts are topped by laterite walls rising 6 metres (20ft) above the outer moat, once overgrown with water hyacinths but now restored.

The ruins of the Old City are contained within the walled boundaries of the **Kamphaeng Phet Historical Park** (daily 8am–4.30pm). Of interest here is **Wat Phra Kaew**, remarkable for its fragile, time-eroded laterite Buddha images. This was the largest and most important temple at this site. Nearby is **Wat Phra That**, represented

IMPERIAL DIPLOMACY

The Shiva image in the Kamphaeng Phet National Museum has an interesting history. Early during the reign of King Chulalongkorn, which extended from 1868 until his death in 1910, an insensitive German visitor had removed the image's head and two hands. Too afraid to arrest a *farang* (Westerner), the governor quickly sent word to Bangkok that the priceless fragments were on their way by boat. Officials in Bangkok detained the German, who declared that he was going to give them to the Berlin Museum. King Chulalongkorn managed to placate the German by promising to send an exact copy of the whole Shiva image to Germany, so that the authentic fragments could remain in Thailand. And so it was done. The copy of the bronze is still in Berlin.

by a substantial circular Sri-Lankan style *chedi* and laterite pillars. To the southeast is the **Kamphaeng Phet National Museum** (Wed–Sun 9am–4pm), housing one of Thailand's finest bronze statues of the Hindu god Shiva. Other exhibits include pre-Sukhothai bronzes, stucco Buddha heads from local monuments, and some ceramics.

ARUNYIK TEMPLES

Kamphaeng Phet's other monuments are found to the northwest of the walled city. The monks who built them were of a forest-dwelling sect, strongly influenced by teachers from Sri Lanka. These *arunik* (or forest) temples, constructed of laterite, are thought to show Ceylonese influence. Most of them, however, underwent major changes during restoration in the Ayutthaya period.

The familiar themes of Buddhist architecture are repeated in the ordination halls of the two main temples. The first, **Wat Phra Si Iriyabot** (daily 8am–6pm), derives its name from Buddha images that are depicted in four postures (*si* meaning four, and *iriyabot*, postures) on the central square *mondop*: walking, standing, sitting and reclining. The standing image is largely intact, with the original stucco coating still on its head and lower part of the body. This is an impressive and unaltered example of Sukhothai sculpture. Unfortunately, the other images are in very poor condition. The whole temple stands on a platform that is encircled by the original laterite railing and walls.

The other temple, **Wat Chang Rawp**, comprises the base of a laterite *chedi* surrounded by a row of elephant buttresses, a theme borrowed from Sri Lanka that claims the universe rests on the backs of these beasts. The row of elephants on the south side is almost complete, but several are missing on the other flanks of the *chedi*. The spire of the great monument has vanished, but the ruins of a crypt on the upper level of the *chedi* can still be seen today.

The pillars of the former *viharn* also remain. Sensitive repair work has restored much of the original form and managed to preserve its character.

Elephant detail at Wat Chang Rawp, Kamphaeng Phet Historical Park.

Wat Chang Rawp.

Scenery on Route 108, near Mae Sariang.

TAK AND MAE HONG SON

The remote mountainous provinces of north Thailand provide an opportunity to get off the beaten track. You can visit Burmese border towns and colourful hill tribe villages, raft down fast-flowing rivers and explore the region's national parks.

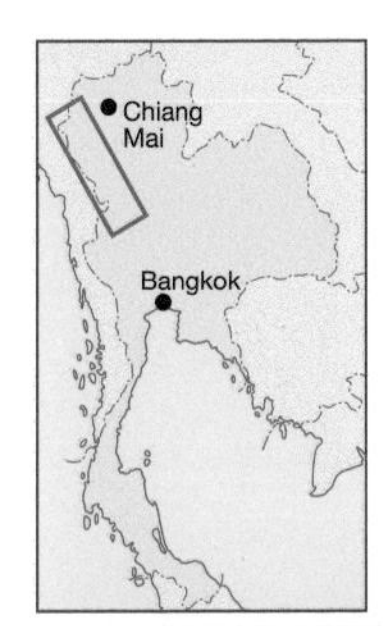

Main attractions

Lan Sang National Park
Mae Sot
Um Phang
Mae Sariang
Khun Yam
Mae Hong Son
Pai

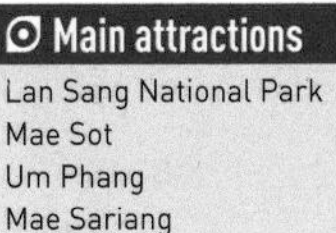
Map on page 290

Tucked away along the Thailand–Myanmar border, in the country's northwesternmost corner, Tak and Mae Hong Son are two of Thailand's least populous provinces. Throughout most of Thai history they were covered by the vast teak forests upon which northern Thai cities such as Chiang Mai and Lampang built their economies. Even as recently as 40 years ago, the Thai government classified this region as "remote", an official euphemism for areas over which Bangkok had little control. The 1968–82 communist insurgency movement thrived here, finding ready recruits among impoverished villagers and hill tribes.

For Mae Hong Son and Tak, the sense of separateness was compounded by their shared economy and cultures with neighbouring Myanmar. There is still much exchange, both legal and illegal, between peoples on both sides of the border.

For visitors, these remote provinces offer many opportunities to get off the beaten tourist track, to enjoy the mountains, rivers and forests, and to encounter a multitude of minority hill-tribe communities and their cultures.

TAK TO MYAWADI

On the banks of the Ping River, the quiet town of **Tak** ⓴, once called Raheng, bills itself as the "gateway to the north". Historically, this was a logging town, from where logs freed from the wild rapids on the upper Ping and Wang rivers were floated down to Nakhon Sawan. Until the railway was completed in the 1920s, the main way north from Bangkok was by boat, agonisingly propelled by poles against the swift currents. Tak served as a provisioning centre, an essential stop for rest and replenishment, on these journeys west into Myanmar and north to Chiang Mai.

In 1964, the rapids were removed by the construction of **Bhumibol Dam**,

A Karen family.

about 60km (37 miles) to the north, which had the effect of permanently sidelining Tak as a river port. At a height of 154 metres (505ft), the dam is the tallest in Southeast Asia and provides both electricity and irrigation to the surrounding area. The shores and islands of the reservoir created by Bhumibol Dam are a favourite canoeing, swimming, fishing and picnicking area for local Thais.

Today, Tak is little more than an administrative and agricultural supply centre for the province, accessed either by Highway 1 from Bangkok, or by an older road that threads through tiny manicured gardens and around a pond near the provincial offices.

Other than views of the Ping River at sunset and the orange suspension bridge resembling a miniature version of San Francisco's Golden Gate Bridge, Tak offers few exceptional sights. A broad esplanade separates the market from the river, and a dyke holds back the river's waters, which are prone to flooding during the rainy season.

The Burmese border at Mae Sot.

LAN SANG NATIONAL PARK

Route 105 leads west from Tak through rugged hills towards Mae Sot, a town on the Thailand–Myanmar border. Around 18km (11 miles) outside of Tak lies **Lan Sang National Park** ㉑ (daily 8am–6pm; http://portal.dnp.go.th), with its rugged mountain peaks and waterfalls that are hidden behind a screen of bamboo groves.

Various species of deer, serow (a type of mountain goat), numerous monkeys, golden cats and a few leopards are still present in these hills. If time allows, stop at the *nikhom*, or "settlement", on Doi Musoe to gain some insight into the life of the Lisu, Lahu and Hmong hill tribes who live in this area.

Freshly brewed, locally grown coffee is sold on Route 105 to passing motorists, as are wild orchids and forest flowers. The road rises to Doi Phawo mountain, where truck drivers make offerings at the elaborate **Chaopho Phawo Shrine** – named in honour of a Karen warrior – for safe passage. Beyond the pass, the road drops through forest into a peaceful valley dotted with small farmhouses, white *chedi* and ornate Burmese-style temples.

MAE SOT

Some 85km (53 miles) from Tak the road reaches **Mae Sot** ㉒, a boisterous border junction inhabited by a diversity of ethnic groups, most of them with family ties and/or business links in Myanmar, which lies just across the Moei River at the town's western limits. Shops around town bear signs in a combination of Thai, Chinese, Burmese and English. With its confusion of narrow streets, sidewalk stalls, Burmese tea shops, bicycles and excited shoppers, Mae Sot has the air of a frontier boom town.

Along with a vigorous smuggling industry (especially in Burmese teak since a 1989 Thai ban on logging), refugee camps on the outskirts of town provide much of Mae Sot's livelihood and contribute to its "not-quite-Thailand" ambience. It is also the centre of the border region's gem trade, specialising in precious and semi-precious stones from Myanmar, particularly jade and rubies.

WAT WATTANARAM

From Mae Sot, it's a 5km (3-mile) drive to the Myanmar border. Worthy of a visit is **Wat Wattanaram** (daily 6am–5pm; free), an ornate Burmese-style temple with tiers of red-tiled rectangular roofs fringed with intricate silverwork that are piled skywards into a tower. Within the sanctuary are four Buddha images, one of which has heavy gold jewellery distending its earlobes.

MYAWADI

Continue to the Moei River, spanned since 1996 by the **Thai-Myanmar Friendship Bridge**. On the far side is **Myawaddy**, a typical Burmese town of dusty streets and glittering pagodas. A riverbank casino here entertains Thai gamblers at weekends.

The border is open from 8.30am to 4.30pm, and foreigners are welcome to tour Myawaddy for the day (charge at the border). A highway from Myawaddy leads west to Mawlamyaing (Moulmein) and Yangon, but for now, foreigners are permitted to travel only as far as Myawaddy.

During the Thai communist insurgency of the late 1970s and early 1980s the high mountains south of Mae Sot were a formidable stronghold for armed guerrillas, making it an area that few tourists dared venture into. After 1982, an amnesty removed the threat and the mountains enjoyed peace once again.

These western mountains harbour more domesticated elephants than anywhere else in Thailand. Local Karen villages still use the sturdy and clever animals for jungle transport, and for various agricultural tasks.

SOUTH TO UM PHANG

Steep and winding Route 1090 meanders through the mountains to **Um Phang** ㉓, a remote, rural district about 150km (90 miles) south of Mae Sot.

Along the way, the road passes two scenic falls, **Pha Charoen Waterfall** and **Thararak Waterfall**, 26km (15 miles) and 41km (24 miles) respectively from Mae Sot, each with picnic areas and short, steep trails following the cataracts.

UM PHANG

The sleepy town of **Um Phang**, with its mostly Karen inhabitants, is a centre for elephant treks and whitewater rafting. One of the most popular local rafting-and-trekking trips follows the Klong River to the lofty 400-metre (1,312ft) **Thilawsu Waterfall**, the largest falls in all of Thailand.

The waterfalls are found in **Um Phang Wildlife Sanctuary**, which was declared a Unesco World Heritage site in 1999 and forms part of Thailand's largest wildlife corridor. Combined with the adjacent Thung Yai Naresuan

Fact

When border skirmishes flare up between Karen insurgents and Myanmar's central government, Myawaddy (across the Moei River in Myanmar) may be closed to foreign visitors for a few days at a time.

Wild elephant in the forest near Mae Hong Son.

Fact

The 150km (93-mile) road between Mae Sot and Um Phang was known as the "Death Highway" during the late-1970s Thai communist insurgency because of the frequent attacks launched on government transport.

Reserve, Huay Kha Kaeng Reserve, Khlong Lan National Park and Mae Wong National Park, the sanctuary is part of one of the most pristine natural forest zones in Southeast Asia.

Following a trail along the Myanmar border, trekkers can hike all the way from Um Phang to **Sangkhlaburi** ㉔ in Kanchanaburi Province. The expedition takes about seven days; experienced guides can be hired through any of the guesthouses in Um Phang. Picturesque Sangkhlaburi is surrounded by high peaks and remains largely untouched by development. It's also a fascinating cultural meeting point: Thai, Burmese, Mon and Karen all live here, mostly involved in border trade, illegal or otherwise. The only route by road to Sangkhlaburi is from Kanchanaburi.

NORTH TO MAE HONG SON

From Mae Sot, Route 105 turns north, staying close to the Myanmar border, and is punctuated by police checkpoints. It passes the limestone cave complex of **Tham Mae Usu** (daily 8am–5pm), near km 94. The main caverns are open to the public, except during the rainy season, when the river that runs through the cave seals its mouth, forcing its closure.

At the end of its winding, 226km (136 miles) -Route 105 reaches **Mae Sariang**, where it joins Route 108, the road to Chom Thong and Chiang Mai.

MAE SARIANG

Hemmed in by high mountains, **Mae Sariang** ㉕ lies along the banks of its namesake Mae Sariang (Sariang River). The district is surrounded by a number of outlying Shan, Karen and Hmong villages. In town, **Wat Uthayarom** (also called Wat Chong Sung) is worth a brief stop for its Shan-style tin-trimmed teak architecture and 19th-century *chedi*. Mae Sariang also offers several pleasant riverside guesthouses and a few shops selling Karen handicrafts.

KHUN YUAM

Route 108 leads north from Mae Sariang, through mountain scenery that is among the most breathtaking in Thailand, reaching **Mae Hong Son** about 170km (100 miles) later. Roughly

Mae Hong Son.

ANCIENT CAVES

The Shan market town of Soppong, 70km (42 miles) northeast of Mae Hong Son, is a jumping-off point for visits to Tham Lot (daily 8am–5pm), 8km (5 miles) away. The most famous limestone cave complex in northern Thailand and one of the longest in Southeast Asia has huge, multiple chambers. When discovered, it contained several ancient teak coffins suspended on wooden scaffolds, suggesting it had been a burial site during prehistoric times. The eight known coffin caves are off limits to visitors. Mandatory guides carrying gas lanterns are included in the entry fee. When the water in a stream running through the three main caverns is high enough, visitors can pass through on bamboo rafts.

midway between Mae Sariang and Mae Hong Son, little-visited **Khun Yuam** 26 has one of the most charming Shan Buddhist monasteries in the province, **Wat To Pae** (daily 6am–6pm; free). Inside the temple and hidden behind curtains is a 150-year-old antique Burmese *kalaga* (embroidered tapestry).

Also in Khun Yuam is the modest **World War II Museum** (daily 8am–5pm) which contains artefacts left behind by Japanese troops retreating from Burma at the end of World War II. An estimated 100,000 Japanese soldiers followed the Skeleton Road (named for the many who died *en route*) from Burma to northern Thailand in August 1945. Many took refuge in Khun Yuam before continuing on to Chiang Mai. The local Shan provided food and medicine to the ailing troops, and turned Wat To Pae into a field hospital. The museum displays a collection of military gear and personal possessions left behind by the Japanese.

MAE HONG SON

Around 75 percent of Mae Hong Son Province consists of forests and mountains. The deep-green peaks that loom over the provincial capital account for **Mae Hong Son Town**'s 27 early-morning fogs, and also separate Thailand from neighbouring Myanmar. Mae Hong Son lies smack in the middle of border-smuggling routes, and the presence of Karen, Hmong, Lawa, Shan, Lisu and Lahu tribespeople, who, taken collectively, easily outnumber the ethnic Thais, adds further romance to the town.

WAT PHRA THAT DOI KONG MU

Doi Kong Mu, a hill that rises a steep 250 metres (820ft) above the town, affords a commanding view of Mae Hong Son and the surrounding countryside. At night, two tall *chedi* at **Wat Phra That Doi Kong Mu** (daily 6am–6pm; free), perched atop the hill, light up like timid beacons. Erected in the 19th century, the temple reflects Shan and Burmese influences.

WAT CHONG KLANG AND WATCHONG KHAM

Nong Chong Kham, a serene lake in the south of Mae Hong Son, is flanked

Fact

Mae Hong Son is famous for its annual Poy Sang Long celebrations, when pre-pubescent boys are temporarily ordained as novice monks. Dressed in mock-royal finery, the boys are paraded on the shoulders of their older family members to a local Buddhist monastery, where they trade their outfits for the ochre-coloured robes of monks.

Thilawsu Waterfall near Um Phang.

A "Welcome to Pai" sign greets visitors. Note that Pai is pronounced as "Bai".

by two picturesque Burmese-Shan temples. **Wat Chong Klang** (daily 6am–6pm; free), built two centuries ago, is the older of the pair. **Wat Chong Kham** (daily 6am–6pm; free) is famous for its painted glass panels and carved wooden figures illustrating episodes from the Buddhist *Jataka* tales. The reflection of the graceful, whitewashed *chedi* of the temples in the lake's mirror-like surface is a favourite photo-op.

Tour agencies, hotels and guesthouses in Mae Hong Son can arrange two- to seven-day treks to mountain valleys, caves and hill-tribe villages in the vicinity. Many visitors travel to nearby "longneck villages" to meet Padaung refugees from Myanmar, whose women traditionally wear heavy brass coils around their necks. Of the three Padaung villages in Mae Hong Son Province, **Nai Soi**, 35km (21 miles) northwest of the provincial capital, is the largest.

SOUTHEAST TO PAI

Route 1095 climbs into pine-forested mountains as it heads southeast from Mae Hong Son towards Chiang Mai, yielding spectacular valley views along the way.

PAI

Heading southeast, the road arrives at **Pai** ㉘, a picturesque and very popular destination that is most often accessed on a four-hour drive from Chiang Mai (see page 269). Once strictly patronised by the backpacking set, Pai has now broadened its appeal and, although still regarded as "alternative", has many more upmarket resorts and restaurants. The original site of the town is a slightly elevated plateau, known nowadays as **Wiang Neua** (northern walled settlement). It still retains parts of Pai's centuries-old earthen city walls and surrounding moat, which are now used for irrigation. Here, most houses are made of wood and the open-air markets are redolent with Shan spices.

Meanwhile, at a lower level of the valley, the newer **Wiang Tai** (southern walled settlement) contains a colourful selection of cafés, bars,

Padaung girl, Mae Hong Son.

"LONGNECK" VILLAGES

Padaung (or Kayan) refugee villages have become a controversial tourist attraction in Mae Hong Son Province because of the traditional brass neck coils worn by many Padaung women. The heavy coils, which typically weigh around 5kg (11lbs) and measure 20–30cm (8–13ins) in height, depress the collarbone and rib cage, making the neck appear unnaturally long. Despite apocryphal claims that the women's necks will flop over if the coils are removed, Padaung women remove the coils regularly for cleaning and bathing.

The origins of these neck coils are not clear; according to the Padaung, the brass coils are a tribute to a mythical female dragon who consorted with the wind god and produced the first Padaung offspring. Other theories postulate that Padaung women used the neck coils to ward off the attentions of men from other tribes.

The villages charge admission, a portion of which goes to the Padaung women, the rest to village administrators, who are not Thai, as is often assumed, but rather Padaung and Karenni. On the one hand the "longneck villages" may appear to be little more than crass human zoos. On the other, the Padaung have fled an ongoing civil war in Myanmar's border regions, and charging visitors to observe their traditions is one of the few ways they have to make a living in a foreign land.

restaurants, travel agencies, galleries, shops and massage centres. The population here is a varied mix of Shan, northern Thai, Chinese Muslim and Lisu, along with a sizeable community of Western expats who relish the peaceful, natural ambience.

Ensconced in a wide, fertile valley, surrounded by low mountain peaks, the town of around 5,000 people has, over the last decade, become a magnet for new-agers, artists and musicians from all over the world.

WAT MAE YEN AND THA PAI HOTSPRINGS

Nearby attractions include a couple of waterfalls, the mountain-top **Wat Mae Yen** (whose buildings have been painted by local Thai artists in a non-traditional but still inspiring fashion), and **Tha Pai Hotsprings** (tel: 053-612 982; daily 8am–6pm), a park with natural mineral springs and fresh-water streams, perfect for soaking year-round. Lahu and Lisu villages lie within moderate walking distance of Wiang Tai.

Two-day **river-rafting** trips on the Pai River are popular with the French-owned **Thai Adventure Rafting**, which maintains high standards (tel: 053 699 111; www.thairafting.com). On the outskirts of Pai Town near the Tha Pai Hot Springs is **Thom's Pai Elephant Camp Tours** (tel: 053-065 778; www.thomelephant.com), which offers short elephant treks into the jungle (unusually, riding bareback), as well as rafting trips.

HUAY NAM DANG N P

From Pai, Route 1095 meanders southeast through the mountains for another 90km (54 miles) to **Mae Malai**, a small market town. A stretch of the route bisects the 1,247-sq-km (748-sq-mile) **Huay Nam Dang National Park** (http://portal.dnp.go.th), a heavily forested sanctuary famous for the "sea of fog" that blankets the area at dawn. It also has a couple of short nature trails, natural hot springs and several waterfalls. From here, Chiang Mai is another hour's drive south along Route 107.

The streets of Pai.

HILL-TRIBE CRAFTS AND CLOTHING

Each hill tribe of Thailand has its own customs, dress, language and spiritual beliefs that are clearly reflected in the crafts they produce.

Textiles and silver jewellery play a very important role in the ceremonial activities of Thailand's hill-tribe communities. Hill-tribe women are defined by what they wear, and their choice of clothing and adornment can reveal not only which tribe they are from, but also their social status, age and even where their home town is located. However, the way of life of Thailand's hill-tribe people is changing as they are slowly assimilated into mainstream Thai society, and abandon many features of their traditional culture. This may be unfortunate for visitors in search of traditional hill-tribe culture, but the process is inevitable and has distinct advantages for these ethnic minorities, as they can now benefit from educational opportunities and medical care.

Padaung women wear brass coils around their arms, legs and necks.

HILL-TRIBE CRAFTS

Hill-tribe craft items started to be made commercially available in the mid-1970s when small craft centres were set up in refugee camps. Authentic items are now rare and expensive, but good-quality crafts can be found in shops all over northern Thailand and in Bangkok.

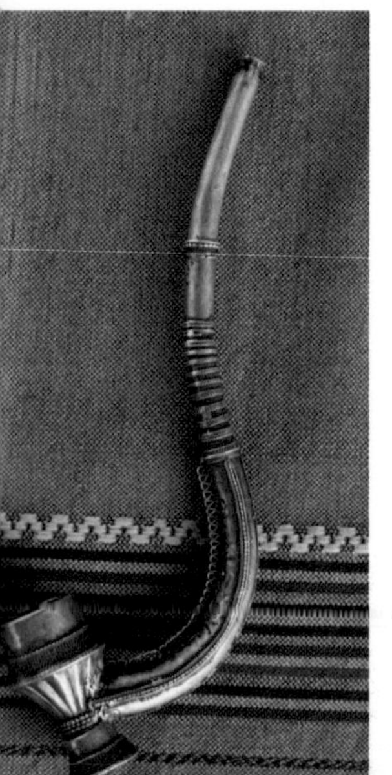

An opium pipe; northwest Thailand lies within the fabled Golden Triangle.

A woman of the Hmong hill tribe, weaving a traditional garment.

Women of the White Karen tribe.

Ikat cloth

The White Karen tribe produce striped-warp *ikat* textiles woven on back-strap looms. *Ikat* is a technique that involves the binding of the cloth with fibre or material, so that in places it becomes resistant to dyeing. Before the cloth is dyed, the weft (yarns woven across the width) or the warp (lengthwise yarns) is pulled tightly over a frame and the threads bound tightly together singly or in bunches. The cloth is then dyed several times using different colours. As a result, beautiful patterns are built up with soft edges on the parts of the cloth not completely covered by the binding materials. The dyeing process is complex, with the dominant colour of the *ikat* dyed first. Cotton yarns are the most suitable for making warp *ikat*, and the dyes used to produce these textiles are natural dyes easily absorbed by cotton. The most popular colours for warp *ikat* are indigo and red. Weft *ikat*, usually made from silk, use mainly yellow turmeric, diluted indigos and a deep crimson red extracted from the lac insect.

Lisu women make distinctive hats and other clothing. In the past, the cloth was woven by hand but machine-made material is now run up on sewing machines.

Women of the Hmong hill tribe spin cotton into thread with a hand spindle, then weave it on a foot-treadle loom.

Married Akha women are famous for their headdresses, decorated with silver coins, which they wear all the time. Unmarried women from the tribe attach small gourds to their headdresses.

Farmers in Loei Province.

NORTHEAST THAILAND

This little-visited region of Thailand is economically poor but rich in attractions, from a sweet-natured people to national parks full of wildlife and stunning temple ruins dating to the Khmer empire.

Scenery near Phu Kradung National Park, Loei Province.

According to official government records, northeast Thailand captures only 2 percent of the country's tourism market. Travellers don't know what they are missing: the northeast is a rich treasure trove of ancient Angkor-era temple ruins, a relatively untouched Lao-Cambodian-Thai culture and beautiful national parks. It is a completely different experience to that offered by Phuket or Bangkok, or even Chiang Mai.

Large parts of the northeast (also known as Isaan) were ruled by the Khmers during the golden 10th-to-13th-century period, when they built the remarkable Angkor Wat (in Cambodia). In the lands to the west and north – present-day northeast Thailand – the Khmers established a number of far-flung satellite towns, each with its own majestic temples and shrines. Their survival leaves a glimpse into one of the world's great civilisations.

Central sanctuary, Prasat Hin Phimai, Nakhon Ratchasima Province.

Northeast Thailand occupies a high plateau (the Khorat) and is home to around one-third of the country's population. Three of Thailand's five largest cities are found here: Khon Kaen, Nakhon Ratchasima (Khorat) and Udon Thani. The region is strongly linked with Lao culture as for long periods it was part of various Lao kingdoms. Today, most northeasterners can trace their ancestry to Laos, across the Mekong River to the north and east. Northeastern Thais retain the Lao quality of passivity in the face of adversity. This quality is useful, for this is not an easy place to live – the soil is thin, there is either not enough rain, or too much, and the Mekong is prone to floods.

Nonetheless, many travellers find the northeast the highlight of their trip. It is the least "touristy" region of the country; the people are genuine and without wiles; the area abounds with natural beauty; and the cultural attraction of many Khmer sites adds to the interest. It is also possible to make forays into neighbouring Laos at several crossings over the Mekong, either by bridge or by boat.

Prasat Hin Khao Phanom Rung.

NAKHON RATCHASIMA TO UBON RATCHATHANI

Heading from west to east takes one from a lush national park, that is easily accessible from Bangkok, to the magnificent Khmer temple ruins of Prasat Khao Phra Viharn, across the border in Cambodia.

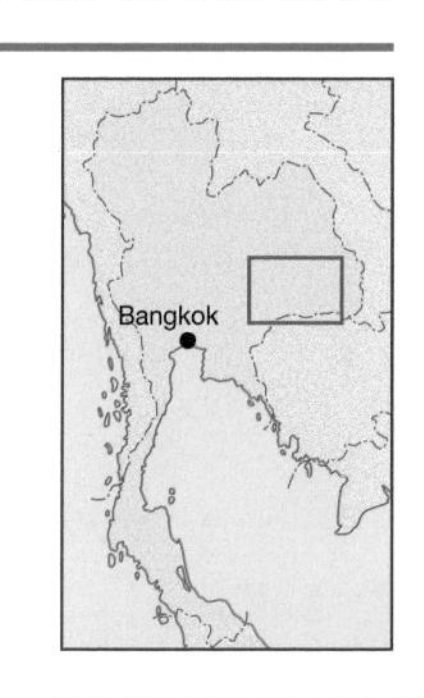

Main attractions

- Khao Yai National Park
- Nakhon Ratchasima (Khorat)
- Pak Thong Chai
- Prasat Hin Phimai
- Prasat Hin Khao Phanom Rung Historical Park
- Surin
- Prasat Khao Phra Viharn
- Ubon Ratchathani
- Kaeng Tanna National Park

Map on page 324

The mountainous Khao Yai area gives way to the Khorat Plateau, considered to be the gateway to Thailand's northeast. Further east lie the provinces of Buriram and Si Saket, with a plethora of Khmer sites, and slightly to the north, the elephant capital of Surin. Beyond, Ubon Ratchathani is the entrance to southern Laos.

Distances between the many out-of-the-way sights are significant, and public transport is patchy. However, roads are relatively good, so the best way to see northeast Thailand is by car.

KHAO YAI N P

One of the region's best-known sights is **Khao Yai National Park** ❶ (daily 8am–6pm; tel: 025-620 760; http://portal.dnp.go.th, more frequently accessed from Bangkok than it is from Nakhon Ratchasima Town). The country's oldest and most visited nature reserve, Khao Yai lies about 200km (175 miles) northeast of Bangkok, and there are several routes from the capital; the most popular is Highway 1 to Saraburi, from where Highway 2 leads to the reserve. The drive from Bangkok should take about three hours.

Khao Yai is Thailand's second-largest national park at 2,168 sq km (837 sq miles), and it cuts across four different provinces. Most of the protected area is located at around 400 metres (1,300ft) above sea level, making it a pleasant escape from the hot, humid lowlands of central Thailand. Those hoping to see wildlife should come in the cool and dry season (October–January) when the animals are most active and trails in the jungle passable. Be sure to bring warm clothes during this period as temperatures can plummet to as low as 10°C (50°F) at night. Visiting in the rainy season isn't out of the question,

Haew Suwat Waterfall, Khao Yai National Park.

Northeast Thailand
0 50 km
0 50 miles
L A O S
CAMBODIA
THIU KHAO PHANOM DONGRAK
PHANG HOEI RANGE
at same scale
Viangchan (Vientiane)
Nong Khai
Udon Thani
Khon Kaen
Kalasin
Maha Sarakham
Roi Et
Yasothon
Sakhon Nakhon
Nakhon Phanom
Mukdahan
Savannakhet
Ubon Ratchathani
Warin Chamrap
Si Saket
Surin
Buri Ram
Nakhon Ratchasima (Khorat)
Chaiyaphum
Loei
Chiang Khan
Phimai
Bua Yai
Phon
Suwannaphum
Amnat Charoen
Aranyaprathet
Phibun Mangsahan
Khong Jiam
Det Udom
Na Chaluai
Nam Yun
Pak Chong
Khao Yai National Park
Haew Suwat Waterfall
Haew Narok Waterfall
Thap Lan National Park
Pang Sida National Park
Phu Kradung N.P.
Phu Luang National Park
Phu Rua N.P.
Tad Ton National Park
Phu Wiang N.P.
Phu Khao N.P.
Than Nga National Park
Phu Phan National Park
Huai Hat National Park
Nam Yoi N.P.
Phu Mu National Park
Phu Pha Thurm N.P.
Pha Taem N.P.
Kaeng Tanna N.P.
Ban Chiang
Wat Phu Thok
Wat Phra That Bang Puan
Phu Phrabat Historical Park
Tham Erawan
Wat Narai Cheng Weng
Wat Phra That Phanom
Prasat Hin Phimai
Prasat Hin Phanomwan
Prasat Peuay Noi
Prasat Hin Khao Phanom Rung Historical Park
Prasat Hin Muang Tam
Prasat Ta Muan Tot
Prasat Khao Phra Viharn
Prang Ku
Ubon Ratana Dam
Sirinthorn Reservoir
Mun
Chi
Khong (Mekong)

but remember to cover up bare legs and arms, as leeches are common.

Often clad in mist, Khao Yai's highest peaks lie in the east along the edge of the Khorat Plateau. **Khao Laem** (Shadow Mountain) is 1,313 metres (4,307ft) high, while **Khao Khiew** (Green Mountain) rises to a height of 1,351 metres (4,432ft). Evergreen and deciduous trees, palms and bamboo blanket the park, and unlike much of Thailand, patches of indigenous rainforest can still be seen here. At lower elevations there are areas of dry deciduous forest and some grassland. Gibbons, macaques and langurs are the most commonly spotted wildlife, while black bears, leopards and other big cats, various species of deer, porcupines and wild pigs also roam the reserve. Khao Yai is home to some 200 elephants and a few tigers, but they are rarely seen. In addition, over 320 species of birds have been identified, with regular sightings of great hornbills.

More than 50km (30 miles) of marked trails crisscross the park, most of them originally forged and still used by elephants. In several clearings, there are observation towers where you can watch animals feed. After-dark safaris by tour companies claim to spot tigers and elephants; in reality such spotlight-led trucks careering around the park are more likely to yield sightings of deer, deer, and yet more deer. Guides are available at the park visitor centre, but you'll have a better chance of getting an English-speaking one if you organise a tour of the park through one of the guesthouses in the area.

Other attractions in the park include the 20-metre (66ft) **Haew Suwat Waterfall** – which featured in the film *The Beach* – east of the park headquarters, and the larger three-level **Haew Narok Falls**, rising to a height of 150 metres (500ft) and located further south.

Near the entrance to the park are numerous lodges and bungalows, including the luxury **Kirimaya**, a boutique resort in the vein of African safari lodges with luxury tented villas. Other pursuits include teeing

Thao Suranari statue in Nakhon Ratchasima.

off at internationally designed golf courses and jungle rides on ATVs (All Terrain Vehicles).

NAKHON RATCHASIMA (KHORAT)

Highway 2 continues northeast up the Khorat Plateau, passing the reservoir of **Lam Takhong**, the area's principal source of water. Soon, the blue lake disappears and scrub brush, typical of the drier northeast, begins to dominate.

The city of **Nakhon Ratchasima** ❷ – more popularly known by its older name, **Khorat** – the richest and largest city in the northeast, is located some 260km (162 miles) from Bangkok. As the capital of **Nakhon Ratchasima Province**, the city was a base for American bombers during the Vietnam War. It now serves as a trade, communications and military centre for the entire northeast.

CITY SIGHTS

Although a busy and important commercial centre with little of obvious architectural value, Nakhon Ratchasima has not forgotten its past. A statue of national heroine **Thao Suranari** (or Khunying Mo) presides over the town square and the whitewashed old city wall, which dates from around the 10th century. Khunying Mo was the wife of an assistant provincial governor in the early 19th century when Prince Anou of Vientiane led his army here. After taking the city, the prince threatened to enslave its residents. Khunying Mo rallied the women, who enticed the Lao soldiers into a drunken revelry and then killed them whilst they slept. Prince Anou, who meanwhile had gone to attack Saraburi, was forced to withdraw his depleted forces back to Vientiane, to the north. The annual **Thao Suranari Festival**, held over 12 days in late March and early April, pays tribute to her victory with colourful parades, live music, outdoor performances of bawdy, traditional folk dance-drama called *likay* and Isaan food vendors. Local residents still place offerings at her statue's feet.

Buddha and offering, Prasat Hin Phimai.

Another tribute to local and regional history can be found at the **Maha Wirawong National Museum** (Wed–Sun 9am–4pm), on the grounds of Wat Suchinda by Thanon Ratchadamnoen. The museum has a fine collection of Khmer and central Thai art and artefacts, as well as exhibits on archaeology and folklore.

OUTSIDE TOWN: PAK THONG CHAI

Silk is one of the region's most important industries, and you will see many shops in Nakhon Ratchasima selling the fabric by the metre as well as ready-made clothing and home accessories like cushion covers and tablecloths. To visit a nearby silk production centre, take Route 304 south towards Kabinburi. After 30km (20 miles) is **Pak Thong Chai** ❸, where about 70 factories weave silk, including the Jim Thompson company, Thailand's famous hand-woven silk enterprise. Silk can be bought direct from the factories or at the many silk shops in the area, although prices are about the same as those in Nakhon Ratchasima or Bangkok.

KHAO YAI WINERIES

Bacchus has discovered Thailand in the past few years, and local vineyards are beginning to grow in popularity and quality. Khao Yai's climate is quite good for grape cultivation, and a number of vineyards around Pak Chong, like **PB Valley Khao Yai** (tel: 081-733 8783; www.khaoyaiwinery.com), **GranMonte Family Vineyard** (tel: 044-009 543; www.granmonte.com) and **Village Farm & Winery** (tel: 044-228 407; www.villagefarm.co.th) have flourished.

The word from connoisseurs is that while these wines are eminently palatable, they still need considerable refinement before they will be ready to compete with international wines. Help from the government – to reduce tax to make local wine significantly cheaper – is also needed. Tours, wine-tastings, meals and even accommodation can all be arranged.

DAN KHWIAN

The ceramics made in the village of Dan Khwian, about 15km (9 miles) southwest of Nakhon Ratchasima on Route 224 are another interesting local handicraft. The kaolin clay mined from the banks of the nearby Mun River here has a high iron content and, after firing in the wood-burning kilns, takes on a natural reddish metallic finish. The items are often cut with elaborate lattice patterns and make good lamps.

A wide variety of wares are on offer, but the trip is really made worthwhile for the chance to view Isaan village life at its most traditional. The name "Dan Khwian" refers to the two-wheeled carts that are made here. For centuries the village has been a traditional rest stop for travellers from Cambodia.

PRASAT HIN PHANOMWAN

Northeast of Nakhon Ratchasima, just beyond the city limits is the peaceful monastery of **Prasat Hin Phanomwan** ❹ (daily 7am–6pm; free). With its trademark heavy stone galleries,

Fact

"Isaan", the common Thai name for northeastern Thailand, derives from Ishanapura, a Sanskrit name for an ancient, pre-Angkor Mon Khmer Hindu kingdom that once ruled the region. Today Isaan covers 19 of Thailand's 76 provinces.

A guardian naga serpent at Prasat Hin Phimai.

Fact

Every November, on the second weekend of the month, Phimai hosts a lively festival celebrating the district's historical legacy. Centred at Prasat Hin Phimai, the festival offers longtail boat races, sound-and-light shows and cultural performances.

it reveals the Khmer penchant for false windows with stone mullions, a method adopted to imitate lathed wood and also to compensate for the soft stone. Look closely and you will see the zigzag patterns embellished over the carved stones.

An uncommon stillness pervades this 11th-century retreat, broken only by the footsteps of resident monks. Unlike the majority of Khmer-era ruins, this one contains an active temple. Behind its well-preserved vaulted entrance, the original, dark sanctuary is filled with many more recent Buddha images of different styles, most of them covered with patches of gold leaf.

PRASAT HIN PHIMAI

Further north the magnificent 11th-century Khmer ruins of **Prasat Hin Phimai** ❺ (daily 8am–6pm) are some 50km (30 miles) from Nakhon Ratchasima on the Mun River, a tributary of the Mekong. Renovated with the help of the same experts who restored Angkor Wat across the border in Cambodia, it has been suggested that Phimai may have been a prototype for Angkor Wat itself, which was built in the following century.

The last of the great Angkor monarchs, King Jayavarman VII, who replaced Hinduism with Mahayana Buddhism as the official religion, knew how to travel in comfort. From his palace to Phimai, which was then at the western extent of his expanding kingdom along a major trade route, a string of 112 rest-houses was constructed along the 240km (150-mile) road to shelter pilgrims and government officials making the same long journey to Phimai. During Jayavarman's reign (AD 1181–1201), Phimai prospered within a walled rectangular area of 1,000 by 560 metres/yds on an artificial island created by linking the Mun River and one of its tributaries by a canal. There were four entrances, with serpents, or *naga*, guarding each. The primary entrance faces south. As with the Angkor temples, the monuments at Phimai were never inhabited. Shops, libraries and houses were built of wood, and therefore disintegrated centuries ago.

Stone lintels at Prasat Hin Khao Phanom Rung.

PHIMAI NATIONAL MUSEUM

The Old City gate, likely the main entrance to the sanctuary, still stands at the end of Phimai's present main street. An original 12th-century water tank, called **Sa Kwan**, has also survived.

Facing Sa Kwan, the large, partially open-air **Phimai National Museum** (Wed–Sun 9am–4pm) displays many of the more beautifully carved lintels and statues found in the area, including an exquisite, Buddha-like stone sculpture of King Jayavarman VII.

SOUTHEAST TO BURIRAM

Backtracking to Nakhon Ratchasima, continue eastwards via Highway 24, running roughly parallel to the Cambodian border, for a good look at rural Isaan country and two significant, but rarely visited, Khmer temple sites in **Buriram Province**.

PRASAT HIN KHAO PHANOM RUNG HISTORICAL PARK

Three full ponds – essential elements of Khmer monumental architecture – and scenic farmland surround **Prasat Hin Khao Phanom Rung Historical Park** ❻ (daily 6am–6pm), which is easily accessed from either Nakhon Ratchasima, Buriram or Surin. Historians believe this temple was an important rest stop between Angkor and Phimai during the 11th and 12th centuries. Many generations must have elapsed during its initial construction, since several of the stone lintels resemble the mid-11th-century Baphuon style, while the *naga* (serpents) date from the later Angkor Wat period. A stone inscription in Sanskrit mentions King Suryavarman II, the ruler behind the construction of Angkor Wat.

The largest and best-restored Khmer monument in Thailand, Prasat Hin Khao Phanom Rung is maintained by monks of the strict Dhammayuti sect. The temple includes a Vishnu lintel, which was spirited out of Thailand by art thieves in the early 1960s. It later surfaced in the US, in a private museum collection. After protracted negotiations, the lintel was returned to Thailand in the early 1990s and placed in its original position over one of the entrances.

The main *prang* of Phanom Rung, and its galleries and chapels, reflect the geometric precision of Angkor architecture: symmetrical doors and windows face the four cardinal points. The monumental staircase, relieved by landings, exudes a sense of mass and power typical of Khmer design. Look for the sandstone bas-reliefs of elephants and enthroned Hindu deities. The 1,000 year-old Phanom Rung Festival every April coincides with the few days each year when the light of the rising and setting suns passes through the temple's 15 aligned doorways. The festival has religious ceremonies, cultural shows and performances.

The remote temple of Prasat Ta Muan Tot is located close to the Cambodian border.

A Burmese-Siamese War re-enactment at the Surin Elephant Roundup.

KHMER LEGACY

Northeast Thailand encompasses a large swathe of former Khmer territory, and over half of the region's Khmer religious sites.

Between the 10th and 14th centuries AD, a large part of mainland Southeast Asia, from the Mekong Delta in the east to around Phetchburi in the west, lay under the control of the Khmer empire. The capital at Angkor was connected to the outlying reaches of empire by a system of highways and religio-political strongpoints such as Prasat Khao Phra Viharn, Wat Phu Champasak, Phanom Rung and Phimai.

By the mid-19th century, when the frontiers of present-day Indochina were effectively fixed by the French, the Khmer empire had long since disappeared, leaving Cambodia much reduced in size. It is true that the crowning glory of the Khmer past, Angkor Wat, still lay within Cambodia's confines, as did – just (though disputed by Thailand) – the magnificent "lofty sanctuary" of Phra Viharn. Yet many other symbolic relics of the Khmer past now lay outside Cambodia's borders, most notably Wat Phu Champasak in southern Laos, and a series of magnificent sites across Thailand's northeast, where they are known as *prasat*. In fact, over 200 Khmer religious sites – over half of the total number – are located in this part of Thailand.

Thailand has long valued these unique historic treasures, traditionally considering them to be temporary homes for Hindu deities and, as such, needing to be consecrated regularly in elaborate ceremonies performed by a class of Hindu priests. Yet only very recently have concerted efforts been made to preserve and promote them. Over the past three decades, several of the most important sites have been painstakingly and successfully restored by the government's Department of Fine Arts.

Khorat and Buriram provinces host the major Khmer complexes: Prasat Hin Phimai, Prasat Phanom Rung and Prasat Muang Tam. All three have been carefully restored, though Phanom Rung is perhaps today the most impressive. Like Angkor Wat itself, these temples were all originally constructed as Hindu temples, dedicated to Vishnu and Shiva, and as such the ruins demonstrate, particularly in their carvings, a deistic diversity and Indic sensuality not evident in more recent, Buddhist structures. It was under Jayavarman VII that Hinduism was replaced by Buddhism, and the temples converted to wats. Until today, their significance to Thai Buddhists remains strong, weakened neither by memories of foreign powers on what is now Thai soil nor by the slightly unfamiliar iconography. Phanom Rung is indeed a regular and important place of Buddhist pilgrimage.

The structure that most immediately identifies a site as Khmer is the tall tapering tower (called *prang*) with longitudinal ridges. These towers were symbolic of Mount Meru, the mythical mountain at the centre of the Hindu universe. Even as far away as Lopburi, Khmer influence is easily recognisable in the three ruined *prang* of Phra Prang Sam Yot, often attributed to Jayavarman VII. And in the vicinity of Phanom Rung are various Khmer *kuti*, or meditation retreats, as well as several other unrestored temple complexes, languishing in the forests and undergrowth.

As recently as 1976, the despotic Khmer Rouge regime was staking a claim to northeast Thailand, promising to "liberate" lost Khmer territories. Fortunately, whilst the local Khmer-speakers are conscious of, and justly proud of, their cultural links with Angkor, they are also loyal Thai citizens.

Hindu motifs feature in this ornate stone carving at Prasat Hin Muang Tam.

Check online for the dates, which change yearly.

PRASAT HIN MUANG TAM

Further east, and downhill a couple of kilometres, is **Prasat Hin Muang Tam** ❼ (daily 8am–6pm), or Lower Temple, sitting on a mossy lawn like an art historian's daydream. Older than Prasat Hin Khao Phanom Rung, its cornerstones were laid in the 10th century, with the temple finished about 100 years later. A Shiva lintel suggests it may originally have been devoted to Hindu worship, and later converted into a Buddhist temple.

Muang Tam, which has five *prang* surrounded by galleries, protected by walls and now shaded by trees, is considered the third-most significant Angkor-period site in the northeast after Phanom Rung and Phimai. It has been beautifully restored. Previously haphazard blocks of masonry and fallen lintels are back in place, and the monumental tank is now rebuilt and filled with water lilies.

The huge rectangular stone blocks that form the outer walls contain drilled circular holes, probably used for stone figures shaped like lotus buds. The rims of the ponds are lined with *naga* serpents, whose many heads rise at the corners, marking the outer boundary of the temple.

SURIN AND SI SAKET

Located on an old Khmer site, the provincial capital of **Surin** ❽ was primarily known for its silk production until 1960, when the first **Elephant Round-Up** was organised. Originally a festival held by the local people, who are known for their abilities in training the animals, the round-up has now been transformed into an elaborate spectacle that takes place on the third weekend of November. These days about 400 elephants will take part in the event, which includes an impressive re-enactment of the famous battle between King Naresuan of Ayuthaya (1590–1605) and the Burmese, which took place in Suphanburi and is a mainstay of Thai patriotic lore. Both men and beasts are elaborately costumed, and the event puts any elephant show you've ever seen to shame. In addition, more prosaic events take place, such as elephant soccer and the obligatory "Miss Elephant Festival" beauty pageant. While these practices have been criticised by animal-rights groups, the centre nevertheless retains its popularity.

The village of **Ban Ta Klang**, located 60km (40 miles) north of Surin, is the true home of elephant culture in Thailand. It is populated by a people known as the Suay (also called Gui), who are originally from Central Asia and settled in this area before the rise of the Khmer empire. They are Thailand's master mahouts and travel throughout Asia as elephant tenders – originally in logging, now in tourism. A visit to Ban Ta Klang is worthwhile for those with a serious

Fact

There were clashes between the Thai and Cambodian militaries at Khao Phra Viharn on several occasions between 2008 and 2011, leading to roughly 40 fatalities. The area has been sporadically closed to visitors since 2010, although tensions have gradually dissipated. In 2013, the International Court of Justice ruled that the temple should remain under Cambodian rule. To check on the current status call the TAT office in Ubon at 045-243 770.

Prasat Khao Phra Viharn overlooks the Cambodian countryside.

interest in elephants and is best arranged with a knowledgeable guide. The elephants taking part in the Surin Elephant Round-Up are trained here, so the best time to visit is in early November, shortly before the event takes place.

PRASAT TA MUAN TOT

South of Surin Town in Ban Ta Miang district, on the Cambodian border, is **Prasat Ta Muan Tot** ❾ (daily 8am–5pm; free), one of the most remote and atmospheric Khmer temple sites in Thailand. Part of a 'healing station' on the route to Angkor Wat, the main sanctuary stands in line with an ornate gate *(gopura)* and prayer hall *(mandapa)* built of sandstone and surrounded by a laterite wall.

PRASAT KHAO PHRA VIHARN

Route 226 and a direct rail line connect Surin with the next province east, **Si Saket** ❿, which borders Cambodia.

Si Saket Province's once main attraction no longer lies in Thailand as the World Court awarded Cambodia the splendid temple complex of **Prasat Khao Phra Viharn** ⓫ (daily 6am–4.30pm) in the early 1960s. Located about 100km (60 miles) southeast of the provincial capital, it used to be easily reached from there or from Surin or Ubon Ratchathani. However, after a long-lasting dispute over the borders between the two countries, the shrine was confirmed as belonging to Cambodia in 2013, and currently, it may only be reached from the Cambodian side. Whether due to Thai dissatisfaction with the World Court ruling or wider political animosities, trouble has regularly flared between Thai and Cambodian soldiers stationed near this site, and it is not always open to visitors. However, when Thai-Cambodian relations are normal, the sanctuary is also accessible from the Thai side and Cambodia does not require visas for visitors to the site.

Prasat Khao Phra Viharn sits on a 500-metre (1,650ft) perch of the Dongrak Mountains overlooking the Cambodian plains. Stretching for almost

The city pillar, Ubon Ratchathani.

1km (0.6 mile), Phra Viharn was constructed in the early 11th century. Its stairs alternate between hewn bedrock and stones put there about 100 years before the days of Angkor Wat. Each layer is marked by an increasingly large *gopura*, or gate, and ends at the topmost sanctuary honouring the god Shiva.

To the east of the first *gopura*, a precarious trail descends through the jungle to the Cambodian plains. The second *gopura*, shaped like a Greek cross, is superbly carved in 11th-century Khmer style. Its lintels show Vishnu in the Hindu creation myth. The stairs continue in a symbolic ascent to heaven, past another purificatory basin, to the first courtyard with its two palaces and *gopura*, and finally up to the second and third courtyards and the main sanctuary. At the end of the long ridge is a breathtaking precipice above the Cambodian countryside, turning a natural site into a stunning work of art.

Since the sanctuary itself is often inaccessible from Thailand, visitors to the **Prasat Khao Phra Viharn National Park** (daily 6am–6pm; http://portal.dnp.go.th), partially reopened in late 2014, must remain satisfied with seeing a bas relief depicting a pair of Khmer figures carved into a sandstone wall about 1,000 years ago in the Pha Mo I Daeng cliff, and a view to Prasat Khao Phra Viharn from the top of the hill.

UBON RATCHATHANI

Called "Ubon" for short, the sleepy northeastern provincial capital of **Ubon Ratchathani** ⓬ lies 700km (430 miles) east of Bangkok and about 60km (40 miles) east of Si Saket. In the 1100s, the area around Ubon belonged to the Khmers, until the Ayutthaya empire supplanted them. Ubon itself is a rather young town, founded in the late 1700s by Lao immigrants. Much of the town's 20th-century growth coincided with the American build-up during the Vietnam War, and the military link is still in evidence today, with many of Ubon's 115,000 inhabitants working for the Thai military. The town's strong trade links with nearby Laos and Cambodia has earned Ubon the moniker "Capital of the Emerald Triangle". A rash of new construction and some of the region's prettiest temples rise behind the banks of the Mun River, which flows east into the Mekong 100km (62 miles) from Ubon.

Mahabodhi Stupa replica at Wat Phra That Nong Bua.

CITY SIGHTS

Established by King Rama III, **Wat Thung Si Muang** (daily 8.30am–4.30pm; free) at Thanon Luang is noted for its scripture library, which is sturdily built of teak and raised on stilts in the middle of a lotus pond.

Ubon Ratchathani National Museum is Isaan's finest museum (Wed–Sun 9am–4pm). Housed in King Vajiravudh's (Rama VI, r. 1910–25) former country residence, it has a collection

The scripture library at Wat Thung Si Muang, Ubon Ratchathani.

of fine artefacts of Thai, Lao, Khmer, Vietnamese and Indian origin.

On the outskirts of town, **Wat Phra That Nong Bua** (daily 8.30am–4.30pm; free) contains a tall *chedi* that is a close replica of the Mahabodhi Stupa in Bodh Gaya, India. **Ko Hat Wat Tai**, a sandy island in the middle of the Mun River, southeast of the town, is a favourite picnic spot during the hot, dry months of March and April when the river recedes and exposes a temporary "beach".

Two temples in nearby **Warin Chamrap** district are well known for their association with the late Ajahn Cha, a famous meditation master. His original monastery, **Wat Nong Pa Phong** (daily 8am–4.30pm; free; www.watnongpahpong.org/indexe.php), lies 10km (6 miles) north of the Ubon train station. This peaceful spot has a small museum dedicated to the famous monk, as well as a *chedi* enshrining his ashes. Many Western monks were ordained and spent time at this monastery studying under Ajahn Cha.

Nearby **Wat Pa Nanachat Bung Wai** (daily 6am–6pm; free; www.watpahnanachat.org) houses another unique Buddhist monastery. Founded by an American monk under Ajahn Cha's tutelage, the tidy, highly disciplined monastery welcomes visitors to stay for meditation and religious talks, although it is always best to contact them before visiting.

KAENG TANNA N P

From Ubon, it's possible to visit **Kaeng Tanna National Park** (daily 8am–6pm; http://portal.dnp.go.th), some 90km (56 miles) to the northeast, near the Mekong River. It has prehistoric cave paintings and rapids where the Mun River squeezes through a gorge before joining the Mekong. The park is also known for its abundance of submerged cave systems. There is basic bungalow accommodation available.

Ubon Ratchathani is also the jump-off point for visiting the scenic peninsula of **Khong Jiam** (see page 349) at the confluence of the Mekong and Mun rivers.

Rock formations at Kaeng Tenna National Park.

Kaeng Tana National Park.

The Phee Ta Khon festival, Dan Sai.

NORTH TO LOEI

Delve deep into the heart of Isaan at Khon Kaen and Roi Et. Then head to Udon Thani, where excavations at nearby Ban Chiang have yielded traces of Thailand's Bronze Age. Further north, Loei is known for its rugged mountain scenery and fertility festival.

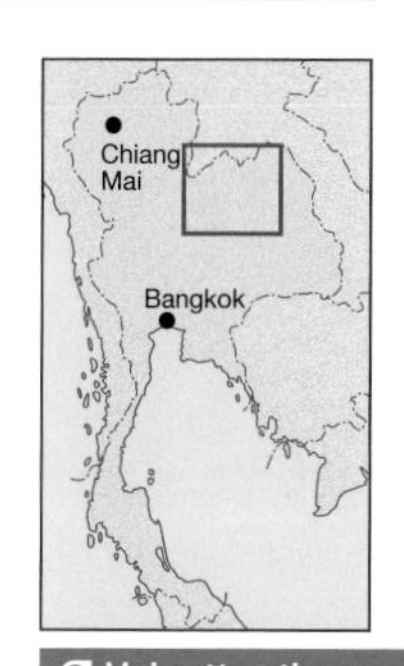

Main attractions

Khon Kaen
Roi Et
Udon Thani
Udorn Sunshine Orchid Farm
Ban Chiang
Loei
Dan Sai
Phu Kradung National Park

From **Nakhon Ratchasima** (Khorat), travellers can continue north on Highway 2 to the heart of the Isaan region in Khon Kaen Province. From Khon Kaen, you can either head east to Roi Et or continue north on Highway 2 to Udon Thani and further until it reaches the northernmost Mekong River town of Nong Khai. Diverting west from Udon Thani leads to the tranquil and mountainous region of Loei.

KHON KAEN AND ROI ET

With a population of 150,000, **Khon Kaen** ⓭ is the Isaan region's second-largest city after Nakhon Ratchasima. It is the only large centre in the eponymous province – an overwhelmingly rural part of Thailand, with farming and textiles being the main livelihoods. Aside from serving as a trade and supply centre for these industries, Khon Kaen is also an important commercial, financial and educational centre.

With its good restaurants and hotels, Khon Kaen makes a fine spot to take a rest from travel in Isaan. Travellers continuing to Laos or Vietnam can also obtain visas from the Lao and Vietnamese consulates in town.

CITY SIGHTS

There are a few attractions in town worth checking out. The well-curated **Khon Kaen National Museum** (Wed–Sun 9am–4pm) at Thanon Lang Sunratchakan has an impressive collection of Dvaravati-period (6th–10th-century) Buddhist art, and ancient Ban Chiang artefacts of bronze and ceramic from the Sukhothai and Ayutthaya periods.

Also of interest is **Wat Nong Wang Muang** (daily 8am–6pm; free) at the southern end of town. The temple is surprisingly grand for Isaan; its beautiful nine-tiered pagoda is said to be designed after the famous Shwedagon Pagoda of Yangon in Myanmar.

Map on page 324

Khon Kaen.

The unique dancing gyrant plant at Udorn Sunshine Nursery.

Khon Kaen town's two large, shallow lakes, **Beung Kaen Nakhon** (Kaen Nakhon Lake), found at the southern limits of the city and **Beung Thung Sang** (Thung Sang Lake) to the north-east, are favourite venues with strollers seeking cool evening breezes and snacks sold by itinerant vendors.

AROUND KHON KAEN

Many visitors to Khon Kaen also use the city as a base to make a day trip to **Chonabot** ⓮, some 57km (34 miles) southwest. This is a well-known centre for the high-quality, traditional north-eastern silk fabric known as *mudmee*. At the small workshops in Chonabot, you can see the silk being woven and dyed, as well as buy the fabrics.

Around 70km (43 miles) southeast of Khon Kaen, via Routes 23 and 2297, **Prasat Peuay Noi** ⓯ (known locally as That Ku Thong) is a little-visited 12th-century Khmer temple site much admired for its large sandstone sanctuary topped by a *prang*. Parts of the original temple walls and gates still stand, along with carved stone pediments and lintels.

EAST TO ROI ET

From Khon Kaen, Route 213 heads east 76km (47 miles) to the small farming centre of **Kalasin**, while Route 214 leads 115km (71 miles) southeast to **Roi Et** ⓰, a worthwhile side trip for anyone interested in Isaan culture, particularly its music.

ROI ET CITY

The city of Roi Et is centred on an artificial lake called **Beung Phlan Chai**. Although once an independent kingdom with 11 city gates, the local architecture today offers little of historic interest.

Wat Burapha (daily 8.30am–4.30pm; free) is a popular pilgrimage point because of its 68-metre (223ft) standing Buddha. A staircase in its base reaches the level of the figure's knees, from where you can take in views of the surrounding townscape.

Nearby **Wat Neua** (daily 7am–7pm; free) contains a very old *chedi* that may date to the Dvaravati period; Dvaravati-style stone ordination markers surround the ordination hall. A stone pillar inscribed in Khmer suggests the

A food stall in the Khon Kaen area.

site was also occupied by the Khmers around the 11th or 12th century.

UDON THANI

Northeast of Khon Kaen, around 50km (31 miles) along Highway 2, look for signs to Ban Khok Sa-nga, or King Cobra Village, which holds snake shows at Wat Si Thamma (donation). Many villagers keep snakes and conduct travelling shows around the countryside. Another 65km (40 miles) on Highway 2 is **Udon Thani** ⓱ (Udon for short, often spelt "Udorn"), a town that grew quickly with the arrival of American airmen during the Vietnam War in the 1960s. The city is unusual for Thailand in that several major avenues are laid out diagonally against a street grid, complete with large traffic circles that might be more at home in a French city.

Aside from the artificial lake, **Nong Prajak**, there is little to see in town. However, just outside to the northwest, off Route 2024, the **Udorn Sunshine Orchid Farm** (daily 7am–6pm) is famous for creating the Thai dancing gyrant, a plant whose leaves sway gently when spoken or sung to. They sell Dancing Tea, apparently prized for its health-giving properties, and several blends of perfume, using aromatic extracts from orchids grown on site.

Udon has many good Isaan diners and local shops sell high-quality Isaan handicrafts, particularly hand-woven cotton and silk textiles.

BAN CHIANG

In Nong Han district in the eastern part of Udon Thani Province lies what is probably the most famous archaeological site in Thailand. The people of **Ban Chiang** ⓲, long used to encountering fragments of pots, beads and even human bones when digging around their houses and farms, had paid scant attention to such finds. Then, in 1966, a University of Pennsylvania anthropology student visited the area. He showed his finds to the archaeology authorities in Bangkok. More comprehensive analysis led to a surprising conclusion; they were much older than had been believed – between 3,500 and 7,500 years old.

Textile weaving.

ROI ET MUSIC

Several villages located around Roi Et specialise in the crafting of a type of mouth organ known as the *khaen*, the lead instrument in *mor lam*, a bawdy and occasionally political northeastern music form. The *khaen* consists of thick hollow reeds bound in two rows to a carved Asian redwood sound chamber, and produces a sound reminiscent of an organ or large harmonica. The rhythmically churning instrument, allied with hand percussion and two stringed instruments (the bowed *so* and plucked *phin*), yields a hypnotic sonic brew that inspires all-night dancing among *mor lam* devotees. The most convenient village to see *khaen*-making is Si Kaew, approximately 15km (9 miles) northwest of Roi Et City.

Wat Burapha, Roi Et.

Shop

Two weaving villages, Ban Na Kha and Ban Thon, 16km (10 miles) and 18km (11 miles) respectively north of Udon Thani and off Highway 2, are well known for their hand-loomed textiles called *khit*. Diamond-shaped motifs woven into weft brocade are *khit* hallmarks. Several shops in the two villages offer the textiles for sale.

Bronze artefacts were also discovered, and dated to around 3,600 BC. This places the appearance of bronze in Thailand centuries earlier than in the Middle East, until then thought to be the earliest location of bronze usage. Equally intriguing is that this dating of Ban Chiang bronze suggests that bronze may have been transmitted from Thailand to China, rather than the other way round, which had hitherto been the theory. Some experts, however, maintain that the dating of 3,600 BC for the appearance of bronze is too early, suggesting that 2,000 BC, or even 2,500 BC, is more accurate. This would put the appearance of bronze in Southeast Asia later than the Middle East, but at around the same time as China.

Even if its antiquity were not authenticated, the beautiful whorl designs of its pottery and the intricacy of its bronze jewellery and implements would make the Ban Chiang culture rather more advanced than most of the early peoples of the earth. In recognition of this, Ban Chiang achieved Unesco World Heritage status in 1992.

Pottery display at the Ban Chiang National Museum.

Many of these artefacts are in the **Ban Chiang National Museum** (Wed–Sun 8.30am–5pm), established with the help of the US-based Smithsonian Institute. One of the original excavation pits, on display at nearby **Wat Pho Si Nai** (daily 9am–4pm) contains 52 human skeletons that were interred with ceremonial pottery.

TOWARDS LOEI

Route 210 runs 150km (100 miles) west of Udon Thani to the ruggedly beautiful **Loei Province**, and the town of the same name. But first, stop midway at **Tham Erawan** ⓳ (daily 8.30am–4.30pm; donation), the Triple-Headed Elephant Cave, about 50km (30 miles) before Loei and a couple of kilometres (1 mile) off the road. Prehistoric artefacts have been found here at the cave, which is ensconced in the side of large and beautiful limestone cliff. It is considered sacred and is part of Wat Tham Erawan, a small complex of shrine rooms and monastic cells in front of the cave. A large sitting Buddha near the mouth of the cave is visible from the plains below. A life-size statue of Erawan, the triple-headed elephant of Hindu-Buddhist mythology, marks the steep 700-step stairway and rocky path to the cave's entrance. The climb is rough, but the views are worth the effort. However, besides the occasional cobra emerging from the rocks, and an elephant's skull, there is little to see inside the actual cave.

LOEI

The city of **Loei** ⓴ is a flourishing centre for the province's cotton trade and its low-level commerce with neighbouring Laos. The usually placid Loei River flows through the centre of town. What is now a traveller's delight was once the civil servant's nightmare, an isolated jungle outpost with fever, cold weather and poor security. Until the 1980s, communist insurgents hid in the surrounding forests.

Loei is somewhat scant on sights, but the surrounding province makes up for this with several lush national parks, rugged mountainous scenery and the chance to witness a unique festival at Dan Sai.

PHU RUA N P

From Loei, Route 203 plunges west into the wilderness to **Phu Rua National Park** ㉑ (daily 5am–8pm; http://portal.dnp.go.th). The 50km (30-mile) road slices through heavy banks of red laterite, past a sawmill and fields of *kenaf* and cotton, the latter being the area's primary source of income. The summit of Phu Rua mountain is 1,370 metres (4,495ft) high. A smooth, winding road leads to the top, from where there are spectacular views of the national forest. Be warned that in winter, the temperature at the summit can drop to freezing point.

DAN SAI

Around 80km (50 miles) southwest of Loei is **Dan Sai** ㉒, famous for its annual **Phee Ta Khon Festival**, possibly Thailand's most raucous celebration. The townspeople don outlandish, clown-like costumes and huge masks with devilish-looking eyes, an oversized wooden nose and a wide, toothy grin.

The festival celebrates the *Mahavessantara Jataka*, a tale in which the Buddha travels to heavenly realms to preach to his deceased mother. The costumed figures represent members of the spirit world who follow the Buddha back to earth after his visit. The figures – women as well as men, children as well as adults – carry large wooden hand totems, carved into graphic phallic shapes (possibly a syncretic blending with a pre-Buddhist fertility festival).

Most of the activities of the three-day festival centre around **Wat Phon Chai**, where the "spirits" circumambulate the main *viharn* (sermon hall) numerous times, dancing to live *mor lam* music. Inspired by copious consumption of *lao khao* (home-distilled moonshine), the circumambulations last hours, reaching a frenzied crescendo after midday. The exact date of the festival changes each year, but it falls in either June or

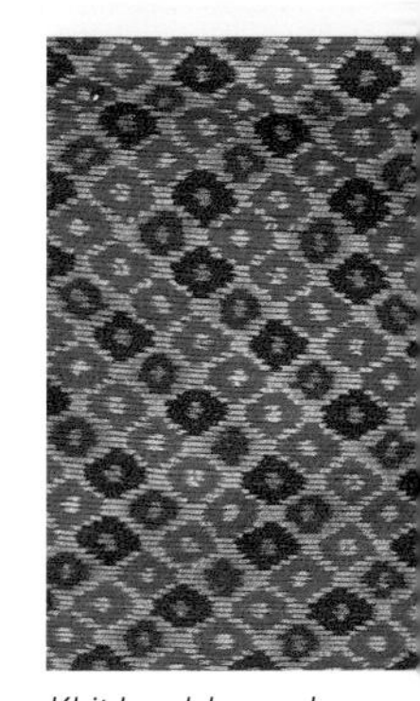

Khit hand-loomed fabric with its distinctive diamond-shaped motifs.

Sunrise view of Phu Rua National Park.

Fact

Loei Province experiences the most extreme weather in Thailand. In the winter, the province consistently records temperatures below freezing, and in the summer months temperatures are often the nation's highest. Enterprising locals have taken advantage of this; in the hot dry months they grow cotton, and in the cooler seasons, at higher altitude, Loei's temperate-species cut flowers are shipped to Bangkok.

July. Just south of town, in the grounds of Wat Phon Chai, the Dan Sai Folk Museum (daily 9am-5pm) has information on the festival and demonstrations of mask making.

AROUND DAN SAI

Just outside Dan Sai is **Phra That Si Songrak** (daily 6am–6.30pm), a highly venerated *chedi* constructed in the four-sided, curvilinear style of Laos and northeastern Thailand. The 30-metre (98ft) monument was erected in 1560 to commemorate the friendship between Thailand and Vientiane, and to mark the border between the two kingdoms.

Northeast of Dan Sai on Route 203 is **Chateau de Loei Vineyards** (daily 9am–5pm; free; www.chateaudeloei.com), the first vineyard in Thailand to produce French-style wines; it has earned a modest reputation for its Chenin Blanc in particular. Self-tours of the vineyards and wine-tasting are available.

The tiny town of **Na Haew**, about 30km (20 miles) northwest of Dan Sai, is a de facto border crossing for locals by raft over the Huang River between Thailand and Laos.

PHU KRADUNG N P

No experience in the Loei area can match the beauty of **Phu Kradung National Park** ㉓ (daily 8am–6pm; http://portal.dnp.go.th), the most memorable escape in this region, some 100km (60 miles) south of Loei. Phu Kradung is a 60-sq-km (24-sq-mile) plateau located between 1,200 and 1,500 metres (4,000–5,000ft) high and with over 50km (30 miles) of marked trails.

The park entrance is along Route 201; about 3km (2 miles) further is the office, where you can arrange for porters and equipment. The park provides bedding and blankets in cabins that hold up to 11 people. It takes three hours to climb the tricky 6-km (4-mile) principal trail, but ladders enable you to negotiate the steepest boulders, and it's well worth the effort. During the March to May hot season, it's best to begin before dawn to avoid the midday heat.

Atop Phu Kradung, clear and mostly level paths crisscross the table. You will

The mighty Mekong river.

encounter rare birds, including various hornbills, woodpeckers and pheasants. Even wild elephants and the occasional tiger make their home on the mountain, along with gibbons, sambars, barking deer and the Asiatic black bear, although few of these species are likely to be seen. As the surrounding forests have been logged indiscriminately in recent years, the authorities close the park in the summer months to permit the ecology to recover.

CHIANG KHAN

From Loei, the road north leads 50km (30 miles) to the Mekong River – where it once again forms the border between Thailand and Laos – and the charming riverside town of **Chiang Khan** ㉔, which is becoming a trendy destination for young Thais. Many of the homes lining the riverbank are built of wood in French-Lao style, and the town's Buddhist temples show a dominant Lao influence. Cycle or catch a taxi about 5km (3 miles) east of town to the **Kaeng Khut Khu** rapids, worthwhile for its raging beauty.

EAST TOWARDS NONG KHAI

From Chiang Khan, Route 211 follows the Mekong east to **Sangkhom** ㉕ village, which has modest accommodation and excellent river views, along with two falls, **Than Thip Waterfall** and **Than Thong Waterfall**, both local picnic spots. Further on along Route 211 beyond Sangkhom, **Wat Hin Mak Peng** (daily 8.30am–4.30pm) is a meditation monastery perched on cliffs overlooking the Mekong. Visitors are welcome to visit the temple if they dress modestly.

Around 20km (12 miles) before Nong Khai, Route 211 passes the town of **Si Chiang Mai** ㉖, directly opposite Vientiane, the capital of Laos, on the other side of the Mekong. Most of its population is of either Lao or Vietnamese descent, and mainly engaged in making the translucent rice-flour skins for Vietnamese-style spring rolls, exported all over the world. All around town, spring-roll wrappers dry on bamboo-lattice racks before being bagged and shipped to wholesalers. A small church serves the town's many Vietnamese Catholic residents.

Tip

Cyclists will enjoy a ride along the Mekong from Chiang Khan to Nong Khai. The traffic is light, climbs are not too difficult and the views are superb. Since there is a village or town with reasonable overnight accommodation every 40km (25 miles) or so, a five-day tour can be done without roughing it too hard. Some guesthouses rent very basic mountain bikes. Need a longer ride? Start in Dan Sai and ride north to the Huang River, then continue east to Chiang Khan and beyond.

Old wooden houses at Chiang Khan.

Sala Kaew Ku Sculpture Park.

ALONG THE MEKONG RIVER

Follow the winding curve of the Mekong River, from Nong Khai in the far north all the way to Khong Jiam in the southeast to experience some of Thailand's most remote sights.

Main attractions

- Nong Khai
- Sala Kaew Ku Sculpture Park
- Phu Phrabat Historical Park
- Wat Phu Thok
- Nakhon Phanom
- Renu Nakhon
- That Phanom
- Mukdahan
- Khong Jiam

From Udon Thani (see page 339), Highway 2 continues north for some 50km (30 miles) to **Nong Khai** ㉗, on the southern bank of the Mekong River. Alternatively, it's also possible (and more exciting) to approach Nong Khai along the Mekong River east from Chiang Khan (see page 343).

NONG KHAI

In 1994, the 1.2km (0.75-mile) **Friendship Bridge** – just 3km (2 miles) west of Nong Khai – opened, connecting Nong Khai with Vientiane, the capital of Laos across the river. A rail link across the bridge opened in 2009, and with daily departures from Bangkok to Nong Khai from where you can board a shuttle train to a stop 13km (8 miles) from Vientiane, the link between capitals is pretty seemless.

Long and narrow, the entire length of Nong Khai Province parallels the Mekong River. From 1353 to 1694, this part of Thailand belonged to the independent Lao kingdoms of Lan Xang and later Vientiane, only becoming a Siamese protectorate in the late 18th century. Nong Khai kept close ties with French-colonised Laos throughout the 19th century, and influences from that period remain in the provincial capital's appealing remnants of Lao-French architecture.

SUNSET CRUISE

To experience the Mekong River fully, take a cruise on the Nagarina, a lovingly restored riverboat operated by the Mut Mee Garden Guest House, which sails from their premises daily at 5pm. Dinner is available – and highly recommended. Alternatively, rough-and-ready grass-topped vessels can be hired throughout the day at Tha Sadet Market (daily 9am–6pm).

During the dry season, when the Mekong shrinks, the "beach" at **Hat Jommani**, 3km (2 miles) west of

Fish farm on the Mekong River at Nong Khai.

Arresting rock formation at Phu Phrabat Historical Park.

Nong Khai, transforms into a local picnic spot.

SALA KAEW KU SCULPTURE PARK

Nong Khai's most popular attraction is the **Sala Kaew Ku Sculpture Park** (daily 8am–5pm; http://garden-buddha-sculpture.blogspot.com), about 4km (2.5 miles) southeast of town via Route 212. Founded by Boun Leua Sourirat, a Hindu-Buddhist guru of Lao descent, the religious park is filled with surreal cement sculptures of Shiva, Vishnu, Buddha and other figures from Hindu and Buddhist mythology.

Born in Laos, Boun Leua fled when the communists took over Vientiane in 1975. Moving to Nong Khai, he began building the giant figures with funds from local donors. The guru died in 1996, but his followers still maintain the park today, along with a small shrine and museum dedicated to the man and his philosophical hybrid fusion of Hinduism and Buddhism.

WAT PHRA THAT BANG PHUAN

Also worth visiting in this area is **Wat Phra That Bang Phuan** (daily 7am–6pm; free) located about 12km (7 miles) south of Nong Khai on Highway 2, and then 11km (7 miles) further west on Route 211. This temple is well known for its elegant 16th-century Lao-style *chedi*, built by King Jaychettha of the Vientiane kingdom. The *chedi* toppled from rain damage in 1970, but was restored a few years later.

PHU PHRABAT HISTORICAL PARK

About 70km (42 miles) southwest of Nong Khai, in Ban Pheu district, is the **Phu Phrabat Historical Park** (daily 8am–4.30pm). This park contains a blend of fascinating prehistoric cave paintings, strange natural rock formations and Buddhist temples. The best way to experience it all is on foot, via a marked trail that takes about two hours to traverse.

ALONG THE MEKONG

It is an exciting journey that few travellers undertake, but it's possible to follow the winding curve of the Mekong River, first northeast, then south all the way to Khong Jiam in Ubon

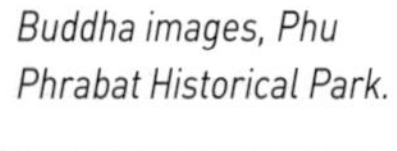

Buddha images, Phu Phrabat Historical Park.

Ratchathani Province. At Khong Jiam, the Mekong first diverts east into Laos and then later south into Cambodia and eventually Vietnam before emptying into the South China Sea.

BEUNG KAN

The first stop is **Beung Kan** ㉘, a long and winding 185km (111 miles) northeast of Nong Khai. Although there is little of historical or cultural note in this small agricultural backwater, it makes for a convenient stopover for long road trips along Thailand's Mekong rim. From Beung Kan, it's possible to take a side trip to **Wat Phu Thok** (also called Wat Chedi Khiri Viharn; daily 6.30am–5pm; closed between 10–16 Apr; free). This is a meditation monastery perched atop a huge sandstone outcrop and an amazing sight. Wooden stairs (best avoided by anyone who suffers from vertigo) lead from ground level to the flat top of the outcrop, 200 metres (650ft) above the surrounding plain, past a number of meditation caves and monastic cells.

NAKHON PHANOM

Following the Mekong River southeast along Route 212, you arrive in **Nakhon Phanom** ㉙ – 270km (162 miles) from Nong Khai and 175km (109 miles) from Beung Kan – the most remote province in northeast Thailand. The Thai name means "city of hills", a reference to the chain of jagged, powder-grey mountains in the distance, across the Mekong River in Laos.

Apart from the pretty views, there is not much to see or do here. Come late October, however, the town is turned into a hive of activity with the onset of the Fireboat Festival.

Nakhon Phanom is also an official Lao–Thai border crossing. The third Thailand-Laos Friendship Bridge opened here in 2011 linking with **Tha Khaek**, a former French colonial outpost. A Lao visa is available on arrival.

RENU NAKHON

From Nakhon Phanom, Route 212 winds gently southwards parallel to the Mekong, at times revealing inspiring views of the Khammuan limestone

Fact

The river known to most Thais as Mae Nam Khong is sometimes shortened to Mae Khong, whence the Western name "Mekong" is derived.

FIRE BOAT FESTIVAL

At the end of the annual three-month Phansa (Buddhist "rains retreat", during which Buddhist monks are required to reside in their home monasteries), usually in late October, Nakhon Phanom becomes the focus of the striking Bun Heua Fai (Fire Boat Festival). In addition to making offerings at Buddhist temples throughout the city, local residents launch homemade "fire boats" on the Mekong River at night. Measuring up to 10 metres (33ft) in length, the elaborate frames and non-functioning "sails" of the curved prow craft are lined with elaborate lanterns, creating a spectacular visual display. The decks are decorated and piled with flowers, balls of sticky rice and cakes, meant as offerings to the Buddhist Devaloka (deity realm).

Mekong River near Renu Nakhon.

Fact

Just east of Nakhon Phanom, in the village of Baan Na Chok, it is possible to visit the 1920s home of Ho Chi Minh (daily 8am–5pm), who was one of many Vietnamese exiles to seek refuge in this part of Thailand. His desk has been preserved, and there is good exhibition of archival photographs. Ironically, during the Vietnam War, Nakhon Phanom was a major US Air Force base.

massif across the river in Laos. Some 44km (26 miles) from Nakhon Phanom, the small town of **Renu Nakhon** 30 is home to the Phu Thai minority, who are much admired for their weaving. Best-known for *mudmee* patterns loom-woven in cotton or silk, the Phu Thai hold a handicraft market every Saturday near the town's main Buddhist monastery.

Wat Phra That Renu Nakhon (daily 6am–7pm; free) in town is worth a quick stop to view its centuries-old and highly revered Lao-style *chedi*. At weekends during the cool season (December–February), the Phu Thai people perform folk dances at the temple.

THAT PHANOM

About 10km (6 miles) further south via Route 212 is a turn-off onto Route 2031, which leads east another 7km (4 miles) to the town of **That Phanom** 31, home to the most famous *chedi* in all of Isaan. **Wat Phra That Phanom** (daily 8am–6pm) towers 57 metres (187ft), and is visible from several kilometres away. The *chedi* was built half a millennium ago, when the province was still part of a Lao kingdom. The four-sided, curvilinear style reflects Lao Buddhist architecture and is similar to several major *chedi* found on the opposite side of the Mekong today.

The short road that leads from the temple into That Phanom Town passes through the **Pratu Chai** (Victory Gate), inspired by Paris's Arc de Triomphe, albeit far smaller and decorated with Lao motifs. Towards the Mekong riverfront, many of the town's worn but quaint shophouses date to the French Indochina colonial period.

Most days, a large **Lao Market** convenes at a spot on the riverbank north of the main ferry pier. Note: the crossing between Laos and Thailand here is open only to Lao and Thai nationals.

A painted cliff at Pha Taem National Park.

MUKDAHAN

Continuing south on Route 212 along the Mekong leads to the district town of **Mukdahan** 32 on the banks of the Mekong and opposite the Lao town of Savannakhet. Mukdahan is a trading centre for Lao timber, agricultural products and gems and is the site of the Thailand-Laos Friendship Bridge II. A visa on arrival in Laos is available. Mukdahan's **Indochina Market** and **Danang Market**, named after the port city of the same name in Vietnam, deal in goods from Laos and Vietnam: the main route into Vietnam runs east from Savannakhet to Danang.

Near the river, the skyline is punctuated by the modern **Mukdahan Jewel Hall** shopping centre, which resembles a tall needle. Take the road to the river, turn right and visit **Wat Si Nongkran**, built by Vietnamese refugees in 1956. The gates present a curious mixture of Thai contours, Vietnamese writing and Chinese-inspired dragons.

Mukdahan National Park (daily 8am–5pm; http://portal.dnp.go.th) – also known locally as **Phu Mu National Park** – is located off Route 2034, about

16km (10 miles) south of Mukdahan. The park is famous for its peculiar rock formations, many in the shape of jagged mushrooms.

AROUND KHONG JIAM

At Mukdahan, Route 212 turns inland towards **Ubon Ratchathani**. From here, head east on Route 217 to the village of **Ban Khon Sai**, where you will find local men forging heavy bronze gongs for temples and traditional Thai music ensembles. Look for open-sided shelters along Route 217, where artisans sit hammering the bronze discs, and then hardening the metal in wood fires.

Several waterfalls can be found in the same general area, the most accessible and unusual of them being one that cascades in front of a cave monastery called **Wat Tham Hew Sin Chai** off Route 2222, southwest of Khong Jiam.

Further west the confluence of the Mekong River and Mun River (or Mae Nam Mun) forms a scenic peninsula on which **Khong Jiam** ㉝ sits. Each river has its own colour (the Mun being muddier than the Mekong), so Thais refer to this section of water as the "Two-Colour River". Longtail boats can be chartered by the hour (B400), with stops at various small river islands.

To the north of Khong Jiam is the **Pha Taem National Park** ㉞ (daily 6am–6pm; http://portal.dnp.go.th), famous for its 200-metre (650ft) cliff that bears murals of fish, elephants and human figures thought to be at least 3,000 years old. A 500-metre (1,640ft) rock trail leads to two platforms for viewing the paintings.

CHONG MEK

Heading south, Route 217 ends at **Chong Mek** ㉟, where a land crossing between Thailand and Laos allows visa on arrival at the Lao side. Another 5km (3 miles) west of Chong Mek is the 288-sq-km (111-sq-mile) **Sirinthorn Reservoir**. A secluded but famous meditation monastery, **Wat Pa Wana** sits on an island in the reservoir.

Lao-style Wat Phra That Phanom.

Traditional Healing Hospital, Chiang Mai.

THAILAND

TRAVEL TIPS

TRANSPORT

Getting There ... **352**
- By Air ... **352**
- By Rail ... **353**
- By Road ... **353**

Getting Around ... **353**
- From Major Airports ... **353**
- Domestic Travel ... **354**
- City Transport ... **355**

A – Z

Accommodation ... **358**
Addresses ... **358**
Admission charges ... **359**
Budgeting for Your Trip ... **359**
Business Hours ... **359**
Business Travellers ... **359**
Children ... **359**
Climate ... **359**
Clothing ... **360**
Crime and Security ... **360**
Customs Regulations ... **360**
Disabled Travellers ... **361**
Electricity ... **361**
Embassies and Consulates in Bangkok ... **361**
Emergencies ... **361**
Entry Requirements ... **361**
Etiquette ... **361**
Festivals ... **362**
Health and Medical Care ... **363**
Hospitals ... **363**
Internet ... **364**
Left Luggage ... **365**
LGBTQ Travellers ... **365**
Lost Property ... **365**
Maps ... **365**
Media ... **365**
Money ... **365**
Photography ... **366**
Postal Services ... **366**
Public Holidays ... **366**
Religious Services ... **366**
Shopping ... **366**
Taxes ... **367**
Telephones ... **367**
Time Zone ... **367**
Tipping ... **367**
Toilets ... **368**
Tourist Offices ... **368**
Websites and Apps ... **368**
Weights and Measures ... **368**

LANGUAGE

Origins and Intonation ... **369**
Pronunciation ... **369**
Thai Names ... **369**
Numbers ... **369**
Useful Words and Phrases ... **370**
- Days of the Week ... **370**
- Basics ... **370**

Directions and Travel ... **370**
Accommodation ... **370**
Shopping ... **370**
Eating Out ... **370**
Other Handy Phrases ... **370**
Glossary of Terms ... **370**

FURTHER READING

General ... **371**
Fiction ... **371**
History and Society ... **371**
Art and Culture ... **371**
Religion ... **371**
Cookery ... **371**
Other Insight Guides ... **371**

TRANSPORT

GETTING THERE

By Air

Bangkok is a key gateway between Asia and the West and a major hub for the rest of Southeast Asia. More than 55 international airlines fly into the city's Suvarnabhumi and Don Mueang Airports. Thailand's other international airports include the tourist destinations of **Chiang Mai**, **Hat Yai**, **Phuket** and **Ko Samui**.

The national airline, **Thai Airways International** (THAI) (www.thaiairways.com), flies to more than 70 cities worldwide. Several airlines, including **Bangkok Airways** (www.bangkokair.com), **AirAsia** (www.airasia.com) and **Orient Thai** (www.flyorientthai.com), operate between Thailand's major tourist centres and other Asian cities.

Flying from the UK, US and Australasia

Even if you don't plan to spend any time in Thailand, Bangkok is the most convenient (and sometimes the only) way to connect to nearby countries like Laos, Cambodia, Myanmar, Malaysia, Singapore and southern China, often with budget airlines.

Passengers from the UK and Europe can fly direct to Bangkok in about 12 hours, though it is usually cheaper to fly via the Middle East. Airlines that fly non-stop include British Airways, Qantas, THAI and EVA Airways. Many travellers to Australia and New Zealand choose Bangkok as a transit point on their journey.

Flying from the US West Coast usually takes around 18 hours (not including transit time) often with a connection in North Asia; Japan, Korea or Taiwan. The East Coast route via Europe takes about 19 hours in the air.

From Australia (Sydney, Melbourne) the flight to Bangkok takes about 9 hours, while Perth is 7.5 hours away. Flight time from New Zealand (Auckland) is 11.5 hours.

Bangkok

Suvarnabhumi Airport

Bangkok's **Suvarnabhumi Airport** (http://airportthai.co.th), pronounced "su-wa-na-poom", and meaning The Golden Land, is 30km (19 miles) east of the city centre. It handles most international flights to Bangkok and some domestic connections.

Suvarnabhumi has one main passenger terminal with seven concourses. Flight delays have been common, particularly when one runway was closed for repairs in 2012 after subsidance (this may be an ongoing problem, as the airport is built on swamp land). Expansion plans for Suvarnabhumi started their construction phase in 2019, with projected completion for 2022.

For flight information, etc., check the airport website or call any of the following numbers for assistance:
Airport Call Centre: 0-2132 1888, hotline 1722
Tourist Information Centre: 0-2134 4079
Lost Property: 0-2132 1880

Don Mueang Airport

In 2012 the government changed its single airport policy and is encouraging low budget carriers to use Bangkok's old **Don Mueang Airport** (tel: 0-2535 1111; www.donmueangairport.com), which was reopened for international flights. Air Asia moved its entire operation to Don Mueang late the same year. A small number of THAI domestic flights and all domestic flights operated by Orient Thai and Nok Air (www.nokair.com) were already using Don Mueang. In 2015, Terminal 2 was officially reopened for domestic flights. A third phase of expansion, with a new international Terminal 3, is underway and due to finish in 2024.

Leave plenty of time for flight connection between Suvarnabhumi and Don Mueang airports, as taxi travel between them could take up to 1.5 hours.

Don Mueang is about 30km (19 miles) north of the city centre, 40 to 45 minutes away by taxi, depending on traffic.

Phuket

Though some visitors to Phuket stop off in Bangkok for a few days at the start of their trip, many also fly in direct to Phuket Airport (www.phuketairportonline.com). There are flights from an increasing number of destinations, including Cambodia (THAI), Hong Kong (Cathay Dragon), Korea (Asiana and THAI), Kuala Lumpur (Malaysia Airlines, AirAsia, Malindo Air and THAI), Istanbul (Turkish Airlines), Sydney (Jetstar Airways), Shanghai (China Eastern Airlines) and Singapore (Air Asia, SilkAir, Singapore Airlines and THAI). Phuket Airport is small and under increasing pressure from expanding markets. An airport expansion was completed in 2015.

Ko Samui

Several airlines land at Samui Airport (www.samuiairportonline.com) from an increasing number of destinations, including Hong Kong (Bangkok Airways), Kuala Lumpur (Bangkok Airways) and Singapore (SilkAir).

Chiang Mai

Airlines flying direct to Chiang Mai Airport (www.chiangmaiairportonline.com) from other Asian cities currently include Kuala Lumpur (AirAsia), Kunming (China Eastern Airlines), Macau (Air Asia), Luang Prabang (Lao Airlines, THAI), Seoul (Korean Air), Taipei (EVA) and

Singapore (Bangkok Airways, Silk Air and Singapore Airways).

By Rail

Trains operated by the **State Railways of Thailand** (hotline 1690; www.railway.co.th) are clean, cheap and reliable, if rather slow. There are three rail entry points into Thailand. Two are from Malaysia on the southern Thai border. The trip north to Bangkok serves as a scenic introduction to Thailand.

Services depart from **Butterworth**, the port opposite Malaysia's Penang Island, at dawn and midday, crossing the border into Thailand and arriving in Bangkok the following day. There are second-class cars with seats that are made into upper and lower sleeping berths at night. There are also air-conditioned first-class sleepers and dining cars serving food. Prices from Butterworth to Bangkok are US$35 and up.

From Bangkok's **Hualamphong Railway Station**, trains leave in the early morning and mid-afternoon for the return journey to Malaysia. A more adventurous but less convenient route travels from Kuala Lumpur up Malaysia's east coast to the northeastern town of Kota Bharu. Take a taxi from there across the border to catch the Thai train from the southern Thai town of Sungai Kolok. Trains leave Sungai Kolok at 11.30am and 2.20pm, arriving in Bangkok at 9.15am and 10.10am the following day.

If you like to travel in style, try the **Eastern & Oriental Express** (www.orient-express.com). Travelling several times a month between Singapore, Kuala Lumpur, Chiang Mai and Bangkok, the 22-carriage train with its distinctive green-and-cream livery passes spectacular scenery. It's very expensive, but worth it.

It is also possible to take a train from close to **Vientiane** (Laos) to Bangkok via Nong Khai.

By Road

Malaysia provides road access into Thailand at crossings near Padang Besar and Sungai Kolok. From Laos, there are four Friendship Bridges located at Mukdahan, Nakhon Phanom and Nong Khai, all in northeast Thailand, and another at Chiang Khong (in Chiang Rai Province).

Suvarnabhumi International Airport, Bangkok.

There is also a land crossing at Huay Kon (in Nan Province).

From **Cambodia**, the most commonly used border crossing is Poipet, which connects to Aranyaprathet, east of Bangkok. Officially, you are only allowed to fly in from **Myanmar**. Land crossings are sometimes allowed from places like Mae Sai and Mae Sot, but these are subject to restrictions and the rules are always in a flux. Thais are permitted entry, but foreigners are usually only allowed into Myanmar territory for the day.

GETTING AROUND

From Major Airports

Suvarnabhumi Airport

The Suvarnabhumi Airport City Rail Link cuts airport–city journey times to just 15 minutes.

Taxis take about 45 to 60 minutes to cover the 30km (19 miles), depending on traffic conditions; the worst time to travel is between 4 and 9pm.

Negotiating an exit from the arrival hall, however, can be more daunting. If you are on a business trip, you'll understand why it is the norm for Bangkok hosts to deploy a personal greeter or escort. Emerging in the arrival hall, you may be harangued by touts both inside and outside the barriers. Avoid giving your name or destination. If you already have a reservation at a hotel, a representative will have your name written on a sign, or at least a sign bearing the name of your hotel. If you haven't made prior arrangements, use one of the following modes to get to the city.

Taxi

Operating 24 hours daily, all taxis officially serving the airport are air-conditioned and metered. When you exit from the arrival hall, take the lift or travelator one level down to the taxi desk, which is located outside the building. Join the queue and tell the clerk at the counter where you want to go to. A receipt will be issued, with the licence-plate number of the taxi and your destination in Thai written on it. Make sure the driver turns on the meter. At the end of your trip, you pay the fare, plus B50 airport surcharge and highway toll fees, which should total about B70 in total to downtown. Depending on traffic, an average fare from the airport to the city centre is around B450 (including toll fees and airport surcharge).

Limousine Service

There are two limousine operators stationed at the arrival hall.

Airports of Thailand Limousines (AOT; tel: 0-2134 2323–5; www.aot-limousine.com) operates a variety of vehicles that can take you to the city centre for about B1,000. Luxury cars like a top-end 7-series BMW will cost B2,200. Rates to Pattaya start at around B2,600, depending on the vehicle used.

THAI Airways Limousines (mobile tel: 08-1652 4444) also operates a premium car service for their passengers. Prices are similar to those charged by AOT.

Airport Express Bus

The airport express bus ceased operations in 2011.The current alternative is Bus Bor Khor Sor (tel. 0-2134-4097-9) with various routes and a flat ticket fare; Bus BMTA with rates from B24 to 35, depending on the route; and public vans. Tickets are available at the Public Transport Centre.

Rail

The high speed Airport Rail Link (ARL; www.srtet.co.th) connecting the airport to the city has two services. The City Line to Phaya Thai calls at eight stations en route – Lat Krabang, Ban Thap Chang, Hua Mak, Ramkhamhaeng, Asoke, Makkasan, Ratchaprarop and Phaya Thai – and takes 30 minutes for the full journey. It links to the Skytrain system at Phaya Thai. The Express Line runs direct to Bangkok City Air Terminal, at Makkasan, where passengers can check in and drop their luggage. Tickets: B15-45 (City Line), B150 (Express Line). Journey time 15 mins to Makkasan, 30 mins to Phaya Thai. Both lines run from 6am–midnight. There have been many complaints about poor service on this line, including lack of escalators, lifts and trolleys. Unless the time-saving is crucial, taxis may be a more comfortable option.

Phuket Airport

Phuket International Airport (www.phuketairportonline.com) is about 32km (20 miles) from Phuket Town. Travel time is about 40 minutes, while Patong beach can be reached in around half an hour.

Taxi

In the arrival hall, airport taxis and limousines can be hired at the fixed rates displayed on a board. After paying the fare, you are issued a coupon that is then given to the driver. Prices start at B200 to B400 for the nearby northern beaches, rising to B550 to B650 for locations further afield. The flat fare for Kata and Karon is B650. Better are the metered red and yellow taxis outside the building. A ride to Phuket Town will take 30 minutes, with the fare around B400. Make sure they turn on the meter.

Minibus

Shared minivans (around B100 to Phuket Town, B150 to Patong) have ticket counters in the arrival hall. If you are part of a large group, book a quicker 8-seater minibus. The fares are around B900 to Phuket Town, B1,200 to B1,500 to Patong and B1,300 to Kata and Karon. Tickets are sold next to the airport limousine counters.

Airport Bus

Tickets for the airport bus can be bought on boarding or from designated booths in the arrival hall. At the time of writing the bus only travels to Phuket Town, every 30 minutes from 8.20am–7.50pm, with several stops along the main route only. It takes at least 45 minutes. Tickets are B90 all the way to town.

Ko Samui Airport

Taxi

Ko Samui International Airport (www.samuiairportonline.com) is located in the northeast of the island. Fixed share-taxi fares from the airport typically cost B150 to Bo Phut and Bangrak, B200 to Mae Nam, B300 to Chaweng, B400 to Lamai and B400 to B500 to Na Thon. Private car transfers start at around B400.

Minivan

Shared minivans also carry passengers to different beaches, though they usually wait until the van is full before leaving. Typical minivan fares are B70 to Bo Phut, B100 to Chaweng and Maenam, and B120 to Nathon and Lamai.

Chiang Mai Airport

Taxi and Bus

Chiang Mai International Airport is about 4km (2 miles) southwest of town. The public green-and-yellow metered taxis available outside the airport will cost around B100 to city centre locations around 15 minutes away. Alternatively, bus No. 4 outside the airport costs B15 and takes around 30 minutes.

Domestic Travel

By Air

Thai Airways International (THAI) operates a network of daily flights from Bangkok to 10 of Thailand's major towns using a fleet of 747s and Airbuses.

The frequency and number of flights change with the seasons, the peak season being November to February. From Bangkok, there are flights to Hat Yai, Phuket, Surat Thani, Ko Samui and Krabi in the south; Chiang Mai and Chiang Rai, in the north; and Khon Kaen, Ubon Ratchathani and Udon Thani in the northeast. Check the website for regularly updated promotional fares.

Another major carrier is **Bangkok Airways**, which has several daily flights from Bangkok to Ko Samui. It also operates from Bangkok to places including Chiang Mai, Krabi, Lampang, Phuket, Sukhothai and Trat. From Ko Samui, destinations include Krabi, Pattaya and Phuket.

Low-cost domestic and international carriers are increasing in number. **AirAsia** has the widest portfolio, connecting Bangkok with various overseas and domestic destinations, including Hat Yai, Narathiwat and Surat Thani. **Nok Air,** partly owned by THAI, serves major tourist destinations such as Chiang Mai and Phuket, but is also a good option for more remote landings at places including Chumphon, Loei, Mae Sot, Nakhon Phanom, Nakhon Si Thammarat and Nan. **Orient Thai Airlines** operates flights from Bangkok to Chiang Mai, Chiang Rai, Hat Yai and Phuket. Thai Smile, launched in 2012 and also owned by THAI, has already started to expand its domestic and international schedule.

For detailed route information, check the airline websites listed below. All these airlines allow you to book tickets and pay online via their websites. The phone numbers given below also allow you to place bookings directly with reservations staff.

AirAsia: tel: 0-2215 9999; www.airasia.com.

Bangkok Airways: tel: 0-2270 6699; Call Centre: 1771; www.bangkokair.com.

Nok Air: tel: 0-2900 9955; Call Centre: 1318; www.nokair.com.

Orient Thai: tel: 0-2229 4100; Call Centre: 1126; www.flyorientthai.com.

Thai Airways International: tel: 0-2356 1111; www.thaiairways.com.

Thai Smile: tel: 0-2356 1111; www.thaismileair.com.

By Rail

The **State Railways of Thailand** (tel: 0-2222 0175, hotline 1690; www.railway.co.th) operates five principal routes from Bangkok's **Hualamphong Railway Station** at Thanon Rama IV.

The **northern line** passes through Ayutthaya, Phitsanulok, Lampang and terminates at Chiang Mai.

The **upper northeastern line** passes through Ayutthaya, Saraburi, Nakhon Ratchasima, Khon Kaen, Udon Thani and terminates at Nong Khai. The **lower northeastern line** branches east at Nakhon

Ratchasima and passes through Buriram, Surin, Sisaket and terminates at Ubon Ratchathani.

The **eastern line** runs from Bangkok to Aranyaprathet on the Thai–Cambodian border.

The **southern line** crosses the Rama VI bridge and stops at Nakhon Pathom, Phetchaburi, Hua Hin and Chumphon. It splits at Hat Yai; one branch runs southwest through Betong and continues to the western coast of Malaysia to Singapore. The southeastern branch goes via Pattani and Yala to the Thai border opposite the Malaysian town of Kota Bharu.

Another railway line leaves **Bangkok Thonburi Station**, on the western bank of the Chao Phraya River, for Kanchanaburi and other destinations in western Thailand.

Express and rapid services on the main lines offer first-class air-conditioned (or second-class fan-cooled) carriages with sleeping cabins or berths and dining carriages. There are also special air-conditioned express day trains that travel to key towns along the main lines. Rail passes (B1,500–3,000) valid for 20 days are available.

Train tickets and rail passes can be bought at Hualamphong Railway Station, at a travel agency.

By Car

Thailand has a good road system, with over 50,000km (31,000 miles) of highways and more being built every year. Road signs are in both Thai and English, and you should have no difficulty following a map. An international driver's licence is required. In Thailand, driving is on the left-hand side of the road. Highway tolls apply to some expressway sections, especially in Bangkok.

Conditions vary depending on the time of day and the route taken, but the roads are generally in good order. However, there is only a rudimentary driving test, so drivers largely learn by intuition. Main routes are very busy and road courtesy is low, with right-of-way determined by size. Tailgating and dangerous overtaking are also common. A 2010 World Health Organisation report ranks Thailand 106th in the world for traffic safety based on number of accidents per 100,000 of population. Government figures show 15 million motorbike riders, who make up most of the 12,000 road deaths every year. All that said, once you are acclimatised, driving in Thailand is not too uncomfortable.

Avis, Budget and numerous local agencies in major tourist centres like Bangkok, Chiang Mai, Pattaya and Phuket offer rental cars with or without drivers, and with insurance coverage. The international companies are more expensive, but they are also more reliable. Car-rental rates range from around B800 per day, but be sure to double-check that insurance is included.

Recommended car-rental agencies in Bangkok are:

Avis: 2/12 Thanon Withayu, tel: 0-2255 5300–4; Suvarnabhami Airport (arrival hall), mobile tel: 08-4700 8157–9; Reservation Centre, tel: 0-2251 1131–2; www.avisthailand.com.

Hertz: 46 North Sathorn Road Silom Bangrak District. tel: 0- 6622 343 230; www.hertz.com.

A safer option is to hire a car or a van with driver. A driver will cost another B300–500 per day, plus a surcharge if an overnight stay is included.

For these try Thai Car Hire (www.thaicarhire.com) or Krungthai Car Rent (tel: 0-2291 8888; www.krungthai.co.th).

You can get to several places outside Bangkok, like Pattaya and Hua Hin, by simply flagging a taxi along a Bangkok street or booking one beforehand. Be sure to negotiate a flat rate before boarding; don't use the meter in such instances.

By Bus

Air-conditioned 42-seater express buses service many destinations in Thailand. VIP coaches with 24 seats and extra leg room and refreshments served on board are best for long overnight journeys.

There is a vast network of both private and government-operated buses in Thailand. The government-run buses are operated by the **Transport Company Ltd** (www.transport.co.th). Known locally as Bor Kor Sor (BKS), its terminals are found at every town in Thailand. Bus tickets can be purchased directly with any BKS station or with a travel agency. Private buses, which are usually more expensive, depart either from BKS terminals or their own stations. In Bangkok, many private buses depart from Thanon Khao San.

In Bangkok, BKS terminals are found at the following locations:

Eastern (Ekamai) Bus Terminal: Thanon Sukhumvit opposite Soi 63 (Soi Ekamai), tel: 023-915 179.

Northern and Northeastern Bus Terminal: Thanon Kampaengphet 2, Northern: tel: 029-362 841-48; Northeastern: tel: 029-362 852–66.

Southern Bus Terminal: Thanon Boromrat Chonnani, Thonburi, tel: 024-351 200.

City Transport

Bangkok

Taxi

Taxis abound in Bangkok. They are metered, air-conditioned, inexpensive, and comfortably seat 3 to 4 persons. Taxis are best hailed along the streets, as those parked outside hotels hustle for a non-metered fair.

The flag-fall charge is B35; after the first 2km (1.25 miles), the meter goes up by B4–B5.50 every kilometre, depending on distance travelled. If your journey involves using a highway to save time, the driver will ask your permission as the toll fee will be borne by you. Note: the toll fee of B20 to B50 is given to the driver at the payment booth, not at the end of the trip.

Before starting any journey, check whether the meter has been reset and turned on. Generally drivers are far better than their reputations in this regard, but will try it on occasionally. This happens particularly if there is heavy rain, when it is sometimes wise to negotiate anyway, as traffic moves more slowly and the meter keeps ticking. Fares, however, can be negotiated for longer distances outside Bangkok: for instance, Pattaya (B1,200), Koh Samet (B1,500) or Hua Hin (B1,500–2,000).

Drivers don't speak much English, but all should know the locations of major hotels. Foreigners frequently mangle Thai pronunciation, so it's a good idea to have a destination written on a piece of paper. Thai drivers can usually understand street addresses written in capital Roman letters.

Siam Taxi: Tel: 1661 (hotline) is one of the more reliable companies that will pick up in Bangkok for a B20 surcharge.

Tuk-Tuk

Tuk-tuk are the brightly coloured three-wheeled taxis whose name comes from the incessant noise their two-stroke engines make. Few tuk-tuk drivers speak English, so it's an idea to have your destination written down in Thai. Unless you bargain hard, tuk-tuk fares are rarely lower than metered taxi fares. Some tuk-tuk drivers loitering around hotels will offer a B10 fare "anywhere". The hitch is that you must stop at a tourist shop where the driver will get petrol coupons in exchange for bringing you in.

Expect to pay B30 to B50 for short journeys of a few blocks or around 15 minutes or less, and B50 to B100 for longer journeys. A B100 ride should get you a half-hour ride across most parts of downtown. Be sure to negotiate the fare beforehand.

Motorcycle Taxi

Motorcycle taxi stands (with young men in fluorescent orange vests) are clustered at the entrances of most *sois* (small side streets) and beside any busy intersection or building entrance. The drivers are experts at weaving through Bangkok's heavy traffic and may cut travel time in half, but do so at your peril.

Hire only a driver who provides a passenger helmet. Fares must be negotiated beforehand, and they are rarely lower than taxi fares for the same distance travelled. Hold on tight and keep your knees tucked in as drivers tend to weave precariously in and out of traffic. Their goal is to get you there as quickly, not as safely, as possible. If the driver is going too fast, ask him to slow down in Thai: *cha-cha*. Thai women usually sit side-saddle and it's common to see whole families on one motorbike.

A short distance, like the length of a street, will cost B10 to B20, with longer rides at B50 to B100. During rush hour (8–10am and 4–6pm), prices are higher. A B80 to B100 ride should get you a half-hour trip across most parts of downtown.

Bus

Bus transport in Bangkok is very cheap but can also be equally arduous, time-consuming and confusing. Municipal and private operators all come under the charge of the **Bangkok Mass Transit Authority** (tel: 184 or 0-2246 0973; www.bmta.co.th).

With scant English signage and few conductors or drivers speaking English, boarding the right bus can be an exercise in frustration. Public buses come in four varieties: micro-bus, Euro II bus, air-conditioned and non-air-conditioned "ordinary". In theory, the routes of both air-conditioned and ordinary buses appear on standard bus maps. In practice, routes change and many bus maps are out of date. The Bus Rapid Transit (BRT) system uses dedicated lanes, but at present is limited to a single route from Chong Nonsi BTS station to Wong Wian Yai on the Thonburi side of the river.

Skytrain

The **Bangkok Transit System**'s (BTS) elevated train service (BTS Tourist Information Centre: tel: 0-2617 7340; hotline: tel: 0-2617 6000; www.bts.co.th), better known as Skytrain, is the perfect way of beating the city's traffic-congested streets.

It consists of two lines. The **Sukhumvit Line** runs from Mo Chit station in the north to Bearing in the southeast. The **Silom Line** runs from National Stadium, near Siam Square, south to Saphan Taksin near Tha Sathorn (or Central Pier), and then across the river to Wongwian Yai in Thonburi. The lines intersect at Siam station, and also connect with the Metro system.

The Skytrain is fast, frequent and clean, but suffers from overcrowding during peak hours. Accessibility, too, is a problem for the disabled and aged as only 12 stations have escalators and lifts. Trains operate from 6am to midnight (3 minutes peak; 5 minutes off-peak). Single-trip fares vary according to distance, starting at B15 and rising to B40. Self-service ticket machines are found at all station concourses. There is also an unlimited ride 1-Day Pass (B130) and a Rabbit Card to which you can add discounted multi-trip packages running from B378 for 15 trips to B1,000 for 50 trips, all available at station counters. There is, however an issuing fee of B50 for Rabbit Cards.

BTS Tourist Information Centres are found on the concourse levels of Siam, Phaya Thai and Saphan Taksin stations (daily 8am–8pm).

Metro (MRT or Subway)

Bangkok's **Mass Rapid Transit** (MRT) system (Customer Relations Centre, tel: 0-2624 5200; www.mrta.co.th/en/) has 2 lines with a total of 35 stations, stretching 44km (27 miles). The Blue Line is between Tao Poon in Bangkok's northern suburbs and the city's main railway station, Hualamphong, near Chinatown. The Purple Line is between Tao Poon and Khlong Bang Phai out of the northwest of the city. The lines are variously referred to as the MRT, Metro or subway. Various extensions and additional stations are in various phases of construction.

Three stations – Silom, Sukhumvit and Chatuchak Park – are interchanges with the Skytrain network.

The air-conditioned trains operate from 6am to midnight, with less than 5 minutes wait at peak times (less than 10 minutes off-peak). Fares range from B16 to B41 for single trip tokens, available at self-service machines in all stations. There are concessions for children and the elderly.

Also available at station counters are unlimited ride passes of 1-Day (B120), 3-Day (B230), 30-Day (B1,400) and the stored-value Adult Card (B230 – includes B80 deposit and issuing fee).

Boat

The most common waterborne transport is the **Chao Phraya River Express Boat** (tel: 0-2623 6001; www.chaophrayaexpressboat.com), which travels from Pakkret in the north and ends at Ratburana in the south. Boats run every 15 minutes from 6am to 8pm (6am–7pm at weekends), depending on the service, denoted by a coloured flag on top of the boat. Yellow-flag boats are fastest and do not stop at many piers, while the orange-flag and no-flag boats stop at most of the marked river piers. If unsure, check before boarding. Fares cost B13–32 and are purchased from the conductor on board or at some pier counters.

The **Chao Phraya Tourist Boat** (http://chaophrayatouristboat.com) operates daily from 9am to 9pm and costs B200 for an all-day pass (for use until 5.30pm) or B60 for a single journey ticket. After 4pm, you can use the ticket on the regular express boats. A useful commentary is provided on board, along with a small guidebook and a bottle of water. The route begins at Tha Sathorn (Central Pier) and travels upriver to Tha Phra Arthit, stopping at eight major piers along the way. Boats leave every 30 minutes, and you can get off at any pier and get onto another boat later on this hop-on-and-off service.

The **cross-river ferries** can be boarded at the jetties located all along the river, often close to Chao Phraya River Express piers. Costing B2.50 per journey, cross-river ferries operate from 5am to 10pm or later.

Longtail boat taxis ply the narrow inner canals and carry passengers from the centre of town to the outlying districts. Many of the piers are located near traffic bridges; remember to stand back from the pier's edge to avoid being splashed by the foul-smelling water. Choose a seat away from the spray, and be sure to tell the conductor your destination, as boats do not stop otherwise. Tickets cost B5 to B30, depending on distance, with services operating roughly every 10 minutes until 6–7pm.

If you wish to explore the canals of Thonburi or Nonthaburi, private **longtail boat rentals** can be negotiated from most of the river's main piers. A 90-minute to 2-hour tour will take you into the quieter canal communities. Ask which route the boat will take and what will be seen along the way; try to avoid major tourist attractions that can be visited independently later. Ask to pull up and get out if anything interests you. Negotiate rates beforehand; an hour-long trip will cost B700 to B800, rising to B1,000 and more for 2 hours. The price is for the entire boat, which seats up to 16 people, not per person.

Phuket

Taxi

There are few metered taxis and those that have meters rarely use them. Taxi fares have to be negotiated, except for those boarded from taxi stands at major shopping centres, the airport, Phuket Bus Terminal 2 and some beaches, where prices are fixed. Phuket Airport Transfer (www.airporttransferphuket.com) is one of few contacts off the street.

Songthaew/Tuk-Tuk

The most common form of transport are small pick-up trucks with a roof over the back and two parallel padded benches. Increasingly, these days, minivans are replacing the older-style trucks. These *songthaew* (often also called tuk-tuk in Phuket) are plentiful, but prices are among the highest in Thailand, costing nearly as much as taxis. Agree on a price before getting into a *songthaew*, and be aware that prices will rise at night and during rainy spells. Prices to beaches from Phuket Town should run from B300. The final rate depends on your negotiating skills.

Motorcycle Taxi

Motorcycle taxis are a cheaper but more risky way to travel, with at least one accident per week from road collisions during the high season.

Bus

Small, blue public buses (*songthaew*) are infrequent and painfully slow but very cheap. They operate between the bus station and beaches for B30-40, from 6am–6pm (return journeys end at 4pm). Phuket Town now also has the Po Thong pink bus network (tel: hotline 1131, 0-7621 0806), which runs around town from 6am–8pm, priced B10–B20 per trip. Local buses go from the central bus terminal on Ranong Road in Phuket Town (tel: 0 3251-1230). Services depart half-hourly between 7am and 6pm to the various beaches, but no buses run from one beach to another. The airport bus (www.airportbusphuket.com) also terminates there. Phuket Bus Terminal 2 on Thepkrasattri Road, Rassada serves inter-regional buses.

Car Rental

Car rental ranges from B700 to B2,500 a day. Use a reputable company, because many of the independent beachfront businesses do not provide insurance.

Budget, 36/1 Moo 6, Thalang, tel: 0-7620 5398.

Phuket Car Rent, 23/3 Moo 1 Sakoo, Thalang, tel: 089-724 2823; www.phuketcarrent.com.

Ko Samui

Songthaew/Tuk-Tuk

Songthaew trucks (sometimes also called tuk-tuk are the island's principal mode of public transport, with vaguely fixed routes, but no fixed stops (just hail one anywhere at roadside). Drivers always try to overcharge, so make sure you hand over the correct fare. A journey down the length of Chaweng beach is B30, from Lamai to Chaweng B50, up to B100 for long journeys, such as Na Thon to Chaweng. Late at night they operate more like taxis, and the fare should be agreed on beforehand.

Taxi

Metered taxis are becoming prevalent on the island but drivers rarely turn on the meter, preferring to quote extortionate rates for relatively short distances. More information can be found on the airport website www.samuiairportonline.com.

Motorcycle Taxi

Motorcycle taxis are cheaper, with fares ranging from B20 to B30 for a short journey, and B150 to B200 for a longer ride from, say, Chaweng to Na Thon. A variety of motorcycles, from mopeds to choppers (B200–500), as well as jeeps (B800–2,000), can be hired at all the main beaches. Motorcycle accidents are frequent, so wear a helmet.

Chiang Mai

Songthaew/Tuk-Tuk

Chiang Mai's *songthaew* – small red pick-up trucks with roofs over the back and two parallel padded benches – ply the city streets day and night, stopping for passengers who flag them down at kerbside. If the driver is going in the direction you want to go, the fare is B20 per person and you will ride with other passengers. If the *songthaew* is empty, the driver may offer the option to charter the truck to your destination. In such cases the fare will vary from B50–150, depending on the distance.

Three-wheeled tuk-tuk operate on a charter basis only and cost B30 to B150, depending on the distance.

Taxi

There are small number of air-conditioned, green-and-yellow metered taxis, which can be booked by telephone (tel: 0-5320-1307; 0-5326-2878). Rates start at B30 for the first 2km, and B4 for each extra km travelled.

Car Rental

Reliable choices are **Budget** (tel: 1-800 283 438 (toll free); www.budget.co.th) and **Journey** (tel: 053-271579; www.journeysmile.com). The latter will deliver and pick up cars. Rates run around B700–B1,500 for economy cars, and B2,500 for luxury models. Discounted weekly and monthly rates are also available.

Bicycle

Most of the city is easily accessible by bicycle. Kiosks and guesthouses around the city rent bicycles from B50 per day. Serious mountain and road bikes go from around B350 a day from dealers like **Velo City Bikes** (Th. Huay Kaew 199/1; tel: 08-1595 5975; www.facebook.com/Velocitythecyclistshop).

A – Z

A

Accommodation

Choosing a Hotel

The top-end hotels in Thailand's major tourist centres are equal to the very best anywhere in the world. The facilities in luxury hotels may include as many as six or more different restaurants serving Western and Asian cuisines, bars, swimming pools, fitness centres, spas, business centres, banquet halls, shopping arcades, Wi-Fi internet access and cable television. Service is very personal. Indeed, many of Thailand's moderately priced lodgings rival what in the West might be considered in a higher class. Even the budget and inexpensive hotels in Thailand will often have a swimming pool and more than one food outlet.

A range of new hotels, high on design and style, both luxury chains as well as independent boutique properties, have opened in recent years in Bangkok and also at popular destinations like Hua Hin, Phuket, Ko Samui, Krabi, Ko Lanta and Chiang Mai. Many have won awards or lavish praise in international surveys and magazines.

Note: A resort does not always have the same connotation in Thailand that it might in the West; often meaning nothing more than it is located in the countryside or by the beach. So if you find a "resort" hotel in some remote corner of Thailand and room rates are a real bargain, don't necessarily have too high expectations.

Guesthouses

Travellers on a tight budget will find numerous clean guesthouses, and many have been upgraded to include air-conditioning and en-suite bathrooms.

In Bangkok, these are mainly in the Khao San Road and Sukhumvit Sois 1–15 areas, in Chiang Mai along the Ping River and around Thanon Moon Muang. In Pattaya and Phuket, guesthouses are less common. Generally, prices start around B500 – Thailand is no longer the ultra-cheap destination of yore – but hunt around and they may drop as low as B200, particularly in the low season, where many hotels will slash prices by more than half.

Prices are cheaper in small towns, where guesthouses are generally family-run, along main streets or close to bus and railway stations. And the low-density islands often have beautifully situated beach huts, where you may only get a fan and a cold shower, but the natural scenery makes up for the scant facilities.

Rates and Bookings

Thailand still has plenty of good-value accommodation, but prices are creeping up. Rates can range widely, particularly in Bangkok, where there is a glut of rooms. Depending on the season, discounts can exceed 50 percent or more off the published rack rate. It pays to shop around. As rates can be so elastic, relative price categories denoting the lowest priced rooms available are used in this section.

During peak holiday periods (holidays, Christmas, New Year, Chinese New Year, Songkran, etc.), generally between November and April, hotels tend to be full and prices are high. Booking well in advance is advisable. For the rest of the year, it is always worth asking for a discount. Alternatively, check online hotel sites, like **Agoda** (www.agoda.com) and **Hotels.com** (www.hotels.com) for better rates. Properties in some beach areas, particularly along the Andaman coast, close for at least part of the low season. This is also the time when properties renovate, so it's always best to enquire about this to avoid unwelcome noise and disruption.

Many hotels include a compulsory (and exhorbitant) gala dinner in Christmas and New Year room rates, which is usually little more than a fancy buffet.

Whether a room rate is quoted in US dollars or in Thai baht, it will be billed on your credit card in baht; the final rate can therefore vary, depending upon the prevailing exchange rates.

Note: Most hotels also charge a value added tax (VAT) of 7 percent to the bill, and at the mid- and top-end hotels, a property service charge of 10 percent as well.

Addresses

Since most of Bangkok developed with little central planning, getting around can be confusing at first, given the size (and flatness) of the city and its many twisting alleyways.

Bangkok is mostly laid out using the *soi* system; smaller streets leading off a main road of the same name, with each *soi* having a number. For example, Sukhumvit Road (or Thanon Sukhumvit) has side streets in sequence such as Sukhumvit Soi 1, Sukhumvit Soi 3, etc. (odd and even numbers on opposite sides). *Sois* may be sub-divided using a slash after the number followed by another number. The same system is used for shop and house addresses, a slash separating the block or building number from the shop. So an address might read 36/1 Sukhumvit 33/1. Most hotels provide business cards with the address written in Thai to show to taxi drivers.

In smaller towns an address might include the word *Moo* (referring to the residential estate) before the name of the road or *soi*, as in 23/3 Moo 1. But many places don't have complete addresses and will just state the beach or general location.

Admission charges

Most temples, museums and historical sites around the country charge an admission fee for entry. Wherever this is not the case, it will be marked as 'free' in this guidebook. In general, foreigners are charged anywhere from five to 10 times more than Thai nationals for tickets, with prices between B40 for most wats to B200-300 for larger historical sites and some of the busier national parks. Usually entry fees will be somewhere between those two extremes. Bangkok's Grand Palace is a notable exception, with tickets costing a hefty B500 for foreign nationals.

B

Budgeting for Your Trip

Although getting more expensive, by Western standards Thailand is still a bargain. Five-star hotels cost half or a third of what they would in New York or London, and at the other end, budget (if a bit dingy) accommodation can be as cheap as B200 per night. Street food can be excellent, and you can have a filling and tasty meal for B30 to B40. Transport is cheap, with bus fares priced from B7–B22, a ride on the Skytrain and Metro from B15–B40. Taxis are inexpensive as well. Drinks in bars cost from B60 to B100 and in clubs from B180 to B300. If you live frugally, you can get by with B500 a day, but the sky is the limit here if you want to live it up at luxury hotels and eat at fine-dining restaurants.

As a general rule, destinations that attract a lot of tourists will be more expensive. Phuket and Ko Samui, for instance, are the most expensive islands, while Ko Phangan, Ko Lanta and Ko Chang are gradually moving up. On the other hand, largely untouched places like Trang and Satun offer the best bargains.

Apart from Chiang Mai, the north and northeast regions have the lowest cost of living in Thailand. In many of these places, you are hard-pressed to find hotels beyond the moderate category.

Business Hours

Government offices in Thailand operate 8.30am to 4.30pm Monday to Friday. Most businesses are open 8am to 5.30pm Monday to Friday, while some are open 8.30am to noon on Saturday. Banks are open 9.30am to 3.30pm Monday to Friday.

Department stores are open 10.30am to 9pm daily, though larger stores are open as late as 10pm. Ordinary shops open at 8.30am or 9am and close between 6pm and 8pm, depending on location and type of business.

Small open-air coffee shops and restaurants open at 7am and close at 8.30pm, though some stay open past midnight. Large restaurants generally have last orders at 10pm. In Bangkok, most hotel coffee shops close at midnight; some stay open 24 hours, and the city has several outdoor restaurants that are open as late as 4am.

Clubs and bars are subject to loosely applied licensing laws and may close anywhere between midnight and 5am, depending on location and political and policing climate. Bangkok's venues generally close by 2am, but outside Bangkok, times may be more flexible. In many resorts – particularly Phuket, Ko Samui, Ko Samet, Ko Phangan and Ko Tao – they don't close until much later.

Business Travellers

Bangkok hosts an increasing number of business travellers from all over the world. Most city hotels have business centres with communications and secretarial services. Outside the capital, such services are limited to places like Pattaya, Phuket, Ko Samui and Chiang Mai, all of which are popular for business conferences and seminars. A good first stop for overseas business people wanting to start a company in Thailand is the **Board of Investment** (BOI), tel: 0-2553 8111; www.boi.go.th.

C

Children

Travelling with children is a breeze in Thailand. Thais love kids, and those with blond hair will receive special attention. It can be a bit overwhelming, but people are just being friendly and it is part of the Thai sense of community.

Footpaths in Bangkok and most Thai cities and towns are not pedestrian-friendly. They are often in disrepair, and inevitably something or somebody obstructs them: leave the buggy at home and bring back- or chest-mounted baby carriers. Many department stores and malls have play areas and baby changing facilities and some upmarket hotels have baby-sitting services. Children should never approach dogs, monkeys or other small animals; those seen in the streets are more feral than back at home, and rabies is still a risk.

The tropical sun is intense, so high SPF sun-block lotion and hats are important. Make sure the kids keep their hands clean, as they can easily pick up stomach bugs.

Climate

There are three main seasons in Thailand: hot, rainy and cool. But to the tourist winging in from more temperate regions, Thailand has only one temperature: hot. To make things worse, the temperature drops only a few degrees during the night, and is accompanied by humidity levels of above 70 percent. Days and nights during the cool season, however, can be pleasant.

The following guideline is a rough indication of Thailand's weather patterns (although you can, and should, expect regional variations in weather). Also, with global warming and erratic weather patterns these days, it's hard to predict with

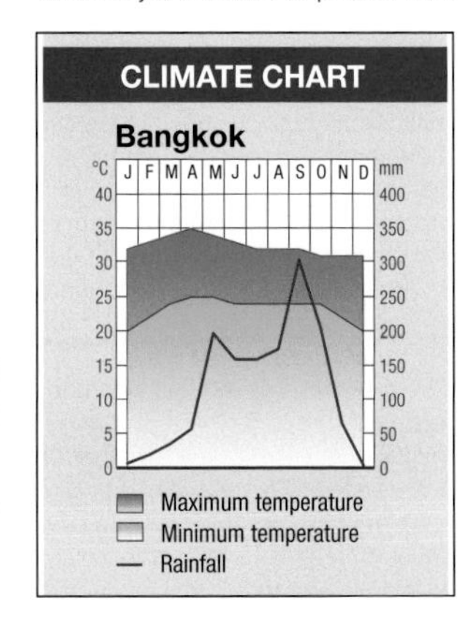

near-certainty the onset (and the end) of the rainy season.
Hot season (Mar to Mid-June): 27–35°C (80–95°F)
Rainy season (June to Oct): 24–32°C (75–90°F)
Cool season (Nov to Feb): 18–32°C (65–90°F), with less humidity.

The countryside is somewhat cooler, but the north and northeast can be hotter in March and April than Bangkok. During these months, the north can also be affected by smoke and haze, as some farmers clear agricultural land by setting fields ablaze. Generally, Chiang Mai enjoys a cooler, less humid climate, and in the cool season, temperatures range between 13°C–28°C (55°F–82°F). In the northern hills, however, temperatures occasionally drop to single digits. In Bangkok, the heaviest rain falls in September.

There are regional variations along Thailand's coastline, but generally the Eastern Seaboard and northern Gulf of Thailand coast have a weather pattern similar to that of Bangkok. The southern Gulf of Thailand coast around Ko Samui is a little different: it receives light intermittent rain from June to October; from November to January, however, the northeast monsoon brings the heaviest rains, with November being the wettest month.

Phuket and the Andaman Coast experience their wettest months from May to October. November can be a bit unstable.

Thailand's peak tourist season runs from November to March and, not surprisingly, roughly coincides with the country's cool season.

Clothing

Clothes should be light and loose; fabrics made from natural fibres are definitely more comfortable than most synthetics. During the height of the rainy season, sandals are preferable to shoes, and it's best to carry an umbrella. Convenience stores sell cheap ones if you get caught out. Sunglasses, hats and sunscreen are recommended for protection from the tropical sun.

Suits are sometimes worn for business in Bangkok but in general Thailand does not have the formal dress code of Hong Kong or Tokyo. A shirt and tie is expected for business appointments, and advisable for any visit to a government office.

Shorts are taboo for both women and men who wish to enter some of the more revered temples and palaces, such as Wat Phra Kaew (Temple of the Emerald Buddha) and the Grand Palace in Bangkok. Women wearing sleeveless dresses and short skirts may also be barred from some temples and mosques.

In some parts of south Thailand, Muslims are in the majority, so dress in deference to the religion and to Thai sensitivities. Although topless sunbathing is common at some beaches in Pattaya, Phuket and Ko Samui, it makes locals uncomfortable. Nudity in public is seen as degrading and generally frowned upon.

Crime and Security

Thailand is a relatively safe country in terms of violent crime. The biggest risk to travellers is from scams and con artists. If you do run into trouble, there are **Tourist Police** (TP) units at the major destinations, which are specially assigned to assist travellers. However, much of the time, there is little they are able to do other than record the details of the crime and provide a report (for insurance purposes). Most members of the force speak some English.

TP National Hotline: 1155; http://touristpolice.go.th

Bangkok Tourist Assistance Centre, 4 Th. Rachadamnoen Nok, tel: 0-2225 7612-4. In Bangkok TP booths can also be found in tourist areas, including Lumphini Park (near the intersection of Th. Rama IV and Th. Silom) and Patpong (at the Th. Surawong intersection).

Common Scams

Touts at Bangkok's Patpong who offer live sex shows upstairs. Once inside, you are handed an exorbitant bill and threatened if you protest. Pay, take the receipt, and go immediately to the Tourist Police, who will usually take you back and demand a refund.

Don't follow touts who offer to take you to a gem factory for a "special deal". The gems are usually synthetic or of substandard quality, and there is no way to get your money back.

Tuk-tuk drivers who offer to take you on a free tour and then stop at every gem, silver and tailor shop along the way where they will collect a commission for wasting your day. A common ruse is to pretend that the attraction you want to visit is closed for a special ceremony. Don't believe them.

People on buses or trains offering sweets, fruits or soft drinks. The items may be drugged and the passenger is robbed while unconscious.

Prostitutes occasionally drug clients (sometimes fatally) and steal valuables, so it is advisable not to consume food or drinks supplied by them in rooms.

Keep in mind that in Thai culture, strangers rarely approach and engage foreigners in conversation, so if you find yourself on the receiving end, be on guard no matter how polite and innocent they appear to be. Feel free to walk away, even if it goes against the rules of polite behaviour.

Drugs

Both hard and soft drugs are easy to procure in Thailand, but it is illegal to possess, consume or trade in them. If caught, the penalties are harsh and the death sentence can apply. Police raids are common at tourist destinations and both plain-clothed and uniformed police will be on the prowl at the infamous full-moon parties at Ko Phangan. Reports of set-ups involving dealers and police are also widespread.

Insurgent Activity

What was initially a low-level Muslim insurgency in the southern provinces closest to the Malaysian border is now a violent separatist movement with regular shootings and bombings. Most governments advise against travel to the provinces of Narathiwat, Pattani and Yala, and to check for updates on the situation in Songkhla.

Women Travellers

Thailand is generally safe for women travellers, even those travelling alone. Thais tend to be non-confrontational, so violent and sexual crimes towards foreign women are not common. That said, like anywhere, it isn't a great idea to be walking alone on quiet streets or beaches late at night.

Customs Regulations

The Thai government prohibits the import or export of drugs, dangerous

⊙ Export Permits

The Thai Department of Fine Arts prohibits the export of all Thai Buddha images, images of other deities and fragments (hands or heads) of images dating from before the 18th century. All antiques must be registered with the department. The shop will usually do this for you. If you decide to handle it yourself, take the piece to the office at Thanon Na Prathat (tel: 0-2226 1661/ 224-2050; www.finearts.go.th) together with two postcard-sized photos of it. The export fee ranges from B50 to B200 depending on the antiquity of the piece. Fake antiques do not require export permits, but airport customs officials are not art experts and may mistake it for a genuine piece. If it looks authentic, clear it at the Department of Fine Arts to avoid problems later.

chemicals, pornography, firearms, ammunition and goods that display the Thai flag. Attempting to smuggle heroin or other hard drugs in or out may be punishable by death. Scores of foreigners are serving very long prison terms for this offence.

Foreign currency exceeding US$20,000 either entering or leaving the country should be declared. Thai currency leaving the country is restricted to B50,000. Foreign guests are allowed to bring in without tax 200 cigarettes and 1 litre of wine or spirits.

It is forbidden to take fragments of Buddha images out of Thailand, even those bought as tourist souvenirs. Antiques, art objects and full Buddha images need Department of Fine Arts clearance, see box.

For more details contact the **National Museum**, Bangkok (tel: 0-2628 5033) or the **Thai Customs Department** (hotline: 1164; www.customs.go.th).

D

Disabled Travellers

Thailand falls short on accommodating the disabled, though this is slowly improving. Pavements are often uneven, studded with obstructions, and there are no ramps; few buildings have wheelchair ramps either. In Bangkok, some major roads have textured brickwork on the paths for the blind. A few Skytrain stations have lifts, but not nearly enough; the Metro has lifts at every station. Getting to many of Thailand's smaller islands often entails taking small boats that are moored at poorly designed piers. It would be a challenge for a disabled traveller to get around Thailand on their own, and a companion is advisable. Online resources are somewhat thin on the ground. There are some companies that can help with things such as accessible hotels and local carers or assistants, as well as planning tours, such as **Wheelchair Holidays Thailand**: www.wheelchairtours.com.

E

Electricity

Electrical outlets are rated at 220 volts, 50 cycles and accept flat-pronged or round-pronged plugs. Adaptors can be purchased at department or hardware stores.

Embassies and consulates in Bangkok

Australia, 181 Wireless Road, Lumphini, tel: 0-2344 6300, http://thailand.embassy.gov.au.
Canada, 15/F, Abdulrahim Place, 990 Th. Rama IV, tel: 0-2646 4300, www.canadainternational.gc.ca/Thailand-thailande/.
New Zealand, M Thai Tower, 14th Floor, All Seasons Place, 87 Wireless Road, tel: 0-2254 2530, www.mfat.govt.nz/en/countries-and-regions/south-east-asia/thailand/new-zealand-embassy/.
Singapore, 129 Th. Sathorn Tai, tel: 0-2384 6700, www.mfa.gov.sg/bangkok/.
UK, 14 Wireless Road, Lumphini, tel: 0-2305 8333, www.gov.uk/world/organisations/british-embassy-bangkok.
US, 95 Wireless Road, tel: 0-2205 4000, https://th.usembassy.gov.

Emergencies

Contact the Tourist Police on 1155
Thailand Emergency Services can be reached at 191.
Direct ambulance number: 1669
Direct fire number: 199
See Crime and Security for more information.

Entry Requirements

Visas and Passports

Travellers should check visa regulations at a Thai embassy or consulate before starting their trip, as visa rules vary for different nationalities. For an updated list, check the Thai **Ministry of Foreign Affairs** website at www.mfa.go.th.

All foreign nationals entering Thailand must have a valid passport with at least six-month validity. At the airport, nationals from most countries will be granted a visa on arrival valid for up to 30 days. Officially you need an air ticket out of Thailand, but this is rarely checked.

Longer tourist visas, obtained from the Thai consulate of your home country prior to arrival, allow for a 60-day stay. People seeking a work permit can apply for a non-immigrant visa, which is good for 90 days. A letter of guarantee is needed from the Thai company you intend to work for, and this visa can be obtained from a Thai consulate at home.

Visas can be extended by 30 days for a fee of B1,000 in Bangkok or at the regional immigration offices, or you can leave the country (even for half an hour) and return to receive another visa on arrival. The 60-day visa can be extended for another 30 days at the same price. In total, tourists can stay in Thailand for a cumulative period not exceeding 90 days within any 6-month period from the date of first entry.

Overstaying your visa can carry a daily fine of B500 to a maximum of B20,000 on leaving the country, but if the police catch you before you leave, you may face imprisonment. Overstaying longer than 90 days is threatened with a ban on re-entering Thailand for at least one year.

In Bangkok, the Thai **Immigration Bureau** is at 120 Moo 3, Th. Chaengwattana; tel: 0-2141 9889; open Mon–Fri 8.30am–4.30pm; www.immigration.go.th. Check the website for contact details of other offices.
Phuket, tel: 0-7622 1905.
Ko Samui, tel: 0-7742 1069.
Chiang Mai, tel: 0-5320 1755.

Etiquette

Thais are remarkably tolerant and forgiving of foreigners'

eccentricities, but there are a few things that are liable to upset them (see also Clothing, page 360).

The Royal Family

Thais have great reverence for the monarchy and disapprove of disrespect towards the institution. Lèse majesté laws, although usually invoked to settle business or political rivalries, can result in jail terms for defaming, insulting or threatening royalty. Standing for the National Anthem is expected in cinemas.

Buddhism

A similar degree of respect is accorded to the second pillar of Thai society, Buddhism. Disrespect towards Buddha images, temples or monks is not taken lightly and, as with the monarchy, public expressions against the institution are considered illegal.

Monks observe vows of chastity that prohibit being touched by (or touching) women, even their mothers. When in the vicinity of a monk, a woman should try to stay clear to avoid accidental contact.

At temples, the scruffy and the underclad are frequently turned away, so dress appropriately.

Terms of Address

Thais are addressed by their first rather than their last names. The name is usually preceded by the word *khun*, a term of honour, a bit like Mr or Ms. Following this to its logical conclusion, Silpachai Krishnamra would be addressed as Khun Silpachai.

Thai Greetings

The common greeting and farewell in Thailand is *sawadee* (followed by *khrap* when spoken by men and *kha* by women). In more formal settings this is accompanied by a *wai*; raising the hands in a prayer-like gesture, the fingertips touching the nose, and bowing the head slightly. However, don't make the mistake of giving a *wai* to all hotel staff, children or the people at the corner shop – it embarrasses them. In these cases, a nod is sufficient. Almost all Thais understand that this is not a part of Western culture and a *wai* is not necessary for foreigners. In business meetings, the *wai* is often followed by a handshake.

Head and Feet

Thai Buddhism regards the head as the wellspring of wisdom and the feet as unclean. For this reason, it is insulting to touch another person on the head, point one's feet at anything or step over another person. In formal situations, when wishing to pass someone who is seated on the floor, bow slightly while walking and point an arm down to indicate the path to be taken, and a path will be cleared.

Public Behaviour

A few decades ago, Thai couples showed no intimacy in public. That has changed due to modernisation and foreign influence on the young, but even these days, intimacy rarely extends beyond holding hands. As in many traditional societies, displaying open affection in public, such as kissing and passionate cuddling, is a sign of bad manners.

F

Festivals

Thais need little excuse for a party, and the kingdom celebrates festivals aplenty. The following are the highlights of the year. As many events are determined by the lunar calendar, it's best to verify exact dates with the TAT in Bangkok (tel: 0-2250 5500) or check www.tourismthailand.org.

January

Bor Sang Umbrella Fair (Bor Sang, Chiang Mai): Celebrates the traditional skill of making gaily painted umbrellas and other handicrafts.

January/February

Chinese New Year (nationwide): Mainly celebrated by the Chinese who visit temples seeking good fortune for the coming year. Shops close in Chinatown areas and family celebrations go on for three days.

Magha Puja (nationwide): The full moon in February marks an event when 1,200 disciples gathered to hear the Buddha preach. When the moon is rising, devotees carrying candles, incense and flowers follow chanting monks around the temple's ordination hall three times before presenting their offerings.

February

Flower Festival (Chiang Mai): This annual event features flower displays, floral floats and beauty contests. It coincides with the period when the province's flowers are in full bloom.

March

Pattaya Music Festival (Pattaya) Thai bands and occasional visiting acts from overseas perform a mix of music styles, modern and traditional, at various Pattaya venues.

April

Songkran (nationwide): 13–15 April. Thailand's official New Year. In days gone by, people would celebrate by visiting temples and sprinkling water on each other's heads. Nowadays it's a different story, as everyone gets wet and wild on the streets with water pistols the size of machine-guns. No one is exempt as revellers career around the streets in open trucks with barrels of water, drenching everyone in sight. It's best to leave your valuables at the hotel. Thanon Khao San in Bangkok is a popular Songkran destination, as many young Thais converge on the backpacker enclave to douse visitors. In the north of Thailand, particularly in Chiang Mai, Songkran is fervently celebrated over several days and attracts many people from Bangkok.

That Phanom Festival (That Phanom): Celebrated by Buddhist pilgrims who make their way to That Phanom in the northeast to honour one of the country's most sacred Buddha images.

May

Rocket Festival (Boun Bang Fai) (Yasothon): This festival is celebrated in the northeast, especially the town of Yasothon near Mukdahan. It's worth the trip to witness the launching of these locally made missiles. They come in all shapes and sizes, some as tall as a person.

Royal Ploughing Ceremony (Bangkok): Held at Sanam Luang in early May. The king presides at this Brahman ritual which marks the start of the rice-planting season. Crimson-clad attendants lead buffaloes drawing a plough over specially consecrated ground.

May/June

Visakha Puja (nationwide): A public holiday at full-moon night in

May that commemorates the birth, enlightenment and death of Buddha. Visakha Puja is celebrated in a similar fashion to Magha Puja.

June/July

Phee Ta Khon (Dan Sai): Possibly Thailand's most riotous festival, Phee Ta Khon is celebrated in this northeastern town near Loei.

July/August

Asalaha Puja (nationwide): The full moon in July witnesses the third-most important Buddhist holiday of the year, marking the occasion when Buddha preached to his first five disciples. It is celebrated in similar manner to Magha Puja and Visakha Puja. It also marks the beginning of the three-month "Buddhist Lent", when Thai monks begin a season of prayers and meditation.

Khao Phansa (nationwide): Celebrated immediately after Asanha Puja and marks the start of the annual three-month "Rains Retreat". This is when young Buddhist novices are ordained at the temple.

Candle Festival (Ubon): The Candle Festival takes place during Khao Phansa in this northeastern town. It celebrates the start of Khao Phansa with a lovely spectacle, during which beautifully embellished beeswax candles are paraded along the streets before being presented to temples.

September

Moon Festival (nationwide): On the first day of the eighth lunar month, Chinese place small shrines laden with fruit, incense and candles in front of their houses to honour the moon goddess, and eat cakes shaped like a full moon stuffed with bean paste and an egg yolk.

October

Vegetarian Festival (Bangkok and Phuket): Held in mid-October, and marked by heaps of vegetarian food, Chinese operatic performances, and elaborate offerings at various Chinese temples in Bangkok and Phuket. In Phuket, devotees go into trance and subject themselves to all kinds of tortuous punishments. Only those wearing all-white attire are allowed in the area of the altar, so dress appropriately.

Ok Phansa (nationwide): Marks the end of the three-month Buddhist Lent, and the beginning of the Kathin season when Buddhists visit temples to present monks with new robes and other necessities. This is also a day of feasting and fun.

Fire Boat Festival (Nakhon Phanom): Marking the end of the Ok Phansa period, this northeastern festival launches a series of gaily decorated "fireboats".

Buffalo Races (Chonburi): Held in late October amid much excitement (and betting on the sidelines).

November

Loy Krathong (nationwide): One of the most beautiful festivals in Asia is held at full moon in November. Thais everywhere launch small candle-laden boats into the rivers and canals to seek blessings, forming a beautiful illuminated mini armada.

Elephant Round-Up (Surin): Thailand's iconic elephants are the subject of this popular festival, attracting visitors from far and wide.

Khon Kaen Silk Fair (Khon Kaen): Silk-weaving demonstrations and a chance to buy silk at this major centre of production in the northeast.

December

River Kwai Bridge Week (Kanchanaburi): A sound-and-light presentation recaptures this dark period of recent history, when thousands of Asians and Westerners died at the hands of the Japanese while building the infamous Death Railway during World War II.

Trooping of the Colours (Bangkok): On 3 December, the royal regiments dressed in brilliantly coloured uniforms march in review before the king on the plaza in front of the old National Assembly building.

King's Birthday Celebrations (nationwide): On 5 December (a public holiday), King Bhumibol celebrates his birthday with a ceremony at Wat Phra Kaew for invited officials and guests. This special day is also regarded as Thailand's very own Fathers' Day.

King's Cup Regatta (Phuket): This long-distance yacht race held off Phuket draws competitors from around the world.

H

Health and Medical Care

Visitors entering Thailand are not required to show evidence of vaccination for smallpox or cholera. Check that your tetanus boosters are up to date. Immunisation against cholera is a good idea, as are hepatitis A and B inoculations. Malaria and dengue persist in remote and rural areas outside Bangkok. When in the countryside, especially in the monsoon season, apply mosquito repellent on exposed skin at all times; dengue mosquitoes are at their most active during the day. At night, be sure to sleep under mosquito netting.

With its thriving nightlife and transient population, Bangkok is a magnet for sexual diseases. Aids and other sexually transmitted diseases are not confined to "high risk" sections of the population in Thailand, so practise safe sex.

Many first-time visitors take a while to adjust to the heat. It is important to drink plenty of water, especially if you've drunk alcohol. Avoid too much sun when out and about and use sun block with a high SPF; the sun is far more powerful at this latitude than in temperate regions.

Tap water in Bangkok has been certified as potable, but take no chances anywhere in Thailand and drink bottled water instead, which is widely available throughout the country. In Bangkok and at reputable hotels and restaurants at Thailand's major tourist centres, ice is clean and presents no health problems.

Stomach upsets are sometimes caused by over-indulgence rather than contaminated food. Many foreigners over-eat and their stomachs react negatively to the sudden switch to a different cuisine. Stick only to freshly cooked food. Establishments catering to foreigners are generally careful with food and drink preparation. They do not, however, always place such a high priority on keeping the environment clean.

Buy travel insurance before travelling to Thailand. Evacuation insurance is not really necessary, as hospitals listed below are of international standard.

Hospitals

The level of medical care in Bangkok and some of Thailand's regional centres is very good. The hospitals listed here all have specialised clinics as well as standard medical facilities. In fact, there has been a growing business in "medical tourism" over the past 15 years, with people coming to Thailand to have procedures performed (including cosmetic and sex-change surgery) that would cost many times more at home or require waiting in a months-long queue. Equipment is up to date and the doctors are usually trained overseas and speak English. By Thai standards, these are considered expensive, but the fees are a fraction of what they are in most Western countries. Note: Most of the hospitals listed here also have dental clinics.

Bangkok

BNH Hospital, 9/1 Th. Convent, Silom, tel: 0-2022 0700; www.bnhhospital.com. This squeaky-clean hospital offers comfortable rooms, top-notch equipment and a large team of specialists. Service is efficient and English is widely spoken.

Bumrungrad International Hospital, 33 Soi 3, Th. Sukhumvit, tel: 0-2066 8888; www.bumrungrad.com. This one is at the top of the heap, and looks more like a five-star hotel than a hospital. Offers a huge range of specialised clinics, excellent staff and a selection of rooms from basic four-bed wards to luxury suites.

Ko Samui

Samui International Hospital, 90/2 Moo 2, Chaweng, tel: 0-7300 394; www.sih.co.th. The best on the island and on a par with the best in Bangkok.

Pattaya

Bangkok Pattaya Hospital, 301 Moo 6, Th. Sukhumvit Km 143, tel hotline: 1719; www.bangkokpattayahospital.com. Part of a network of well-equipped modern private hospitals that also has a branch in Phuket.

Pattaya International Hospital, Pattaya Soi 4, tel: 0-3842 8374–5; www.pattayainterhospital.com. This hospital is equipped to deal with emergencies and elective surgical procedures, including sex changes.

Phuket

Bangkok Hospital Phuket, 21 Th. Hongyok Utis, Phuket Town, tel: 0-7625 4425; www.phukethospital.com. Popular with foreign tourists who come for health checks and surgical procedures.

Phuket International Hospital, 44 Th. Chalermprakiat, tel: 0-7624 9400; www.phuketinternationalhospital.com. Probably the best healthcare facility on the island and familiar with the needs of international patients.

Chiang Mai

Chiang Mai Ram Hospital, 8 Th. Bunruangrit, tel: 0-5392 0300; www.chiangmairam.com. The city's premier hospital, with efficient staff and modern facilities.

Lanna Hospital, 1 Th. Sukkasem, tel: 0-5399-9777; www.lanna-hospital.com. Another hospital with a fine reputation.

McCormick Hospital, Th. Kaew Nawarat, tel: 0-5392-1777; www.mccormick.in.th. Former missionary hospital with a good reputation.

Medical Clinics

All the major hotels in Bangkok and at Thailand's main tourist centres have doctors on call, or clinics they can recommend. Some international hotels also have an on-premises clinic.

Badalveda (www.facebook.com/Badalveda) is a network of dive medicine centres, with branches in Phuket, Ko Tao, and Bangkok. As well as having hyperbaric chambers, they are experienced in treating other dive-related ailments.

Dental Clinics

Apart from the dental clinics at the international hospitals listed here, the **Dental Hospital** at 177 Community, Soi On Nut 1/1, tel: 0-2092 2000; www.dentalhospitalbangkok.com, is highly regarded in Bangkok. It looks more like a hotel than a dental hospital and has the latest equipment.

In the major tourist centres, head to the recommended hospitals, all of which offer dental services.

Pharmacies

These are found everywhere in downtown Bangkok, as well as at most island and beach destinations. In recent years, official control on prescription drugs has been more strongly enforced and requires the presence of a licensed pharmacist on the premises, especially in Bangkok. Nonetheless, most antibiotics and many other drugs that would require a prescription in the West are still available without one in Thailand.

Check the expiry date on all drugs you buy, and wherever possible, purchase them from an air-conditioned pharmacy. There are several branches of **Boots** and **Watsons** pharmacies in central Bangkok.

I

Internet

Wireless surf zones (WiFi), at Bangkok Airport and in hotels, malls and some branches of Starbucks in Bangkok, are a growing trend.

All major hotels in Thailand offer broadband/WiFi internet services, including in the rooms, mostly for free, although if not, these are generally more expensive than at the public internet cafés. These days, even the smallest bungalow outfits in relatively remote towns and beaches have WiFi for guests to use. Connection speeds at such places, however, can be slow.

In Bangkok, remaining internet cafés charge B30–60 per hour for broadband services. Be warned, though, that – in Bangkok at least – they tend to be full of teenagers

Khao San Road, Bangkok.

playing violent games online and can be quite noisy. The Khao San area has more internet cafés than in any other area in Bangkok, but the Silom and Ploenchit areas have some internet cafés as well. Ask your hotel reception desk for advice.

L

Left Luggage

There are two left-luggage facilities at Suvarnabhumi Airport. One is on Level 2 (near Exit 4) of the arrival hall, and the other is on Level 4 behind check-in line Q of the departure hall. The fee is B100 per bag per day. The airports at Phuket, Ko Samui and Chiang Mai also have left-luggage facilities; enquire at the information desks at the respective airports.

Most hotels and guesthouses offer a left-luggage service; usually it is free, but some may levy a small daily fee.

LGBTQ Travellers

The LGBTQ community is quick to discover that Thailand is one of the most tolerant countries in the world. The LGBTQ nightlife scene in Bangkok, Pattaya and Phuket is huge. Bangkok also hosts an on-off annual Bangkok Gay Pride Festival, while similar events take place in Pattaya and in Phuket (www.gaypatong.com). Chiang Mai has a small LGBTQ scene as well, but it's a bit more discreet.

Utopia at www.utopia-asia.com is a major online resource for the community throughout the region. It's a good place to make contacts and to find out what's going on.

Purple Dragon is a travel agency that caters exclusively to LGBTQ travellers. It is located at 942/58 Issara Tower 1, Rama IV Road, tel: 0-2236 1776; www.purpledrag.com.

Lost Property

If you lose any valuable property, report it as soon as possible to the **Tourist Police** (1155) to get an insurance statement.

Suvarnabhumi Airport: For property lost at Bangkok Airport, contact tel: 0-2132 1888.

Public Transit: BMTA **city bus service**, tel: 0-2246 0973; **BTS Skytrain**, tel: 0-2617 6000; **MRTA Metro**, tel: 0-2624 6200, **Hualamphong Railway Station**, tel: 1690.

Taxis: Bangkok taxi drivers frequently listen to a radio station (**JS100 Radio 100FM hotline**: 1137), which has a lost-property hotline; it's surprising how often forgetful passengers get their lost items back.

M

Maps

Basic maps of Bangkok are available for free at the offices of the **Tourism Authority of Thailand** (TAT) offices and at big hotels. More detailed ones can be found at bookshops. Insight Guides Fleximap series includes laminated, detailed maps of Bangkok and Thailand, ideal even in wet weather. Other useful and off-beat insights to Bangkok's attractions can be found in Nancy Chandler's *Map of Bangkok* and Groovy Map's publications on Bangkok, Pattaya, Phuket and Samui, with sections on bars, dining, culture and shopping. At the major tourist centres like Phuket, Ko Samui and Chiang Mai, free maps are available at hotels and tour agencies.

Media

Magazines

There are several what's on and listings publications in English that cover events, nightlife, art galleries, restaurants, etc., although most are sparsely filled, unreliable and often consist of advertising copy disguised as editorial. The best free sheet is the weekly *BK* (http://bk.asia-city.com). The glossy small-format monthly *Bangkok 101* (www.bangkok101.com) costs B100, and has a good run down of art shows and venues, along with events and restaurant and nightlife reviews.

New regional magazines geared towards the tourist market are constantly appearing and disappearing. Recommended is Chiang Mai's *City Life Magazine* (www.chiangmaicitylife.com).

Newspapers

Thailand has two longstanding English-language dailies, the *Bangkok Post* (www.bangkokpost.com) and *The Nation* (www.nationmultimedia.com). Both are quite conservative by Western press standards, but have some informative writers and are often more opinionated about government policies than in the past. Many big hotels furnish one or the other for free with the room, or they can be purchased at newsstands for B30.

Regional, advertisement-driven newspapers include *The Thaiger* (the surviving online presence of the now-defunct *Phuket Gazette;* http://thethaiger.com), *Pattaya Mail* (www.pattayamail.com), *Pattaya Today* (www.pattayatoday.net) and *Chiang Mai Mail* (www.chiangmai-mail.com), and the monthly *Hua Hin Today* (www.huahintoday.com).

Radio

AM radio is devoted entirely to Thai-language programmes. FM frequencies include several English-language stations with the latest pop hits. Some frequencies have bilingual DJs and play a mixture of Thai and English songs in the same programme.

97 MHZ: Radio Thailand has 4 hours of English-language broadcasts each day.

105.5 MHZ: Tourism Authority of Thailand offers useful tips to tourists every hour.

Fat FM **104.5**: Has the latest on Thailand's thriving indie music scene.

Eazy FM **105.5**: As the name suggests, mostly easy-listening middle-of-the-road music.

FMX **95.5**: Contemporary dance and pop hits.

Television

Thailand has six Thai-language terrestrial television channels: ITV or Independent Television specialises in news and documentaries. The rest mainly air soaps and game shows with a sprinkling of mostly domestically oriented news. There is also Truevision, a cable television network that provides subscribers with an increasing choice of Thai and international channels, including BBC World News, HBO, ESPN and MTV Thailand.

Money

The *baht* is the principal Thai monetary unit. Though it is divided into 100 units called *satang*, this is becoming outdated; only 50 and 25 *satang* pieces are used.

Banknote denominations include 1,000 (light brown), 500 (purple), 100 (red), 50 (blue) and 20 (green). There is a 10 *baht* coin (brass centre with silver rim), a 5-*baht* coin (silver), a 2-*baht* coin (copper coloured), a 1-*baht* coin (silver), and two small coins of 50 and 25 *satang* (both brass-coloured).

In 2019, US$1 was worth B32, £1 sterling B41, and 1 Euro equalled B36.

Changing Money

Banking hours are from 9.30am to 3.30pm Monday to Friday, but nearly every bank maintains money-changing kiosks in the tourist areas of Thailand. Better hotels almost always have exchange facilities at their reception desks, but generally give poor exchange rates when compared to banks. ATM machines are widely available, except on smaller islands.

Credit Cards

American Express, Diner's Club, MasterCard, JCB and Visa are widely accepted throughout Bangkok and major resort towns like Phuket, Ko Samui, Hua Hin and Pattaya. Smaller establishments, however, may impose a 3 percent surcharge on card transactions. Credit cards can be used to draw emergency cash at most banks. If you lose your credit card, contact your card company as soon as possible so that your card can be cancelled.

American Express, tel: 0-2273 5222.
Diner's Club, tel: 0-2238 3660.
MasterCard, tel: 001-800-11-887-0663
Visa, tel: 001-800-441-3485.

Warning: Credit card fraud is a major problem in Thailand. Don't leave your credit card in safe-deposit boxes. When making a purchase, make sure that you get the carbon slips and dispose of them. When your card is swiped through the machine, make sure it is done in your presence, and **never** let the card out of your sight.

Travellers' Cheques

Travellers' cheques are gradually becoming less common and harder to change. They can be cashed at most exchange kiosks and banks, and generally receive better exchange rates compared to cash. There is a nominal charge of B25 for each travellers' cheque cashed.

P

Photography

With more than 10 million visitors per year, Thailand gets its photo taken an awful lot. The country and its people are very photogenic, and everything the photographer may need is readily available. However, some ticketed sites may charge extra for the use of a camera, although with smart phones this is getting harder to police.

Postal Services

The Thai postal service is reasonably reliable, though mail seems to go astray more frequently outside Bangkok and at Christmas time. The odds for domestic mail can be improved by registering or sending items by EMS for a fee of B20 for a business-sized letter. EMS is supposed to guarantee that a letter reaches a domestic destination in one day, and it generally does, particularly in Bangkok. If you wish to send valuable parcels or bulky documents overseas, it is better to use a courier service.

In Bangkok, the **Central Post Office** at Thanon Charoen Krung, tel: 0-2233 1050, is open from Monday to Friday 8am to 8pm, Saturday until 4pm, and Sunday and holidays until 1pm.

Post offices elsewhere in Bangkok and Thailand usually open at 8am and close at 4pm on weekdays. Postal services are found at all tourist centres, even on small islands like Ko Samet.

In Bangkok, you can find mini post offices in some office buildings and hotels. Look for a red sign in English. These outlets offer basic mail services and accept small packages, but have no telecommunications services.

Courier Services

The usual global courier services are available in Bangkok. You can call direct or book online.

DHL: www.dhl.co.th; **Bangkok**, tel: 0-2631 2621; **Pattaya**, tel: 0-3871 1274; **Phuket**, tel: 0-7625 8500; **Chiang Mai**, tel: 0-5332 6553.
Fedex: www.fedex.com/th; **Bangkok**, tel: 0-2229 8800; hotline: 1782; toll free: **Outside Bangkok**, tel: 1800-236 236.
UPS: www.ups.com/th; **Bangkok**, tel: 0-2762 3300; **Phuket**, tel: 0-7626 3987; **Chiang Mai**, tel: 0-5375 5030.

Public Holidays

Public holidays related to religion or royalty are often accompanied by restrictions on the sale of alcohol. This will not affect hotels, but may affect bars and shops, depending on local policing.

1 Jan: New Year's Day
Jan/Feb: (full moon) Magha Puja. Note: Chinese New Year is not an official holiday, but many businesses close for several days
6 Apr: Chakri Day (or following Monday if the 6th falls on a weekend)
13–15 Apr: Songkran
1 May: Labour Day
Late May/June: (full moon) Visakha Puja
28 July: H.M. King's birthday
Late July/August: (full moon) Asalaha Puja
12 Aug: Queen's Birthday
14 Oct: The passing of King Bhumibol
23 Oct: Chulalongkorn Day
5 Dec: King's Birthday
10 Dec: Constitution Day

R

Religious Services

Though it is predominantly Buddhist, Thailand has historically been tolerant of other religions. According to government census, 94 percent of people are Theravada Buddhists, 3.9 percent are Muslims, 1.7 percent Confucians, and 0.6 percent Christians (mostly hill-tribe people living in the north).

Buddhists will find no lack of places of worship, but in Bangkok, there are Christian churches (both Catholic and Protestant), Hindu temples, mosques and synagogues. Outside the capital, the options are fewer. The further south you venture the more mosques you will find. Check with your hotel reception desk for addresses of places of worship and timings of services.

S

Shopping

Whatever part of your budget you have allocated for shopping, keep a tight grip on your wallet or you will find yourself being seduced by the low prices and walking off with more than you can possibly carry home.

The range of Thai handicrafts for sale is stupendous. While regional products were once found only in the towns that produced them, today, due to ease of distribution, it's possible, for instance, to buy Chiang Mai umbrellas in Phuket. The widest range of handicrafts is found in Bangkok, Phuket and Chiang Mai. If you don't have a chance to leave Bangkok, despair not; nearly everything you might want to buy in small towns can be found in the capital.

In Bangkok, especially, shopping has become an obsessive leisure activity for many. Teenagers, young couples and families love meandering through the new mega malls and department stores. At weekends it all gets extremely crowded.

Most malls and department stores in the large cities open daily from 10am–10pm and participate every June to July and December to January in the Thailand Grand Sales. Many also offer a 5 percent tourist discount year-round; simply show your passport at the point of purchase. Alternatively, you can claim the 7 percent VAT refund at Suvarnabhumi Airport.

T

Taxes

Thailand has a Value-Added Tax (VAT) of 7 percent. This is added to most goods and services (but not goods sold by street vendors and markets). You can get the VAT refunded at the airport on anything you purchase in designated stores costing at least B2,000.

All major hotels add to the room rate at least 10 percent service charge and at least 7 percent tax (made up of VAT and hotel tax). At top-class restaurants, VAT and 10 percent service charge is added to the bill.

Telephones

International Calls

The **country code** for Thailand is 66. When calling Thailand from overseas, dial your local international access code first, followed by 66 and then the number (without the 0 prefix) in Thailand.

To make an international call from Thailand, dial 001 before the country and area codes, followed by the telephone number. If you need international call assistance, dial 100. Peak-hour calls made from 7am to 9pm are the most expensive, so it pays to call during non-peak hours from 5am to 7am, and 9pm to midnight. The lowest call rates are from midnight to 5am.

Prepaid international phone cards (called Thaicard) of B300, B500 and B1,000 value can be used to make international calls. These can be bought at post offices, certain shops that carry the Thaicard sign or the office of the **Communications Authority of Thailand** in Bangkok, tel: 0-2104 3000;www.cattelecom.com.

Local Calls

The prefix 0 must be dialled for all calls made within Thailand, even when calling local numbers within the same city. Therefore when in Bangkok, dial 0 first, followed by the local 8-digit number; if you need local directory assistance, dial 1133. Some services also have four-digit hotline numbers, which require no code.

Mobile Phones

Any local telephone number that begins with the prefix 08 denotes a mobile phone. Just like fixed-line phones, dial the prefix 0 for all calls made within Thailand but drop the zero when calling from overseas.

Only users of GSM 850 or GSM 900 mobile phones with international roaming facility can hook up automatically to the local Thai network. Check with your service provider if you're not sure, especially if coming from the US, Korea or Japan. Your phone will automatically select a local service provider and this enables you to make calls within Thailand at local rates. However, if someone calls your number, international call rates will apply. Charges will be billed to your account in your home country.

If you're planning to travel in Thailand for any length of time, it's more economical to buy a local SIM card with a stored value from a mobile-phone shop. You will be assigned a local number, and local calls to and from the phone will be at local rates. International rates will apply to overseas calls.

VAT Refunds

It is possible to get the 7 percent VAT refunded from your shopping if you purchase goods from stores displaying the "VAT Refund for Tourists" sign and leave from an international airport within 60 days of purchase. Refunds can only be claimed on single purchases of B2,000 or more, with a minimum overall expenditure of B5,000. At the time of purchase, present your passport and ask the sales assistant to complete the VAT refund form. Before departure at Suvarnabhumi Airport, present your goods with the VAT refund form and sales invoice to the Customs officers for inspection. After approval, present your claim to the Revenue officers at the airport's VAT Refund Counter.

Refunds not exceeding B30,000 will be made in cash (in Thai baht) or by bank draft or credited to your credit-card account. Refunds over B30,000 cannot be made in cash. In addition, there is an administrative fee of B100 for cash refunds; bank drafts and credit-card refunds will incur extra charges. See www.customs.go.th for more details.

Public Phones

Even though Thais are heavy users of mobile phones, there are still a few coin- and card-operated telephone booths in cities. Public telephones accept B1, B5 and B10 coins. Phone cards for local calls in denominations of B50, B100, B200 and B400 can be purchased at 7–11 convenience shops throughout the city.

Time Zone

Thailand is 7 hours ahead of GMT. Since it gets dark between 6pm and 7pm uniformly throughout the year, Thailand does not observe daylight savings time.

Tipping

Tipping is not a custom in Thailand, although it is becoming more prevalent. A service charge of 10 percent is included in the more expensive restaurants and is usually, though not always, divided among the staff.

Do leave a small tip when service charge has not been included. Porters are becoming used to being tipped, but will not hover with their hand extended. Do not tip taxi or tuk-tuk drivers unless the traffic has been particularly bad and he has been especially patient. In most cases, though, people will leave loose change left over from their bill or taxi fare.

Toilets

There are not a great deal of public toilets in Thailand, though Bangkok is beginning to address this issue in tourist areas. Public restrooms are usually dirty and sometimes of the squat-toilet variety, a tricky experience for the uninitiated. Your best bet is to make use of the facilities at fast-food outlets, which are very easy to find. Shopping malls usually have clean toilets as well, particularly near the food courts. Sometimes a small fee of a few baht applies.

Tourist Offices

The **Tourism Authority of Thailand** (TAT) spends billions of baht every year to promote tourism domestically and abroad. They have information outlets in several countries and service kiosks within Thailand that offer maps and other promotional materials as well as advise on things to do and places to see. The main website www.tourismthailand.org has hundreds of pages of information.

Bangkok

TAT **Call Centre**, tel: 1672. Open daily 8am–8pm.
Tourism Authority of Thailand Main Office, 1600 Th. Phetchaburi, Makkasan, Bangkok, tel: 0-2250 5500. Open daily 8.30am–4.30pm.
TAT **Tourist Information Counter**, Arrival Hall, Suvarnabhumi Airport, tel: 0-2504 2701. Open daily 8am–10pm.
TAT **Tourist Information Counter (Ratchadamnoen)**, 4 Th. Ratcha-damnoen Nok, tel: 0-2282 9774. Open daily 8.30am–4.30pm.

Overseas Offices

UK, 1st Floor, 17-19 Cockspur Street, Trafalgar Square, London, tel: 020 7925 2511, www.tourismthailand.co.uk.
US, 61 Broadway, Suite 2810, New York, NY 10006, tel: 1-212-432 0433; and 611 North Larchmont Blvd, 1st Floor, Los Angeles, CA 90004, tel: 1-323-461 9814.
Australia, Australia 2002, Level 20, 56 Pitt Street, Sydney 2000, tel: 61-2-9247 7549, www.tourismthailand.org/au.

Regional Offices

Ayutthaya, 108/22 Moo 4, Th. Pratuchai, tel: 0-3524 6076–7.
Chiang Mai, 105/1 Th. Chiang Mai-Lamphun, tel: 0-5324 8604/8607.
Chiang Rai, 448/16 Th. Singhaklai, tel: 0-5371 7433.
Hat Yai, 1/1 Soi 2, Th. Niphat Uthit 3, tel: 0-7424 3747.
Kanchanaburi, Th. Saengchuto, tel: 0-3451 1500.
Khon Kaen, 15/5 Th. Prachasamoson, tel: 0-4324 4498–9.
Loei, Old District Office, Th. Charoenraj. tel: 0-4281 2812.
Lopburi, Th. Ropwat Phrathat, tel: 0-3642 2768–9.
Nakhon Phanom, 184/1 Th. Sunthornvichit, tel: 0-4251 3490–1.
Nakhon Ratchasima, 2102–2104 Th. Mittraphap, tel: 0-4421 3666.
Nakhon Si Thammarat, Sanam Na Muang, Th. Ratchadamnoen, tel: 0-7534 6515–6.
Pattaya, 609 Moo 10, Th. Phra Tamnak, tel: 0-3842 8750.
Phetchaburi, 500/51 Th. Phetchkasem, tel: 0-3247 1005–6.
Phitsanulok, 209/7–8 Surasi Trade Center, Th. Boromtrailokanat, tel: 0-5525 9907.
Phuket, 191 Th. Thalang, tel: 0-7621 1036/7138.
Songkhla, 1/1 Soi 2, Th. Niphatuthit 3, tel. 0-7423 1055/8518.
Sukhothai, 130 Th. Charot Withithong, tel: 0-5561 6228-9.
Surat Thani, 5 Th. Talat Mai, tel: 0-7728 8818–9.
Surin, 355 Th. Thessaban, tel: 0-4451-4447.
Tak, 193 Th. Taksin, tel: 0-5551 4341.
Trat, 100 Moo 1, Th. Trat-Laem Ngop, tel: 0-3959 7259–60.
Ubon Ratchathani, 264/1 Th. Khuan Thani, tel: 0-4524 3770.
Udon Thani (Loei), 16/5 Th. Mukmontri, tel: 0-4232 5406–7.

W

Websites and apps

Thailand

www.tourismthailand.org
The official website of the Tourism Authority of Thailand.
www.bangkokpost.com
Daily news from the *Bangkok Post* daily newspaper.
www.nationmultimedia.com
Daily news clips from *The Nation* newspaper.
www.boi.go.th
The Thailand Board of Investment.
www.customs.go.th
The Thai Customs Department.
www.langhub.com/en-th
Audio and video files to learn Thai.

Bangkok

www.khaosanroad.com
Backpacker resource with accommodation, forums, etc.
www.timeout.com/bangkok/restaurants
Reviews of restaurants and bars in Bangkok by *Time Out*.
www.bangkok-translation.com
Interpreter and translation services in Bangkok.
www.bangkoktourist.com
Information on Bangkok from the Bangkok Tourist Bureau.
www.bkmagazine.com
Nightlife and restaurant listings, plus what's new and hot in Bangkok.

Weights and Measures

Thailand uses the metric system, except for their traditional system of land measurement (1 rai = 1,600 sq metres) and the weight of gold (1 *baht* = 15.2 grammes).

LANGUAGE

ORIGINS AND INTONATION

For centuries, the Thai language, rather than tripping from foreigners' tongues, has been tripping them up. Its roots go back to the place Thais originated from in the hills of southern China, but these are overlaid by Indian influences. From the original settlers come the five tones that seem designed to frustrate visitors. One sound can have five different tones: mid, high, low, rising and falling, and each of these means a different thing from the other.

Therefore, when you mispronounce a word, you don't simply say a word incorrectly: it is another word entirely. It is not unusual to see a semi-fluent foreigner standing before a Thai and running through the scale of tones until suddenly a light of recognition dawns on his companion's face. There are the misinformed who will tell you that tones are not important. These people do not communicate with Thais – they communicate at them in a one-sided exchange that frustrates both parties.

PRONUNCIATION

The way Thai consonants are written in English often confuses foreigners. An *h* following a letter like *p* and *t* gives the letter a soft sound; without the *h*, the sound is more explosive. Thus, *ph* is not pronounced *f* but as a soft *p*; without the *h*, the *p* has the sound of a very hard *b*. The word *thanon* (street) is pronounced *tanon* in the same way as *Thailand* is not meant to sound like *Thighland*. Similarly, final letters are often not pronounced as they look. The letter *j* at the end of a word is pronounced as *t*, while *l* is pronounced as an *n*. To complicate matters further, many words end with *se* or *r*, which are not pronounced; for instance, *Surawongse*, one of Bangkok's main thoroughfares, is simply pronounced *Surawarong*.

Vowels are pronounced as follows: **i** as in *sip*, **ii** as in *seep*, **e** as in *bet*, **a** as in *pun*, **aa** as in *pal*, **u** as in *pool*, **o** as in *so*, **ai** as in *pie*, **ow** as in *cow*, **aw** as in *paw*, **iw** as in *you*, **oy** as in *toy*.

In Thai, the pronouns *I* and *me* are the same word, but it is indicated differently for males and females. Men use the word *pom* when referring to themselves, while women say *di chan*. Men use *khrap* at the end of a sentence when addressing either a male or a female to add politeness, or in a similar manner as "please" (the word for "please", *karuna*, is seldom used directly), ie *pai nai, khrap* (Where are you going sir?). Women add the word *kha* to their statements, as in *pai nai, kha*.

To ask a question, add a high tone *mai* to the end of the phrase ie *rao pai* (we go) or *rao pai mai* (shall we go?). To negate a statement, insert a falling tone *mai* between the subject and the verb ie *rao pai* (we go), *rao mai pai* (we don't go). "Very" or "much" are indicated by adding *maak* to the end of a phrase ie *ron* (hot), *ron maak* (very hot), or *phaeng* (expensive), *phaeng maak* (very expensive), and the opposite *mai phaeng* (not expensive).

THAI NAMES

Thai names are among the longest in the world. Every Thai person's first name and surname has a meaning. Thus, by learning the meaning of the name of everyone you meet, you would acquire a formal, but quite extensive, vocabulary.

There is no universal transliteration system from Thai into English, which is why names and street names can be spelled in three different ways. For example, the surname Chumsai is written Chumsai, Jumsai and Xoomsai, depending on the family. This confuses even the Thais. If you ask a Thai how they spell something, they may well reply, "How do you want to spell it?" So, Ratchadamnoen is also spelled Ratchadamnern. Ko Samui can be spelled Koh Samui. The spellings will differ from map to map, and from book to book.

To address a person one has never met, the title *khun* is used for both male and female. Having long and complicated surnames, Thais typically address one another by their first name only, preceded by the title *khun* for formality, ie Hataichanok Phrommayon becomes *Khun* Hataichanok. Thais usually adopt nicknames from birth, often accorded to their physical or behavioural attributes as a baby, ie *Lek* (small), *Yai* (big), etc. If the person is familiar – a friend, relative, or close colleague – then according to the age relationship between both persons, they are addressed *Pii* (if older), or *Nong* (if younger). So an older friend would be addressed *Pii Lek*, and if younger *Nong Lek*.

NUMBERS

0 *soon*
1 *nung*
2 *song*
3 *sam*
4 *sii*
5 *haa*
6 *hok*
7 *jet*
8 *bet*
9 *kow*
10 *sip*
11 *sip et*
12 *sip song*
13 *sip sam* and so on
20 *yii sip*
30 *sam sip* and so on
100 *nung roi*
1,000 *nung phan*

USEFUL WORDS AND PHRASES

Days of the Week

Monday *Wan Jan*
Tuesday *Wan Angkan*
Wednesday *Wan Phoot*
Thursday *Wan Pharuhat*
Friday *Wan Sook*
Saturday *Wan Sao*
Sunday *Wan Athit*
Today *Wan nii*
Yesterday *Meua wan nii*
Tomorrow *Prung nii*

Basics

Yes *Chai*
No *Mai chai*
Hello/goodbye *Sawadee* (a man then says *khrap*; a woman says *kha*: thus *sawadee khrap* or *sawadee kha*)
My name is… *Pom cheur…* (man); *Di chan cheur…* (woman)
How are you? *Khun sabai dii, mai?*
Well, thank you *Sabai dii, khopkhun*
Thank you very much *Khopkhun maak*
Sorry *Kor toet*
Can you help me? *Chuay pom noy dai mai?*
Never mind *Mai pen rai*
Do you speak English? *Kun poot par sar ang grit dai mai?*
I don't understand *Pom mai kow jai*

DIRECTIONS AND TRAVEL

Go *Pai*
Come *Maa*
Where *Thii nai*
Right *Khwaa*
Left *Sai*
Turn *Leo*
Straight ahead *Trong pai*
Stop here *Yood thii nii*
Fast *Raew*
Slow *Cha*
Hotel *Rong raem*
Street *Thanon*
Lane *Soi*
Bridge *Saphan*
Police station *Sathanii Dtam Ruat*
Ferry *Reua*
Longtail boat *Reua haang yao*
Taxi *Taihk see*
Train *Rot fai*
Bus *Rot may*
Skytrain *Rot fai faa*
Metro/subway *Rot fai tai din*
Pier *Tha reua*
Bus stop *Pai rot may*
Bus station *Sathanii rot may*
Train station *Sathanii rot fai*
How do I get to…? *Pom ja pai tee… pai yang ngai?*
Can you show me on the map where I am? *Chuay chee nai pairn tee hai doo noy war torn nee pom yoo tee nai?*
Where's the tourist office? *Sam nak ngarn torng teaw yoo tee nai?*

ACCOMMODATION

The air-conditioning doesn't work *Air mai tam ngarn*
The light doesn't work *Fai far mai tam ngarn*
There's no hot water *Mai mee narm rorn*

SHOPPING

Do you have…? *Mii… mai?*
How much? *Thao rai?*
Expensive *Phaeng*
Do you have something cheaper? *Mii arai thii thook kwa, mai?*
Can I try it on? *Kor lorng noy dai mai?*
Too big *Yai kern pai*
Too small *Lek kern pai*
I'll take it *Pom ow an nee la*
I don't want it *Mai ao*
Do you have another colour? *Mii sii uhn mai?*

Colour (sii)

White *sii kao*
Black *sii dum*
Red *sii daeng*
Yellow *sii leung*
Blue *sii num ngern*
Green *sii keeow*
Orange *sii som*

EATING OUT

May I have the menu, please? *Kor doo rai garn ar harn noy dai mai?*
Nothing too spicy, please *Mai ow rot jat na krap (ka)*
I'm vegetarian *Pom pehn mang sawi rat*
Hot (heat hot) *Ron*
Hot (spicy) *Phet*
Cold *Yen*
Sweet *Waan*
Sour *Prio*
Delicious *Aroy*
Water *Narm*

OTHER HANDY PHRASES

Do you have…? *Mi… mai?*

The Five Tones

Mid tone: Voiced at the speaker's normal, even pitch.
High tone: Pitched slightly higher than the mid tone.
Low tone: Pitched slightly lower than the mid tone.
Rising tone: Sounds like a questioning pitch, starting low and rising.
Falling tone: Sounds like an English-speaker suddenly understanding something: "Oh, I see!"

Can I pay by credit card? *Jai duay bat krey dit dai mai?*
Where's the toilet? *Horng narm yoo tee nai?*
I do not feel well *Mai sabai*
Can you get me a doctor? *Chuay dtarm mor mar hai noy dai mai?*
Is it safe to swim here? *Tee nee plort pai por tee ja wai narm dai mai?*
Is it all right to take pictures? *Tai roop tee nee dai mai?*

GLOSSARY OF TERMS

ao **gulf/bay**
baht **Thai unit of currency**
ban **house or village, short for *mooban***
bot **ordination hall in a Thai temple**
chao lay **indigenous sea gypsies**
chedi **relic tower, also called *stupa***
doi **mountain (in the north)**
guti **monks' living quarters**
hat **beach**
ho trai **Buddhist scripture library**
Isaan **a term for northeast Thailand**
kathoey **"lady-boy" or transvestite**
khao **hill or mountain**
klong/khlong **canal**
ko/koh **island**
mae nam **river**
mor lam **northeastern music tradition**
muay thai **Thai boxing**
mudmee **northeastern Thai silk**
namtok **waterfall**
phipat **classical Thai music**
prang **Khmer-style tower**
soi **lane or small street**
tham **cave**
thanon **street**
tuk-tuk **motorised three-wheeled taxi**
viharn **sermon hall in Buddhist temple**
wai **palms clasped together in a Thai-style greeting**
wat **temple or monastery**

GENERAL

Bangkok Found: Reflections on the City by Alex Kerr. An incisive look into the traditions underpinning Bangkok as well as the often quirky results of mixing old and new in this city of fusion.
Bangkok's Waterways by William Warren and R. Ian Lloyd. A heartfelt guide to the essence of Bangkok; the canals and rivers that wind through the city. Beautifully written and photographed.
Travelers' Tales Thailand edited by James O'Reilly and Larry Habegger. A stimulating collection of observations and true stories contributed by some 50 writers.

FICTION

Bangkok 8 by John Burdett. A best-selling story about a half-Thai, half-American policeman who avenges his partner's death.
Fieldwork: A Novel by Mischa Berlinski. A thriller set in the north, refreshingly free of bar-girl subplots.
A Killing Smile by Christopher G. Moore. A gripping thriller set in the capital city of Thailand. Moore has written many books based on his experiences with Bangkok's seamier side.
Many Lives (Lai Chiwit) by Kukrit Pramoj. Insight into Buddhist thoughts from the famous Thai polymath.
Monsoon Country by Pira Sudham. One of the best books to come out of Thailand in recent times gives a unique glimpse of rural Thai life.
Probability (Kwam Na Ja Pen) by Prabda Yoon. The collection of short stories that launched the career of this highly rated Thai author.

HISTORY AND SOCIETY

A Journalist in Siam by Andrew A Freeman. Take a trip back in time with this 1920's travelogue by the then editor of the *Bangkok Daily Mail* newspaper.
Borderlines by Charles Nicholl. ***A History of Thailand*** second edition by Dr Pasuk Phongpaichit and Chris Baker. Concise and well-informed history of the country, mainly from the Rattanakosin period.
The King Never Smiles by Paul Handley. A serious but controversial analysis of the monarchy's role in Thailand. Unavailable in the kingdom.
Thailand: A Short History by David K. Wyatt. Despite the title, this is a scholarly, wide ranging history of the country from the first millennium AD.

ART AND CULTURE

Architecture of Thailand by Nithi Sthapitanonda and Brian Mertens. Explores Thailand's unique architectural lineage, from the simple bamboo hut to teak mansions and religious edifices.

Send us your thoughts

We do our best to ensure the information in our books is as accurate and up-to-date as possible. The books are updated on a regular basis using local contacts, who painstakingly add, amend and correct as required. However, some details (such as telephone numbers and opening times) are liable to change, and we are ultimately reliant on our readers to put us in the picture.

We welcome your feedback, especially your experience of using the book "on the road". Maybe you came across a great bar or new attraction we missed.

We will acknowledge all contributions, and we'll offer an Insight Guide to the best letters received.

Please write to us at:
Insight Guides
PO Box 7910
London SE1 1WE

Or email us at:
hello@insightguides.com

The Grand Palace by Nngnoi Saksi, Naengnoi Suksri and Michael Freeman. A beautifully illustrated and detailed account of Bangkok's Grand Palace.
Thai Folk Wisdom: Contemporary Takes on Traditional Proverbs by Tulaya Pornpiriyakulchai & Jane Vejjajiva. Dual language coffee table book that looks at society through 50 proverbs illustrated with paintings by leading Thai artists.

RELIGION

A History of Buddhism in Siam by Prince Dhani Nivat. Written by one of Thailand's most respected scholars.

COOKERY

Green Mangoes and Lemongrass: Southeast Asia's Best Recipes From Bangkok To Bali by Wendy Hutton. Presenting the rich diversity of Southeast Asian cuisine, accompanied by striking photographs.
Thai Food by David Thompson. Almost 700 pages of traditional recipes with background on food and social fabric from the chef at Europe's first Michelin starred Thai restaurant.

OTHER INSIGHT GUIDES

Titles that highlight Thailand include: *Insight Guides Thailand's Beaches and Islands* picks the very best of the country's coastal locations with insightful text and stunning photography.
Insight Guides Explore Bangkok offers a range of easy-to-follow walking tours of the city and its surroundings.
Insight Fleximap Thailand is a handy map with a weatherproof laminated finish, with clear mapping and useful travel information.

CREDITS

PHOTO CREDITS

A Good/IBL/Rex Features 238
akg-images/British Library 33R
Alamy 71, 183, 210, 251, 258
Aleenta Resorts 190
Amari Resorts 180T
Apa Publications 30
Austin Bush/Apa Publications 255, 257T, 259, 260, 261
Bigstock.com 202
BPK, Berlin/Photo Scala, Florence 37L
Corbis 12/13, 31, 38, 45, 58/59T, 70, 94/95, 96/97
David Henley/Apa Publications 7BL, 274, 276T, 277, 293, 294, 295T, 297T, 298, 304, 306B, 306T, 307, 308B, 309T, 311, 316T, 316B, 321T, 325, 328, 329T, 331, 333T, 338T, 340, 341T, 343, 344, 345, 346B, 347, 349
Dominique Dalbiez 330
Dreamstime.com 26, 59BR, 92/93T, 121B, 252, 286T, 348
Fotolia 8B, 93ML, 220BL, 333B
Francis Dorai/Apa Publications 112T, 115T
Getty Images 6BR, 9TR, 29, 40, 42, 43, 46, 47, 58BR, 59TR, 60, 72, 104, 137B, 140/141, 159, 168/169, 206, 212, 268, 278, 288, 292, 296, 299, 318/319T, 318BL, 319BL
Hans Fonk 129
iStock 4, 7TR, 7MR, 7ML, 8T, 24, 32, 39, 66BL, 67BR, 67BL, 87, 89L, 93BR, 100, 101T, 105T, 111, 115B, 120, 126, 127B, 143T, 153B, 154BC, 154/155T, 154BR, 155BR, 155ML, 155BL, 155TR, 160, 161, 162T, 167T, 173, 182, 189, 198B, 201, 203, 215T, 216, 220BR, 220MR, 220/221T, 221BL, 221BR, 221TR, 228T, 237, 243, 249, 253, 257B, 262, 267T, 267B, 272, 273, 295B, 297B, 300, 301, 302, 303, 305, 308T, 319BR, 319TR, 329B, 334, 335, 341B, 364, 371
Jason Lang/Apa Publications 52, 54, 64L, 64R, 88, 90, 132T, 139T, 148T, 188T
Joe Cummings/Apa Publications 315
John W. Ishil/Apa Publications 10BR, 21, 25, 51, 55R, 66BR, 67ML, 135, 174, 178, 181, 188B, 191B, 191T, 192, 195, 196, 197, 199, 200B, 200T, 205T, 207, 208, 209, 213, 214, 215B, 217, 233B, 234T, 235, 239, 240, 244B, 244T, 245, 247, 248, 250
JW Marriott Resort & Spa 228B
Kevin Foy/Rex Features 205B
M.C.Piya Rangsit 41
Mandarin Oriental Hotel Group 131
Marco Bottigelli/AWL images 1
Marcus Wilson-Smith/Apa Publications 19T, 76, 78, 92BR, 93BL, 93TR, 113T, 198T, 246
Nikt Wong/Apa Publications 7TL, 9BR, 10TR, 218, 219T, 222, 223, 225, 227, 230, 231, 233T, 234B, 236T, 236B
Peter Stuckings/Apa Publications 6M, 6BL, 7ML, 14/15, 16/17, 18, 48/49, 55L, 56, 57, 58BL, 61, 63, 66/67T, 68, 69, 74, 75, 77, 79, 80, 81, 82, 83L, 83R, 84L, 84R, 85, 86L, 86R, 91, 92BL, 98/99, 105B, 108, 109, 112B, 113B, 114, 116, 117, 118, 119, 121T, 122, 123, 125B, 127T, 128B, 128T, 130, 133, 134, 136, 137T, 142, 143B, 145, 149, 150, 151, 156, 157, 158, 162B, 164T, 187, 264/265, 266, 269, 275, 310, 312, 313, 314, 317, 320, 323, 326, 327, 332, 339B, 339T, 350, 352, 353, 358, 369
Public domain 34, 35, 36, 37R, 44, 67TR
Shutterstock 7BR, 8BL, 9TL, 10BL, 11T, 11B, 19B, 20B, 20T, 22, 23, 27, 50, 53, 59BL, 62, 65, 73, 89R, 101B, 110, 124, 132B, 138, 139B, 144, 147, 148B, 152, 153T, 163, 164B, 165, 166, 167B, 170, 171T, 171B, 172, 175, 177, 179, 180, 184, 185, 193, 194, 211, 219B, 229, 232, 241, 254, 263, 271, 276B, 279, 280, 281B, 281T, 282, 283, 284, 285, 286B, 287, 289, 291, 309B, 318BR, 321B, 322, 336, 337, 338B, 342, 346T
Superstock 319ML
The Metropolitan Museum of Art/Art Rsource New York/Scala, Florence 28
The Philadelphia Museum of Art/Art Resource/Scala, Florence 33L

COVER CREDITS

Front cover: Wat Phra Kaeo Temple, Bangkok *SuperStock*
Back cover: Similan island *iStock*
Front flap: (from top) Diamond Beach, Ko Samed *Shutterstock*; Wat Chang Rawp *Shutterstock*; Bird *iStock*; Tuk Tuks, Chiang Mai *iStock*
Back flap: Phanan Choeng, Ayuthaya *Peter Stuckings/Apa Publications*

INSIGHT GUIDE CREDITS

Distribution
UK, Ireland and Europe
Apa Publications (UK) Ltd;
sales@insightguides.com
United States and Canada
Ingram Publisher Services;
ips@ingramcontent.com
Australia and New Zealand
Woodslane; info@woodslane.com.au
Southeast Asia
Apa Publications (SN) Pte;
singaporeoffice@insightguides.com
Worldwide
Apa Publications (UK) Ltd;
sales@insightguides.com
Special Sales, Content Licensing and CoPublishing
Insight Guides can be purchased in bulk quantities at discounted prices. We can create special editions, personalised jackets and corporate imprints tailored to your needs.
sales@insightguides.com
www.insightguides.biz

Printed in China by CTPS

First Edition 1978
Eighteenth Edition 2019

www.insightguides.com

Editor: Zara Sekhavati
Updater: Paul Stafford
Author: Howard Richardson
Head of DTP and Pre-Press: Rebeka Davies
Managing Editor: Carine Tracanelli
Picture Editor: Aude Vauconsant
Cartography: original cartography Berndtson & Berndtson, updated by Carte

CONTRIBUTORS

This new edition of Insight Guide Thailand was updated throughout by travel writer **Paul Stafford**. This edition builds on the efforts of those involved in previous editions of the guide: Howard Richardson, Ed Peters, Peter Holmshaw, Sarah Rooney, Connelly La Mar, Andrew Forbes, Steven Pettifor, Lauren Smith, Austin Bush and Joe Cummings.

This edition was commissioned by **Helen Fanthorpe** and edited by **Zara Sekhavati** at Insight Guides.

ABOUT INSIGHT GUIDES

Insight Guides have more than 45 years' experience of publishing high-quality, visual travel guides. We produce 400 full-colour titles, in both print and digital form, covering more than 200 destinations across the globe, in a variety of formats to meet your different needs.

Insight Guides are written by local authors, whose expertise is evident in the extensive historical and cultural background features. Each destination is carefully researched by regional experts to ensure our guides provide the very latest information. All the reviews in **Insight Guides** are independent; we strive to maintain an impartial view. Our reviews are carefully selected to guide you to the best places to eat, go out and shop, so you can be confident that when we say a place is special, we really mean it.

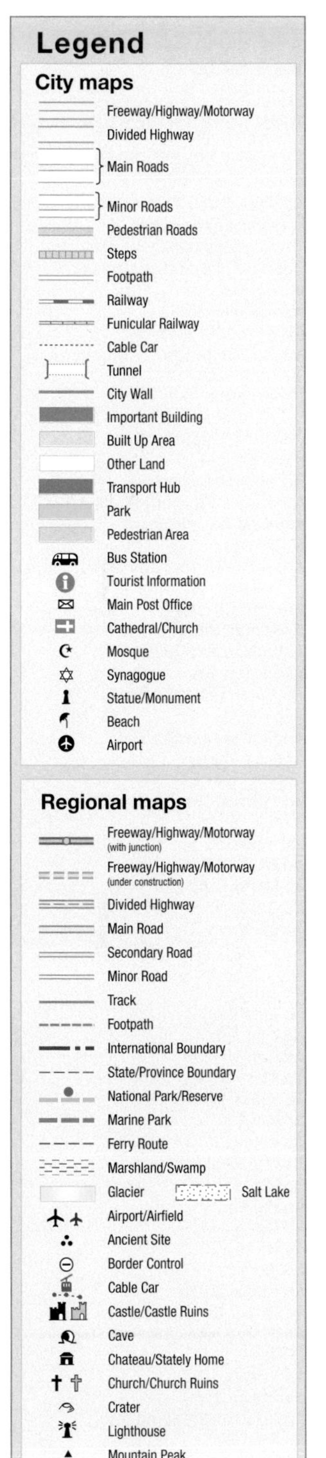

INDEX

MAIN REFERENCES ARE IN BOLD TYPE

A

Abhisek Dusit Throne Hall 124
accommodation 358
rates and bookings 358
Adang-Rawi Archipelago 259
addresses 359
agribusiness 155
Air Force Museum 137
air pollution 25
air travel 354
domestic 354
left-luggage facilities 365
Aisawan Thipphaya-at 157
Akha people 57
Allied War Cemetery 150
Amphawa Floating Market 148
amulets 63, 308
amulet market 114, 115, 120
Anantara Resort and Spa Golden Triangle 295
Ancient City 166
Andaman Coast 211
Andaman Sea 23, 24
Ang Kaew Reservoir 276
Angkhang Nature Resort 291
Angkor 34
Angkor monarchs 328
Angkor Thom 30
Angkor Wat 111
Ang Thong Marine National Park 201
antiques 75
Ao Bai Lan 181
Ao Bang Thao 228
Ao Batok 234
Ao Chalong 233
Ao Chao, 178
Ao Hin Khok 178
Ao Jak 259
Ao Kantiang 251
Ao Kao 182
Ao Karang 178
Ao Khao Khwai 213
Ao Khlong Chak 251
Ao Kui 179
Ao Lek 212
Ao Mai Phai 251
Ao Manao, 192
Ao Molae 259
Ao Nang 243
Ao Nuan 178
Ao Pansea 229
Ao Pattaya. 260
Ao Phai 178
Ao Phang Nga National Park 24, 218
Ao Phra Ae 250
Ao Phrao 178
Ao Po Grand Marina 235
Ao Rusi 259
Ao Sa Lad 182
Ao Sone 259
Ao Suan Yai. 182
Ao Taloh Wow 259
Ao Thian 179
Ao Thung Makam Noi, 192
Ao Tub Tim 178
Ao Wong Deuan 179
Ao Yai 212, 213
Aphaimani, prince 73
architecture 88
contemporary 91
temples 88
traditional houses 89
Western influences 90
Arporn Phimok Prasat 113
art 75
Buddha images 66, 78
contemporary art 78
temple art 78
Arts of the Kingdom 123
Arunyik temples 309
Asiatique 131
Assumption Cathedral 131
Atsadang Bridge 174
Ayutthaya 34, 73, 76, **158**
Historical Park 159
museums 163
temples 162

B

Baan Bayan 190
Baan Dum 293
Baan Na Chok 348
Baan Sao Nak 284
Baan Talay Dao 190
Baan Vichayen 165
Baiyoke II Tower 129
Ban Bang Bao 181
Ban Bo Phut 198
Ban Bu 117
Ban Chiang 29, 339
Ban Chiang National Museum 340
Bang Bae Waterfall 237
Bangkok 20, 19
Abhisek Dusit Throne Hall 124
addresses 358
airport 353
Amarin Vinitchai Throne Hall 113
Ananta Samakhom Throne Hall 123
Angkor Wat 111
Arporn Phimok Prasat 113
Art and Culture Centre 128
Asiatique 131
Assumption Cathedral 131
Baiyoke II Tower 129
Ban Bu 117
Banglamphu 119
Bangrak 131
boat trips 117, 122
Chao Phraya Express 117
Borombhiman Hall 113
botanical garden 124
Buddhaisawan Chapel 114
Calypso Cabaret 132
canals 122
Central World, 129
Chakri Maha Prasat 113
Chinatown 125
Chitralada Palace 123
Coins and Decorations Museum 114
Democracy Monument 120
Dusit 121
Zoo 124
Dusit Maha Prasat 113
Dusit Park 123
Emerald Buddha 112, 118
Emporium area 134
Erawan Bangkok 130
Erawan Shrine 130
Gaysorn 130
Giant Swing 119
Golden Buddha 127
Golden Mount 120
Grand Palace 110, 112
Ho Phra Montien Tham 111
Ho Phra Nak 111
hospitals 364
International Buddhist Meditation Centre 115
Jim Thompson's House 129
Joe Louis Theatre 132
Kamthieng House 134
Khao San Road 120
khlongs
Bangkok Noi 117, 122
Bangkok Yai 117
Banglamphu 119
Om 117
Ong Ang 119
Saen Saep 122, 128, 129
Kukrit Pramoj's Home 133
Lak Muang 114
Loha Prasat 120
Lumphini Park 130
Lumpinee Boxing Stadium 138
Madame Tussaud's 129
Maha Chulalongkorn Rajavidyalaya University 115
Maha Uma Devi 132
Mahboonkrong 128
Mandarin Oriental Hotel 131
markets
amulet market 115, 120
floating markets 117, 122
Flower Market 126
night market 132
Pahurat 126
Pratunam 129
Saphan Phut t 126
Talad Kao 127
Talad Mai 127
Taling Chan 117
Wat Sai 117
Narayana Phand 130
National Museum 114
Old City 119
Pak Khlong Talad 126
Panthip Plaza 129

Pathumwan 128
Patpong 132
Patravadi Theatre 71
Phra Mondop 111
Phra Nakorn 109
Phra Si Rattana Chedi 111
Phra Sri Sakyamuni Buddha 119
Platinum Fashion Mall 129
Prasat Phra Thep Bidom 111
Pratunam 129
Pridi Banomyong Institute 71
Queen Saovabha Memorial Institute 130
Queen Sirikit Museum of Textiles 110
railway station 353, 354
Rattanakosin 109
Rattanakosin Exhibition Hall 120
Reclining Buddha 116
Red House 114
Royal Barge Museum 118
Royal Dusit Garden Palace 124
Royal Plaza 121
Sampeng 125
Sanam Luang 114
Siam Centre 129
Siam Discovery Centre 129
Siam Museum 116
Siam Ocean World 129
Siam Paragon 129
Siam Square 128
Silom 131
Silom Soi 4 133
Sirocco 132
Sivamokhaphiman Ha 114
Skytrain 126
Snake Farm 130
Soi Itsaranuphap 127
Soi Thaniya 133
Soi Thonglor 134
Sri Guru Singh Sabha 126
State Tower 132
Statue of King Chulalongkorn 121
Suan Pakkad Palace 129
Sukhumvit 134
Thai History Gallery 114
Thai Traditional Massage School 116
Thanon Khao San 119
Thanon Na Phra Lan 110
Thanon Ploenchit malls 130
Thanon Rama I 128
Thanon Ratchadamnoen 119
Thanon Sanam Chai 114
Thanon Sathorn 131
Thanon Silom 131
Thanon Sukhumvit 134
Thanon Yaowarat 127
Thonburi 109, 116
tourist office 368
transport 354, 355
universities 110
Viharn Yot 111
Vimanmek Mansion 123
Wat Arun 118
Wat Benjamabophit 124
Wat Bowonniwet 121
Wat Mahathat 115
Wat Mangkon Kamalawat 126
Wat Pho 115
Wat Phra Kaew 110
Wat Phra Kaew Museum 114
Wat Ratchabophit 119
Wat Ratchanatdam 120
Wat Saket 120
Wat Sisudaram 117
Wat Suthat 119
Wat Suwannaram 117
Wat Traimit 127
Weapons Museum 113
Yaowarat Chinatown Heritage 128
Bangkok Opera 70
Bangkok Symphony Orchestra 70
Bangkrajao 139
Bang Laen River 216
Bang Leap Nam Waterfall 215
Bang Makok 38, 39
Bang Pa-In 40, 157
Bangrak 131
Bang Saen 173
Bang Saphan Yai 192
Ban Hat Sai Ree 208
Ban Khai 203
Ban Khon Sai, 349
Ban Khrua 129
banking 366
Ban Krut, 192
Ban Kwan Chang 181
Ban Mae Hat 208
Ban Na Kha 340
Ban Phe 177
Ban Pinsuwan Benjarong 148
Ban Puen Palace 187
Ban Sala Dan 249
Ban Tai 203
Ban Ta Klang 331
Ban Thawai 282
Ban Thon, 340
Ban Wan 282
Barang, Marcel 73
bars and pubs
opening hours 359
beach party 202
beauty products 78
beer 86
***bencharong* ceramics** 76
Beung Kaen Nakhon (Kaen Nakhon Lake) 338
Beung Kan 347
Beung Thung Sang (Thung Sang Lake 338
Bhumibol Adulyadej, king 44
Bhumibol Dam 311
bicycles 343, 357
Big Buddha beach 199
birds' nests 248
Black House 293
Bloody May 45
boats
Bangkok city transport 356
longtail boat trips 148
Boonma, Montien 79
Bo Sang 281
Boun Leua Sourirat 346
Brahman rituals 61, 64
brassware 78
Bridge on the River Kwai 149
bronze artefacts
Ban Chiang 340
bronze statues 78
Buddha images 66, 78
mudras 66, 67
Buddhaisawan Chapel 114
Buddhism 29, 30, 32, 61, 330
and contemporary art 79
Chinnarat Buddha 308
Eightfold Path 112
Emerald Buddha 110, 112, 118
etiquette 362
festivals 58
Golden Buddha 127
International Buddhist Meditation Centre 115
Mahayana 62
Phansa (rains retreat) 347
Phra Buddha Sihing 114
Phra Sri Sakyamuni Buddha 119
Reclining Buddha 116
temple life 62
Theravada 32, 32, 61
budgeting 359
buffalo fighting 262
Bun Heua Fai (Fire Boat Festival) 347
Burdett, John 72
Buriram 329
Burma 33
Burma Banks 211, 213
Burmese 35, 37
buses 355, 356, 357
airport 353, 354
business hours 359
business travellers 359
Butterfly Farm 286

C

Cambodia 32, 331
Cambodia
border crossings 353
canals 357
cars
airport limousines 353, 354
car hire 355, 357
driving in Thailand 355
Cartoon Network Amazone 177
Cathedral of St Joseph 160
censorship 72, 73
Central Plain 22
Central World, 129
ceramics 76
Cha-am 188
Chakri, Chao Phaya 37
Chakri Day 111
Chakri Dynasty 34, 37, 38
Chanthaburi 37
Chantharakasem National Museum 163
Chanthara Phisan Pavilion 164
chao khao 270
Chaopho Phawo Shrine 312
Chao Phraya 34
Chao Phraya Express 117
Chao Phraya River 22, 109, 122
Chateau de Loei Vineyards 342
Chatuchak 136
chedi 139, 146
Cheow Lan Lake 216

Chiang Dao 287
Elephant Training Centre 287
Chiang Khan 343
Chiang Khong 294
Chiang Mai 33, 31, 269
airport 352, 354
Ang Kaew Reservoir 276
Arts and Cultural Centre 272
cuisine 270
culture 269
Healing Hospital 275
history 270
hospitals 364
Mahachulalongkorn Buddhist University 276
markets 274
National Museum 277
Phra Satang Man 272
Phra Sila Buddha 272
Phra Singh Buddha 273
Phra That Chang Lom 272
Phra Viharn Lai Kham 272
Three Kings Monument 272
transport 357
Tribal Museum 277
University 276
Wat Bupparam 274
Wat Chedi Luang 273
Wat Chiang Man 271
Wat Jet Yot 276
Wat Phan Tao 273
Wat Phra Singh 272
Wat Prasat 273
Wat Srisuphan 275
Wat Suan Dok 275
Wat U Mong 274
Wiang Kum Kam 277
Zoo and Arboretum 276
Chiang Mai Night Safari 280
Chiang Rai 289, **292**
Chiang Saen 293
children 359
Chinatown 125
Chinese immigrants 50
Chinese pottery 32
Chinese temples 226
Chinnarat Buddha 308
Chitralada Palace 123
Chonabot 338
Chong Mek 349
Chuan Leekpai 45
Chulalongkorn, king 40, 125, 157, 308
Chulalongkorn University 41
Chumphon 192
Chung Kai Allied War Cemetery 151
cinema 72
city pillars 63
city transport 355
classical Thai music 71
climate 19, **359**
clothing 360
coastal geography 24
Coins and Decorations Museum 114
communist insurgency 313
Coral Island 175
coral reefs 24
country music (luk thung) 72
coups 41, 46
courier services 366
crafts 75
hill-tribe crafts 318
Isan handicrafts 339
shopping for handicrafts 367
Crazy Horse Buttress 281
credit cards 366
crime 360
Crystal Lagoon 242
cuisine. *See* food and drink
customs regulations 360
cycling 343, 357

D

Damnoen Saduak 148
Danang Market (Mukdahan) 348
dance
contemporary 71
dance drama 69, 326
khon 69, 71
lakhon 70
Dan Khwian 327
Dan Sai 341
Dan Sai Folk Museum 342
Death Railway 148, 150
deforestation 23, 25
democracy 45
Democracy Monument 120
dental clinics 364
disabled travellers 361
diving and snorkelling 24
Ko Lanta 252
Ko Phangan 206
Ko Phi Phi 248
Ko Tao 209
Similans 217
Surin islands 213
Doi Ang Khang 289
Doi Chiang Dao 287
Doi Inthanon National Park 282
Doi Kong Mu 315
Doi Phu Kha National Park 298
Doi Pui 280
Doi Saket 291
Don Hoi Lot 147
Dream World 137
dress code 110
drugs 267, 293, 360
prescription drugs 364
Duchanee, Thawan 79
dugong 257
durian 154
Dusit 121
Maha Prasat 113
Park 123
Zoo 124
Dusit Palace 40
Dutch 36
Dvaravati kingdom 30

E

Eastern & Oriental Express 353
Ekatotsarot, king 35
electricity 361
Elephant Camp 286
Elephant Cave 340
Elephant Conservation Centre 284
Elephant Round-Up 331
elephants 23
Elephant Training Centre 287
elephant treks 181
Elephant Village 176
Emerald Buddha 110, 112, 118
entry requirements 361
Erawan Bangkok 130
Erawan Museum 166
Erawan National Park 151
Erawan Shrine 130
ethnic mix 50
etiquette 53, **361**
greetings 51, **362**
head and feet 362
Europeans 35

F

Fang 287, 289
fauna 23
Feroci, Corrado 79
ferry services 247
cross-river ferries 356
festivals 58, **362**
Boon Bang Fai 87
film festivals 72
Phee Ta Khon Festival 341
films
The Beach 246
The Bridge on the River Kawi 149
Fire Boat Festival 363
Fisherman's Village. 198
flag 54
Flight of the Gibbon 281
flooding 25
flora 22, 23
flower market 126
food and drink 81
chillies 82
desserts 86
eating Thai food 81
insects 84
local specialities 84
meat 85
noodles 85
Northeastern cuisine 82
Northern cuisine 82
refreshments 86
rice 82, 87
Royal Tai cuisine 83
Southern cuisine 82
spring rolls 343
water 363
forests 23
Forum of the Poor 52
French 36
Friendship Bridge 345
fruit 154
Full Moon Party 202

G

Garland, Alex 73
Gaysorn 130
gemstones 77
Ghost's Skull Cave 241
Giant Swing 119
Gibbon Rehabilitation Centre 237
Golden Buddha 127

Golden Mount 120
Golden Triangle 267, 293, 296
golf 191
gopura 333
Grand Palace 110, 112
guesthouses 358
Gulf of Thailand 171

H

Hang Dong 282
Hariphunchai National Museum 284
Hat Bangrak 198
Hat Bo Phut 198
Hat Chang Lang 256
Hat Chaweng 199
Hat Choeng Mon 199
Hat Hin Ngam 252
Hat Jommani 345
Hat Jomtien 175
Hat Kai Bae 180, 182
Hat Kamala 229
Hat Karon 230
Hat Karon Noi 230
Hat Kata Noi 231
Hat Kata Yai 231
Hat Khlong Dao 249
Hat Khlong Khong 250
Hat Khlong Muang 242
Hat Khlong Nin 250
Hat Khlong Phrao 180
Hat Laem Sala 192
Hat Laem Set 200
Hat Lamai 199
Hat Maenam 197
Hat Mai Khao 227
Hat Nai Harn 232
Hat Nai Thon 228
Hat Nai Yang 228
Hat Naklua 175
Hat Na Ko 259
Hat Noppharat Thara 243
Hat Pak Meng 256
Hat Patong 229
Hat Pattaya 175
Hat Phu Noi 192
Hat Railay East 244
Hat Railay West 243
Hat Rawai 232
Hat Rin 204
Hat Sai Khao 182
Hat Surin 229
Hat Taling Ngam 200
Hat Tham Pang 174
Hat Tham Phra Nang 244
Hat Tha Nam 181, 182
Hat Ton Sai 245
Hat Yai 261
Hat Yao 181
health 363
Hellfire Pass 149
Heroines' Monument 236
Hill Tribe Museum 292
hill tribes 270
  crafts 318
Hin Bai 206
Hin Daeng 252
Hinduism 29, 330
Hin Luk Bat 182
Hin Muang 252
Hin Ta 200
Hin Yai 200
Hi-So society 51
Hmong people 56
Ho Chi Minh
  home of 348
hospitals 363
hotels 358
Hot Springs Waterfall 241
Houei Sai 295
houses, traditional 89
Hua Hin 188
Huay Nam Dang National Park 317
Huay Toh Waterfalls 241

I

ikat **textiles** 319
Indian influence 29
Indigenous literature 73
Indochina Market (Mukdahan) 348
Ing River 291
insurgent activity 360
International Buddhist Meditation Centre 115
Internet 364
  websites 368
Isaan 22
  village life 327
Islam. *See* Muslims

J

James Bond Island 219
Jayavarman VII 30, 328, 330
Jazz Festival 191
JEATH War Museum 150
Jesuit missionaries 36
jewellery 77
Jim Thompson's House 129
Judhadhut Palace 174
Jui-Tui 226
Jui Tui Temple 226
Jumbo Queen contest 146
jungle trails 215

K

Kaeng Khut Khu rapids 343
Kaeng Krachan Dam 188
Kaeng Krachan National Park 188
Kaeng Tanna National Park 334
Kalasin, 338
Kamjorndet, Jadet 73
Kamphaeng Phet 308
Kamthieng House 134
Kanchanaburi 148, 151
  Allied War Cemetery 150
Karen people 56
Karon 231
Kata 231
Kata Hill Viewpoint 231
kathoey 178
Kayan people 57
Kengtung 297
Khao Hin Lek Fai 190
Khao Khad Viewpoint 235
Khao Khien 219
Khao Khiew 325
Khao Laem 325
Khao Lak 216
Khao Nor Chu Chi Wildlife Sanctuary 242
Khao Phanom Bencha National Park 241
Khao Phra Thaeo National Park 237
Khao Saen, 261
Khao Sam Roi Yot National Park 191
Khao San Road 120
Khao Sok National Park 215
Khao Takiab 190
Khao Tang Kuan 261
Khao Tao 190
Khao Wang 186
Khao Yai National Park 23, 323
Khlong Chao Waterfall 182
Khlong Phrao National Park 212
Khlong Phu 181
Khmer empire 30, 31, 33, 31, 321, 330
Khmer Rouge 330
khon **dance drama** 69, 71
Khong Jiam 334, 349
Khon Kaen 337
Khon Kaen National Museum 337
Khorat 321
Khorat Plateau 22
Khun Yuam 314
Killing Fields 190
King Buddhalertla Naphalai Memorial Park 148
King Cobra village 339
King Cruiser wreck 248
Kirimaya 325
Klai Kangwon Palace 189
Ko Adang 259, 260
Ko Bon 233
Ko Bubu 253
Ko Chang 171, 179, 212
  archipelago 182
  beaches 180
  nightlife 182
  sights and activities 181
Ko Damui
  activities 200
Ko Hae 233
Ko Hai 257
Ko Hat Wat Tai 334
Ko Hin Sorn 260
Ko Jum 253
Ko Kaeo 233
Ko Khai 213
Ko Khlum 182
Ko Klang, 213
Ko Kradan 257
Ko Kret 137
Kok River 291
Ko Krok 175
Ko Kut 182
Ko Lanta 248
Ko Lanta Yai 248
Ko Larn 175
Ko Libong 257
Ko Lipe 259
Ko Mak 182
Ko Man Wichai 175
Ko Matlang 199
Ko Muk 257

Ko-Nakkerd 233
Ko Ngam Noi 192
Ko Ngam Yai 192
Ko Panyi 219
Ko Phangan 201, 202
diving and snorkelling 206
east-coast beaches 204
Hat Rin 204
inland attractions 205
nightlife 206
north-coast beaches 205
west coast beaches 205
Ko Phayam 212
Ko Phi Phi. 246
Ko Phi Phi Don 246
Ko Phi Phi Ley 246, 247
Ko Phi Phi National Park 25
Ko Ping Kan 219
Ko Racha 234
Ko Racha Noi 234
Ko Racha Yai 234
Ko Rang 182
Ko Rattanakosin 38
Ko Rawi 260
Ko Ri 213
Ko Rin 175
Ko Rok, 252
Ko Sak 175
Ko Samet 177
beaches 178
sights and activities 179
Ko Samet National Park 24
Ko Samui 195
airport 197, 354
hospital 364
transport 357
Ko Si Chang 173
Ko Sireh 235
Kositpipat, Chalermchai 79
Ko Sukorn 258
Ko Surin Nua 213
Ko Surin Tai 213
Ko Talu 179
Ko Tao 24, 192, 207
diving and snorkelling 209
east-coast beaches 208
nightlife 209
north coast beaches 208
south-coast beaches 208
west-coast beaches 207
Ko Tapu 219
Ko Tarutao 259
Ko Tarutao Marine National Park 258
Ko Thalu 192
Ko Wai 182
Ko Wua Talab 201
Ko Yang 260
Ko Yippon. 201
Ko Yo 261
Kra 22
Krabi Province 239
beaches 242
Four Islands tour 245
Hot Springs Waterfall 241
islands 245
karsts 239
Khao Nor Chu Chi Wildlife Sanctuary 242
Khao Phanom Bencha National Park 241
Ko Lanta 248
mangroves 240
monsoon 240
Mu Ko Lanta Marine National Park 252
Mu Ko Phi Phi National Park 246
Thanboke Koranee National Park 241
Tha Pom 241
Wat Tham Seua 240
Krabi Town 239
Krue-on, Sakarin 79
Kuden Mansion, 258
Kukrit Pramoj's Home 133
Kwan Phayao 291

L

lacquerware 75, 271
lady-boys 53
Laem Ngop 180
Laem Phan Wa 234
Laem Phra Nang 243
Laem Promthep 232
Laem Tanode 252
Laem Yai 197
Lahu people 56
lakhon dance drama 70
lakhon dance drama 70
lak muang 114
Lalvani, Gulu 235
Lampang 285
Lamphun 283
Lamyai Fruit Festival 58
Lam Takhong 326
Lamyai Festival 283
language 369, 51
Lanna culture 31, 33
Lan Sang National Park 312
Laos 296
border crossings 342, 343, 347, 348, 353
left luggage 365
legal code 34
likay 70
limestone karsts 24, 239
Lisu people 57
literature
indigenous 73
Thai 73
Loei 340
climate 342
logging 25
Loha Prasat 120
longtail boats 357
Lopburi 34, 163
lost property 365
Loy Krathong festival 58, 303
Luang Pho Chuang 233
Luang Pro Chaem 233
Lumphini Park 130
Lumpinee Boxing Stadium 138

M

Madame Tussaud's 129
Mae Chaem 283
Mae Fah Luang Art & Culture Park 292
Mae Hong Son 314, 315
Mae Klang 282
Mae Sa 286
Mae Sai 296
Mae Salong 291
Mae Sariang 314
Mae Sot 312
magazines 365
Mahachulalongkorn Buddhist University 276
Maha Chulalongkorn Rajavidyalaya University 115
Maha Uma Devi 132
Mahavessantara Jataka 341
Maha Wirawong National Museum 327
Mahayana Buddhism 62
Mahboonkrong 128
mahouts 331
Malacca 36
Malaya 29
Malay witch doctors 65
Mandarin Oriental Hotel 131
Mangrai, king 270, 273
Mangrai of Lanna, king 33
maps 365
marine life 25
Marine Turtle Foundation 228
marionette theatre 71
markets 127
Amphawat 148
amulet market 115, 120
Chatuchak 136
Chiang Mai 274
Damnoen Saduak 148
floating markets 117, 122
flowers 126
Mukdahan 348
night market 132
Pahurat 126
Pattaya 177
Pratunam 129
Saphan Phut 126
Talad Kao 127
Talad Mai 127
Talad Rod Fai 137
Taling Chan 117
That Phanom 348
Trang 256
Wat Sai 117
Maruekhathayawan Palace 188
massages 116
Mechudhon, Patravadi 71
media 365
medical care 363
Mekong River 293, **346**
sunset cruise 345
Melayu, 29
Mien people 56
minibuses/minivans
airports 354
Mini Siam 176
Miss Elephant Festival 331
mobile phones 367
Moei River 313
Moklen community 214
monarchy 34, 44, 19, 51, 362
royal cremations 114
money 365
Mongkut, king 39
monkeys 189
monks 62, 233, 347

Mon people 30, 31, 33, 284
monsoon 19, 197
Monthathon 281
mother-of-pearl decoration 78
motorcycle taxis 356, 357
Mukdahan 348
Mukdahan Jewel Hall 348
Mukdahan National Park 348
Mu Ko Lanta Marine National Park 252
Mu Ko Phayam National Park 212
Mu Ko Phi Phi National Park 246
Mun River 327, 328, 333, 334
mural painting 78
museums
Air Force 137
Ban Chiang National Museum 340
Chantharakasem National Museum 163
Chiang Mai National 277
Chiang Saen 294
Coins and Decorations 114
Dan Sai Folk Museum 342
Death Railway 150
Erawan 166
Hariphunchai 284
Hellfire Pass 149
Hill Tribes 292
JEATH War 150
Jim Thompson's House 129
Kamphaeng Phet 309
Kamthieng House 134
Khon Kaen National Museum 337
Kukrit Pramoj's Home 133
Maha Wirawong 327
Nakhon Si Thammarat 262
Nan 297
Narai National Museum 165
National Museum 114
Opium 280
Phimai 328
Phra Pathom Chedi 146
Phuket Seashell Museum 233
Prasart 138
Queen Sirikit Museum of Textiles 110
Ramkhamhaeng 302
Rattanakosin Exhibition Hall 120
Royal Barges 118
Satun National Museum 258
Siam Museum 116
Songkhla National Museum 261
Thai History Gallery 114
Thaksin 261
Thalang 236
Thavorn Hotel Lobby Museum 226
Tribal Museum 277
Ubon Ratchathani 333
Wat Phra Kaew 114
Weapons 113
World War II 149, 315
music
classical Thai music 71
modern music and film 72
mor-lam 339
Muslims 29, 44, 51, 61, **65**
separatist movement 360
Muslim separatist insurgency 255
Myanmar 297, 353
Thai-Myanmar Friendship Bridge 313
Myanmar border 22
Myawadi 313

N

Na Dan 178
Naga Pearl Farm 235
Na Haew 342
Nai Saen Pom 35
Nai Soi 316
Nakhon Pathom 145, 146
Nakhon Phanom 347
Fire Boat Festival 347
Nakhon Ratchasima 326
Nakhon Si Thammarat 262
names 369
Nam Tok 149
Na Muang Waterfall 200
Nan 296
Nangyuan Island Dive Resort 209
Narai, king 36
Narai National Museum 165
Narathiwat 51
Narayana Phand 130
Naresuan the Great 35
Na Thon 197
National Museum 114
national parks
Ang Thong 201
Ao Phang Nga 24, 218
Doi Inthanon 282
Doi Phu Kha 298
Doi Suthep/Doi Pui 279
Erawan 151
Huay Nam Dang 317
Kaeng Krachan 188
Kaeng Tanna 334
Khao Phnom Bencha 241
Khao Phra Thaeo 237
Khao Sam Roi Yot 191
Khao Sok 215
Khao Yai 23, 323
Khlong Phrao 212
Ko Phi Phi 25
Ko Samet 24
Ko Tarutao 258
Lan Sang 312
Mukdahan (Phu Mu) 348
Mu Ko Lanta 252
Mu Ko Phayam 212
Mu Ko Phi Phi 246
Phu Kradung 342
Phu Rua 341
Prasat Khao Phra Viharn 333
Sai Yok 153
Similan Islands 217
Sirinat 227
Surin Islands 213
Thanboke Koranee 241
Than Sadet 206
Navaratree Festival 132
newspapers 365
Ngao Waterfall 212
nielloware 78
Nong Khai 345
Nong Nooch Tropical Garden & 177
Nonthaburi 137
novels 73
numbers 116

O

Ocean World 129
opera 70
opium 293, 296
Opium Museum 280
Oriental Hotel 131

P

Padaung 316
Pahurat Market 126
Pai 287, 316
Pak Bara 259
Pak Khlong Talad 126
Pak Thong Chai 327
palaces
Baan Vichayen 165
Bang Pa-In 157
Ban Puen 187
Chitralada Palace 123
Grand Palace 110, 112
Judhadhut 174
Klai Kangwon 189
Maruekhathayawan 188
Phra Narai Ratchanivet 164
Phu Phing 280
Royal Dusit Garden Palace 124
Sanam Chandra 146
Suan Pakkad Palace 129
Wang Luang 161
Wehat Chamrun 157
Pala-U Waterfall 188
parks
Chatuchak 137
Dusit Park 123
King Buddhalertla Naphalai Memorial Park 148
Lumphini Park 130
Rama IX Royal Park 139
passports 361
Pathumwan 128
Patong 230
Patpong 132
Pattani 51
Pattaya 171, **174**
beaches 175
hospital 364
land attractions 176
nightlife 177
pearls 235
People's Alliance for Democracy (PAD) 46
People's Party 41
performing arts 69
Petchkasem Highway 185
Pha Charoen Waterfall 313
Phaeng Waterfall 206
Phanoen Tung 188
Phanom Rung Festival 329
pharmacies 364
Pha Taem National Park 349
Phaulkon, Constantine 37
Phayao 291
Phaya U Thong 34
Phee Ta Khon Festival 341
Phetchaburi 185, 186

Phetchaburi's 186
Phimai 328
Phimai National Museum 328
Phiman Mongkut Pavilion 165
***phipat* orchestras** 71
Phitsanulok 307
Phom Phet 160
photography 366
Phra Buddha Sihing 114
Phrae 298
Phra Nakhon Khiri Historical Park 186
Phra Nakorn 109
Phra Narai Ratchanivet 164
Phra Pathom Chedi 146
Phra Phuttha Chinnarat 307
Phra Ruang 31
Phra Siam Devadhiraj 32
Phra Sri Sakyamuni Buddha 119
Phra That Si Songrak 342
Phra Thinang Khuha Kharuhat. 192
Phuket 171
- airport 354
- Aquarium and Marine Biological Research Centre 235
- Chinese population 225
- East Coast 234
- Gibbon Rehabilitation Centre 237
- hospitals 364
- Khao Phra Taew National Park 237
- Ko-Nakkerd 233
- markets and malls 227
- Naga Pearl Farm 235
- Orchid Garden and Thai Village 226
- people and economy 223
- Royal Phuket Marina 235
- Siam Niramit 227
- South Coast 232
- Southern Islands 233
- temples 226, 233
- Thalang 236
- transport 357
- Vegetarian Festival 59
- West Coast 227

Phuket Seashell Museum 233
Phuket Town 225
- Chinatown 225
- markets 227

Phu Kradung National Park 342
Phu Mu National Park 348
Phu Phing Palace 280
Phu Phrabat Historical Park 346
Phu Rua National Park 341
Pibul 43
Ping River 269
Pisai Sayalak 163
PlaekPhibunsongkhram 41
Ploughing Ceremony (Rack Na) 61
pok pok 189
popular music 72
Portuguese 35
postal services 366
pottery 75
Poy Sang Long celebrations 315
Prachuap Khiri Khan 192
Prajadhipok, king 41, 43
Pramoj, Kukrit 73
Pranburi 191
Prang Sam Yot 165
Prasart Museum 138
Prasat Hin Khao Phanom Rung Historical Park 329
Prasat Hin Muang Tam 331
Prasat Hin Phanomwan 327
Prasat Hin Phimai 328
Prasat Khao Phra Viharn 332
Prasat Muang Singh 152
Prasat Peuay Noi 338
Prasat Ta Muan Tot 332
Prasat Thong, king 35
Pratu Chai 348
Pridi Panomyong 41
pronunciations 20
prostitution 135
public holidays 366
Punyaban Waterfall 211
puppet shows 262
Put Jaw 229
Put Jaw Temple 229

Q

Queen Saovabha Memorial Institute 130
Queen Sirikit Botanic Gardens 286
Queen Sirikit Museum of Textiles 110

R

radio 365
Railay Bay 243
rail travel 353, 354, 356
- Bangkok airport 354

Raksawarin Park 211
Rama I 37, 109
Rama II 38
Rama III 38
Rama IV 39, 115
Rama IX Royal Park 139
Ramakien 71, 73
Ramathibodi I 34, 35
Ramathibodi II 35
Rama V 40
Rama VI 41
Rama VII 41
Rama VIII 43
Rama V, statue 121
Ramkhamhaeng, king 32, 301
Ramkhamhaeng National Museum 302
Ranong 211
Ratchadaphisek 136
Ratchprabha Dam 216
Rattanakosin 109
- Exhibition Hall 120

Rawai 232
Reclining Buddha 116
Red House 114
Red Shirts 47
religious services 366
Renu Nakhon 347
rice 82
Richelieu Rock 213
Ripley's Believe It or Not 176
river cruises 117, 122
- Chao Phraya Express 117

roads 353, 355
rock climbing 245
Roi Et 338
Royal Barges Museum 118
royal cremations 114
Royal Dusit Garden Palace 124
Royal Thai cuisine 83
Ruen Mai Rim Talay 174
rural villages 52, 55

S

Safari World 138
Sai Nam Phung Orchid and Butterfly Farm 286
Sai Yai 281
Sai Yok National Park 153
Sala Kaew Ku Sculpture Park 346
Salak Phet 181
samlor 189
Samnak Song Nai Harn monastery 232
Samoeng Loop 287
Sampeng 125
Samphran Elephant Ground 145
Sampran Riverside 145
Samui Aquarium & Tiger Zoo 200
Samui Archipelago 195
Samui International Regatta 201
Samui Monkey Theatre 198
Samut Prakan Province 166
Samut Sakhon 147
Samut Songkhram 147
Sanam Chandra Palace 146
Sanam Luang 114
Sanctuary of Truth 176
Sangkhlaburi 153, 314
Sangkhom 343
Sanjao Pho Khao Yai 174
Sanjao Sam San 226
Sanjo-Sam-San 226
San Luang 304
Santikhiri 291
Sao Din 298
Saphan Phut Market 126
Satun 258
Sawankhalok 304
Sawan Waterfall 215
scams 360
sea cow 257
sea gypsies 214
sexual attitudes 53
sex workers 135
shadow-puppet theatre 71
Shan people 57
Shark Point 179
Shell Fossil Beach 244
Shinawatra, Thaksin 44, 46, 52
shopping 366
- opening hours 359
- VAT refunds 367

Siam Centre 129
Siam Discovery Centre 129
Siam Museum 116
Siam Ocean World 129
Siam Paragon 129
Siam Society 134
Si Chiang Mai 343
silk 76, 129, 327

Silom 109, 131
Similan 24
Similan Islands 216
Sip-et Chan Waterfall 216
Si Racha 173
Siributr, Jakkai 79
Sirinat National Park 227
Siriphum 282
Sirocco 132
Si Saket 332
Si Satchanalai 304, 306
Sitthiket, Vasan 79
Skytrain 129, 356
slash-and-burn farming 22
Snake Farm 130
snakes 24
snorkelling. *See* diving and snorkelling
soap operas 55
socialising 53
social problems 54
Soi Thonglor 134
Sok River 215
Songkhla 260
Songthaew/Tuk-Tuk 357
Songtham, king 35
Soppong 314
Sop Ruak 295
spirit houses 64, 89
spirits 63
Sri Guru Singh Sabha 126
Srivijaya civilisation 29, 30
Sriwanichpoom, Manit 79
star sapphires 77
State Tower 132
Suan Pakkad Palace 129
Suan Son 190
Sucharitkul, Somtow 70
Suchart Subsin's Shadow Puppet Workshop 262
Suchinda Krapayoon 44, 45
Sudham, Pira 73
Sukhothai 34, 301
  Historical Park 302
  Ramkhamhaeng National Museum 302
  Wat Chana Songkhram 304
  Wat Chetupon 305
  Wat Mahathat 303
  Wat Pa Mamuang 306
  Wat Phra Phai Luang 304
  Wat Saphan Hin 306
  Wat Sa Si 304
  Wat Si Chum 305
  Wat Si Sawai 304
  Wat Trakuan 304
Sukhothai Buddha images 32
Sukhothai kingdom 29, 31, 301
Sunthorn Phu 73, 117, 177
Suphanburi 331
Surin 24, 331
Surin Islands Marine National Park 213
Surin Phuket 229
Suriyothai Chedi 161
Suryavarman II 30
Suvarnabhum 29

T

Tachilek 297
Tai people 30
Tais/Thais 31
Tak 311
Taksin, king 37, 38
Talad Rod Fai 137
Talay Nai 201
Tamarind Retreat 197
Tamil community 132
Tarutao Archipelago 259
taxes 367
taxis 355, 357
  airport 353, 354
  longtail boats 357
telephones 367
television 55, 365
temples **62**
  architecture 88, 92
  art 78
  etiquette 362
  murals 93
  spirit worship 64
terms of address 362
textiles 76
  khit 340
Tha Bon 174
Thai boxing 138
Thai History Gallery 114
Thai literature 73
Thai-Myanmar Friendship Bridge 313
Thai names 369
Thai Traditional Massage School 116
Tha Khaek 347
Thaksin administration 46, 47
Thaksin Folklore Museum 261
Thalang 236
Tham Bua Bok 201
Tham Chiang Dao 287
Tham Erawan 340
Tham Kaew 192
Tham Khao Luang 187
Tham Lod 219, 257
Tham Lot 314
Tham Luang 296
Tham Mae Usu 314
Tham Mai Kaeo caves 253
Thammaracha, king 35
Tham Morakot 257
Tham Muang On 281
Tham Nam Talu 216
Tham Pha Plong Monastic Centre 287
Tham Phraya Nakhon 191
Tham Sai 192
Thanboke Koranee National Park 241
Than Mayom 181
Thanon Bangla 230
Than Praphat Waterfall 206
Than Prawet Waterfall 206
Than Sadet National Park 206
Than Sadet Waterfall 205
Than Thip Waterfall 343
Than Thong Waterfall 343
Thao Suranari Festival 326
Tha Pai Hotsprings 317
Tha Pom 241
Thararak Waterfall 313
Thaton 291
That Phanom 348
theatre
  contemporary 71
  dance drama 69
  puppet theatre 71
Theravada Buddhism 32, 32, 61
Thilawsu Waterfall 313
Thompson, Jim 76, 129
Thonburi 37, 38, 109, 116
Thonburi Wreck 182
Thong Sala 203
Tho Thip Waterfall 188
Three Kings Monument 272
Thung Wua Laem, 192
Tiger Cave Temple 240
tigers 23, 25
tiger zoo 200
time zone 367
tipping 367
Tiravanija, Rirkit 79
Toe Boo Cliff 259
toilets 368
Ton Gloy Waterfall 215
Tongsai Bay 199
Ton Sai Waterfall 237
tourism 25
tourist offices 368
trains 353, 356
  Bangkok airport 354
Traitrung 35
Trang 255
  beaches 256
  coffee shops 258
  islands 257
transgenders 178
transport 352
Trat Province 180
travellers' cheques 366
Tribal Museum 277
Triple-Headed Elephant Cave 340
tropical rainforest 23
tuk-tuk 124, 355, 357
turtles 227

U

Ubon Ratchathani 333, 349
Udon Thani 19, 339
Udorn Sunshine Nursery 3 39
Um Phang 313
Underwater World 176
universities 110, 115
Urak Lawoi 214

V

Vajiravudh, king 41
Vegetarian Festival 59
Vegetarian Festival **363**
venom-milking 130
Vientiane (Laos) 345
Viewpoint Hill 253
Viharn Phra Mongkhon Bophit 162
Viking Cave 248
Vimanmek Mansion 123
vineyards 327, 342
visas 361
Vongburi House 298

W

Wachiratan 282
Wangbadan Cave trail 152
Wang Luang 161
Warophat Phiman Hall 157
Wat Arun 39, 118
Wat Atsadang Nimit, 174
Wat Benjamabophit 124
Wat Bowonniwet 121
Wat Buak Khrok Luang 281
Wat Bunthawi 187
Wat Bupparam 274
Wat Burapha 338
Wat Chai Wattanaram 160
Wat Chalerm Phra Kiet 137
Wat Chalong 233
Wat Chama Thewi 284
Wat Chana Songkhram 304
Wat Chang Lom 306
Wat Chang Rawp 309
Wat Chedi Jet Thaew 307
Wat Chedi Luang 273, 294
Wat Chedi Sao 285
Wat Chetupon 305
Wat Chiang Man 271
Wat Chom Sawan 298
Wat Chong Kham 315
Wat Chong Klang 315
Wat Chong Lom 147
water 363
Wat Hin Mak Peng 343
Wat Hua Khuang 297
Wat Jet Yot 276
Wat Kamphaeng Laeng 186
Wat Khao Lad 190
Wat Khao Phanom Pleung 307
Wat Khao Suwan Khiri 307
Wat Khunaram 200
Wat Kow Tahm International Meditation Center 206
Wat Mae Yen 317
Wat Maha Samanaram 186
Wat Mahathat 115, 187, 303
Wat Mangkon Kamalawat 126
Wat Matchimawat 261
Wat Nang Phya 307
Wat Na Phra Men 161
Wat Neua 338
Wat Niwet Thamma-prawat 157
Wat Nong Pa Phong 334
Wat Nong Wang Muang 337
Wat Pa Daet 283
Wat Pa Mamuang 306
Wat Pa Nanachat Bung Wai 334
Wat Pa Sak 294
Wat Pa Wana Phothiyan 349
Wat Phanan Choeng 159
Wat Phan Tao 273
Wat Pho 115
Wat Phon Chai 341
Wat Phon Chai, 341
Wat Pho Si Nai 340
Wat Phra Kaew 38, 110, 292, 308
Wat Phra Kaew Don Tao 285
Wat Phra Kaew Museum 114
Wat Phra Mahathat 162, 262
Wat Phra Phai Luang 304
Wat Phra Ram 162
Wat Phra Si Iriyabot 309
Wat Phra Singh 272, 292
Wat Phra Si Rattana Mahathat 164, 307
Wat Phra Sri Sanphet 161
Wat Phra That 308
Wat Phra That Bang Phuan 346
Wat Phra That Chae Haeng 298
Wat Phra That Chang Kham 297
Wat Phra That Cho Hae 298
Wat Phra That Chom Kitti 294
Wat Phra That Doi Kong Mu 315
Wat Phra That Doi Suthep 279
Wat Phra That Doi Wao 296
Wat Phra That Hariphunchai 283
Wat Phra That Lampang Luang 286
Wat Phra That Nong Bua 334
Wat Phra That Renu Nakhon 348
Wat Phra That Si Chom Thong 282
Wat Phra Thong 236
Wat Phra Yai, 199
Wat Phumin 297
Wat Phu Thok 347
Wat Phutthaisawan 160
Wat Plai Laem 199
Wat Poramaiyikawat 137
Wat Prasat 273
Wat Ratchabophit 119
Wat Ratchaburana 162
Wat Ratchanatdam 120
Wat Rong Khun 293
Wat Saket 120
Wat Saphan Hin 306
Wat Sa Si 304
Wat Si Chum 305
Wat Si Khom Kham 292
Wat Si Nongkran 348
Wat Si Sawai 304
Wat Srisuphan 275
Wat Suan Dok 275
Wat Suthat 39, 119
Wat Suwan Dararam 160
Wat Suwannaram 117
Wat Tham Erawan 340
Wat Tham Erwan 340
Wat Tham Hew Sin Chai 349
Wat Thammamongkhon 139
Wat Tham Mangkhon Thong 151
Wat Tham Seua 240
Wat Thung Si Muang 333
Wat Traimit 127
Wat Trakuan 304
Wat U Mong 274
Wat Uthayarom 314
Wat Wattanaram 313
Wat Yai Suwannaram 186
Weapons Museum 113
weather 187
  monsoon 197
websites 368
Weera-sethakul, Apichatpong 72
Wehat Chamrun Palace 157
weights and measures 368
Wiang Kum Kam 277
Wiang Neua 316
Wiang Tai 316
wine 327
Withun Thatsana 157
women in Thai life 63
women travellers 360
woodcarving 76, 77
World War II 41, 43
World War II Museum 149, 315

Y

Yala 51
Yaowarat Chinatown Heritage 128
Yellow Shirts 46
Yellow Submarine 177
Yingluck 47

Z

zoos 124
  Chiang Mai 276
  Safari World 138
  Samphran Elephant Ground 145
  Samui Aquarium & Tiger Zoo 200

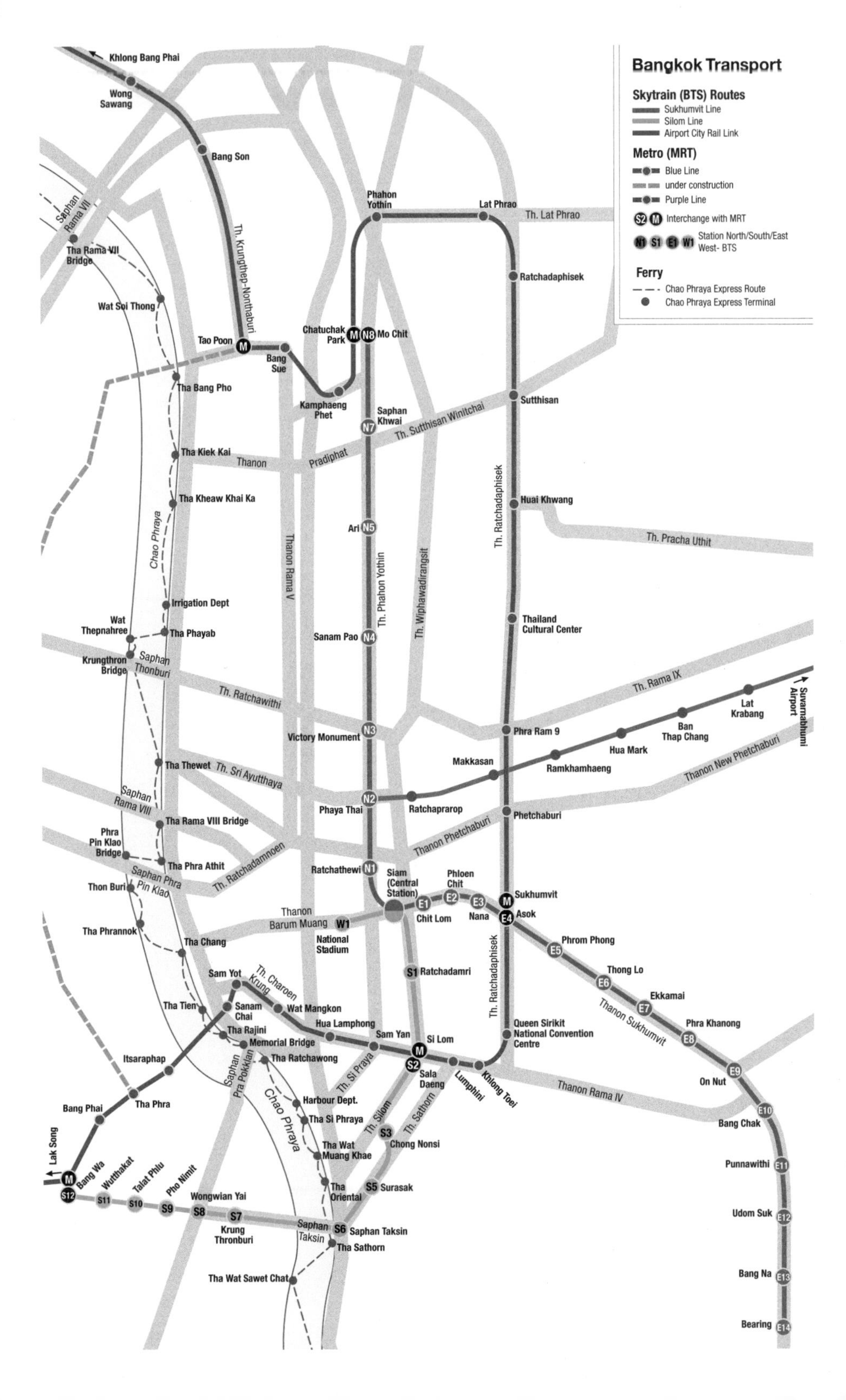
Bangkok Transport
Skytrain (BTS) Routes
Sukhumvit Line
Silom Line
Airport City Rail Link
Metro (MRT)
Blue Line
under construction
Purple Line
Interchange with MRT
Station North/South/East West- BTS
Ferry
Chao Phraya Express Route
Chao Phraya Express Terminal
Khlong Bang Phai
Wong Sawang
Bang Son
Th. Krungthep-Nonthaburi
Tao Poon
Bang Sue
Chatuchak Park
Mo Chit
Kamphaeng Phet
Phahon Yothin
Lat Phrao
Th. Lat Phrao
Ratchadaphisek
Sutthisan
Huai Khwang
Th. Pracha Uthit
Thailand Cultural Center
Th. Rama IX
Phra Ram 9
Saphan Rama VII
Tha Rama VII Bridge
Wat Soi Thong
Tha Bang Pho
Tha Kiek Kai
Tha Kheaw Khai Ka
Chao Phraya
Irrigation Dept
Wat Thepnahree
Tha Phayab
Krungthron Bridge
Saphan Thonburi
Th. Ratchawithi
Saphan Khwai
Th. Sutthisan Winitchai
Thanon Pradiphat
Thanon Rama V
Ari
Th. Phahon Yothin
Th. Wiphawadirangsit
Th. Ratchadaphisek
Sanam Pao
Victory Monument
Tha Thewet
Th. Sri Ayutthaya
Saphan Rama VIII
Tha Rama VIII Bridge
Phra Pin Klao Bridge
Tha Phra Athit
Saphan Phra Pin Klao
Thon Buri
Tha Phrannok
Tha Chang
Th. Ratchadamnoen
Phaya Thai
Ratchaprarop
Makkasan
Ramkhamhaeng
Hua Mark
Ban Thap Chang
Lat Krabang
Suvarnabhumi Airport
Thanon New Phetchaburi
Thanon Phetchaburi
Phetchaburi
Ratchathewi
Siam (Central Station)
Phloen Chit
Chit Lom
Nana
Sukhumvit
Asok
Thanon Barum Muang
National Stadium
Ratchadamri
Phrom Phong
Thong Lo
Ekkamai
Thanon Sukhumvit
Phra Khanong
On Nut
Bang Chak
Punnawithi
Udom Suk
Bang Na
Bearing
Sam Yot
Th. Charoen Krung
Sanam Chai
Tha Tien
Tha Rajini
Wat Mangkon
Hua Lamphong
Sam Yan
Si Lom
Memorial Bridge
Tha Ratchawong
Th. Si Praya
Sala Daeng
Lumphini
Khlong Toei
Queen Sirikit National Convention Centre
Thanon Rama IV
Itsaraphap
Tha Phra
Bang Phai
Saphan Pra Pokklao
Harbour Dept.
Tha Si Phraya
Th. Silom
Th. Sathorn
Chong Nonsi
Tha Wat Muang Khae
Tha Oriental
Surasak
Lak Song
Bang Wa
Wutthakat
Talat Phlu
Pho Nimit
Wongwian Yai
Krung Thonburi
Saphan Taksin
Tha Sathorn
Tha Wat Sawet Chat

BANG PHLAD
Th. Lukmahadthai
Charan Sanit Wong Soi 40
Nonthaburi
Soi Suwannin
Thanon Somdet Phra Pin Klao
Amarin
Th. Arun Amarin
THA WASUKRI
Wat Rachathiwas
THA THEWET
National Library
Wat Thewarat Kunchon
Chao Phraya
Saphan Rama VIII
Th. Samsen
Th. Uthong Nok
Samsen Soi 12
Th. Sri Ayutthaya
Thanon Phitsanulok
Th. Ratchasima
Vimanmek Mansion
National Assembly (Parliament)
Abhisek Dusit Throne Hall
SUANSAT DUSIT
Ananta Samakhom (Royal Throne Hall)
DUSIT
Uthong Nai
Gate
AMPORN PARK
Prem Prachakon
Thanon Rama V
Chitralada Palace
King Chulalongkorn
Parusakkawan Palace
Thanon Sri Ayutthaya
Royal Turf Club
Wat Benjamabophit (Marble Temple)
Government House
Nakhon Pathom
THA RONG LAD
Wat Dao Wadung
Th. Wisut Kasat
THA WISUTH KASAT
Wat Sam Phraya
THA WAT SAM PHRAYA
Wat Sangwet
Wat Indra Wiharn
Wat Mai Amatarot
Thanon Samsen
Samsen Soi 4
Th. Prachathipatai
Krung Kasem
Wat Mongkrut
Krasat Thiyaram
Ratchadamnoen Boxing Stadium
Wat Sommanat
Thanon Ratchadamnoen
Thanon Nakhon Sawan
Phadung Krung Kasem
Thanon Phitsanulok
Th. Luk Luang
Th. Arun
Ansorel Sunnah
THA WAT DAO DUNG
THA PHRA ATHIT
UNICEF
Th. Phra Athit
Saphan Phra Pin Klao
Bangkok Noi/Thonburi Railway Station
Banphak Rotfai
THA RAILWAY
Wat Chai Chana Songkhram
Th. Chakrabongse
Phra Sumen
Banglamphu
Wat Bowonniwet
Th. Chao Fa
National Gallery
Th. Khao San
National Theatre
National Museum
Thammasat University
THA SIRIRAJ
THA PHRACHAN
Th. Phra Chan
Thanon Phrannok
THA MAHARAJ
Th. Mahathat
Wat Mahathat
Th. Na Phra That
SANAM LUANG
Th. Ratchadamnoen Klang
14 October Monument
Democracy Monument
Th. Dinso
Th. Phra Sumen
Th. Parinayok
Rattanakosin Exhibition Hall
Thanon Lan Luang
Th. Lan Luang
Phong Chakkaphatdi
Th. Damrong Rak
Saen Saep
Th. Krung Kasem
Th. Khlong Lan Pak
Th. Atsadang
Th. Rachini
Wat Mahan
Loha Prasat
Wat Ratchanatda
Wat Saket
Phu Khao Thong (Golden Mount)
Th. Boriphat
Soi Ban Chang Lo
Th. Na Phra Lan
Wat Phra Kaew (Emerald Buddha)
Lak Muang (City Pillar)
City Hall
Sao Ching Cha (Giant Swing)
Th. Tanao
Th. Maha Chai
Th. Rong Liang Dek
Th. Anantanak
Wat Phra Yai
Wat Bomonniwet
Wat Chamni Hatthakan
THA CHANG WANG LUANG
Grand Palace
Kanlaya Namit
Wat Ratchapradit
Wat Suthat
Ban Baat
Thanon Barum Muang
RATTANAKOSIN
Th. Maharat
Wat Ratchabophit
Th. Fuang Nakhon
Th. Ti Tong
Thanon Dev Mandir Temple
Th. Luang
S. Ban Baat
Th. Wora Chak
Th. Ditsamak
Th. Yukhol 2
S. Yotsi
Phla Chai
Th. Rama I
Thanon Thai Wang
Th. Sanam Chai
Th. Atsadang
Charoen Krung
Sam Yot
Wat Thepsirin
THA TIEN
Wat Pho (Reclining Buddha)
Th. Ban Mo
Nakhon Kasem (Thieves' Market)
Th. Chakrawat
Th. Chao Khamrop
Suapa
Th. Phlab
Th. Luang
Wat Phlapphla Chai
Phadung Krung Kasem
Thanon Rong Muang
Wat Arun (Temple of Dawn)
THA WAT ARUN
Sanam Chai
Museum of Siam (Discovery Museum)
Sri Guru Singh Sabha
Pahurat Market
Chak Phet
Charoen Krung (New Rd)
Wat Kanikaphon
Wat Mangkon Kamalawat
Maitri
Th. Wang Doem
Pak Khlong Talad (Flower Market)
Th. Chakkaphet
Wat Ratchburana
Thanon Wanit 1
Wat Chakrawat
Th. Yaowarat
Wat Mangkon
Talad Mai
Chit
Vichaiprasit (Old Fort)
THA RAJINI
Th. Saphan Phut
Saphan Pra Pokklao
Thanon O-Sathahon
CHINATOWN
Soi Itsaranuphap
Shanghai Mansion
Talad Kao (Sampeng Lane)
Song Sawat
Th. Krung Kasem
Hualamphong Railway Station
Thanon Itsaraphap
Wat Kalayanamit
THA SAPHAN PHUT
THA RATCHAWONG
Thanon Songwat
Wat Traimit
Chinatown Heritage Museum
Rama IV
Hua Lamphong
Itsaraphap
Itsaraphap Soi 28
Th. Thetsaban Sai 1
Wat Prayunwongsawat
Th. Thetsaban Sai 2
Th. Thetsaban 2
S. Somdet Chao Praya 3
THA DIN DAENG
Th. Tha Din Daeng
Tha Din Daeng S. 18
THA SONG SAWAT
Songwat
Wat Pathuma Kongkha
Th. Traimit
Th. Kao Lan
Th. Charoen Krung (New Rd)
S. Charoen Phanit
Th. Maha Phrutharam
Itsaraphap Soi 21
Thonburi Christian Hall
Soi 15
Thanon Itsaraphap
Thanon Prachathipok
Th. Somdet Chao Praya
Wat Thong Thammachat
Th. Chiang Mai
THA WAT THONG
THA KROM CHOTHA
Soi 10 Somdet Chao Praya Soi 12
Patchamid Fort
River City Shopping Complex
Bang Sakai
Bangkok Yai
Wat Yai Si Suphan
S. Khang Rong Rap Chamnan
Th. Itsaraphap
Th. Tha Din Daeng
THA KLONG SAN
Royal Orchid
THA SI PHRAYA
BANGRAK
Th. Inthraraphitak
Wongwian Yai (King Taksin Monument)
Thanon Lad Ya
Soi 13
Soi 3
Th. Charoen Nakhon
Soi 2
Soi 5
THA KROM PRISANEE
Th. Charoen Krung
Charoen Krung Soi 43
2nd Stage Expressway
Soi Wiset San
Thanon Charoen Rat
KHLONG SAN
THA WAT MUANG KHAE
Soi 3
Soi 2
Soi 1
Wongwian Yai Railway Station
Soi 2
Soi 4
Soi 8
Soi 10
Soi 7
Soi 9
Mandarin Oriental
Mahasak
Thanon Thoet Thai
Tr. Yenchit
Wat Thong Phleng
Wat Suwan Ubasikaram
Peninsula Hotel
THA ORIENTAL
Assumption Cathedral
Th. Silom
Suanphlu
S. Saksin
Soi 1
Soi 3
Soi Charoen Nakhon 14
Krung Thonburi
THA SHANGRI-LA
State Tower
Shangri-La
Number 1 Gallery
Silom Soi 21
Th. Surasak
Soi 13
THA DUMAKE
Soi 15
Wongwian Yai
Thanon Krung Thonburi
Thanon Krung Thonburi
Th. Charoen Krung
Pho Nimit
Soi Saraphi 3
Thanon Somdet Phra Chao Taksin
Saphan Taksin
Soi Charoen Nakhon 18
Th. Sathorn
Surasak
THA SATHORN